D1878321

ELEMENTS
OF
HINDU ICONOGRAPHY

ELEMENTS
OF
HINDU ICONOGRAPHY

BY

T. A. GOPINATHA RAO, M.A.
SUPERINTENDENT OF ARCHAEOLOGY, TRAVANCORE STATE.

Vol. II—Part I.

GYAN

Published by

GYAN

Gyan Publishing House
5, Ansari Road
Daryaganj, New Delhi-110002
Phone: 011-47034999, 9811692060
E-mail: books@gyanbooks.com

Distribution Network
gyanbooks.com
India, USA, Canada, UK, Australia, France

© Publisher

All rights reserved. No part of this work may be reproduced, stored, adapted, or transmitted in any form or by any means, electronic, mechanical, photocopying, micro-filming, recording or otherwise, or translated in any language, without the prior written permission of the copyright owner and the publisher.

ISBN : 978-81-212-2694-3 (Set)
ISBN : 978-81-212-2697-4 (HB)
First Published, 1916

2nd Impression 2021

Printed at: Gyan Press, Delhi.

The book is sold subject to the condition that it shall not, by way of trade or otherwise, be lent, resold, hired out, or otherwise circulated without the prior publisher's written consent.

Elements of Hindu Iconography Vol. II–Part I
Author: T. A. Gopinatha Rao

ELEMENTS

OF

HINDU ICONOGRAPHY

BY

T. A. GOPINATHA RAO, M.A.

SUPERINTENDENT OF ARCHÆOLOGY, TRAVANCORE STATE.

Vol. II—Part I.

THE LAW PRINTING HOUSE
MOUNT ROAD :: :: MADRAS
1916

DEDICATED

WITH KIND PERMISSION

To

HIS HIGHNESS SIR RAMAVARMA,

Sri Padmanabhadasa, Vanchipala, Kulasekhara Kiritapati,
Manney Sultan Maharaja Raja Ramaraja Bahadur,
Shamsher Jang, G.C.S.I., G.C.I.E.,

MAHARAJA OF TRAVANCORE,

Member of the Royal Asiatic Society, London,
Fellow of the Geographical Society, London,
Fellow of the Madras University, Officer de L'Instruction Publique.

By

HIS HIGHNESS'S HUMBLE SERVANT

THE AUTHOR.

PREFACE.

In bringing out the Second Volume of the Elements of Hindu Iconography, the author earnestly trusts that it will meet with the same favourable reception that was uniformly accorded to the first volume both by *savants* and the Press, for which he begs to take this opportunity of tendering his heart-felt thanks. No pains have of course been spared to make the present publication as informing and interesting as is possible in the case of the abstruse subject of Iconography. Though the illustrations appearing in the present volume are by no means inadequate for the main purpose of the work, yet they are not so full and exhaustive as in the first, and a word of explanation in that connection may not be out of place. To the great regret of the author, the liberal pecuniary help offered for the preparation and publication of the first volume has been, owing to the somewhat straitened finances of the Travancore State at present, withheld from him on the present occasion and he has, in consequence, not been able to embody as many illustrations as he had intended personally to gather for the purpose from various parts of India with a view to present to the public a series representative of the varied sculpture of the different parts of this country. But the Travancore Durbar have, in gracious consideration of the trouble and labour involved in the preparation of the present volume, been pleased to permit its publication by the author himself, for which he begs to offer his respectful and grateful thanks to the Dewan, Mr. Dewan Bahadur M. Kṛishṇa Nāir, B.A., B.L.

Mention may here be made of a few points worthy of notice in the book. In the Introduction is given a collective description of all the peculiarities of the tenets and observances of some of the Śaiva sects of which the general public has hitherto been practically ignorant, and of certain other cults that have died out without a trace. The nature of *Liṅga* worship has been examined critically in the light of original texts gathered from such important sources as the Śaivāgamas, Śaiva philosophical treatises, Purāṇas and Itihāsas, and with reference to the extant sculpture of all ages of this symbol of worship, and the matter has been thoroughly discussed and, what the author ventures to claim to be, an impartial conclusion arrived at. In the body of the book, several matters, which will be seen to be quite new even to the informed Hindu, have been dealt with ; to cite an instance, everybody knows that Śiva begged for food with the broken skull of Brahmā as an expiation for the sin of having cut off one of Brahmā's heads, but it is doubtful if it is known why this curious sort of penance should have been resorted to by Śiva to get rid of His sin. Again, it has been found possible with the help of the knowledge derived from a close study of the bulk of the science of *Nāṭya-Śāstra* together with commentaries thereon to elaborate and treat fully the manifold dances of Śiva, though only eight or nine modes are described in the *āgamic* and other works. The reader will, it is hoped, come across many other instances of fresh information being furnished on matters that have remained more or less obscure hitherto.

The author cannot be too thankful to the Proprietors of the Law Printing House for the extraordinary care and trouble they have bestowed upon the printing and general get up of the books and for their readiness in coming forward and generously offering their timely help but for which the volume could not have been brought out. The author cannot also omit to express his sense of gratitude to Dr. A. K. Ānandakumāraswāmi, M.A., D. Sc., for the ready and willing permission granted to him for reproducing the valuable article on the dance of Śiva, contributed some time ago to the *Siddhānta-Dīpikā* by the learned Doctor. He has also very great pleasure in recording here his high appreciation of the help cheerfully rendered by his Paṇḍit Mr. V. Śrīnivāsa Śāstri, Smṛitiviśārada, but for whose untiring industry and intelligent collaboration this work could not have been brought to a successful completion so soon. Messrs. Longhurst, Stoney, Kay and Beardsell, have been so very kind as to assist the author with photographs of images in their respective collections and to accord their gracious permission to reproduce them: to these gentlemen, the author offers his grateful thanks.

For reasons which need not be explained here, it was not possible for the author personally to supervise the printing of the work throughout so as to ensure the presentation of an absolutely correct text; he had therefore to entrust the task to the printers themselves. In spite of the care and trouble ungrudgingly bestowed by them in the midst of their multifarious duties, a number of errors have unavoidably crept in. Though such of them as have been subsequently noticed are noted in the errata list, it is likely many more have escaped detection, for which the author craves the indulgence of his readers.

MADRAS,
January 1916.

THE AUTHOR.

CONTENTS.

CONTENTS.

LIST OF ILLUSTRATIONS.*

* T.S.A. Trivandram School of Arts; A.S.M. Archæological Survey of Madras; A.S. My. Archæological Survey of Mysore; A.S. Bo. Archæological Survey of Bombay; A.S.I. Archæological Survey of India; I.M. India Museum and A.S.U.P. Archæological Survey of United Provinces. The photographs and drawings which are not followed by any of the abbreviations given above belong to the author's collection.

PLATE | TO FACE PAGE

LIST OF ILLUSTRATIONS.

PLATE | TO FACE PAGE

LIST OF ILLUSTRATIONS.

PLATE — TO FACE PAGE

PLATE TO FACE PAGE

LIST OF ILLUSTRATIONS.

LIST OF ILLUSTRATIONS.

LIST OF IMPORTANT WORKS CONSULTED OTHER THAN THOSE MENTIONED IN THE FIRST VOLUME.

Atharvaśirasōpanishad.
Bharata-nāṭya-śāstra.
Brahma-mīmāmsā-śāstra.
Dakshiṇāmūrtyupanishad.
Dharmasūtras of Āpastamba with Haradatta's commentary.
Hālāsya-māhātmya.
Harivaṁśa.
Jīrṇōddhāra-daśakam.
Kōyil-purāṇam (Tamil).
Kūrma-purāṇa.
Kuvalayānanda.
Mallāri-māhātmya.
Mālatī-mādhava.
Manu-dharma-śāstra.
Mayamata.
Nāṭyavēda-vivṛiti.
Periyapurāṇam (Tamil).
Prabōdhachandrōdayam.
Prasthānabhēda.
Pratyabhijñasūtras.
Śaṅkara-vijaya (Anantānandagiri's).
Śarabhōpanishad.
Sarvadarśana-saṅgraha.
Śatarudriya.
Śivajñānasiddhiyār (Tamil).
Śiva-liṅga-pratishṭhā-vidhi.
Śiva-tatva-ratnākara.
Sūta-saṁhitā.
Tiruvaruḷpayaṉ (Tamil).
Tiruvāchakam (Tamil).
Yaśōdharakāvyam.

ERRATA.

Page	Line	For	Read
5	5	... was	... were
9	8	... Śrīkanṭha-Śivā-chārya	... Śrikānthā-Śivā-chārya
9	12	... gamatvat	... gamatvāt
17	12	... Pati	... *Pati*
19	6	... Ātharva	... Atharva.
32	4	... was	... were
35	15	... though unnecessary to be detailed here	... though it is unnecessary to detail them here
41	24	... to have attempted	... to attempt
42	22	... Gaṇgā	... Gaṅgā
43	14	... an	... a
44	26	... Mahāndēva	... Mahādēva
44	27	... Iāśna	... Īśāna
48	12	... the stomach of Śiva	Śiva's stomach
48	13	... the throat of Śiva	... Śiva's throat
48	16	... "	... "
50	14	... Thou King	... Thou, King
53	12	... the *vaidika*	... the Vaidika
58	25	... *Mārkaṇḍēya*	... Mārkaṇḍēya.
62	11	... Śankara is	... Śankara who is
65	1 & 2	... which are believed by Mr. Banerji	... which Mr. Banerji believes
65	2	... might	... may
81	11	... Vāmadēva	... Nigamajñānadēva
81	15	... "	... "
81	25	... "	... "
82	25	... *Vāmadēvasivā-chārya.*	... Vāmadēvasivā-chārya.
85	21	... Vindhyāparvata	... Vindhyaparvata.

Page	Line		For		Read
86	20	...	Sthāvarā lingas	...	Sthāvara lingas
105	19	...	towhich	...	to which.
110	20	...	are sculptured against	...	are not sculptured in accordance with
111	1	...	Fig 2, Pl. XIV	...	Fig 1, Pl. XIV.
113	8	...	and and the skull	...	and the skull
119	16	...	*makara-kuṇḍala*	...	*makara-kuṇḍala,*
121	18	...	The first comes	...	The first, fig. 1, Pl. XV
125	19	...	carry on	...	carry an
131	4	...	a utpala flower	...	an utpala flower
137	11	...	with creeper orna-ment	...	with a creeper ornament.
140	20	...	catching hold of	...	catching hold
145	2	...	or a pacific,	...	or as a pacific,
148	5	...	of Śiva	...	of Kāma by Śiva.
148	20	...	and in the com-pany	...	and being in the company
150	5	...	said to have told	...	said to have men-tioned
152	17	...	piece of sculpture,	...	piece of sculpture, Pl. XXX,
157	12	...	says, to Tirukka-ḍavūr	...	says, Tirukkaḍavūr
161	20	...	see later on, the	...	see later on that the
163	6	...	with hands	...	with his hands
164	12	...	they desired and	...	they desired and that
165	9	...	with a half of	...	with one half of
165	10	...	stronger than all other	...	stronger than all the other
166	16	...	who destroyd	...	who destroyed
168	10	...	upon Apasmāra-purusha	...	upon the Apas-mārapurusha

ERRATA.

Page	Line	For	Read
168	16	... *Apasmāra* ...	Apasmāra
168	20	... should be held so... as the	should be held that
168	26	... *Apasmārapūrusha* .	Apasmārapūrusha
170	3	... and padmāpāśa ...	the padma-pāśa
171	24	... belongs to the... modern times.	belongs to modern times.
172	14	... skin of Narasiṁha,	skin of Narasiṁha
173	5 & 6	... as carrying with... two of his legs Narasiṁha	as carrying Narasiṁha with two of his legs.
174	11	... and a face of the... lion	and the face of a lion
175	5	... and wearing an ...	and wearing a
176	5	... learnt at the ...	learnt by the
176	8	... Srītatvanidhi ...	*Srītatvanidhi.*
176	16	... in the garments ...	in garments
177	26	... as that of its master.	as its master
178	1	... so far for the ...	so much for the
179	17	... should have an ...	should have
184	26	... of demons which ...	of demons who
185	18	... made to the ...	made for the
187	3	... as his underwear ...	as underwear.
189	1	... by dēvas ...	by the dēvas.
189	4	... to Vishṇu about... their lot	about their lot to Vishṇu
189	6	... extorted Vishṇu's ...	evoked Vishṇu's
191	4	... and the feet of Śiva.	and his feet
192	7	... in his ears white, ...	in his ears white
201	15	... stay away in their... midst	stay in their midst
201	17	... stopped away at ...	stopped at
201	20	... Lalitōpākhyāna ...	*Lalitōpākhyana.*
205	3	... a Anugrahamūrti...	an Anugrahamūrti.
206	16	· ... was offering ...	was offering to

Page	Line	For	Read
211	16	... the other two ones...	the other two
214	11	... a utpala flower ...	an utpala flower
217	6	... Kubēra was ...	Kubēra, was
218	15	... return to Lanka ...	to return to Lanka.
218	15	*insert* " at the time" *after* " he cried"	
220	7	... praising him. ...	praising Mahādēva.
225	9	... and stand ...	and these stand
226	10	... with ...	holding
227	1	... a tortoise shell ...	tortoise shell.
229	12	... Apasmārapurusha...	the Apasmārapurusha
231	3	... Siva ...	Śiva
231	8	... ,, ...	,,
231	9	... turmed ...	turned
231	13	... and if ...	and, if
235	27 (f.n.)	... wears ...	wears.
252	10	... extorts ...	evokes
252	16	... The second photograph, Pl. LVII, the original of which was ...	The original of the second photograph, Pl. LVII, which was
252	17	... in earth ...	in the earth
252	18	... and is ...	is
256	22	... to carry ...	should carry
257	13	... but rest ...	but should rest
258	6	... dance ...	dancing
260	11	... is known ...	known
260	27	... other ...	others
263	1	... arms ...	hands
263	3	... arm ...	hand.
269	15	*omit* 'and' *after* 'side'	
269	18	... on the left ...	to the left
269	19	... Pl. LXIX, ...	Pl. LXIX
269	26	... Kailāsanatha-svmin ...	Kailāsanatha-svāmin.

ERRATA.

Page	Line	For	Read
270	10	... is	... are
273	13	... have	... has
278	20	... has its	... has as its
279	4	... descend	... descends
284	7	... a *utpala*	... an *utpala*
286	7	... to be	... that it is
286	14	... arm	... arms
286	24	... is	... has been
286	25	... Śaṅkarāchārya ;	... Śaṅkarāchārya.
286	25	... on	... On
287	22 (f.n.)	... with thin coat	... with a thin coat
289	2	... *vīnā*,	... *vīnā* ;
290	21	... are added also	... are also added
291	2	... on the	... on a
295	21	... accepted	... and accepted
297	14	... *kūrma-purāṇa*	... *Kūrma-purāṇa*
299	24 (f.n.)	... intimated	... informed of
300	5	... brāhmaṇa	... Brāhmaṇa.
300	6	... "	... "
301	5	... at	... as
301	18	... brāhmaṇas	... Brāhmaṇas
305	27	... according	... according to
307	8	*omit* 'the' *after* 'under'	
308	19	... have	... has
315	7	*omit* 'to' *after* 'Gaṅgā'	
315	16	*omit* 'the' *before* 'Gaṅgā'	
317	25	... arm	... hand
318	3	... "	... "
318	4	... "	... "
320	11	*omit* 'also' *after* 'is'	
322	2	... Thitherto	... Until then
322	27	*omit* 'over' *after* 'covered'	
324	21	*insert* 'be' *after* 'may'	
324	21	... by	... in
327	3	... Pl. XCIII	... Pl. XCIV

Page	Line	For	Read
328	8	... quite	... quiet
334	23	*insert* 'that' *after* 'right'	
335	18	... isa	... is a
337	6	*omit* 'by' *after* 'but'	
338	5	*insert* 'even in rendering help' *after* 'meant'	
338	5	... by others	... by any other
338	6	*omit* 'that of' *before* 'her'	
338	6	*omit* 'even in helping others'	
338	7	... was standing	... stood
338	19	... that of Śiva	... his
339	9	... in	... at
339	20	*omit* the comma *after* 'gods.'	
340	19	... to age	... of age
341	6	... for	... to
341	20	*omit* 'that.' *after* 'and'	
341	27	... with	... in
342	22	*insert* 'the' *after* 'of'	
345	25	*omit* 'in.' *after* 'busy'	
347	18	*omit* 'got' *after* 'not'	
347	27	... to obtain the hand of Śiva	... to become Śiva's spouse
348	19	*insert* 'she' *after* 'reluctance'.	
348	21	... held	... holds it
349	21	*omit* 'even' *before* 'during'	
349	21	... two !!	... two !!.
350	1	... by	... of
350	2	... but	... and had
350	14	... outstretched fingers	... fingers outstretched.
353	27	... carrying	... should carry
353	27	... a *utpala*	... an *utpala*.
354	2	... done	... sculptured
355	25	*insert* 'it' *after* 'find'	
356	7	*insert* 'hand' *after* 'right'	
356	20	... considered	... regarded as

ERRATA.

Page	Line		For		Read
357	9	...	sight	...	gaze
357	11	...	going	...	about
358	6	...	to be	...	to have been
362	14	...	destruction, (saṁhāra)	...	destruction (saṁhāra),
365	10	...	otherwise Īśvara	...	otherwise called Īśvara
365	15	...	lengh	...	length
366	22	...	beautiful	...	beautiful,
367	2	...	and is with a smiling countenance	...	and a smiling countenance
367	4	...	have	...	has
371	23	...	ordinary mortals	...	ordinary mortals,
372	2	...	heads be adorned	...	heads should be adorned
372	17	...	Pl. CXII	...	Pl. CXIII
373	20	...	and since	...	and, since
376	8	...	authority	...	authority,
377	14	...	*khaṭvāṅga*	...	*khaṭvāṅga*,
391	21	...	an	...	a
400	12	...	S. India,	...	S. India
400	15	...	whose photograph	...	and a photograph of it
404	20	...	*Īśvara*	...	Īśvara
417	25	...	an	...	a
419	26	...	was	...	were
420	1	...	it	...	them
420	14	...	Agni Rudra	...	Agni, Rudra
429	15	...	the *yajñōpavīta*	...	a *yajñōpavīta*
433	9	...	with rubies,	...	with rubies;
438	5	...	Tārakāri,	...	Tārakāri
456	18	...	as also	...	and also
458	5 & 6	...	They informed this sad news to the father of the boy.	...	They informed the father of the boy of this sad news.

HINDU ICONOGRAPHY.

Page	Line	For	Read
463	2	attained to	attained
508	6	an	a
509	6	a	an
509	15	ana *kshamālā*	an *akshamāla*
516	23	and that	and it is also stated that
518	2	of	in
521	4	an	a
521	4	adorns	adorn
529	14	at the present	at the present time
529	21	an	a
542	26	had become	became
543	20	in	at
549	13 & 14	Besides, the present compilation being a close following of	Besides, since the present compilation closely follows
551	24	*Omit* 'they requested' *after* 'whom'	
551	27	being disposed	having been disposed
552	1	*Omit* 'then' *after* 'they'	
554	10	man	men
554	14 & 15	Svāyambhuvamanvantara	*Svāyambhuvamanvantara.*
556	12	hands	palms
561	16	pointed	pointed out
561	16	being	was
562	4	are	is
562	15	are	is
568	2	are	is
569	3	and is	and it is
569	4	to be given	to give it

INTRODUCTION.

ONE of the oldest as also the most widely spread cult in India is that of Śiva. It consisted once of several sects, of which only a few have survived to the present day. Some of them had the sanction of the Vēdas while others were classed as outside the Vēdas or as opposed to them; again, some of them had milder forms of worship, while others practised horrible and shocking rites. The ideas about life, action and liberation differed from sect to sect. It will not be without interest to examine in some detail the history, the main tenets and the ceremonies of a few of the leading sects of Śiva in the following paragraphs.

First, as regards the origin of the sects classed as outside the pale of the Vēdas, the following account taken from the *Varāha-purāṇa* will be of interest. In the forest of Daṇḍaka, situated in the middle of *Bhāratavarsha*, the *ṛishi* Gautama had his *āśrama* (hermitage), round which, he had abundant food-giving plants and trees. There once raged a twelve years' famine during which a number of *ṛishis* from various other *āśramas* flocked to that of Gautama for food and shelter, and were received with all kindness and treated with great hospitality by Gautama. After the famine abated and the country became again fertile, the *ṛishis* desired to start out on a pilgrimage to the several famous *tīrthas;* one of the *ṛishis* named Marīcha, thinking that they should not leave the *āśrama* without informing Gautama, but fearing at the same time that he might, in his extreme kindness and hospitality, refuse permission for the pilgrimage, created from *māyā* an enfeebled, old cow and let it graze near Gautama's *āśrama.* Gautama went near the cow to water it; as he went near the cow, it fell down and died. The ungrateful *ṛishis* attributed to Gautama, the sin of killing a cow and refused to stay any longer in the abode of such a sinful one. Gautama, who did not know this trick of the *ṛishis*, really believed that he had committed the sin and asked them how he could raise the cow from death. Advising him to sprinkle on it water brought from the Ganges, they departed on their projected pilgrimage. Gautama repaired to the Himālaya and prayed to Śiva a hundred years and got from his *jaṭāmaṇḍala* a small quantity of the water of the Gaṅgā which he sprinkled on the dead cow. The water of this divine river revived the cow and itself began to flow as the river Gōdāvarī. Gautama at last perceived through his mind's eye that the death of the cow and other incidents connected therewith were a clear deceit practised on him by the *ṛishis* and cursed them to become *Vēdabāhyas* or those outside the pale of the Vēdic religion. On their entreaty to abate his anger against them, he was pleased to assure them that though they were outside the Vēdic cult, they would rise to heaven through *bhakti* or devotional love of God. The fallen *ṛishis* went to Kailāsa and prayed to Śiva to grant them some *śāstras* which had a few Vēdic rites at least. Thereupon, the *ṛishis* were decreed to be born to the Raudras, the lovers of spirituous liquors and flesh, who sprang up from the sweat-drops which flowed from Śiva while he was in the aspect of Bhairava, and to these he gave the *Pāśupata Śāstra*.

From the above account one fact becomes clear, namely, that some at least of the followers of the Pāśupata and other non-Vēdic sects were at first followers of the Vēdic religion and gave it up and joined the *avaidika* cults. That the Pāśupata and a few other sects are indeed very ancient may be inferred from ancient authorities. The *Atharva-śiras Upanishad* describes the Pāśupata rite thus: "This is the Pāśupata rite: 'Agni is ashes, Vāyu is ashes, water is ashes, dry land is ashes, the sky is ashes, all this is ashes, the mind, these eyes are ashes.' Having taken ashes while pronouncing these preceding words, and rubbing himself, let a man touch his limbs. This is the Pāśupata rite, for the removal of the animal bonds." Again the Bhīta liṅga and the Guḍimallam liṅga bear clear sculptural evidence of the antiquity of the Śaiva cults. From the summary of the philosophy of a few of the important Śaiva sects given below it would be clear that they have played a prominent part in the Religious History of India.

History of the Agamanta Saivas.

Let us take first the Āgamānta or the Śuddha Śaiva sect. In the Āgamānta Śāiva works it is stated that the Śaivas flourished in a place called Mantra-kāḷi situated on the banks of the Gōdāvarī river, that there were four *maṭhas*, beginning with the Āmarddaka *maṭha*, surrounding the temple of Mantrakāḷēśvara, that when Rājēndrachōḷa went to the Ganges on his victorious march in the north he met there these Śaivas, whom he, on his way back to his capital, induced to come and settle down in his kingdom and that from that time the Śaivas immigrated into the Toṇḍaimaṇḍala and the Chōḷamaṇḍala. Since then an impetus was given to the spread of Śaivaism and a very large number of original works belonging to the Āgamānta school of Śaivaism was written. The Āmarddaka *maṭha* mentioned above is a famous one and had its branches all over India. For instance, mention is made of this in the *Siddhāntasārāvaḷi* and the *Kṛiyākramadyōtini*, as also in a number of inscriptions.

The members of some of these *maṭhas* were great authors and exerted considerable influence over the sovereigns of various countries. The *Kṛiyākramadyōtini* of Aghōraśivāchārya, the *Siddhāntasārāvaḷi* of Trilōchanaśivāchārya, the *Jīrṇoddhāra-daśakam* of Nigamajñānadēva, son of Vāmadēvaśivāchārya and many another work will bear testimony to the above statement regarding the literary activity of the Śaiva Brāhmaṇa settlers in the Drāviḍa country. The first of these lived in the Śaka year 1080, the second lived sometime later, for he quotes the former, and the third in the beginning of the fourteenth century A.D. The great Rājarāja, the builder of the Bṛihadīśvara temple at Tanjore, is stated to have appointed a Sarvaśiva Paṇḍita-Śivāchārya as the priest of that temple and to have ordered that thenceforth the *śishyas* and their *śishyas* alone, belonging to the Āryadēśa, the Madhyadēśa and the Gauḍadēśa, shall be eligible for the office of chief priest.(1) Again, some of these Śaivāchāryas became *rājagurus* or the preceptors of kings, and appear to have wielded such great influence and power that they have sometimes set aside even the royal commandments and acted on their own authority. For example, Kulōttuṅgachōladēva III appointed two Śaivāchāryas for the service of the temple at Tirukkaḍavūr, but Svāmidēvar, the king's *guru*, cancelled the order and appointed two others, in recognition of their hereditary rights.(2) All the Āgamas declare that the Śaivāgamas flourished to the south of the Vindhya ranges, which is corroborated by the statement made by Aghōraśivāchārya; and it therefore appears quite certain that Rājēndrachōḷadēva implanted in the south a large colony of Śaiva Brāhmaṇas of Middle India.

These Śaivas should be carefully distinguished from the Vēdānta Śaivas, who base their philosophy on the Vēdas and the Upanishads. These two schools are diametrically opposed to each other

(1) S.I.I., Vol. II, Part II, p. 153.

(2) No. 40 of 1906 of the Madras Epigraphist's collection. For an account of the origin and development of the Śaiva *maṭhas*, see *Kṛiyākramadyōtini*, *Śiddhāntasārāvaḷi* and other works.

on many points. From the statement, *Yasya-niśvasitam-vēdāh*, of the Advaitins the followers of the Āgamānta considered Vēdas as inferior to the Āgamas; for they assert that the former came out of Śiva as unconsciously as His breath, whereas the twenty-eight Āgamas were personally and consciously dictated by Śiva. Besides, the Āgamāntins consider the Advaitins and the Mīmāṁsakas as *paśus* or unevolved souls and to be therefore unfit for receiving *Śaiva dīkshās* or initiations. The Āgamāntins are in their turn reviled by the Vaidikas as being heterodox; Kumārilabhaṭṭa classes them among atheists and we read Amarasiṁha accordingly classing Dēvalas who are generally the Pāśupatas, the Pāñcharātras and other Tāntrikas that are addicted to image worship, among Śūdras.[1] At any rate, these Śaivas did not evidently hold a high place in the system of castes; the *Sūta-saṁhitā* also states that very low classes of Brāhmaṇas alone underwent the *dīkshā* or initiatory ceremony in the Pāśupata, the Pāñcharātra and other *tantras*. It is therefore clear that inferior Brāhmaṇas embraced some of the non-Āryan cults and became Pāśupatas and Pāñcharātras. At a later stage of their history,

---

(1) Amarakōśa, Kāṇḍa II, Śūdravarga.

they probably adopted a few of the *hōmas* and the *mantras* appropriate to them from the *Gṛihya-sūtras* and created for themselves some others in imitation of the *mantras* of the Vēda. This explains the eagerness with which these *anārya-sampradāyas* were somehow classed in the *ārya-sampradāyas*. But, their system of *dīkshā*, Ankurārpaṇa with which the ceremonies are begun, the philosophy of *Shaḍadhvās* (1) and many others are not found in the Vaidik religions and therefore mark off Āgamānta as being different in essentials from the Vaidik religion. The Āgamānta has freely borrowed the philosophy of the Sāṅkhya and the Yōga schools. Unlike the Vēdāntins the Āgamāntins do not shut out women, Śūdras, and the Pratilōmas from participating in religious rites and ceremonies. They freely allow women to meditate upon the *pañchākshara-mantra*, and grant *dīkshā* to Śūdras, who might, in their turn, give *dīkshā* to others among them. "If the Śūdra is a *naishṭhika* (one who passes into *sannyāsa* without undergoing the intermediate stage of *gṛihastha)* he is entitled to consecrate the *svārtha-chala-liṅgas*, offer *dīkshā* to Śūdras, might recite

(1) For an explanation of this and of a summary of the Śaiva philosophy see the beginning of the Chapter on Miscellaneous Aspects of Śiva (Xth).

with proper *svaras* all *mantras*, and study *Śiva-jñāna*. If he is a *gṛihastha*, he is privileged to utter the *nityēshti mantras*, and that too without proper intonation or *nāda*." Though the Avaidika Śaivaism was essentially different in tenets at the beginning, attempts have been made at later times to identify Avaidikas with the Vaidikas. Srīkaṇṭha-Śivāchārya who wrote a *Bhāshya* on the *Brahma-sūtras* in accordance with the Āgamānta Śaiva teachings exclaims, *na vayam vēda-śivāgamayōrbhēdam paśyāmah vēdasyāpi śivāgamatvat*, (we do not perceive any difference between the Vēdas and the Śivāgamas, Vēdas are also as authoritative as the Śivāgamas); and at a later stage, that is, about the time of Appayya-dīkshita (16th century A. D.), the Vēdantins began to study the Āgamānta philosophy and adopted several of their customs; at this day several of the anthropomorphic aspects of Śiva, which might, with propriety, be called peculiarly Āgamāntic, are worshipped by the Vēdic Śaivas, and they also get themselves initiated into the meditation on the *Pañchākshara mantra*. But they do not receive Tāntric *dīkshā*, nor do they interdine with those Tāntric Brāhmaṇas who are at present only priests in Śiva temples; the latter are always considered as low in the scale of Brāhmaṇas. The multiplication of images, both Śaiva and Vaishṇava, is due to the Tāntrikas who have devoted a great deal of attention to the description of images in their Tantras. The Vaidikas do not appear to have possessed so large a number of images for worship at the earlier stages at any rate.

Saiva dikshas.

The one great peculiarity of all the *avaidik* Śaivas is their *dīkshā*. In performing this ceremony they need different shaped *kuṇḍas* or receptacles for fire and *maṇḍalas* or drawings, all of which are described in their works in great detail. They also invoke Śiva in *kumbhas* or vessels (filled with water), and perform different kinds of *hōmas* or fire offerings. It is their faith that he who has not received the *Śaiva dīkshā* does not attain *mōksha* or liberation. They believe that Śiva personally presents Himself before the disciple in the form of an *āchāryā* for granting him *Śiva-dīkshā*. This *dīkshā* ceremony varies with the *recipient*. He who has renounced family life and is expectant of gaining *mōksha* by constantly adoring his *guru* is the fittest person for *dīkshā*. For attaining this state of mind he requires the divine grace of Śakti. The bestowal of this grace by *Śakti* on the aspirant for *dīkshā* is technically known as *Śakti-pātam*. The grace of *Śakti* is of four kinds, instantaneous, rapid, slow and very slow, and the *dīkshās* to be given differ with the modes, noted above, in which the grace of Śakti is received. To him who gets this grace very slowly, that kind of

Samaya diksha.

dīkshā called the *samayadīkshā* should be given. In this, the *guru* should invoke through *mantras* Śiva in his own person and perform several ceremonies; the *śishya*, with flowers in hand kept in the *añjali* pose, is taken out, blind-folded, so that he might not see sinners, round the *maṇḍapa* wherein is set up the *kumbha* or vessel in which is invoked Śiva, and after a certain number of rounds are gone through, his eyes are opened to light upon the *kumbha*, which he is asked to worship with the flowers in his hands. Before he begins the worship, the *guru*, considering his own right hand as *tējōrūpa* or the embodiment of enlightenment, and also as the hand of Śiva himself, and uttering the *mūla-mantra*, should place it on the head of his *śishya*. By this act of placing the hand which is the embodiment of enlightenment, first on the head, then over the whole body of the disciple the *pāśas*, bonds, the darkness of ignorance which enveloped him, are dispelled. After this ceremony the *guru* directs the *śishya* to throw the flowers which he holds in his hands on the *kumbha*. The disciple shall receive his *dīkshā-nāma* or the name bestowed on him on his initiation, according as the flowers fall on the top or on any one of the four cardinal directions round the *kumbha*, which correspond to the position of the Īśāna, Tatpurusha, etc., aspects of Śiva; the suffix, Śiva or Dēva, is to be added to the names according as the disciple is a Brāhmaṇa or a Kshatriya, and *gaṇa* if he is a Vaiśya or a Śūdra. Thus, if the flowers fall on the side of Īśāna, the disciple should be called Īśānaśiva if he is a Brāhmaṇa, Īśānadēva if a Kshatriya, and Īśānagaṇa if a Vaiśya or a Śūdra. If the disciple is a female, she should be called Īśāna or Īśāśiva-śakti, Īśadēvaśakti, Īśagaṇaśakti according as, she is of the Brāhmaṇa, Kshatriya, or, Vaiśya or Śūdra caste. Those that have undergone this *dīkshā* are known as *Samayis* and will attain Rudrapada. To these are prescribed the performance of duties contained in the *charyāpāda* of the *āgamas*. The description given above of the *Samaya-dīkshā* reads like a page from the ceremonials of the Freemasons of the present day; the claims of freemasonry to remote antiquity do not after all appear to be a pretension. It is perhaps an echo of a really ancient institution, like the ancient Āgamānta Śaivaism, that it is after all an Eastern institution engrafted upon Western soil.

The second kind of *dīkshā* is called the *Viśēsha dīkshā* and is conferred upon those to whom the grace of Śakti comes more rapidly than in the previous case. In all its details, it is similar to the *dīkshā* ceremony already described; but the *guru* in this case is supposed to join the soul of the *śishya* from the *Māya-garbhā* to *Śakti-garbha*, and is made to contemplate in his mind on the external union of Vāgīśvarī with Vāgīśvara. After this the *guru* teaches his disciple the *samayāchāras* or the creeds of his faith. They are: abstinence from reviling Śiva, Śivaśāstras, Śivāgni, and the *guru*, from crossing even the shadow of these and from eating oneself or presenting to others for eating the food offered to Śiva: doing *pūjā* to Śivāgni and to the *guru* to the end of one's life and so on. He who has received the *viśēshadīkshā* would attain after death the Īśvara-pada; he is known during his lifetime as *putraka*. These are enjoined to observe the ceremonies and duties prescribed in the *charyā* and the *kṛiyāpādas* of the *āgamas*. The conduct and duties of the life of the *Samayi* are called the *dāsamārga*. From these descriptions of the *samayis* and *putrakas*, it appears to be clear that those who collect flowers and knit them into garlands for the temple services, that is, people of the class of *Paṇḍārams* etc., are to be considered as *Samayis* or *Tādars* (Dāsas), while those that go by the distinct appellation of Piḷḷais or Piḷḷaimārs, as *putrakās*.

The *dīkshā* prescribed for those to whom the grace of Śakti comes instantaneously or rapidly is called *Nirvāṇa dīkshā*.

In this kind of *dīkshā*, the fiction is that the bonds (*pāśas*) are cut off even when the *śishya* is in his material body; for this purpose, a few strands of string are taken and suspended from the tuft of his hair to the toe of the right foot; in these strings, the *chaitanya* (or energy) of the *śishya* is invoked and the *guru* conceives in his mind as having undergone, even then, the several births which the *śishya* has otherwise to take to absolve himself from the various bonds known as *mala*, *māyā*, *karma* and *kalā*, and then cuts the strings into pieces. To check the further growth of these *pāśas* or bonds, the *guru* throws the bits of strings into the fire. After these ceremonies are over, the soul of the *śishya* is believed to have become equal to Śiva in purity. Another formality is also gone through to establish this identity of the soul with Śiva, namely, the *guru* yokes on to the soul of the *śishya*, the six qualities which distinguish Śiva, namely *Sarvajñatva*, (omniscience), *pūrna-kāmatva* (filled with love) *anādi-jñana* (beginningless knowledge), *apāraśakti* (unbounded power) *svādhīnatva* (perfect freedom) and undiminishing power. There are still a few other minor ceremonies belonging to the *dīkshā* which need not be detailed here.

Those that have undergone the *nirvāṇa-dīkshā* are divided into two classes, the *sādhakas* and the *āchāryas*, and for being called by these names they should once again undergo the ceremony of anointment as *sādhakas* and *āchāryas*. The *sādhakas* are supposed to have attained the eight *siddhis* or powers, beginning with *aṇimā*, so well-known through the Yōga system ; the *sādhakas* are entitled to observe the *nityakarmas* or daily observances such as bath, *pūjā*, *japa*, *dhyāna* and *hōma*, and *kāmyakarmas* only ; whereas, the *āchāryas* are entitled to perform, in addition to these, *naimittika* ceremonies such as performing the *dīkshā* ceremony on others, and *pratishṭhā* ceremony or consecrating images.

The above described *nirvāṇa-dīkshā* is of two classes, respectively known as *lōkadharmiṇi* or *bhautiki* and *Śivadharmiṇi* or *naishthiki*. Those that have undergone the latter or the *Śivadharmiṇi dīkshā* should wear the tuft of hair on the top of the head, covering the *brahma-randhra*, whereas those that have undergone the former or the *lōkadharmiṇi dīkshā* need not cut off the hair.

The Śaivas may observe both the Vaidika and the Śaiva duties, but if some of the former are opposed to the teachings of the Śaiva *tantras*, they should be abandoned. Those that have undergone the *bhautiki* and *naishṭhiki dīkshās* may even abandon the Vaidik *sandhyā* ceremony but never the Śaiva *sandhyā*.

The *Āgamas* are always divided into four parts, the *Kṛiyāpāda*, the *Charyāpāda*, the *Yōgapāda* and the *Jñānapāda* the study and observance of the rules laid down in one, two, three or all four of these are enjoined upon the *Samayis*, the *putrakas*, the *bhautikis* and the *naishṭhikis* respectively. The paths pursued by these are also known respectively by the names *dāsamārga*, *putramārga*, *sahamārga* and the *sanmārga*; that is, the persons who have been initiated in the *samayi* and other *dīkshās* conduct themselves towards the Lord as a servant, a son, a friend or as the Lord himself. The paths prescribed are of varying grades suitable to souls at various stages of religious evolution.

These *dīkshās* were described in some detail, in order to give the readers an idea of the religious ceremonials which are common to all sects of the Śaivas; it is meant also to give scope for the comparative study of the religious ceremonial institutions of India and of other countries, more especially with Freemasonry. As the philosophy of this branch of Śaivaism is dealt with elaborately by various authors elsewhere, it need not be given here.

The Pasupatas.

The Pāśupatas are the next important class of Śaivas. According to Rāmānujāchārya it included the Kāḷāmukhas the Kāpālas, and the Āgamānta Śaivas. There is some justification for Rāmānuja including all the four under one name, the Pāśupata religion; for all these four sectarians called the *Jīvātman*, *paśu* and the *paramātman*, Pati. The Āgamānta Śaivas also class these as *agachchamayams* or sects included in Śaivaism. As regards the antiquity and history of the Pāśupata sect, little is known. In later times the Pāśupata sect is known as the Lakuḷisa Pāśupata or the Pāśupata sect founded by Lakuḷīśvara, who is considered as an incarnation of Śiva himself. An attempt has been made by Dr. Fleet to fix the age of Lakuḷīśvara, the founder of the Pāśupata sect. It is a matter for surprise that even such a circumspect scholar as Dr. Fleet has, perhaps in his desire to arrive at some conclusion, proceeded upon baseless premises which have naturally led him to incorrect results. Because the name Lakuḷīśvara-paṇḍita occurs in an inscription at Mēlpāḍi and in another at Baḷigāmi, and because tradition asserts that he propagated his faith in Kāyārōhaṇa in N. India, Dr. Fleet concludes that Lakuḷīśvara, the founder of the sect which goes by his name, began his activities first in Mēlpāḍi, wherefrom he drifted on to Baḷigāmi and then eventually settled down at Kāyārōhaṇa in Northern India, and that he lived in the first quarter of the eleventh century A. D. The two individuals bearing the name Lakuḷīśvara Paṇḍita, mentioned in the two inscriptions referred to above were two distinct personages and were named after the founder of their faith; the conclusion of Dr. Fleet is untenable for the following reasons. Śaṅkarāchārya, whose age is believed to be the last quarter of the eighth century, reviews the Pāśupata philosophy in his Śārīraka Bhāshya. Says he, "The Māhēśvaras (Śaivas) maintain that the five categories, *viz*, effect (*kārya*) cause (*kāraṇa*), union (*yōga*), ritual (*vidhi*) and the end of pain (*duhkhānta*), were taught by the Lord Paśupati (Śiva) to the end of breaking the bonds of the animals (*paśu*, *i.e.*, the souls). Paśupati is, according to them, the Lord, the operative cause." In his masterly treatise on the different systems of philosophy that were in existence in his time, Vidyāraṇya gives the same five categories given above as those held by the Lakuḷīśa

Pāśupatas ; the later author, Madhusūdana Sarasvati, also reiterates the same statement in his *Prasthānabhēda.** The Pāśupata sect as known by the name Lakuḷiśa Pāśupata is older than Śaṅkara at least, or perhaps even as old as the *Ātharvaśirasōpanishad.* The authors of the famous Dēvāram hymns have sung the praises of the Śiva temples at Nāgapaṭṭaṇam (Negapatam) and Kumbhakōṇam, which were known even in their times by the name of Kāyārōhaṇa or Kārōṇa, so named evidently after the more famous place of that name in Northern India. The age of these hymnists, is settled to be the middle of the seventh century. This fact pushes the limit of the age of Lakuḷiśa by one more century. Hence, Lakuḷiśa the founder of the faith, should not be confounded with his namesakes of Mēlpāḍi and Baḷigāmi, nor can his date be taken as the first quarter of the eleventh century. The Kāḷāmukhas also appear to be a subdivision of the Pāśupatas, as we have seen above. To substantiate this, we have not only the authority of Rāmānuja, but also that of some others. The Śaivāgamas sometimes divide Śaivism into Śaiva, Pāśupata, Sōmasiddhānta and Lākuḷa ; and in other places divide Śaivas into Śaiva, Pāśupata,

---

*The *Uttara-Kāmikāgama* also states that *Lākuḷa* had five categories and they are the same as given above.

Kāpālika and Kāḷāmukha. In the above groupings we see that the first two sects are identical in both cases; we learn from the *Prabōdhachandrōdayam* that Sōmasiddhānta is the authoritative text-book of the Kāpālikas and the remaining Lākuḷa may be inferred to be the same as Kāḷāmukha. In praising certain Kāḷāmukha *gurus*, the Baḷigāmi inscriptions use the phrase "a very Nakuḷīśvara in the knowledge of the Siddhāntas", which clearly proves that the Kāḷāmukhas were identical with Lakuḷīśa Pāśupatas.*

---

*Regarding the antiquity of the Śaiva teacher Lakuḷīśa and the faith that he was an *avatāra* of Śiva, the following may be quoted:—

'महादेवावताराणि कलौ श्रुणुत सुव्रताः ।

....

महायामो मुनिः शूली डिण्डमुण्डीश्वरः स्वयम् ।
सहिष्णुः सोमशर्म्मा च नकुलीश्वर एव च ॥ and
वैवस्वतेऽन्तरे शम्भोरवतारास्त्रिशूलिनः ।
अष्टविंशतिराख्याता ह्यन्ते कलियुगे प्रभोः ।
तीर्थे कायावतारे स्याद्देवेशो नकुलीश्वरः ।

Kūrmapurāṇa, Chap. 53, Vv. 1, 9 & 10.

दिव्यां मेरुगुहां पुण्यां त्वया सार्द्धं च विष्णुना ।
भविष्यामि तदा ब्रह्मँल्लकुली नाम नामतः ॥ ४७ ॥
कायावतार इत्येवं सिद्धक्षेत्रं परं तदा ।
भविष्यति सुविख्यातं यावद्भूमिर्धरिष्यति ॥ ४८ ॥

The tenets of the Lakuḷīśa Pāśupatas as we gather from the *Sarvadarśana-Saṅgraha*, stated very briefly, are as follows:—

The end of pain, their fifth category, is of two sorts the *anātmaka mōksha* and the *sātmaka moksha.* Of these, the former is defined as the absolute freedom from pain. The possession of Kṛiyāśakti and Jñānaśakti, which are the attributes of Paramēśvara and which are described below, is called *sātmakamōksha.* Perception of even the smallest, the most distant matters, hearing of every kind of sound, being well versed in all *śāstras*, the possession of these and similar powers is called Jñānaśakti. The accomplishment of every object, quickly assuming every form according to one's own desire, is known as Kṛiyāśakti. These two Śaktis constitute, as stated just now, the *sātmaka mōksha*.

In every other system a *kārya* or effect is defined as that which follows a *kāraṇa* or cause;

तत्रापि मम ते शिष्या भविष्यन्ति तपस्विनः ।
कुशिकश्चैव गर्गश्च मित्रः कौरुष्य एव च ॥ ४९ ॥
योगिनो ब्राह्मणा वेदपारगा ऊर्ध्वरेतसः ।
प्राप्य माहेश्वरं योगं गमिष्यन्ति शिवं पुरम् ॥ ५० ॥

Śivapurāṇa, Tritīya-Śatarudra-Samhitā, Chap. 5.

Also compare pages 190 and 191, Director General of Archæology's Annual for the year 1906-07.

the Pāśupatas call all dependent objects as effect; in conformity with this their definition of *kārya*, they bring *Jīvātman* or *paśu*, which they admit as eternal, under the category of *kārya* because it is dependent upon the *paramātman* or *Pati*. The Being who is endowed with the powers of creation, destruction and protection, the Lord Paramēśvara, is known to their philosophy as the *kāraṇa*. His attributes are Jñānaśakti and Kṛiyāśakti, which are eternally with him, not as are acquired after a stage by the perfected human souls.

The Pāśupatas believe also in divine dispensation which need not be based upon the good or evil *karma* of the soul.

The category called *Yōga* or union of the soul with Pati, may be attained in two ways. In the first, it is attained through *japa*, *dhyāna*, and other *karmas;* while in the second by exercising strict control over the senses. By this *Yōga* the two kinds of *mōksha* mentioned above could be obtained.

Vidhi or the rules of conduct of the Pāśupatas is the most interesting part of their religion. Bathing their bodies thrice a day in ashes, lying down on ashes, making noise like *ahā ahā*, singing loudly the praises of their god, dancing either according to the science of dancing or in any manner, curling the tongue and roaring like bulls,—this noice is called *huḍukkāra* or noise like *huḍu huḍu*, making prostrations and circumambulation, repeating the names of Śiva—all these constitute their *vrata* or daily observances. But these strange acts are strictly forbidden to be practised in places where there are other persons present. Besides these, the Pāśupatas are advised to behave actually like mad men. For instance, pretending to be asleep when not actually sleeping, begging for food, shaking the limbs as when attacked by paralysis, walking like one with rheumatic pain in his legs, or like a lame man, exhibiting signs of lust at the sight of women, doing other acts befitting lunatics such as making meaningless noise—these are enjoined upon the Pāśupatas. To get rid of fastidiousness, they are enjoined to beg for food, eat the remnants of the dishes of others and do similar objectionable acts.*

---

*It appears quite probable that this *vidhi* of the Pāśupatas is responsible for the origin and existence of obscene sculptures in Hindu temples. In the majority of cases, such sculpture consists of the figure of a stark naked male with his *membrum virile* erect, standing with his legs kept separated from each other and with his hands held in the *añjali* pose over his head, and his head always covered with long *jaṭās*, hanging down on either side. In front of this figure is its counterpart,

The Kalamukhas and Somasiddhantins.

The Śaivāgamas arrange the Śaiva sects in the following order of superiority, namely, the Śaivas, the Pāśupatas, the Sōmasiddhāntins and the Lākuḷas. Again we learn that the Kauḷas worship the *ādharachakra*, the *Kshapaṇakas* the actual *yōni* and the *trikōṇas* (or triangular *yantras*), and the *Kāpālikas* and *Digambaras* both the objects worshipped by the first mentioned two sects. The various sects of Śaivas hold the view that as there is no difference between one animal and another, there is none whatsoever between man and man and *dīkshā* might be given to all alike. The

---

a female one, whose clothing is represented as slipping down the waist, thereby leaving the *pudendum* exposed. It is more than certain that the matted haired naked man could represent no other than a Śaiva devotee belonging to one of the indecent sects of the Śaiva religion, putting to practice the rules of the *vidhi* taught by his philosophy.

In almost all the later additions to more ancient temples and in all the temples built after the 14th century A.D., one could meet with figures of men in all manner of capering attitudes—with ill-kept, but amusing faces and with the body twisted and bent in most astounding postures: one such is reproduced on Pl. 69 in his *Viśvakarma* by Dr. Ānanda-kumārasvāmi. This sort of sculpture recognised by the name of *kōṇāṅgis* has also its origin in the *vidhi* of the Pāśupata philosophy.

Kāḷāmukhas appear to be so called because they marked their forehead with a black streak, and they are said to be born of *nara* (human) and *rākshasa* (demoniacal) parents.

The Kapalikas.

The Kāpālikas appear to be also an ancient but an extremist sect of Śaivas. They have rites and ceremonies which are more revolting than those of the Kāḷāmukhas. About the various Śaiva sects Rāmānuja says:—"The *Sūtras* now declare that, for the same reasons, the doctrine of Paśupati also has to be disregarded. The adherents of this view belong to the four classes—Kāpālas, Kāḷāmukhas, Pāśupatas and Śaivas. All of them hold fanciful theories of Reality which are in conflict with the Vēda, and invent various means for attaining happiness in this life and the next. They maintain the general material and the operative cause to be distinct, and the latter cause to be constituted by Paśupati. They further hold the wearing of the six *mudrā* badges and the like to be means to accomplish the highest end of man.

"Thus the Kāpālas say, 'He who knows the true nature of the six *mudrās*, who understands the highest *mudrā*, meditating upon himself as in the position called *bhagāsana*, reaches *Nirvāṇa*. The necklace, the golden ornament, the ear-ring, the head-jewel, ashes, and the sacred thread are called the six *mudrās*. He whose body is marked with these is not born here again. Similarly, the Kāḷāmukhas teach that the means of obtaining all desired results in this world as well as the next are constituted by certain practices such as using a skull as a drinking vessel, smearing oneself with ashes of the dead body, eating the flesh of such a body, carrying a heavy stick, setting up a liquor-jar and using it as a platform for making offerings to the Gods, and the like. 'A bracelet made of Rudrāksha-seeds on the arm, matted hair on the head, a skull, smearing oneself with ashes etc.,'—all this is well known from the sacred writings of the Śaivas. They also hold that by some special ceremonial performance men of different castes may become Brāhmaṇas and reach the highest *āśrama*: 'by merely entering on the initiatory ceremony (*dīkshā*) a man becomes a Brāhmaṇa at once; by undertaking the *Kāpāla* rite a man becomes at once an ascetic."

We learn a little more about the Kāpālikas from stray mention made of them in a number of books. For instance, Krishṇamiśra in his *Prabōdhachandrōdaya* introduces a Kāpālika as a character in that drama who describes himself in the following words: " My necklace and ornaments consist of human bones; I live in the ashes of the dead and eat my food in human skulls. I look with my eyes made keen with the ointment of *yōga* and I believe that though the different parts of the world are different, yet the whole is not different from God. O! Digambara! listen to our rites: after fasting we drink liquor from the skulls of Brāhmaṇas; our sacrificial fires are kept up with the brains and lungs of men which are mixed up with their flesh, and the offerings by which we appease our terrific God are human victims covered with gushing blood from the horrible cut on their throats. I contemplate on the lord of Bhavānī, the mighty God who creates, preserves and destroys the fourteen worlds whose glory is revealed in the Vēdas as well as in his deeds." The *Śaṅkara-vijaya* of Anantānandagiri states that when *Śaṅkara* went to Ujjayini, the foremost men of all the sects living there came for a religious disputation with him. Among them one sect of Kāpālikas had the following characteristic feature and doctrines. They wore *sphaṭika* (crystal beads), the *arddha-chandra* (an ornament shaped like the crescent moon) and the *jaṭā* (or matted heir). Their God is Bhairava, the author of creation, protection and destruction; they believe that all other gods are subservient to him. Bhairava has eight different aspects namely

Asitāṅga, Ruru, Chaṇḍa, Krōdha, Unmatta Bhairava, Kāpāla, Bhīshma and Saṁhāra-Bhairava corresponding to Vishṇu, Brahmā, Sūrya, Rudra, Indra, Chandra, Yama and the Supreme Being respectively. This class of Kāpālikas was taken by Śaṅkarāchārya, states Anantānandagiri, into the fold of Brahmanism. But another subject of Kāpālikas headed by one Unmatta-Bhairava came to wrangle with Śaṅkara; he had smeared his body with the ashes of the dead and wore a garland of skulls; his forehead was marked with a streak of black stuff. The whole of the hair of his head was turned into *jaṭās*. He wore a *kaṭisūtra* and a *kaupīna* consisting of tiger's skin and carried in his left hand a skull and in the right a bell. He was calling out the names of Śambhu, Bhairava and Kāḷīśa. He said that their *mōksha* consisted in joining Bhairava after death. Śaṅkara rejected this class of Kāpālas as incorrigible. Living with one's wife happily in this world as does Chandraśēkhara (Śiva) with his consort Pārvatī in heaven, is also considered by the Kāpālikas as *mōkshā*. It is certain that this sect of Śaivas were freely indulging in human sacrifices, for there are literary evidences to this effect. Bhavabhūti introduces in his drama *Mālatī-Mādhava* a Kāpālika who, for having attained *mantra-siddhi*, attempted to sacrifice Mālatī to his god. Vādirajasūri in his *Yaśōdharakāvya* describes the preparations for two human sacrifices for which two pretty little children were decoyed and taken to the altar but fortunately saved from the catastrophe.

Kṛishṇamiśra says that the Digambaras and the Kāpālikas quitted all other countries and gradually retired to the Māḷava and Ābhira countries, which are inhabited by low class men (*pāmaras*).

The Śaivagamas inform us that the Śaivas worship Śiva in the aspect of Tāṇḍava-bhūshaṇa; the Pāśupatas, Śiva smeared with ashes and wearing *jaṭāmakuṭa*, the Mahāvratas, Śiva wearing a garland of bones; the Kāḷāmukhas, Śiva wearing *sphaṭikā* and *putradīpa* (?) beads; the Vāmāchāras, Śiva wearing the sacred thread and carrying fire and the Bhairavas, Śiva carrying *ḍamaru* and wearing anklets; and that all these aspects of Śiva should have three eyes.

From all that has been said of the various sects of Śaivas the following conclusion about Śaivaism naturally suggests itself. The prototype of all the *ghōra* forms of Śaivaism is the personality of Śiva himself; dancing and singing in a wild manner on the burning ground and smearing himself with the ashes of the dead and adorning himself with the skulls and bones of the dead; or going about naked in the streets of householder ṛishis and tempting their womenfolk, living in bliss also with his own consort; or performing severe austerities; wearing his hair in *jāṭas;* drinking and eating from human skulls; killing, maiming and otherwise destroying animal life—all these acts of Śiva were closely followed by such sects as the Kāpālas, the Kāḷāmukhas and the Vāmāchāras. These sects which considered living in close imitation of Śiva and who considered living happily with women in this life *mōkshā* or bliss, are perhaps really old. Their teachings afforded ease and pleasure, indulgence in flesh-food, drinking liquor and promiscuous intercourse; and at a time when, as a result of the preaching of the Buddha and Mahāvīra, the Vaidikas practically gave up flesh and liquor, some of its members with a taste for lower passions not finding their surroundings congenial to their tastes might have turned renegades and joined the ranks of the Śaivas, as we hear from the *Varāhapuraṇa* and the *Sūta-saṁhitā*, and have undergone the *dīkshā* and other rites peculiar to Śaivaism. This state of moral depravity attended with conduct unfit for any society could not be tolerated by others and in the long run by the members of even the Śaiva sects themselves. Therefore, after the fresh glamour passed away, these degraded Brāhmaṇas apparently set themselves to cleanse their faith of its filth, evolve a system of philosophy for it and a line of conduct for its adherents and claim a purer status equal to or identical with that of the Vaidikas. In this evolved Śaivaism, also known as Śuddha Śaivaism, we do not meet with any one of the evils complained of. Those that persisted in it, the Kāpālas and the Kāḷāmukhas, have gone to the wall in the contest and are lost for ever.

The Vaidikas at first never paid so much attention to the details of temple building, setting up in them of innumerable images and performing pompous ceremonials, but had one or two small images in their own houses their *ishṭa dēvatās* and *kula dēvatās*, and they were enjoined to meditate in silence upon the Supreme Brahman as residing in the image; they took to resorting to temples and attending to elaborate ceremonials held in them at a later stage when the *avaidika* cults were purged of their objectionable practices. And when the non-Āryan Śiva was beyond contention welded on the Āryan Rudra or Agni, even *liṅga* worship was adopted by the Vaidikas as identical with the worship of Rudra or Agni and at the present time all Vaidika or Smārta Brāhmaṇas are worshipping the *liṅga* and are even seen dancing and making *huḍukkāra* noise while worshipping in temples, a strange survival of the Pāśupata customs.

The orgies and revels in lascivious acts was also the characteristic feature in all countries in which phallic worship was practised; in Greece, in Alexandria, in fact the whole of the Mediterranean Coast the revelries differed in no way from those in existence among the early Indian Śaiva sects. The initiation and other ceremonies belonging to these Priaptic cults, might possibly have been refined by such intellectual and moral men as Socrates, Pythogoras and others, and very likely the reformed cults have descended to or been copied by the modern Freemasons.

We have till now been discussing the earlier forms of Śaivaism; but India has not been idle since then. Newer sects of Śaivaism sprang from time to time and gathered a large following. Two such stand out prominently, namely the Vīraśaivas of Southern India and the Pratyabhijñas of Kashmere. The former was started by Basava, a Brāhman who occupied a high position in the Court of the Kaḷachūri, king Bijjaṇa or Bijjaḷa. Basava was born of Brāhmaṇa parents but refused to undergo the *Upanayana* ceremony, proclaiming that he was a special worshipper of Śiva and that he was born to destroy the caste system. Basava taught the adoration of the *liṅga* as the chief feature of his system; his followers were taught the importance of veneration to the *guru;* the *liṅga* and the *Saṅgha.* They were also taught that, as soon as a Śaiva dies, he becomes one with Mahēśvara; child-marriage was discountenanced and post-puberty marriage was the general rule among them; widow re-marriage was also permitted. The Liṅgāyatas or the followers of Basava carry about their person a small *liṅga* either encased in a silver casket and hung about the neck or tied up in a silk cloth which is bound round the right arm or on the neck. Under no circumstances should this *liṅga* leave the person of the wearer; it is like the *yajñōpavīta* of the Brāhmaṇa never to be removed during the life-time of the wearer. The Liṅgayatas are supposed to have no caste distinction, but there are among them Brāhmaṇas who are known by the name of Ārādhyas; nor is an Ayyanōru (their priestly class) known to interdine with low caste Jaṅgamas (or congregation). They have a number of curious customs among them which it is not possible to deal with here.

The Pratyabhijña school had its origin, as we have already stated, in Kashmere. It appears that the most important of their religious works are five in number; of these the *Pratyabhijña-sūtras* is the oldest and is said to have been composed by Utpalāchārya, the son (or disciple) of Udayakara. The basis of the work was the *Śiva-drishṭi śāstra* of Sōmānandanātha. The Pratyabhijña system is believed to be an easy and new system of religious philosophy. Though comparatively new, the Pratyabhijña school has its foundation in older works. The great Abhinavaguptāchārya has written two commentaries on the *sūtras*, which are known as the *Laghu-Pratyabhijñavimarśani* and the *Bṛihat-Pratyabhijña-vimarśani*. From the internal evidences available in the various works, it is inferable that this school became prominent in the 10th century A.D.

The power of recognising an object originally known to us but which had been lost sight of for long is called *Pratyabhijña*. According to the followers of this school, Paramātman or Paramēśvara is that which exists always and is pervading everywhere, is absolutely free and is the embodiment of energy and of blissful light. There is no distinction between Paramēśvara and the Jīvātman. But the latter is covered by the darkness of *māyā*. If one realises, by the help of his *guru*, his own omniscience, omnipotence etc., he recognises in him the Paramātman. This recognition by the

Jivātman of the Paramātman as identical with itself is illustrated by an example. A husband is separated from his wife. The wife learns everything about her husband and *vice versa* by means of news of each brought to the other. But when the husband returns after a very long time and stands before his wife, she is unable to recognise him and till she is able to realise in him her husband, she is not conscious of the presence of her husband near her. Since the Pratyabhijña philosophy does not involve severe practices like *prāṇāyāma* it is held by Abhinavaguptāchārya to be an easy religion. All castes are equally admitted into it. Its categories and their philosophy are also easy enough though unnecessary to be detailed here.

Regarding the caste marks of the various schools of Śaivas, Anantānandagiri says as follows: —The *Śaivas* make marks of the *liṅga* on both the shoulders; the *Raudras* mark their forehead with the *triśūla;* the *Ugras* mark their shoulders with the *ḍamaru;* the *Bhaṭṭas* mark their forehead with the *liṅga;* the *Jaṅgamas* mark their chest with the *triśūla* and wear on it the *liṅga* and the *Pāśupatas* mark the forehead, the two shoulders, the chest and the navel with the *liṅga.*

ŚIVA.

ŚIVA.

ONE of the most interesting chapters in Hindu Mythology is the history of Śiva, the god of destruction among the Hindu Trinity. In the *Ṛigvēda*, the *Vājasanēyi-saṁhitā* of the *White Yajur-vēda* and in the *Atharvaṇa-vēda*, the word *Śiva*, meaning the auspicious, occurs as an epithet of Rudra. It is only Rudra, (and not Śiva) who is praised in all hymns; he is represented in these hymns as a malevolent deity causing death and disease among men and cattle and is therefore specially prayed to by the hymnists for allaying his wrath towards them, sparing them their families and cattle, and attacking and damaging their enemies and their belongings. The physical description of Rudra is found in a number of hymns in great detail. For instance, in some places he is said to be tawny in colour and in others of a very fair complexion, with a beautiful chin, wearing golden ornaments, youthful and having spirally braided hair on his head. He

Early references to Rudra.

carries in his hands a bow and arrows and is described, in some hymns, as wielding the thunderbolt. He is, throughout the Vēdic period, identified with Agni and is also said to have given birth, by his contact with Pṛishṇi (the earth), the Maruts (the winds). In the *Atharvaṇa-vēda* it is stated, that "Bhava (Rudra) rules the sky, Bhava rules the earth and Bhava hath filled the vast atmosphere"; in the same work we come across the names Bhava, Sarva, Sahasra-bāhu, Mahādēva, Paśupati, Rudra the slayer of Ardhaka (the Andhaka of the Purāṇic period), Ugra and Īśāna used as synonyms of Rudra; these names are also found in the *Śatarudrīya* along with Aghōra, Giriśa, Nīlagrīva, Kapardin, Sabhāpati, Gaṇapati, Sēnāni, Bhīma, Sitikaṇṭha, Śambhu and Śaṅkara. It might be remarked here that all the names given above are applied at the present time to Śiva-Rudra, who is a later addition to the Hindu triad. In the *Śatapatha-Brāhmaṇa* we learn "Agni is a god. These are his names: Śarva, as the eastern people call him, Bhava, as the Bāhikas call him, Paśūṇāmpati, Rudra and Agni. The names other than Agni are ungentle (*aśānta*), Agni is his gentlest designation (*śāntatma*)."

From the descriptions of Rudra given above it is patent that Agni, who is the same as Rudra, had his abode in the sky as the sun, in the atmosphere as the lightning and on the earth as fire; in other words, the sky, the atmosphere and the earth give birth to Agni in his triple aspect of the sun, the lightning, and fire; hence he receives the name Tryambaka or Three-mothered. By the heat of the sun received by the earth winds are produced, a physical fact well-known even to school-boys. It is this natural phenomenon, the production of winds on the surface of the earth by sun's heat, that is poetically expressed in the Vēdic hymns as the sun begetting on the earth the Maruts. The winds cause the clouds to accumulate in the atmosphere and lightning and storm follow next; all these phenomena are traceable to Agni or Rudra. The stormy winds, the dark masses of clouds with flashing lightning in their midst are all sufficiently terrifying in their effect, and Rudra or Agni who is the cause of all these fearful phenomena is naturally treated as a terrific and malevolent deity always requiring propitiation. The sufferings caused to man and beast by storms, thunder and rain should naturally have induced the Vēdic bards to have attempted to appease the wrath of this fearful deity and to protect themselves and their possessions by praises and offerings.

References to Rudra in the Mahabharata.

The identity of Agni and Rudra also appears from the Mahābhārata. In narrating the birth of Skanda, it is stated in the Vana-parvan, that Svāha, the wife of Agni, assumed on six consecutive days the forms of the wives of six out of the seven *ṛishis* and enjoyed the company of her husband, who had previously abandoned her and retired to the forest, because he could not succeed in securing for himself the company of the wives of the *ṛishis* with whom he had fallen in love. The seed of Agni gathered on the six days by Svāha was deposited in a pit and covered with *kuśa* grass. On the sixth day the seed assumed the form of Kumāra (that is, Skanda). Again, later on, it is also said that Rudra, who was dallying with his consort Umā for a long time, was prayed to by the gods to assume his other functions; he let drop his seed on the earth. Agni was asked to take it in and develope it, but its burning effect was so great that he could not bear it; he dropped it in the river Gaṅgā and Skanda was born therefrom. From these two statements, the only conclusion possible is that Rudra, who was the same as Agni was the father of Skanda.

From occupying the minor position of Agni in the Vēdic period, Rudra emerges into one of the supreme deities in the Purāṇic period; and he is often found to claim superiority over Vishṇu and Brahmā. In the Purāṇic period also Rudra retains his attributes as the destroyer and the terrific; he is described as "assuming the forms of the gods Vishṇu and Brahmā, of men, of *bhūtas* and other beings, of beasts and of birds; he is the soul of the universe; and pervades through it; he dwells in the heart of all creatures and knows all their desires; he carries a discus, a trident, a club, an axe and a sword; he wears a girdle of serpents, ear-ornaments composed of serpents and an *Yajnōpavīta* of serpents; he laughs, sings and dances in ecstacy, and plays on a number of musical instruments; he leaps, gapes and weeps and makes others weep; speaks like a mad man or a drunkard, as also in sweet voice............He dallies with the daughters and wives of the *ṛishis;* he has erect hair, looks obscene in his nakedness and has an excited look." "Rudra has braided hair and matted locks, frequents cemeteries and performs awful rites; he is now a mild *yōgi* and is also very terrible. He is said to possess in every age the nature of Nārāyaṇa, that is, his *tāmasic* nature." Such descriptions form the basis of the several *purāṇic* legends

Rudra in the Puranic period.

regarding Śiva, as also of the various images of this deity. For instance, Śiva is represented as dancing in an ecstacy; he is then known by the name of Naṭarāja; as a naked figure engaged in begging for cooked rice, when he is called the Bhikshāṭana-mūrthi; and so forth. We are therefore concerned immediately with the various aspects of Śiva described in the *Purāṇas*.

Birth of Rudra in the Brahmanas.

The birth of Rudra is given in the *Śatapatha-brāhmaṇa* as follows: "Prajāpati (the lord of beings), who is identified with the Sun and also the year, (the beings of whom he is lord being the seasons), desired to have a son; he consorted, for that purpose, with Ushas and a son (Kumāra) was born. As soon as he was born the boy wept. The father asked why he wept. He replied he had got no name to take away the evil from him. Prajāpati gave him the name Rudra. Inasmuch as he gave him the name, Agni became his form, for Rudra is Agni; he was Rudra because he wept (*arōdīt*, from *rud*, to weep). The boy said 'I am greater than one who does not exist, give me another name'. Prajāpati replied 'thou art Śarva'. Thus he obtained from Prajāpati the names Rudra, Śarva, Paśupati, Ugra, Aśani, Bhava, Mahāndēva, and Īāśna—eight names which are associated respectively with the *tattvas* of *agni*, (the fire), *jala* (the water), the plants, *vāyu* (the winds), *vidyut* (the lightning), *parjanya* (the rain), *chandramas* (the moon) and *āditya* (the sun). These are the eights forms of Agni and Kumāra is the ninth. This is the threefoldness (*trivṛitta*) of Agni. Since there are eight forms of Agni and the Gāyatri metre has eight syllables, men say 'Agni pertains to Gāyatri'. This boy Kumāra entered into the forms. Men do not see Agni as a boy: it is these forms that they see: for he entered into these forms." The same story is found in the *Sāṅkhāyana* and the *Kaushītaki-Brāhmaṇas*. This story forms the foundation for all the later accounts given in the Purāṇas of the birth of Rudra, as also of the Ashṭa-mūrtīśvaras of the *Śaivāgamas*.

In the Puranas.

The account of the birth of Ṛudra as found in the *Vishṇu-purāṇa* which is almost identical with that given in the *Mārkaṇḍēya-purāṇa* runs thus: At the beginning of the *kalpa* (æon) Brahmā was meditating upon begetting a son similar to himself. At once a boy of blue and ṛed colour was seen sitting on his lap and weeping loudly. Brahmā asked him why he was weeping. The boy answered 'Give me a name'. Brahmā conferred upon him the name Rudra. But the boy wept again and again for seven times more and obtained seven more names, Bhava, Śarva, Īśāna, Paśupati, Bhīma, Ugra and Mahādēva.

Another version of the birth of Rudra is also given in the *Vishṇu-purāṇa.* Sanandana and others who were first created by Brahmā for the purpose of creating the various beings became absorbed in meditation, attained all kinds of knowledge and became free from love and hatred. They neglected the business for which they were brought into existence by Brahmā. Seeing the indifference of his sons towards the creation of the worlds, Brahmā grew very angry and from the frowned forehead of this deity was born a son as resplendent as the sun. The body of this newly born being was half male and half female and it was terrific and large in size. Brahmā, commanding him to divide, disappeared. This being, known as Rudra, divided himself into two parts, of which one was male and the other female. The male portion further divided itself into eleven bodies of which some were pacific and some terrific in nature; in a similar way, the female portion divided itself in many forms some of black and others of white colour. Here is the origin of the Ēkādaśa Rudras and the multiform Śaktis of the later period of Hindu Mythology.

A third account of the birth of Rudra is as follows: When Madhu and Kaiṭabha, the two demons, attempted to kill Brahmā when he was created by Vishṇu in the lotus that issued from his navel, Brahmā prayed to Vishṇu that he might be saved from the demons. Pleased with the prayers of Brahmā, Vishṇu grew fiercely angry with the *Rākshasas;* from the frowned brows of Vishṇu sprang forth a being named Śambhu, wielding a trident and possessing three eyes. Thus we see, as in the case of many other deities, there are various accounts of the birth of Rudra.

Before proceeding with the systematic description of the images of Śiva, it will be well to look into the import of the various names given to this god. When Śiva was besought by the gods to destroy the demons who were the dwellers of three castles, the Tripurāsuras, he sought and obtained one half of their strength from all the gods; he was thenceforth known among the gods as Mahādēva or Mahēśvara, because he became the greatest among them. Since he consumes flesh, blood and marrow (as Agni), is fiery and glorious, he is called Rudra. He is termed Dhūrjaṭi from his smoky colour, and since he makes

Explanation of the different names of Siva.

Mahadeva.

Rudra, Dhurjati, Siva.

men prosper in all their actions, he bears the appellation Śiva (the auspicious). Śiva is known as Nīlakaṇṭha and Sitikaṇṭha. The following are the stories connected with these names: When the ocean of milk was churned for obtaining ambrosia for the gods, the first thing that came up from it was the all-destroying poison; the gods afraid of

Nilakantha.

this dreadful poison withdrew from the churning; Śiva in his kindness to the gods, took up the poison and swallowed it; but Pārvatī who was near her consort would not permit the poison to get into the stomach of Śiva lest it should kill him; she pressed the throat of Śiva and the poison remained there. From that time the blue poison became visible through the fair skin of the throat of Śiva, and lent it a blue lustre, which accounts for his being known as Nīlakaṇṭha.* Again it is said in the *Mahābhārata* that when Śiva destroyed the sacrifice of Daksha, he

---

* In the *Aitarēya-brāhmaṇa*, Rudra is said to have drunk water (*visha*, which also means poison). Of the two meanings of the word *visha*, the latter seems to have given birth to the *purāṇic* legend of the later period. The statement made in the Brāhmaṇa is a poetic rendering of the physical phenomenon of Rudra, that is, the Sun or the fire drying up water.

thrust his flaming trident again and again at Daksha and the assembled gods, and thus burnt everything with it. The trident having done its duty flew and fell near the *āśrama* (hermitage) of the *ṛishis* Nara and Nārāyaṇa at Badari with terrific force. The glow of the weapon was so great that the hair on the head of Nārāyaṇa turned green like the *muñja* grass. Nārāyaṇa thereupon repelled the trident, which returned to its owner howling. Śaṅkara, in anger, ran up to Nārāyaṇa, when the latter, fearing injury at the hands of Śiva, seized him by his throat. Hence the name Sitikaṇṭha (*mamapāṇy-aṅkitaś-chāpi śrīkaṇṭas tvam bhavishyasi*).

Sitikantha.

Śiva has three eyes; the third eye came into existence under the following circumstances. Śiva was sporting with his consort Pārvatī on the slopes of the Himālayas, when she playfully closed with her hands the two eyes of Śiva. The whole universe was at once submerged in cosmic darkness and all activity was suspended; sacrifices stopped and gods became quiescent. Mahādēva dispelled the darkness, by the fire bursting out of his forehead, in which a third eye, as luminous, as the sun, was formed.

Trinetra.

In a number of places in the *purāṇic* literature we see a sort of fierce denunciation of Śiva and the

Śaiva cult; this is perhaps on account of some of the revolting rites connected with the worship of Śiva. A graphic description of these rites as has already been mentioned, is given by Bhavabhūti in his *Mālati-Mādhava*.

Conflict between the Vedic and the Saiva cults.

At the time of the *Mahābhārata*, animals seem to have been offered systematically as sacrifices in the temple of Śiva, for, we hear Kṛishṇa admonishing Jarāsandha for his cruelty to other kings: says he, "what pleasure can those princes have in existence, when they have been consecrated for slaughter and kept as victims in the temple of Paśupati....Thou king, hast set apart for sacrifice to Mahādēva Kshatriya princes........In so far as you have resolved to offer these kings to Rudra, the guilt committed by you by slaughtering them will also attach to us........and we have never seen such a thing as offering human beings in sacrifice and thou seekest to sacrifice to Śaṅkara human victims." Daksha in his rage, denounces Śiva as the "Proud abolisher of rites and demolisher of barriers, such as by teaching the word of the Vēda to the Śūdras....," as "roaming about in cemeteries attended by the host of *bhūtas* (goblins), like a mad man, naked and with dishevelled hair. He is seen laughing, weeping, covered with ashes gathered from the funeral pyres and wearing a garland of human skulls and ornaments of human bones: he pretends to be the auspicious (*Śiva*) while in reality he is *aśiva ;* he is insane and is liked by the insane ; and he is the lord of the Pramathagaṇas, beings whose nature is essentially darkness............Let this Bhava, the lowest of the gods, never receive at the worship of the gods like Indra, Upēndra and others, any portion of the oblations with them." It might be noted here that the conscious neglect of Daksha to offer a portion of the sacrifice to Śiva in his great *yajña* was certainly due to his hatred for Śiva and his cult. Mahādēva himself admits that from the beginning he was not given any oblations in sacrifices : addressing Umā, he says " the old practice of the gods has all along been that no portion should be offered to me in any sacrifice. By this custom, which is established by the earliest arrangement, the gods legitimately (*dharmatah*) decline to give me a share in the sacrifices." From these statements we are led to infer that the Vēdic Indian looked upon Śiva as a low class deity and was not offering him any oblations along with Indra and other gods. By the entreaties of his wife Pārvatī, Śiva establishes for the first time in the *yāga* of Daksha, his right to receive oblations ; this " lowest of the gods " gets up to the level of the Vēdic gods at a later period and is reconciled with the Vēdic Hindu. That the ways of the adorers of Śiva were indeed revolting is seen in the imprecation of Bhṛigu found in the *Śrī Bhāgavata*. He says " Let those performers of the rites of the Śaiva cult be heretics and opponents of the true *Vēdas*. Having lost their purity and misled in their understanding, wearing matted hair, ashes and bones, let them undergo the Śaiva initiation, in which liquor is the deity. Since you, the followers of the Śiva cult, revile the *Vēda* and the Brāhmaṇas, who are the only safeguards keeping intact the straying humanity, you have become heretics. For, the *Vēda* is the auspicious (*Śiva*) and the eternal path of the people, which has been followed by the ancients and of which Janārdana is the authority." We obtain a glimpse of the real state of affairs at that time from the quotation from the *Śrī Bhāgavata* given above. People, including some Brāhmaṇas, left the fold of the Vēdic religion and joined the cult of Śiva, reviled the Vēdic religion, took to spirituous liquors and became celibate mendicants, daubing their bodies with the ashes of the cemeteries and adorning themselves with bones. They threw off the study of the *Vēdas* and violated their sanctity by teaching them to Śūdras and others. The conditions of the Vēdic Brāhmaṇas of that period is mirrored in the counter imprecation pronounced by Nandīśvara, a devout follower of the Śiva cult. He tells us that the revilers of Śiva are sunk, out of the love of carnal pleasures, in domestic life, in which bad morals are not infrequent; they practise a number of ceremonies without understanding their real import and are degraded by the rules of the *Vēdas*. They smell strongly of liquor. Nandīśvara heaps up on the heads of the followers of the Vēdic religion the curse that these be ever sunk, deluded by the words of the *Vēdas*, in the mire of ceremonial ignorance. The complaint of the *Śaiva* against the *vaidika* is that the latter pays greater regard to the life of a house-holder and that he performs a number of ceremonies without understanding their meaning. It is in fact a rebellion against the ignorance of Vēdic rites and a denunciation of family life.

With the admission of Śiva into the fold of the higher gods, there seems to have come over the followers of both the Vēdic and Śaiva cults a strong desire for a sort of reconciliation. Thus, we see Arjuna praising Śiva, in the *Vana-parvan* of the *Mahābhārata*, as follows: "Adoration to Śiva in the form of Vishṇu, to Vishṇu in the form of Śiva.........to Hari-Rudra." Again, in the *Śānti-parvan*, we see it stated by Kṛishṇa that, when the god of gods, Mahēśvara, is worshipped, the god

Nārāyaṇa, the Lord, will also be worshipped, that he who knows and loves Rudra knows and loves Nārāyaṇā and that Rudra and Nārāyaṇā are but one in principle, divided into two and operating in the world in manifested forms. The same spirit of conciliation, by which Hari and Hara are viewed as one, is also found in the *Harivaṁśa* wherein we hear Mārkaṇḍēya saying to Brahmā: "When you show me this auspicious vision, I perceive that there is no difference between Śiva who exists in the form of Vishṇu and Vishṇu in the form of Śiva........He who appears as Vishṇu is Rudra............Bestowers of boons, creators of the worlds, self-existent, they are the (composite being) half male and half female (Ardhanārīśvara)....And just as fire entering into fire becomes nothing other than fire, so Rudra entering into Vishṇu should possess the nature of Vishṇu........Vishṇu, the highest manifestation of Rudra, and Śiva, the highest manifestation of Vishṇu, are only one god, though divided into two and move continually in the world. Vishṇu does not exist without Śaṅkara nor Śiva without Kēśava; hence, these two, Rudra and Upēndra (Vishṇu) have formerly attained oneness." This reconciliation of Śiva with Vishṇu seems to be based upon the re-discovery of the identity of Rudra, Agni with Āditya, another modification of Agni, as found residing in the sky. The Vēdic Agni becomes Rudra or Śiva and the Vēdic Āditya becomes Vishṇu, in the Purāṇic period.

The hatred of the followers of the Vēdic cult towards the Śaivas seems to have been also attributable to the worship by the latter of the phallic emblem. The very touch of the Śaiva was considered by the Vaidika as imparting pollution, because the former set up, from the earliest known times, material representations of the *phallus* in their temples and offered worship to them. That the phallic worship is foreign to the Vēdic religion becomes quite clear from the references we meet with in the *Ṛig-Vēda*. In one place it is stated "The glorious Indra defies the hostile kings; let not those whose god is the *śiśna* approach our sacred ceremony" and in another we read "Proceeding to the conflict, and desiring to acquire them, he has gone to, and in hostile array besieged, inaccessible places, at the time when, irresistible, slaying those whose god is the *śiśna*, he by his craft conquered the riches of the city with a hundred gates."* The worship of the Phallus

* "But, Śāyaṇa, following Yāska, interprets the word *śiśnadēva* of these two passages as referring to those who

which the non-Aryans of India shared with other nations who inhabited on the borders of the Mediterranean sea, has survived in India to this day. The *Dhruvabēras* in all Śiva temples is the *Liṅga* surmounted upon the *Yōni* or the *piṇḍikā* (pedestal). It is only in very rare instances we meet with the anthropomorphic representations of Śiva set up as the principal deity in Śiva temples. This non-Āryan phallic emblem seems to have been identified at a later period with Skambha of the Vēdas, wherein Skambha is conceived as co-extensive with the universe and comprehends in him the various parts of the material universe, as also the abstract qualities, such as, *tapas*, faith, truth and divisions of time. He is distinct from Prajāpati, who founds the universe upon him. " The thirty-three gods are comprehended in him and arose out of non-entity, which forms his highest member, as well as entity is embraced within him ". The gods who form part of him do homage to him. In the praise of Skambha we meet with the following passages, namely, " Where Skambha, generating,

---

sport with the *śiśna, i.e.*, unchaste men. Durgāchārya also gives the same meaning: he says that the name is applied to those who are always dallying carnally with prostitutes, forsaking Vēdic observances."

brought Purāṇapurusha into existence" and "Skambha in the beginning shed forth that gold (*hiraṇya*, out of which Hiraṇyagarbha arose) in the midst of the world" and lastly " He who knows the golden reed standing in the waters is the mysterious Prajāpati." From the first two of the three passages quoted above, we see that one of the functions of Skambha is, to beget Hiraṇyagarbha, or Purāṇapurusha, the god of reproduction. He pours forth his golden seed in begetting Prajāpati. The original of the third passage runs thus: *Yō vētasam hiraṇyayam tishṭhantam salilē vēda sa vai guhyah Prajāpatih.* In the *Ṛig-vēda* and the *Śatapatha-Brāhmaṇa*, the word *vaitasa* has the sense of *membrum virile.* Hence the word *vētasa* in the present passage also might be understood to refer to Liṅga and the non-Aryan worshippers of the phallus might have based the identity of the Liṅga with the Skambha of the texts of the *Atharvaṇa vēda* quoted above. It is this same Skambha that has given birth to the *purāṇic* story of Śiva's appearance as a blazing pillar between Brahmā and Vishṇu when they were quarrelling about the superiority of the one over the other. At a later time a sort of philosophical clothing is given to the primitive Liṅga; by a section of scholars the Liṅga and its pedestal are viewed, with some justification, as the representation of the *araṇis*, the two pieces of wood which were rubbed together by the Vēdic Indian in making fire. At that period the upper stick was considered as male and the lower as female, by the co-operation of which fire was generated. If this explanation is to be taken, the object generated is the fire, which the Vēdic Indian identified with Rudra, same as Śiva of the later mythology and the objects that gave birth to Rudra cannot represent the hermaphroditic form of Rudra. Hence, it is undoubted that the Liṅga and the Yōni represent the Great Generative Principles of the Universe, Purusha and Prakṛiti. That in its earlier stages Liṅga worship was purely phallic can be established by means of a number of Sanskrit texts from various works of authority.

References to Linga worship.

The earliest references to the phallic worship are, as we have seen above, to be found in the *Ṛig-vēda*, where the phallus is called *śiśnadēva*. When we come to the later or the *purāṇic* period the references are fuller and more explicit. In the *Markaṇḍēya-Purāṇa* there occurs the following story: *Mārkaṇḍēya* says that Rudra and Vishṇu are the creators of the Universe and they form the Ardhanārīśvara aspect of the former deity. Here the allusion is to the Haryardha form of Śiva, in which the female generative principle is identified with Vishṇu. That the male and the female principles are inseparable and are ever found together in cosmic evolution is the real import of the Ardhanārīśvara or Haryardha forms of Śiva; the same idea is also conveyed in a brief way by the symbols the *liṅga* and the *yōni*. In the *Bhāgavata-Purāṇa* (second *skanda*) Mahādēva is described by Brahmā as, "the Parabrahman, the lord of Śakti and Śiva, who are the womb and seed respectively of the universe, who, like a spider, forms it in his sport, through the agency of Śakti and Śiva, (who are one with himself), preserves and re-absorbs it." The *Liṅga-purāṇa* also states that Pradhāna (nature) is called the Linga and Paramēśvara is called the Liṅgin (the sustainer of the Liṅga) and that the pedestal of the Liṅga is Mahādēvī (Umā) and the Liṅga is the visible Mahēśvara. A more express allusion to the generative power of the *Liṅga* and the *yōni*, the emblems of the Śaiva cult, is found in the *Vishṇu-purāṇa*, wherein we are told that Brahmā asked Rudra, born of his anger, to divide himself; thereupon Rudra divided himself into two, a male and a female portion. The epithet *mahāśēpha* in *Ūrddha-kēśō mahāśēphō nagnō vikṛita lōchanah* occurring in the *Mahābhārata* is also worth noting in this connection. A further quotation from the same work is also to the point: "And since, standing aloft, he consumes the lives of men, and since he is fixed, and since his Liṅga is perpetually fixed, he is called Sthāṇu . . . and when his Liṅga remains continually in a state of chastity, and people reverence it, this is agreeable to the great God Mahādēva. The worshipper of the Liṅga who shall adore the image (*vigraha*) or the Liṅga of Mahādēva, enjoys continually great prosperity. It is the Liṅga, raised up, which the *ṛishis*, gods, *gandharvas* and *apsarases* worship;" and "He whose seed is raised up, whose Liṅga is raised up, who sleeps aloft, who abides in the sky....... The Lord of the Liṅga, the lord of the *suras* (gods)......the lord of the seed, the producer of the seed." Śaṅkarāchārya in his *Saundaryalahari* (verse 1) also says "When Śiva is united with Śakti, he is able to create, otherwise he is unable even to move." The *Kuvalayānanda* of Appayya Dikshita begins with "We praise the ancient pair, the parents of the universe; each is the end attained by the penance of the other." In a work called *Ānandānubhava* it is stated that Śakti is of the form of the pleasure derivable from *Guhya* (the female organ) and that Śiva is the Liṅga; from the union of these two is the cause of the joy that is found in the universe.* Again, in an inscription found in the Mysore State, the following salutation to Śiva and his Dēvī is given.† "The only god, victorious is Śiva, the

---

*गुह्यानन्दात्मिका शक्तिः लिङ्गरूपः शिवः परः ।
तयोर्मिथुनकौशल्यं जगदानन्दकारणम् ॥

†एको देवः स जयति शिवः केवलज्ञानमूर्त्तिः
देवी सा च त्रिभुवनमिदं यद्विभूतेः प्रपञ्चः ।
यत्कूटस्थं मिथुनमविनाभावसम्बन्धयोगात्
मिश्रीभूतं तदखिलजगज्जन्मवीजं नमामि ॥

No. 242, Shikaripur Taluk, Shimoga District, Mysore.

Other references to the phallic nature of the *linga* are :—

1. वचनाद्वो महाभागाः प्रणम्योमां तथा भवत् ।
सा भगाख्या जगद्धात्री लिङ्गमूर्तेस्त्रिवेदिका ॥
लिङ्गस्तु भगवान्द्वाभ्यां जगत्सृष्टिर्द्विजोत्तमाः ।
लिङ्गमूर्तिः शिवो ज्योतिस्तमसश्चोपरि स्थितः ॥
लिङ्गवेदिसमायोगादर्धनारीश्वरोऽभवत् ॥

Liṅgapurāṇa, ch. 100, Vv. 6 & 7.

2. जाने त्वं ईशमीशं विश्वस्य जगतो योनिविजयोः ।
शक्तेः शिवस्य च परं यत्तद्ब्रह्म निरन्तरम् ॥
त्वमेव भगवन्नेचच्छिवशक्त्योः सरूपयोः ।
विश्वं सृजसि पास्यत्सि क्रीडन्नूर्णपटो यथा ॥

Bhāgavatapurāṇa.

3. योनिलिङ्गप्रकारेण जगत्सृष्ट्यर्थकारणम् ।
तथासंयोगभावेन कर्मरूपमुदाहृतम् ॥

Vātuḷaśuddhāgama.

form of all wisdom, and also Dēvī; whose possession are the three worlds, unchangeable in the universe, ever united, through whose union the essence of all things is mingled, the seed from which the world is born—do I reverence." In the *Śiva-Liṅga-Pratishṭhā-vidhi*, the author Aghorā-Śivāchārya gives a *mantra* which runs thus: *Umāyai bhaga-rūpiṇyai liṅga-rūpadharāya cha Śaṅkarāya namastubhyam........*; and which means I salute Umā who is in the form of *bhaga* and Śaṅkara is in the form of Liṅga. We learn from the *Siddhāntasārāvaḷi* that the bringing about the union of the *pīṭha* which is the symbol of Śakti and the *liṅga*, that of Śiva, in accordance with the rules laid down in Śaiva śāstras is called *pratishṭhā*.* We

4. In marking the lines (*sūtras*) on the surface of the stone *liṅga*, it is stated that the part marked out thus should resemble the nut of the (human) *liṅga* :—

"..............................लिङ्गमूर्द्धेव मूर्द्धा"

Similarly in describing the form of the *pīṭha* for the *Liṅga*, it is required to be made in the shape of the *bhaga* (the human *pudendum*) :—

"पीठेलक्ष्म भगाकृतिस्तु पुरतस्तूर्ध्वाग्रकं पिण्डिका रन्ध्रस्यापि गुणांशभागयुगळे मूले भ्रमद्वंद्वयुक्..................................."

Siddhāntasārāvaḷi.

उमायै भगरूपिण्यै लिङ्गरूपधराय च ॥

Kāmikāgama.

*पीठं लिङ्गमुमाशिवस्तयोर्योग: प्रतिष्ठोदिता विध्युक्त:....................

can quote several such texts, but those already given are more than ample to show the phallic nature of liṅga worship. So much about the evidences gathered from literature. Let us now turn our attention to sculptural evidences.

The earliest known Liṅgas, so far as we know at present, are two; one comes from Bhiṭa and is, now preserved in the Lucknow Museum. It has been described in a brief account contributed by Mr. R. D. Banerji to the Annual of the Director General of Archæology for 1909—1910. About this *liṅga* of Bhitā Mr. Banerji writes, "The top of it is shaped as the bust of a male holding a vase in his left hand, while the right is raised in the *abhaya mudrā* posture. Below this bust, where the waist of the figure should have been, are four human heads, one at each corner. From the mode of dressing the hair and the large rings worn in the lobes of the ears, it appears that these are the busts of females. They are more or less defaced, but still retain sufficient detail to admit of identification. The upper part of the head of the male is broken, only the portion below the nose being extant. The male figure wears a cloth which is thrown over the left shoulder, the folds being shown by a double line running over the breast. The vase held in the left hand resembles to some extent, the ointment vessel found in the figures of Bōdhisatvas of the Gāndhāra school. The left ear of the male figure bears the circular pendants, which may be earrings. In front, immediately below the heads of two females, the phallus is marked by deeply drawn lines. To the proper left of this is the inscription to which I have already referred. The lower part of the stone has been shaped as a tenon to be fitted in a mortice.

"The inscription is in a good state of preservation, and with the exception of the last three letters, can be deciphered very easily." The translation of the inscription is given by Mr. Banerji as follows: "The Linga of the sons of Khajahuti, was dedicated by Nāgasiri, the son of Vāsēṭhi. May the deity be pleased."*

From the description given by Mr. Banerji it is evident that it is a *Mukhaliṅga* having five faces corresponding to the Īśāna, Tatpurusha, Aghōra, Vāmadēva and Sadyōjāta aspects of Śiva. In the description of *Mukhaliṅgas* given elsewhere in this book, it will be seen that the face representing Īśāna should be on the top, while the other four should face the east, south, west and north respectively.

---

* The text of this inscription reads as follows: *Khajahuti-putanam l[iṁ]gō patiṭhāpitō Vāsēṭhi-putēna Nāgasirinā piya-ytā[ṁ] d[ē]vatā.*

PLATE I.

Three different views of the Bhiṭa Liṅgam : Stone.

The four faces on the four corners which are believed by Mr. Banerji might be of females are really those of male figures. (See Pl. I.)

The palæography of the inscription found engraved at the bottom of this Liṅga is its most important feature, for, it enables us to determine the approximate age of this most interesting antiquarian object. With the help of the characters, Mr. R. D. Banerji has correctly guessed the age of the Liṅga to be the first century B.C.

The second most ancient Liṅga is the one discovered by me at Guḍimallam some years ago and which has not been described in detail hitherto. It is one of the most perfect pieces of sculpture of its class and is of great value in connection with the history and nature of the *liṅga* worship. Guḍimallam is a village situated at a distance of six miles to the north-east of Rēṇiguṇṭa, a railway junction station on the Madras and Southern Mahaㅡratta Railway. In this place, there is an ancient temple with several inscriptions in it; the god of that temple, the Liṅga under consideration, is known from ancient times by the name of Paraśurāmēśvara and the liṅga is still in *pūjā*. Being a badly managed temple, scarcely any oil is spent upon bathing the images, a fact which accounts for the liṅga being in the same condition as when it was carved; there is no oily dirt on it and the high polish is in no way lost; but there are a few chips here and there, and it is not known if they have existed from the beginning or came into existence at a later period. It is very probably the latter. The liṅga is made of a reddish igneous rock, very brittle and compact in its composition which takes very high polish and which is found in the Tirupati hills which pass near the temple of Paraśuramēś-vara. The Liṅga is set directly on the floor of the central shrine and the *piṇḍikā* or the pedestal is cut out in the form of a quadrangular ridge on the ground; it is exactly five feet in height and bears upon its front portion a beautiful figure of Śiva. This figure of Śiva has two arms, in the right one of which a ram is held by its hind legs and with its head hanging downwards (see fig. 4, Pl. V); in the left one is held a water-pot (fig. 3, Pl. V), and a battle-axe (*paraśu*) rests upon the left shoulder (fig. 2, Pl. V). On the head of the figure of Śiva is a covering, resembling a turban, of plaited,—not matted,—hair (see Pl. III and fig. 9, Pl. IV). The face is distinctly Mongoloid in its features, with a somewhat snub nose, high cheek-bones, narrow forehead and oblique eyes. This last item agrees well with Virūpāksha (he with oblique eyes), one of the

PLATE II.

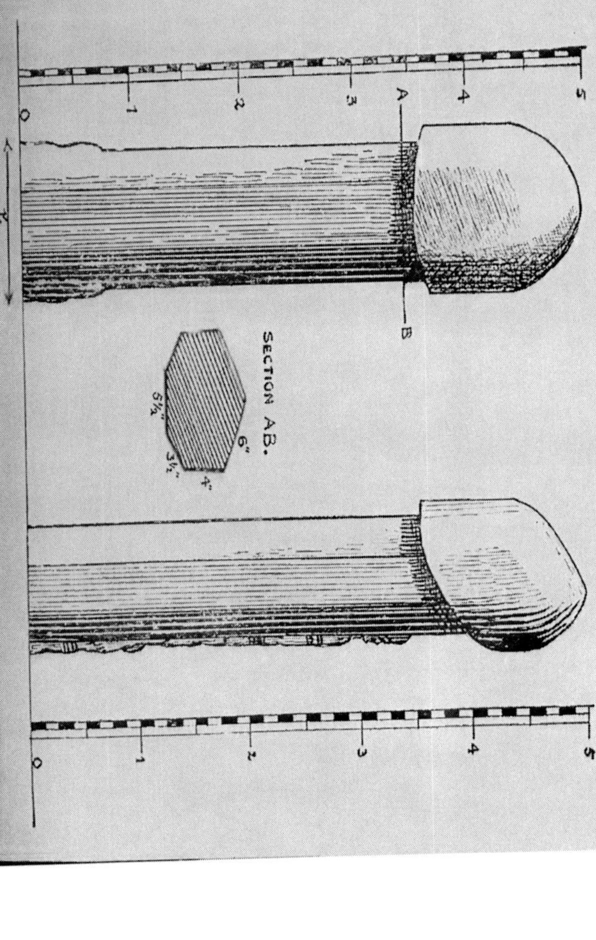

[To face page 66.]

PLATE III.

Bust of the image of Śiva on the Guḍimallam Liṅga.

[To face page 66]

PLATE IV.

Details of ornaments in the Guḍimallam Sculpture.

Fig. 1.

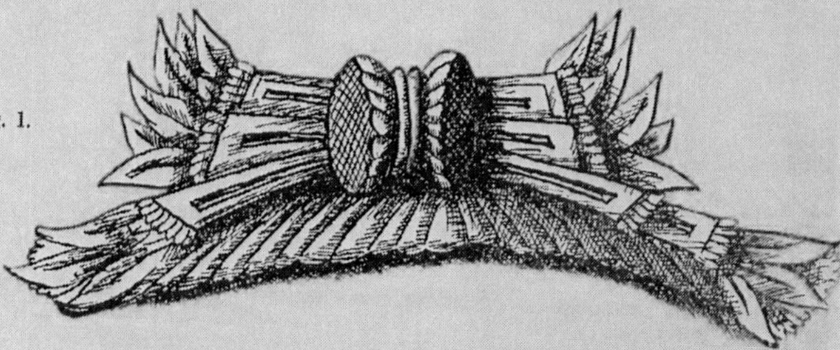

Fig. 2.

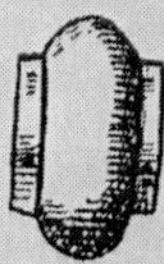

Fig. 5.

Fig. 3.

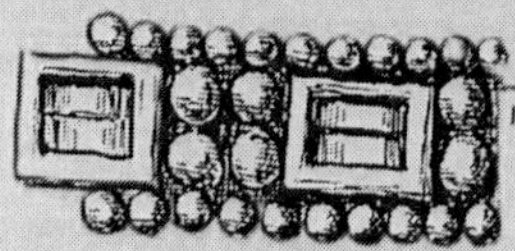

Fig. 6.

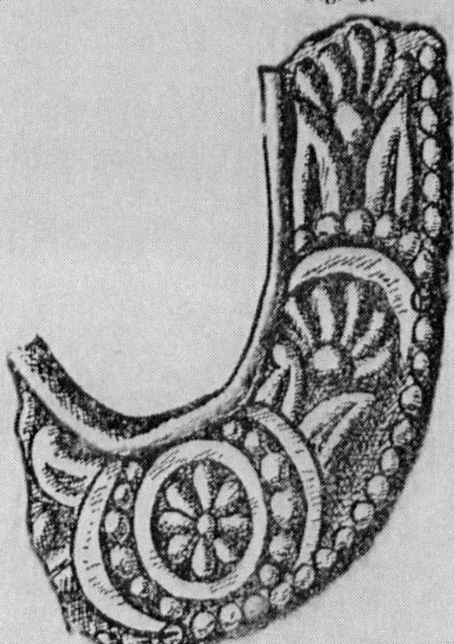

Fig. 4.

Fig. 7.

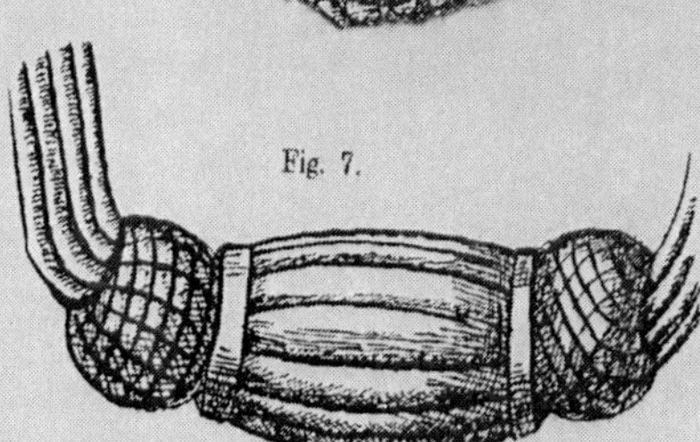

[To face page 67.]

names of Śiva. There are *kuṇḍalas* in the ears (fig. 1, Pl. IV), the lobes of which are distended so as to hang down as far as the shoulders; on each of the upper-arms is a highly finished ornamental band (*aṅgadā*) and on the forearms five bracelets of different patterns (see figs. 2—7, Pl. IV). Round the neck is to be seen a necklace of rare workmanship (fig. 8, Pl. IV); it is noteworthy that there is no *yajñōpavīta*, the Brāhmanical sacred thread, which is insisted upon in all *Āgamas.* The image wears a cloth on the loins, which, from its sculpture, appears to be of a very fine texture, for the thighs and the organ are visible through it very distinctly. The creases and smaller folds of the cloth running across the thighs are very well executed, and the larger and heavier folds flow down between the two legs.

The figure of Śiva stands astride upon the shoulders of a Rākshasa—the Apasmāra-purusha—who is sitting on the ground on his haunches and supporting himself with his hands which are planted on the ground near the feet. He too has a sort of *jaṭāmakuṭa* on his head and a *hāra* of beads round his neck. He is swarthy and burly in the build of his body, possesses a pair of pointed animal ears and is, withal, jolly and happy, as is evidenced from the broad grin on his face.

The Linga itself is composed of two parts, the nut and the shaft of the *membrum virile*, each of them shaped exactly like the original model, in a state of erection. On Pl. II are given the front, the side and the back views of the Liṅga, a reference to which will enable the reader to form an excellent idea of the exactitude with which the sculptor has modelled this Liṅga in imitation of the human *phallus*. The longitudinal facets on the erect organ (*ūrddhava-rētas*) are also represented in this Liṅga.

There is a very close resemblance of the figure of Śiva on this Liṅga to that of a *yaksha* in the Śāñchi Stūpa, figured on page 36 of Grunwedel's "Buddhist Art in India" (translated by Gibson and Burgess); the face, the ear and the ear-ornament, the arms and the ornaments thereon, the necklace the details of the workmanship of these jewels and the peculiar arrangement of the drapery, particularly the big folds that descend between the legs,—all these are exactly alike both in the image of Śiva on the Liṅga at Guḍimallam and in the picture of the *Yaksha* referred to above. The date of the sculpture represented in the latter picture has been fixed to be the second century B.C.*

* "143 Before Christ (*cir.*). Probable date of Sanchi gateways." Grunwedel, p. 5.

PLATE V.

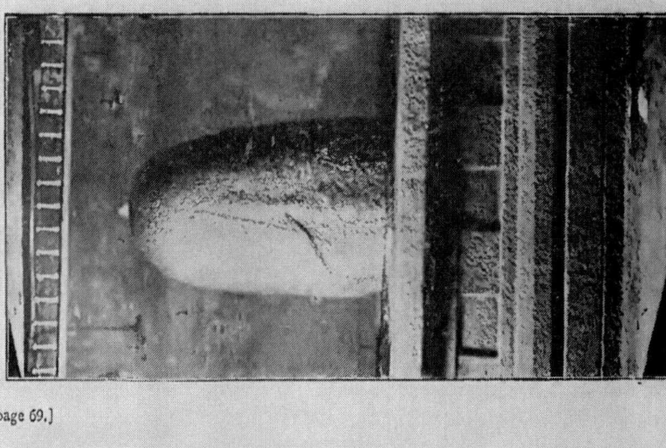

(Fig. 1.)

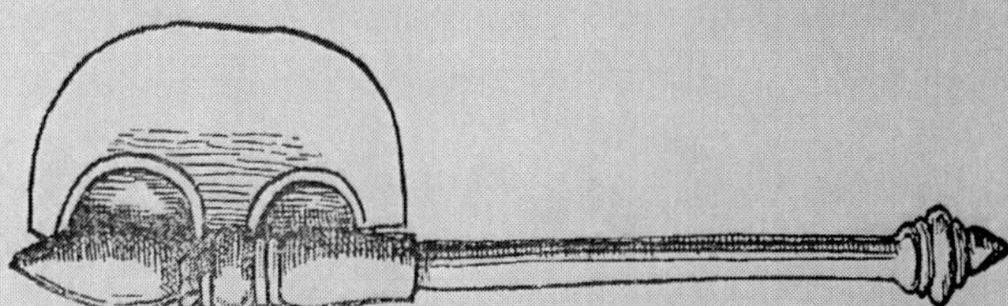

(Fig. 2.)

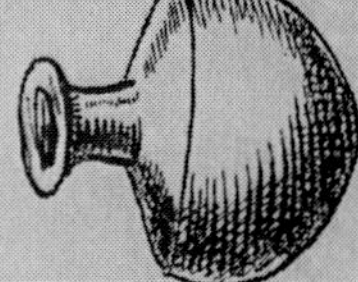

(Fig. 3.)

(Fig. 4.)

[To face page 69.]

This naturally leads us to the inference that the image of Śiva might also belong to the first century at least of the Christian era, if not to a still earlier period. Again, from the exact likeness of the Guḍimallam Liṅga to the human phallus, it is certain that Liṅga worship was not of a mere symbol (*liṅga*), nor of a simple pillar (*sthāṇu*), but is beyond doubt phallic in its nature.* That this is the real origin of Liṅga worship even at the present day is easily seen from the rules laid down in the *Āgamas* for making a Liṅga, as also from the innumerable sculptures of Liṅga, found throughout the length and breadth of India. (For an exhaustive treatment of Liṅga, see the Chapter on Liṅgas).

Because it is established to be phallic in its nature, some may be inclined to consider Liṅga worship obscene and immoral. There is nothing in it to be ashamed of; the two great Generative Principles of the Universe, Śiva and Śakti, or Purusha and Prakṛiti, the father and mother of all creations, the energy and matter of the physical scientist, is symbolised briefly in the form of the

---

* For a third ancient liṅga which is also sculptured like the human phallus, see fig. 1, Pl. V. It is set up in the central shrine of the Śiva Temple at Chennittalai, a village in Central Travancore.

liṅga and the *yōni.* For the past two thousand years at least, the Hindus, males and females, have been offering worship to this symbol of the Great Architect of the Universe, without in the least adverting to or feeling conscious of the so-called obscenity of this pure symbol of the fatherhood and motherhood of the supreme deity; to them it is a symbol and nothing more; there is nothing obscene in connection with its worship; the simplest and the purest materials, such as water from a well reserved for ceremonial purposes, flowers, incense and freshly cooked rice and cakes, are used in the worship of the Liṅga. If there be any the slightest lack of cleanliness and purity on the part of the officiating priest, it would be passed over unnoticed in a Vishṇu temple; but never in a Śiva temple, where absolute purity and cleanliness are rigorously demanded from the *pūjāri.* Thus, whatever might have been the original setting and the import of the symbolism, at the present time they are forgotten and lost; and the worship of the *Liṅga* and the *yōni*, is absolutely* and thoroughly

* The attention of the reader may here be drawn to a little book entitled "Primitive Symbolism as illustrated in Phallic Worship" by Hodder M. Westrop, published by Messrs. Geo. Redvay in London. In this, the author has collected information about the existence, in the past and

free from even the remotest associations of any kind of immorality or indecency.

The great antiquity of Śiva worship is established by a number of references in ancient inscriptions; some of these references are given on page 8 of the General Introduction in Volume I of this publication.

Having considered at some length the history and nature of Śiva worship, I now proceed to a systematic description of the various images of Śiva in the subsequent chapters.

---

present, of phallic worship in several countries—Greece, Egypt, Rome, Assyria, Ancient Amercia, &c. Liṅga worship or worship of Priapus, or *fascinum* or Pripe-gala continued to exist, according to Boudin, till the 12th century A.D. in Germany, Slavonia and France. In Franco a document entitled *Sacerdotal Judgments on Crimes*, of the 8th century A.D. is said to contain the following: "If any one performs enchantments before the *fascinum*, let him do penance on bread and water during three lents."

LINGAS.

LIṄGAS.

SIVA is worshipped in a number of anthropomorphic forms, as also in the symbol of Liṅga. The more common representation is the latter. As has been said already, the chief image in the central shrine of a Śiva temple, is, in a large majority of instances, the Liṅga. Very rarely do we meet with anthropomorphic images of Śiva in the central shrines, and where they are seen, as in some temples of the Pallava period in South India, they occupy a position subordinate to the Liṅga.

Liṅgas are broadly divided into two classes, namely, the *chala-liṅgas* and the *achala-liṅgas*, that is, the moveable and the immoveable Liṅgas. To the latter class belong the large and heavy stone Liṅgas which are permanently set up in the central shrines of Śiva temples. A description of the different varieties of the *chala-liṅgas*, had better be given first before proceeding to deal with the important class of *achala-liṅgas*.

The Chala or Jangama Lingas.

The *chala-liṅgas* are divided into *mṛiṇmaya* (those made of earth), *lōhaja* (of metals), *ratnaja* (of precious stones), *dāruja* (of wood), *śailaja* (of stone) and *kshaṇika liṅgas*, (those made for the occasion and disposed of immediately their use is over).

The Mrinmaya Lingas.

The *mṛiṇmaya liṅgas* may be of baked or unbaked clay. For making an unbaked clay *liṅga* it is stated in the *Kāmikāgama* that white clay, gathered from pure places, such as the tops of hills and banks of rivers, should be mixed with milk, curds, ghee, as also the flours of wheat and barley, the barks of milky trees, powdered sandal paste, mercury, etc., and the whole mass is then well mixed up and kneaded and kept for a fortnight or, at the most, a month. The *liṅga* is then shaped according to the instructions given in the *Āgamas* for that purpose. The baked clay *liṅga* is used for *ābhichārika* purposes; that is, for incantations such as those made to bring about the destruction of an enemy.

The Lohaja Lingas and the Ratnaja Lingas.

The *lōhaja liṅgas* may be made of the following eight metals, namely, gold, silver, copper, bell-metal, iron, lead, brass and tin. Similarly, the *ratnaja-liṅgas* may be carved in pearls, coral, cat's-eye (*vaiḍūrya*) quartz crystal, topaz (*pushyarāga*), emerald and bluestone; that is, the *ratnas* or precious stones employed in making *liṅgas* are seven in number. The Dāruja liṅgas are made of

The Daruja Lingas.

the timber of the *śami*, *madhūka*, *karṇikāra*, *maṇḍūka*, *tinduka*, *arjuna*, *pippala*, and *udumbara* trees; besides these, the timber of all such trees as have barks which exude a milky latex when cut, is also mentioned as good for making *liṅgas;* one such tree is the jack and it is very largely employed in the Malabar Coast for carving very fine specimens of images. The *Kāmikāgama* adds many more trees, such as the *khadira*, the *chandana*, the *sāla*, the *bilva*, the *badara* and the *dēvādaru*, the timber of which is also fit for making liṅgas.

The Sailaja Lingas.

The stone *liṅgas* included in the class of *chala-liṅgas* are perhaps those small ones which are worn on the person by the people of the sect of Śaivas known as the Jaṅgamas, Liṅgavantas or Lingāyats, or Vīra Śaivas. The *kshaṇika-liṅgas* are those that

The Kshanika Lingas.

are made then and there for *pūjā* and are, after the *pūjā* is over, cast away. They may be made of *saikatam* (sand), uncooked rice, cooked rice, river-side clay, cow-dung, butter, *rudrāksha* seeds, sandal paste, *kūrcha* grass, flowers, jaggery, and flour. It is said that worshipping a *liṅga* made of gold grants wealth (śrīpradam) *; one of uncooked rice, *vibhava*; a *liṅga* made of cooked rice, grants the worshipper plenty of food; a *liṅga* made of clay gathered from river banks, grants landed estates; of cow-dung, removes all disease; of butter, gives one a jovial temper; of *Rudrāksha* seeds, grants knowledge; one of sandal paste, is prescribed for those who desire *saubhāgya*, while that of *kūrcha* grass for seekers after soul-liberation; a *liṅga* composed of flowers grants long life; one made of jaggery confers all desired ends and that made of flour strength.

Effect of worshipping various kinds of Lingas.

* In the *Uttara-kāṇḍa* of the *Rāmāyaṇa* it is stated that wherever Rāvaṇa went, he carried with him a golden *liṅga* for his worship: placing that *liṅga* in the midst of a pedestal of sand, Rāvaṇa made *pūjā* to it with incense and flowers of fine smell (*yatra yatra cha yātisma Rāvaṇō rākshasēśvara jāmbūnadamayam liṅgam sthāpya Rāvaṇah archayāmāsa gandhaiśchāmṛita gandhibhih*). The commentator remarks " that the golden *liṅga* was intended for constant worship. He worshipped it from the desire of sovereignty. For it is prescribed in the *Tantras* that a golden *liṅga* should be worshipped when any one desires sovereignty. (*Tal-liṅgam jāmbunadamayam nitya-pūjā liṅgam aiśvarya kāmanāya hi tal-liṅga-pūjā Rāvaṇasya aiśvarya kāmasya sauvarṇa-liṅga-pūjāyastantrēshūktah.*)

It is further stated that the *liṅgas* made of metals, precious stones etc., should have only the *pūjā-bhāga* or the portion which is projecting above the pedestal in *achala-liṅgas*, together with the *piṇḍikā* or the pedestal; in other words, these *liṅgas* need not be made with the *Brahmabhāga* and the *Vishṇu-bhāga* and then set up in a separate *piṇḍikā*; the *piṇḍikā* and that portion of the *liṅga* which is to be visible and which is known by the name of the *Rudra-bhāga* are to be either carved out of a single block of precious stone or cast in metals. No rules need be observed, as in the case of *achala-liṅgas* in shaping the *chala-liṅgas* and they need not bear on them the lines that are required to be marked on the *achala-liṅgas*.

The Achala or Sthavara Lingas.

The *achala* or *sthāvara-liṅgas* are, according to the *Suprabhēdāgama*, classified under nine heads, namely, the Svāyambhuva, the Pūrva (or Purāṇa), the Daivata, the Gāṇapatya, the Asura, the Sura, the Ārsha, the Rākshasa, the Mānusha, and the Bāṇa liṅgas.* Of

---

*The *Mānasāra* has another classification according to which the *achala-liṅgas* are of six kinds, namely, Śaivaliṅga, Pāśupata-Liṅga, Kāḷāmukha-Liṅga, Vāma-Liṅga, Bhairava-Liṅga and a variety which is not mentioned; but it gives no description of any of these liṅgas. लिङ्गमानविधिं सम्यग्लक्षणं वक्ष्येऽधुना । शैवं पाशुपतं चैव कालामुखमुदाहृतम् ॥ वामं च भैरवं चैव लिङ्गमानंतु षड्विधम् ।

these, the Svāyambhuva, are said to belong to the *uttamōttama* (most superior) variety of liṅgas; those belonging to the Daivata and the Gāṇapatya classes, are of the *Uttamamadhyama* (middling superior) variety; whereas the Asura, the Sura and the Ārsha liṅgas belong to the *uttamādhama* (lowest among the superior) variety. The *Mānushaliṅgas* belong to the *madhyamādhama* (middling among the inferior) variety.

Their classification.

The *Makuṭāgama* recognises only four classes of *sthira-liṅgas*, namely, the Daivika, the Ārshaka, the Gāṇapa, and the Mānusha liṅgas, whereas the most authoritative of all the Śaiva *Āgamas*, the *Kāmikāgama* states that the *sthāvara-liṅgas* are divided into six classes, the Svāyambhuva, the Daivika, the Ārshaka, the Gāṇapatya, the Mānusha and the Bāṇa liṅgas. Though there is apparent diversity among the statements of the various *Āgamas* in the classification of the *sthāvara* liṅgas, practically there is no difference at all in them; some of them include the minor varieties under the major heads and swell the list, while others are somewhat more rigorous in keeping apart the major and the minor divisions among the *sthāvara liṅgas*.

The Svāyambhuva Liṅga is described in the *Kāmikāgama* as one which rose up and came in into existence by itself and had existed from time immemorial. As such, even if these are slightly damaged by causes such as fire, wild elephants, inundation or encroachment of rivers, enemies of religion like the Tulushkas, * madmen or men possessed by devils, they need no re-setting up (*jirṇōddhāra*). If anything at all is necessary, it

The Svayambhuva Linga.

---

*While commenting on the word *ripavah*, Nigamajñānadēva, son of Vāmadēvasivāchārya says, *ripavah śatruvastulushkādaya :* Vāmadēva was a contemporary and protege of a king called Śambhuvarāya. There are three or four Śambhuvarāyas, (that is, members of a dynasty of chiefs who styled themselves Śambhuvarāyas), of whom the Śambhuvarāya, the patron of Vāmadēva seems to be Rājanārāyaṇa Śambhuvarāyar, whose initial date is A. D. 1322-23. In one of the inscriptions discovered by me at Tiruvāmāttūr and which is dated 1335-6 A.D., it is said that the Turukkar invaded some time previously and caused ruin to the country and that the *pūjā* in the Śiva temple at Tiruvāmāttūr was suspended for want of funds and that Rājanārāyaṇa Śambhuvarāyar granted some lands and money to revive the *pūjās.* This Rājanārāyaṇa constructed a *gōpura* in the Aruṇāchalēśvara temple at Tiruvaṇṇāmalai ; sitting in this *gōpura,* Vāmadēva wrote the original and commentary of the *Jīrṇōddhāra daśaka.* Hence, the invasion and havoc caused to the temples by the Mussalmans under Malik Kafur, the general of Alla-ud-din Khilji, were fresh in the mind of the author who, therefore, includes in the term *ripavah*, the Tulushkas.

is but a few ceremonials that might be done to purify the liṅga from pollution. If a portion of the Svāyambhuva Liṅga is broken, the broken part is required, if possible, to be bound with the main part with bands of gold or copper; if however, the damage is such as to prevent the pieces being bound together the broken part may be thrown away. If, however, a Svāyambhuva Liṅga is, by some cause or other, completely removed from its setting and thrown out, the event would cause the king his destruction as also of his kingdom, perhaps because he and his officers, responsible for the safety of such objects of hoary antiquity, were negligent in their duty. In fact, a Svāyambhuva Liṅga is considered so sacred that it is above all the rules laid down in the *Āgamas* for the other classes of Liṅgas. If such indeed be the superiority of the Svāyambhuva Liṅgas over others, it is no wonder that every village claims the Svāyambhuva nature for the Liṅga set up in its temple. Sixty-eight places, which are situated in various parts of India, are said to possess Svāyambhuva Liṅgas and a list of these places, is given in the commentary on his *Jirṇōddhāra-daśakam* by Nigamajñānadēva of Vyāghrapura, son of *Vāmadēvaśivāchārya.**

---

* The sixty-eight places wherein Svāyambhuva Liṅgas are said to be found are:—

The Daivika Liṅgas are recognised, according to the *Makuṭāgama*, by their characteristic shapes. They may

The Daivika Liṅga.

No.	Place.	Name of the deity.
1	Vārāṇasi ...	Mahādēva.
2	Prayāga ...	Mahēśvara.
3	Naimiśa ...	Dēvadēvēśa.
4	Gayā ...	Prapitāmaha.
5	Kurukshētra ...	Sthāṇu.
5-*a*	Prabhāsa ...	Śaśibhūshaṇa.
6	Pushkara ...	Ajōgandha.
7	Vimalēśvara ...	Viśva.
8	Aṭṭahāsa ...	Mahānāda.
9	Mahēndra ...	Mahāvrata.
10	Ujjayini ...	Mahākāḷa.
11	Mahākōṭe ...	Mahōtkaṭa.
12	Śaṅkukarṇa ...	Mahātējas.
13	Gōkarṇa ...	Mahābala.
14	Rudrakōṭi ...	Mahāyōgi.
15	Mahāliṅgsthala ...	Īśvara.
16	Harshaka ...	Harshaka.
17	Viśvamadhya ...	Māhēśvara.
18	Kēdāra ...	Īśāna.
19	Himālaya ...	Rudrarudra.
20	Svarṇāksha ...	Sahasrāksha.
21	Viśvēśa ...	Vṛishabhadhvaja.

be of the shape of a flame or resemble a pair of

No.	Place.	Name of the deity.
22	Bhadravaṭa ...	Bhadra.
23	Bhairava ...	Bhairava.
24	Kanakhāla ...	Rudra.
25	Bhadrakarṇa ...	Sadāśiva.
26	Dēvadāruvana ...	Daṇḍi.
27	Kurujāngala ...	Chaṇḍēśa.
28	Trisandhi ...	Ūrdhvarētas.
29	Jāngala ...	Kaparddi.
30	Ēkagrāma (?) ...	Kṛittivāsas.
31	Mṛitakēśvara ...	Sūkshma.
32	Kālañjara ...	Nīlakaṇṭha.
33	Vimalēśvara ...	Śrīkaṇṭha.
34	Siddhēśvara ...	Dhvani.
35	Mṛitakēśvara ...	Gāyatri.
36	Kāśmīra ...	Vijaya.
37	Makuṭēśvara ...	Jayanta.
38	Kṛitēśvara ...	Bhasmakāya.
39	Kailāsāchala ...	Kirāta.
40	Vṛishasthāna ...	Yamaliṅga.
41	Karavīra ...	Kṛitaliṅga.
42	Trisandhi (?) ...	Tryambaka.
43	Virajā ...	Trilōchana.
44	Dīpta ...	Māhēśvara.
45	Nēpāḷa ...	Paśupati.

hands held in the *añjali* pose; they may have rough

No.	Place.	Name of the deity.
46	Kārōhaṇa ...	Lakuḷi.
47	Ambikā ...	Umāpati.
48	Gaṅgāsāgara ...	Amara.
49	Hariśchandra ...	Hara.
50	Mahēśvara ...	Ōṁkāra.
51	Kuruchandra ...	Śaṅkara.
52	Vāmēśvara ...	Jaṭila.
53	Makuṭēśvara ...	Sauśruti.
54	Saptagōdāvara ...	Bhīma.
55	Nagarēśvara ...	Svayambhū.
56	Jalēśvara ...	Triśūli.
57	Kailāsa ...	Tripurāntaka.
58	Karṇikāra ...	Gajādhyaksha.
59	Kailāsa (?) ...	Gaṇadhipa.
60	Hēmakūṭa ...	Virūpāksha.
61	Gandhamādana ...	Bhūrbhuva.
62	Himasthāna ...	Gaṅgādhara.
63	Bāḍabāmukha ...	Anala. Dānavāri (?)
64	Vindhyāparvata ...	Varāha.
65	Koṭitīrtha ...	Ugra.
66	Ishṭikāpura (in Lanka?).	Varishṭa.
67	Pātāḷa ...	Hāṭakēśvara.
68	Liṅgēśvara ...	Varada.
69	Gajapriya ...	Jalaliṅga.

exterior with elevations and depressions, deep hollows and scars resembling *ṭaṅka* (chisel) and *śūla* (trident). The Daivika Liṅgas do not possess the *brahma* or the *pārśvasūtras*.

The Ganapa Lingas and the Arsha Lingas.

The Gāṇapa-liṅgas are those that are believed to have been set by Gaṇas. They are of the shape of the fruits of cucumber, citron, wood-apple or palm. The Ārsha Liṅgas are those set up and worshipped by Ṛishis; they are spheroidal in shape, with the top portion less broad than the lower portion ; in other words, they are like an unhusked cocoanut fruit. Both the Gāṇapa liṅgas and the Ārsha liṅgas, like the Daivika liṅgas, are without the *brahma-sūtras*. The *Kiraṇāgama* informs us that the Svāyambhuva, the Ārsha and the Daivika liṅgas have no shape (*rūpa*) and no measurements (*māna*) and are recognised only by their respective shapes.

The Manusha Lingas.

The largest number of the *achala* or the *sthāvarā* liṅgas, are of the class of Mānusha liṅgas. As the name indicates, this class of liṅgas consists of those set up by human hands. They are sculptured in accordance with the rules definitely laid down in the *Āgamas* and consist of ten classes. The measurement of the Mānusha Liṅgas depend upon any one of the following, namely, the height of door-way of the central shrine, the length of one side of the central shrine (which is generally cubical in shape) or the natural unit, the *hasta* or the cubit. The Mānusha liṅgas are made up of three parts, namely, the lowest which is square in section and is known as the Brahma-bhāga, the middle of octagonal section, known as the Vishṇubhāga and the topmost, of generally circular section, known as the Rudrabhāga; the lengths of these parts vary with the different classes of liṅgas. On the Rudrabhāga of all Mānusha liṅgas are carved certain lines called *brahma sūtras*, and the tops of the liṅgas technically known as *śirōvarttana* are fashioned in a number of forms; the rules for tracing the *brahma-sūtras* and for making the *śirōvarttanas* will be described in a subsequent portion of this chapter.

Lengths of the Sarvadesika Linga.

The *liṅgas* whose measurements depend upon the length of the side of the central shrine are called the *Sārvadēśika liṅgas*; different proportions which are fractions such as three-fifths, five-ninths, or half, of the length or breadth of the central shrine are prescribed for the lengths of the liṅgas, which are further classed under *uttama*, *madhyama* and *adhama* or the superior, the middling and the inferior varieties.

Of Sarvasama Linga.

The second class of the Mānusha liṅgas is called the *Sarvasama liṅga*. It is also called Sarvatōbhadra in the *Mayamata* and the *Kāmikāgama*.

Of Varddhamana Linga.

In the Sarvasama* class of liṅgas the brahmabhāga, the Vishṇubhāga and the Rudrabhāga are equal in length; whereas in the class known as the Varddhamāna liṅga,† which is also known, according to the *Siddhāntasārāvaḷi*, as the Surēḍhya liṅga, the proportion of the Brahmabhāga, the Vishṇubhāga and the Rudrabhāga are as 4, 5, 6 or 5, 6, 7, or 6, 7, 8, or 7, 8, 9. Of these the proportion 4, 5, 6 is prescribed for *Brāhmaṇas* and the other three for the Kshatriyas, the Vaiśyas and the Śūdras respectively.

Of Saivadhika Lingas.

The lengths of the Brahmabhāga etc., in the Śaivādhika‡ liṅgas are according to the *Kāmikāgama*, the *Kāraṇāgama* and the *Mayamata* are 7, 7, 8 or 5, 5, 6 or 4, 4, 5 or 3, 3, 4, respectively; and are meant for the four castes respectively beginning with the Brāhmaṇas.

---

* Literally '*all-equal*'.

† Literally '*of ascending order of lengths.*'

‡ Literally 'with the Śaiva part of larger length.'

Of Svastika Lingas. This class appears to be the same as the Anāḍhya liṅga of the *Siddhāntasārāvaḷi.* The proportion of the lengths of the *Brahmabhāga* and other parts in the Svastika liṅga, is given in the *Kāmikāgama* and the *Mayamata* as 2, 3, 4 respectively. In the class known

Of Trairasika Lingas. as the Trairāśika or Traibhāgika liṅgas, the lengths of the various parts are given as follows: dividing the whole length of the liṅga into nine equal parts, the periphery of the Brahmabhāga should be equal to eight of these parts, that of the Vishṇubhāga seven and that of the Rudrabhāga six. It should be noted here that the diameter of the *liṅga* is not given and we have to deduce it from the periphery; supposing that the total length of the *liṅga* is nine feet, the length of each division is one foot. If, as we have already said, the periphery of the square section of the *brahmabhāga* is eight times one division, the length of a side of the square will be two feet. The same is the length of the diameter of the octagon and the circle inscribed in this square. Mathematically the proportions of the periphery of the square, and the octagon and the circle inscribed in it are approximately 8, 6.624*

* $8r$, $16 \tan 22^{\cdot}5^{\circ}$ and $2\Pi r$, respectively where r=the radius of the circular Rudrabhāga, which we have assumed to be=1.

and 6.3 times one division. (See fig. 1, Pl. VII.) Thus there is a slight discrepancy between the proportions laid down in the *Āgamas* and those obtained mathematically. All the works, such as the *Kāmikāgama*, the *Kāraṇāgama*, the *Suprabhēdāgama* and the *Mayamata* are uniform in giving the same proportions to the three parts of the Trairāśika-liṅga. There is yet one more class of *liṅgas*, the Āḍhya-liṅga of the *Siddhāntasārāvaḷi:* the lengths of the Brahmabhāga, the Vishṇubhāga and the Śivabhāga of this variety are given as 8½, 8 and 7½ respectively. So far about the lengths of the various classes of *liṅgas.* I shall now proceed to the general rule regarding the width of *liṅgas.*

Of the Adhya Linga.

The *Siddhāntasārāvaḷi* lays down the following rule for fixing the widths of the Āḍhya, the Anāḍhya, the Surēḍhya and the Sarvasama *liṅgas:* divide the total length of the *liṅga* into sixteen equal parts; the width of the Āḍhya *liṅga* should be six of these parts; that of the Anāḍhya *liṅga*, five; that of the Surēḍhya *liṅga*, four; and lastly of the Sarvasama *liṅga*, five; the width of the three parts having the square section, the octagonal section and the circular section of the *liṅga* is obviously the same throughout.

Widths of Lingas.

The *Mayamata* gives the widths of the various *liṅgas* in greater detail.

The central shrines of Hindu temples are roughly divided according to their ground plans and superstructure into three classes, namely, the Nāgara, the Drāviḍa, and the Vēsara classes.

Of the Nagara Lingas.

The width of the *liṅga* to be set up in the central shrine of the Nāgara variety is given in the *Mayamata* as follows: divide the total length of the *liṅga*, (which itself depends upon the length of one side of the central shrine),* into sixteen equal parts: the widths of the liṅga that is to be set up in it might be 5, 4 or 3 of these parts. The one with a width of five parts is known as the *Jayada*

* The central shrines of all Śiva temples are square in plan. The length of the *adhamādhama* or the most inferior *liṅga* that might be set up in the Nágara type of central shrine is .5 of the length of one side of the central shrine and that of the *Uttamōttama* or the most superior *liṅga* is .6. Between these two extreme limits are seven varieties of *liṅgas*, the *adhama-madhyama*, *adhamōttama*; *madhyamādhama*, *madhyama-madhyama*, *madhyamōttama*; *uttamādhama* and *uttama-madhyama*; these have lengths obtained by adding a seventh part of the difference in length between the *uttamōttama* and the *adhamādhama* varieties, which in the case of the Nāgara temples is .1.

or the victory-bestowing variety; that with a width of four parts is of the *Pāushṭika* or the strength-bestowing variety and that of a width of three parts, the *Sārvakāmika* or the all-desires-bestowing variety.

Of Dravida Lingas.

In the case of the *liṅgas* to be set up in the Drāviḍa form of central shrines, the following rule gives their widths: divide the total length of the *liṅga** into twenty-one equal parts: the *liṅga* whose width is six of these parts is called the *Jayada liṅga;* that whose width is five parts is *Paushṭika* and that whose width is four parts is *Sārvakāmika.*

Of Vesara Lingas.

The *Jayada*, *Paushṭika* and *Sārvakāmika liṅgas* set up in the Vēsara class of central shrines have the following proportions: if the total length of the *liṅga*† is

---

* The length of the *Uttamōttama* class of the *liṅga* set up in the Drāviḍa temple is 13/21, part of the length of one side of the central shrine; that of the *adhamādhama* is 10/21 and the difference is 3/21 or 1/7. Dividing this difference into seven equal parts and adding one, two, etc., of these latter smaller parts to the length of the *adhamādhama liṅga* we obtain the seven varieties of *liṅgas* of intermediate lengths.

† The length of the *Uttamōttama liṅga* of the Vēsara type of the *garbha-griha* is 16/25 of the side of the central shrine; that of the *adhamādhama*, 13/25 and the difference in their lengths is 3/25 ; this difference is divided into seven equal parts; by the

PLATE VI.

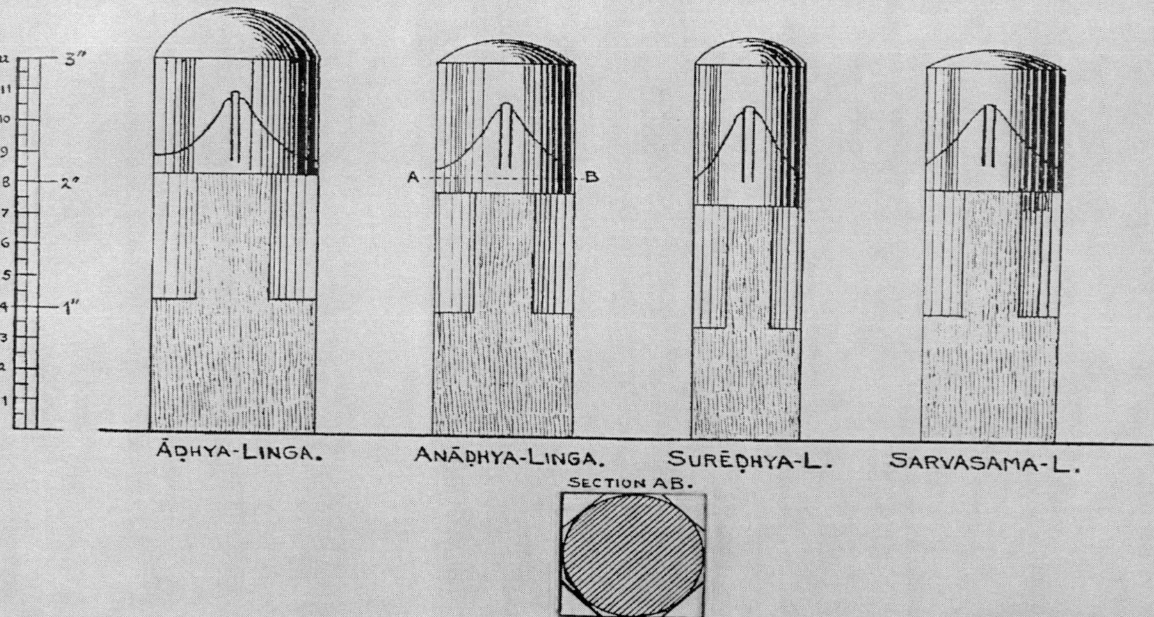

[To face page 93.]

divided into twenty-five equal parts, the width of the *Jayada liṅga* is eight parts; that of the *Paushṭika*, seven parts; and of the *Sārvakāmika*, six parts.

A few of the *liṅgas* described above are drawn to scale and are reproduced on Pl. VI; it might be noticed that they have different types of tops, some resembling a half-moon; some, the top of an umbrella and others, shaped like the egg. The process of rounding of these tops is technically known as the making of the *śirōvarttana.* Minute rules are laid down for producing the various tops, about which it is necessary to give here a brief account.

The tops of Lingas.

The tops of *liṅgas* are of several kinds, the most important of which are five, according to the *Mayamata*, and four according to the *Siddhāntasārāvaḷi.* They are named respectively *chhatrākāra*, *tripushākāra*, *kukkuṭāṇḍākāra*, *arddha-chandrākāra* and *budbuda-sadṛiśa* meaning the umbrella-shaped, the cucumber-shaped, the egg-shaped, the half-moon-shaped and the bubble-like respectively. The last named variety has been omitted by the *Siddhāntasārāvaḷi*, probably because its author is

---

addition of one, two, etc., of these smaller parts to the *adhamādhama* variety we get seven *liṅgas* of intermediate lengths.

inclined to include it in the *arddha-chandrākāra* class. These different forms represent different conic sections and the rules relating to their formation are of greater interest to the mathematician than to the iconographer; they are of great use to the sculptor. These rules would help an investigation into the various curves known to the Hindus and furnish some materials for the study of the History of Hindu mathematics. As these rules are extremely minute and are not quite easy to understand they have been omitted here; but the original texts have been inserted in the appendix for the benefit of those who can make any use of them.

Brahma-sutras.

There is yet one more detail in the making of a *liṅga*, without which the *liṅga* does not become complete and fit for worship; it is the tracing of certain lines known as the *brahma-sūtras* on the *liṅga*. Two vertical lines are engraved on the surface of the *Rudrabhāga* (or the *pūjābhāga*, as it is often referred to in the *Āgamas*). The length of these lines* should be, according to the *Siddhāntasārāvaḷi*, determined by the

* These lines are called by the name of *lakshaṇōddhāraṇa* in *Mayamata*; *maṇirēkhā*, *pārśva-sūtrā*, etc., are also other names of these.

PLATE VII.

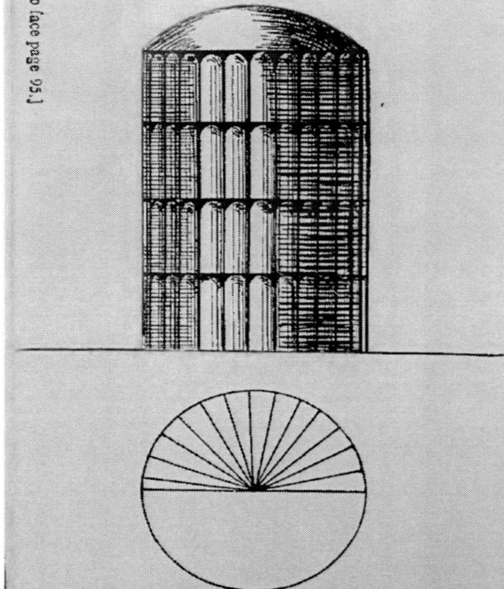

Fig. 2. Ashṭōttara-śata Liṅga.

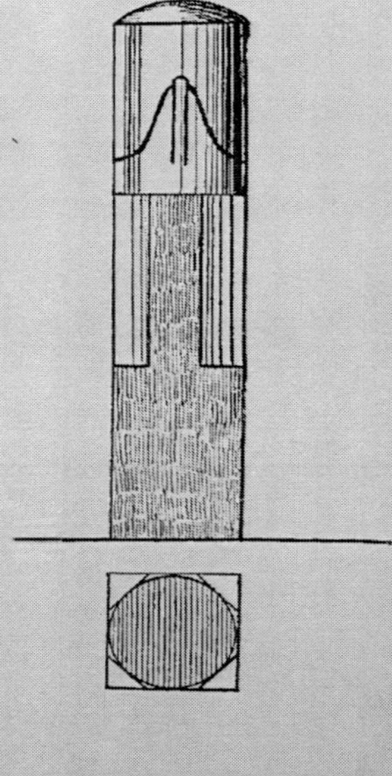

Fig. 1. Trairāśika Liṅga.

Fig. 3. Mukhaliṅga.

[To face page 95.]

following rule : divide the length of the *pūjābhāga* of the *liṅga* into three equal parts : divide further the two lower parts into eight equal divisions : now the distance between the two parallel vertical lines should be one of these smaller divisions ; the thickness and depths of the lines, should be one-ninth of this division : two lines are to be traced, one on either side, which should begin from near the tops of the vertical lines, descend sloping down and removed farther and farther from the central double parallel lines until they reach a distance which is two divisions from the lowest portion of the *pūjābhāga ;* then the two sloping side-lines, (*pārśva sūtras*), should be traced in a horizontal plane so as to meet each other at the back. (See fig. 1, Pl. VI, Pl. VII and fig. 1, Pl. X). The two central vertical parallel lines should be joined at their tops by a curved line whose curvature should resemble that of the top or (*śiras*) of the *liṅga.*

The Ashtottara sata Linga.

Among the Mānusha-liṅgas are included five more varieties, namely, the *Ashṭōttara-śata-liṅga*, the *Sahasra-liṅga*, the *Dhāra-liṅga*, the *Śaivēshṭyaliṅga* and the *Mukha liṅga.* Of these, the first, the *ashṭōttara-śata-liṅga* or the 108 miniature *liṅgas* are required to be carved on the *pūjābhāga* of the Surēḍhya *liṅga.* They are produced by cutting four equidistant horizontal deep lines on the surface of the *pūjābhāga*; at right angles to these and parallel to the axis of the *liṅga* are to be carved twenty-seven deep lines. The portions of the surface of the main *liṅga* formed by the intersection of the vertical and horizontal lines are small oblongular blocks, which are later on shaped into the form of the *pūjābhāga* of the ordinary *liṅgas* by rounding the sides and the top. Thus are formed a hundred and eight *liṅgas* (practically half-*liṅgas*) attached on the back to the main *liṅga* (See fig. 2, Pl. VII, and fig. 1, Pl. VIII).

The Sahasra Linga.

The *Sahasra-liṅga* is obtained in exactly the same manner as the *ashṭōttara-śata-liṅga*. The carving of the thousand and one *liṅgas* should be done on the surface of the *pūjābhāga* of an Āḍhya-liṅga. In the case of the Sahasra-liṅga the horizontal lines are eleven and the vertical lines ninety-nine (See fig. 2, Pl. VIII).

The Dhara Linga.

The *Dhārā-liṅgas* are *liṅgas*, the *pūjābhāga* of which has round it vertical fluted facets ranging from five to sixty-four in number. The *Suprabhēdāgama* prescribes 5, 7, 9, 12, 16, 20, 24 and 28 facets for Dhārā liṅgas, while the *Kāraṇāgama* mentions only 16 facets. But the *Māyamata* lays

PLATE VIII.

Fig. 1. Ashṭōttara-śata liṅga : Stone : Tiruvoṟṟiyūr.

Fig. 2. Sahasra-liṅga : Stone : Tiruvoṟṟiyūr.

PLATE IX.

Fig. 1. Mukhaliṅga : Stone :
Charchoma, Kotale District : Marwar.

Fig. 2. Mukhaliṅga :Stone.
Chakodi : Jodhpur District, Marwar.

[To face page 97.]

down the rule that the number of facets in the *Brahmabhāga*, the *Vishṇubhāga* and the *Rudrabhāga* should be either 4, 8 and 16; 8, 16 and 32; or 16, 32 and 64 respectively. The text of the *Kāmikāgama* is corrupt and hence what rule it lays down on this point is unintelligible. The *Dhārāliṅgas* should be made out of the Sarvasama liṅgas.

The Mukhalinga.

The Mukhaliṅga is one of the varieties of Mānusha-liṅgas and is distinguished from all other *liṅgas* in that it bears one or more human faces sculptured on it. Regarding the making of a Mukhaliṅga all the *Āgamas* and *Tantras* have detailed descriptions. The substance of these is that a Mukhaliṅga should be made on the *pūjābhāga* of the Sarvasama-liṅga and that it might have one, two, three, four or five faces corresponding to the five aspects, Vāmadēva, Tatpurusha, Aghōra, Sadyōjāta and Īśāna, of Śiva. If the central shrine has only one door-way in its front or the east side, there should be carved only one face and that on the front side of the *liṅga* facing the door-way (See fig. 1, Pl. IX); if it has two door-ways one in front and the other at the back of the central shrine, that is, on the eastern and western sides, there should be two faces carved on the front and back of the *liṅga*; there should be three faces on the *liṅga*, if there are three door-ways, that is, on all sides except the west (See fig. 2, Pl. IX); if, lastly, there are four doorways, there should be four faces or five; in the former case, the faces are turned in the four directions of the quarters; in the latter case, in addition to the four faces, there is to be one on the top of the *liṅga* and facing the east. The Īśāna aspect of Śiva is represented by the face on the top of the *liṅga;* the Tatpurusha, by that facing the east, the Aghōra, by that facing the south; the Sadyōjāta, by that facing the west and the Vāmadēva, by that facing the north. In the case of the four faces carved on the four sides of the Mukhaliṅga they should be attached to bodies which ought to be represented only as far as the chest (*stana-sūtra*) (See fig. 3, Pl. VII, Pl. XI and Fig. 2, Pl. X). Each of these figures should have only one pair of arms and be fashioned in all other respects in conformity with the rules laid down for the making of images.

From the descriptions of the Mānusha *liṅgas* given above, it is easily seen that the symbol represents a phallic emblem, of which the part projecting above the *pīṭha* is the representation of the *membrum virile* and the *brahmasūtra* makes of the nut from the shaft and the rounded top completes its likeness to the human phallus. The

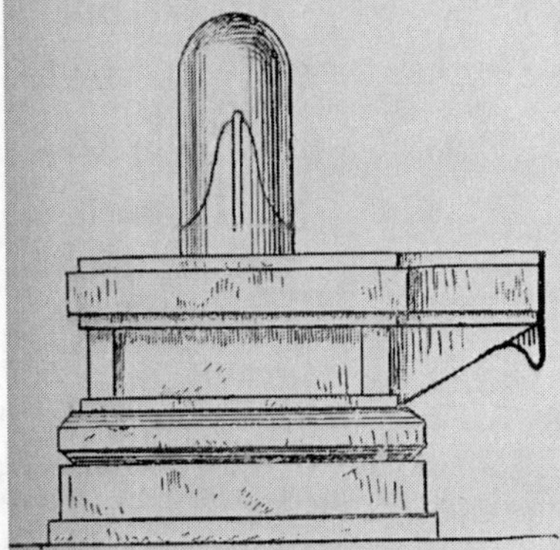

Fig. 1.

Fig. 2. Mukhaliṅga : Marble : Nasik.

Fig. 3. Dhārā-liṅga : Stone : Tirūvoṟṟiyūr.

[To face page 98.]

PLATE XI.

Mukhaliṅga : Stone. Joti, (Cuddapah District.)

[To face page 98.]

Brahmabhāga and the *Vishṇubhāga* are only designed to fix the *liṅga* firmly in the pedestal. Of the component parts of the *pīṭha*, that slab of stone with a square hole, in which the square portion of the *liṅga* fits in and which forms the lower member of the *pīṭha*, prevents its rotation. The second slab with an octagonal hole in it and which is the second or upper member of the *pīṭha* restricts the vertical motion of the *liṅga*.

Pithas.

Liṅgas are almost always set up in pedestals known as the *piṇḍikās* or *pīṭhas*. These may be square, oblongular, octogonal, elongated octagon, hexagon, elongated hexagon, duodecagon, elongated duodecagon, 16 sided, regular or elongated, circular, elliptical, triangular and semi-circular, in plan.[1] In a square *pīṭha*, which is the

Forms of the plans of pithas.

---

(1). The *Mānasāra* lays down the rule that the form of the *pīṭha* that should be used in the Nāgara, Drāviḍa and Vēsara forms of *vimānas* (central shrines) is the *nāgara*, *drāviḍa* and *vēsara* respectively and it defines that the *nāgara pīṭha* is square; the *drāviḍa pīṭha*, octagonal and the *vēsarapīṭha* circular in plan.

कुर्यात्तु नागरे लिङ्गपीठं नागरमेव च ।
द्राविडे द्राविडं प्रोक्तं वेसरे वेसरं तथा ॥
धारालिङ्गं तु सर्वेषां धारापीठं प्रकल्पयेत् ।
* * * * *
नागरं चतुरश्रं स्यादष्टाश्रं द्राविडं तथा ।
वृत्तं च वेसरं प्रोक्तमेतत्पीठाकृतिस्तथा ॥

Length of the side of the pithas.

one commonly met with, the length of one side of it may be twice the length of the *pūjābhāga*, or equal to the total length of the *liṅga ;* in other words two-thirds of or equal to the total length of the *liṅga*. The *pīṭha*, the length of whose side is equal to the total length of the *liṅga* is said to belong to the *Uttamōttama* class and that whose side is equal to two-thirds the total length of the *liṅga*, *adhamādhama.* Dividing the total length of the *liṅga* into twenty-four equal parts, the following classification of the *pīṭhas* is obtained.

Adhamādhama	piṭha's side		16	parts.
Adhamamadhyama	,,	,,	17	,,
Adhamōttama	,,	,,	18	,,
Madhyamādhama	,,	,,	19	,,
Madhyamamadhyama	,,	,,	20	,,
Madhyamōttama	,,	,,	21	,,
Uttamādhama	,,	,,	22	,,
Uttamamadhyama	,,	,,	23	,,
Uttamōttama	,,	,,	24	,,

Or, dividing the total length of the *liṅga* into 32 parts, the nine above-mentioned varieties are obtained by taking the same number of parts as in the above case; then the *Uttamōttama* variety of *pīṭha* has a side whose length is, three-fourths of the total length of the *liṅga* and the *adhamādhama* variety, one-half of the total length of the *liṅga*.

PLATE XII.

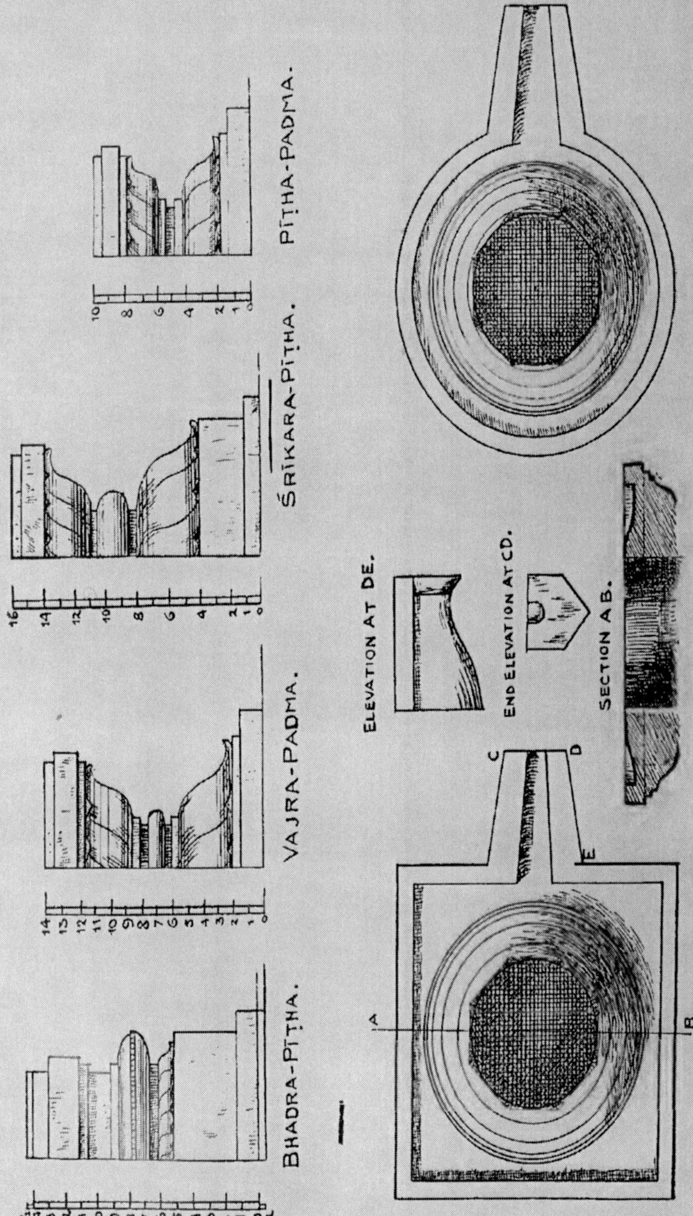

[To face page 101.]

The length of a side of the *pīṭha* may also be equal to three times the diameter of the *liṅga* or equal to the periphery of the *pūjābhāga* or equal to the periphery of the *Vishṇubhāga*.

The height of the pitha

The height of the *pīṭha* may come up as far as the upper end of the Vishṇu-bhāga of the *liṅga*; or it might cover up the *pūjābhāga* to a height equal to a quarter or even half the height of the *Vishṇubhāga*. These *pīṭhas* are made of one, two or three slabs of stones placed one over another and they are shaped with various kinds of ornamental mouldings which are arranged in tiers one over another. They are named according to the number and form of the different kinds of mouldings as Bhadrapīṭha, Mahāmbuja-P., Śrīkara-P., Vikara-P., Mahāvajra-P., Saumyaka-P., Śrīkāmya-P., Chandra-P., and Vajra-P. The various items of the mouldings are known as *upāna*, *jagati*, *kumuda*, *padma*, *kampa*, *kaṇṭha*, *paṭṭikā*, *nimna* and *ghṛitavāri*. Drawings made to scale of a few of the *pīṭhas* are given on Pl. XII. The upper surface of the *pīṭha* from which the *pūjābhāga* of the *liṅga* juts out is so shaped as to allow a free flow of water towards the water spout, which is generally found attached

Kinds of pithas.

Nala or the water-course.

to the side of the *pīṭha* on the left of the *liṅga*, as the worshipper faces it. (See the plan and section of a *pīṭha* reproduced on Pl. XII). The length of this water spout or water-course which is known in Sanskrit as the *nāḷa*, as also its width at its origin, is required to be one-third or one-fourth of the length of the side of the *pīṭha*, and its breadth at the free end, three-fourths of its breadth at the origin. The side view of the *nāḷa* should be like the lip of an elephant. (See the end elevation at C.D., Pl. XII).

The *liṅga* should be made out of *pum-śilā* or the male stone, while the *piṇḍikā* or *pīṭha* of *strī-śilā* or female stone. A very elaborate dissertation on the male, the female or the neuter nature of stones, timber, and other objects, is given in all *āgamas*, but it is perhaps unnecessary to detail their descriptions here.

LINGODBHAVAMURTI, CHANDRASEKHARAMURTI, PASUPATAMURTI AND RAUDRAPASUPATAMURTI.

LIṄGŌDBHAVAMŪRTI AND CHANDRA-ŚEKHARAMŪRTI.

HAVING described the various forms of *liṅgas*, let me now proceed to a description of the Liṅgōdbhavamūrti. This is one of the common icons in Southern India, which according to the *Āgamas* is required to be placed in the niche in the western wall of the *garbha-gṛiha* or the central shrine. Śiva is said to have appeared in the form of a blazing pillar of immeasurable size to quell the pride of Brahmā and Vishṇu. The story, which is almost identically given in the *Liṅga-purāṇa*, the *Kūrma-purāṇa*, the *Vāyu-purāṇa* and the *Śiva-purāṇa*, runs as follows :—Vishṇu at the end of a *kalpa* was slumbering on the deep abyss of waters; a great illumination occurred then near Vishṇu and from it emerged Brahmā. Brahmā saw before him another person Vishṇu ; Brahmā approached Vishṇu and introduced himself to Vishṇu as the creator of the whole universe and demanded of Vishṇu who he was ; towhich Vishṇu replied that he was

14

also the architect of the universe. Brahmā could not brook the statement of Vishṇu and a quarrel ensued between them both. At this juncture there appeared a *liṅga* resembling the great cosmic fire, with hundreds of tongues of flames blazing out of it. Instead of quarrelling with each other Brahmā and Vishṇu set about to find out the top and bottom respectively of this huge mass of fire, for which purpose the former assumed the form of a swan (*haṁsa*) and flew up in the air; while the latter took the form of a boar and burrowed down into the earth. The attempt of these two gods to discover the reality and measure of this fiery pillar proved futile. They then came to realise that there certainly was something far greater than themselves; whose top or bottom they could not find out: thus humiliated they approached this pillar of fire and began to praise it. Pleased with their prayers Śiva manifested himself to them in the body of this fiery *liṅga* with a thousand arms and legs, with the sun, the moon and the fire as his three eyes, bearing the bow called the *pināka*, clad in the hide of an elephant, carrying the *triśūla*, wearing the *yajñōpavīta* made of snakes and with a voice resembling the rumbling of the clouds or the noise of the drum, addressed Brahmā and Vishṇu thus:—" You both are born from me, Brahmā having come from my right loin and Vishṇu from the left loin; all three of us are really one, but are now separated into three aspects, namely, Brahmā, Vishṇu and Mahēśvara. Brahmā will in the future be born of Vishṇu and at the beginning of a *kalpa*, I myself will be born from the angry brow of Vishṇu." Thus declaring, Mahēśvara disappeared. From this time the *liṅga* came to be worshipped by all men.

While searching for the top of the pillar of fire, Brahmā came by a petal of the *kētaki* flower and asked it wherefrom it was descending; to this the petal answered that it was falling from the head of Mahēśvara, for what length of time it could not remember. Taking hold of this petal, Brahmā descended and lied to Vishṇu that he had discovered the head of Mahēśvara and from it had brought this petal of the *kētaki* flower. For uttering this piece of falsehood Brahmā was cursed not to receive any worship from men on earth. Hence, it is stated, Brahmā is never enshrined in a separate temple and offered worship.

In the *Aṁśumadbhēdāgama* is found the following description of the Liṅgōdbhavamūrti: The figure of Śiva in the aspect of Chandraśēkharamūrti should be carved on the front of a *liṅga*. It is stated in the *Kāraṇāgama* that one-fifth part of the *liṅga* should be left out on the top and at the bottom respectively without any sculpture. The legs below the knees of the figure of Chandraśēkhara carved on the *liṅga* should be invisible, that is, should be left unsculptured. On the right of the *liṅga* and near its top Brahmā should be represented in the shape of a swan (*haṁsa*) while Vishṇu should be carved in the form of a boar on the left at the foot of the *liṅga*. The figures of Brahmā and Vishṇu should be sculptured on the right and left respectively of the *liṅga* and also facing it, with two hands held on the chest in the *añjali* pose. The colour of the figure of Śiva should be red, that of Vishṇu black and that of Brahmā golden yellow. Over and above this description, a few additional details are found in the *Kāmikāgama*. The size of the swan, it is stated, should be the same as that of the face of Śiva, while that of the boar, twice that of the face of Śiva. The figure of the boar should be worked out as digging into the earth. The figures of Vishṇu and Brahmā should be expressive of submission and be sculptured beautifully ; or they may be altogether omitted from the panel ; in this latter case, the swan and the boar should necessarily be there. The *Śilparatna* adds that Śiva should carry the *śūla* in one of his hands ; whereas, the *Kāraṇāgama* requires that of the four hands, one should be in the *abhaya* pose,

PLATE XIII.

Liṅgōdbhavamūrti : Stone :
Kailāsanāthasvāmin Temple : Conjeevaram.

[To face page 109.]

another in the *varada* pose, a third should carry the *paraśu* and the fourth a *kṛishṇa-mṛiga* (a black buck) and that the digit of the moon (*chandra-kalā*) should adorn the crown of Śiva. Such is the description of the Liṅgōdbhavamūrti, which is illustrated with three pictures. The first photograph (Pl. XIII) is that of the Liṅgōdbhavamūrti found in the Kailāsānāthasvāmin temple at Conjeevaram and is over twelve hundred years old. This piece of sculpture is very much at variance with the textual descriptions. The figure of Śiva-Chandraśēkhara has eight arms of which some are seen carrying the *paraśu*, the *śūla*, an *akshamālā* and some other objects, while one is held in the *abhaya* pose and another is resting upon the hip (*kaṭyavalambita*). Then again the one-fifth part of the *liṅga* on the top is not left unsculptured, nor is the part of the *liṅga* lower than the knees of the figure of Śiva, equal to a fifth of the total length of the *liṅga*. But the sculpture agrees with the Sanskrit texts in that the legs of Śiva below the knees are left out unsculptured; the digit of the moon is shown on the crown of Śiva; the boar-*avatāra* of Vishṇu, with four hands out of which two are shown as digging the earth and the other two as carrying the *śaṅkha* and the *chakra*, and not an ordinary boar, as stated in the *Āgamas*, is carved out at the bottom space of the panel; Brahmā is seen flying in the air in his own form instead of as a swan; one of his legs, as also that of the other deities on the left of the *liṅga*, is horizontal, while the figures of Brahmā and Vishṇu each having four arms are sculptured on the right and left of the *liṅga*; they have each one arm lifted up in the pose of praising, while the other rests upon the hip, and the remaining ones carry their characteristic weapons. The top of the niche has got a highly artistically carved *makara-tōraṇa*.

The second photograph, Fig. 2., Pl. XIV, represents the Liṅgōdbhavamūrti in the temple of Śiva at *Ambar Māgāḷam*. In this, the *liṅga* has a wreath of flowers thrown over its top; the figure of Śiva is shown with four arms, one of which is held in the *abhaya* pose, the other in the *kaṭyavalambita* pose (resting upon the hip), and the remaining two carry the *paraśu* and the black buck. The legs of the figure of Śiva below the knees and up to the ankles are sculptured against the rules laid down in *Āgamas*; the feet alone are kept hidden in the *liṅga*. On the right of the *liṅga* and on its top is to be seen the swan whose beak is prominently visible; below and on the left of the *liṅga* is to be seen the boar, half man and half beast, burrowing the earth. This piece of sculpture belongs to the mediæval Chōḷa period, that is, to the 11th or 12th century A.D.

PLATE XIV.

Fig. 1. Liṅgōdbhavamūrti : Stone : Daśāvatāra Cave : Ellora.

Fig. 2. Liṅgōdbhavamūrti : Stone : Ambar-Māgāḷam.

[To face page 110.]

The third picture, (Fig. 2, Pl. XIV), is a pen and ink sketch of the Lingōdbhavamūrti from the Daśāvatāra Cave at Ellora. The whole panel is a remarkable piece of artistic work; it consists of the blazing pillar of fire at the centre, with the figure of Śiva emerging from the middle of it, having one hand in the *abhaya* pose, another resting on the hip, while the others are carrying perhaps the *paraśu* and *mṛiga* (deer). Since Śiva is said in some *purāṇas* to have presented himself before Brahmā and Vishṇu as a flaming pillar (the *Skambha* of the *Atharvaṇa-vēda*), the artist has shaped the *liṅga* like a pillar with a capital. Flames are bursting out in tongues on both sides of the pillar. Brahmā with four faces is seen flying in the air, and Vishṇu as Varāha is digging the earth with his hands and snout. On the right and left are seen Brahmā and Vishṇu respectively standing in a reverential attitude, with two hands clasped in the *añjali* pose and the other two carrying the characteristic objects such as the *śankha*, the *chakra*, the *kamaṇḍalu*, etc., of these two deities. The details in this sculpture are executed in the most exquisite manner. It might be observed that in all these cases, the figure of Śiva is enclosed in a lenticular aperture on the surface of the *liṅga*.

CHANDRAŚĒKHARAMŪRTI.

THE name Chandraśēkharamūrti implies an image which has Chandra (the moon) as its head-ornament. How Śiva came to possess snakes on his body, the black buck and the *paraśu* in his hands, the Apasmāra-purusha or the demon under his feet, to wear the skins of the lion and the tiger on his loins and and the skull and the moon tucked up in his crown is described in the *Suprabhēdāgama* thus :—When Śiva was passing by the slopes of the mountain Mēru without any garments, the wives of the Ṛishis fell in love with him and lost their chastity. The Ṛishis, wild with rage, performed incantations to kill Śiva, the seducer of their wives; from their ceremonial ground there came snakes, a *kṛishṇa-mṛiga*, an *Apasmāra-purusha*, a *paraśu*, a bull, a tiger, a lion and several other things. For destroying Śiva all these were discharged by the Ṛishis against him. The latter took into his hands

General characteristics of the images of Siva.

for his sports the black-deer, the snakes and the *paraśu ;* the *Apasmāra-purusha* was trampled under his feet and is always serving him as a foot-stool ; the lion and the tiger were killed by Śiva and their skins worn by him as his garments, while the skull and the digit of the moon were placed on his *jaṭāmakuṭa* as ornaments. The *Suprabhēdāgama* adds further that all figures of Śiva should have the following characteristics, namely, three eyes, four arms, the crescent moon, the *dhurdhura* flowers, (*dātura*), snakes on the crown (*jaṭāmakuṭa*), the tiger-skin garment, the *hāra*, the *kēyūra*, *yajñō-pavita* and *kuṇḍalas* adorning his person. Special figures of Śiva may have other objects about them than those mentioned just now.

In addition to these, other characteristic features of the images of Śiva are given in a manuscript added at the end of the *Śilparatna* whose name is not known. It is stated therein that the colour of the figure of Śiva, if it is painted on a wall, should be white or of the red colour of the sun or golden yellow. The image should possess high shoulders, long arms and eyes like the petals of the lotus ; there should be three waist zones or *kaṭi-sūtras.* The appearance of the figure of Śiva should be that of a youth of sixteen years of age, with a blue throat, handsome countenance, and wearing *kuṇḍalas* in the ears; the neck should be somewhat stout. The figure may have four, eight, ten, sixteen or eighteen arms. The image is said to be a *śānta-mūrti* or pacific in nature, when it has four arms:—in this case, of the four arms two should carry the *triśūla*, and the *ḍamaru*, while the remaining two should be kept in the *varada* and the *abhaya* poses. If the image has eight arms—(it is not mentioned in the text in what aspect Śiva should have eight arms)—it should carry all the objects which are in the hands of the image of Śiva with ten arms, except the *khaḍga* and the *khēṭaka*. The image of Śiva, when he is in the act of killing the *Gajāsura*, should have ten arms; when it has ten arms, the right hands should carry an *akshamālā*, a sword, the *śaktyāyudha*, the *daṇḍa* and the *śūla*; whereas the left hands should carry the *khaṭvāṅga*, a snake, a skull, the *khēṭaka* and the deer. Śiva in the act of destroying the three-castle (*Tripura-dahana*) should possess sixteen arms. In this instance, the following six objects should be carried in addition to those mentioned in connection with the image of Śiva with ten arms; namely, the *bāṇa*, the *chakra* and the *gadā* in the right hands and the bow, a bell and the *śaṅkha* in the left hands. In the aspect of Bhairava, Śiva has eighteen arms; the additional hands hold the *ḍamaru* and the *śaṅkha* (?)*

---

* महादेवं प्रवक्ष्यामि यथा लेख्यस्स भित्तिषु ।
शुक्लोऽर्करश्मिसङ्काशस्तप्तस्वर्णनिभोऽपि वा ॥
उन्नतांसो महावाहुः कमलायतलोचनः ।
द्वीपिचर्मपरीधानवृत्तर्ण्णघो(?)रुमण्डलः ॥
केयूरहारसंपन्नः कटिसूत्रत्रयान्वितः ।
नवेन्दुकलिता(का ?)कान्तनवजूटविराजितः ॥
भ्राजितः फालनेत्रेण नागाभरणभूषितः ।
व्यष्टवत्सरदेशीयो नीलकण्ठो मनोहरः ॥
कुण्डली पीनगण्डस्स्यादष्टभिर्बाहुभिर्युतः ।
दशभिर्बाहुभिर्वाथ भुजैष्षोडशभिः क्वचित् ॥
अष्टादशभुजं क्वापि चतुर्बाहुरथापि वा ।
ते शस्त्राणि प्रवक्ष्यामि भुजेषु च यथाक्रमम् ॥
अक्षमालामासिं शक्तिं दण्डं शूलं च दक्षिणे ।
खट्वाङ्गं भुजगं चैव कपालं खेटकं तथा ॥
परुणं (हरिणं ?) च तथा हस्ते वामभागे निवेशयेत् ।
गजासुरवधेनाढ्ये बाहुभिर्दशभिर्युतः ॥
पुरत्रयस्य दहने भुजैष्षोडशभिर्युतः ।
बाणं चक्रं गदां चैव दक्षिणेऽभ्यधिकं भवेत् ॥
धनुश्चैव तथा घण्टा शङ्खं वामेऽधिकं भवेत् ।
दशपूर्वा भुजाः प्रोक्ता षोडशैवं निरूपिताः ॥
स्व(?)श्च भैरवाकारे बाहवोऽष्टादश स्मृताः ।
डमरुं च तथा शङ्खमधिकं तु प्रकल्पयेत् ॥
त्रिशूलं डमरुं चैव वरदं चाक्षमालिकाम् ।
चतुर्बाहोर्महेशस्य शान्तमूर्तेस्समालिखेत् ॥

The *Pūrva-Kāraṇāgama* states that the figures of Śiva in the Bhikshāṭana, the Kaṅkāḷa, the Haryarddha, the Arddhanārīśvara, the Sukhāsana, the Kāmāntaka and the Dakshiṇāmūrti aspects should not have near them the figure of the Dēvī; while in all other aspects the Dēvī should be found near Śiva. The height of the figure of the Dēvī, in company with that of her consort Śiva, should be up to the ear of Śiva, if the figure of the Dēvī is of the *uttama* class; up to his mouth, if of the *madhyama* class, and up to his uplifted hand, if of the *adhama* class.

The colour, according to the *Kāraṇāgama*, of the Nṛittamūrti, of the Kaṅkāḷamūrti and of the Dakshiṇāmūrti is to be white; while that of all other aspects of Śiva, coral red.

The image of Chandraśēkharamūrti is divided into three classes, namely, the Kēvalamūrti, the Umāsahitamūrti and the Āliṅganamūrti. All these three classes are usually found in the temples of Southern India and their descriptions are contained in all *Āgamas*. For instance, the *Aṁśumadbhēdāgama* says that the Kēvalamūrti should have one of his right hands

Kevala-murti.

अन्यस्य दशहस्तस्य भवेयुर्हेतयः क्रमात्
अष्टबाहोर्महेशस्य न स्यातां खड्गखेटकौ ॥
(शिल्परत्नसंयोजिते कस्मिंश्चिद् ग्रन्थे)

held in the *abhaya* pose, one of his left hands in the *varada* pose, the other right hand should carry the *ṭaṅka* and the remaining left hand a black buck; Śiva should be standing erect, without any bends in his body, that is, in the attitude known as *samabhaṅga*. He should be shown as wearing on his head a *jaṭāmakuṭa* ornamented with a crescent moon; also, he should have three eyes, a beautiful face, and be adorned with all ornaments; he should be clad in yellow garments (*pītāmbara*), the ends of which should descend as far below as the knees, while the bigger folds should pass between the two legs. If the hand held in the *varada* pose happens to be completely stretched out as in fig 5, Pl. V. of Vol. I, it should be kept so as to make the wrist reach the height of the hip, while the tips of the fingers should reach the *mēḍhramūla-sūtra*. If the hand has its fingers slightly bent, as in fig. 4, on the same plate, the back of the hand should be raised as far as the *nābhi-sūtra*. The *samabhaṅga* attitude is expressive of the *rājasa-guṇa* of the image. The deer and the *ṭaṅka* should be held in the hands kept in the *kartari-hasta* pose; and the deer may be facing the figure of Śiva or be away from it. The crescent of the moon may be attached to the right or the left of the *jaṭāmakuṭa*. The colour of the figure of Śiva should be red.

To the above description, the *Uttara-kāmikāgama* adds, that the right front hand may be held in the *simhakarṇa*, *kaṭakahasta* or the *kaṭyavalambitahasta* pose. The two back hands which are held in the *kartari-hasta* pose should not go higher than the *hikkā-sūtra*, that is, above the shoulders and the tops of the *ṭaṅka* and the *mṛiga*, higher than the *karṇa-sūtra* or the ear. While the deer might face the figure of Śiva or be away from it, the head of the *ṭaṅka* should always be turned away from it. In the left ear of the image of Śiva-Chandraśēkhara there should be either the ear-ornament named the *ratna-kuṇḍala*, the *śaṅkha-patra* or the *padma-patra ;* whereas in the right ear there may be either the ornament named the *makara-kuṇḍala* the *simha-kuṇḍala*, or the *patra-kuṇḍala*. The curls of hair should hang at the back as far down as the ear, while the *jaṭās* or the braids or plaits of hair should hang on the right and left of the image as far as the shoulders. The figure of Chandraśēkhara should be ornamented with several pearl necklaces (*muktāhāra*) and jewelled necklaces (*ratnahāras*), with well designed medallions (*padakas*) attached to them ; and there should also be *yajñōpavīta* and the *chhannavīra* and *udarabandhana*. Besides, there should be *kēyūras* and other bracelets (*kaṭakas*) on the arms; and the fingers should be adorned with rings and the waist with a zone, and the ankles with anklets. The figure of Chandraśēkhara should be standing upon a *padma-piṭha*.

The second variety of Chandraśēkharamūrti is, as we have mentioned above, known as the Umāsahitamūrti. If the image of Chandraśēkhara has that of the Dēvī by his side, either on the same pedestal (*piṭha*) or a different one, it is said to be Umā-sahitamūrti, or Chandraśēkhara with Umā.

Uma-sahita-murti.

The third variety of Chandraśēkharamūrti is known as the Āliṅgana-mūrti. In this aspect, Chandraśēkhara is to be represented as embracing the Dēvī with one of his left arms: this arm might rest upon the left side of the Dēvī just below her breast, or it may be placed upon the left arm of the Dēvī, outside the *pārśva-sūtra;* the Dēvī should keep in her right hand a red lotus flower. Or, the right hand of the Dēvī may embrace Śiva, in which case the hand of the Dēvī should rest on the right side of Śiva a little above the waist zone; and the left hand of the Dēvī should carry a flower. Or, the two figures of Śiva and Umā may be embracing each other, the one with the left and the other with

Alinganamurti.

PLATE XV.

Fig. 1. Kēvala-Chandraśēkharamūrti :
Bronze : Tiruppālatturai (Tanjore Dt.)

Fig. 2. Umāsahita-Chandraśēkharamūrti :
Bronze : Agaram-Śettūr.

[To face page 121.]

the right hand. Thus there are three modes in which the figure of Āliṅgana Chandraśēkhara may be sculptured.

In all the above instances Chandraśēkharamūrti whether in company with his consort or not, should have around him the *prabhā-maṇḍala.* It must also be noted that this image of Siva should always be a standing one.

The *Śrītatva-nidhi* adds that the colour of Śiva in this instance should be that of coral, while the colour of Dēvī, black. The Dēvī is here said to possess three eyes and is required to be standing with three bends in her body (*tribhaṅga*); her right leg should be planted firmly on the pedestal and the left leg, slightly bent. She should carry in her right hand the *nīlōtpala* flower.

In illustration of the descriptions given above ten photographs are given. The first comes from Tiruppālatturai in the Tanjore district. The artist who produced this image of the Kēvala Chandraśēkharamūrti has followed in every detail the descriptions of the *Āgamas;* the image is standing perfectly erect on a *padma-pīṭha;* its *varada-hasta* and the *abhaya-hasta* as also those carrying the *paraśu* and *mṛiga* are placed in the exact positions required by the *Āgamas.* In fact, the sculptor is seen to exhibit in this piece of work such scrupulous care to be true to the descriptions of *Āgamas* that he has subordinated his artistic instinct, if he had it in any degree, and the result is not quite pleasant. The long *jaṭā-makuṭa* and the unhappy looking countenance of Śiva together with its ill-shaped legs, stamp the work as being really of an inferior kind. The second photograph, Pl. XVI, is that of a figure of Kēvala Chandraśēkharamūrti carved in wood. It is found in the Bhagavatī temple at Ōṇakkūr in North Travancore. The figure is about four feet in height. It holds the *paraśu* and the *mṛiga* in the back right and left hands respectively, while the front right and left hands are in the *varada* and the *abhaya* poses respectively. The ornaments and the drapery of the image are carved out very elaborately. This image is one of the best specimens of wood-carving of the medieval period found in Travancore. The third photograph, Pl. XVII, is of the Umāsahita-Chandraśēkharamūrti belonging to the Śiva temple at Tiruvoṟṟiyūr near Madras. The rules of the *Āgamas* are very carefully carried out but not so as to mar the beauty of the image; the execution of the work is excellent. The head of the *paraśu*, it will be observed, is turned away from the figure of Śiva and the deer has its face turned towards Śiva. The height of Umā comes up to the shoulders of

PLATE XVI.

Kēvala-Chandraśēkharamūrti.
Wood : Ōṇakkūr (Travancore State).

[To face page 122.]

PLATE XVII.

Umāsahita-Chandraśēkharamūrti.
Bronze: Tiruvoṟṟiyūr.

[To face page 122]

PLATE XVIII.

Fig. 1. Umā-sahita-Chandraśēkharamūrti.
Bronze: Madeour.

Fig. 2. Āliṅgana-Chandraśēkharamūrti.
Stone: Māyavaram.

[To face page 123]

Śiva and the Dēvī is therefore of the *adhama* class. Both the Dēva and the Dēvī are standing upon *padmāsanas* as required by the Sanskrit texts. The fourth is a photograph of the Umā-sahita-mūrti to be found in the Śiva temple at Agaram Śēttūr (See fig. 2., Pl. XV). In this case, the figures of Śiva and Umā are standing each on a separate pedestal and are each surrounded by a *prabhāmaṇḍala* of elaborate workmanship. The Dēvī has three bends in her body and keeps in her right hand a *nīlōtpala* flower. The figure of Śiva is almost similar to the one first described; the left hand, instead of being held in the *varada* pose, is held in the *siṁhakarṇa* pose. The artistic merit of this group of images is also far from excellent. Fig. 1, Pl. XVIII is the photograph of the Umā-sahita-mūrti of the temple at Madeour. This is a fine piece of sculpture correctly conceived and very neatly executed. In this group Śiva and Umā stand on two *padmapīṭhas* which are fixed on a *bhadrapīṭha* and are both surrounded by a single *prabhāmaṇḍala*.

The next photograph, fig. 2, Pl. XVIII, represents the Āliṅgana-Chandraśēkhara to be found in the Mayūranāthasvāmin temple at Māyavaram. Śiva, in this piece of sculpture, carries in his two back hands the *paraśu* and the *mṛiga*, while he keeps the front right hand in the *abhaya* pose. The front left hand is carried behind the Dēvī and is resting on her body below her breast. The Dēvī carries in her right hand a flower. The figures of Śiva and Umā are both shown with three bends in their bodies (*tribhaṅga*). This excellent piece of sculpture belongs to the Chōḷa period (of approximately 10th or 11th Cent. A.D.) In the image of Paṭṭīśvaram reproduced as fig. 1, Pl. XIX, which resembles closely the Kēvalamūrti of Tiruppālatturai (fig. 1, Pl. XV), and which appears to be the handiwork of the same sculptor, has its left arm taken near the waist of the Dēvī; whereas in the sculptures of Marudāntanallur and Kōvilūr, figs. 2 and 3 respectively of Pl. XIX, the left hand of Śiva rests upon the left shoulder of the Dēvī—that is, about the *pārśva-sūtra* of the figure of Dēvi. The original of the photograph of the Āliṅgana Chandraśēkharamūrti reproduced on Pl. XX, belongs to the Chālukya-Hoysaḷa school and comes from Āṅgūr in the Bellary District and is an extremely beautiful piece of art. The image of Śiva carries an *akshamālā*, a *triśūla* and a *ḍamaru* in three of its hands and the fourth is thrown over the shoulder of the Dēvī; the figure of Dēvī has its right arm placed on the right shoulder of Śiva and carries in its left hand a lotus flower. On the right and the left, near the feet of Śiva and Umā

PLATE XIX.

Fig. 1.
Āliṅgana-Chandraśēkharamūrti.
Bronze : Paṭṭīśvaram.

Fig. 2.
Āliṅgana-Chandraśēkharamūrti.
Bronze : Marudāntanallūr.

Fig. 3.
Āliṅgana-Chandraśēkharamūrti.
Bronze : Kōvilūr.

[To face page 124.]

PLATE XX.

Āliṅgana-Chandraśēkhara-mūrti :
Stone : Āṅgūr : Bellary District.

[To face page 124.]

respectively are seated their two sons, Gaṇapati on the floor and Subrahmaṇya on his peacock. The highest praise is due to the artist for the excellent pose in which he has sculptured the two images, the well-proportioned features of the male and female figures, and the splendid effect they produce on the observer.

Pasupatamurti and Raudrapasupatamurti.

Closely allied to the Chandraśēkharamūrti are the Pāśupatamūrti and a slightly different aspect of it, the Raudrapāśupatamūrti. The Pāśupatamūrti should also be standing erect (*samabhaṅga*) as in the case of the Chandraśēkharamūrti, should have three eyes, four arms and hair standing on the head upright on all sides, and a large well-proportioned body. One of the right hands should be held in the *abhaya* pose, while the other, should carry a *śūla*. One of the left hands should be kept in the *varada* pose and the remaining hand should carry on *akshamālā*. The figure must be decorated with all ornaments; and it must have a good look with a gentle smile playing upon its lips. The *Aṁśumadbhēdāgama* states that the image of Pāśupata-mūrti may be either standing or sitting, whereas the *Śilparatna*, wants it to be a standing figure and substitutes the *kapāla* in the place of *akshamālā* in the above description. According to the *Aṁśumadbhēdāgama*, the Pāśupatamūrti is to be used for the daily services (*nityōtsavas* in temples).

If, in the above description of the Pāśupatamūrti, the following alterations are made, it becomes the Raudrapāśupatamūrti: The colour of the body as also the eyes of the Raudrapāśupatamūrti is to be fiery red, the image of this aspect of Śiva should have sharp tusks, curling eye-brows, *yajñōpavīta* made of snakes, flaming head and red garments; in one of its hands there should be *triśūla* held head downwards, and another hand should carry a *kapāla.* Or, in the front hands must be held the *triśūla* in a horizontal position and the other two hands should hold the *ṭaṅka* and the sword. Meditating upon this aspect of Śiva even once, destroys all enemies, but this aspect should not be worshipped in actual images, but in certain symbols such as a *pīṭha.*

SUKHASANAMURTI, UMASAHITAMURTI, SOMASKANDAMURTI AND UMAMAHESVARAMURTI.

SUKHĀSANAMŪRTI, UMĀSAHITAMŪRTI, SŌMĀSKANDAMŪRTI AND UMĀMAHĒŚVARAMŪRTI.

THE four varieties of the images of Śiva known as the Sukhāsanamūrti, the Umāsahitamūrti, the Sōmāskandamūrti and Umāmahēśvaramūrti are usually met with in all Śiva temples which lay claim to some importance in Southern India. Of these, the Sukhāsanamūrti is described as follows in the *Śilparatna*, which is practically the same as the description given in all other authorities. The image of Sukhāsanamūrti is a seated figure with four arms, three eyes, a very handsome appearance suggestive of the *rajōguṇa* and of coral red complexion. The image should be seated erectly upon a *bhadra-pīṭha* with its left leg bent and resting upon the seat and the right one hanging below it. It must be clad in the skin of the tiger and also in silk garments; in its back right hand is to be the *paraśu*, and in its back left hand the *mṛiga*; the front right hand should be held in the *abhaya* pose, while the front

Sukhasanamurti.

left hand may be either in the *varada* or the *simhakarṇa* pose. In the right ear there should be either a *makara-kuṇḍala* or a *simha-kuṇḍala* and in the left ear, a *patra-kuṇḍala;* or there may be *vṛitta-kuṇḍalās* in both the ears. The head is adorned with a *jaṭāmakuṭa*, the fore-arms with *kaṅkaṇas* or bracelets shaped like serpents (*sarpa-kankaṇas*) and the chest with *yajñōpavīta;* besides these, the image should be decorated with all other ornaments. It is imperative that neither Dēvī nor Skanda should be near the Sukhāsanamūrti. The *Pūrva-Kāraṇāgama* differs from the above description in one small detail, namely, it states that the right leg of the image should be bent and be resting upon the seat and the left one hanging.

When seated alone as described in the previous paragraph, the image of Śiva is known as the Sukhāsanamūrti. If the figure of the Dēvī is also seated on the same seat by the side of the image of Śiva and faces the latter, the group is known as the Umāsahitamūrti. The position of the Dēvī is to the left of Śiva. She should have only two arms; in her right hand she should keep a lotus flower, while she may hold her left hand either in the *simhakarṇa* pose or keep it straight resting on the seat. Her head is to be adorned with a *karaṇḍa-makuṭa*. The left

Umasahitamurti.

leg of the Dēvī should be hanging down the seat, while the right one is to be bent and kept resting on the seat. The *Śilparatna* states that the right hand of the Dēvī should keep a *utpala* flower and the left hand held in the *varada* pose, or the left hand might rest on the *pīṭha* a little to the left of the left thigh of the Dēvi, and that the colour of the Dēvī should be grass-green. The Dēvī is required to be adorned with all ornaments, *hāras* and *makuṭa* and be clad in red silk garments. The *Pūrva-Kāraṇāgama* adds that the figure of the seated Dēvī should be as high as the shoulder of that of Śiva. The aspect of Śiva and Umā seated on the same seat and under the same *prabhā-maṇḍala* as described above is known as the Umā-sahitamūrti.

In the case of the Sōmāskandamūrti, the same relative positions are maintained by the figures of Śiva and Ūmā, but between these, there is the additional figure of the child Skanda. The figure of Skanda may be standing, sitting on the seat or on the lap of Umādēvī, or dancing; it should have a single face with a pair of eyes and two arms; and be adorned with a *karaṇḍa-makuṭa* on the head, *nakra-kuṇḍalas* in the ears, and *chhannavīra* on the body. The child Skanda should have a waist zone and bracelets. The figure of Skanda if it is standing simply, may carry in its right hand a lotus flower and keep the left hand hanging; or the two hands may keep lotus flowers in them; or as the *Śilparatna* would have it, the left hand should be held in either the *varada*, or the *siṁha-karṇa* pose and the right hand carrying a book. There should be no clothing on the person of the child Skanda. If the figure of Skanda is represented as dancing, it should carry in its left hand a fruit and the right one should be kept in the *sūchi* pose; or the left hand might be kept stretched out and be without the fruit.

The height of the figure of Skanda, says the *Uttara-Kāmikāgama*, may vary from one-tenth to four-tenths of the height of that of Śiva; and according to the *Kāraṇāgama* one-eighth to a quarter of the height of Śiva. The *Śilparatna* states that it should be as high as the bent hand or the breasts of the Dēvi.

The *Kāraṇāgama* adds that the gods Brahmā and Vishṇu together with their respective consorts should be standing on either side of the Sōmāskandamūrti.

Umamahesvaramurti.

The *Vishṇudharmōttara* and the *Rūpamaṇḍana* give the description of the Umāmahēśvaramūrti. The former authority states that in this aspect, the image of

PLATE XXI.

Fig. 1. Umā-sahita Sukhāsanamūrti.
Stone : Madeour.

Fig. 2. Umā-sahita Sukhāsanamūrti.
Bronze : Agaram Śāttūr.

[To face page 133]

Śiva and Umā should be seated on a seat, embracing each other. Śiva should have the *jaṭā-makuṭa* on his head with the crescent moon stuck in it; he should have two arms, in the right one of which there should be a *nīlōtpala* flower and the left one should be placed in embrace on the left shoulder of Umā. Umādēvī should have a handsome bust and hip; she should have her right hand thrown in embrace on the right shoulder of Śiva and should keep in her left hand a mirror. The figures of Śiva and Umā should be sculptured very beautifully.

The *Rūpamaṇḍana* informs us that Śiva should have four arms and that in one of the right hands there should be the *triśūla* and in the other a *mātuluṅga* fruit (a kind of citron); one of the left arms should be thrown on the shoulder of Umā and there should be a snake in the other left hand. The colour of Śiva should be red like the coral. The Dēvī should be as in the description of the *Vishṇudharmōttara* given above. There should be in this group the *Vṛishabha* or the bull of Śiva, Gaṇēśa, Kumāra and a lean emaciated figure of the *ṛishi* Bhṛiṅgi dancing, all arranged in an artistic composition.

Figs. 1 and 2, Pl. XXI, are to illustrate the aspects known as the Umā-sahita-mūrti, as also the Sukhāsanamūrti. If the Dēvī were absent in both the instances, the image of Śiva would have passed for the Sukhāsanamūrti; as they are, they are Umāsahita-mūrtis. In both the instances the back right hand keeps the *paraśu* and the back left hand, the *mṛiga ;* whereas the front right hand is in the *abhaya* pose and the front left hand in the *siṁhakarṇa* pose. In the one case, the left hand of the Dēvī is kept resting on the seat, whereas in the other it is held in the *siṁhakarṇa* pose. The stone image is older than the bronze one. Figs. 1 and 2, Pl. XXII are two splendid pieces of sculpture; the first belongs to the Śiva temple at Madeour and the second was recently discovered as a treasure trove in Nellore. Both of them are very good specimens of the Sōmāskanda-mūrti. The textual descriptions are carried out with scrupulous accuracy and the workmanship is superb. In the first piece, the left hand of the Dēvī rests on the *pīṭha* and in the second piece, it is held in the *varada* pose. In both, the child Skanda is in the dancing attitude, with both his hands held in the *siṁhakarṇa* pose. Attention may be drawn to the *makara-kuṇḍala* in the right ear and the *patra* or *vṛitta-kuṇḍala* in the left ear of Śiva in both the pieces of sculpture. Illustrations beginning from Pl. XXIII to XXIX

Fig. 1. Sômâskandamûrti. Bronze: Madeour.

Fig. 2. Sômâskandamûrti.
Bronze: Treasure Trove found in Nellore.

[To face page 134.]

PLATE XXIII.

Umāmaheśvaramūrti : Stone :
Bāgaḷi : Bellary District.

[To face page 135.]

PLATE XXIV.

Umāmahēśvaramūrti : Stone : Aihoḷe.

[To face page 135.]

represent Umāmahēśvaramūrti. Pl. XXIII is the reproduction of the image at Bāgaḷi in the Bellary District. In this, Umā is seated upon the left lap of Śiva and has her right hand taken round in embrace and resting upon the right side of the chest of Śiva, and carries in her left hand a *mātuluṅga* fruit. The front right hand of Śiva is held in the *abhaya* pose and the front left hand is placed on the left shoulder of Umā. In the back right and left hands are the *triśūla* and the *ḍamaru* respectively. The Dēvī wears on her head the hair dọne up in a fine side-knot. On the *prabhāvaḷi* are sculptured minutely the figures of the *ashṭa-dik-pālas* or the guardians of the eight quarters. It should be noted that in this case the figures of Gaṇēśa, Kumāra, the rishi Bhṛiṅgi and the bull are not sculptured. Pl. XXIV is the photograph of a piece of sculpture to be found in Aihole. Here, Śiva is carrying in two hands snakes, and in one hand the *triśūla ;* the remaining hand embraces Umā and rests on her shoulder. Umā keeps her right hand on the left thigh of Śiva ; her other arm is broken. On the left side of the seat on which Śiva and Umā are seated, is the figure of the child Kumāra who seems to be holding in his left hand three lotus flowers by their stalks and keeping some fruit in the right one. Below the seat are two *Apasmāra-Purushas* and the *ṛishi* Bhṛiṅgi. The figure of Gaṇēśa which ought to be on the right of Bhṛiṅgi appears to be lost. Pl. XXV is one of the very best pieces of ivory carving executed in the School of Arts at Trivandram. The delicacy of the workmanship, the beauty of the conception and execution, the grandeur of the effect it produces are beyond praise. Śiva is here represented as seated on a *bhadrāsana* under a tree and carries the *paraśu* and the *mṛiga* in his back hands; he holds his front right hand in the *abhaya* pose and embracing the Dēvi with his left arm, keeps that hand in the *varada* pose. Umā is embracing Śiva with her right hand and keeps in her left one a lotus flower. There is a profusion of snake ornaments—on the crown, in the ear-lobes, on the arms, and round the chest, of Śiva. On the right and left are the two children of Umā, the elder, Gaṇapati, having an underwear and the younger, Kumāra, standing naked. Gaṇēśa has four arms in which he keeps the *aṅkuśa*, the *pāśa*, the *danta* and the *mōdaka* and behind him is his vehicle, the mouse. Kumāra has two arms; in the left of which he holds the *śakti* and with his right arm he embraces the neck of his favourite vehicle, the peacock. In front of the seat of Śiva is the seated figure of Nandi, the bull vehicle of Śiva.

PLATE XXV.

Umāmahēśvaramūrti: Ivory: Trivandram School of Arts.

[To face page 136]

PLATE XXVI.

Fig. 1. Umāmahēśvaramūrti : Stone : Haveri, Dharwar District.

Fig. 2. Umāmahēśvaramūrti : Stone : Ajmere Museum, Ajmere.

[To face page 137.]

Fig. 1, Pl. XXVI, represents Umāmahēśvara as found in the temple at Haveri. In this also Umā is seated on the left lap of Śiva and embraces him with her right hand, which rests upon the right side of his body; she appears to have held a flower in her left hand, which is unfortunately broken. Śiva carries in three out of the four of his hands the *śūla*, the *ḍamaru* and an *akshamālā* and the remaining hand is thrown in embrace over the left shoulder of Umā. Around Śiva and Umā is a nicely carved *prabhāvali* with creeper ornament; in each of the circular loops of the creeper is carved a *dik-pāla*. At the right extremity of the *bhadrāsana* on which are seated Śiva and Umā is a tiny figure of a seated Ganēśa with four arms, carrying as usual the *ankuśa*, the *pāśa*, the *danta* and a *mōdaka*. In front of him sits Nandi, the bull of Śiva. Corresponding to these, are to be seen on the left side of the seat the figures of Kumāra with six heads seated upon his peacock vehicle, and an alligator, the vehicle of Umā-Pārvatī. The whole work is executed very skilfully and tastefully.

Fig. 2, Pl. XXVI is another group almost similar to the one described above. Śiva is, in this sculpture, seen carrying a lotus, the *śūla*, and a snake in three of his hands and the remaining one is embracing Umā about her chest. Both Umā and Śiva are wearing *śankha-patra kuṇḍalas*, that is, sections of conch-shells. Round the head of Śiva is a very well executed *prabhā-maṇḍala* while the hair of the head of Umā is fashioned into an artistic knot behind. The Dēvī keeps her right hand resting on the left foot of her lord and appears to have carried a flower in her left hand which is broken. On the top right hand corner of the panel is seated Brahmā in the *yōgāsana* attitude and carrying in his hands the articles peculiar to him. The middle face of this deity has a peaked beard. Correspondingly on the left is the figure of Vishṇu who, in three of his hands carries the *gadā* the *chakra* and the *śaṅkha* and keeps the remaining hand in the pose of praise. Both Brahmā and Vishṇu are seated each on a full blown lotus. There is a distinctly noticeable smile on the faces of Brahmā and Vishṇu. Below are the figures of Gaṇēśa and two others, who are unidentifiable, on the right; the *ṛishi* Bhṛiṅgi, in a dancing attitude, in the middle; and Kumāra on the left. Both Gaṇēśa and Kumāra are represented as children and are nude. There is also the bull behind Bhṛiṅgi. The grouping of the members in the composition of this piece of sculpture and its execution are indeed very good. Pls. XXVII-XXIX are the characteristic pieces of sculpture of the cave-temples of the Bombay Presidency. A certain amount

PLATE XXVII.

Umāmahēśvaramūrti. Stone panel: Elora.

[To face page 139.]

of family likeness could be noticed in these three pieces of elaborately carved panels. The Dēva and the Dēvī, the central figures are shaped rather larger than the others, seated in the middle; and around them a number of other deities attending upon them. In the lower section is the big bull of Śiva tended or rather overtended, by the most humourously carved impish *gaṇas*. The artists of these master-pieces have spared no pains to cover the panels with a profusion both of vigorous figure sculpture and minute ornamental designs. Nothing short of the highest praise is due to the long gone artists who executed these immortal pieces of art. In Pl. XXVII Śiva has four arms, the left one of which is holding the right arm of Umā andanother is seen resting upon the seat. What the two right hands carried cannot be guessed, as they are broken; evidently, the one resting upon the right thigh was left empty and the other perhaps carried a snake as in fig. 2, Pl. XXVI. Between the figures of Śiva and Umā stands Kumāra, who keeps both his hands crossed on the chest. Gaṇēśa is standing on the right of Śiva. There are two lady attendants, one carrying a *chāmara* and another a water-vessel (?) On either side of the panel are standing two divine figures, who cannot be identified as Vishṇu and Brahmā, because both of them have *jaṭā-makuṭas* on their head and because neither of them has four faces. They are in all probability two *dvārapālakas.* Pl. XXVIII is almost similar to the previous plate. Herein there are sculptured a number of Dēvas, shown as hovering in the air carrying different kinds of offerings in their hands. It is worthy of notice that to the left of Umā is seen standing a dwarfish woman servant. This dwarfish woman is a characteristic feature of the sculptures at Ellora. In the lower section of the panel is the bull in the centre. The dwarfish *gaṇas* are taking care of it; one peculiarity worth noticing is that these *gaṇas* are supporting the legs of the bull—an idea apparently borrowed from the Buddhist sculptures wherein the hoofs of the horse of Buddha are borne by *dēvas* lest they, treading on the earth, might produce noise and awaken the guards and stop Buddha from renouncing the world. The sculptors of all these panels are curiously agreed in representing one of the *gaṇas* as biting the tail of the bull, another as catching hold of of its horns, others tumbling about and playing with each other. In Pl. XXIX one is seen in the extreme left and behind the figure of a lady, widening his eyes with both his hands, thereby to frighten all others, while another in the extreme right over the figure of another lady is exposing his back in an obscene manner. Of the lady attendants in this

PLATE XXVIII.

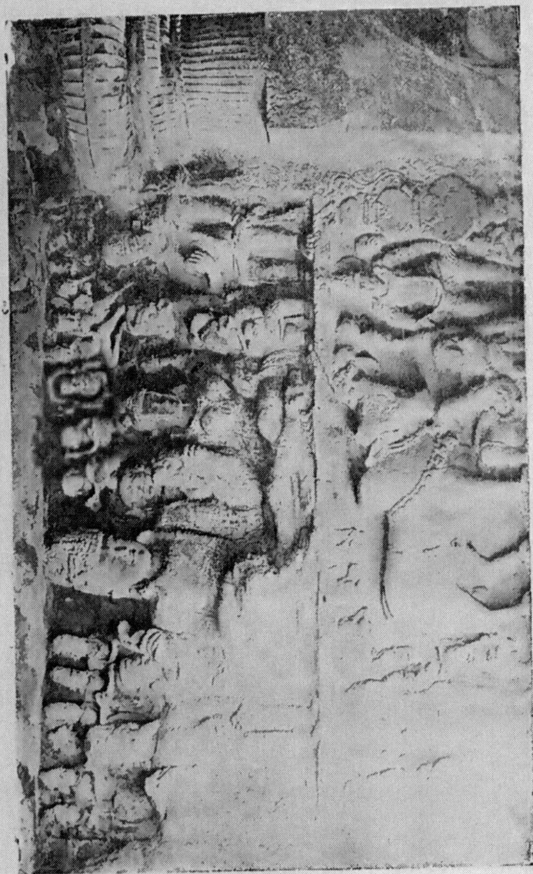

Umāmahēśvaramūrti. Stone panel: Ellora.

[To face page 140]

PLATE XXIX.

Umāmahēśvaramūrti. Stone panel: Ellora.

[To face page 141.]

panel one is fanning Śiva and another is taking hold of the hair of Umā and dressing it up. Śiva is herein holding in one of his left hands the upper part of the garment of his consort and keeps one of his right hands in the *sūchi* pose and the other appears to be carrying a book. He is evidently giving out to Umā one of the *purāṇas*, which are supposed to have been addressed by Śiva to Pārvatī.

SAMHARAMURTIS.

SAṀHĀRAMŪRTIS.

SIVA is represented in sculptures either as a terrific, destructive deity or a pacific, boon-conferrer. In the former aspect he is known by several names, each one being indicative of the destruction of a particular malevolent and troublesome demoniacal being; for example, he is known as the Gajahāmūrti, having killed an elephant-formed *asura ;* Kālārimūrti, as having killed Kāla, the God of Death; Kāmāntakamūrti, because, he burnt down the God of Love who came to meddle with his austerities; and so on. In the latter or the pacific aspect, Śiva is represented as seated with his consort,—be it noted that the company of the Dēvī is always to keep Śiva in a pacific turn of mind—, bestowing boons and blessings on his deserving votaries. The various boon-bestowing aspects of Śiva are called the *anugrahamūrtis :* for example, Śiva is called Chaṇḍēśānugrahamūrti, because he conferred on Chaṇḍēśvara the boon of being the steward of the household of Śiva ; Vishṇvanugraha-mūrti, because he restored an eye to Vishṇu, who had plucked the same for offering it to Śiva, and for which act Śiva also presented Vishṇu with the *chakra* or the discus ; and so forth. Śiva is a great master in the arts of dancing and music, besides being the greatest *Yōgi* and philosopher. Being well-versed in the art of dancing, he is often represented as dancing any one of the hundred and eight modes of dances detailed in the *Nāṭyaśāstras ;* as a master of music also he is portrayed as sitting or standing and playing upon the *vīṇa*, the most perfect of stringed Indian musical instruments. In this capacity he is known as the Vīṇādhara-Dakshiṇāmūrti. As a *yōgi* and philosopher, he is known as Vyākhyāna-Dakshiṇāmūrti, etc. Besides the aspects above described there are many others of smaller or greater importance. To sum up, the images of Śiva are of five classes, namely, the *Saṁhāramūrtis* (or destructive aspects), the *Anugrahamūrtis* (or boon-conferring aspects), the *Nṛitta-mūrtis* (or dancing aspects), the *Dakshiṇā-mūrtis* (or the *yōgic*, musical and philosophic aspects), and other minor aspects. Let me now deal with each one of these aspects under a separate chapter, noticing the various forms comprised in each of these different aspects.

SAṀHĀRAMŪRTIS.

The circumstances under which Śiva is said to have destroyed Kāma, the god of love, are described as follows in the *Liṅga-purāṇa*. After Dākshāyaṇī, otherwise also known as Satī, the first wife of Śiva committed suicide by plunging into the fire, because her father slighted her Lord Śiva by not offering oblations to him, Śiva sat upon the Himālaya and began to practice severe penance. The daughter of Himavān, Pārvatī, who was none other than Satī, who was reborn to Himavān, began to attend upon Śiva, the great *yōgi*. In the meantime the *asura* Tāraka began to do havoc to the gods; they knew that the only person who could destroy this demon would be a son born to Śiva. Since Siva had to be diverted from his austerities and be induced to beget a son for the purpose of destroying Tāraka, Kāma, the god of love was deputed to create lascivious thoughts in the mind of Śiva. Kāma approached Śiva and attacked him with his flowery arrows. Incensed at the disturbance caused by Kāma in his mind, Śiva opened his frontal eye and emitted flames of fire and reduced Kāma to ashes; but all the same, he fell in love with Pārvatī, married her and begot Kumāra or Subrahmaṇya and through the latter got Tārakāsura killed, thereby satisfying

1. Kamantaka-murti.

the wishes of the gods. At the entreaties of Ratī, the wife of Kāma, Śiva promised her that Kāma would be reborn as Pradhyumna. In the Tamil country it is believed that this act of destruction of Śiva took place in a village called Tirukkurukkai in the Tanjore district.

Descriptions of the Kāmāntakamūrti are given in the *Ūttara-Kāmikāgama*, the *Suprabhēdāgama* and the *Pūrva-Kāraṇāgama*. Śiva should be represented in this aspect exactly similar to the figure of Yōga-Dakshiṇāmūrti, before which the figure of Manmatha or Kāma should be sculptured as having fallen down at the mere glance of Śiva. The height of the figure of Manmatha may range from one to seven-tenths of that of Śiva; he should be shown as decorated with golden ornaments; his complexion should also be golden yellow. He is required to be represented as carrying in his hands the five different flowery arrows and the bow made of sugar-cane and in the company of his dear consort Ratī. There should also be with him his companions, Dēvabhāga (?) and Vasanta (or the spring season). The names of the five arrows of Manmatha are given as the *Lambinī*, *Tāpinī*, *Drāviṇī*, *Māriṇī* and *Vēdinī*.* The arrows should

* The *Kāraṇāgama* calls these, *Tāpanī*, *Dāhanī*, *Viśvamōhinī*, *Viśvamardinī* and *Mādinī*.

be held by Manmatha in the right hand and the bow in his left. The figures of the companions of Manmatha may or may not be represented; so also, instead of five arrows, he may be shown as carrying only one. To this description the *Pūrvakāraṇāgama* adds that the figure of Śiva should have three eyes and four arms; his head should be covered with a *jaṭā-makuṭa;* he should have a terrific look and carry a snake and an *akshamālā* in two out of his four hands: the remaining right arm should be shown as held in the pose of *patākā-hasta* (or the hand held banner-wise)* and the remaining left hand in the pose known as the *sūchi-hasta*. In all other respects, it should be similar to Yōga Dakshiṇāmūrti. This authority prescribes that the height, of Manmatha should be one-half of that of Śiva; and that he may be represented as being on a *pīṭha* or pedestal or in a chariot (*ratha*). The banner of Manmatha should bear on the chariot the device of a fish. The names of the companions of Manmatha are given in the *Kāraṇāgama* as Mada, Rāga, Vasanta and Śiśiraṛitu (the cold season).

The story of the destruction of an elephant-

* Or, should carry a banner.

asura by Śiva and his wearing the skin of the elephant as his garment is found in the *Kūrmapurāṇa* while describing the *liṅga* named Kṛittivāsēśvara in Kāśi (Benares). Sūta is said to have told that Śiva came out of this *liṅga*, when an *asura*, who assumed the shape of an elephant, came near it to disturb the meditations of several Brāhmaṇas who had gathered round it, and killed the elephant and made its skin his upper garment. But the *Varāhapurāṇa* gives quite a different account which is already given elsewhere.* Another version of the story is that found in the *Suprabhēdāgama* which is also noticed in one of the earlier chapters of this volume.† So, the accounts found in different authorities, as usual, differ from each other, but the fact that Śiva killed an elephant and had the elephant-skin as his clothing is common to all. A village in the Tanjore district called Vaḻuvūr is associated, in the Tamil country, with this destructive act of Śiva and this is perhaps the only place which has a beautiful metal image of Gajahāmūrti.

2. Gajasura-samharamurti.

Descriptions of the image of Gajahāmūrti or Gajāsurasaṁhāramūrti are found in the

---

* Hindu Iconography, Volume I. p. 379.

† Do. Volume II, p. 114.

Aṁśumadbhēdāgama, the *Śilparatna* and other *Śaivāgāmas*. In the former it is said that the image of Śiva in this aspect may possess four or eight arms; if there are only four arms, one of the right hands should hold the *pāśa*, and the other the skin of the elephant, while the two left hands should hold the tusk of the elephant and the skin respectively. If, on the other hand, there are eight arms, three out of the four right hands should carry the *triśūla*, the *ḍamaru* and the *pāśa* and the fourth hand should be holding the skin of the elephant; one of the left hands should be held in the *vismaya* pose, another catching hold of the skin of the elephant and the remaining two carrying a *kapāla* and the tusk of the elephant respectively. The left leg of Śiva should be planted firmly on the head of the elephant; while the right one should be bent and lifted up above the thigh of the other leg. The tail of the elephant should be visible over the *makuṭa* of Śiva and the artist might arrange on either side the position of the four legs of the elephant in any artistic manner which suggests itself to him. The skin of the elephant should be so arranged as to look like a *prabhāmaṇḍala* to the image of Śiva. The image of Śiva should be adorned with all ornaments and have the garments made of silk and tiger's skin; the colour of Śiva in this instance is deep red. This is one of the descriptions given in the *Aṁśumadbhēdāgama ;* the other one runs as follows:—In the right hands of Śiva there should be the *triśūla,* a sword, the tusk of the elephant and in the last the skin of the elephant; while in the left hands, a *kapāla,* the shield, a *ghaṇṭa* and the skin of the elephant. The left leg of Śiva must be kept firmly on the head of the elephant and the right one bent and held as in the *utkuṭikāsana* posture.

On the left side of the Gajāsurasaṁhāramūrti there should be standing the Dēvī with Skanda in her hands, trembling with fear at the ferocity of her lord.

To illustrate the descriptions of the Gajāsurasaṁhāramūrti five photographic reproductions are given. Of these, the first piece of sculpture, is to be seen in the *mahānāsika* or the ornamented facade of the Amṛitēśvara temple at Amṛitapura in the Mysore Province. In this, Śiva has sixteen arms, a large number of hands being broken; from what remains it is seen that they must have held the *pāśa, danta, triśūla, akshamālā* and *kapāla ;* two of the hands are seen holding the skin of the elephant. Surrounding the figure of Śiva is the skin of the elephant in the form of a *prabhāmaṇḍala.* On the top of this skin, and beginning from the right

PLATE XXX.

Gajāsura-saṁhāra-mūrti : Stone.
Amṛitapura (Mysore).

[To face page 152.]

and ending on the left are the figures of the *ashṭadik-pālas* or the guardians of the eight quarters. On the right of Śiva is the four-faced Brahmā playing on the *viṇā* with two hands and carrying in the other the *kamaṇḍalu* and the *sruk* and *sruva*. To the left of Brahmā is a four armed person, who cannot be identified (because the objects in the hands are not clearly visible in the photograph) sounding the drum called *jaṇṭha*. To the left of Śiva is standing Vishṇu with six hands: two are playing upon the flute, while the remaining four carry the *śankha*, *chakra*, *padma* and *gadā*; there is also another four-armed figure standing to the left of Vishṇu, which is also not identifiable. All these four figures are so carved as to suggest the notion of dancing. Within the fold of the skin of the elephant are the Dēvī and Gaṇēśa to the right of Śiva, and Nandi, the bull and Bhṛiṅgi, to the left. At the foot of Śiva lies the head of the elephant killed by him. The head of Śiva is ornamented by a *maṇḍala* of *jaṭās* and the *jaṭāmakuṭa* he wears, is adorned with a garland of skulls: a similar garland is also worn on the neck. A large number of very nicely executed ornaments are on the person of the image of Śiva. This is a unique piece of patiently and elaborately carved sculpture.

The second illustration, Pl. XXXI, is taken from the Śiva temple at Vaḻuvūr, the reputed place of the destruction of Gajāsura. The bronze, of which the illustration is a photograph, is a remarkable piece of artistic work, both for its size and the excellence of its execution. The very well-carved face has a pair of round eyes, a pair of side tusks, both indicative of the *terrific* nature of the deity; surrounding the head is a *jaṭāmaṇḍala* in which are seen on the left the crescent of the moon and on the right a snake. In the *jaṭāmakuṭa* are the skull, *durddhura* flowers and other ornaments. The image of Śiva has eight arms; one of the right hands holds the elephant-skin, another two carry a very artistically shaped *triśūla*, and a *khaḍga* respectively, while what is held in the fourth is not clear in the photograph. Each of the left hands carry the *kapāla*, *khēṭaka* and *ṭaṅka* (?). Below the right foot of Śiva is the head of the elephant, while its tail is visible on the top. One leg of the elephant is shown as hanging in front above the left hands of Śiva. On either side of Śiva stands a *gaṇa* each with four arms and playing upon the drum and other musical instruments.

The third illustration fig. 1, Pl. XXXII, comes from Dārāśuram in the Tanjore district. Śiva in this sculpture is represented with eight arms. In the right hands of Śiva are seen the *ḍamaru*, *khaḍga*, *triśūla* and the elephant's skin; in three out of the four left hands are the *kapāla*, *pāśa* and the

PLATE XXXI.

Gajāsura-samhāra-mūrti. Bronze: Vaḻuvūr.

[To face page 154.]

PLATE XXXII.

Fig. 1. Gajāsura-saṃhāra-mūrti.
Stone: Dārāśuram.

Fig. 2. Gajāsura-saṃhāra-mūrti.
Stone: Tiruchcheṅgāṭṭaṅguḍi.

[To face page 155.]

elephant's skin, while the fourth is held in the *sūchīhasta* pose. As in the previous instances there is the *jaṭāmaṇḍala* on the head of Śiva, in which is tied up a skull; and the whole person of Śiva is adorned with a large number of well carved ornaments such as the *kuṇḍalas*, *hāras*, *udarabandha*, *kēyūras* and *kaṭakas*. As in the image of Vaḻuvūr, the right leg is planted on the head of the elephant and the left held up bent is an *utkuṭikāsana* in direct opposition to the descriptions given in the *Āgamas*. This deviation from the *Āgamas* appears to be a peculiarity of this aspect of Śiva belonging to the sculptures of the Chōḷa period and country, as might be seen also in the figure of Tiruchcheṅgāṭṭaṅguḍi (see fig. 2, Pl. XXXII). In the Dārāsuram sculpture, the artist has kept the two legs and the tail of the elephant vertically over the head of Śiva. Towards the left of Śiva stands the Dēvī with the child Subrahmaṇya seated on her loins; both of them are looking with awe at Śiva. The Tiruchcheṅgāṭṭaṅguḍi image of Gajāsurasaṁhāramūrti is almost exactly similar to the Dārāsuram image; in his right hands Śiva holds the *ḍamaru*, the *pāśa*, the *śūla* and the elephant's skin; one of the left hands is held in the *vismaya* pose, another seems to carry a deer (?), the third having a *kapāla* in it is held in the *sūchī* pose, while the fourth is holding the skin of the elephant.

The fifth photograph, Pl. XXXIII, is that of an image to be found in the Hoysaḷēśvara temple at Haḷēbīḍu. Like the first illustration, this one also has sixteen arms, which carry a very large number of objects such as the *khaḍga, aṅkuśa, vajra, ḍamaru, bāṇa, gadā, khaṭvāṅga, ṭaṅka ghaṇṭā, sarpa, dhanus* and *kapāla*; the two hands are seen holding the elephant's skin. As in the sculpture of Āmṛitapura the right leg of Śiva is made to rest upon the head of the elephant and the left is bent and held slightly lifted up. The skin of the elephant is kept like a *prabhā-manḍala*. On the right of Śiva are four famishing goblins (*ḍākiṇīs*) praising Śiva; and on the left of Śiva are a few male and female musicians sounding drums and other musical instruments. Like the first illustration this belongs to the Hoysala style of sculpture of the 13th Century A.D.

3. Kalarimurti.

Śiva once got angry with Kāla, the god of death and kicked him on his chest. The circumstances under which this act was performed by Śiva are given in the *puraṇas* thus:—The Ṛishi Mṛikaṇḍu was long without a son. He prayed to God that he may be blessed with sons. God appeared to him and asked him if he would like to have a large number of useless sons or only one remarkably intelligent but with his life limited to

PLATE XXXIII.

Gajāsura-saṁhāra-mūrti. Stone: Halebid.

[To face page 156.]

sixteen years. The *ṛishi* chose the latter alternative and in due time his wife Manasvinī bore him a son who was called Mārkaṇḍēya. The child grew up to be a very intelligent boy : even as his intelligence and behaviour grew to be more and more remarkable, the hearts of the parents began to be weighted with sorrow, for at the sixteenth year of his age he was fated to die. The news of the short duration of his life, reached Mārkaṇḍēya's ears. He resolved to offer *pūjās* to the gods at all important places of pilgrimage, and, in the course of his perigrinations, reached, the tradition says, to Tirukkaḍavūr and was intently absorbed in worshipping the *liṅga* enshrined in its temple. Just then the call from the lord of death, Yama, came. His emissaries approached Mārkaṇḍēya to bind his soul and carry it to their master ; not finding it possible for them to do so, they reported the fact to Yama, who proceeded in person to conduct operations against the life of Mārkaṇḍēya which was not destined to continue longer than sixteen years. He all but succeeded in binding the Brāhmaṇa lad, but Śiva burst out of the *Liṅga* in great anger, and administered a kick on the chest of Yama, which almost killed him. Yama came to his senses, realised that this great devotee of Śiva ought not to have been submitted to the same rules as other ordinary mortals and went away the wiser for his visit to Tirukkaḍavūr. Śiva then blessed Mārkaṇḍēya to be ever of sixteen years of age, so that the destiny that he should die at the expiry of his sixteenth year might not operate on him and he is believed to exist as one of the *chirañjīvīs* (immortals). Śiva in the act of chastising Yama is known as Kālārimūrti. This beautiful story is often seen perpetuated in stone and colour in many a temple. In the Tamil country it is believed that this incident took place in Tirukkaḍavūr in the Tanjore district.

The descriptions of Kālārimūrti are given in all the *āgamas*. The image of Kālārimūrti is to have its right foot placed upon a *padma-piṭha* and the left leg being lifted up so far high as to reach the chest of the figure of Yama, over which the toe of Śiva should rest. The figure of Śiva should have three eyes, lateral tusks, the *jaṭāmakuṭa* adorning the head and four or eight arms. If the image has only four arms, one of the right hands carrying a *śūla* should be lifted up as far as the ear ; the other right hand may carry the *paraśu* or be held in the *varada* pose ; if the hand holds the *paraśu* the edge of the instrument should be turned towards the person of Śiva and the height at which this hand is to be kept raised is that of the *hikkāsūtra*. The front left hand should be held with the palm in front, at the height of the navel and this hand should be in the *sūchī* pose. The back left hand should be kept in the *vismaya* pose ; in this case, the ring-finger of the hand should be raised as high as the *ushṇīsha* or the lower portion of the crown. If, however, the image of Śiva has eight arms, the right ones should bear in them the *śūla*, the *paraśu*, the *vajra* and the *khaḍga ;* in two of the left hands there should be the *khēṭaka* and the *pāśa*, while the two remaining hands should be held in the *vismaya* and the *sūchī* poses respectively. The colour of Śiva in this aspect is also red, though of the coral, and he should be adorned with all ornaments.

Kāla, Yama or the god of death should be represented with two arms and two legs, with side tusks and with a *karaṇḍa-makuṭa* on his head. One of his hands should carry the *pāśa* and with this and the remaining hand he should be doing *añjali* to Śiva, his body covered with blood and trembling with fear ; his legs should be standing apart from each other (as though he is attempting to steady himself). Kāla must also be looking up to Śiva for his grace.

The above description of Kālārimūrti according to the *Aṁśumadbhēdāgamā* is supplemented by the *Kāmikāgama* thus : the right leg should be shown, according to this authority, in the act of kicking Yama and the left one should be placed on the ground. In the right hands of Śiva there must be the *śūla* and the *paraśu* and in one of the left hands the *nāgapāśa*, while the remaining hand should be held in the *sūchi* pose. The eyes of Śiva should be so sculptured as to suggest the idea that their sight is directed towards Kāla and the *śūla* should be turned head downwards and piercing the neck of Yama. In this work Kāla is required to be represented as fallen down fainted with eyes filled with tears. He should be clothed in red garments, should have red eyes, red hair both on the head, the moustache and the brows; he should have side tusks also. The height of Yama should reach up to the navel of Śiva and his figure must be shaped according to the *nava-tāla* measure.

There is another description given in the *Kāmikāgama* according to which the figure of Śiva may be represented as rising from the Liṅga which Mārkaṇḍēya was worshipping and the figure of Yama fallen prostrate on the ground. In this instance, the *liṅga* and the image of Śiva should be sculptured as in the Liṅgōdbhavamūrti already described above. The body of Śiva should be covered with white ashes (*vibhūti*).

Mārkaṇḍēya should be seated near the *liṅga* with flowers for offering and his features should

PLATE XXXIV.

Kalāri-mūrti : Stone panel : Daśāvatāra Cave : Ellora.

[To face page 161]

indicate the fear due to the approach of death rather than happiness at the appearance of Śiva for his rescue.

The *Kāraṇāgama* adds that the two front hands of Śiva which are to hold the down-turned trident must be in the *kaṭaka* pose. Evidently, this rule is meant to be applicable to bronze images in which such implements, which are wrought separately and not cast with the original image itself, and are generally inserted whenever they are wanted. The *kaṭaka-hasta* pose will be seen in all metal images in whose hands different articles are meant to be inserted at the will of the worshipper. For example, in the case of the goddesses who stand near their consorts, one hand is held in the *kaṭaka* pose to receive a natural flower every day in it; the hands of Rāma and Lakshmaṇa are kept in the same pose for inserting in them the bow and the arrow; in the case also of Viṇādhara Dakshiṇāmūrti, we shall see later on, the hands are held in the *kaṭaka* pose.

Five illustrations are given of Kālārimūrti. The first of these, Pl. XXXIV, is a drawing of the Kālārimūrti to be found in the Daśāvatāra cave in Ellora. In this panel Śiva is represented as issuing from the *liṅga*, in front of which is seen the boy Mārkaṇḍēya kneeling with his arms folded on his bent knees. One of the right hands and one of the left hands of Śiva grasp a stout handled, sharp trident which is aimed at the abdomen of Yama. The remaining right hand rests on the hip (*kaṭyavalambita hastā*) and the remaining left hand is held in the *vismaya* pose. The right leg of Śiva is buried up to the knee in the *liṅga* and the left leg is represented as kicking Yama. The person of Śiva is adorned with many ornaments. Yama has apparently fallen down; in this miserable plight he praises Śiva with his right hand uplifted and in the left hand he still grasps the *pāśa* with which he had bound the neck of Mārkaṇḍēya.

The second sculpture, Fig 1, Pl. XXXV, also belongs to Ellora, and is found in the Kailāsa temple. It is almost similar in its details to the panel described above. Here Yama stands praising Śiva with one hand uplifted and holds in the other the *pāśa* bound to the figure of Mārkaṇḍēya. The image of Śiva issues from the top of a *liṅga* before which is seen seated the figure of Mārkaṇḍēya with the head broken and lost. The action of Śiva in kicking Yama with his foot and piercing him with his *śūla* is portrayed vigorously.

The third illustration, Fig. 2, Pl, XXXV, belongs to Paṭṭīśvaram in the Tanjore district. Herein the treatment of the subject is quite

PLATE XXXV.

Fig. 1. Kālāri-mūrti: Stone: Kailāsa temple: Ellora.

Fig. 2. Kālāri-mūrti: Stone: Paṭṭīśvaram.

[To face page 162.]

PLATE XXXVI.

Fig. 1. Kālāri-mūrti : Stone : Tiruchcheṅgāṭṭaṅguḍi.

Fig. 2. Kālārimūrti : Bronze : The Collection of Mr. R. F. Stoney.

[To face page 163]

different. Śiva is standing with his left leg resting upon the body of the fallen Yama and is kicking him with the right foot on his chest. He carries in his hands the *śūla* with its head turned downward, the *paraśu*, the *mṛiga* and the *kapāla*. Mārkaṇḍēya stands to the right of Śiva with hands in the *añjali* pose praising Śiva.

The next illustration, Fig. 1, Pl. XXXVI, is of an image to be found in Tiruchcheṅgāṭṭaṅguḍi and is almost similar to the Paṭṭīśvaram sculpture described above. The only differences between the two are that in the former the left leg of Śiva is lifted up to kick Yama, whereas in the latter, it is the right leg that is lifted for that purpose; the right foot is planted firmly on the body of Yama in Tiruchcheṅgāṭṭaṅguḍi sculpture, while in the Paṭṭīśvaram sculpture, the left foot is so placed. The head of Yama is on the left of Śiva in the Tiruchcheṅgāṭṭaṅguḍi image and on the right in the Paṭṭīśvaram one. The last illustration, Fig. 2, Pl. XXXVI, is the reproduction of the photograph of a bronze image kept in the collection of Mr. R. F. Stoney, Executive Engineer, P. W. D., Madura. In this instance, Śiva is seen emerging from a *liṅga*, within which his right leg is buried up to the thigh. The other leg is lifted up in the act of kicking Yama (whose image seems to have been sculptured as a separate piece). The back hands carry the *paraśu* and the *mṛiga*, while the front ones are so kept as to hold in them a *triśūla*.

On one occasion Śiva killed three *asuras* who dwelt in three forts constructed of metals and who caused great damage to the *suras* and the *ṛishis*. The story is given in detail in the Karṇaparvan of the *Mahābhārata*, an abstract of which is given below. The three sons of Tārakāsura*, having performed great penances, obtained from Brahmā the boons that they should occupy three castles wherefrom they should move as they desired and after a thousand years the three castles should unite into one and should be only destructible with a single arrow. The *asura* architect Maya built them the three castles, one of gold which was in heaven, another of silver in the air and a third of iron on the earth : each one of these was appropriated by one of the *asuras*, and they started out on their tour of harassing the gods. Indra attacked them with his *vajra* but did not succeed in putting them down. The gods then repaired to Brahmā to consult him as to the means of destroying these *asuras*. He told them that they could only be

Tripurantaka-murti.

* These were named Vidyunmālī, Tārakāksha and Kamalāksha.

killed with a single arrow and such a weapon could be wielded only by Mahādēva and directed them to pray to him for help. They prayed accordingly and succeeded in inducing him to undertake the task of killing the *asuras.* Mahādēva then demanded of them one half of their powers (*sākti*) to add to his own strength, as, otherwise, it was impossible to kill those strong demons. They consented and parted with a half of their strength. Mahādēva became now stronger than all other gods and hence came to be known by the name Mahādēva, the great god. The various gods served Mahādēva in other capacities also. Vishṇu, became his arrow, Agni its barb and Yama its feather. Mahādēva made the *Vēdas* his bow and Sāvitri his bow-string. Brahmā became his charioteer. With the three-barbed arrow consisting of Sōma, Agni and Vishṇu the castles with their inhabitants were destroyed by Mahādēva.

The *purāṇik* account of the destruction of the three castles by Mahādēva is based upon very much older accounts found in the *Saṁhitās* and *Brāhmaṇas.* For instance, in the commentary of the *Vājasanēyi Saṁhitā* of the *Yajurvēda,* it is stated that the *asuras* being defeated by the gods, performed austerities and built three castles, which were destroyed by Agni. Similarly in the

Śatapatha-Brāhmaṇa we are told that the gods and the *asuras* fought together, though born of the same father, Prajāpati. The latter built for themselves three castles which excited the envy of the gods. For destroying them Indra is said later on to be preparing his thunderbolt with Agni as the shaft, Sōma as the iron and Vishṇu as the point. The *Taittirīya Saṁhitā* somewhat amplifies the story thus: The *asuras* had three castles, the lowest being made of iron, the next higher of silver and the highest of gold. The gods were unable to conquer them; therefore they made an arrow, consisting of Agni as the wooden shaft, Sōma as the iron and Vishṇu as the point. But then they needed one to wield this weapon; their choice fell upon Rudra, the cruel, who destroyed the castles and drove out the *asuras* from these regions. Similar references to the destruction of three metallic castles are found in the *Aitarēya-Brāhmaṇa* and other ancient authorities.

Tripurāntakamūrti is described in great detail in almost all the *āgamic* authorities.

No less than eight different descriptions of the Tripurāntakamūrti are given in the *Aṁśumadbhēdāgama* alone; but there are not many points of material difference between one form and the other given in this work; however, since a distinction has been made by this authority, let me adhere to its descriptions. In the first form of this aspect of Śiva, the right leg of the image of Śiva should be kept a little in front, while the left one, slightly bent, should be behind. One of the right hands should be held in the *simhakarṇa* pose at about the height of the *nābhi-sūtra* and be holding the bow string in which the arrow is set. The thickness of the arrow should be that of the little finger of Śiva; one of the left hands should be grasping the bow and raised up in a horizontal position; the thickness of the bow ought to fit in exactly into the closed fist of Śiva and should be tapering at both the ends. The bow should be painted beautifully with various colours. It may have three bends (see fig. 3, Pl. II, in Vol. I) or be like the crescent moon and may be of wood or metal. The thickness of the bow string is given as one-third of the thickness of the bow and its length as seven-eighths of the length of the bow. The remaining hands should be held in the *kartari-hasta* pose; in the right hand there should be the *ṭaṅka* and in the left, the *krishṇa-mṛiga*. The figure should be adorned with the *jaṭā-makuṭa* and all ornaments should be of red colour. On the left of that of Śiva, there should be the figure of the Dēvī.

The *Uttarakāmikāgama* adds to the above description the following: the image of Śiva should have three eyes; in its right ear there should be the *makara-kuṇḍala ;* from the non-mention of any ornament for the other ear, we have perhaps to infer that it has to be adorned by none. This authority states that Śiva may have four hands or even two; in the latter case, they should carry the bow and the arrow. The body of Śiva should be in the *samabhaṅga* attitude.

In the second form of Tripurāntakamūrti the left foot of Śiva must be kept upon Apasmāra-purusha, while the rest of the description is exactly similar to the first. In the third form, the left leg of Śiva should be kept standing vertically while the right should be slightly bent. In the fourth it is stated that the left foot should be placed upon the *Apasmāra ;* this is evidently a mistake for the right foot, for, as it is, it is the description of the second form given above. The front right and left hands of Śiva, in the fifth form, should be held, so as the palm of the latter might be facing up and that of the former turned down, grasping the point and tail of the arrow; in the back right and left hands there should be the *ṭaṅka* and the *mṛiga* or *dhanus* respectively. The legs should be somewhat bent but there should not be the *Apasmārapūrusha* in this form. There should be the Dēvī to the left of Śiva. In all these five forms of Tripurāntakamūrti there should be only four arms and no more.

In the sixth form, Śiva as the Tripurāntakamūrti should have eight arms, in the four right ones of which there should be the *bāṇa*, the *paraśu*, the *khaḍga* and the *vajra;* whereas two of the left hands should be held in the *vismaya* and the *kaṭaka* poses respectively, while the remaining two should carry the *dhanus* and the *khēṭaka*. There should be several bends in the body of Śiva (*atibhaṅga*) which should add grace to the general beauty of the figure. There should also be the Dēvī to the left of Śiva. In the seventh form, there should be ten arms; in the right hands they should carry the *bāṇa*, the *chakra*, the *śūla*, the *ṭaṅka* and the *vajra;* and in three out of the five left hands there should be the *dhanus*, the *śaṅkha* and the *khēṭaka :* the remaining hands being in the *vismaya* and the *sūchī* poses respectively.

In the eighth form, Śiva is to be represented as driving in a chariot. His right leg should be slightly raised and be resting on a part of the chariot, whereas the left one should be planted in the middle of the chariot. In the chariot there should be a part called the *mukuḷa*, which is not quite intelligible. It is stated that this *mukuḷa* should be tied up with a rope, and Brahmā, the charioteer should be seated in the middle of this *mukuḷa*, with a bamboo stick in one right hand and *kamaṇḍalu* in the other; and *padma-pāśa* (?) in one left hand and the *kuṇḍikā* (a kind of water-vessel) in the other. Below the *mukuḷa* there should be standing a white bull. This bull is Vishṇu who got down from the arrow temporarily to steady the chariot which was giving way under the feet of Śiva; and after steadying the chariot Vishṇu returned to the arrow. The chariot should be shown as sailing in the air.

The common features of the eight forms of the Tripurāntakamūrti are that they are all of red complexion, have one face and three eyes, and have the Dēvī on the left side. In this aspect Śiva is guided by a passion composed of the *satva* and the *rajō guṇas*.

Four illustrations are given of Tripurāntakamūrti. The first two are to be found in Ellora and another in the Kailāsanātha temple at Conjeevaram. Of the two sculptures of Ellora, the first is in the so-called Daśāvatara cave, Pl. XXXVII. In this, Śiva stands in his chariot with his right leg kept forward and the left one, behind; the body of Śiva is turned away from the objects aimed at, but his face and arms are turned in the direction of the three castles which he is about to destroy. He seems to

PLATE XXXVII.

Tripurāntakamūrti : Stone. Daśāvatāra Cave : Ellora.

[To face page 170]

PLATE XXXVIII.

Tripurāntakamūrti : Stone : Kailāsa Temple : Ellora.

[To face page 171]

PLATE XXXIX.

Tripurāntakamūrti : Stone : Conjeevaram.

[To face page 171]

PLATE XL.

Tripurāntakamūrti : Stone : Madura.

[To face page 171]

have had ten arms; those that still remain unbroken are carrying the sword, and the shield, a third arm is holding the arrow strung in the bow-string, while a fourth holds the bent bow. Brahmā is driving the chariot which is yoked to two horses.

The second illustration, Pl. XXXVIII, is the photograph of the sculpture to be found in the Kailāsa cave in the same place. In this, Śiva has only two arms; the right hand bears the arrow while the left one the bow. On the right shoulder is a quiver of arrows. Brahmā is seen sitting in the front portion of the chariot and driving the two horses yoked to it. In front of Tripurāntakamūrti are the *asuras* fleeing before their pursuer.

In the third illustration, Pl. XXXIX, Śiva is seated in the *ālīḍhāsana* posture in the chariot and has eight arms, in which there ought to be the bow, arrow and other implements of war. As in the previous instances, Brahmā is driving the chariot.

The last illustration, Pl. XL, is the reproduction of the photograph of the beautiful sculpture found in the maṇḍapa in front of the central shrine of the Sundarēśvara temple at Madura, which belongs to the modern times.

Once Śiva assumed the form of a mythical animal called *Śarabha*. The circumstances under which he was obliged to take this form are given as follows: Vishṇu, in his Nṛisiṁhāvatāra, destroyed the *asura* Hiraṇyakasipu who was causing great annoyance to the gods. Even after the destruction of the *asura*, Vishṇu did not abate his terrific attitude, which was causing damage to the inhabitants of the world. They approached Śiva for succour and Śiva promised them his help. He at once assumed the form of a *śarabha*, an animal with two heads, two wings of resplendent beauty, eight legs of the lion with sharp claws, and a long tail; making dreadful noise the Śarabha approached Nṛisiṁha, caught hold of him and tore him up; the skin of Narasiṁha, he wore as his garment and the head was worn on his chest or, as some accounts have it, on his *makuṭa* as an ornament. Vishṇu came to his proper senses and retired, after praising Śiva, to his own abode, the Vaikuṇṭha. Śiva came thenceforth to be known as Śarabhēśamūrti or Siṁhaghnamūrti.

5. Sarabhesa-murti.

Śarabhēśamūrti is described in the *Kāmikāgama* as follows: The body of Śarabhēśa is that of a bird of golden hue; it should have two wings which should be uplifted: Śarabhēśa has two red eyes, four legs resembling those of the lion resting upon the ground and four others with sharp claws kept lifted upwards, and an animal tail; the body above the loins should be that of a human being but having the face of a lion which should be wearing upon its head a *kirīṭa-makuṭa.* There should also be side-tusks and on the whole a terrific appearance. Śārabhēśa is to be shown as carrying with two of his legs Narasiṁha. The figure of Narasiṁha should be the ordinary form of a human being with the hands held in the *añjali* pose.

The *Śrītatvanidhi* gives a somewhat different description. It requires that the figure of Śārabhēsa should have thirty-two arms, in the right ones of which are to be found *vajra*, *mushṭi*, *abhaya*, *chakra*, *śakti*, *daṇḍa*, *aṅkuśa*, *khaḍga*, *khaṭvāṅga*, *paraśu*, *akshamālā*, a bone, *dhanus*, *musala*, and *agni;* whereas the left hands ought to keep the *pāśa*, *varada*, *gadā*, *bāṇa*, *dhvaja*, another kind of sword, a snake, a lotus flower, *kapāla*, *pustaka*, *hala* and *mudgara* and one hand should be embracing Durgā.

The *Uttarakāraṇāgama* says that by consecrating this image, all enemies will be destroyed, battles won, all ailments cured and every good achieved; and that the three eyes of this aspect of Śiva are the sun, the moon and the fire; that his tongue is the subterranean fire known as the *baḍavānala;* that his two wings are Kāḷi and Durgā; his nails, Indra, the belly, Kālāgni; the thighs, Kāla and Mṛityu; and his gigantic strength

Mahāvāyu. Again, in the *Śarabhōpanishad* it is stated that *śara* means the *Jīva* or soul; Hari is shining in the limbs of Śarabha, and that Hari himself is Śarabha who is capable of granting *mōksha*.

An illustration of the Śarabhēśamūrti is given in Vol. I, Pl. E, Introduction. It is a bronze image to be found in the Śiva temple at Tribhuvanam in the Tanjore district. In this piece of sculpture Śarabha is represented as having three legs, the body and a face of the lion, a tail and four human arms; in the right upper hand is the *paraśu*, in the lower right one, the *pāśa*, in the upper left one, the *mṛiga* and in the lower left one, *agni*. With the front leg, Śarabhamūrti has pinioned Nṛisiṁha, who is struggling against his adversary with his eight arms.

The following account is found in the *Varāha-purāna* regarding the cutting off of the fifth head of Brahmā by Śiva. Brahmā created Rudra and addressing him as Kapāli, asked him to protect the world. Because he was insulted as Kapāli, Śiva cut off the fifth head of Brahmā with his left thumb-nail; but this head stuck to his hand and would not fall off from it. Then Brahmā was requested by Rudra to tell him how he could get

6. Brahmasira-schchhedaka-murti.

rid of the head stuck up in his hand, for which Brahmā prescribed to Rudra the observance of the Kāpālika life for twelve years, at the end of which he promised that the head would fall off. Then Rudra repaired to Mahēndragiri and wearing an *Yajñōpavīta* made of hair, a garland of beads made of bone and a piece of the skull tied up as an ornament in the *jaṭāmakuṭa* on his head and carrying a skull filled with blood in his hand, went round the earth visiting all places of pilgrimage. At the end of twelve years he arrived at Vārāṇasi, where, by the followers of Sīmachāri (?) the skull of Brahmā was removed from the hand of Rudra. The place where the head fell obtained the name of Kapāla-mōchana. Rudra then bathed in the Ganges, worshipped Viśvēśvara at Kāśi and returned to Kailāsa.

A somewhat different version is found in the *Kūrmapurāṇa.* Once upon a time the *rishis* asked Brahmā as to who was the origin of the universe. Brahmā arrogated it to himself. Just then Śiva appeared on the scene and claimed to be the originator of the universe; upon this there ensued a dispute between Brahmā and Śiva. Even though the Vēdas came to declare that Śiva was the greatest of all Gods, Brahmā would not accept their verdict. Then appeared in space a huge illumination in which was discernible the figure of Śiva. Śiva then ordered Bhairava to cut off that fifth head of Brahmā which spoke to him with haughtiness and disrespect. By the power of his *yōga*, Brahmā escaped death and he also learnt, at the sacrifice of one of his heads, the superiority of Śiva.

The following description of Brahmaśiraśchchhēdakamūrti is found in the Śrītatvanidhi. The figure of this aspect of Śiva should be of white complexion, with three eyes, four arms and a *jaṭāmakuṭa* on the head and the *patrakuṇḍala* in the right ear and the *nakrakuṇḍala* in the left one. In the right hand are to be the *vajra* and the *paraśu* and in the left ones, the skull of Brahmā and the *śūla*. It should be draped in the garments made of tiger's skin.

The *Śiva-purāṇa* calls Bhairava the *pūrṇarūpa* or the full form of Śaṅkara and that those whose intellect is darkened by *māyā* are not able to understand the superiority of this aspect of Śiva and decline to worship it. Bhairava is so called because he protects the universe (*bharaṇa*) and because he is terrific (*bhīshaṇa*). He is also known as Kālabhairava for even Kāla (the god of death) trembles before him ; Āmarddaka because he kills bad persons(*marddana*) and Pāpabhakshaṇa, because he swallows the sins of his *bhaktas* or devotees. He is the lord of the city of Kāśi.

(a) Bhairava.

The description of Bhairava is found in the *Vishṇudharmōttara*. It is there stated that Bhairava should have a flabby belly, round yellow eyes, side-tusks and wide nostrils, and should be wearing a garland of skulls. He should be also adorned with snakes as ornaments; besides these there should be other ornaments also. The complexion of Bhairava is dark as the rain-cloud and his garment the elephant's skin; he should have several arms carrying several weapons. He should be represented as frightening Pārvatī with a snake.

Bhairava has many forms such as the Vaṭuka-bhairava, Svarṇākarshaṇabhairava and so forth. The features of each one of these forms are described below.

(b) Vatuka-Bhairava.

Vaṭuka-Bhairava should have eight arms in six of which are to be the *khaṭvāṅga* the *pāśa*, the *śūla*, the *ḍamaru*, the *kapāla* and a snake; while one of the remaining hands should carry a piece of flesh and the other should be held in the *abhaya* pose. By the side of this Bhairava there should be a dog of the same colour as that of its master. Meditation upon this form of Bhairava is said to secure all the wishes of the votary. So far for the description given in the *Rūpamaṇḍana* ; the following is the description found in the *Vaṭuka-Bhairavakalpa*. This aspect of Bhairava should have *jaṭās* of red colour, three eyes and a red body. He should carry in his hands the *śūla*, the *pāśa*, the *ḍamaru* and the *kapāla* and be riding upon a dog. Vaṭuka-Bhairava should be stark naked and be surrounded on all sides by a host of demons.

Four illustrations of Vaṭuka-Bhairava are given, in none of which is Bhairava seen with eight arms as given in the *Rūpamaṇḍana*. The South Indian image of Paṭṭīśvaram, Pl. XLI, carries the *śūla*, the *ḍamaru*, the *pāśa* and the *kapāla* and is naked. It has *jvālās* or flames surrounding its *jaṭāmakuṭa* and wears round its neck a long necklace made of small bells, besides a number of well-wrought golden and other necklaces. Round the loins is the *kaṭisūtra* or waist zone consisting of a snake. To show the terrific aspect of this deity, the eyes of the image are made round and there are shown large side-tusks. Immediately behind the figure of Bhairava is a dog also adorned with a number of necklaces and other ornaments. This image belongs to the later Chōḷa period (12th and 13th centuries A.D.).

The two Northern Indian images as also the one of the Chālukya style, figs. 1, 3 & 2, Pl. XLII,

PLATE XLI.

Bhairava: Stone: Paṭṭīśvaram.

[To face page 178]

PLATE XLII.

Fig. 1. Bhairava : Stone : Indian Museum, Calcutta.

Fig. 2. Bhairava: Stone : Madras Museum.

Fig. 3. Bhairava : Stone : Museum of the Royal Asiatic Society, Bombay.

[To face page 179]

are alike in their execution. They all carry the *śūla*, the *khaḍga*, the *pāśa* and the *kapāla*, have their *jaṭās* arranged in a circle (or *maṇḍala*,) and are naked. They wear garlands of skulls and are of terrific appearance. The image belonging to the Indian Museum, Calcutta, fig. 1, Pl. XLII, alone is smiling, whereas that belonging to the Museum of the Bombay Branch of the Royal Asiatic Society, fig. 3, Pl. XLII, has a scorpion attached as a *lāñchhana* or mark on the front face of the pedestal; and these two images are surrounded by emaciated *piśāchas*. The sword in the hand of the image of the Madras Museum (fig. 2, Pl. XLII), is a short dagger held with its point downwards. All these three images stand on sandals, which are absent in the case of the South Indian image.

(c) Svarnakarshana Bhairava.

Svarṇākarshaṇa Bhairava should have an yellow coloured body, with four arms and three eyes and should be clothed in yellow garments. He should be adorned with all kinds of ornaments and be praised by all gods. The appearance of this aspect of Bhairava should be one which suggests perfect happiness coupled with masterful authoritativeness. He should be carrying in his hands a vessel filled with gold and precious gems, a *chāmara* and a *tōmara* and a large *śūla* should be resting upon the shoulder.

(d) The sixty-four Bhairavas.

We have already seen in the introduction that Bhairava's aspect has eight different forms, named Asitāṅga, Ruru, Chaṇḍa, Krōdha, Unmatta-Bhairava, Kāpāla, Bhīshaṇa and Saṁhāra. Each one of these forms is divided further into eight subordinate forms, thus making sixty-four in all. All these are grouped into eight groups and are described in the *Rudra-yāmaḷa.*

In the group coming under Asitāṅga are included Viśālāksha, Mārttāṇḍa, Mōdaka-priya, Svachchanda, Vighna-santushṭa, Khēchara and Sacharāchara. All these are of golden complexion and have good looking limbs, and carry the *triśūla,* the *ḍamaru,* the *pāśa* and the *khaḍga.*

The group headed by Ruru consists of Krōḍa-damshṭra, Jaṭādhara, Viśvarūpa, Virūpāksha, Nānārūpadhara, Vajrahasta and Mahākāya. The colour of the Bhairavas of this group is pure white; they should all be adorned with ornaments set with rubies and should carry an *akshamālā,* the *aṅkuśa,* a *pustaka* and a *vīṇā.*

Chaṇḍa, Pralayāntaka, Bhūmikampa, Nīlakaṇṭha, Vishṇu, Kulapālaka, Muṇḍapāla and Kāmapāla constitute the third group. All these are to be of blue colour and have good looks. They should carry in their hands *agni, śakti, gadā* and *kuṇḍa.*

In the group headed by Krōdha are included Piṅgalēkshaṇa, Abhrarūpa, Dharāpāla, Kuṭila, Mantranāyaka, Rudra and Pitāmaha. All these are of smoke colour and should carry *khaḍga*, *khēṭaka*, a long sword and *paraśu*.

In the Unmatta-Bhairava group are Vaṭukanāyaka, Śaṅkara, Bhūta-vētāḷa, Triṇētra, Tripurāntaka, Varada and Parvatāvāsa. Their colour is white and they are all to be of good looks and carry in their hands the *kuṇḍa*, the *khēṭaka*, the *parigha* (a kind of club) and *bhinḍipāla*.

Kāpāla, Śaśibhūshaṇa, Hasticharmāmbaradhara, Yōgīśa, Brahmarākshasa, Sarvajña, Sarvadēvēśa and Sarva-bhūtahṛidi-sthita form a group and are all to be of yellow colour and carry the same weapons as in the previous group.

The seventh group consists of Bhīshaṇa, Bhayahara, Sarvajña, Kālāgni-Mahāraudra, Dakshiṇa, Mukhara and Asthira. They all carry the same weapons as in the above group and are of red colour.

In the group of Saṁhārabhairava are Atiriktāṅga, Kālāgni, Priyaṅkara, Ghōranāda, Viśālāksha, Yōgīśa and Dakshasamsthita; all these are to be of the colour resembling the lightning and to carry the same weapons as in the previous group. Pl. XLIII, represents the Atiriktāṅga aspect of

Bhairava and is found sculptured in one of the cave-temples of Ellora. Seated near his foot is the emaciated figure of Kāḷī; round him are a number of blood-thirsty goblins and on his right stands a brahmaṇa votary with his hands held in the *añjali* pose. Though grotesque, the sculptor has executed his work with great skill.

7. Vīrabhadra-murti.

Vīrabhadra is a form of Śiva assumed at the time of the destruction of the *yajña* (sacrifice) of Daksha. The following account of the destruction of the sacrifice of Daksha occurs in the *Kūrma-purāṇa*. On one occasion Daksha with his consort, paid a visit to the house of Śiva. In spite of the solicitous attentions of Siva, Daksha became displeased with his son-in-law, and returned to his quarters. On another occasion Śiva's wife Satī went to her father Daksha's house. Daksha reviled Śiva in the presence of Satī and also abused her and directed her to quit his house. This insult offered to her in his own house by Daksha smote Satī so hard that she burnt herself to death; she was afterwards born to Himavān as his daughter under the name of Pārvatī. Learning the demise of his consort, Śiva cursed Daksha to be born as a Kshatriya and to commit incest with his own daughter in that birth. Daksha was born as king

PLATE XLIII

Atiriktāṅga Bhairava: Stone Panel: Ellora.

[To face page 182]

Prāchētas and was performing a *yāga* at Gaṅgādvāra, but owing to the hatred he conceived for Śiva in his former existence he declined to dedicate a portion of the offering to Śiva. All other gods who had received their portions did not intercede on behalf of Śiva. But one Dadhīchamaharishi alone remonstrated against the injustice of Daksha's neglect of Śiva but in vain. Then Dadhicha cursed all those who were present to become *vēdabāhyas* and lovers of lower religious systems and even to lose the favour of Vishṇu on which they so much counted. He then invoked there the presence of Śiva. Just then Pārvatī also was requesting Śiva to destroy the irregular sort of *yāga* that was being performed by Prāchētas. He acceded to her request and created Vīrabhadra with a thousand heads, a thousand eyes, powerful shoulders, a thousand arms, and resembling in brightness the fire that devours the universe at the end of an æon; having side-tusks, carrying the *śaṅkha*, the *chakra* and a bow and besmeared with ashes; this Vīrabhadra was sent to destroy the *yāga* of Prāchētas. Pārvatī, in her turn, created Bhadrakāḷi and sent her also with Vīrabhadra, with a body of *gaṇas* to help them. Vīrabhadra destroyed the *yāga* and in the action that ensued put out the eyes and plucked the teeth of Sūrya, cut off the hands and the tongue of Agni, cursed Indra's arm, that had been lifted up to strike, to remain stiff in the same position. Chandra was crushed by the toe of Vīrabhadra and Vishṇu's vehicle Garuḍa had to flee for life. Daksha came to his senses and prayed to Śiva, who became pleased with him and promised the headship over the *gaṇas* at the end of that æon and disappeared.

An altogether different tale is found in the *Varāhapurāṇa.* Rudra was born from the anger of Brahmā; the latter asked him to create beings, which he did not care to do, but lay in inactivity. Brahmā therefore created Daksha and six other Prajāpatis. Daksha begot a lot of children and grand-children. Indra and other Gods, the grand-children of Daksha, began to perform sacrifices for the pleasure of Daksha. Meanwhile Rudra who was sunk in inactivity came and created four species of animals; in a short time the voices of Indra and other gods came to be heard by Rudra who got angry at the creation of these beings by some one else before he himself took up the act of creation. This anger of his glowed in the form of tongues of fire issuing from his ears and from this fire came a number of demons which went against the Dēvas, attacked and destroyed their sacrifices and compelled them to offer him also a portion of the offerings. Daksha prayed to Rudra to appease his anger and gave his daughter Gaurī in marriage to Rudra. Brahmā then allotted to Śiva and his consort a place in Kailāsa.

The *Bhāgavata-purāna* gives a fuller account of the enmity between Daksha and Rudra. The gods and the *ṛishis* were assembled at a sacrifice. Daksha entered the hall when all the assembly, excepting Brahmā and Mahādēva, rose up. Daksha made his obeisance to Brahmā and sat down at his command. But he did not like Mahādēva being seated when he entered the hall and so reviled Mahādēva in very strong and highly objectionable language alluding to his roaming in cemeteries and other repulsive acts and cursed him that he should never be given thenceforth a portion in the offerings in *yāga* made to the delectation of the gods. Śiva departed from the hall of sacrifice. Some years after, Daksha began to perform the sacrifice known as the Bṛihaspatisava. All the gods with their wives were seen going to attend the sacrifice; seeing which Satī, the wife of Śiva, pressed him to take her to her father's house for the sacrifice. He informed her of the insult offered to him by her father and advised her not to persist in going to the sacrifice. But she persisted in going, and, as was predicted by her husband, was slighted by her father. On being treated with scant courtesy, she committed suicide. The news of the death of his spouse reached Śiva, who in his anger tore a lock from his matted hair; this lock of hair took a gigantic form. Bidden by Śiva, this Being completely destroyed the sacrifice of Daksha and brought him to submission to Śiva.

The *Śrītatvanidhi* contains a description of the image of Vīrabhadramūrti. It should have four arms, three eyes and a terrific face with fierce side tusks. In the left hands should be held a bow and a *gadā* and in the right ones a *khaḍga* and a *bāṇa*. It should be wearing a garland of skulls and should be standing on a pair of sandals. By the side of the figure of Vīrabhadra there should be the figure of Bhadrakāḷi also. On the right side of Vīrabhadra there should be the figures of Daksha with a goat's head, two eyes and two horns, and with hands held in the *añjali* pose.

The *Kāraṇāgama* has a somewhat different description of Vīrabhadramūrti. It says that the figure of Vīrabhadra should have four arms, three eyes, head covered with *jaṭās* which emit fire, side tusks, and wearing garlands composed of bells and skulls and those made of scorpions, a *yajñōpavīta*

Fig. 1. Vīrabhadramūrti: Bronze: Madras Museum.

Fig. 2. Vīrabhadramūrti: Stone: Teṉkāśi.

[To face page 187]

of snake, and adorned with beautiful anklets; it should be standing upon a pair of sandals and should have short drawers as his underwear. The colour of Vīrabhadra should be red; he should have a face indicating great anger and should look terrific. He should carry the *khaḍga*, the *khēṭaka*, the *dhanus* and the *bāṇa*. The setting up of this image is believed to remove all great sins and to cure people of all their ailments.

Two photographs are reproduced in illustration of Vīrabhadramūrti. The first, fig. 1, Pl. XLIV, is of a bronze image belonging to the Madras Museum; its hands are broken and therefore the objects carried in them cannot be made out. The figure has round eyes and side-tusks indicating the terrific nature of this aspect of Śiva. It stands upon a pair of sandals. The second photograph, fig. 2, on the same plate, is that of an image carved on a pillar in the *maṇḍapa* in front of the Śiva temple at Teṅkāśi and is of the 15th century A.D. In this piece of sculpture Vīrabhadra has ten arms; three out of the five right hands carry the *bāṇa*, the *paraśu* and the *khaḍga*; of the remaining two hands, one holds a long sword (partly broken) which is thrust into the neck of Daksha and the other pulls out an arrow from the quiver. The left hands keep in them the *dhanus*, the *musala* (?), the *pāśa*, a round shield and an oblong one with a beautiful device on it. The *jaṭāmakuṭa* has round it tongues of flames. Vīrabhadra is standing upon the prostrate body of Daksha-Prajāpati.

Fig. 1, Pl. XLV, represents Daksha-Prajāpati and his wife; this piece of sculpture is to be found in Āṅgūr in the Bellary district and belongs to the Chālukya-Hoysaḷa school and is executed very well. It is to be noted that Daksha has the face of a goat.

8. Jalandhara-haramurti.

The *Śiva-purāṇa* gives the account of the destruction by Śiva of the *asura* named Jalandhara. The fire that emanated from the forehead of Śiva at the time of the destruction of the three castles of the Tripurāsuras was let into the sea where Sindhu joins it. This rose up as a child named Jalandhara. When he grew old he loved and married Brinda, the daughter of Kālanēmi and became reputed as the most powerful king in the world. Once upon a time Rāhu, with his maimed body came to the court of Jalandhara; he was asked about the cause of his deformation to which Rāhu replied that when the Milky Ocean was churned, he misconducted himself and was therefore punished, and added that the gods then took away from the ocean a great quantity of gems. The news of

PLATE XLV.

Fig. 1. Daksha-Prajāpati and his wife : Stone : Āṅgūr, Bellary District.

Fig. 2. Andhakāsuravadhamūrti : Stone Panel : Daśāvatāra Cave : Ellora.

[To face page 188]

the possession by *dēvas* of a lot of riches induced Jalandhara to wage war against them and he began in right earnest to attack them. The gods complained to Vishṇu about their lot, who fought hard but unsuccessfully with Jalandhara; meanwhile Jalandhara's might extorted Vishṇu's admiration, as a consequence of which, Vishṇu asked Jalandhara to ask for any boon he desired. The *asura* took this opportunity to request Vishṇu and his consort Lakshmī, to come and reside in his capital. Vishṇu was therefore obliged to repair to the city of Jalandhara. The gods then desired that Śiva should become hostile to the *asura* and kill him. For this purpose, they induced Nārada to kindle enmity between the *asura* and Śiva. Nārada went straight to the palace of Jalandhara and told him that such a pretty damsel as Pārvatī, the consort of Śiva, was alone the fittest partner in life to Jalandhara and that he should therefore make every attempt to possess her. Thus incited by Nārada, Jalandhara despatched immediately messengers to Śiva to surrender Pārvatī to him. Śiva forthwith set out for battle with this impudent *asura*, but very soon the *gaṇas* of Śiva were put to flight by the *asura*. Śiva then appeared in person for a combat, but did not succeed well. In the meantime Jalandhara created, with his *māyā*, a host of very pretty

Gandharvas and Apsarasas and made them sing and dance before Śiva, who became absorbed in the dance and music; he became unaware of the fact that his weapons dropped down from his hands. Seeing that that was the best opportunity for him, Jalandhara assumed the form of Śiva and proceeded to Pārvatī to ravish her. But she knew the person who was disguised as Śiva and invoked Vishṇu to come to her help. Vishṇu appeared on the scene; Pārvatī requested Vishṇu to ravish Brindā, the wife of Jalandhara. Pārvatī's wishes were carried out immediately. Brinda not being able to bear the indignity offered to her committed suicide and died, cursing Vishṇu that in one of his *avatāras* he should suffer the loss of his wife by abduction by another. Jalandhara could not find Pārvatī at her abode, hence he returned. Śiva had also recovered from the spell of the music; a battle ensued in which Jalandhara was killed with the Sudarśana-chakra which Śiva obtained from the sea. Thus ended the life of the *asura* Jalandhara.

The description of the image of Jalandhara-haramūrti is given as follows: The colour of Śiva in this aspect is red; he should have three terrific looking eyes, and only a single pair of arms; in the right hand he should carry an umbrella and in the left a *kamaṇḍalu*. On his head should be a dishevelled *jaṭābhāra* containing in it the crescent moon and Gaṅgā. He should be adorned with *kuṇḍalas* in the ears, *hāras* on the neck and anklets on his legs and the feet of Śiva should rest on a pair of sandals. The posture of Śiva should be such as to indicate his desire to move quickly.

Jalandhara should be represented with two arms, and be adorned with *kirīṭa*, *kaṅkaṇa* (bracelets) and all other ornaments. He must have a sword tucked up below his forearm, while the two hands should be held in the *añjali* pose. On the hands thus held there should be the Sudarśanachakra. The colour of Jalandhara should be yellow.

9. Mallari Siva.

Anantānandagiri in his *Śaṅkaravijaya* states that there was a quarter called Malla in Ujjayini. In it dwelt a sect of people who were adoring Śiva in the aspect of Mallāri and conducting themselves like dogs, after the fashion of the dog-vehicle of Mallāri, barking like it and putting on the appearance of the dog, adorning their necks with garlands made of shells. They believed that Mallāri was the origin of the whole universe and were offering *pūjā* to him as the Supreme Being. Śaṅkarāchārya proved to them that their appearing like dogs and barking like them and other characteristic customs of theirs were opposed to the *śāstras* and converted them to the religion of the Brāhmaṇas.

The aspect Mallāri that is referred to above is described in the *Mallāri-māhātmya* thus: Mallāri is to be of the colour of gold, wearing on his *jaṭā-makuṭa*, the crescent moon, in his ears white, shining *kuṇḍalas*, and round his neck, necklaces of rubies and pearls and a garland of flowers. In his arms there should be bracelets of snakes and he should be clad in yellow silk garments. The ornaments of Śiva should be hidden here and there by the hoards of snakes and there must be a smile playing upon the lips of Śiva. In the hands are to be seen a *ḍamaru* and a *khaḍga*. His vehicle is to be a white horse and he must be surrounded by seven dogs.

10. Andhakasuravadha-murti.

The *paurāṇic* story of the destruction by Śiva of the great demon Andhakāsura has already been given in connection with the Sapta-Mātṛikās on pages 379-382 in Volume I. To illustrate the descriptions of the aspect of Śiva as Andhakāsura-vadha-mūrti, three photographs are reproduced, all of which belong to the Cave-temples of the Bombay Presidency. The sculptures represented on Pls. XLV—XLVII, belonging as they do to

Andhakāsuravadhamūrti : Stone Panel : Elephanta.

[To face page 192]

PLATE XLVII.

Andhakāsuravadhamūrti: Stone Panel:

Kailāsa Temple: Ellora.

[To face page 193]

one school, bear a strong family likeness; the artists have dwelt upon the subject in exactly the same manner and it is therefore sufficient to describe one of these pieces of sculpture. In all the three instances, Śiva has eight arms, in two of which he carries a *triśūla*, at the end of which is pinned the body of Andhakāsura and from it blood drops down. The goddess Yōgēśvari, squatting on the ground, holds in her hand a cup in which she catches the blood-drops as they trickle down. Śiva himself bears the *kapāla* in one of his hands to collect in it the blood flowing down from the body of Andhakāsura. In the other hands of the sculpture of the Daśāvatāra cave, Śiva is seen keeping the *ḍamaru* and the *khaḍga;* two other hands of his hold stretched the skin of the elephant in the shape of a *prabhāmaṇḍala* and the remaining hand is held in the *tarjanī* pose.

Yōgēśvari or Kāḷi carries in her other hand a short curved dagger: her body is represented as very emaciated and her head is surrounded by a *jaṭāmaṇḍala.* Just above the head of Kāḷi is the figure of a *ḍākiṇi*, half human and half bird, sitting waiting for her prey of human flesh.

On the right of Kāḷi is the Dēvī, seated upon a *padmāsana* and viewing with awe the events that are taking place before her.

The sculpture belonging to the Kailāsa at Ellora and that belonging to the Elephanta Cave are not different in their description, but it must be noted that the latter is one of the finest pieces of workmanship of the period to which it belongs; in this sculpture, one hand of Śiva carries a *ghaṇṭā* instead of the *ḍamaru*.

OTHER UGRA FORMS OF SIVA.

OTHER UGRA FORMS OF ŚIVA.

AMONG the rites and ceremonies that are prescribed for kings for attaining success against their enemies is the adoration of Aghōramūrti. The description of the rites that have to be performed is given in the *Liṅgapurāṇa*. A priest who has attained *mantra-siddhi* or the power of efficaciously using *mantras*, should for that purpose repair to a place where there is a corpse or where there is a temple dedicated to the Saptamātṛikas (or the seven mothers), and construct five *kuṇḍas* (receptacles for fires), one on each cardinal point and one in the centre. On the fourteenth day of the dark fortnight * the ceremonies

11.Aghoramurti.

* The fourteenth *tithi* of the dark fortnight of the month of Phalguni is known as Aghōra-chaturdaśi; it is said that those who worship Śiva in the aspect of Aghōra on this day will be taken to Śiva's abode.

भाद्रमास्यसिते पक्षे ह्यघोराख्या चतुर्दशी ।
तस्यामाराधितश्शम्भुर्नयेच्छिवपुरं ध्रुवम् ॥

(Apte's Sanskrit Dictionary.)

ought to be begun and continued to the eighth day in the succeeding bright half of the next month. During this period the priest with four of his disciples, who have also attained *mantra-siddhi*, should sit in front of the *kuṇḍas*, himself occupying the middle and the four disciples the four quarters, before the *kuṇḍas* and perform *hōma* sacrifices in the fire concentrating their thought upon Aghōra. Then they should make a wooden effigy of the enemy king, place it in one of the *kuṇḍas* with the head downwards and burn it with the fire brought from the burning ground. There are a few other minor ceremonies of no great interest.

The following is the description of the Aghōra who is required to be meditated upon. The figure of Aghōra should have eight arms; in the hands are to be seen the *śūla, ḍamaru, pāśa, kapāla, daṇḍa, dhanus, bāṇa* and *khaḍga;* the neck of Aghōra should be blue and his complexion black. He should be naked, or be clad in the skin of the elephant and the lion and be adorned with ornaments composed of snakes and scorpions, and be covered with the ashes of the dead bodies of human beings. His face should be terrific in appearance and should have side tusks. A snake should bind his hair and he should be surrounded by demons and goblins.

Another description, according to which the Aghōramūrti is generally sculptured and set up in temples, is found in the *Kāraṇāgama*. In this work he is known as the Aghōrāstramūrti and it is stated therein that the image of this aspect of Śiva is set up for gaining victory, for destroying such great sins as *brahmahatyā* or brahmanicide and for granting riches. Aghōrāstramūrti should have three eyes, eight arms and be of terrific look, with side tusks. The colour of this aspect of Śiva is dark. He is to be draped in red clothes, adorned with garlands of red flowers, ornaments set with rubies, a garland of skulls, and another composed of short daggers (*khaḍgamālā*) and a third of scorpions. His hair should be flaming and his forehead marked with ashes in the shape of the crescent moon. In his two hands he should carry a *triśūla* horizontally as though about to charge with it, and the other hands should hold a *vētāḷa*, *khaḍga*, *ḍamaru*, *kapāla* and *khaḍga* (*ghaṇṭā* ?).

A third description is given in the *Śivatatvaratnākara*. According to this, Aghōra has a single face, and thirty-two arms; on the head is a *jaṭā-makuṭa* and in it the crescent moon. He should have three eyes. In his right hands are to be *abhaya*, *khaḍga*, *śūla*, *chakra*, *ḍamaru*, a bone, *bāṇa*, *gadā*, a lotus flower, *kapāla*, *jñānamudrā*, *kuṇḍa*, *aṅkuśa*, *akshamāla*, *khaṭvāṅga* and *paraśu;* in the left hands, *varada*, *kavacha* (shield), *ṭaṅka*, *pāśa*, *mudgara*, a snake, *agni*, *mṛiga*, *ghaṇṭā*, *dhanus*, *kaṭyavalambita-hasta*, *ratnas* or gems, a water lily, a pitcher, *musaḷa* and *pustaka*. This Aghōramūrti should have also a garland of skulls and be standing upon the severed head of Kāla. An image of the above description is believed to grant all protection to its votaries.

12. Dasabhuja Aghoramurti.

Aghōramūrti with ten arms is described as possessing three eyes and a terrific countenance. The colour of his body is blue and that of the garments red. There are to be snake ornaments all over the body. In his ten hands he should carry the *paraśu*, *ḍamaru*, *khaḍga*, *khēṭaka*, *bāṇa*, *dhanus*, *śūla* and *kapāla* and the remaining hands should be held in the *varada* and *abhaya* poses.

Two photographs, figs. 1 and 2 on Pl. XLVIII, are reproduced in illustration of Aghōramūrti, both of which belong to Southern India. The first image is to be found in the Śiva temple at Tirukkaḻukkunṟam and the other in the Śiva temple at Paṭṭiśvaram. Both of them are almost similar to each other; in these pieces of sculpture two front hands bear the *triśūla* in a horizontal position, while the other hands carry the *ghaṇṭa*, the *pāśa*, the *khēṭaka*,

PLATE XLVIII.

Fig. 1. Aghōramūrti : Stone : Paṭṭīśvaram.

Fig. 2. Aghōramūrti : Stone : Tirukkaḻukkuṉṟam.

[To face page 200]

kapāla, the *khaḍga* and the *ḍamaru*. The head is surrounded by tongues of flames and the face, with its round eyes and the side-tusks, indicates the terrific nature of this image. Round the neck is a large garland of skulls reaching down to the ankles and the *prabhā-maṇḍala* surrounds the figure.

13. Mahakala with Mahakali.

An *asura* named *Dūshaṇa* was giving trouble to the Brāhmaṇas residing in and near Ujjayini. They prayed to Śiva to relieve them from the visitations of the cruel *asurā*. Śiva pleased with the prayers of the Brāhmaṇas, appeared on the spot and with a breath of his reduced Dūshaṇa to ashes. The Brāhmaṇas then prayed to Śiva to stay away in their midst; Śiva assumed the form of a *Jyōtirliṅga* and the name *Mahākāḷa* and stopped away at Ujjayini. Such is the account of Mahākāla of Ujjayini as given in the *Śivapurāṇa*.

The description of the image of Mahākāḷa with his consort Mahākāḷi is found in the *Lalitōpākhyāna*. It is stated therein that Mahākāḷa should be embracing Mahākāḷi and be wearing a black coat. The colour of Mahākāḷa is black. His eyes should be red on account of the excessive drink in which he is indulging; he should be drinking from the *brahmāṇḍa* (the colossal shell from which Brahmā was born) used as a vessel to hold the liquor. His sight must itself be resting fondly on his dark coloured consort Mahākāḷi, and both of them should be seated upon a *siṁhāsana*. Mahākāḷa, swallower of the Universe, should have by his side Kāḷa and Mṛityu. He should also be meditating upon Lalitā, doing *pūjā* to her and bestowing long life on her devotees.

ANUGRAHAMURTIS.

ANUGRAHAMŪRTIS.

AS we have already stated Śiva possesses also the faculty of affording grace to his votaries and that in this aspect he is said to be a Anugrahamūrti. Let me proceed with the description of some of the *anugrahamūrtis* of Śiva.

In the village of Śeyñalūr on the bank of the river Maṇṇi in the Chōḷa country **1. Chandesanugrahamurti.** there lived a pious and learned Brāhmaṇa named Yajñadatta of the Kāśyapagōtra. He had a son by name Vichāraśarman of great intelligence. One day when the lad was going to the school, he saw a cowherd assaulting brutally a cow, that sacred animal which deserves being worshipped. Incensed at the behaviour of the cowherd, young Vichāraśarman took upon himself the duty of tending the cows of the village, to which the villagers acceded. From that day the cows became happy and began to yield much more milk than their udders could hold and naturally the extra milk began to flow out. Vichāraśarman seeing that the milk was wasted, collected it in vessels, set up *liṅgas* made of sand and began to bathe them with this extra milk, with intense piety for Śiva. The cowherd who lost his position on account of this Brāhmaṇa boy, found this a fine cause for denouncing him and immediately repaired to the village and reported to the villagers that the boy Vichāraśarman was wantonly milking the cows, drinks milk with his chums and spills the rest on mounds of sand. The complaint thus often repeated, made one of the villagers go and see for himself the truth of the accusation preferred by the cowherd and to his surprise he saw young Vichāraśarman actually pouring milk on sand mounds, but he did not pause to investigate and see that it was only the extra milk that the boy, in his intense devotion to Śiva, was offering the sand-made symbol of the *liṅga*. Forthwith he complained to the father of the boy, Yajñadatta, about the wickedness of his son. On this complaint the father also went one day to the river side to see what his boy was doing and found him in the act of spilling milk in the sand. He approached the boy and stood near him, but, in his deep devotion the proximity of the father was not perceived by Vichāraśarman. On seeing the apparent mischief of his son, Yajñadatta, in anger, kicked the mound of sand; whereupon the son woke up from his reverie and cut off with his axe the leg that kicked the object of his worship with the result that Yajñadatta fell. Śiva who was pleased with the devotion of this boy Vichāraśarman appeared on the scene with his consort Pārvatī and offered him his grace. Śiva told the boy that in his intense love for himself (Śiva) he even went to the extent of cutting off the leg of his father, and promised him that thenceforth he would be in *loco-parentis* to him, embraced him and made him the head of his *gaṇas* and the steward of his household under the name of Chaṇḍēśa. Śiva commanded that thenceforth the offerings made to him must be given to Chaṇḍēśvara, the clothes worn by him should be set aside for his devotee and in token of his favour he also tied round the head of Vichāraśarman the flower garland then worn by him.

The scene representing Śiva as offering to Chaṇḍēśa his grace is described in the *Aṁśumadbhēdāgama*. Śiva should be seated with Pārvatī as in the case of Umāsahitamūrti described already. But his face should be turned a little to the left; his right hand should be held in the *varada* pose and the left hand be placed on the head of Chaṇḍēśa. With hands folded in the *añjali* pose Chaṇḍēśa should be standing on a *padmāsana* in front of

Śiva; the colour of Chaṇḍēśa is golden yellow. The *Uttarakāmikāgama* states that Śiva and Umā should be seated as in the case of Chandraśēkhara-mūrti and Chaṇḍēśvara with hands in the *añjali* pose should be either standing or sitting before Śiva, who with his right hand should be holding the end of a flower-garland and with the left hand tying it round the head of Chaṇḍēśa. The height of the figure of Chaṇḍēśa may be up to the knee, thigh, navel, breast, neck or mouth of that of Śiva and it should be made in accordance with the *adhama-daśa-tāla* measurement. The *Pūrvā-kāraṇāgama* and the *Śilparatna* have practically the same description as that found above.

Four pictures are reproduced to illustrate the description given above. The first fig. 1, Pl. XLIX, is of a sculpture to be seen in the big Śiva temple at Gaṅgaikoṇḍaśōḻapuram, built by Rājēndraśōḻa, the son of Rājarāja the great. In this is seen Śiva seated with his wife Pārvatī on a seat, below which is seated Chaṇḍēśa. In the two back hands of Śiva are the *paraśu* and the *mṛiga*; the right front hand holds the end of a flower garland and the left front one is tying it round the head of Chaṇḍēśa. This fine piece of sculpture belongs to the Chōḷa period and is of the first quarter of the eleventh century A.D.

PLATE XLIX.

Fig. 1. Chaṇḍēśānugrahamurti : Stone : Gaṅgaikoṇḍaśōḻapuram.

Fig. 2. Chaṇḍēśānugrahamūrti : Stone : Conjeevaram.

[To face page 208]

The original of the second illustration, fig. 2, Pl. XLIX is found in the Kailāsanātha temple at Conjeevaram. In this Śiva is standing on his right leg, while the left one is resting upon a raised seat. He has four hands, the right one of which is held in the *varada* pose; it is not quite clear from the photograph what objects are kept in the remaining hands. To the right of Śiva stands Chaṇḍēśvara with the axe with which he cut down the leg of his father resting upon his right shoulder. Below him and fallen on the ground is the father of Chaṇḍēśa, with his left hand held in the *vismaya* pose. The sculpture is in a highly damaged condition. It belongs to the reign of the Pallava King Rājasiṁha and is of the 7th century A.D. The third and the fourth illustrations, figs. 1 and 2, Pl. L, are of the Chaṇḍēśānugrahamūrtis sculptured on the base of the *gōpura* in front of the Sthāṇunāthasvāmin temple at Suchīndram and on the pillar in the front *maṇḍapa* of the Mīnākshī-Sundarēśvara temple at Madura respectively. They both resemble the sculpture at Gaṅgaikoṇḍaśōḻapuram.

2. Vishnvanugrahamurti, or Chakradanamurti.

Vishṇu obtained through the grace of Śiva the *chakra* and the circumstances thereof are narrated in the *Śiva-puraṇa*. On one occasion Vishṇu found himself unable to conquer certain *asuras*, and prayed to Śiva for the grant of the *chakra* which was in Śiva's possession. To his prayer he added a *pūjā* in which he employed a thousand lotus flowers daily. One day he sat for *pūjā* with the required number of flowers but at the end he missed one flower, which, to test the strength of his devotion Śiva had secreted; Vishṇu at once plucked one of his eyes which are always compared to lotuses, (*kamala-lōchana*) and threw the same in offering on Śiva. Śiva became so pleased with the devotion of Vishṇu that he presented him with the *chakra* which was originally in his possession. This fact is also alluded to in the *Mahābhārata*.

The *Uttarakāraṇāgama* and the *Śrītattvanidhi* give the description of the Chakradānamūrti. The first authority states that Śiva should have three eyes, four arms, a pacific appearance, and the *jaṭāmakuṭa* on the head. The left leg should be bent and be resting on the seat, while the right one should hang down. In the right hands are to be the *ṭaṅka* and the *chakra*, the left ones being in the *varada* pose and holding a *kṛishṇa-mṛiga*. Surrounding the head of Śiva is to be a *prabhāmaṇḍala* and a *śiraśchakra*. On the left of Śiva should be seated Pārvatī and on the right Brahmā should be standing. Vishṇu, with hands

PLATE LI.

Fig. 1. Vishṇvanugrahamūrti (or Chakradānamūrti): Stone: Conjeevaram.

Fig. 2. Vishṇvanugrahamūrti: Stone: Madura.

[To face page 210]

PLATE L.

Fig. 1. Chaṇḍēśānugrahamūrti : Stone : Madura.

Fig. 2. Chaṇḍēśānugrahamūrti : Stone : Suchīndram.

[To face page 211]

folded in the *añjali* pose, should be worshipping or doing *pūjā* to Śiva with lotuses and his eye.

The *Śrītattvanidhi* is not particular about the *taṅka* in the hand of Śiva, but gives the alternative of carrying the *paraśu.* In this work it is stated that Vishṇu ought to be standing to the left of Śiva in such a manner as to indicate his readiness to receive the boons and the *chakra*, after finishing his *pūjā* of Śiva with lotuses and his eye. Śiva should be seen presenting Vishṇu with a *pītāmbara* (a yellow garment), the *kaustubha* (an ornament) and the *chakra*, as also the name Kamalāksha to Vishṇu. Vishṇu should be black in colour, clad in yellow garments and adorned with all ornaments. In two of his hands should be the *śaṅkha* and the *chakra* and the other two ones should be held in the *añjali* pose.

Two illustrations of Vishṇvanugrahamūrti are reproduced. The first of these, Pl. LI, fig. 1, belongs to the Kailāsanātha temple at Conjeevaram. Śiva is seated on a raised seat with his consort, having his two back hands raised up in astonishment (*vismaya* pose), the right front hand rests upon the seat, the remaining left hand being held in the *simhakarṇa* pose. Behind Śiva stands an attendant and below the seat is seen Vishṇu kneeling; with one of his left hands he is plucking out his eye, the other left hand holding the last remaining lotus flower; the front right one is held in the *kaṭaka* pose, while the remaining hand is not visible in the photograph. The second illustration, fig. 2, Pl. LI, is of a piece of sculpture found in the Mīnākshi-Sundarēśvara temple at Madura. In it, Śiva and Pārvatī are seated upon a *bhadrāsana* and Śiva is seen presenting the *chakra* to Vishṇu, who is standing reverently and receiving it.

3. Nandisanugrahamurti.

Nandikēśvara is an important adjunct to the family of Śiva. His history is given in detail under Nandikēśvara or Adhikāra-Nandi elsewhere in this volume. When Nandi's tenure of life on earth was coming to an end, he prayed intensely to Śiva to grant him a longer lease of life. Śiva appeared and granted him his prayer, as also the command over a portion of his *gaṇas*, and complete exemption from old age and pain. He then took the boy near him and threw round his neck the flower garland that was gracing his own. At once he became a duplicate of Śiva, with three eyes and ten arms. Śiva took a quantity of the water of the Ganges which he had tied in his *jaṭā* and sprinkled it upon Nandi. It began to flow as the river Jaṭōdaka. Śiva ordered his consort Pārvatī to treat Nandi thenceforth as her own son. She also smelled the top of the head of Nandi* and milk began to flow from her breast and fall in three spouts on the head of Nandi; this milk also became a river under the name Trisrōtas. Nandi out of joy bellowed then like the bull. This noise also gave rise to a river named Vṛishadhvani. Śiva still more pleased with Nandi presented him with his own golden *makuṭa* and ear-rings set with precious gems. Sūrya seeing that Nandi was thus honoured and loved by Śiva sent a cool downpour of rain. The water having come in contact with the gold of the *makuṭa*, began to flow as two rivers named Svarṇōdaka and Jāmbūnadi. Thus near Japyēśvara the place where all these events occurred, five rivers began to flow. Nandi was afterwards crowned as the lord of the *gaṇas* and was married to Suyaśa the daughter of the Marut gaṇas.

4. Vighnesvaranugrahamurti.

In this aspect of Śiva, Vighnēśvara seems to have been blessed by Śiva immediately after he was restored to life by placing on his shoulders the head of an elephant. (For this account of Gaṇēśa, see Vol. I, pp. 36-39). Śiva should have, as usual, four arms, three eyes and the head adorned with a *jaṭā-makuṭa* and he should be seated with his

* An instinctive practice of mothers in regard to their children.

consort Pārvatī. Śiva should have one of his right hands in the *abhaya* pose and placed on the head of Vighnēśvara; the corresponding left hand should be in the *varada* pose and the remaining hands should be shown as carrying the *paraśu* and the *mṛiga*. The right leg of Śiva should be bent and be resting on the seat while the left one should be hanging down. The colour of Śiva is to be black and there should be all ornaments on his person. Near him on the left should be seated Pārvatī, smiling and keeping in her right hand a *utpala* flower and holding the left hand in the *varada* pose. Curiously enough, it is stated here that Pārvatī should have three eyes. She too has her right leg bent and the left one hanging.

Vighnēśvara, of red colour, adorned with a *kirīṭamakuṭa* on his head, and carrying in his hands the *pāśa* and *aṅkuśa*, should be standing reverently before Śiva with his other two hands held in the *añjali* pose.

5. Kiratarjuna-murti.

Arjuna was presented by Śiva with the powerful weapon named the *pāśupatāstra* to fight successfully against the Kauravas. The account of the gift of the weapon by Śiva is narrated in the *Vanaparvan* of the *Mahābhārata* thus: Arjuna being advised by Indra to beseech Śiva to grant him the powerful *pāśupatāstra*, went north to the Himalaya mountain, where he began to observe severe austerities for pleasing Śiva. The *ṛishis* were alarmed at the severity of the austerities of Arjuna and reported the matter to Śiva. Śiva being already aware of the reason for the penance of Arjuna, pacified the *ṛishis* and himself assuming the form of a *kirāta* (hunter) approached Arjuna. Just at that moment an *asura* in the form of a boar was about to attack Arjuna; Arjuna having seen the boar coming against him aimed his arrow against it, but the *kirāta* disputed the right of Arjuna to shoot the boar which he was the first to aim at. Arjuna not consenting to the claim of the *kirāta*, they both simultaneously shot the boar and killed it. Arjuna then reviled the *kirāta* as an unsportsman-like person, upon which a fight ensued between the *kirāta* and Arjuna, in which the latter was uniformly unsuccessful, and at the end fell exhausted. After he regained his senses, he recognised in the *kirāta* Śiva himself and fell at his feet and praised him. Śiva in his turn admired the strength and courage of Arjuna and promised the most powerful weapon which Arjuna was praying for and was fit to employ, namely the *pāśupatāstra*. Thus did Arjuna procure from Śiva the *pāśupatāstra*.

The Kirātārjunamūrti is described as having four arms, three eyes and a *jaṭāmakuṭa* on the head. He is adorned with all ornaments and wears nice garments and a *yajñōpavita*. His colour is red. He is to be standing perfectly erect (*samabhaṅga*) carrying in his hands the *dhanus*, the *bāṇa*, the *paraśu* and the *mṛiga*. Arjuna is to be seen standing on the right of Siva and Gaurī on the left. Arjuna should be represented as having only one face, set with two eyes and standing with his hands held in the *añjali* pose. His head should be adorned with a *jaṭāmakuṭa* and his person with all ornaments.

Two illustrations are given of the Kirātamūrti. The first belongs to the Śiva temple at Tiruchcheṅgāṭṭaṅguḍi, in which Śiva and Pārvatī stand together. The former carries the *paraśu*, the *mṛiga* and a bow. The photograph is of an image to be found in Śrīśailam. In this is seen Śiva portrayed in the act of giving the weapon *pāśupatāstra* to Arjuna. (See Pl. LII, figs. 1 and 2).

The weapon *pāśupatāstra* is described in the Saivāgamas as a person thus:—The Pāśupatāstra should have four faces each with three eyes; it should have four arms and terrific faces with awful tusks, stiff hair and fierce moustache, all lending strongly the impression that it is a *terrific* aspect

PLATE LII.

Kirātamūrti : Stone : Tiruchcheṅgāṭṭaṅguḍi.

Fig. 2. Pāśupatāstradānamūrti : Stone : Srīśailam.

[To face page 216]

of Siva. In the four hands there should be the *śakti*, the *mudgara*, the *śaṅkhā* and the *khaḍga*. This image representing the *Paśupatāstra* should be seated upon a *padmāsana*.

Rāvaṇa, king of Laṅka, having gone to defeat Kubēra was returning after achieving his purpose. On his way he came to Śaravaṇa, the place in which Kārttikeya was born. He ascended the hill, from the top of which he saw a much more pleasant garden whither he drove his *vimāna* Pushpaka. But when it neared the place it would not move any further. At this place Rāvaṇa met a tawny coloured, monkey-faced and powerful dwarf, by name Nandikēśvara, one of the strong adherents of Śiva, who, on being asked why the car was unable to move further, told Rāvaṇa that Mahādēva with his consort Umā was sporting on the mountain and had prohibited all, even the gods, from crossing that way. In great anger Rāvaṇa asked who that Mahādēva was and laughed contemptuously at the monkey-faced Nandikēśvara. Nandikēśvara, who was no other than a form of Śiva, grew incensed at the insult offered to him by Rāvaṇa and cursed that he should be destroyed by monkeys like himself in appearance and strength. Not being able to proceed further and being cursed by Nandikēśvara, Rāvaṇa

5. Ravananugrahamurti.

determined to pluck up the mountain Kailāsa, from its very roots, threw his ten arms round the mountain and began to lift it up. He was able to move it, so that those that were on it trembled and Umā actually began to shake out of fear and clung to her lord. Śiva, learning the real cause, pressed the mountain with the great toe of his foot, which fixed the mountain firmly as of old and also pinned down Rāvaṇa underneath it. Rāvaṇa seeing his own miserably helpless condition, and advised by his counsellors to propitiate Mahādēva wept for a thousand years, singing hymns in praise of Śiva; the latter was at last pleased with Rāvaṇa, whom he presented with a sword at his request and let him return to Lanka. Because he cried, he was given the name Rāvaṇa.

Three photographs are reproduced in illustration of this legend. The first and second, Pls. LIII and LIV belong to the Ellora rock caves and the third to Bēlūr in the Mysore State. The first which is to be found in the Daśāvatāra cave is one of the finest pieces of sculpture extant in India. The natural proportions of each image in the group, the great realism in their moulding and the expression on the face of many a figure in it, especially the fright of Pārvatī, all these are admirably worked out. In this group,

PLATE LIII.

Rāvaṇānugrahamūrti : Stone Panel : Ellora.

[To face page 218]

PLATE LIV.

Rāvaṇānugrahamūrti : Stone Panel: Ellora.

[To face page 219]

PLATE LV.

Rāvaṇānugrahamūrti:
Stone: Bēlūr.

[To face page 219]

Śiva and Pārvatī are seated upon the mountain Kailāsa which the artist has in the conventional manner represented as a pile of rhomboidal pieces. Surrounding this pair are seen two of his own attendants and two female attendants of Pārvatī and on either side are two of the *gaṇas*, dwarfish little fellows standing in a very reverential attitude. Below the mountain is to be seen Rāvaṇa, of mighty strength trying to up-root the Kailāsa hill. His posture is suggestive of the display of his strong muscular energy. Pārvatī, in great fear, embraces the well-proportioned and well-built body of Śiva, who is calm and unperturbed, and is seen in his turn embracing and reassuring his frightened consort.

The second panel which is found in the so-called Dhumar Lena Cave, is almost similar to the above described sculpture, but utterly lacks the spirit and realism of the former. The other differences between the two are that in the latter there are more *gaṇas* and a number of gods with their consorts praising Śiva and Pārvatī.

The original of the third photograph is sculptured on the south wall of the central shrine of Chennakēśavasvāmin temple at Bēlūr. It is a most elaborately carved piece of sculpture and is characteristic of the Hoysaḷa style. The Kailāsa mountain is so minutely carved as to accommodate in it a large number of gods and goddesses and all sorts of animals, from the elephant down to the snake. On the top and in a finely carved *maṇḍapa* are seated Mahādēva and Pārvatī, surrounded by a number of other deities who are praising him. Below the mountain is to be seen Rāvaṇa in a kneeling posture trying to lift up the mountain, as in the other photographs. He has a sword in his hands, perhaps the one presented to him by Śiva.

NRITTAMURTIS.

NṚITTAMŪRTIS.

SIVA, we have already said, is a great master in the art of dancing. He was often dancing in ecstacy on the burning ground with great glee, accompanied by sweet music in which also he was a great expert. The *Bharata-Nāṭyaśāstra* mentions a hundred and eight different kinds of dances and in the Śaivāgamas it is stated that Śiva danced in a hundred and eight modes. Perhaps the one hundred and eight kinds of dances mentioned in the *śāstra* are identical with the one hundred and eight modes of dances of Śiva. The *Nāṭya-śāstras* distinctly mention the necessity of dancing for both males and females; in the case of the former, dancing is said to give a suppleness to the limbs, which is very useful in warfare. It is very curious that all the one hundred and eight kinds of dances are sculptured on either side of a *gōpura* in the Naṭarāja temple at Chidambaram with their descriptions in Sanskrit as they are found in the *Bharata-Nāṭya-śāstras* engraved below each one of them. These sculptures and the texts are reproduced in the Madras Epigraphist's Annual Report for 1913-14.

The *Śaivāgamas*, state that Śiva danced in a hundred and eight modes but content themselves with the description of nine modes only as it is very difficult to describe all. Of these the first variety is the one which we see associated with the figure of Naṭarāja, commonly found in all Śaiva temples of importance. According to the *Aṁśumadbhēdāgama* the image of Naṭarāja should be sculptured according to the *Uttama-daśa-tāla* measurement. The front left hand should be held in the *daṇḍahasta* or the *gajahasta* pose across the body, and the back left hand should carry *agni* either in a vessel or upon the palm itself. In either case the *agni* should be at the end, middle or the root of the middle finger. The front right hand should be held in the *abhaya* pose, the top of the middle finger of which should be just touching the *hikkā-sūtra*. On the fore-arm of this hand, there should be the *sarpa-valaya*, a description of which is given on page 23 in the Chapter on Definition and description of terms in Vol. I; it is there called *bhujaṅgavalaya* and means the same thing as *sarpavalaya*. The back right hand should keep a *ḍamaru*. The right leg should be slightly bent and placed upon the back of the Apasmārapurusha and the knee should reach the *nābhisūtra*. The left leg should be lifted up, somewhat turned towards the right leg and kept across it. On the head of Śiva there should be the *jaṭāmakuṭa* adorned with flower garlands, *dhurdhura* and *arka* flowers, a snake, jewelled ornaments, a grinning human skull and the crescent moon tied on the left side. From this *jaṭāmakuṭa* should issue on either side five, six, seven or eleven *jaṭās* and stand either horizontally or arranged in a circle. The body of Śiva should be adorned with a *yajñōpavita*, a *urassūtra* (a chest band), rings on all fingers except the middle ones, on all toes except the middle one and anklets on the ankles. The face should be smiling. The chest should be smeared with saffron paste and the rest of the body with ashes. The garment must be made of tiger's skin.

The Apasmāra-purusha who is trodden on by Śiva should have his head on the right side and his legs on the left side of Śiva. He should be black in colour and be playing with a snake, by keeping all his fingers in a cuplike shape, and resembling the hood of a snake (*nāga-mudrā*).

On the left of Naṭarāja should be standing his consort Pārvatī, in the manner described in Umā-sahita-Chandraśēkharamūrti.

The measurements of the position of the various limbs of this image are given in Appendix A.

This is the first mode of dancing of Śiva as found in the *Aṁśumadbhēdāgama*. The *Uttara-Kāmikāgama* gives a somewhat detailed description, of which only those that are not already given above are noticed here. Śiva, according to this authority, should have four arms kept in the poses described and with the objects mentioned above, three eyes and two legs disposed as in the above description. The *jaṭās* should be spread around the *jaṭāmakuṭa*. These *jaṭās* might vary from five to thirty, each one being separated from one another. In the intervals between the *jāṭās* might be the flowers of *dhurdhura*, *arka* and other plants. The colour of these *jaṭās* should be brownish red. In the *jaṭās* on the right side there should be the figure of Gaṅgā with the upper half shaped in the form of a woman and the lower half like running water, standing with hands in the *añjali* pose; on the *jaṭās* on the left side there should be the crescent moon. Round the neck of Śiva there should be necklaces of different sorts; one should be made of pearls, another should be of snakes, a third of *vakuḷa* flowers and a fourth composed of sea-shells, boar's tusks, tiger's claws and beads, with a pendant of a tortoise shell. On his left shoulder there should be an upper garment made of tiger's skin, a deer's skin, or a very fine-textured cotton cloth. On his left earlobe there should be a *patra-kuṇḍala* and on the right one a *nakra-kuṇḍala ;* on the ankles, anklets made of tiny bells and another set composed of ornamental designs. The colour of Śiva-Naṭarāja should be milky-white. The rest of the description is exactly that given in the *Aṁśumadbhēdāgama.*

The Apasmāra should be made in the *chatus-tāla* measurement, with two arms, two eyes, with the face downcast or looking up and should be holding in his left hand a cobra with uplifted hood.

The height of Gaṅgā should be equal to that of the face of Śiva. She should have three (?) eyes, two arms held in the *añjali* pose, adorned with the *karaṇḍa-makuṭa* and all other ornaments.

On the right side of Naṭarāja there should be either the *ṛishi* Bhṛiṅgi or Bhadrakāḷī.

This dance, it is said, is known as *Bhujaṅga-trāsa.* If the foot of the uplifted leg is kept higher than the knee of the standing leg, the dance is said to be *Bhujaṅga-lalita.*

In the *Nāṭya-Śāstra* however that particular dance which is known by the name of *bhujaṅgatrāsa* is defined as follows: one leg being bent in a triangular fashion and lifted up while the body about the hip and knee being slightly turned on one side, is called *bhujaṅgatrāsa*. Abhinavaguptāchārya, the commentator of the *Bharata-Nāṭya-śāstra*, explains the term *bhujaṅgatrāsa* in his *Nāṭya-vēda-vivṛiti*, thus: 'This kind of dance is called *bhujaṇgatrāsa*, because in it the dancer suddenly lifts up his leg as though he discovered a snake very near him, and appears to be of an unsteady gait. In this, one arm should be in the *dōla-hasta* pose and the other in the *kaṭaka* pose; * and the *dōla-hasta* pose is defined in the *Bharata-Nāṭya-śāstra* thus:— If the hand hangs down freely from the somewhat drooping shoulder, in the form of the *patākā-hasta*, it is called *dōla-hasta* pose. †

The *Śilparatna* adds to the foregoing descriptions of the Nṛittamūrti the fact that surrounding

---

* कुञ्चितं पादमुत्क्षिप्य त्र्यश्रमूरु विवर्तयेत् ।
कटिजानुविवर्तौ च भुजङ्गत्रासितं भवेत् ॥

नृत्तस्यानादिसिद्धत्वात्करणमिदमुक्तरूपम् । असंकितदृष्टनिकटतस्सर्पत्रासाविष्टस्येव गतिसंवर्ते भुजङ्गत्रासितम् । क......................दवशाद्वा वर्तितपरिवर्तितौ भवतः । क्रमेणैको दोलहस्तः परं खटकाख्य इति करणम् । एतत्सादृश्यात्तु भुजङ्गत्रासिता वारिवक्ष्यते । एवं करणतुल्यनामा सर्वेचारिषु वाच्यम्॥
(नाट्यवेदविवृतिः ॥)

† अंसौ प्रशिथिलौ मुक्तौ पताकौ तु प्रलम्बितौ ।
यदा भवेतां करणे स दोल इति संज्ञितः ॥

the figure of the dancing Śiva there should be a *prabhāmaṇḍala* resembling the orb of the sun; and the *Pūrva-Kāraṇāgama* states that the eyes of Śiva should resemble the shape of the bird *kurari*, that in the right ear of Śiva there should be the *nakra-kuṇḍala* and in the left ear *patrakuṇḍala*, that the garment of Siva should be a tiger's skin, that the *agni* in the left hand should have three tongues or flames and that between the two left hands there should be a piece of tiger's skin to serve as the upper garment. It further adds that the figure of Apasmārapurusha should be made in the *chatustāla* measurement and should have three bends in its body.

The descriptions given above of the first form of the Nṛittamūrti, refer to the figures of Naṭarāja commonly occurring everywhere in Southern India. In all Śiva temples of importance a separate place is allotted to Naṭarāja which is known as the *Naṭana-Sabhā* or simply *Sabhā*. The most important of these *Sabhās* is that at Chidambaram. From the earliest times Chidambaram has been held very sacred by the Śaivas who call it "the temple". In the days of Tirujñānasambandha, the Śaiva saint, that is, in the middle of the seventh century A. D., it was already very famous. Further from time immemorial the god in the temple at Chidambaram had been the family deity of the Chōḷas who were strongly Śaiva in their persuasions. They had covered the *Sabhā* with gold and hence it came to be known as the *Kanakasabhā* (or the golden hall) and the image of Naṭarāja as Kanakasabhāpati. The *Sabhā* at Madura, the capital of the Pāṇḍyas, had a covering of silver and was known as the *Rajatasabhā*. The Chōḷas might have desired to out-do the Pāṇḍyas in their regard for their family deity and hence covered the *Sabhā*, not with silver as the Pāṇḍyas had done, but with gold; and in the days of the king Parāntaka Chōḷa I, the roof of the *Sabhā* was regilt. (A.D. 908-948). At the present day the Nāṭṭukkōṭṭaichetṭis have once again covered the temple with gold. Chidambaram has been maintaining its importance from the earliest times and has always been the seat of activity of several Śaiva scholars. For instance, the *Periyapurāṇam* describing the lives of the sixty-three Śaiva saints was written and published by Śēkkiḻār in this .temple; many a work on Śaiva Siddhānta was written and published there. The saint Māṇikkavāchaka spent the evening of his life in Chidambaram and such great Śaiva saints as Jñānasambandha, Nanda and others are said to have been absorbed in the figure of Śiva at Chidambaram. On account of such holy associations, the temple at Chidambaram is clothed with extraordinary sanctity and mysticism, and a good deal of philosophical significance is attributed to the dancing immage of Siva that graces the *Sabhā* in the temple.

The significance of the mystic dance is explained in several ways. The same materials which were gathered by me for the purpose of explaining the mystic nature of the dance of Siva have been turmed to account by Dr. A. K. Anandakumarasvami in writing independently a very beautiful article which he contributed to the *Siddhānta-Dipikā* (Vol. XIII, July 1912). Since the work has already been done by him and if I may respectfully say so, in quite a splendid manner, my task is lightened and I have much pleasure in reproducing with his kind permission, the whole of the article here.

THE DANCE OF ŚIVA.

"The Lord of Tillai's Court a mystic dance
performs: what's that, my dear?"—
Tiruvāchagam, XII, 14.

A great master-of-dancing (Naṭarāja) is Śiva! The cosmos is His theatre, there are many different steps in His repertory, He himself is actor and audience—

> When the Actor beateth the drum,
> Everybody cometh to see the show:
> When the Actor collecteth the stage properties,
> He abideth alone in His happiness.

How many various dances of Śiva are known to His worshippers I cannot say. No doubt the root idea behind all of these dances is more or less one and the same, the manifestation of primal rhythmic energy: Śiva is the Eros Protogonos of Lucian, when he wrote:

> It would seem that dancing came into being at the beginning of all things, and was brought to light together with Eros, that ancient one, for we see this primeval dancing clearly set forth in the choral dance of the constellations, and in the planets and fixed stars, their interweaving and interchange and orderly harmony.

I do not mean to say that the most profound interpretation of Śiva's dance was present in the minds of those who first danced in frantic, and perhaps intoxicated energy, in honour of the pre-Āryan hill-god, afterwards merged in Śiva. A great motif in religion or art, any great symbol, becomes all things to all men; age after age it yields to men such treasure as they find in their own hearts.

Whatever the origins of Śiva's dance, it became in time the noblest image of *activity* of God which any art or religion can boast of. Of the various dances of Śiva I shall only speak of three, one of them alone forming the main subject of interpretation. One is an evening dance in the Himālayas, with a divine chorus, described as follows in the *Śiva Pradōsha Stōtra*—

"Placing the Mother of the Three Worlds upon a golden throne, studded with precious gems, Śūlapāṇi dances on the heights of Kailās, and all the gods gather round Him:"

"Sarasvatī plays on the *vīṇā*, Indra on the flute, Brahmā holds the time-marking cymbals, Lakshmī begins a song, Vishṇu plays on a drum, and all the gods stand round about:"

"Gandharvas, Yakshas, Patagas, Uragas, Siddhas, Sādhyas, Vidhyādharas, Amaras, Apsaras and all the beings dwelling in the three worlds assemble there to witness the celestial dance and hear the music of the divine choir at the hour of twilight."

This evening dance is also referred to in the invocation preceding the *Kathā Sarit Sāgara*.

In the pictures of this dance, Śiva is two-handed, and the co-operation of the gods is clearly indicated in their position of chorus. There is no prostrate Asura trampled under Śiva's feet. So far as I know, no special interpretations of this dance occur in Śaiva literature.*

The second well-known dance of Śiva is called the *Tāṇḍava*, and belongs to His *tamasic* aspect as Bhairava or Vīrabhadra. It is performed in cemeteries and burning grounds, where Śiva, usually in ten-armed form, dances wildly with Dēvī, accompanied by troops of capering imps. Representations of this dance are common amongst ancient sculptures, as at Ellora, Elephanta, and also at Bhuvanēśvara. This *tāṇḍava* dance is in origin that of a pre-aryan divinity, half-god, half-demon, who holds his midnight revels in the burning ground. In later times, this dance in the cremation ground, sometimes of Śiva, sometimes of Dēvī, is interpreted in Śaiva and Śākta literature in a most touching and profound sense.

Thirdly, we have the Nādānta dance of Naṭarāja before the assembly (*sabhā*) in the golden hall of

---

* It is not known upon what authorities the varieties of dances referred to here and the descriptions of images made in these dancing postures, are based. I am not aware of any texts which mention a two handed figure of Śiva employed in the act of dancing. (T.A.G.).

Chidambaram or Tillai, the centre of the Universe, first revealed to gods and *ṛishis* after the submission of the latter in the forest of Tāraka, as related in the *Kōyil-Purāṇam*. The legend, which has after all, no very direct connection with the meaning of the dance, may be summarised as follows:

In the forest of Tāraka dwelt multitudes of heretical *ṛishis*, followers of the Mīmāmsa. Thither proceeded Śiva to confute them, accompanied by Vishṇu disguised as a beautiful woman, and Ādi-Śēsha. The *ṛishis* were at first led to violent dispute amongst themselves, but their anger was soon directed against Śiva, and they endeavoured to destroy Him by means of incantations. A fierce tiger was created in sacrificial fires, and rushed upon Him; but smiling gently, He seized it and, with the nail of His little finger stripped off its skin, and wrapped it about Himself like a silken cloth.* Undiscouraged by failure, the sages renewed their offerings, and produced a monstrous serpent, which, however, Śiva seized and wreathed about His neck like a garland. Then He began to dance; but there rushed upon Him at last a monster in the shape of a malignant dwarf, Muyalaka (the

* A similar story is elsewhere related about an elephant and these account for the elephant or tiger skin, which Śiva wears

Apasmārapurusha). Upon him the God pressed the tip of His foot, and broke the creature's back, so that it writhed upon the ground; and so, His last foe prostrate, Śiva resumed the dance, witnessed by gods and ṛishis.

Then Ādi Śēsha worshipped Śiva, and prayed above all things for the boon, once more to behold this mystic dance; Śiva promised that he should behold the dance again in sacred Tillai, the centre of the Universe. The dance of Śiva in Chidambaram or Tillai forms the motif of the South Indian copper images of Śri Naṭarāja, the Lord of the Dance. These images vary amongst themselves in minor details, but all express one fundamental conception. Before proceeding to enquire what these may be, it will be necessary to describe the image of Śri Natarāja as typically represented. The images then, represent Śiva dancing, having four hands, with braided and jewelled hair of which the lower locks are whirling in the dance. In his hair may be seen a wreathing cobra, a skull, and the mermaid figure of Gaṅgā; upon it rests the crescent moon, and it is crowned with a wreath of cassia leaves. In His right ear He wears a man's ear-ring, a woman's in the left; He is adorned with necklaces and armlets, a jewelled belt, anklets, bracelets, finger and toe-rings. The chief part of His dress consists of tightly fitting breeches, and He wears also a fluttering scarf (*aṅgavastram*) and a sacred thread. One right hand holds a drum (*ḍamāru*, *uḍukkai*), the other is uplifted in *abhaya mudrā* (do not fear): one left hand holds fire, the other points downward to the lifted foot. The right foot is pressed down upon the *asura* Muyalaka, a dwarf holding a cobra; the left foot is raised. There is a lotus pedestal, from which springs an encircling arch of glory, (*tiruvāśi*), fringed with flame, and touched within by the hands holding drum and fire. The images are of all sizes, rarely if ever exceeding four feet in total height.

Even without reliance upon literary references, the interpretation of this dance would not be difficult. Fortunately, however, we have the assistance of a copious contemporary literature, which enables us to fully explain not only the general significance of the dance, but equally, the details of its concrete symbolism. Some of the peculiarities of the Naṭarāja images, of course, belong to the conception of Śiva generally, and not to the dance in particular. Such are the braided locks, as of a *yōgi*: the cassia garland: the skull of Brahmā: the figure of Gaṅga, the Ganges fallen from heaven and lost in Śiva's hair: the cobras: the different ear-rings, betokening the dual nature of Mahādēva, 'whose half is Umā ': the four arms. The drum also, is a general attribute of Śiva, belonging to his character of *yōgi*, though in the dance, it has further a special significance. What then is the meaning of Śiva's dance, as understood by Śaivas? The dance is called Nādānta. Its essential significance is given in texts such as the following:

"Our Lord is the Dancer, who, like the heat latent in firewood, diffuses His power in mind and matter, and makes them dance in their turn."*†

The dance, in fact, represents His five activities (*Pañchakṛitya*), *viz.*, Srishṭi (overlooking, creation, evolution), Sthiti (preservation, support), Saṁhāra (destruction, evolution), Tirōbhava (veiling, embodiment, illusion, and also, giving rest,) Anugraha (release, salvation, grace). These, separately considered, are the activities of the deities Brahmā, Vishṇu, Rudra, Mahēśvara and Sadāśiva.

---

* காட்ட அனல்போல் உடல் கலந்து உயிரையெல்லாம்
ஆட்டுவிக்கும் நட்டுவன் நம்மண்ண லெனவெண்ணாய்.

† Kaḍavuḷ Māmunivar's *Tiruvātāvūrār Purāṇam* Puttaraivātil-veṉṟa-śarukkam, stanza 75, translated by Nallasvāmi Piḷḷai, *Śivajñānabōdham*, p. 74. This could also be rendered;

Like heat latent in firewood, he fills all bodies:
Our Father dances, moving all souls into action, know ye!

Compare Eckhart, "Just as the fire infuses the essence and clearness into the dry wood, so has God done with man."

This cosmic activity is the central motif of the dance. Further quotations will illustrate and explain the more detailed symbolisms. *Uṇmāi Viḷakkam*, verse 36, tells us:

"Creation arises from the drum: protection proceeds from the hand of hope: from fire proceeds destruction: the foot held aloft gives *mukti*." Here *mukti* is the same as *anugraha*, release. It will be observed that the fourth hand points to this lifted foot, the refuge of the soul.

We have also the following from *Chidambara Mummaṇi Kōvai*.

"O my Lord, Thy hand holding the sacred drum has made and ordered the heavens and earth and other worlds and innumerable souls. Thy lifted hand protects the Chētana and Achētana Prapañcha which Thou hast created. All these worlds are changed by Thy hand bearing fire. Thy sacred foot, planted on the ground, gives an abode to the tired soul, struggling in the toils of *karma*. It is Thy lifted foot that grants eternal bliss to those that approach Thee. These Five-Actions are indeed Thy handiwork."

The following verses from the *Tirukūttu Darśana* (Vision of the Sacred Dance), forming the ninth *tantra* of Tirumūlar's *Tirumantram*, expand the central motif further :

" His form is everywhere : all-pervading is His Śiva-Śakti :

Chidambaram is everywhere, everywhere His dance :

As Śiva is all and omnipresent,

Everywhere is Śiva's gracious dance made manifest.

" His five-fold dances are in *sakaḷa* and *nishkaḷa* form,

His five-fold dances are His *Pañchakṛitya :*

With His grace He performs the five acts,

This is the sacred dance of Umā-Sahāya.*

" He dances with Water, Fire, Wind and Ether,

Thus our Lord dances ever in the court†

" Visible to those who pass over Māyā and Mahāmāyā,

---

* ஆனநடமைந்தகளசகளத்த
ரானநடமாடியைங்கருமத்தாக
வானதொழிலருளாலைந்தொழிற்செய்தே
தேன்மொழிபாகன் றிருநடமாடுமே.

† காளியோடாடிக் கனகாசலத்தாடிக்
கூளியோடாடிக் குவலயத்தேயாடி
நீடியநீர்தீகால்நீள் வானிடையாடி
நாளுறவம்பலத்தே யாடுநாதனே.

Our Lord dances His eternal dance.*
" The form of the Śakti is all bliss (*ānanda*)—
This united bliss is Umā's body:
This form of Śakti arising in *sakaḷa*
And uniting the twain is the dance "†
" His body is Ākāś, the dark cloud therein is Muyalaka,
The eight quarters are His eight arms,
The three lights are His three eyes,
Thus becoming, He dances in our body as the assembly (*sabhā*) ".‡

This is His dance. Its deepest significance is felt when it is realised that it takes place within the heart and the self: the kingdom of God is within. Everywhere is God: that Everywhere is the heart. Thus also we find another verse:

---

* தீமுதலைந்துந் திசையெட்டுங்கீழ்மேலு
மாயுமறிவினுக் கப்புறமானந்த
மாயைமாமாயை கடந்துநின்றார்காண
நாயகனின்று நடஞ்செய்யும் வாறே.

† சத்திவடிவுசகலவானந்தமு
மொத்தவானந்தமுமையவள்மேனியாஞ்
சத்திவடிவுசகளத்தெழுந்திரண்
டொத்தவானந்தமொருநடமாமே.

‡ ஆகாசமாமுடலங்கார்முயலக
னேகாசமாந்திசையெட்டுந்திருக்கைகண்
மோகாயமுக்கண்கள்மூன்றொளிதானாக
மாகாயன்மன்றுள்நடஞ்செய்கின்றானே.

"The dancing foot, the sound of the tinkling bells,
The songs that are sung and the varying steps,
The forms assumed by our Dancing Guru-para—
Find out these within yourself, then shall your fetters fall away."*

To this end, all else but the thought of God must be cast out of the heart, that He alone may abide and dance therein. In *Uṇmai Viḷakkam*, we find:

"The silent *jñānis* destroying the threefold bond are established where their selves are destroyed. There they behold the sacred and are filled with bliss. This is the dance of the Lord of the assembly, "whose very form is Grace."†

With this reference to the 'silent *jñānis*' compare the beautiful words of Tirumūlar:

---

* ஆடியகாலுமதிற்சிலம்போசையும்
பாடியபாட்டும்பலவானநட்டமுங்
கூடியகோலங்குருபரன்கொண்டாடத்
தேடியுளேகண்டுதீர்ந்தற்றவாறே.

† மோனந்த மாமுனிவர் மும்மலத்தை மோசித்துத்
தானந்த மானிடத்தே தங்கியிடு—மானந்த
மொண்டருந்தி நின்றாடல் காணுமண்ரு மூர்த்தியாய்க்
கொண்டதிரு வம்பலத்தான் கூத்து.

"When resting there they (the *yōgis* who attain the highest place of peace) lose themselves and become idle....Where the idlers dwell is the pure Space. Where the idlers sport is the Light. What the idlers know is the Vēdānta. What the idlers find is the deep sleep therein".*

Siva is a destroyer and loves the burning ground. But what does He destroy? Not merely the heavens and earth at the end of a *kalpa*, but the fetters that bind each separate soul. Where and what is the burning ground? It is not the place where our earthly bodies are cremated, but the heart of the *bhakta*, the devotee, laid waste and desolate. He brings not peace but a sword. The place where their selves are destroyed signifies the place or state where their egoity or illusion and deeds are burnt away: *that* is the crematorium, the burning-ground where Śrī Naṭarāja dances, and whence He is named Suḍalaiyāḍi, Dancer of

---

* இருந்தார் சிவமாகி யெங்குந்தாமாகி
இருந்தார் சிவன் செயலியாவையு நோக்கி
இருந்தார் முக்காலத்தியல்பைக் குறித்தங்
கிருந்தாரிழவு தெய்திய சோம்பே.
சோம்பர் இருப்பது சுத்த வெளியிலே
சோம்பர் கிடப்பது சுத்த வொளியிலே
சோம்பர் உணர்வது சுருதி முடிந் திடம்
சோம்பர் கண்டார்ச் சுருதிக்கட் டூக்கமே.

the burning-ground. In this simile, we recognize the historical connection between Śiva's gracious dance as Naṭarāja, and His wild dance as the demon of the cemetery.

This conception of the dance is current also amongst Śāktas especially in Bengal, where the Mother rather than the Father-aspect of Siva is adored. Kāḷi* is here the dancer, for whose entrance the heart must be purified by fire, made empty by renunciation. A Bengali Hymn to Kāḷi voices this prayer :

"Because Thou lovest the Burning-ground,
I have made a Burning-ground of my heart—
That Thou, Dark One, haunter of the Burning-ground,
Mayest dance Thy eternal dance."†
"Nought else is within my heart, O Mother:
Day and night blazes the funeral pyre:
The ashes of the dead, strewn all about,
I have preserved against Thy coming,
With death conquering Mahākāla neath Thy feet

* *Vide* article on "What is Kāḷi ?" in, *S.D.* Vol. III, p. 13,—*Ed. S.D.*

† உலகமே யுருவமாக யோனிகளுறுப்பதாக
விலகுபேரிச்சா ஞானக்கிரியை யுட்கரணமாக
வலகிலா உயிர்கட்கெல்லா மிருபயனுக வைத்து
நலமிடு தொழில்களோடு நாடக நடிப்பன் நாதன்.

Do Thou enter in, dancing Thy rhythmic dance,

That I may behold Thee with closed eyes".

Returning to the South, we find that in other Tamil texts the purpose of Śiva's dance is explained. In *Śivajñāna Siddhiyār*, Supaksha, Sūtra v. 5, we find,

" For the purpose of securing both kinds of fruit to the countless souls, our Lord, with actions five, dances His dance". Both kinds of fruit, that is *Iham*, reward in this world, and *Param*, bliss in *Mukti*.

Again, *Uṇmai Viḷakkam*, vv. 32, 37, 39 inform us

" The Supreme Intelligence dances in the soul ....for the purpose of removing our sins. By these means, our Father scatters the darkness of *Māyā*, burns the thread of *Karma*, stamps down *Mala* (*āṇava*, *avidyā*), showers Grace, and lovingly plunges the soul in the ocean of bliss (*Ānanda*). They never see rebirths, who behold this mystic dance".*

---

* எட்டு மிரண்டுமுருவானவி லிங்கத்தே
நட்டம்புதல்வா நவிலக்கேள்—சிட்டன்
சிவாயநம வென்னுந் திருவெழுத்தஞ்சாலே
யவாய மற நின்றாடுவான்.
மாயை தனையுதறி வல்வினையைச் சுட்டு மலஞ்
சாயவ முக்கியருள்தானெடுத்து—நேயத்தால்

The conception of *Līlā*, the world-process as the Lord's sport or amusement, is also prominent in the Śaiva scriptures; thus, Tirumūlar writes: " The Perpetual Dance becomes His Play".

This aspect of His activity appears to have given rise to the objection that He dances as do those who seek to please the eyes of mortals; to which the answer is given that He dances to maintain the life of the cosmos and to give release to those who seek Him.

In another way, more arbitrary, the Dance of Śiva is identified with the Pañchākshara, the five syllables Śi-vā-ya-na-ma, which have a peculiar and special significance in Śaiva symbolism. In *Uṇmai Viḷakkam*, vv. 33-35 they are identified in the dance as follows:

" In His feet is *na ;* in His naval is *ma ;* in His shoulders is *Śi ;* in His face is *vā ;* in His head is *ya*".*

ஆநந்தவாரிதியி லான்மாவைத்தா னழுத்தல்
தானெந்தையார் பாதந்தான்.
உரையுணர்வுக் கெட்டா வொருவன் மிடபெஞ்சாக்
கரத்தால் வரைமகடான்பாதி—பரையிடமாய்க்
காணும்படியே கருணையுருக் கொண்டாடல்
பேணுமவர்க்குண்டோ பிறப்பு.

* ஆடும்படிகேள் நல்லம்பலத்தா னையனே
நாடுந் திருவடியிலே நகரம்—கூடு
மகரமுதரம் வளர்தோள் சிகரம்
பகருமுகம் வாமுடியப்பார்.

A second way of contemplating the Pañchākshara is also given, as follows:

"The hand holding the Drum is *śi;* the hand held out is *vā;* the hand holding out protection (*abhaya*) is *ya;* the hand holding fire is *na;* the foot holding down Muyalaka is *ma*".*

The text continues:

"The meanings of the five letters respectively are God, Śakti, Soul, Tirōbhava and Mala....If this beautiful Five-Letters be meditated upon, the soul will reach the land where there is neither light nor darkness, and there Sakti will make it One with Sivam".†

Another verse of *Uṇmai Viḷakkam* explains the fiery arch (*tiruvāsi*): The Pañchākshara and the Dance are identified with the mystic syllable Ōm, the arch being the *kombu* or hook of the

---

* சேர்க்கும் துடிசிகரம் சிக்கனவாவீசுகரம்
ஆர்க்கும் யகரமபயகரம்—பாக்கிலிறைக்
கங்கி நகரமடிக்கீழ் முயலகனார்
தங்கு மகரமது தான்.

† ஈசன் அருள் ஆவி யெழிலார் திரோதமலம்
மாசிலெழுத்தஞ்சினடைவாம்.
அண்ணல் முதலாயழகா ரெழுத்தைந்து
மண்ணிலிராப் பகலற்றின்பத்தே—நண்ணி
யருளானது சிவத்தே யாக்குமணுவை
யிருளானது திரவின்று.

ideograph of the written symbol : "The arch over Srī Naṭarāja is Ōmkāra; and the *akshara* which is never separate from the Ōmkāra is the contained splendour. This is the Dance of the Lord of Chidambaram".*

The *Tiru-Aruḷ-Payan*, however, (Ch. IX. 3) explains the *tiruvāśi* more naturally as representing the dance of Nature, contrasted with Siva's dance of wisdom.

"The dance of matter (*Prakṛiti*) proceeds on one side : the *jñāna* dance on the other. Fix your mind in the centre of the latter".†

I am indebted to Mr. Nallasvāmi Piḷḷai for a commentary on this :

The first dance is the action of matter—material and individual energy. This is the arch, *tiruvāsi*, Omkāra, the dance of Kāḷi. The other is the Dance of Śiva—the *akshara* inseparable from the Omkāra—called *ardhamātra* or the fourth letter of the *Praṇava*, *Chaturtam* and *Turīyam*. The first dance is not possible unless Śiva wills it and dances Himself.

---

* ஓங்காரமே நற்றிருவாசி யுற்றதனின்
நீங்காவெழுத்தே நிறை சுடராம்—ஆங்காரம்
அற்றார் அறிவாரணி யம்பலத்தானாடலிது
பெற்றார் பிறப்பற்றார் பின்.

† ஊன நடன மொருபா லொருபாலா
ஞான நடந்தானடு.

The general result of this interpretation of the arch is, then, that it represents matter, nature, *prakṛiti;* the contained splendour, Śiva dancing within and touching the arch with head, hands and feet, is the universal omnipresent Purusha. Between these stands the soul, as *ya* is between *Śi-va* and *na-ma.*

Now to summarise the whole interpretation, we find that *The Essential Significance of Śiva's Dance is threefold: First, it is the image of his Rhythmic Activity as the Source of all Movement within the Cosmos, which is represented by the Arch: Secondly, the Purpose of his Dance is to Release the Countless souls of men from the Snare of Illusion: Thirdly the Place of the Dance, Chidambaram, the Centre of the Universe, is within the Heart.*

In these notes I expressly refrain from all æsthetic criticism and have endeavoured only to translate the central thought of the conception of Śiva's dance from plastic to verbal expression, without reference to the beauty or imperfection of individual works. In conclusion, it may not be out of place to call attention to the grandeur of this conception itself as a synthesis of science, religion and art. How amazing the range of thought and sympathy of those rishi-artists who first conceived such a type as this, affording an image of reality, a key to the complex tissue of life, a theory of nature, not merely satisfactory to a single clique or race, nor acceptable to the thinkers of one century only, but universal in its appeal to the Philosopher, the Bhakta, and the artist of all ages and all countries. In these days of specialisation, we are not accustomed to such a synthesis of thought; but for those who 'saw' such images as this, there could have been no division of life and thought into water-tight compartments. Nor do we always realise, when we criticise the merits of individual works, the full extent of the creative power which, to borrow a musical analogy, could discover a *rāga* so expressive of fundamental rhythms and so profoundly significant and inevitable.

Every part of such an image as this is directly expressive, not of any mere superstition or dogma, but of evident facts. No artist of to-day, however great, could more exactly or more wisely create an image of that Energy which science must postulate behind all phenomena. If we would reconcile Time with Eternity, we can scarcely do so otherwise than by the conception of alternations of phase extending over vast regions of space and great tracts of time.*

[* Oliver Lodge, Hibbert Journal, Vol. X, No. 2, 1911.]

Especially significant, then, is the phase alternation implied by the drum, and the fire which 'changes,' not destroys. These are but visual symbols of the theory of the day and night of Brahma!

In the night of Brahma, Nature is inert, and cannot dance till Śiva wills it: He rises from His rapture, and dancing sends through inert matter pulsing waves of awakening sound, and lo! matter also dances, appearing as a glory round about Him. Dancing, He sustains its manifold phenomena. In the fulness of time, still dancing, he destroys all forms and names by fire and gives new rest. This is poetry: but none the less, the truest science.

Again, this Naṭarāja is not only Truth, but Love: for the purpose of His Dance is Grace, the giving of freedom to countless individual souls. Lastly, also, how supremely great in power and grace this dancing image must appear to all those who as artists have striven in plastic forms to give expression to their intuition of Life!

It is not strange that the figure of Naṭarāja has commanded the adoration of so many generations past: we, familiar with all scepticisms, expert in tracing all beliefs to primitive superstitions, explorers of the infinitely great and infinitely small, are worshippers of Śri Naṭarāja still.

A. K. C."

Five photographs are given in illustration of the Bhujaṅgatrāsa mode of dance of Śiva. The first, Pl. LVI, is that of the beautiful figure of Naṭarāja discovered at Tiruvālaṉgāḍu and now preserved in the Madras Museum. It is one of the finest specimens of bronze casting in South India and extorts our admiration for the excellence of its design and execution. The *prabhāmaṇḍala*, the *jaṭas*, the upper cloth tied round the chest and the *ḍamaru* are broken and lost. The head is ornamented with peacock feathers, the *dhurdhura* flowers, a skull, a cobra and the crescent moon. The second photograph, Pl. LVII, the original of which was found buried in earth at Kōṭṭappāḍi and is at present kept in *pūjā* in the temple at that village. As required by the *āgāmas*, the Dēvī is sculptured as standing near Naṭarāja, but on a separate pedestal. There are five *jaṭās* on each side and between each pair of them are worked out flowers and the figure of Gaṅgā. The Dēvī is standing in the *tribhaṅga* posture and has her left hand let down and the right arm bent and held in the *kaṭaka* pose. The illustration, fig. 1, LVIII, comes from Rāmēsvaram. The image has not got

PLATE LVI.

Naṭarāja; Bronze: Madras Museum.

[To face page 252]

PLATE LVII.

Naṭarāja with Dēvi : Bronze : Koṭṭappādi.

[To face page 252]

PLATE LVIII

Fig 1. Naṭarāja : Bronze : Rāmēśvaram.

Fig 2. Naṭaraja Ivory : Trivandram.

[To face page 252]

PLATE LIX.

Naṭarāja with Devi: Bronze: Paṭṭiśvaram.

[To face page 253]

the *jatās* round the head; the head is adorned with a *kirīṭa* like *jaṭāmakuṭa* and the back hands are not fully stretched out as in the previous illustrations. The work lacks the vigour of action which is well portrayed in the other instances, and does not appear to be altogether a commendable piece of art. Fig. 2 on the same plate is a piece of ivory carving executed in the School of Arts, Trivandram, which is made in utter disregard of the *agāmic* rules. Pl. LIX is a pretty piece of sculpture belonging to the temple at Paṭṭīśvaram.

The second, the third and the fourth varieties of Nṛitta are not very different from the first. In the second form of dance, the *Aṁśumadbhēdāgama* states, there should be the figure of Gaṅgā standing on the *jaṭās* flowing on the right side of Śiva with hands held in the *añjali* pose; and that the height of this figure of the river Gaṅgā should be sixteen *aṅgulas*, an *aṅgula* being a hundred and twentieth part of the total height of the figure of Śiva. In the third kind of dance it is stated that the left foot of the Nṛittamūrti should be placed on the body of the Apasmāra-purusha and the right leg lifted up. A *jaṭābhāra* or *jaṭāmaṇḍala* spread round the crowned head of the figure of Śiva in the form of a circular disc is required in the fourth form of *Nṛitta* or dance.

The fifth form of the dance of Śiva is somewhat different from the previous ones. In this the right leg is to be lifted straight up to the crown of the head and the left leg, somewhat bent, should be resting upon the Apasmāra-purusha; Śiva in this aspect has eight arms; in three out of the four right hands are to be seen the *śūla*, the *pāśa*, and the *ḍamaru*, while the last one should be kept in the *abhaya* pose; one of the left hands is to be held crosswise, from left to right in the *gajahasta* pose, and the three other hands are to carry the *kapāla*, the vessel of fire and a bell (*ghaṇṭa*).

In the sixth variety of dance, the legs of the figure of Śiva should be as in the case of the fifth variety described above; but Śiva is to be represented here as having sixteen arms; one of the right hands is required to be held in the *abhaya* pose and the remaining right ones to carry the *ḍamaru*, *vajra*, *śūla*, *pāśa*, *ṭaṅka*, *daṇḍa* (*hasta*?) and a snake; or, *abhaya*, *śūla*, *pāśa* *khaḍga*, *ḍamaru*, *dhvaja* (*patāka-hasta*?), *vētāḷa* and the *sūchī* pose. One of the left arms should be held in the *gajahasta* pose, being held across the body from left to right, while the remaining ones carrying either *agni*, *mithuna* (a double headed instrument like the *vajra*?), *valaya* (quoit),

PLATE LX.

Naṭarāja : Stone : Teṅkāśi.

[To face page 259]

a banner,* *ghaṇṭā*, *khēṭaka* and *kapāla ;* or *agni*, *gajahasta*, *khēṭaka*, the *vismaya* pose, *ghaṇṭa*, *kapāla*, *khaḍga* and the *sūchī* pose.

To the left of the dancing Śiva should be standing his consort, carrying in her left arm Skanda and keeping her hands in the *añjali* pose, while the child Skanda should, out of fear at the sight of the ecstatic dance of his father, be catching hold of the breast and abdomen of his mother, the Dēvī. On the face of the Dēvī the emotions of fear and wonder and yet a friendly feeling should be brought out by the skilful artist.

The photograph reproduced on Pl. LX, in illustration of the sixth mode of dance belongs to a series of well-carved life-size stone images in the Śiva temple at Teṇkāśi. In this, one of the left hands is shown as carrying a *dhvaja* with the bull, the characteristic totem of Śiva's banner, sculptured on it. To the right and left of the figure of Śiva are the *ṛishis* Vyāghrapāda and Patañjali respectively with hands folded on their chests in the *añjali* pose. This piece of sculpture is one of the

* Here the word may be understood to mean a banner or the hand held in the form of a banner, *patāka-hasta*. In fact, these two different senses are taken and sculptures executed accordingly. See the description of the illustrations to the sixth *nṛitta*.

best specimens of the later Pāṇḍya period and is in an excellent state of preservation.

In the seventh form of *nṛitta*, the image of Śiva is required to possess eight arms, three eyes and an out-spreading *jaṭāmaṇḍala ;* the left leg of Śiva should be placed upon the Apasmārapurusha and the right leg lifted up fully stretched, as far as the head. One of the right hands should be held in the *abhaya* pose, the others carrying the *śūla*, the *pāśa* and the *ḍamaru.* Two of the left arms should be kept in the *gajahasta* and the *vismaya* poses, respectively; the remaining two carrying a *kapāla*, and an *agnipātra* (or vessel of fire). There should be a bend in the body of ten *aṅgulas* from the medial line (*madhya sūtra*). To the left of the dancing figure of Śiva should stand that of the Dēvī.

If in the seventh mode of dance there be substituted six hands in the place of eight, we get the eighth form of the Nṛittamūrti. In this, one of the right hands ought to be held in the *abhaya* pose and the remaining ones to carry the *ḍamaru* and the *śūla ;* and one of the left arms is to be kept in the *gajahasta* pose, another in the *vismaya* pose and the third should carry a *kapāla.*

Here it must be particularly noted that the images of the fifth and sixth forms of the

PLATE LXI.

Nṛittamūrti : Stone : Tiruchchengāṭṭaṅguḍi.

[To face page 257]

Nṛittamūrtis should possess only two eyes, whereas all the rest, described hitherto and hereafter, should have three eyes.

The ninth form of Nṛittamūrti is described as follows:—The image of Śiva should have four arms, three eyes and a *jaṭāmakuṭa* on the head. One of the right hands is to be held in the *abhaya* pose and the other should carry a *ḍamaru*, whereas one of the left arms is to be held in the *gajahasta* pose and the other hand ought to carry fire in it. In this particular dance, Śiva's left foot should not be placed upon the back of the Apasmārapurusha but rest upon a *pīṭha* and should be somewhat bent. The great toe of the right foot should also rest upon the *pīṭha*. A photograph, Pl. LXI, the original of which is found in the Śiva temple at Tiruchcheṅgāṭṭaṅguḍi, is reproduced here in illustration of this, the ninth dance of Śiva. There is a very close adherence to the description in the making of this image and the work is well executed.

From a study of the so-called nine different forms of the Nṛittamūrtis it becomes patent that these do not really represent nine varieties of dances as described in the *Nāṭya-śāśtra*. We find the dance of the common form of Naṭarāja to be what is technically known as the *bhujaṅgatrāsa* mode of dancing. Besides these nine varieties of the Nṛittamūrtis described in the *Aṁśumadbhēdāgama*, we meet with several different images of Naṭanamūrtis in actual sculpture. Some of them do, as a matter of fact, represent a few of the modes of dance whose descriptions are found in the *Bharata Nāṭya-śāstra.* Since the art of dancing, which was very popular till so recently as twenty years ago, is fast going out of fashion owing to the notion of a large section of the English-educated people of India that *nautch* ought to be discouraged owing to its association in practice with dancing girls who have, quite contrary to the original lofty ideals of the institution, degenerated into professional prostitutes, the study and practice of one of the Fine Arts of India is gradually dying out and is least understood by the educated classes at the present day. The works dealing with the science have almost perished for want of appreciation, and it is very difficult to meet a scholar who is really well versed with the *Nāṭya-śāstra* in its theoretical and practical aspects. Consequently the explanations of the few modes of dance of Śiva met with in actual sculpture which are attempted below are, it is feared, likely to be somewhat inaccurate, but endeavour is made, with the help of the only commentary on the subject written by the great

PLATE LXII.

Kaṭisama mode of Dance of Śiva : Stone Panel : Ellora.

[To face page 259]

Abhinavaguptāchārya,* to describe them as correctly as possible.

Katisama dance.†

Plate LXII exhibits a mode of dance which is called the *Kaṭisamam* in the *Nāṭya-śāstra*. In this mode, according to the text of the *Nāṭya-śāstra*, the legs are required to be in the pose known as the *svastikāpasritam*, while one of the hands should be near the navel and the other on the hip; and the pelvis should be in the *udvāhita* pose. The term *svastikāpasritam* is explained in the *Nāṭya śāstra*;

---

* There is only one copy of this rare work hitherto discovered and this one also is here and there damaged. It is now in the custody of the Curator of the Sanskrit Manuscripts in Trivandram. If other copies are found, the work deserves being published by a competent scholar of the *Nāṭya-śāstra*.

† स्वस्तिकापसृतः पादः करौ नाभिकटिस्थितौ ।
पार्श्वमुद्वाहितं चैव करणं तत् कटीसमम् ॥

स्वस्तिकादनन्तरं.......... ....इत्यनेनाक्षिप्ताया। अनन्तरमुपक्रान्तायाः प्रयोगमाह—चकारेण करौ च स्वस्तिकौ अवधूतौ । तत एका नाभिस्थः कनक एव मपटः कर्षद्यामर्धचन्द्रः। तदेव पार्श्वं व्यानतमपरमुद्वाहितं द्वितीयेनाङ्गेनाकुञ्चितं पादमुत्क्षिप्य व्याक्षिप्यत्वं चितं न्यसेत् "जङ्घा स्वस्तिकसंयुक्ता प्रक्षिप्ता नाम सा स्मृता" "उत्क्षिप्य चक्रा तु यदानामिका साकनीयसी। अस्यैव तु कपित्थस्य तदसौ कटकामुखं" "यस्याङ्गुलेन चापवत्सोऽर्धचन्द्रः" "ऊर्ध्वाहितमूर्ध्वीकृतमुरो ज्ञेयं प्रयोक्तृभिः" इति । पार्श्वमप्युद्वाहितं वैष्णवं चात्र स्थानकं कटिर्लभ्यते ॥

(नाट्यवेदविवृतौ ॥)

but it is easier to make out the meaning of the term from a number of sculptures and from the etymology of the term. Two legs kept crossing each other is known as the *svastika* pose; in this pose if the legs are kept a little apart from each other, that is, without touching each other, they are said to be *svastikāpasrita* pose. Again, if the hands are kept as described in the text quoted above, the pose is, according to the *Nāṭya-vēda-vivṛiti*, the commentary on the *Bharata-nāṭya śāstra* by Abhinavaguptāchārya, is known as the *svastika* pose. In this pose, Abhinavaguptāchārya says, the hand that is near the navel should be kept in the *kaṭaka-hasta* pose and the other hand in what is known as the *arddha-chandra* pose: in the latter pose the thumb and the other fingers should be kept so as to resemble a bow. Again, *udvāhita* pose of the pelvis is that in which one side of it is raised and the other lowered proportionately. The mode of standing in the *kaṭisama* dance is technically known as the *vaishṇavasthānam*, which Abhinavaguptāchārya describes as follows: In the *vaishṇavasthāna* one leg should be resting firmly on the ground and the other bent and placed across the first at a distance of two and a half *aṅgulas*. This sort of posture is prescribed for men when they are conversing with other or throwing the discus.

In the illustration given on Pl. LXII, Śiva has eight arms. Of these, one of the right hands is carrying a *ḍamaru;* another is held near the navel in the *kaṭaka* pose, a third is lowered down and on it is thrown a fine cloth, the upper garment of Śiva, and the fourth is broken. One of the left arms is raised in the *tripatāka* pose, another is resting on the thigh, and the hands of the third and fourth are broken. The legs are in the *svastikāpasrita* pose. The head is adorned with an extremely well executed *jaṭāmakuṭa* and is surrounded with a *prabhāmaṇḍala.* The upper arms wear beautiful spiral bands resembling snakes. On the chest and around the neck hangs a necklace of rare beauty and a *yajñōpavīta* is seen lying across the chest. Besides these, there are the *udarabandha* and *kaṭisūtra* on the abdomen and the loins. The under-wear of Śiva is silk and tiger's skin, the latter of which is sculptured very distinctly and accurately. Pārvatī is seen standing to the left of Śiva with the baby Skanda in her arms. Between her and her lord are two female musicians playing upon two musical instruments. Behind Pārvatī stands a man with a big *jaṭābhāra* bearing on its front a fillet and has a pair of long moustaches; perhaps he is one of the attendants of Śiva. Over his head are the four *Dikpālas,* Yama, Indra, Nirṛuti and Agni. To the right of Śiva are three or four male musicians of whom one is playing upon the flute, another is sounding the drum. The head of the elephant-headed Gaṇēśa, the first son of Śiva, is peering through from the background. Over his head are the remaining Dikpālas. This is also one of the finest pieces of sculpture of its period.

Lalita dance.

The next mode of dance is technically called *Lalitam.** In this, the left arm should be held in the *gajahasta* pose and the right in the *pravartita* pose. The former has already been described and should be familiar to those who have studied the first volume of this treatise. According to the Naṭyā-śastras, *gajahasta* is a combination-pose in which both hands are employed to produce the required effect and this is described thus : in the case of a human

---

* करिहस्तो भवेद् वामो दक्षिणश्च प्रवर्तितः ।
[बहुशःकुट्टितःपादो] ज्ञेयं तल्ललितं बुधैः ॥

समुन्नतो लता..................................यो दक्षिणं विविधं कृत्वा बहुशो वर्तितस्ते " बाहुशीर्षाद् विनिष्क्रान्तौ नितम्बौ," " केशदेशाद् विनिष्क्रान्तौ परिपार्श्वोत्थितौ सदा । तथा विज्ञेयौ केशबन्धौ " इत्येवं प्रकारनृत्तहस्तयोजनया वर्तितः चकाराद् वनान्ते पताको वरः कर्ण इति करिहस्ता पादश्च हस्तवस्तानुसारेण निकुट्टितः पुन.......................... स्त्रिसंविद्वासनृत्तविषयमेतदन्त एव ललितामन्नामकरणम् ॥

(नाव्यवेदविवृतौ ॥)

PLATE LXIII.

Lalita mode of dance of Siva: Stone Panel: Ellora.

[To face page 262]

being who has only two arms, if one hand is stretched right across the chest towards the other shoulder and if the other arm is bent thrice in the *tripatāka* pose, that is, the upper arm lifted up as high as the shoulder horizontally and the forearm held at right angles to it vertically and the palm of the hand bent at right angles to the forearm and facing upwards, the double-hand pose is called *gajahasta* according to the Naṭya-śāstra. This definition is, no doubt, different from the explanation found in Volume I of this treatise, but the one given here is applicable to the combination-pose of both the arms. *Pravartita hasta* simply means uplifted arm. The leg pose required for the *Lalita* dance is technically called *kuṭṭitam*, which is described in the *Nāṭya-vēdavivriti* thus: if one leg rests firmly on the ground and the other, resting upon the toe, strikes the ground with the heel, the leg pose is called *nikuṭṭitam.*

In the illustration, Pl. LXIII, Śiva is represented as dancing in a vigorous manner. The trunk of his body is thrown on one side and to the back, with the left side of the pelvis lifted and the right side depressed. His left leg is standing on the ground and the right resting on the toe is stamping the ground with the heel. One of the right hands carries the *ḍamaru*, another the *paraśu*, a third is broken and the fourth is held in the *gajahasta* pose; while one arm is kept in the *tripatāka* pose, another in the ordinary *patāka* or streamer pose (in which it is kept stretched horizontally, away from the shoulder), the third appears to be held in the *tarjanī* pose and the last in the *sūchī* pose. A pretty *jaṭāmakuṭa* adorns the head while the ears are ornamented with *kuṇḍalas*. There is the *yajñōpavīta*, the *hāra*, the *udarabandha* and a snake employed as *kaṭisūtra*. On either side are groups of four Dikpālas. To the left of Śiva is Pārvatī holding in her right hand the hand of her boy Skanda, while with her left hand she holds a portion of her garment. Near her to her left is standing a *gaṇa*. To the right of Śiva is Nandi sounding the drum, another playing on the flute and a third doing something which is not clear. On the seat on which Śiva dances, there is the famished figure of Kāḷī seated in an easy pose and witnessing the dance of her lord. This panel is remarkable for its vigorous action. This one and the previous panel, belong to the rock temples at Ellora.

Pls. LXIV-LXV exemplify the dance called *Lalāṭa-tilakam.** In this mode of dance one of

* वृश्चिकं चरणं कृत्वा पादस्याङ्गुष्ठकेन तु ।
ललाटे तिलकं कुर्याल्ललाटतिलकं तु तत् ॥

PLATE LXIV.

Fig. 1. Lalāṭa-tilaka mode of dance of Śiva : Stone : Tiruchcheṅgāṭṭaṅguḍi.

Fig. 2. Lalāṭa-tilaka mode of dance of Śiva : Stone : Conjeevaram.

[To face page 261]

PLATE LXV.

Fig. 1. Lalāṭa-tilaka mode of dance of Śiva : Stone : Teṉkaśi.

Fig. 2. Lalāṭa-tilaka mode of dance of Śiva : Stone : Tāramaṅgalam.

[To face page 265]

the legs is to be lifted up (technically known as the *vriśchika* pose) as if going to mark the forehead with its toe with a *tilaka* mark. Abhinavaguptāchārya informs us that that leg pose in which the leg is lifted up behind is called the *vrischika* pose, for it then resembles the tail of a scorpion. In Fig. 1, Pl. LXIV, Śiva is seen standing on the Apasmārapurusha on his left leg, while he has his right leg lifted in the *vriśchika* pose; one of the left arms is lifted up in the *patāka* pose, while the other holds a *kapāla*. One of the right hands bears a *ḍamaru* and the other is kept in the *abhaya* pose. On the left of Śiva is seen the figure of Bhairava dancing in the Lalita mode; on the right is a figure (who might be Nandi) sounding the drum. This piece of sculpture is to be found in the Śiva temple at Tiruchcheṅgāṭṭaṅguḍi and is of the same age as the figure on Pl. LXI illustrating the ninth mode of dance of Śiva.

The sculpture reproduced as fig. 2, on Pl. LXIV, is to be found in the Kailāsanāthasvāmin temple at Conjeevaram. In this Śiva has eight arms carrying various objects such as the ·*śūla*, the *valaya* and

---

पादस्य तस्यैव पश्चाद्भागामितस्याङ्गुष्ठेन तिलकं तिलकक्रियाहेतुभूतत्वेन लक्षितं संश्लेषितं कुर्यादित्यासिकमेतत्करण .... विषये प्रयुज्यते ॥

(नाट्यवेदविवृतौ ॥)

the *dhvaja ;* one of his right hands is in the *abhaya* pose. The left leg of Śiva is planted firmly on the ground, while the right one goes up, from behind, as far as the top of the crown. To the immediate left of Śiva is Nandi, also dancing, but in the Lalita mode ; and immediately to the right is a *kinnara*, half man and half bird playing apparently on a stringed instrument. On the right and left niches adjoining the central one of Śiva are the figures of Brahmā and Vishṇu standing and praising Śiva.

The third illustration, Pl. LXV, fig. 2, belongs to the Kailāsanāthasvāmin temple at Tāramaṅgalam and is a very recent production. Here, the figure of Śiva has sixteen arms carrying various objects. The right leg of Śiva is lifted up as far as the crown while the left one is somewhat bent and resting upon the back of the Apasmārapurusha. One of the left hands holds a *ḍamaru* which is sounded by one of the right hands ; also one of the left arms is lifted up to the head in the *patāka* pose. To the right of the figure of Śiva is that of Brahmā sounding the cymbals and to the left is the figure of Vishṇu sounding the drum. Between Brahmā and Śiva is a figure of a *ṛishi ;* who it is, is not clear. The Apasmārapurusha is lying with his head towards the right and the legs towards the left of Śiva and holds in his hands a snake.

PLATE LXVI.

Fig. 1. Chatura mode of dance of Śiva : Stone : Bādāmi.

Fig. 2. Chatura mode of dance of Śiva : Bronze : Tiruvaraṅguḷam.

[To face page 267]

PLATE LXVII.

Front View.

Back View.

Chatura mode of dance of Śiva : Bronze : Nallūr (Tanjore Dt.)

[To face page 267]

Another mode of dance commonly met with in the sculpturing of the dancing Śiva is known as *chaturam.** The *Bharata-Nāṭya Śāstra* defines this mode thus: 'The left arm should be in the *añchita* pose, the right one in the *chatura* pose, and the right leg in the *kuṭṭita* pose.' Abhinavaguptāchārya seems to be giving the term *alapallava* as a synonym of *añchita* and explains *alapallava* as follows: that pose of the hand in which the fingers are kept separated and all turned towards the palm, is called *alapallava.* Again, the *chatura* pose, according to the same authority, is one in which the little finger is kept vertical, the three others stretched at right angles to the little finger, while the thumb is placed in the middle of the three fingers.

Figs. 1 and 2, Pls. LXVI and LXVII, illustrate in a manner the dance called *chaturam.* Of these,

---

* अञ्चितः स्यात् करो वामः समश्चतुर एव तु ।
दक्षिणः कुट्टितं पादश्चतुरं तत् प्रकीर्तितम् ॥

अन्वि(ञ्चि ?)त इत्यलपल्लवस्तिस्रःप्रसारिता यत्त तथा चोर्ध्वा कनीयसी तासां मध्ये स करश्चतुरः स्मृतः । एवकारेण वक्षःक्षेत्राद् द्वयोरप्यलं, तु शब्देन संनिवेशाधिक्यं केवलमिति सूच्यते। कुट्टित इति 'स्थित्वा पादतलाग्रेण पार्ष्णि भूमौ निपात्यते'। इद्धट्टितांशरूपं एतद् विदूषकस्य सविस्मयसूच्याभिनयादौ यथा सानुरेखण्डसवर्मामिसा सा ।

(नाट्यवेदविवृतौ ॥)

the first is the reproduction of a very well executed piece of sculpture to be found in the lower cave at Bādāmi. In this, the central figure of Śiva has sixteen arms in which are seen such objects as the *śūla*, the *paraśu* and a snake. One left arm is in the *gajahasta* pose and the lowermost right hand is in the *chatura* pose whereas the third right hand from above is in the *añchita* pose. The figure of Śiva is adorned with various ornaments and a *prabhā-maṇḍala* graces the head, which is surmounted with a neatly carved *jaṭā-makuṭa*. The left leg is in the *kuṭṭita* pose. Behind and on the right of Śiva is seen his bull-vehicle; on his left is Gaṇēśa, also attempting to dance. There are two drums to the left of Gaṇēśa one of which is being sounded by a male, perhaps Nandīśvara.

Fig. 2 is almost exactly similar to fig. 1.

One other mode of dance represented in sculptures of Śiva is known by the name of *talasamsphōṭitam**. In this mode of dancing the dancer stamps vehemently the ground in front of him with

---

* द्रुतमुत्क्षिप्य चरणं पुरस्तादथ पातयेत् ।
तलसंस्फोटितौ हस्तौ तलसंस्फोटितौ स्मृतौ ॥

अतिक्रान्तया चार्या दय.................णमुत्क्षिप्तं कृत्वा तथैवाग्रे निपातयेत् तत्समकालं च पताकौ हस्तौ संश्लेषितशब्दादभिहित इति तलसंस्फोटितं तस्यैतद्विषय एव यथा तालीद्देवी सुसुख सुभस इजणु इत्यादौ ॥

(नाट्यवेदविवृतौ ॥)

PLATE LXVIII.

Talasamsphōṭita mode of dance of Siva: Stone: Kailāsanāthasvāmin Temple: Conjeevaram.

[To face page 268]

PLATE LXIX.

Talasamsphōṭita mode of dance of Śiva: Stone:
Cheṅgunnūr: Travancore State.

[To face page 269]

PLATE LXX.

Nṛittamūrti : Stone : Conjeevaram.

[To face page 269]

one of his feet lifted fairly high. In this mode of dance the hand pose *patāka hasta* is also insisted upon, according to the commentary *Nāṭyavēda-vivṛiti*. *Talasamsphōṭita* mode of dance is exemplified in Pls. LXVIII and LXIX. The original of the first photographic reproduction is in the Kailāsanāthasvāmin temple at Conjeevaram. The right leg of Śiva is lifted up as high as the knee of the left one and is in the act of thumping the ground; the left is somewhat bent and is resting upon the ground. Of the eight arms of Śiva, one is held in the *patāka* pose, another in the *abhaya* pose while the rest are in various other *nāṭya* poses. From the *jaṭāmakuṭa* of Śiva issues one *jaṭā* on the left side and on which is seated Gaṅgā with hands folded in the *añjali* pose. Her head is shaded with the hood of a five-headed cobra. Pārvatī is seated on a seat on the left of Śiva. The photograph reproduced on Pl. LXIX, is also of this class and is of a piece of sculpture to be found in the Śiva temple at Chengunnūr in Travancore.

The last illustration, Pl. LXX, is of a kind of dance, which it is not easy to identify with any one of the hundred and eight standard modes of dance enumerated in the *Nāṭya Śāstra*. In this sculpture, also found in the Kailāsanathasvmin temple at Conjeevaram, Śiva is seen suddenly assuming in the middle of his dance, a posture similar to the *ālīḍhāsana*. He has eight arms, of which one carries the *śūla*, another the *paraśu*, a third one a snake and so on. One of the hands is in the *gaja-hasta* pose, another in the *patāka* pose and a third in the *chatura* pose. On the left side there are three niches in one of which is seen Pārvatī seated, in another the bull of Śiva couchant, and in the third an elephant; similarly on the right are three niches in which is a figure which is unidentifiable, some musical attendants and an elephant respectively. In a niche below the central one are three *gaṇas* imitating the dance of their lord.

DAKSHINAMURTI.

DAKSHIṆĀMŪRTI.

WE have already stated that Śiva is a great master of *yōga*, music and dancing and have described in detail his dances in the chapter on "Nṛittamūrtis." As a teacher of *yōga*, music and other sciences he is known by the name of Dakshiṇāmūrti. One account gives an explanation regarding the etymology of this name; it states that because Śiva was seated facing south when he taught the *ṛishis yōga* and *jñāna* he came to be known as Dakshiṇāmūrti. This aspect of Śiva is always invoked by students of science and arts. The great Śaṅkarāchārya, among several other celebrities, have sung the praise of this aspect of Śiva, which is as remarkable for its peacefulness as the Nṛittamūrti is for joyfulness.

Dakshiṇāmūrti is viewed in four different aspects namely, as a teacher of *yōga*, of *vīṇā*, of *jñāna* and as also an expounder of other Śāstras (*Vyākhyānamūrti*). Of these, the last form is the one which is most frequently met with in temples. It has already been mentioned elsewhere that in all Hindu temples, both Śaiva and Vaishṇava, the niche on the south wall of the central shrine should have the figure of Dakshiṇāmūrti enshrined in it.

VYĀKHYĀNA DAKSHIṆĀMŪRTI.

As an expounder of the *Śāstras*, Dakshiṇāmūrti should be represented as seated on a secluded spot on the Himālayas, under a banyan tree, on a seat covered with a tiger's skin; or, as another account has it, on a white lotus (*padmāsana*). The right leg of Dakshiṇāmūrti should be hanging below the seat while the left one bent and rested across on the right thigh. The kind of sitting posture adopted here is called the *vīrāsana*. The leg hanging down may or may not rest on the back of the *Apasmārapurusha*. Dakshiṇāmūrti should have three eyes and four arms: of these the front right one is held in the *jñānamudrā* or the *sandarśanamudrā** pose and the front left hand may be kept in the *varada* pose or stretched straight in the *daṇḍa* pose, the elbow resting upon the left knee in that latter posture. Even when the hand is in the *varada* pose it should rest upon the left knee but with the back of the hand touching it. The back right hand should hold the *akshamālā*, while in the back left hand there should be either *agni* (fire) or a *sarpa* (snake). In one account it is stated that one of the left hands may be, as already stated, in the *varada* or the *daṇḍa*

* This is known as the *saṁdaṁśa* in the Nāṭya-śāstras, a name which occurs also in the *āgamas*.

pose; if it is in the former pose, it might keep a book, the other left hand holding a snake, fire or a lotus or *nīlōtpala* flower. The various parts of the body of Dakshiṇāmūrti should be free from bends—a rigidity indicative perhaps of the resolute will and force of thought of the god in the aspect of the teacher. His head might be adorned with a *jaṭābhāra*, *jaṭābandha*, *jaṭāmaṇḍala* or *jaṭā-makuṭa;* or the *jaṭās* might be held together with a *paṭṭa-bandha.* In any case the mass of *jaṭās* should be embellished with the flowers of the *durdhura* (*dhatura*) and other wild plants, as also with a serpent on the left and with small tinkling bells, the *kapāla* and the crescent moon on the right side. In the middle of the *jāṭābhāra* there should be visible the smiling face of the river-goddess *Gaṅgā.* The complexion of Dakshiṇāmūrti is pure white, resembling a *sphaṭika* (crystal); according to another account the colour of Dakshiṇāmūrti may be white, red, yellow or black. His person should be adorned with all ornaments, clothed with perfectly white clothes and tiger's skin, should wear a white *yajñōpavīta* and have on his chest a coat of white sandal paste. In his left ear there should be a *Śaṅkhapatra* and in the right ear a *kuṇḍala*, or there may be only the *śaṅkha-patra* or the *kuṇḍala* in both the ears. A garland of *rudrākshas* should be hanging round the neck and descending as far down as the chest. The countenance of the god should be absolutely free from even a trace of mental perturbation. His sight must be fixed upon the tip of the nose; according to the *Kāraṇāgama* the sight must be fixed on the tip of the toe. The *Śilparatna* adds that this aspect of Śiva which preaches the *dharma* or law is very auspicious to the devotees and grants all good to its worshipper.

Surrounding the great teacher-god, are to be *ṛishis* eager to learn the *śāstras*. The names of the *ṛishis* are given differently in different works; for example, the *Aṁśumadbhēdāgama* mentions the *ṛishis* Nārada, Jamadagni, Vasishṭa, Bhṛigu, Bhāradvāja, Sanaka and Agastya. The *Kāmikāgama* mentions the names Kauśika, Kaśyapa, Bhāradvāja, Atri and Gautama and omits the names of two others though it gives the number of *ṛishis* as seven. The *Kāraṇāgama* gives the names of Agastya, Pulastya, Viśvāmitra and Āṅgirasa only. These *ṛishis* should have *jatāmakuṭas* on their heads, the garland of *rudrāksha* seeds round their neck and white *yajñōpavītas* on their person. Their bodies should be covered with ashes (*vibhūti* or *bhasma*) and be clothed in white garments. The height of these *ṛishis* should not exceed that of the chest of

Dakshiṇāmūrti. It is stated in the *Kāmikāgama* that the complexion of the *ṛishis* Kauśika and Kaśyapa should be dark, of two others (unmentioned in the text) yellow, of Bhāradvāja red and of Atri and Gautama a mixture of dark and red. In grouping them on a panel around the figure of Dakshiṇāmūrti, two may be placed on one side and three on the other, or three and three on each side, or three and four on either sides.

The god Dakshiṇāmūrti should be adored by *kinnaras*, *dēvas* and others.

The Apasmāra-purusha should hold his right hand in the *sarpa-mudrā* pose, that is, hold the palm of his hand in the form of the hood of a cobra, in front of the cobra which he should hold in his left hand.

The *Dakshiṇāmūrti Upanishad* and the *Sūta-saṁhitā* give the esoteric meaning of the figure of Dakshiṇāmūrti. It is stated that He is the supreme god who, at the end of an æon (*kalpa*) absorbs within himself the whole universe and remains resplendent with joy. Dakshiṇāmūrti is such a deity. *Jñāna* (knowledge) is known also as *dakshiṇā* and since *dakshiṇā* is ever in front of Śiva and is gazing at him in the aspect of Dakshiṇāmūrti, he is called Dakshiṇāmukha. The Apsmāra-purusha under his foot is the personification of the ignorance of the living beings, which he keeps under subjection under the tread of his foot. The book he holds in his hand contains all wisdom and illuminates the souls of beings. The *akshamālā* which he carries in his hand is the representation of the *tatvas*. His body is composed of eternal bliss and eternal energy; the wide-spreading banyan tree casting deep shade is the symbol of *māyā* (illusion) and the *vṛishabha* of Śiva is *dharma* (law). Dakshiṇāmūrti is teaching the *rishis* who are already deeply versed in the Vēdas the *ātma-vidyā* (knowledge of self and soul) and rescuing them from *saṁsāra* (bondage). He is himself imperishable, without birth or death and the *kamalāsana* or the lotus-seat upon which he is seated is the symbol of the sacred syllable *Ōm*.

Eight photographs are reproduced in illustration of the above description. Of these the first illustration, Pl. LXXI, comes from Deogarh and represents a very fine piece of sculpture. This panel has its central figure Dakshiṇāmūrti seated on a raised platform placed under a tree, with his left leg hanging and the right one bent and rested upon the seat. On his head is a *jaṭābandha*; the back right hand carries an *akshamālā* and the front right hand is held in the *jñānamudrā* pose. The back left hand carries a long object which is not easy to identify; perhaps it represents a cadjan

PLATE LXXI.

Jñāna-Dakshiṇāmūrti: Stone Panel: Deogarh.

[To face page 278]

manuscript : or a bundle of *kuśa* grass (*kūrcha*) the front left hand carries a pot, perhaps an *amṛita-ghaṭa*, as required in the *Vishṇudharmōttara*. He wears round his loins a garment which descend as far down as the knees ; on his left shoulder and descending below as far as the left thigh and lying on it is a *kṛishnājina* (or deerskin), the head and front legs of the deer being clearly visible there : this skin is worn in the *upavīta* fashion. The whole figure is slightly bent forward and a few *jaṭās* are seen descending over the shoulders. The face portrays beautifully the calmness that is insisted upon by the *āgamas* and the sight is fixed below.

Below his seat and near his left leg are seen two deer, also listening to this exposition of *dharma*. This brings to mind the analogy of the representations of Buddha's preaching the *dharma* wherein also the same animals are introduced as members of the audience. Behind stands an ascetic with crossed arms and legs and carrying on his left hand an *akshamālā ;* he has a tapering beard and his *jaṭās* are tied up in a knot on the crown of his head.

To the left of Dakshiṇāmūrti is seated a person as tall as himself. He is also seated underneath a tree on a rocky seat. This may either be a *ṛishi* or

Śiva himself in the aspect of the Vyākhyāna-Dakshiṇāmūrti; on the latter supposition the other person (seated to the right) must be taken to be Yōga-Dakshiṇāmūrti. However it is not possible to say definitely whom this figure represents. The right hand of this image though carrying an *akshamālā* is held in the *chin-mudrā* pose, while the left hand is held in the *bhū-sparśamudrā* pose. Its head is adorned with a neatly executed *jaṭāmakuṭa*, and its body is covered with a deer skin in the *upavīta* fashion. The right leg is let down the seat and is resting on the ground and the left leg is bent and kept on the seat. The garment covering the lower portion of the body descends as far below as the knees. As in the case of the other figure there is behind it a smaller one, also an ascetic, whose right hand, holding an *akshamālā*, is kept in the *chinmudrā* pose and the left hand carries a water pot. Below the seat of this image is a lion couchant with its head resting upon its forelegs which are kept crossed over each other.

There are *dēvas* and *gandharvas*, who are shown as flying in the air over the heads of these two central figures carrying flower garlands in their hands. Higher up and in a separate compartment is sculptured Brahmā as seated on a *padmāsana*; as usual, he has four heads; but only two arms;

PLATE LXXII.

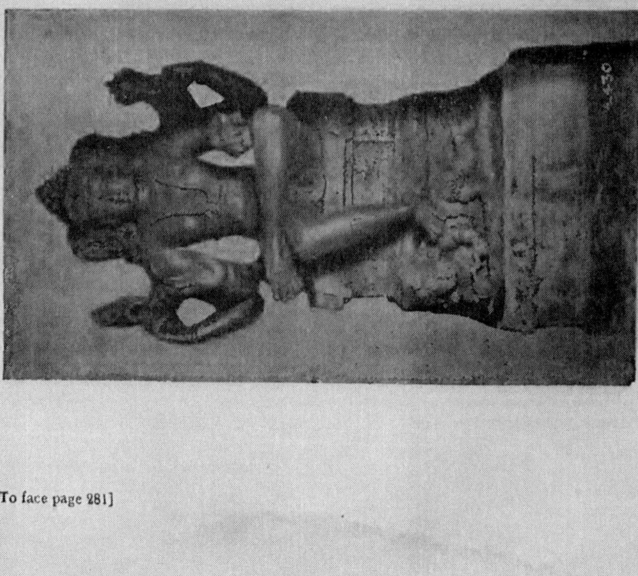

Fig. 1. Jñāna-Dakshiṇāmūrti: Āvur (Tanjore District).

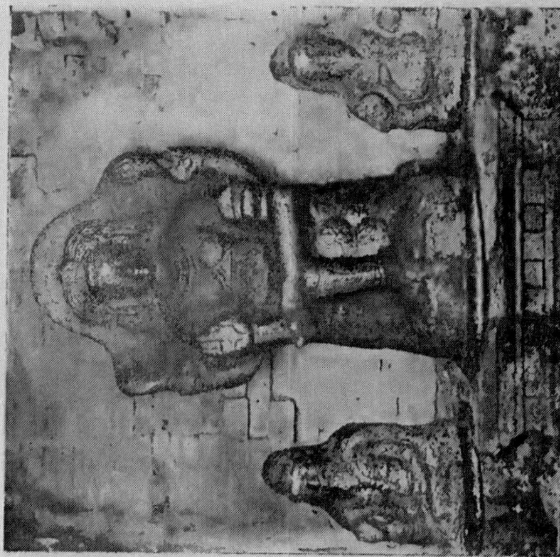

Fig. 2. Jñāna-Dakṣiṇāmūrti: Stone:

[To face page 281]

PLATE LXXIII.

Jñāna-Dakshiṇāmūrti : Stone : Tiruvoṟṟiyūr.

[To face page 281]

the right hand is kept in the *chinmudrā* or *abhaya* pose and the left carries a *kamaṇḍalu.* On both sides of Brahmā are a *dēva* and his *dēvī*, flying in the air and praising him.

The second image whose photograph is reproduced as fig. 1, on Pl. LXXII, is to be found in the Śiva temple at Āvūr in the Tanjore district. It is also a well executed piece of sculpture. In this image the *jaṭās* are bound together by a *lalāṭa-paṭṭa* of elaborate workmanship. In the left ear is a *patrakuṇḍala* and in the right a *nakrakuṇḍala ;* on the chest are the *yajñōpavīta* and a necklace of *rudrāksha* seeds; there are also the *chhannavīra* and the *udarabandha* and a cloth worn in the *upavīta* fashion. The front right hand is kept in the *chinmudrā* pose and the front left hand, which rests on the left knee, bears a book. In the back right hand is the *sarpa* (snake) while in the back left hand is *agni* (fire). The right leg hangs down the seat and is placed upon the Apasmārapurusha and the left foreleg rests upon the right thigh. This image belongs to the early Chōḷa period.

The photograph reproduced on Pl. LXXIII is of a comparatively modern sculpture to be found in a Śiva shrine built in the second *prākāra* of the temple at Tiruvoṟṟiyūr. It is coarse in its execution and lacks effect. The *jaṭās* in this case are spread fanwise and are bound at their base by a *lalāṭa-paṭṭa*. The image has the same objects in its hands as the one noticed above (Pl. LXXII, fig. 1). But there is in addition the figure of a *ṛishi* seated below the seat of Dakshiṇāmūrti, with its hands held in the *añjali* pose. The seat on which Dakshiṇāmūrti is seated in fig. 1, Pl. LXXII, is a *bhadrapīṭha* while in Pl. LXXIII it is the mountain represented in the usual conventional manner.

The fourth illustration, fig. 2, Pl. LXXII, is exactly similar to the third; but there are two *ṛishis* sculptured separately and seated on either side of the central figure.

The fifth illustration, fig. 1, Pl. LXXIV, is from Suchindram in South Travancore. The image is of a comparatively recent date. It has on its head a carefully worked up *jaṭāmakuṭa ;* and a few stray *jaṭās* are seen flowing down on the shoulders. The posture assumed herein is the *vīrāsana.* In the right back hand is seen a lotus flower, in the back left hand a *sarpa*, while the front right hand is held in the *chinmudrā* pose and the front left hand carries a book.

Fig. 2, Pl. LXXIV, is the photograph of the figure of Dakshiṇāmūrti found in Kāvēripakkam

Fig. 1. Jñāna-Dakshiṇāmūrti : Stone : Suchīndram.

Fig. 2. Jñāna-Dakshiṇāmūrti Stone : Kāvēripākkam.

[To face page 282]

PLATE LXXV.

Fig. 1. Jñāna-Dakshiṇāmūrti : Stone : Tiruvēṅgavāśal.

Fig. 2. Jñāna-Dakshiṇāmūrti : Bronze : Collection of Mr. Kay, Madras.

[To face page 283]

and belongs to the Pallava period. Herein, the deity has on his head heavy curls of hair constituting the *jaṭābhāra;* he carries the *akshamālā* in his back right hand, *agni* (?), in the back left hand and a book in the front left hand; the front right hand is held in the *vyākhyāna-mudrā* pose. The right leg is hanging below the seat, while the left one is kept bent in the *utkuṭikāsana* posture. Round the neck are two *hārās* (necklaces) on the chest, the *yajñōpavīta* and in one ear a *vṛitta-kuṇḍala;* the other ear wears no ornament. Below the seat are to be seen a deer and a cobra listening to his discourse.

Fig. 1, Pl. LXXV, is the reproduction of a photograph of the Jñāna-Dakshiṇāmūrti kept in the southern niche of the central shrine of the Śiva temple at Tiruvengavāśal in the Pudukottah State. In this case, the deity is represented as seated with his left leg kept in the *utkutikāsana* posture and on it is stretched the front left arm. Fig. 2, on the same plate is that of a bronze statuette belonging to the collection of Mr. Kay, Madras. It is almost similar to the figure on Pl. LXXIII; the only difference is that in the figure belonging to Mr. Kay, the back right hand keeps *agni* and the back left one, a snake, whereas in the Tiruvoṟṟiyūr image the order is reversed.

JÑĀNA-DAKSHIṆĀMŪRTI.

There is not much difference between the Vyākhyānamūrti and the Jñānamūrti. In the latter the general posture of Siva is exactly the same as in the former, but in the back right hand there should be the *akshamālā*, and in the back left hand a *utpala* flower. The front right hand should be held in the *jñānamudrā* pose, whereas the front left hand may be kept in the *abhaya* or the *daṇḍa* pose.

YOGA-DAKSHIṆĀMŪRTI.

This form of Dakshiṇāmūrti may be sculptured in three different ways. In the first, the two legs of the image should be crossed as in the *svastikāsana;* while the front right hand should be held near the chest in the *yōgamudrā* pose and the front left hand should rest upon the lap in the characteristic *yōgic* posture. In the back right hand there should be the *akshamālā*, and in the back left hand a lotus flower. The gaze must be fixed on the tip of the nose: and a few *jaṭās* should hang over the shoulders. This image of Dakshiṇāmūrti should be surrounded by *ṛishis* who should be adoring him.

In the second mode of representation of Yōga-Dakshiṇāmūrti the left leg of the figure should be bent in the *utkuṭikāsana* posture; surrounding the

PLATE LXXVI.

Yōga-Dakshiṇāmūrti (locally known as Gauḷīsvara) : Stone : Tiruvoṟṟiyūr.

[To face page 285]

body of the figure and its left leg should be a *yōga-paṭṭa*. The right leg should be hanging down the seat. The front left arm should be kept stretched and be resting by the elbow on the knee of the bent left leg. The rest of the description is identical with that given for the first form.

The third form is required to be sculptured thus: The two legs are bent and crossed in a more or less vertical position (as in the figure of Yōga-Nārasiṁha), and round these and the body is passed a *yōgapaṭṭa* to keep the legs in position. The front two arms are stretched and kept resting on the knees. In the back right hand there should be the *akshamālā* and in the back left hand a *kamaṇḍalu.* The *jāṭas* should be disposed of in the form of a *jaṭāmaṇḍala* and in it should be the crescent moon, a snake and other objects. The colour of the body of this aspect of Dakshiṇāmūrti is white, but his neck should be represented as of black colour. The image should be adorned with all ornaments including a number of snake ornaments.

The illustration on Pl. LXXVI, is a well-carved figure of Śiva in the *yōgāsana* posture. It is enshrined in a fane situated in the south *prākāra* of the Śiva temple at Tiruvoṟṟiyūr. The inscriptions on the walls of this shrine refer to the image set up in it as Paḍampakkanāyinār and state that it was set up in the fifth year of the reign of the Chōḷa king Vīrarājēndradēva (about A.D. 1067-8). From the position of this shrine with reference to the main central shrine, that is, to the south side of it, and from the posture and other features of the image itself enshrined therein, it may, without fear of contradiction, be stated to be the first form of Jñāna-Dakshiṇāmūrti described above. The figure has a well executed *jaṭā-makuṭa* ornamented with jewelled discs and bands round it; *kuṇḍalas* in the ears; and *hāra* and necklace of *rudrāksha* seeds and *yajñōpavīta* on the chest. The forearms are adorned with a number of bracelets and the upper arm with *kēyūras*. The legs are crossed one over the other so as to bring the soles up; this is exactly the *yōgic āsana* called the *svastikāsana*. In the back right hand there appears to have been a *śūla*, whose shaft alone now remains, the head being broken; in the back left hand is the *kapāla;* the front right hand is held in the *chinmudrā* pose and the front left hand also in the pose characteristic of an expounder of sciences. This image now goes by the inexplicable name of Gauḷīśvara and near it and to its proper right is set up in more recent times the figure of Saṅkarāchārya; on the base of the seat of this latter are carved the figures of his four great disciples.

Yōga-Dakshiṇāmūrti: Stone: Conjeevaram.

[To face page 287]

The second form is illustrated by Pl. LXXVII. The original of this photograph is in the Kailāsanāthasvāmin temple at Conjeevaram. In this sculpture Śiva has his left leg bent and rested vertically on the seat and this leg and the body are bound together by the *yōgapaṭṭa*. The front right hand is held in the *yōgamudrā* pose, while the front left hand is in the *abhaya* pose. The back right hand keeps an *akshamālā*, and the back left hand *agni* or a lotus flower.* The right leg is hanging down the seat. Śiva is as in the previous instances, seated under the shade of a banyan tree and below his seat are deer lying, with their heads lifted up to Śiva. Below his right elbow is a cobra with an uplifted hood, also gazing at the enchanting figure of Śiva. Above the head of Śiva are seen seated a pair of *bhūtas* on either side. On three niches situated on either side respectively of Dakshiṇāmūrti (not shown in the picture) are *ṛishis* sitting

* At some later period of the history of this temple, when the surface of the stones of which the sculptures are composed began to peel off, they have all been covered with thin coat of plaster. The plasterer not being able to make out the exact nature of some badly injured objects has shaped slightly different things in their stead: thus, a lotus flower that is required by the *āgamās* seems to have been evidently mistaken for the most likely object in the back left hand of Śiva, namely, *agni*.

and listening to the preaching of the *Dharma* or *Yōga* by Śiva.* The image whose photograph is reproduced as Pl. LXXVIII is almost similar to that on Pl. LXXVII; the back right hand, in this instance, carries a cobra. Dakshiṇāmūrti is seen sitting here upon a *bhadrapiṭha* placed upon a hill.

Pl. LXXIX is the photograph of the image of Dakshiṇāmūrti to be found in the Siva temple at Nañjangōḍu in the Mysore Province. This represents, only so far as its sitting posture goes, the third form the Yōga-Dakshiṇāmūrti. The *āsana* assumed is that form of *utkuṭikāsana* described under the third form. The legs are bound with the body with a *yōgapaṭṭa*. But in fact the image is a combination of all aspects of Dakshiṇāmūrtis—namely, the Yōga, the Vīṇā-dhara and the Vyākhyāna forms; it is the Yōga form because its sitting posture is the *yōgic*;

---

* Mr. Alex. Rea in his "*The Pallava Architecture*" describes a panel containing the images of Dakshiṇāmūrti and the *ṛishis* thus: "in this panel, eleven seated sages are listening to the exhortations of Śiva, who is represented in a panel on the north side of the central shrine. He is armed with different symbolical weapons, and seems to be preaching war" (!) Such mistakes are fairly common in his publications and hence need no serious refutation; nor are his drawings reliable, for, to quote an instance, a *śaṅkha* in the hand of an image is wrongly represented in the drawing as a *padma*.

Yōga-Dakshiṇāmūrti : Stone : Conjeevaram.

[To face page 288]

the Vīṇādhara because it carries in its back left hand a *vīṇā*, and Vyākhyāna because its front right hand is in the *chinmudrā* pose and the front left hand carries a book. The figure is seated below a banyan tree and the *lāñchhana* (the totemistic emblem), the bull, is carved in a counter-sunk surface on the pedestal, in front. Below the seat and in the middle of it is seated a Lingāyat priest who holds in his left hand a *liṅga*. On either side of this *guru* are his disciples with their hands in the *añjali* pose. A *prabhāvaḷi* is placed behind the figure of Dakshiṇāmūrti on the jambs of which are standing one on each side a *ṛishi* with the hands in the *añjali* pose.

VĪṆĀDHARA-DAKSHIṆĀMŪRTI.

As a great teacher of music, both instrumental and vocal, Śiva is worshipped in the form of Vīṇādhara-Dakshiṇāmūrti. The description of the image of this aspect of Dakshiṇāmūrti is found in the *Kāmika*, the *Aṁśumadbhēda* and the *Kāraṇāgamas*. The *Aṁśumadbhēdāgama* states that the left leg should be kept in the *utkutika* posture and the two front hands should hold the *vīṇā;* the rest should be exactly similar to the description of the Vyākhyānamūrti. According to the *Kamikāgama* the Gāna-Dakshiṇāmūrti should have his front right and left hands held in the *kaṭaka* pose, the former with its palm facing below and the latter facing above. The *kaṭaka* pose being slightly different in form, the *Kāmikāgama* calls the pose the *sarpa-kara*. The left arm should be lifted up and the right arm lowered below, so as to hold in proper position the long-handled musical instrument, the *vīṇā*. The *vīṇā* should be held at the top by the left hand and by the right hand at the lower end; the resonating body of the instrument should rest on the right thigh. The lower right hand should be manipulating the strings of the instrument.

The measurement of the *vīṇā* is next given as follows: the *vīṇā* should be projecting three *aṅgulas* beyond the right thigh and four *aṅgulas* above the left *kaṭaka-hasta*. The distance between the two points specified above is the length of the *vīṇā-daṇḍa* or the hollow shaft of the instrument whose width at the top should be two *aṅgulas*. The gourd resonator attached at the lower end should be six *aṅgulas* in diameter and three *aṅgulas* in height.

A few general observations are added also about the figures of Dakshiṇāmūrti. It is stated that the face of Dakshiṇāmūrti should be turned towards the hand held in the *sandarśanamudrā* pose; also the gaze of the god may be fixed on this hand. Surrounding the figure of Dakshiṇāmūrti there should be different kinds of animals and reptiles, sages (*munis*)

PLATE LXXX.

Viṇādhara-Dakshiṇāmūrti: Bronze: Madras Museum.

[To face page 291]

PLATE LXXXI.

Vīṇādhara-Dakshiṇāmūrti: Bronze: Vaḍaraṅgam.

[To face page 291]

and ascetics (*siddhas*), *vidyādharas*, *bhūtas* and *kinnaras ;* Śiva should be seated in a place on the mountain where all sorts of flowering trees and plants grow luxuriantly and under a banyan tree, on the right side of its trunk, on a jewelled *pīṭha* covered with a tiger's skin and he should present a benign look: and the *ṛishis* the ancestors of the *Śivadvijas* (Śaiva brāhmaṇas) should be seated round him. The figure of Dakshiṇāmūrti may be sculptured as seated or standing surrounded or not by *ṛishis*, with his legs either resting or not upon the Apasmāra-purusha and with or without the banyan tree, *bhūtas* and others mentioned above.

Two photographs, Pls. LXXX and LXXXI, are reproduced in illustration of the Vīṇādhara-Dakshiṇāmūrti ; both of them are identical in shape and in the details of moulding.* Śiva is seen standing

* These two images figure on Pls. XV and XVI of Mr. O. C. Gangoly's *South Indian Bronzes.* Besides these, he has reproduced two other photographs of the same aspect of Śiva on Pls. I and XIV. In every detail all the four figures agree ; for instance, in all, the right leg stands straight on the ground while the left one is slightly bent ; all four have four arms, the back hands of which carry the *paraśu* and the *mṛiga* and the two front hands are held in the *kaṭaka* poses required in the *āgamas* and are evidently meant to keep a *viṇā* in them ; the very same ornaments, head-gear and clothing are to be seen on all the images. In the case of Pl. I, there is a slight divergence from

with his right leg kept firmly on the ground, while the left leg is placed a little forward slightly bent. The front two hands are held in the *kaṭaka* pose, the left one looking up and the right one looking down. Evidently a separately cast *vīṇā* was intended to be inserted in the hands whenever wanted and hence this instrument is not to be seen in either image. The back right hand carries a *paraśu* and the back left one a *mṛiga*. There are all sorts of elaborately sculptured ornaments on the person of the figures. The first figure (Pl. LXXX) belongs to the Madras Museum, while the second (Pl. LXXXI) is to be found in the temple at Vaḍaraṇgam in the Tanjore district. The second, an earlier piece of sculpture, is of very high artistic value; the first is of rather inferior workmanship.

---

the description of the *āgamās*, namely, the left leg, instead of being placed directly on the ground, is held supported on its head by a *bhūta*—which deviation is one of the artistic embellishments of the master-sculptor. In spite of the striking similarity, nay identity among the four images, they are called by different names: thus, the figure on Pl. I is said to be Kālasamhāra or Kālakālamūrti; that on Pl. XIV, Gaṅgādhara, that on Pl. XX, Chandraśēkhāra or Sōmadhāri; and lastly; that on Pl. XVI, Pramēswara Swami (*sic*). It is not quite clear either from the *dhyāna-ślōkās* quoted or from the short descriptive notes added to each if the identifications are justifiable at all.

KANKALAMURTI AND BHIKSHATANAMURTI.

KAṄKĀḶAMŪRTI.

Once upon a time the great *ṛishis*, desirous of learning as to who was the real author of this Universe went to the top of the mountain Mēru and put Brahmā, who was seated thereon, the question which was engaging their thought. In his vanity, forgetting the real creator, he boasted that he himself was the great Architect of the Universe. Meanwhile, Śiva appeared on the scene and justly claimed the place for himself. Though his own position was reasonably defended by Śiva, Brahmā would not yield ; the Vēdas and the Praṇava (the sacred syllable *Ōm*) also interceded on behalf of Śiva in vain. At last, through the will of Śiva, there appeared near by a huge pillar of illumination, which demonstrated the greatness of Śiva, but Brahmā remained still obstinate. Incensed with anger at the thoughtless conduct of Brahmā, Śiva ordered Bhairava to cut off that one out of the five heads of Brahmā, which reviled him. Brahmā suffered temporary death, but, soon revived by the power of his austerities, accepted the superiority of Śiva. However, the sin of having killed Brahmā (the major sin called *brahmahatyā*) possessed Bhairava (a form of Śiva). Bhairava requested Brahmā to suggest to him some penance to get rid of this sin ; Brahmā advised him to beg food in the skull of the head cut by him till he met Vishṇu who would devise means for wiping off the sin. Till then, said Brahmā, the sin would assume the form of a woman and be ever pursuing him. Bhairava surrounded by a host of *bhūtas* (goblins) went from place to place begging for food. All the women of the houses he visited fell in love with him and set out, singing and dancing, to accompany him. Last of all he reached the abode of Vishṇu and attempted to enter it, but Vishvaksēna, the gate-keeper, would not allow him to enter. A fight ensued in which Vishvaksēna was killed and added one more sin of *brahmahatyā*. Bhairava, fixing the body of the gate-keeper of Vishṇu on his trident, got into the interior of Vishṇu's mansion and begged for food. Vishṇu cut open an artery on the forehead of Bhairava and told him that the blood that flowed from it was the fittest food for him. Bhairava next requested Vishṇu to assist him in washing off his sin. Vishṇu pleaded on behalf of Bhairava to the personified female form of Brahmahatyā to quit him but she would not leave him. However, the thought occurred to Vishṇu that if Bhairava went to Vārāṇasi the sin would leave him off and he advised him to go to this sacred place for being freed from his sins. Dancing with joy Bhairava wended his way to Vārāṇasi (or Kāśi) with the body of Vishvaksēna and as soon as he reached that place, the sin left him and plunged into the nether world. The skull of Brahmā and the dead body of Vishvaksēna also left him and he once again became pure Mahēśvara and returned to Kailāsa. Vishvaksēna was restored to life and he joined Vishṇu's service as usual. Such, in short, is the account we meet with in the *kūrma-purāṇa* regarding the bearing of the skull and the dry bones (*kaṅkaḷa*) of Vishvaksēna by Śiva and also regarding his begging expedition. There is a confusion here about Śiva and a particular aspect of his, Bhairava; also the sin of the slaughter of Vishvaksēna is imposed upon the shoulders of Śiva which were already groaning under that of the cutting off of the head of Brahmā.

The reason for Śiva having begged so is revealed by a study of the *Dharma-Śāstras.* It is therein laid down that if a Brāhmaṇa happens to kill another of great learning and good conduct (such a learned person is called a *bhrūṇa*), the sin could be expiated by following the course of conduct prescribed thus: the sinner should, with his own hands, erect for himself a hut in the forest, hoist on it as a flag the head of the man he killed [and live therein, having for his upper garment the skin of a horse or an ass, which he should wear with the hairy side appearing outside. His underwear should be made of threads of the hemp and when worn it should not descend below the knee. Carrying a skull in one hand, as his begging bowl and one of the long bones of the arm (*khaṭvāṅga*) of the deceased as a stick he should start out begging for his food saying "who is there who would feed the murderer of a *bhrūṇa*." He should not visit more than seven houses for making his living and if any day he does not succeed in getting food from them, he should go without it that day. He should take his food and drink from this skull. At home in his hut, he should observe the vow of silence and be contemplating upon the sin committed. He may undertake to tend the cows belonging to a Brāhmaṇa village and on that account and on account of receiving food alone he can enter the village. At other times he should conduct himself like one belonging to one of the classes considered to be untouchable. While walking on a public way if he meets an Ārya on the road he should, like a pig, move away to the very edge of the road, leaving it clear for the Ārya to go by. Thus should he spend twelve years only to absolve himself from the sin and no more; from the day he committed the murder he ceases to be fit for the society of the Āryas; by this course of conduct alone, he wipes off the sin and prepares himself for a better birth in the future. If, however, the life prescribed above in the Dharmaśāstra is unendurable, he may end it in one or other of the following ways. In those days, there were cattle-raids committed often for political reasons.* He may fight against the raiders and suffer death in their hands; or, if he is unfortunately successful in his attempt at driving away the raiders, he may still attempt on future occasions with a view to die in the same cause. If thrice he comes out successful in repelling the cattle-raiders, he is absolved from the sin. Or, he

* War is divided into two classes in Tamil literature, namely, *aṟa-ppōr* and *maṟa-ppōr*, that is, righteous or *dharma-yuddha* and unrighteous or *adharma-yuddha*. In declaring a righteous war against an enemy king, notice is given to good men and women, children, mendicants and ascetics, and cows to quit the place which is to be attacked. Since cows cannot be intimated the intentions of the invading king, they are carried away by the army of the invader preparatory to war and this act is considered sufficient notice to all the others to leave the place as early as practicable. In the *maṟa-ppōr* no such notice is given.

might get into the thick of a battle seeking to be shot dead; it then becomes, the Dharma-śāstra says, incumbent on the soldiers to kill this murderer of a *bhrūṇa*. Such, in short, is the punishment meted out to the brāhmaṇa murderer of a learned brāhmaṇa.*

---

* सू॰—अथ भ्रूणहाऽश्वाजिनं खराजिनं वा बहिर्लोम परिधाय पुरुषशिरः-प्रतीपानार्थमादाय ॥

हरदत्तव्याख्या—षडङ्गस्य वेदस्याध्येता तदर्थवित् प्रयोगशास्त्रस्य च सव्याख्यानस्य चार्थवित् कर्मणोऽनुष्ठाता अनुष्ठापयिता च ब्राह्मणो भ्रूणः........ ....पुरुषस्य शिरः यस्य कस्यचिन्मृतस्य शिरः प्रतीपानार्थं छान्दसं दैर्घ्यं पानमेव प्रतीपानं पानग्रहणमुपलक्षणं भोजनमपि तत्रैव............

Āpast. Dharma-sūtra, Haradatta's Comm. 1st Praśna, 10th Paṭala, 29th. Khaṇḍikā.

सू॰—खट्वाङ्गं दण्डार्थे कर्मनामधेयं प्रब्रुवाणश्चंक्रम्येत को भ्रूणघ्ने भिक्षामिति ॥

Ap. Dh. Sū., Har. Com. I, 10, 29.

सू—अरण्ये कुटिं कृत्वा वाग्यतः शवशिरध्वजोऽर्धशाणीपक्षमधोनाभ्युपरिजान्वाऽऽच्छाद्य ॥

हरदत्तव्याख्या—कृत्वेति वचनान्न परकृता कुटी ग्राह्या.............. शवशिरो ध्वजो यस्य स शवशिरध्वजः सलोपश्छान्दसः स्वव्यापादितस्य ब्राह्मणस्य शिरोध्वजदण्डस्याग्रे प्रोतं कृत्वेत्यर्थः। यस्य कस्यचिच्छवस्येत्यन्ये। आयामविस्तारयोरुभयोरप्यर्धम्। अधोनाभ्युपरिजानु च यथा भवति तथाऽऽच्छाद्य तावन्तं प्रदेशमाच्छाद्य सापेक्षत्वाद् ग्रामे प्रतिष्ठेतेति वक्ष्यमाणेन संबन्धः। मध्ये क्रियान्तरविधिः।

Āpastambha-Dharma-sūtra, with Haradattāchārya's

Now, the Purāṇas and other authorities are one in asserting that Śiva cut off the head of Brahmā, the most learned of all beings in the Vēdas and Śāstras and hence a veritable *bhrūṇa* of *bhrūṇas*. The sin of *brahmahatyā* stuck, at it ought, to him and he underwent the course of conduct prescribed for a *bhrūṇaghna* (murderer of *bhrūṇa*). With the skull for his drinking and eating vessel, with bones for his staves, he went about begging for food and, be it noted, he went to the seven houses of the seven great *ṛishis* and also he never lived in any town or village, but made the burning ground outside the village his abode. From all accounts about Śiva found recorded in the ancient literature we see that the course of conduct followed by Śiva was exactly that prescribed, in the early *Dharma-śāstras*, to a *bhrūṇaghna*. Having committed the murder of Brahmā, the best of brāhmaṇas, it is to be conjectured that Śiva should have become unfit for the society of the Āryas; if so, the question arises whether it was this disqualification on the part of Śiva that made him hateable to the

---

commentary on it named Ujjvala, 1st Praśna, 9th Paṭala, 24th Khaṇḍikā.

Cf. Manu Smṛiti, XI, 72—86, Gautama, XXII, 2—10, Kūrma-Purāṇa, XXXth chapter end.

Āryas, as he is said to ḥave been in the earlier literature (See the Introductory chapter).

There is another slightly different account concerning the act of begging for food associated with Śiva and this account serves only the purpose of explaining why, in his aspect known as the Bhikshāṭanamūrti, he is seen stark naked when going out abegging. The *Liṅgapurāṇa* states that in the forest of Dāruvana even women and children took to the performance of austerities and forgot the worldly ways of living (*pravṛitti-mārga*). To make them feel the need also of the worldly ways, Śiva started out to beg in their quarters; for this purpose, he became a black, ugly looking being and naked he went into their midst. The appearance of this notable figure drew the attention of all the inhabitants of the Dāruvana and through his *māyā* the residents of this forest took to all sorts of bad ways of this world. Angered by the bad example set up by the new comer, the *ṛishis* cursed him, but, instead of being affected by it, he disappeared. The *ṛishis* became aware that the intruder was no other than Śiva and repented their inability to have offered him worship when they had the good fortune to have in their midst his human embodiment. Brahmā advised them to worship his *liṅga* studiously if they desired to see him in person once again. They followed his advice and were rewarded for their devotion by Śiva appearing before them once again and blessing them.

The images of the Kaṅkāḷamūrti and the Bhikshāṭanamūrti are generally found in almost all Śiva temples of importance throughout Southern India and all the Śaivāgamas contain more or less detailed descriptions of these images. The *Aṁśumadbhēda*, the *Kāmika* and the *Kāraṇa āgamas*, as also the *Śilparatna* describe them as follows:—

Kankalamurti.

The figure of the Kaṅkāḷamūrti should be a standing one, with the left leg planted firmly on the ground and the right slightly bent and kept a bit forward suggesting that the figure is in the act of moving. The colour of the body of Śiva in this aspect is pure white. He should be wearing red-coloured upper garments while his under-wear should be composed of silk and tiger's skin. The head should be ornamented with the *jaṭāmakuṭa ;* on the left side, it should be adorned with a few *durdhura* (*dhatura*) flowers and a snake and on the right with the crescent moon. His face should be beautiful and beaming with the feeling of happiness, smiling and singing sweet songs. The pearly teeth of Śiva should be half visible and the ears adorned both with ordinary *kuṇḍalas* or with a *makara-kuṇḍala* in the right ear and a *śaṅkhapatra* in the left one. There should be the *yajñōpavīta* on his chest. Of the four hands, the front right one should keep the *bāṇa*—here the term *bāṇa* seems to mean a short resined stick used in exciting the membrane of a sort of drum,—while the front left one should keep a drum known by the name of *ḍhakka*. The back right arm should be stretched out and its hand held in the *kaṭaka* pose near the mouth of his pet animal, the deer; and in the back left hand should be the *kaṅkāḷa-daṇḍa* or the staff on which the bones of the arms and the legs of the murdered person are tied up together by a rope and ornamented with the feathers of the peacock and a banner. The bones should be dry and of blackish colour and be free of flesh; but there should be traces of blood on them and on the small jingling bells tied to the staff. This *kaṅkāḷadaṇḍa* should be placed horizontally on the left shoulder, one end being held, as already noticed, by the back left hand. In the girdle round the loins of Śiva there should be tucked up a dagger made of gold, with a silver handle; he should be wearing a pair of wooden sandals on his feet and the whole of this curious get-up should be finished with a number of snake ornaments distributed all over the body. The Kaṅkāḷamūrti should be surrounded by a number of women and the *bhūtagaṇas* (goblins) represented variously as dancing, singing and in other attitudes; one of the *bhūtas* should carry on his head a large vessel for storing in the food received in alms and be situated on the left of Śiva. Of the women who surround Śiva some should appear to be completely possessed of irrepressible love for him, some eager to embrace him, some others blessing him, while still others serving in his vessel food ladled out from another with a spoon. Out of lust for Śiva the clothes of the women should appear slipping down their loiṇs. There should also be hosts of *ṛishis*, *dēvas*, *gandharvas*, *siddhas* and *vidyādharas* everywhere around Śiva, with arms crossed on the chest in the *añjali* pose. The god Vāyu should sweep the streets before Śiva, Varuṇa should sprinkle them with water, the other *dēvas* should shower flowers on him, the *ṛishis* should praise him by repeating the *Vēdas*, Sūrya and Chandra should carry umbrellas over his head and the celestial musicians Nārada and Tumburu should sing songs to the accompaniment of musical instruments. The height of the women who are keeping company with Śiva may be that of the chin, chest or the navel of Śiva; the height of the *bhūtas* should be equal to three or three and a half times the length of the face of Śiva and they should be shaped according the *pañcha-tāla* measure.

Bhikshatana-murti. In the case of the image of the Bhikshāṭanamūrti, the general posture of Śiva is the same as in the Kaṅkāḷamūrti aspect; that is, the left leg standing firmly on the ground and the right slightly bent suggesting walking. The front right hand and the back left are held as in the case of the Kaṅkāḷamūrti, whereas the front left hand should carry a *kapāla* and the back right one a *ḍamaru.* The head may have the *jaṭās* dishevelled (*jatābhārā*) or arranged in the form of a circle (*jaṭāmaṇḍala*) with the crescent moon in it. The forehead should be adorned with a *paṭṭa* or ornamented band; there should also be the other ornaments all over the body. But there should be no kind of clothing on the person of Śiva, not even the waist zone. Instead of this latter there should be a snake tied round the waist; besides this, there should be other snake ornaments in appropriate places on the person of Śiva. On the chest is to be seen a white *yajñōpāvīta.* The neck of Śiva should be of blue colour and his forehead should be beautified with the *tripuṇḍra* mark. In this aspect he should not carry the *kaṅkāḷa-daṇḍa,* but in its place there should be the *śūla* decorated with a lot of peacock-feathers. There should be a pair of wooden sandals on his feet; sometimes it might be omitted also. The hand that bears the *kapāla* should be lifted as high as the navel, whereas the one that carries the *ḍamaru* should be raised as far as the ear and the distance between the wrist of this arm from the ear is to be sixteen *aṅgulas*. As usual, Śiva should possess in these two aspects three eyes. The rest of the description of the Bhikshāṭanamūrti is identical with that given already under the Kaṅkāḷamūrti.

The *Suprabhēdāgama* adds that the *kapāla* held by Śiva is that of Brahmā and the *kaṅkāḷa* that of Vishṇu; herein the Paurāṇic story of the murder by Śiva of both Brahmā and Vishvaksēna, an aspect of Vishṇu, is accepted and followed.

A number of photographs are reproduced in illustration of the Kaṅkāḷamūrti and the Bikshāṭanamūrti; unfortunately all of them belong to South India, a fact which seems to point out that these two aspects of Śiva were more favoured by the Southern people than the Northerners, who worshipped the equally naked Bhairava more freely instead. All the images of the Kaṅkāḷamūrti as also those of the Bhikshāṭanamūrti are practically similar to one another, and it will therefore be sufficient to give the description of any one of each aspect.

On the whole eleven photographs are reproduced in illustration of the descriptions of the Bhikshāṭana and the Kaṅkāḷamūrtis (Pls. LXXXII —LXXXIX). Of these, five are of Bhikshāṭana and five of Kaṅkāḷamūrti ; and the remaining one may be taken either as the one or the other, because it does not conform strictly to the description of either. It might be noticed that the left back hand of all the bronze images of the Bhikshāṭana and the Kaṅkāḷamūrtis are held in the *kaṭaka* pose ; they are so held as to permit of being inserted in them a separately cast *kaṅkāḷadaṇḍa* or a *śikhipiñchha*, if necessary. The dead body of Vishvaksēna is clearly visible in the photographs of the Kaṅkāḷamūrti images in temples of Nagēśvarasvāmin, Tiruchcheṅgāṭṭaṅguḍi and Suchīndram. The pet deer of Śiva is seen with all the stone representations of the Kaṅkāḷa and the Bhikshāṭanamūrtis given here, but have been left off while the photographs of some of the bronze figures were taken. The sculpture belonging to the Kailāsanāthasvāmin temple at Conjeevaram has only two arms, in one of which is a *śikhipiñcha* and the other keeps an *akshamālā* and is held in the *chinmudrā* pose ; it is doubtful if it is wearing any clothes and it has no *jaṭāmakuṭa* on its head ; and from the general appearance it is to be inferred to be a Bhikshāṭanamūrti rather

PLATE LXXXII.

Kaṅkāḷamūrti : Stone : Dārāsuram.

[To face page 308]

PLATE LXXXIII.

Kaṅkāḷamūrti : Bronze : Teṉkāśi.

[To face page 308]

PLATE LXXXIV.

Kaṅkāḷamūrti : Stone : Suchīndram.

[To face page 308]

PLATE LXXXV.

Fig. 1. Kaṅkāḷamūrti : Stone : Kumbhakōṇam.

Fig. 2. Kaṅkāḷamūrti : Stone : Tiruchcheṅgāṭṭaṅguḍi.

[To face page 303]

PLATE LXXXVI.

Fig. 1. Bhikshāṭanamūrti : Stone : Conjeevaram.

Fig. 2. Bhikshāṭanamūrti : Stone : Tiruchcheṅgāṭṭaṅguḍi.

[To face page 309]

PLATE LXXXVII

Fig. 1. Bhikshāṭanamūrti : Stone : Kumbhakōṇam.

Fig. 2. Bhikshāṭanamūrti : Bronze : Tiruveṇkāḍu.

[To face page 309]

PLATE LXXXVIII.

Bhikshāṭanamūrti : Bronze : Vaḻuvūr.

[To face page 309]

PLATE LXXXIX.

Bhikshāṭanamūrti : Bronze : Paṇḍaṇanallūr.

[To face page 309]

than the Kaṅkāḷamūrti. The cut of the face of the image of Bhikshāṭanamūrti of Vaḻuvūr is in striking similarity with that of the image of the Vṛishavāhanamūrti of Vēdāraṇyam, which makes us believe that the artist (*sthapati*) who made these two images was perhaps one and the same person. All the images are made very well indeed, but we should separate from these the bronze statue of Bhikshāṭanamūrti of Tiruveṇkāḍu and the stone figure of the same of the Nāgēśvarasvāmin temples for the special notice of the readers. Both of them are gems of art. The extremely easy and natural posture, the remarkably well-proportioned limbs, and the smile which the artist has eminently succeeded in depicting on the countenance of the bronze Bhikshāṭanamūrti are noteworthy. In the stone image the posture and the general effect are splendid. One other peculiarity which is not found in the *āgamic* descriptions but found in the sculpture is a tiny bell tied by a string just below the knee of the right leg ; it is found in the majority of the instances reproduced in this chapter.

OTHER IMPORTANT ASPECTS OF SIVA :—

Gangadharamurti, Ardhanarisvaramurti, Haryardhamurti, Kalyanasundaramurti, Vrishavahanamurti and Vishapaharanamurti.

OTHER IMPORTANT ASPECTS OF ŚIVA.

THE king Sagara had, by his first wife Kēśinī, a son named Asamañjasa and sixty thousand others by the second wife Sumatī. Asamañjasa was from his childhood a wicked man and his example affected the other children of Sagara and made them equally bad. The gods who could not bear the evil ways of the sons of Sagara asked the *ṛishi* Kapila, one of the aspects of Vishṇu, as to what would be the fate of all the wicked sons of Sagara, to which the *ṛishi* replied that in a short time they would all perish. Sagara arranged for a horse-sacrifice, for which purpose he let loose a horse. It was stolen by Indra and hidden in the *Pātāḷa-lōka.* Tracing the foot-prints of the horse the sixty thousand sons of Sagara excavated the earth till they reached the *Pātāḷa-lōka* and there found the horse in the hermitage of Kapila. These wicked sons of Sagara mistaking Kapila for the thief rushed on him to kill him. But Kapila by the power of his penance reduced them to ashes. Having waited long for the

Gangadhara-murti.

return of his sons in vain, Sagara sent his grandson Aṁśumat (son of Asamañjasa) to search for the horse as also his uncles. He too traced his way into the *Pātāḷa-lōka* and found the horse near Kapila. Being, unlike his uncles and father, a well-behaved boy, he implored Kapila to permit him to take away the horse; the *ṛishi* pleased with the boy gave over the horse to him, informed him of the fate of his uncles and conferred upon him the boon that they would all go to heaven in the life-time of his grandson. The horse-sacrifice was celebrated by Sagara and after sometime he passed away. The son of Aṁśumat was Dilīpa and his son was Bhagīratha. The *ṛishi* Kapila had told Aṁśumat that if the water of the Gaṅgā was sprinkled on the ashes of his uncles they would go to heaven. Bhagīratha performed severe austerities to bring down the celestial river Gaṅgā; the latter was pleased with Bhagīratha and asked him who could resist the force of her fall on earth from heaven; if none could, the fall would cause the earth to be pierced in the middle. He replied that Rudra, the powerful, would be able to bear the force of her descent and began to address his penances to Rudra for granting him the boon of receiving Gaṅgā on his (Rudra's) head. Śiva, being satisfied with the austerities of Bhagīratha, went to the

Himālayas to receive Gaṅgā. At first Gaṅgā thought Śiva would be unable to bear her descent and came down in great volume and with enormous force. Śiva, indignant at her haughty behaviour towards him, determined to humble her. Having received her on his mighty head covered with matted hair, Śiva made Gaṅgā to wind through the labyrinth of his locks of hair for a long time before she was able to reach the earth. Being once again requested by Bhagīratha, Śiva let the river Gaṅgā flow down on the earth. Bhagīratha led Gaṅgā to where his ancestors' ashes lay and made them attain heaven by the contact of the waters of the holy river Ganges. It is under the circumstances described above that Śiva came to wear on his head the Gaṅgā and thence became known as Gaṅgādharamūrti. The story of the descent of Gaṅgā for the sake of Bhagīratha is given in the *Vishṇu-purāṇa*, the *Bhāgavata-purāṇa* and the *Rāmāyana.*

The image of Gaṅgādharamūrti is described in the *Aṁśumadbhēdāgama*, the *Kāmikāgama* and the *Kāraṇāgama*. It is stated that the figure of Śiva should be standing with his right leg planted vertically on the earth and the left one slightly bent. The front right hand should be placed near the chin of his consort Umā, whom he should be embracing with his left front arm; the back right arm being lifted up as high as the *ushṇīsha* or the crown on the head, should be holding a *jaṭā* or a lock of matted hair, on which should be the figure of the goddess Gaṅgā; the back left hand should carry a *mṛiga*.

On the left of Śiva there should be Umā standing in a state of mental uneasiness * which emotion must be portrayed on her face by the sculptor. The right leg of Umā should be somewhat bent, while the left one should be straight. Her right hand should be hanging down freely and the left one should be carrying in it a flower; or, the right hand might be holding a few folds of the cloth about her thigh.

On the left should be Bhagīratha in company with a number of *ṛishis*, praising Śiva. The group of figures described above constitute the panel of Gaṅgādharamūrti. The central figure of Śiva may also be called Gaṅgā-viśarjanamūrti.

The following are the additional facts found in the *Kāmika* and the *Kāraṇāgamas*. The figure of Śiva should have four arms and three eyes; of these, the front right hand should be in the *abhaya* pose and the front left one in the *kaṭaka* pose. The

* This is the feeling of jealousy due to Śiva trying to favour another lady with his attentions.

PLATE XC.

Gaṅgādharamūrti : Stone Panel : Elephanta.

[To face page 317]

other two hands should be carrying the *paraśu* and the *mṛiga*. The hand that touches the *jaṭā* (this must be the one which keeps the *paraśu*), should be lifted as high as the ear. The height of the figure of Bhagīratha should be that of the navel, the chest or the neck of that of Śiva and it should be made according to the *ashṭa-tāla* measurement. The figure of Bhagīratha should be draped with the garment made of barks of trees; the matted hair of the head of Bhagīratha should be dishevelled and flowing down and he should have only two eyes and two arms and these latter should be held in the *añjali* pose on his chest or over his head.

Five illustrations of the Gaṅgādharamūrti are given; of these the first, Pl. XC, is to be found in the rock-cut cave at Elephanta and is executed in a very admirable manner. In the centre of this fine panel are the figures of Śiva and Umā. The back right hand is holding a *jaṭā* from which a female, whose figure is broken and whose legs alone are visible at present, seems to be descending: near the end of this *jaṭā* is Brahmā seated upon a *padmāsana*. The front right hand of Śiva is kept in the *abhaya* pose. Even though the forearm of the back left arm is broken it is easy to find that it must have been directed towards the chin of Umā; it is not easy to say what there was in the front left hand of Śiva. To the left of the figure of Śiva is seen standing that of Umā, whose left arm is let down hanging, while the right is bent and held up; the forearm of this arm is broken; it is very likely that this hand held in it a flower. Near the shoulder of the goddess Umā is seen Vishṇu seated upon his vehicle, the Garuḍa. On the right and near the foot of Śiva is seated Bhagīratha with flowing *jaṭās* and facing the lord Śiva. His arms are broken; perhaps they were in the *añjali* pose. Between Śiva and Umā and to the left of Umā are two dwarfish *gaṇas* or attendants of Śiva. On the head of Śiva is a triple headed goddess who is in all probability the triple river Gaṅgā after she was joined by the Yamunā and the Sarasvatī branches. On a level with the head of Śiva are sculptured a number of *dēvas*, all flying in the air, which is shown in the conventional manner of a cumulus cloud. This, like the other pieces of sculpture in the large cave at Elephanta, is of rare workmanship and is remarkable for its gigantic size.

The second photograph, Pl. XCI, is that of a large panel sculptured on the west wall of the rock-cut cave at Trichinopoly. In this Śiva is standing with his left leg placed straight upon the ground and the right bent and placed upon the Apasmāra-purusha (or a *gaṇa*). His back right arm is lifted

PLATE XCI.

Gaṅgādharamūrti : Stone Panel : Trichinopoly.

[To face page 318]

PLATE XCII.

Fig. 1. Gaṅgādharamūrti : Stone : Kailāsa, Ellora.

Fig. 2. Gaṅgādharamurti : Bronze : Vaidyīśvaraṉkōyil.

[To face page 319]

up and bent to take hold of one *jaṭā* issuing from his head; at the end of this *jaṭā* is the river goddess Ganges seated with hands folded on her chest in the *añjali* pose. The front right hand holds a snake in it; whereas the back left hand is meant to keep a *mṛiga*, which is actually shown at a distance from this hand; the remaining hand is resting upon the hip of Śiva. Bhagīratha on the right and another *ṛishi* on the left are holding up their hands in an attitude of praise. On either side of Śiva is a *dēva* also praising him. Besides these, there are some other beings also praising the lord. The whole panel is supported by an ornamental platform; both the panel and the base are exquisitely carved. The age of this piece of sculpture is the middle of the seventh century and it was carried out by the order of the Pallava King Mahēndravarman.

The third piece of sculpture given as fig. 1, Pl. XCII, is to be found on the south wall of the central shrine of the famous Kailāsa temple at Ellora. Śiva is seen here also as letting down the river goddess Gaṅgā from one of his *jaṭās*, which he holds with his front right hand and his back right one rests upon the hip. The front left arm is kept bent upwards as if to carry either the *paraśu* or the *mṛiga;* the back left arm which is broken, was apparently near the chin of Umā. The river Gaṅgā is descending upon the head of a *ṛishi* seated with crossed legs supported by the *yōga-paṭṭa*, evidently Bhagīratha. From near him it flows to where the deceased Sagaras are, that is, below the foot of Śiva; they are all sculptured as seated cross legged and with arms folded in the *añjali* pose. Above these Sagara-putras are sculptured an elephant and a horse, for what purpose, it is not possible to say. At the foot of Śiva is a figure bending lowly in obeisance; it is also perhaps that of Bhagīratha who expresses his gratitude to Śiva after his ancestors reach heaven. Above and near the head of Śiva are two or three celestial figures praising Śiva. Near Śiva and to his left stands Umā with one arm resting upon her hip and the other holding a flower. Her left leg is planted firmly on the ground and the right is kept bent and crossing the left one.

The fourth illustration, Pl. XCIII, belongs to the Kailāsanāthasvāmin temple at Tāramaṅgalam in the Salem District of the Madras Presidency. It is of comparatively modern date (*circa* 15th century A. D). In this sculpture Śiva is standing in a very solicitous attitude towards his consort who is angry with him for having sheltered another woman, Gaṅgā. He is pacifying her with the

Gaṅgādharamūrti : Stone : Tāramaṅgalam.

[To face page 320]

front right hand placed near her chin; with one of his left arms he is embracing her. In his back left hand which is kept in the *kartari hasta* pose he holds Gaṅgā who is descending from a *jaṭā* of his head; and she is flowing down in the form of water and the river thus descending is swallowed by a bull, which is seated on the pedestal on which Śiva and Umā are standing. In the remaining hand of Śiva is to be seen (rather faintly in the photograph) the *mṛiga*. The right leg of Śiva is planted firmly on the ground and the left one is somewhat bent; the left leg of Umā is straight while the right one is somewhat bent. In her left hand is a flower and the right hand rests upon her thigh.

The fifth illustration (fig. 2, Pl. XCII) is that of a bronze belonging to the Śiva temple at Vaidyēśvarankōyil (Tanjore district) which is exactly similar to the sculpture of Tāramangalam, just described.

Arddhanarisvaramurti.

It is stated in the *Śiva-purāṇa* that Brahmā first begot a number of male beings, the Prajāpatis, and commanded them to create various other beings. They were found later on to be unfit for the task for which they were intended and Brahmā, feeling uneasy at the slow progress of creation, contemplated on Mahēśvara. The latter appeared before him in the composite form of a male-female and asked him to cease feeling distressed. Thitherto it did not occur to Brahmā to create a female also, and at the sight of this composite form of Mahēśvara he realised his error; thereupon he prayed to the female half of Mahēśvara to give him a female to proceed with the act of creation: Brahmā's request was complied with and the creation went on aferwards very well. This story accounts for the Arddhanārīśvara form of Śiva. The real meaning of this aspect has already been adverted to in the Chapter on Liṅgās.

There is yet another account of the appearance of Śiva in the Arddhanārīśvara form. On a certain occasion when Śiva was seated with his consort Pārvatī on the top of the Kailāsa mountain, the dēvas and *ṛishis* went there to pay their homage to him. All of them except the *ṛishi* Bhṛiṅgi, went round both Śiva and Pārvatī in their circumambulations and also bowed to both. This *ṛishi* had a vow of worshipping only one Being, that is, Śiva; in conformity with his vow, he neglected to go round or bow down to Pārvatī. Pārvatī growing angry with Bhṛiṅgi, desired in her mind that all his flesh and blood should disappear from his body and instantly he was reduced to a skeleton covered over with only the skin. In this state he was unable to support himself in an erect position. Seeing his pitiable plight Śiva gave him a third leg so as to enable him to attain equilibrium; Bhṛiṅgi became pleased with his lord and out of joy danced vigorously with his three legs and praised Śiva for his grace. The design of Pārvatī to humble Bhṛiṅgi thus failed and the failure caused great annoyance to Pārvatī who returned to do penance for obtaining a boon from Śiva. At the end of the penance, Śiva, pleased with his consort, granted her wish of being united with his own body. Thus was the Arddhanārīśvara form assumed by Śiva, for offering difficulty to the *ṛishi* Bhṛiṅgi in circumambulating, or bowing to Śiva alone. But, undaunted by this impediment Bhṛiṅgi assumed the form of a beetle pierced a hole through the composite body of Śiva and circumambulated Śiva alone to the great wonder and admiration of even Pārvatī, who became reconciled to his vow and bestowed her grace upon the pious *ṛishi* for his steadfastness to his vow.

The description of the image of Arddhanārīśvara is given in the *Aṁśumadbhēdāgama*, the *Kāmikāgama*, the *Suprabhēdāgama*, the *Śilparatna*, the *Kāraṇāgama* and a few other works. As the name indicates, the form of this image should be half man and half woman. The right half is male, that is, Śiva and the left half is female, that is, Pārvatī. The male half should have a *jaṭāmakuṭa* on the head, which should be adorned with the crescent moon. In the right ear there should be the *nakra-kuṇḍala, sarpa-kuṇḍala* or an ordinary *kuṇḍala* and the right half of the forehead should have one half of an eye sculptured in it. The image of Arddhanārīśvara may have two, three or four arms. If there are four arms, one of the right hands should be held in the *abhaya* pose and the other should keep the *paraśu ;* or one hand may be in the *varada* pose the other carrying a *śūla ;* or there may be a *ṭaṅka* in one hand, and the other may be held in the *abhaya* pose ; or one of the arms may be somewhat bent and rested upon the head of his bull-vehicle and the other hand held in the *abhaya* pose ; or there may be the *śūla* and the *akshamālā* in the two right hands : if there are only two arms, the right one should be held in the *varada* pose ; or there may the *kapāla* held by it. The whole of the right side should be adorned with the ornaments peculiar to Śiva and the chest on the right side should be that of a man. On the right side the garment should cover the body below the loins only up to the knee and the material of the garment is the tiger's skin and silk. On the right half of the chest there should be the *nāga-yajñōpavīta* and on the loins of the same side, the *sarpamēkhala* (or girdles of snake). The whole of the right side should be covered with ashes. The right leg should be somewhat bent (or it may also be straight) and be resting upon a *padma-pīṭha*. The right half might be terrific in appearance and should be of red colour. So much about the Śiva half of Arddhanārīśvara. The left or the Pārvatī half of the Arddhanārīśvara image, is as described below.

On the head of the female half or the left side there should be a *karaṇḍa-makuṭa* or a fine knot of hair well-combed and divided, or both. On the forehead of this half a half *tilaka* mark, contiguous with the half eye of Śiva should be shown. The left eye should be painted with collyrium. In the left ear there should be a *kuṇḍala* known as *vāḷikā*.* If the image of Arddhanārīśvara has four arms, of the two left ones, one is to be bent and rested upon the head of the bull of Śiva and the other kept in the *kaṭaka* pose, holding a *nīlōtpala* in it; or the latter may be let down hanging below.

* This is the rendering of the Tamil word *vāḷi*, which is the name of an ear-ornament; such words are common in the Āgamas, and indicates distinctly the fact that the authors of the bulk of the *āgamas* were residents of the Tamil country.

If there be only three arms in the image of Arddhanārīśvara, there should be only one on the left side. This hand may keep in it either a flower, a mirror or a parrot and it must be adorned with *kēyūra*, *kaṅkaṇa* and other ornaments; if, on the other hand, there are only two arms, the left one may be hanging below, or keeping in it a mirror, a parrot or a flower, or it may be bent and resting upon the head of the bull. The parrot may be sculptured as perching upon the wrist of Pārvatī. On the left side there should be the bosom of a woman with a round well-developed breast; on this side of the chest and the trunk there should be sculptured *hāras*, and other ornaments made of diamonds and other gems. The female half should be smeared with saffron, draped in multicoloured silken female cloth, covering the body down to the ankles; or, the garment may consist merely of white silk. The garment may be held in position on the loins by three girdles. On the left ankle there should be an anklet and the left foot tinged red with the leaves of henna (Tam. *Marudāṇi*). The left leg might be somewhat bent or stand erect upon the *padmāsana*. The colour of the left half may either be parrot-green or dark, and should be of pacific appearance.

PLATE XCIV.

Arddhanārīśvara: Stone Panel: Bādāmi.

[To face page 327]

Eight photographs are reproduced to illustrate the description of Arddhanārīśvara given above. Of these, Pl. XCIII is of a fine panel to be found in the rock-cut temple at Bādāmi. In this sculpture, Arddhanārīśvara has four arms; in one of the right hands he holds the *paraśu*, wriggling round which is to be seen a snake, one of the favourite animals of Śiva; the same arm has a *sarpa-valaya* round it. The remaining right and one of the left hands hold a *vīṇā* in them and play upon it. On the right upper arm there is a snake ornament; there is a *sarpa-kuṇḍala* in the right ear. On the right half of the head is the *jaṭāmakuṭa* bearing on it the crescent moon, the skull and other ornaments. An exceedingly well wrought necklace adorns the neck. There is also the *yajñōpavīta* on the chest. This side is draped from the loins down to the knees with deer's skin. The right leg is somewhat bent and is resting upon an ornamented platform. The female half has a *karaṇḍa-makuṭa*, a knot of hair with bands of jewelled ornaments running across it, a large number of *kaṅkaṇas* on each forearm and a well executed *kēyūra;* there are *mēkhalas* or girdles keeping in position the silk garment which descend down to the ankles. On the foreleg is an anklet. The other left hand holds a *nīlōtpala* flower. The whole of the head is surrounded with a *prabhāmaṇḍala.* To the left of Arddhanārīśvara is a female attendant standing with the right arm hung down and the left arm bent and carrying in it a vessel; she is also beautifully adorned with all ornaments and is draped in a fine cloth. Her hair is done up in a knot, *dhammilla.* To the right of the central image is the bull of Śiva, meek and quite, with its eyes casting glances on the ground before it. Behind the bull is a human figure with a thoroughly emaciated body; it may be representing either Bhairava or the *ṛishi* Bhṛiṅgi. Its hands are held in the *añjali* pose. On the right and left of the head of the central figure are the representations of Dēvas with their consorts, flying in the air and praising Śiva. Below the platform on which stands the figure of Arddhanārīśvara, are sculptured small figures of the *gaṇas,* some dancing and others playing upon different musical instruments.

The second illustration, fig. 2, Pl. XCV, belongs to Mahābalipuram. The figure of Arddhanārīśvara reproduced here is sculptured on the Dharmarāja-ratha. In this, the image has four arms; one of the right hands holds a *paraśu* and the other is kept in the *abhaya* pose. The right half is shaped male and the left half female; of the two arms on the female half one is hanging down and the other one

PLATE XCV.

Fig. 1. Arddhanārīśvara : Stone : Kumbhakōṇam.

Fig. 2. Arddhanārīśvara : Stone : Mahābalipuram.

[To face page 348]

bent and lifted up holding a flower. The forearm of this last mentioned arm has a number of bracelets. In the right ear there is an ordinary small *kuṇḍala* while the left ear bears a big disc of a *patra-kuṇḍala*.

The third illustration, fig. 1, Pl. XCV, the original of which is to be found in the Nāgēśvarasvāmin temple at Kumbhakōṇam, represents that class of the image, with the bull at the back. This piece of sculpture is one of the finest of the Chōḷa period and is remarkable for the exactness of the proportions both of the male and the female portions of the torso and the excellence of its artistic effect. The figure in this instance has three arms, two on the right and one on the left; of the right arms one is bent and placed upon the head of the bull and the other bent and lifted up carrying the *paraśu*. The left hand keeps a mirror towards which the head of the image is slightly turned; the left forearm bears a number of bracelets. On the left the hip and the pelvis are shaped larger than on the right and bring out beautifully the relative proportions of the male and female pelvises. The garment on the right side does not descend below the knee, whereas that on the left side descends as far as the ankle and has a many-folded portion tucked up in front near the loins.

On the whole, this is one of the many excellent pieces of sculpture in the Nāgēśvarasvāmin temple.

The fourth illustration, fig. 2, Pl. XCVI, is exactly similar to the third and belongs to about the same period. The original of this is to be found set up in the circuit round the Śiva temple at Tiruchcheṅgāṭṭaṅguḍi in the Tanjore district.

The fifth illustration is a photograph of a bronze preserved in the Madras Museum (see fig. 1, Pl. XCVI). It is noteworthy in some points : the back right arm is bent and lifted up and carries a *paraśu ;* the front right hand is held in the *kaṭaka* pose, apparently to hold a *triśūla.* Of the two left arms, the back one is bent and kept raised and holds in it a *nīlōtpala* flower, whereas the front one has on its wrist a parrot. In other details, it resembles the other images described above.

The sixth illustration is entirely different from all the others noticed above (see Pl. XCVII). The original stone sculpture is a loose piece lying in the first *prākāra* of the Kailāsanāthasvāmin temple at Conjeevaram and is as old as the middle of the seventh century A.D. In this, the image of Arddhanārīśvara has three arms ; the front right hand is seen carrying a *triśūla* by its lower end and the back one is raised up as high as the head and holds a cobra by its tail ; the

PLATE XCVI.

Fig. 1. Arddhanārīśvara : Bronze : Madras Museum.

Fig. 2. Arddhanārīśvara : Stone : Dārāsuram (?)

Fig. 3. Arddhanārīśvara : Stone : Tiruchchengāṭṭangudi.

[To face page 330]

Arddhanārīśvara : Stone : Conjeevaram.

[To face page 330]

PLATE XCVIII.

Arddhanārīśvara : Stone : Madura.

[To face page 331]

reptile hangs down and lifts up its hood near the hand holding the *triśūla*. The left hand, that of the female half, holds a *vīṇā* in it; it is bent and its elbow is resting upon the head of the bull upon the back of which the figure of Arddhanārīśvara is seated. Nowhere in the authorities quoted in the beginning is it stated that the figure of this composite aspect of Śiva may be a seated one and this particular piece of sculpture is noteworthy for its breach of the rule in this respect. The bull is also seated, an unusual attitude for this animal, especially in the presence of its master.

The seventh illustration, Pl. XCVIII, comes from Madura and belongs to the time of Tirumala-Nāyaka (A. D. 17th century). In its details, it agrees closely with the Mahābalipuram sculpture; the workmanship exhibits peculiarities which were common to the age to which the sculpture belongs, namely, a conventional mode of standing, sharp-pointed nose, artificial disposition of the drapery etc. However, it is a strikingly fine piece of workmanship.

The eighth and the last illustration, fig. 3, Pl. XCVI, is an exceedingly interesting and extraordinary piece of sculpture; in this Arddhanārīśvara has three faces and eight arms. The heads are surrounded by a *prabhā-maṇḍala* and the hands carry in them the *akshamālā*, the *khaḍga*, the *pāśa*, the *musala* (?), a *kapāla*, a lotus flower and other objects. The right side of the figure is male and represents Śiva and the left side is female and represents Pārvatī. In no Sanskrit work that has been examined do we meet with a description of Arddhanārīśvara which agrees with the image whose photograph is reproduced here.

Having described the image of Arddhanārīśvara it is easy to describe the figure of Haryarddhamūrti. Before proceeding with its description it is necessary to say a few words regarding the origin of this aspect of the deity; it is related in the *Vāmana-purāṇa* that Vishṇu is reported to have said to a *ṛishi* that he and Śiva were one and that in him resides Śiva also and manifested himself to the *ṛishi* in this dual aspect of his. In the Arddhanārīśvara form the left half is occupied by the Dēvī or Prakṛitī and Purusha and Prakriti are united with each other for the purpose of generating the universe; the same idea is, as we have already noticed, represented by the *liṅga* and the *yōni*. Umā, Durgā or Dēvī is also considered to be a female aspect of Vishṇu. It is necessary in this connection to draw the attention of the readers to the fact that Durgā, the consort of Śiva,

Haryarddhamurti or Hariharamurti.

is represented in all sculptures with the *saṅkha* and the *chakra*, the weapons characteristic of Vishṇu. In one instance, she is also called the sister of Vishṇu. Vishṇu is also viewed as the *prakṛiti-tatva* and hence we see Vishṇu substituted in the place occupied by Dēvi in the Arddhanār-īśvara aspect of Śiva.

Again, it appears likely that the sculpturing of the Haryarddhamūrti and its worship as a chief image in many temples came into existence after the conflicts between the partizans of the cults of Śiva and Vishṇu had abated and a compromise was arrived at, namely, that Śiva is Vishṇu and Vishṇu is conversely Śiva and that they are essential for the creation, protection and destruction of the Universe. It is gratifying to note that during the *mahōtsavas* in the temples of Harihara, the vehicles, decoration and ceremonies are alternately those that are peculiar to Śiva and to Vishṇu respectively and these festivals are attended by both Vaishṇavas and Śaivas.

In the figure of Harihara or Haryarddhamūrti, the description of the right half or the Śaiva portion is exactly identical with the description given under Arddhanārīśvara. The left half or the Vaishṇava portion is described in the Sanskrit texts as follows: On the left side of Harihara there should be two arms, of which one should be carrying the *chakra*, the *śaṅkha* or the *gadā* and the other held in the *kaṭaka* pose near the thigh. On the head, in the Vaishṇava half, there should be a *kirīṭa* set with precious stones and of excellent workmanship; there should be a *makara-kuṇḍala* in the left ear. The arms on this side should be adorned with *kēyūra*, *kaṅkaṇa* and other ornaments. On the right foreleg there should be an anklet shaped like a snake while that on the left leg should be set with all precious stones. The Vaishṇava half is to be draped with a yellow silk garment. The colour of the Śaiva half is snow-white and that of Vishṇu either green or bluish brown. It is also stated that the two legs of Harihara should be kept without any bends in them. The right half should be terrific and the left half pacific. On the Śaiva portion of the forehead the third eye of Śiva must be half visible and behind the head of the image of Harihara there should be a *śiraśchakra* or halo. The *Vishṇudharmōttara* adds that to the left of the figure of Harihara there should be sculptured that of Garuḍa and to the right, of Nandi.

Of the two photographs given in illustration of the Haryarddhamūrti one, Pl. XCIX, belongs to the panel found in the lower cave temple at Bādāmi. The central figure in this panel is

PLATE XCIX.

Haryarddhamūrti (or Harihara, Śaṅkara-Nārāyaṇamūrti) : Stone Panel : Bādāmi.

[To face page 334]

Harihara; a clear vertical line of demarcation between the *jaṭāmakuṭa* of Śiva and the *kirīṭa-makuṭa* of Vishṇu is visible in the head-gear. In the right ear is a *sarpa-kuṇḍala* whereas in the left one there is a *nakrakuṇḍala.* In the right back hand the image carries a *paraśu* with a snake round it: and the back left hand keeps a *śaṅkha.* The front right hand, though broken, appears from its position to have been held in the *abhaya* pose: the corresponding left hand is resting upon the thigh. There is a *śiraśchakra* surrounding the crown of the head and the legs stand straight. On the right and left are two goddesses, evidently Pārvatī and Lakshmī, the consorts respectively of Śiva and Vishṇu. Between Pārvatī and Harihara is a short figure of the bull-faced Nandi carrying in his right hand a *daṇḍa;* and on the left between Lakshmī and Harihara is a dwarfish figure of Garuḍa. Below the panel and in a long horizontal niche in the platform, over which the figures of Harihara and others stand, are carved a number of *gaṇas,* some playing upon musical instruments and others dancing.

On the top of the panel and on both sides of the head of Harihara are shown two celestial beings with their wives as flying in the air and carrying in their hands a flower garland each.

The second photograph, Pl. C, is that of a beautiful image of the Chālukya period preserved in the Office of the Superintendent of Archæology, Western Circle. In all details regarding the ornaments and dress this is not different from the first. In this sculpture the hands in the Śaiva half carry the *triśūla* and the *akshamālā*, whereas those on the Vaishṇava half keep the *gadā* and perhaps a *śaṅkha*, (this hand is broken and hence the object carried cannot be correctly guessed). As in the previous illustration here also there are the two *dēvīs*, Pārvatī and Lakshmī each one carrying a fruit and a flower in the two hands. Garuḍa is kneeling on the left and Nandi, here represented wholly in the form of a bull, is standing on the right. The sculpturing of this image is excellent; great credit is due to the sculptor for the remarkably minute carving of the ornaments. At the back of the central figure is a *prabhāvaḷi*. Even here distinction is shown between the Śaiva and Vaishṇava halves, the right half being an ordinary *prabhāvaḷi* and, the left being one-half of an expanded hood of a five-headed snake; but on the top of the *prabhāvaḷi* the central figure is the face of a lion. On the right and near the blades of the *triśūla* might be observed the figure of Brahmā seated crosslegged, with hands in the usual

PLATE C.

Harihara : Stone : Poona.

[To face page 336]

poses and carrying the objects characteristic of this deity.

Satī, the daughter of Daksha and the consort of Śiva was dead. The *asura*, Tāraka, was offering great annoyance to the *dēvas* and *brāhmaṇas* and could not be disposed of by any one but by one born of Śiva. In the absence of a wife Śiva can have no progeny and the gods became interested in the marriage of Śiva. Satī was already born to the god of the Himālaya (Himavān) as Pārvati and was herself performing austerities to be joined to her lord once again. It was at such a moment that, induced by the *dēvās*, Kāma the god of love, tried his artifices upon Śiva and met with his end. But when once the mind of Śiva was disturbed he could not at once gather his mental determination and he yielded to the prayers of the gods; he resolved to enter marital life. He wanted to try the steadfastness of Pārvatī. The *Varāha-purāṇa* is alone in giving the following account of how he tested it. Śiva assuming the form of an old, decrepit *brāhmaṇa*, approached Pārvatī, who was absorbed in her austerities, and begged to be supplied with food, as he was feeling very hungry. Pārvatī was pleased to ask him to finish his bath and other ablutions and come for meals. The old man went to the river very near the

Kalyanasundaramurti.

hermitage of Pārvatī and as soon as he got down into the water contrived to be caught by a crocodile. He called out to Pārvatī for help. Prāvatī came to the riverside, but she could not stretch her arm, which was never meant to be held by others than that of her lord, Śiva, even in helping others. Perplexed with this feeling she was standing still for some moments but the danger of the guest being swallowed by the crocodile very soon became patent to her and she was obliged to give up her vow of not being touched by a hand other than that of Śiva; she stretched out her arm and took hold of that of the old *brāhmaṇa* and pulled him out of the water and the crocodile also left him. Pleased with Pārvatī, Śiva showed his real self to her and she was immensely gratified with her lord for having saved her from being held up to obloquy for having caught hold of a hand other than that of Śiva. She dedicated herself to Śiva and the regular marriage was celebrated later on. The details of the celebration and the description of the images of the gods and goddesses that are to be represented as having taken part in it are found in the *Āgamas*.

In the composition of the scene of the marriage of Pārvatī with Śiva there should be Śiva and Pārvatī forming the central figures facing the east.

Vishṇu and his consorts Lakshmī and Bhūmī as the givers—acting the parts of the parents in a *brāhmaṇa* marriage—of the bride should be there; of these Lakshmī and Bhūmī should be standing behind the back of the bride, touching her at the waist indicative of handing her over to her lord; and Vishṇu should be standing in the back-ground, between Śiva and Pārvatī with a golden pot of water ready to pour it in the ceremony of giving the bride to the bridegroom; then, there should be Brahmā in the foreground, seated and performing the ceremony of *hōma* or making offerings to the fire. In the back-ground and at various distances should be seen the eight *Vidyēśvaras* (or the lords of learning), *Ashṭadikpālakas* (or the guardians of the eight quarters), *Siddhas* (persons who have attained the eight great powers), *Yakshas* (semi-divine beings), *ṛishis* (sages), *Gandharvas* (another class of semi-divine beings), the *Mātṛikās* (or the seven mothers) and a host of other gods, with their respective goddesses, all of them standing with arms folded in the *añjali* pose, and with the feelings of pleasure, happiness and wonder portrayed in their faces. Such are the details of the general composition of this remarkable scene and the individual figures are described in detail as follows:—

Śiva should be sculptured as standing firmly

on the left leg and with the right one resting upon the ground somewhat bent; or, the left leg may be represented as slightly bent and the right straight and standing firmly on the ground. The front right arm should be stretched out to receive the right arm of the bride, Pārvatī; the front left hand should be held in the *varada* pose. In the back right hand there should be the *paraśu* and in the back left one the *mṛiga.* There should be three bends in the body of Śiva, that is, should be of the *tribhaṅga* posture. The head of Śiva should be adorned with a *jaṭāmakuṭa* with the crescent moon tucked up in it, and all other parts of the body, with their appropriate ornaments such as the *hāra*, the *kēyūra*, the *udarabandha* and the waist zone. The snake Vāsuki should serve Śiva as the *sarpa-kuṇḍala*, Takshaka as the waist band and Pushkara as the *hāra.* The figure of Śiva should be that of a young man who has just come to age. The colour of Śiva should be red. As usual Śiva should have three eyes.

To the left of the figure of Śiva * should be standing that of Pārvatī, of dark complexion, with

---

* Some authorities state that Pārvatī should be standing to the right of Śiva and there are sculptures representing Pārvatī as standing both on the right and on the left sides of Śiva.

her right arm stretched out to receive that of Śiva, in the act of *pāṇigrahaṇa* (the ceremony of taking hold of the hands) and with her left hand keeping a *nīlōtpala*. Her head should be slightly bent down in shyness and her person should be adorned with all ornaments appropriate for the occasion. The figure of Pārvatī should be as high as the eye, the chin, the shoulder or the chest of Śiva and she should be represented as a well-developed youthful maiden, with two eyes and two arms and draped in silk garments.

In front of Śiva and seated on the ground should be the figure of Brahmā doing *hōma* or making offerings to the fire. The figure of Brahmā should be as high as the chest of Śiva. The *Pūrva-Kāraṇāgama* gives numerical proportions for the height of the figures of Brahmā and Vishṇu. It is therein stated that the height of Vishṇu might be seven-twelfths, eleven-twelfths, three-fourths or two-thirds of the height of Śiva and that the height of Brahmā either equal to or one-sixth, one-seventh or one-eighth less than that of Vishṇu.

Brahmā must be seated upon a *padmāsana* facing the north, with, in front of him, a *kuṇḍa* in which the fire is burning with tapering flames. As usual he should be represented with four faces, four arms and as being busy with the performance of the *hōma* ceremony. He should be adorned with a *jaṭāmakuṭa* and the body with a *yajñōpavīta*, a girdle made of *muñja* grass, and all other ornaments; he should wear an upper cloth. In his front right and left hands he should hold the *sruva* and *sruk* respectively, and in the back right and left hands there should be the *akshamālā* and the *kamaṇḍalu* respectively. The colour of Brahmā should be red like the fire.

The size of the sacrificial *kuṇḍa* is then given as follows: the *kuṇḍa* should have three *mēkhalas* (broad tiers going round the central pit in which the fire is kindled) each of twelve *aṅgulas* in width and the extreme length of the whole *kuṇḍa* including the *mēkhalas* being 22 *aṅgulas*. In the pit of the *kuṇḍa*, the fire should be shown as possessing seven or five *jvālas* or tongues of flame which ought to be a fourth of the height of Brahmā; and the breadth of the flames of fire must be half their height. The *aṅgula* mentioned here is the *dēha-labdha-aṅgula* of the central figure of Śiva.

On the north of *hōma-kuṇḍa* should be standing the figure of Vishṇu, whose height should come up to that of the nose, shoulder or chest of Śiva. If it is as high as the nose, it is said to be a *uttama* figure; if as high as the chest, *adhama*. Dividing the distance between the nose and the chest into eight equal divisions, we shall get the nine classes, composed of the *uttama*, *madhyama* and *adhama* forms of Vishṇu, that is, *uttamōttama*, *uttama-madhyama*, *uttamādhama* and so forth. Vishṇu should be adorned with a *kirīṭa-makuṭa* on his head and all other ornaments in their proper places. In the back right and left hands he should bear the *chakra* and the *śaṅkha*, while the front right or left hands should carry a golden pot, held ready for pouring water from in the act of giving the bride Pārvatī to the bridegroom Śiva. The colour of Vishṇu should be, as usual, dark.

The figure of Lakshmī is required to be as high as the chin or the shoulder of Vishṇu, with arms resembling the trunk of an elephant adorned with *kēyūras*, *kaṅkaṇas* and other ornaments. The hip of Lakshmī should be broad and graceful and she should be draped in richly embroidered silk cloth.

Such are the descriptions of the individual figures composing the picture depicting the favourite theme of the Indian artist, as given in the *Aṁśumadbhēdāgama*, *Uttara-kāmikāgama* and the *Pūrva-Kāraṇāgama*. Let me now turn to the descriptions of the actual sculptures found in the various parts of India, whose photographs are reproduced on Pls. CI to CVII.

Seven photographs are given in illustration of the marriage scene of Śiva with Pārvatī; the original sculptures are of varying degrees of complexity and consist in one instance of barely Śiva and Pārvatī standing hand in hand, while in others with all the divinities surrounding them and each doing a duty in connection with the marriage. Let me therefore describe each of them separately.

The first photograph, Pl. CI, is that of the bronze images of Śiva and Pārvatī in the act of taking hold of each other's hand in marriage. The original image of Śiva is nearly three feet in height and has four arms and three eyes. The front right hand is held out to receive that of Pārvatī, while the back right one carries a *paraśu* with its head turned away from the face of Śiva. The front left hand is held in the *abhaya* pose and the back left one carries a *mṛiga*. The right leg of the image of Śiva is placed firmly on the ground and the left one is slightly bent and is resting upon the ground. There are two bends (*dvibhaṅga*) in this image. On the head of this image is a *jaṭāmakuṭa* adorned with very nicely executed ornaments; the *hāra* and the *yajñōpavīṭa*, the *kēyūra* and the *kaṭakas* the *udarabandha* and the *kaṭibandha*—all these are also artistically made. The image is apparently draped in tiger's skin and on the feet are the

Kalyāṇasundaramūrti : Bronze : Tiruvoṟṟiyūr.

[To face page 344]

PLATE CII.

Kalyāṇasundaramūrti : Stone Panel : Ratanpūr (Bilāspūr District).

[To face page 345]

anklets. The figure is standing upon a *padmāsana*. The image of Pārvatī, with its face slightly bent down in shyness, stands by the right side of that of Śiva, with the right arm stretched out to receive that of Śiva, while the left hand is kept in the *kaṭaka* pose. On the head of Pārvatī is a *karaṇḍa-makuṭa* and her person is adorned with a large number of ornaments of good workmanship; she wears an exquisitely embroidered cloth which descends in flowing folds on either side and is held on the loin by *mēkhalas* (a kind of belt). The figure of Pārvatī is also standing on a *padmāsana* with two bends in its body. This piece of sculpture appears to belong to the early Chōḷa period (A. D. 1000-1100).

The second sculpture whose photograph is reproduced on Pl. CII, comes from Ratanpur in the Bilaspur district of the Central Provinces. In this panel Śiva stands with his front right hand stretched out to receive that of Pārvatī, who in this instance alone, stands to the left of Śiva. His front left hand rests upon the right shoulder of Pārvatī. In the back hands he carries perhaps the *sūla* and the *ḍamaru*. Brahmā is seen seated before the fire, on the right of Śiva and is busy in making fire-offerings; the fire is burning in a cup placed in front of him. Near the *kuṇḍa* or cup of fire stands the bull of Śiva. Surrounding the central figures of Śiva and Pārvatī are a large number of gods and goddesses, several in the *añjali* attitude and some with their arms resting upon their hips (*kaṭyavalambita*).

The next illustration, CIII, is to be found in the Cave temple at Elephanta. It is a remarkably well-executed panel, but very unfortunately here and there mutilated. But what remains is sufficient to disclose the master-hand of the artist who sculptured this most interesting scene. Śiva is standing with Pārvatī to his right; his front right hand is as usual stretched out to receive that of Pārvatī. The figure of Pārvatī is of striking beauty; her slightly bent head and down-cast look depict an amount of shyness: her narrow waist and the broad hip, the well-formed bosom and the easy posture of the legs all lend a charm to the figure which is all its own. Brahmā is making *hōma* to the left of Śiva and Lakshmī is seen standing behind Pārvatī with her hands touching her back and behind Lakshmī stands her consort Vishṇu with a large pot of water for pouring water at the ceremony of giving the bride to the bride-groom. The figure of a very well built man is to be seen standing behind Pārvatī with his right hand bent and resting upon the right shoulder of

PLATE CIII.

Kalyāṇasundaramūrti : Stone Panel : Elephanta.

[To face page 346]

PLATE CIV.

Kalyāṇasundaramūrti : Stone Panel : Ellora.

[To face page 347]

PLATE CIV.

Kalyāṇasundaramūrti : Stone Panel : Ellora.

[To face page 347]

PLATE CV.

[To face page 947]

Subrahmaṇya teaching Śiva : The scene of marriage between Śiva and Pārvatī : Pārvatī doing penance to obtain the hand of Śiva in marriage.

Stone Panel : Ellora.

Pārvatī. From the size of the figure and from the fact that it has only two arms, as also from a sort of inferior head-gear, one may presume it represents Parvatarāja, the father of Pārvatī. If that is he, it is indeed noteworthy to find him in the panel. Below the right hand of this figure is a large drum, also very well-carved. A number of gods with their respective goddesses are seen in the air in the attitude of flying and praising the married couple. In point of size also this panel is most remarkable; the height of the figure of Pārvatī is 8 feet and 6 inches and the panel itself measures approximately 10¾ feet square.

The photograph reproduced on Pl. CIV is of the panel found in the Dhumar Lena Cave at Ellora. In its details the panel is exactly similar to that of the Elephanta Cave, though its workmanship has not got the latter's fineness and artistic finish.

The large panel whose photograph is given on Pl. CV belongs to the Cave temple of Rāmēśvara at Ellora. It is divided into three sections, the two on the left are depicting scenes from the marriage of Pārvatī with Śiva. In the extreme left section and at its right end is seen Pārvatī standing erect on the mountain between two fires, performing penance to obtain the hand of Śiva in marriage. Her left hand rests upon her thigh, while the right one is counting the beads of an *akshamālā*. To her left stands a woman carrying a box; a male figure, with outstretched right hand as though asking for something from Pārvatī, is seen standing to the left of the tall girl with the box in her hand. It is the figure of Śiva as a hungry beggar asking for food. A little to the left, the scene changes: the beggar, who was asked by Pārvatī, according to the *Varāha-purāṇa*, to go to the river to bathe and return for meals, is in knee deep water, the surface of which is covered with lotus flowers and leaves; his left leg is caught hold of by a *makara* and he is calling out for help. Pārvatī who repairs to the spot to see what has become of her guest, sees him in this miserable plight; after hesitating for a moment if she should now offer her hand or not to this beggar, and with great reluctance, tries at last to lift him up with her left hand—note, she keeps her right one far away from the man and held in the *vismaya* pose. To save her from the tongue of slander Śiva appears to her in his real person, represented in the panel, just above the head of the beggar. His *jaṭā-makuṭa* and other ornaments readily proclaim his identity. It should be noted here that water, fire and mountain are represented in the conventional manner described elsewhere. Proceeding then to the next scene, that of the actual marriage ceremony, which is depicted in the middle section of the panel, it is seen that Pārvatī, standing to the right of Śiva is offering her right hand to him, who receives the same in his right hand. At the background and between the bride and bridegroom is Vishṇu standing with a pot of water ready to pour in the hands of Śiva, in making the gift of the bride. Lakshmī's face is seen behind the head of the bride and she is standing behind Pārvatī and presenting her to her lord, Śiva. Behind the bride are two female attendants, one of them carrying a box and behind the bridegroom are two *dēvas* and a *gaṇa*, the latter being easily recognised by his size and head-gear. Brahmā, assisted by a *ṛishi*, is seen performing the fire-offering (*hōma*). The strangest thing in the panel is the anachronistic presence of Gaṇēśa and Kārttikēya, the two sons of Śiva and Pārvatī, even during the marriage of the two!! The little Gaṇēśa is standing between the legs of Śiva and Pārvatī and Kārttikēya between those of Śiva and the *gaṇa*. The latter appears to carry in his left hand a *kukkuṭa* (cock) whose tail is visible in the photograph. The presence of these two children is, in all probability, meant to indicate that they were not born by the union of the couple but had existed from eternity like all gods, but at a later period assumed the position of the sons of Śiva and Pārvatī.

The remaining portion of the panel represents another scene in the life of Śiva. He is seen learning the significance of the mystic syllable *Ōm* from his son Subrahmaṇya. An account of this event will be found given in the chapter on Subrahmaṇya. Subrahmaṇya with six heads (of which three are visible in the sculpture) is seated on a high pedestal with a *ṛishi;* one of his right hands is held in the *chin-mudra* pose, while the other is kept with outstretched fingers. One left hand is resting upon his lap. He wears the cloth in the *upavīta* fashion; the legs are hanging below the seat and resting upon the ground. The *ṛishi* has also both his legs hanging down the seat and seems to have his hands kept in the *añjali* pose. In front of Subrahmaṇya is seated cross-legged on the ground Śiva with his right hand held in the *jñāna-mudrā* pose and the left one resting, in the *yōga-mudrā* pose, on his lap. He also wears his upper garment in the *upavīta* fashion. Behind him is seen standing Pārvatī, his consort.

Below this remarkable composite panel is a row of most humourous *gaṇas* some with animal

PLATE CVI.

Kalyāṇasundaramūrti : Stone : Madura.

[To face page 351]

Kalyāṇasundaramūrti : Stone : Madura.

[To face page 351]

faces, others with animal-mouthed bellies (*vṛikōdaras*) and the rest like human beings taking active part, with great cheerfulness, in the arrangements in connection with the marriage festivities. The two first on the right end are seen carrying each a banner and the third a mace ; the fourth is dancing. Three *gaṇas* are seen carrying a four-footed article resembling a table, which is evidently a raised seat. On the left of this group another *gaṇa* is seen playing upon the flute ; next to him is a lion faced *gaṇa* playing upon a stringed musical instrument. Adjoining this, there is a bear-faced *gaṇa* carrying something on his head ; another, tiger-faced, holds in his left hand something kept in a round leaf, apparently that of the lotus. The fourth from the left is a *vṛikōdara ;* the rest are carrying some article or other in their hands.

The next two illustrations, Pls. CVI and CVII, are from South India. They are found in Madura, the one in the *Pudu-maṇḍapa* and the other in the *maṇḍapa* in front of the central shrine of Sundarēśvara temple ; the first belongs to the reign of Tirumalai Nāyaka and the second, a copy, made some forty years ago. In these the principal figures are Pārvatī, who is being given to Śiva in marriage by Vishṇu pouring water in the hands of Śiva ; and Śiva standing on the left with his right hand stretched out to receive the gift; in front of and between him and Vishṇu is seen, with the head bent down in shyness, Pārvatī keeping her right hand lifted up so as to be taken hold of by Śiva; and on the left is Vishṇu pouring water from a vessel on the hand of Śiva. Below, and in a countersunk panel is seen Brahmā making fire-offering. The whole subject is treated with great cleverness and the effect is very striking. There is not that elaborateness which one meets with in the Cave temples of Northern and Western India, but the very simplicity of the sculpture carries a great charm with it. The shyness depicted on the countenance of the bride is very noteworthy.

One of the favourite modes in which Śiva is represented in sculpture is known as the Vṛisha-vāhana or Vṛishabhārūḍhamūrti; that is, Śiva seated upon the bull, his vehicle. It is in this aspect which is held in high veneration by the people that Śiva has often appeared in person before his devotees. One day, among the ten days' festival in any Śiva temple in South India, the image of Śiva is seated upon a bull and carried round the streets in procession and that day is held by people as the most important of all the days of the

Vrishabha-rudhamurti.

festival. Hence also this form of the image of Śiva is described in great detail in all the important *āgamas*.

Vṛishavāhanamūrti should be standing with his right leg placed firmly on the ground and the left slightly bent; the left arm should be bent and its wrist resting on the head of the bull; the hand of this arm may be hanging fully open so that the tip of the middle finger may reach the level of his own navel. The right hand should carry a *vakra-daṇḍāyudha* (a crooked stick like the one carried by Śāsta, Mannannār Kṛishṇa, etc.). This stick should be of the thickness of the small finger and should have three bends at its top end and its length equal to the distance between the *hikkā-sūtra* and the knee. In the back right hand there must be the *ṭaṅka* or *paraśu* and in the back left hand the *mṛiga*. The head might be adorned with a *jaṭāmakuṭa*, or a hanging *jaṭābhāra* or a *jaṭā-bandha*, the choice of which is left to the sculptor. The figure should be adorned with all ornaments; the colour of Śiva, as also that of his garments is to be red. On the right side or the left should be the figure of Dēvī, standing with the right leg kept firmly on the ground and the left one slightly bent. The right arm of the Dēvī should be bent and that hand carrying a *utpala* flower. The left hand should be hanging down freely. The figure of Dēvī should be done according to the measurements given in the *āgamas* for female images; the direction of the bends in its body would depend upon its situation to the right or left of the image of Śiva.

The *ṛishabha* (bull) should be standing behind Śiva and should be of the height either of the chest, navel, root of the penis or even the thigh or the foreleg. (Evidently in the last two or three instances the animal should perhaps be sculptured as sitting on the ground).

The illustrations which fit in almost exactly with the description given above are the images of Vṛishavāhanamūrti of Vēdāraṇyam, that reproduced from the *Viśvakarma* and that of Tāramaṅgalam, whose photographs are given as Pls. CVIII, CIX and CX respectively. In the first instance, as in others, it is not the left arm that is resting on the head of the bull but the right. The left arm is let down and its hand is resting upon the thigh and not as required, held in the *kaṭaka* pose. The tip of the middle finger of the right hand held in the *patāka-hasta* reaches, as is required by the *āgamas*, the level of the navel. It is to be noted that the figure of Śiva in the present instance has only two instead of four arms. The left leg stands firmly on the ground and the right one is slightly bent and resting

PLATE CVIII.

Vṛishavāhanamūrti : Bronze : Vēdāraṇyam.

[To face page 354]

PLATE CIX.

[To face page 355] Vṛishavāhanamūrti : Bronze : Viśvakarma (Dr. A. K. K.)

PLATE CX.

Vṛishavāhanamūrti : Stone : Tāramaṅgalam.

[To face page 355]

PLATE CXI.

Vṛishavāhanamūrti : Stone : Mahābalipuram.

[To face page 355]

PLATE CXII.

Fig. 2. Vṛishavāhanamūrti : Stone : Madura.

Fig. 1. Vṛishabhārūḍhamūrti : Stone : Haḷebiḍu.

[To face page 355]

on the ground on its toes. The bull is as high as the thighs of Śiva. Pl. CIX is true to the very description given in the *āgamas*.* Its left arm rests on the head of the bull and the right hand is held in the *kaṭaka* pose to receive in it a separate metallic or wooden crooked stick. The right leg is kept firmly on the ground and the left one is kept slightly bent. In the image of Tāramaṅgalam, Pl. CX, the front right hand is kept in the *abhaya* pose, but in other respects it is exactly similar to the one on Pl. CIX.

The third photograph reproduced on Pl. CXI is that of the sculpture to be found on the wall of one of the so-called *rathas* at Mahābalipuram. It almost resembles the image represented on Pl. CVIII. The image of Śiva has four arms. The left hand is in a manner held in the *kaṭaka* pose. On either side of this Vṛishavāhanamūrti is a Dēva, with his consort, praising Śiva.

The photographs reproduced as figs. 1 and 2 on Pl. CXII are similar in treatment. The *āgamic* description agreeing with this mode of representation of the Vṛishavāhanamūrti is not available at present. So, we should be satisfied with the description as we find recorded in the sculptures.

---

* Mr. V. A. Smith calls this image " Siva in sandhyānṛitta dance."

Here, Śiva and Pārvatī are seated exactly as in the aspect of Umāsahita-āliṅganamūrti, or Sōmāskanda-mūrti, on a seat placed upon the back of a full sized bull. In fig. 1, Śiva is embracing Pārvatī and in fig. 2, he is not. In the first piece of sculpture Śiva carries in his back hand the *śūla* and the *ḍamaru* and the front right is kept in the *abhaya* pose and the front left is thrown on the shoulder of Pārvati; in the second sculpture the back hands carry the *paraśu* and the *mṛiga* and the front hands are in the *abhaya* and the *varada* poses respectively. An elaborately carved *prabhāvaḷi* is seen surrounding the figures of Śiva and Pārvatī. The first piece of sculpture belongs to the Hoyasaḷa School and the second to the modern Naṭṭukkōṭṭai artisans and the former is fitted up now in the reconstructed Kēdārēśvara temple at Haḷebīḍu and the latter in the Sundarēśvara temple at Madura.

Vishapaharana-murti.

The aspect of Śiva known as the Vishāpaharaṇāmūrti appears to be considered a kind of *anugrahamūrti;* since it is not definitely mentioned as such in the *āgamas* it is included in this chapter. We have already mentioned that Śiva swallowed the dreadful poison that emerged from the ocean, when it was churned by the Dēvas and the Dānavas for obtaining ambrosia (*amṛita*) from it. We have a description of this *mūrti* in the *Kāraṇāgama;* therein it is stated that Śiva, as usual, should have a face with three eyes on it, wearing a *jaṭāmakuṭa* and having four arms. In two of his hands there should be the *paraśu* and the *mṛiga;* in one of the remaining hands there should be the cup containing the poison and the fourth hand should be held in the *varada* pose. His sight must be fixed upon the poison and the general attitude should be such as to indicate that he is going to sip the poison immediately. He should be adorned with all kinds of ornaments. On the left of Śiva there should be his consort Pārvatī embracing her lord about the neck with her right arm and appearing highly perplexed and distressed. Her complexion should be dark, she should have two eyes, two arms and be standing in the *tribhaṅga* posture, (with three bends in her body), with her right leg placed vertically on the ground and the left one kept slightly bent. Another description adds to the above the following details: that the appearance of Śiva should be made terrific (*ugra*) by the addition of side tusks; his complexion should be white as the full-moon and he should be draped in garments made of tiger's skin; there should be a garland made of small bells, and along with the other usual ornaments, there should be some others composed of scorpions (*vṛiśchika*). In the right hands of Śiva there should be the *triśūla* and a beaked vessel (*gōkarṇa*) containing the poison; and in one of the left hands the *kapāla*. Since no object is mentioned as being in the fourth hand, it appears that this arm may be taken to be employed in the act of embracing the Dēvī. In the first description Śiva and Pārvatī are required to be standing, but in this one, they are said to be seated on the bull-vehicle of Śiva.

ELEMENTS
OF
HINDU ICONOGRAPHY

ELEMENTS
OF
HINDU ICONOGRAPHY

BY

T. A. GOPINATHA RAO, M.A.
SUPERINTENDENT OF ARCHAEOLOGY, TRAVANCORE
STATE.

Vol. II—Part II.

GYAN

Published by

Gyan Publishing House
5, Ansari Road
Daryaganj, New Delhi-110002
Phone: 011-47034999, 9811692060
E-mail: books@gyanbooks.com

Distribution Network
gyanbooks.com
India, USA, Canada, UK, Australia, France

© Publisher

All rights reserved. No part of this work may be reproduced, stored, adapted, or transmitted in any form or by any means, electronic, mechanical, photocopying, micro-filming, recording or otherwise, or translated in any language, without the prior written permission of the copyright owner and the publisher.

ISBN : 978-81-212-2694-3 (Set)
ISBN : 978-81-212-2698-1 (HB)
First Published, 1916

2nd Impression 2021

Printed at: Gyan Press, Delhi.

The book is sold subject to the condition that it shall not, by way of trade or otherwise, be lent, resold, hired out, or otherwise circulated without the prior publisher's written consent.

Elements of Hindu Iconography, Vol. II–Part II
Author: T. A. Gopinatha Rao

ELEMENTS

OF

HINDU ICONOGRAPHY

BY

T. A. GOPINATHA RAO, M.A.,
SUPERINTENDENT OF ARCHÆOLOGY, TRAVANCORE STATE.

Vol. II—Part II.

THE LAW PRINTING HOUSE
MOUNT ROAD :: :: MADRAS
1916

MISCELLANEOUS ASPECTS OF SIVA:—

Sadasivamurti and Mahasadasivamurti, Panchabrahmas or Isanadayah, Mahesamurti, Ekadasa Rudras, Vidyesvaras, Murtyashtaka and Local Legends and Images based upon Mahatmyas.

MISCELLANEOUS ASPECTS OF ŚIVA.

(i) SADĀŚIVAMŪRTI AND MAHĀSADĀŚIVAMŪRTI.

THE idea implied in the positing of the two gods, the Sadāśivamūrti and the Mahāsadāśivamūrti contains within it the whole philosophy of the Śuddha-Śaiva school of Śaivaism, without an adequate understanding of which it is not possible to appreciate why Sadāśiva is held in the highest estimation by the Śaivas. It is therefore unavoidable to give a very short summary of the philosophical aspect of these two deities as gathered from the *Vātuḷaśuddhāgama.* According to the Śaiva-siddhāntins there are three *tatvas* (realities) called Śiva, Sadāśiva and Mahēśa and these are said to be respectively the *nishkalā*, the *sakalā-nishkalā* and the *sakalā*[1] aspects of god: the word *kalā* is often used in philosophy to imply the idea of limbs, members or form; we have to understand, for instance, the term *nishkalā* to mean

Sadasiva-murti.

(1) Also *sūkshma, sthūla-sūkshma* and *sthūla*, and *tatva, prabhāva* and *mūrti*.

that which has no form or limbs; in other words, an undifferentiated formless entity. Now the Śiva-tatva mentioned above is identified with the *nishkalā* aspect of the Supreme god, because in this state all created beings merge their bodies, which they had obtained for the purpose of the enjoyment of actions of the pure and impure kinds, in the primeval cause, and therein suppress all activities. In the *nishkalā* state the Supreme Being has no beginning, no limit or boundary and is pervading everywhere, is indestructible, incomparable, extremely subtle and supreme, and is unknowable by any mode of proof. At the end of an aeonic destruction, (*saṁhāra*) for the purpose of creating the *śuddha-tatvas*, the *suddha-bhuvanas*, and for the removal of dirt (*mala*) from *Yōgis*, five Saktis evolve as follows: when Śiva in his boundless mercy wills, a thousandth part of his self emerges out of him as Parāśakti; from a thousandth part of this Parāśakti comes out Ādiśakti, a thousandth part of Ādi-śakti gives rise to Ichchhāśakti; from this latter are produced in a similar manner Jñānaśakti and Kṛiyāśakti. These five Śaktis are also known as

Parāśakti=Śāntyātītaśakti,
Ādiśakti=Śāntiśakti,
Ichchhāśakti=Vidyāśakti,

Jñānaśakti=Pratishṭhāśakti and
Kṛiyāśakti=Nivṛittiśakti

in the technology of the Śaiva philosophy. Because it produces the faculty in souls of the enjoyment of *karmas* (good and bad actions) the Kṛiyāśakti is called *nivṛitti*; because it yokes to the *purusha tatvas* which are naturally inert and supremely subtle, the Jñānaśakti is called *pratishṭha*; because it understands *māyā*, the objects ushered into existence by the *māyā* and the distinction of the soul from the above two, the Ichchhāśakti is called *vidyā*; because it destroys *mala*, *māyā* and *karma*, the Ādiśakti is called *śānti*; and because it is the source through which souls attain the knowledge of the *sat-chit-ānanda svarūpa* of the Supreme Being, the Parāśakti is called *śāntyātita*.(1) From the five Śaktis mentioned just now appear the five different Sadāśiva-tatvas as follows :—

1. From a tenth of Parāśakti comes the first Sadāśiva-tatva, Śivasādākhya, known also by the name of Sadāśiva; because it is born of Parāśakti and is pure, it is called Śiva; and it exists everywhere as a subtle divine light, bright as the

(1) See also verse 27, Chap. 14 of the *Yajña-khaṇḍa* of the *Sūta-saṁhitā* and the commentary thereon.

lightning and pervading the space in the universe;

2. from a tenth portion of Ādiśakti is evolved the second Sadāśiva-tatva, Amūrtta-sādākhya, known also as Īśāna. Because Ādiśakti, like Parāśakti, is also formless, this second *tatva* is called the *amūrtta;* that is, this is also *nishkalā*. This *sādākhya* exists as a luminous pillar whose lustre is equal to that of a crore of suns put together. This pillar is called the Divya-liṅga or the Mūla-stambha. As everything takes its origin from the *mūla-stambha* and ends finally in it, it was called the *liṅga;* (1)

3. from a tenth of Ichchhāśakti is produced the third Sadāśivatatva, Mūrttasādākhya, known also as Brahmā. Because this *tatva* has form it is called *mūrtta;* in other words it is *sakalā*. This *tatva* exists in the form of a Divyaliṅga with the brightness of fire and having flames of fire playing round it. On the top of

(1) लयं गच्छान्ति भूतानि संहारे निखिलं यतः।
सृष्टिकाले पुनस्सृष्टिस्तस्माल्लिङ्गमुदाहृतम् ॥

Suprabhēdāgama.

this *liṅga* there is a figure with a beautiful face having three eyes, four arms and all other limbs. It carries in two out of its four hands the *paraśu* and the *mṛiga* and the remaining hands are held in the *varada* and the *abhaya* poses ;

4. from a tenth part of Jñānaśakti proceeded the fourth *ṭatva*, Kartṛisādākhya, otherwise Īśvara. Because Jñāna is the characteristic of the *kartā* (doer) this *tatva* received the name Kartṛisādākhya. Usually it is believed to exist in the form of a Divyaliṅga of immeasurable lengh and girth : the characteristic quality of this *liṅga* is its crystal clearness. On this liṅga resides Śiva, the origin of all existence, in the form of a figure having four faces, twelve eyes, eight ears and arms, and two legs. In the right hands of this figure are *śūla*, *paraśu*, *khaḍga* and *abhaya*, whereas in the left ones are *pāśa*, *sarpa*, *ghaṇṭā* and *varada* and is adorned with all ornaments ; and similarly

5. from a tenth part of Kṛiyāśakti emerged the fifth *tatva*, Karmasādākhya, known

also as Īśāna.[1] It is called *karma* because it is of the nature of *kṛiyā*. This *tatva* exists as the *liṅga* set upon the *pīṭha*. As the act (*karma*) of the conjunction of these two objects is the condition precedent to creation, the *tatva* received the name of Karmasādākhya.

Each one of these *tatvas* is dependant upon its immediate predecessor; for example, the *amūrttasāda* depends upon the *śivasāda*, the *mūrtta* on the *amūrtta* and so on. Therefore, the *Karmasādatatva* is to be taken as containing in it all the five *sādākhyas*. The deity Īśāna representing the *Karmasāda* has a perfectly white body resembling the flower of the *kunda* (a kind of jasmine) or the full moon; having five heads adorned with *jaṭāmakuṭas;* bearing on each face three eyes, ten arms and two legs. He is standing on a *padmāsana* and keeps in his right hands the *śūla*, *paraśu*, *khaḍga*, *vajra* and *abhaya* and in the left ones the *nāga*, *pāśa*, *aṅkuśa*, *ghaṇṭa*, and *agni*. He is beautiful

(1) The names of these five aspects corresponding to the five *sādākhyas* are usually known as Vāmadēva (=Īśa), Tatpurusha (=Īśāna), Aghōra (=Īśvara), Sadyōjāta (=Brahmā) and Īśāna (=Sadāśiva) and they face the north, east, south, west and the top respectively.

adorned with all ornaments, draped in fine clothes and is with a smiling countenance full of peacefulness. The significance of the articles in the hands of all these deities have already been explained in the Chapter on "Āyudhapurushas" in Vol. I of this work. Of the five faces of this deity, the one facing the east is that of Īśāna; that facing the south, of Īśvara; the west, of Brahmā; the north, of Īśa and the top of Sadāśiva. All ceremonials, such as installation (*sthāpana*), should be done only for the Īśāna face and not for the other faces. The other faces are meant for the meditation of those who have attained perfection in *yōga*, *mantra-siddhi*, etc. It is from these five faces the *Śaivāgamas* were given out to the world[1]. From a thousandth part of this

---

(1) The Āgamas that were proclaimed to the world by the Sadyōjāta face are:—

1. Kāmikāgama,
2. Yōgajāgama,
3. Chintyāgama,
4. Kāraṇāgama and
5. Ajitāgama;

those by the Vāmadēva face are:—

1. Dīptāgama,
2. Sūkshmāgama,
3. Sahasrāgama,
4. Aṁśumānāgama and
5. Suprabhēdāgama;

Karmēśa, there came into existence Mahēśamūrti, who is the direct agent in the acts of *sṛishṭi* (creation), *sthiti* (protection) and *laya* (reabsorption): (1) he must therefore be understood as a

---

those by the Aghōra face are:—

1. Vijayāgama,
2. Niśvāsāgama,
3. Svāyambhuvāgama,
4. Analāgama and
5. Vīrāgama;

those by the Tatpurusha face are:—

1. Rauravāgama,
2. Makuṭāgama,
3. Vimalāgama,
4. Chandrajñānāgama and
5. Mukhabimbāgama;

and those by the Īśāna face are:—

1. Prōdgītāgama,
2. Lalitāgama,
3. Siddhāgama,
4. Santānāgama,
5. Narasiṁhāgama,
6. Pāramēśvarāgama,
7. Kiraṇāgama and
8. Vātuḷāgama,

making in all twenty-eight in number.

(1) In connection with the five aspects of Śiva, it is interesting to compare the Śaktimaya-vyūha of Vaishṇavaism given on pp. 235—237, Vol. I, as also the five Bōdhisatvas, namely,

sakala-mūrti. It is this Mahēśamūrti that manifests himself to the devotees in different forms, performing several sports (*līlās*) as seated or standing, dancing or riding upon vehicles, as terrific (*ugra*) or pacific (*saumya*) and so on. This Mahēśa has one face set with three eyes, the head adorned with a *jaṭā-makuṭa*, four arms, and is standing on a *padmāsana.* In two of his hands are the *mṛiga* and the *paraśu* and the remaining two hands are held in the *abhaya* and the *varada* poses. The *Līlāmūrtis* of Mahēśa are twenty-five in number and they are :—

1. Chandraśēkharamūrti.
2. Umāsahita M.
3. Vṛishabhārūḍha M.
4. Nṛitta M.
5. Kalyāṇasundara M.
6. Bhikshāṭana M.
7. Kāmadahana M.
8. Kālāntaka M.
9. Tripurāntaka M.
10. Jalandharavadha M.
11. Gajāri M.

Ratnapāṇi, Vajrapāṇi, Samantabhadra, Padmapāni and Viśvapāṇi, of the Bauddha Mahāyana philosophy, who also possess similar powers and functions as their parallels in the Śaiva and Vaishṇava philosophies.

12. Vīrabhadra M.
13. Śaṅkara-Nārāyaṇa M.
14. Ardhanārīśvara M.
15. Kirāta M.
16. Kaṅkāḷa M.
17. Chaṇḍēśanugraha M.
18. Vishāpaharaṇa M.
19. Chakradāna M.
20. Vighnēśvarānugraha M.
21. Sōmāskanda M.
22. Ēkapāda M.
23. Sukhāsana M.
24. Dakshiṇāmūrti and
25. Liṅgōdbhavamūrti.

Again, from Mahēśvara were produced the following: Rudradēva who is a thousandth portion of Mahēśa; Vishṇu who is one part out of a crore of Rudra; Brahmā who is one part out of a crore of Vishṇu and the three luminaries the sun, the moon and the fire, from the three eyes of Mahēśa; the wind from his nose; *jñāna* from his mouth; Gaṇēśa from his neck; Shaṇmukha from his chest; fifty crores (!) of divine beings from his navel; and several crores (!) of *ṛishis* from his hair. Such in short is the philosophy of the five *sādākhyas*, the five *mūrtis* and the *tatvas* of the Śaiva-siddhānta.

From the above we can very well understand that Sadāśiva is the highest and the Supreme Being, formless, beyond the comprehension of any one, subtle, luminous and all pervading; not contaminated by any qualities (*guṇas*) and above all actions (*karmas*). It is from this Supreme Being all else have their origin, being and end at his will. This Sadāśiva-tatva is said to be *sakala-nishakala*, for this reason, namely:—after a cosmic destruction, a cosmic evolution has to follow; for, those souls that have not been cleansed of their dirt of actions (*karma-mala*) should be made to undergo once again worldly bondage (*saṁsāra*) thereby enabling them to rub down the effects of their bad *karmas* done in past births and accumulate in the present existence those of good *karmas* and finally be relieved of mundane existence. For the purpose of creation, the Supreme Being attempts to cause the movement of the *bindu* (sperm) and it is in this state that he is considered as *sakala-nishkala*. This abstruse conception of the Sadāśivamūrti, which the *Āgamas* themselves declare cannot be comprehended by ordinary mortals has fortunately been idolised in a material form for the benefit of men and the description of this image is found in all Śaivagamas.

The *Uttara-kāmikāgama* states that the colour of Sadāśivamūrti should be of white colour and be standing upon a *padmāsana*. There should be five faces and the heads be adorned with *jaṭāmakuṭas*, whose *jatās* are required to be of brown colour. Sadāśiva should have ten arms; in the five right hands there should be the *śakti*, *śūla*, *khaṭvāṅga*, *abhaya* and *prasāda* (?) and in the five left ones, the *bhujaṅga* (a snake), *akshamālā*, *ḍamaru*, *nīlōtpala* and a fruit of the *mātuḷuṅga*. Or, Sadāśiva may be conceived as having only one face set with three eyes which represent the Ichchhāśakti, the Jñānaśakti and the Kṛiyāśakti; with the Chandrakalā (the crescent moon), which stands as a symbol of *jñāna* (wisdom), tucked up in the *jāṭamakuṭa* and adorned with all ornaments such as the *yajñōpavīta*. Manōnmanī, the Supreme goddess, should be standing by his side.

Figs. 1 and 2, Pl. CXII and Pl. CXV illustrate the description of Sadāśivamūrti. The seated figure has five heads each of which is adorned with a *jaṭā-makuṭa*; it has ten arms; one of the right hands is held in the *abhaya* pose and a corresponding left one in the *varada* pose. The other hands carry the *akshamālā*, *pāśa*, *khaḍga*, *ṭaṅka* (or *paraśu*), *kamaṇḍalu* and other objects not quite clear in the photograph. The standing figure (fig. 2, Pl. CXII), also possesses five heads of which the topmost has tongues of flames playing round it;

PLATE CXIII

Fig. 1. Sadāśivamūrti : Bronze :
Collection of Mr. W. A. Beardsell, Madras.

Fig. 2. Sadāśivamūrti : Bronze :
Collection of Mr. K. Kay, Madras.

[To face page 372]

Sadāśivamūrti : Stone : Elephanta (from *Viśvakarma*).

[To face page 378]

some of the faces have side-tusks and the figure is nude; all these are characteristic features of a terrific (or *ugra*) aspect of the deity. There are eighteen arms, the hands of which are seen to carry such objects as the *śūla*, *pāśa*, *khaḍga*, *khētaka*, *musala*, *paraśu*, *ghaṇṭa*, *kapāla* and others. The figure is adorned with various necklaces of which one is long enough to descend as far as the ankle and is composed of tiny bells. Both these images appear to be modern.

The beautiful figure of Sadāśivamūrti reproduced on Pl. CXV is said to have been discovered in Elephanta and is badly damaged. Like all other pieces in the caves at Elephanta this one also is carved splendidly. The very well executed *jaṭā-makuṭas* adorned with finely wrought discs, the row of small curls of hair fringing the forehead (*ushṇīsha*), the necklaces, the *yajñōpavīta*, the girdle round the loins are all very nicely worked out. The figure has four faces and since all its arms are broken, it is not possible to say how many it originally possessed.

Mahasadasiva-murti.

Mahāsadāśivamūrti is conceived as having twenty-five heads and fifty arms bearing as many objects in their hands. The five heads of Sadāśivamūrti which represent the five aspects of Śiva (the Pañchabrahmās), who are the lords of creation, protection, etc., are each substituted by five heads, making on the whole twenty-five; which stand for twenty-five *tatvas* of philosophy. The *Mānasāra* states that Mahāsadāśiva should be represented with twenty-five faces, having on the whole seventy-five eyes and fifty arms. The heads should be adorned with *jaṭā-makuṭas* and the ears with *kuṇḍalas*, and there should be a number of snake ornaments (*sarpālaṅkāra*). One of the hands should be held in the *abhaya* and another in the *varada* pose respectively. A representation such as this is rarely found portrayed in sculpture; one instance is found in Vaittīśvarankōyil (Tanjore District) made of brick in mortar. In this, one other peculiarity is also observable, namely the heads are arranged in tiers in arithmetical progression. The topmost tier has only one head, the next one below has three, the next five and so on till the last tier has nine heads. Only those heads which are on the borders of this triangle of heads could be adorned with *jaṭāmakuṭas* and they alone are actually ornamented with these in the sculpture. Surrounding the image are two flower garlands so put on as to represent a sort of *prabhāvaḷi*. Out of the large number of hands, one is held in the *abhaya* and another in the *varada* poses.

(ii) PAÑCHABRAHMĀS OR ĪŚANĀDAYAH.

The five aspects of Śiva known collectively as the Pañchabrahmās and whose individual names are Īśāna, Tatpurusha, Aghōra, Vāmadēva and Sadyōjāta are, as we have already said, emanations from the *nishkala*-Śiva (the formless, unmanifested Parabrahma of the Vēdāntins and Vāsudeva of the same state of existence according to the Vaishṇavāgamas).

The *Pādmapurāṇa* also states that Rudra when he cried to Brahmā to give him (Rudra) names, the latter conferred upon him the eight names Bhava, Śarva, Īśāna, Śiva, Paśupati, Bhīma, Ugra and Mahādēva. These eight aspects of Rudra became the presiding deities over the sun, the water, the fire, the earth, the air, the ether (*ākāśa*), the brāhmaṇas who had performed sacrifices and the moon respectively. The names of the consorts corresponding to these eight aspects of Śiva are Suvarchalā, Ushā, Vikēśi, Śivā, Svāhā, Diśā, Dīkshā and Rōhiṇī and those of their sons, Sanaiśchara, Śukra, Lōhitāṅga (Mars), Manōjava, Sarga, Śunda, Santāna and Budha.

The figures representing these five aspects are described in the *Āgamas*, the *Vishṇudharmōttara* and the *Rūpamaṇḍana*. The descriptions of these according to the *Āgamas* have already been given in the summary of the Śaiva philosophy added at the beginning of this chapter.

The *Vishṇudharmōttara* states that these aspects should have each five faces and ten arms: it omits describing one aspect, which is perhaps the Īśāna considered to be above all the other four. The colours of Tatpurusha, Aghōra, Vāmadēva and Sadyōjāta, according to this authority should be white, yellow, black and red respectively and they may also be considered to belong to the four *varṇas* (castes) namely, the Brāhmaṇa, the Kshatriya, the Vaiśya and the Sūdra. They should keep in their hands the *khaḍga*, *khēṭaka*, *dhanus*, *bāṇa*, *kamaṇḍalu*, *akshamālā*, *varada*, *abhaya*, *śūla* and *padma*.

Iśāna, according to the *Rūpamaṇḍana*, should have the colour as pure as that of the crystal; his head should be adorned with a *jaṭāmakuṭa* ornamented with the crescent moon and his hands should have the *akshamālā*, *triśūla*, *kapāla* and *abhaya*. The colour of the garment and the *yajñōpavīta* of Tatpurusha is to be yellow and in his left hand there is to be a *mātuḷuṅga* fruit and in the right one an *akshamālā*. The face of Aghōra should be of terrific look, set with three yellow coloured eyes and the mouth having side tusks; on the head there should be a garland of human skulls and a snake, and snake ornaments everywhere; two snakes serving as the ear-rings, two others as *kēyūras*, one as *hāra*, one as *yajñōpavīta*, one as *kaṭisūtra* (the waist-zone), the snakes Taksha and Pushṭika as anklets, and so on; there should also be a garland composed of scorpions (*vṛiśchika*). The colour of the body of Aghōra should be blue like the *nīlōtpala*, and that of the *jaṭās*, yellow, and these should be adorned with the crescent moon. The general look of this aspect of Śiva should resemble that of Kāla (the god of death) and appear as though terrifying a host of enemies. The left hands should bear in them the *khaṭvāṅga* the *kapāla*, the *khēṭaka* and the *pāśa* while the right ones, the *triśūla*, the *paraśu*, the *khaḍga* and the *daṇḍa*. The colour of the body, the eyes, garments, the head-gear, the *yajñōpavīta*, the garland, the sandal-paste and ear-ornament of Vāmadēva should be red. As usual, the crescent moon should be adorning the *jaṭāmakuṭa* of this deity also. He should have three eyes and a prominent nose, be decorated with all ornaments and carry in his hands the *khaḍga* and the *khēṭaka*. The colour of the body, garland, sandal-paste and the garments of Sadyōjāta should be white. His head should be adorned with a *jaṭamakuṭa*, ornamented with the crescent moon. He should have a good-looking face expressive of joy, three eyes and two arms: the two hands should be held in the *varada* and the *abhaya* poses.

The *Śrītatvanidhi* gives somewhat different descriptions of the Pañchabrahmās. For Īśāna there should be, according to this work, five faces, and four for each of the rest; each of these faces should have three eyes; the colour of Īśāna, Tatpurusha, Aghōra, Vāmadēva and Sadyōjāta, are respectively white, golden-yellow, blue, red and white. They ought to face the top, east, south, north and west respectively. Īśāna should have in his hands *abhaya*, *varada* (?) (*ishṭa* in the original), *aṅkuśa*, *pāśa*, *ṭaṅkā*, *kapāla*, *ḍhakka* (a musical instrument), *akshamāla* and *śūla*. In two out of the four hands of Tatpurusha there should be *kuṭhāra* (a sort of axe) and *vidyā* (*jñāna-mudrā* or a book) and the remaining two should be held in the *abhaya* and the *varada* poses; whereas there should be the *paraśu*, *vēda* (a book ?), *aṅkuśa*, *pāśa* *śūla*, *kapāla*, *ḍhakka* and *akshamālā* in the hands of Aghōra. Two of Vāmadēva's hands should be held in the *varada* and the *abhaya* poses and the two remaining ones should hold in them the *akshamālā* and the *ṭaṅka*; while similarly two of those of Sadyōjāta are to be held in the *varada* and *abhaya* poses and the two remaining ones keep the *vēdas* and the *akshamālā*. But Sadyōjāta is distinctly required to be sculptured so as to appear of greater importance than the rest.

(iii) MAHĒŚAMŪRTI.

Mahēśamūrti, we have been told by the Śaivāgamas, is the fully manifested Supreme Śiva and is the cause of creation, protection and destruction. The figure of this deity is described at some length in the *Suprabhēdāgama*. It is stated therein that Mahēśa should have five heads, the faces of four of which alone should be visible ; each of these faces should possess three eyes besides a mouth, a nose and a pair of ears and should be placed above a neck each. Mahēsa should have two legs and ten arms ; two of his hands are to be held in the *varada* and the *abhaya* poses, while the remaining four right ones should keep the *śūla*, *paraśu*, *vajra* and *khaḍga* ; and the remaining left ones the *khēṭaka*, *aṅkuśa*, *pāśa* and *ghaṇṭa*. The complexion of this aspect of Śiva should be crystal clear, having the lustre of the sun, but cool as the dew or the moon ; Mahēśa must be clothed in white garments and should wear a white *yajñōpavīta* and should be adorned with all ornaments.

By his side should be the figure of Śakti also. It should have three eyes, and four arms. On the head there should be a *karaṇḍa-makuṭa* and on the person all ornaments appropriate to women. The waist of the figure should be slender, and the pelvis broad; similarly there should be two well-developed high breasts on thē chest. Two of the hands should each hold a *nīlōtpala* and an *akshamālā*, while the other two should be kept in the *varada* and *abhaya* poses. The figure must be clothed in silk garments and must be standing on the same seat and under the same *prabhāvaḷi* as Mahēśa on his left side.

Four photographs are reproduced in illustration of the Mahēśa aspect of Śiva: the first, Pl. CXVI, is a beautiful figure of stone lying in a field opposite a ruined Śiva temple at Mēlchēri near Kāvērippākkam in the N. Arcot District. It has suffered damage at the hands of the Mussalmans during the troublous days of the contest for the succession to the Nabobship of the Karnatic. It has, as required, four faces, three of which are visible in the photograph. On the crown of the left face could be distinctly seen a big human skull and just below it is the hood of a cobra, whereas the middle head has a beautifully tied up *jāṭāmakuṭa* ornamented with jewelled discs, flower garlands and the inevitable crescent moon; at the base of this *makuṭa* may be noticed a row of five or six spherical

PLATE CXVI.

Mahēśamūrti : Stone : Kāvēripākkam.

[To face page 380]

objects which appear to be the skulls composing a garland. The third eye is very clearly marked on the forehead of the central face. There are as usual *hāras*, *udarabandha* and *yajñōpavīta*. Close to the neck is also a *hāra* composed of a snake. In the unbroken right hand is visible the *ḍamaru*; one other hand seems to have held a long sword whose upper part is visible on the crown, near the human skull; this latter itself appears to be the head of the *khaṭvāṅga* held by the image in one of its right hands; for, it might be noticed that there is a base attached to the skull; and this base is the capital of the handle of the *khaṭvāṅga*. (See fig. 10, Pl. II, Vol. I.) Perhaps one hand was held in the *abhaya* pose; it is impossible to say what the remaining two other hands might have held: in the unbroken left hands are to be seen the *pāśa*, the *khēṭaka*, a *kapāla* and something which resembles a fruit. One of the left hands should also have carried a long handled object—perhaps a *triśūla* or *paraśu* (?). There are also two legs as described in our authority. The image is seated in a comparatively rare posture. The right and the left faces are pacific, while the middle face is terrific. Its circular eyes, surmounted with a pair of knitted eye-brows, its wide mouth having side tusks—all these indicate, according to the rules of the *āgamas*, the terrific (*ugra*) aspect, which, in this instance, is that of the Aghōra face of the Mahēśa. This fine piece of sculpture belongs to the later Pallava period, perhaps to the reign of Nandivarman, son of Dantivarman (about A. D. eighth century).

The figure of Mahēśamūrti whose photograph is shown on Pl. CXIV as fig. 1 is found near the Gokak Falls in the Belgaum district. It is seated in the *yōgāsana* posture and has four faces (of which three are visible) and six arms. The front face is of the terrific aspect and the two side ones are pacific. The hands carry the *śūla*, *akshamālā*, *ḍamaru*, a fruit and some other objects not clear from the photograph.

The next illustration is the celebrated "Trimūrti" of the famous Elephanta Cave. (See Pl. CXVII.) I am of opinion that it is unmistakeably the representation of Mahēśamūrti and not of Trimūrti. My reasons therefor are:—

(1) There are no texts to be found in the whole of the *Āgamic* or the *Paurāṇic* literature which agree with this piece of sculpture.

(2) The three heads bear only *jaṭāmakuṭas* which are the characteristic head-gears of Śiva and Brahmā only. Vishṇu should, under no circumstances, wear a *jaṭāmakuṭa*, his appropriate

PLATE CXIV.

Fig. 1. Mahēśamūrti: Stone: Gokak Falls (Belgaum Dt.).

Fig. 2. Mahāsadāśivamūrti: Brick in Mortar: Vaithiśvarankōyil (Tanjore Dt.).

[To face page 382]

PLATE CXVII

Mahēśamūrti (wrongly called Trimūrti) : Stone : Elephanta.

[To face page 332]

head dress being a *kirīṭa-makuṭa*. Hence, even if it is supposed that two out of the three faces are those of Brahmā and Śiva, because they wear the *jaṭāmakuṭas*, the third cannot be identified with that of Vishṇu for the very reason that its head bears a *jaṭāmakuṭa*.

(3) Brahmā is nowhere as he is under no circumstances represented in sculpture or even in literature as possessing only one head. His figure should always be sculptured with four heads. So, the supposition that one of the heads is that of Brahmā is also clearly untenable.

(4) The descriptions of Trimūrti as found are very clearly different from these sculptured representations and have a number of material illustrations in corroboration of the description given of them in the *āgamas*. (See under Trimūrti or Ēkapādamurti below.)

(5) The central position occupied by this sculpture in the cave-temple with reference to the other manifestations of Śiva (the *līlāmūrtis*), such as those of Arddhanārīśvara, Kalyāṇasundara, Rāvaṇānugraha, Gaṅgādhara and other *mūrtis*, found surrounding him, bear incontrovertible evidence to the conclusion that the sculpture represents only the Mahēśa or the most important aspect of Śiva.

Now, the face on the left side has a severe look on its countenance, with cruel eyes, curling moustaches and a beard and a *jaṭāmakuṭa* serving as an abode for several snakes, which are seen wriggling through the *jaṭās*. The human skull ornament is also seen on the *jaṭāmakuṭa;* the ear belonging to this face has a *sarpa-kuṇḍala,* the hood of a cobra constituting it being visible. This is certainly the face that represents Aghōramūrti. The central face is calm and dignified. In the ears belonging to this face are to be seen *makara-kuṇḍalas.* This is perhaps the face representing Sadyōjāta. The face on the right side is also a calm and pacific one. In its ear there appears to have been a *śaṅkha-patra* which is broken, but a sufficient portion of it still remains for it to be recognized. The three different kinds of ear-ornaments are sufficient proof against the sculpture being that of Trimūrti. There are only six arms represented in the sculpture, that is, as many pairs as there are faces visible. One of the right hands carries a cobra which has its hood widened out, the hand holding it being also kept in the *sarpa-mudrā* pose; another hand appears to have been held in the *abhaya* pose or to have kept an *akshamālā,* but it is badly broken; the front left hand is seen keeping a *mātuḷuṅga.* It is not possible to say

Mahēśamūrti: Stone: Chitorgarh (Udaipur, Marwar).

[To face page 385]

what other objects are held in the other hands. Copies of this piece of sculpture are to be seen in one or two other caves at Ellora and other places. A personal study of more than one such sculpture will settle once for all the question of the identity of this image.

The next illustration comes from Chitorgarh, in the Udaipur State, Marwar (Pl. CXVIII). Though it is not a good specimen of art, it is very valuable in settling definitely the question of the nature of the image in favour of my hypothesis. In this also there are three faces, the one on the left and the central one being of a pacific and that on the right of a terrific type. The third eye is clearly visible in the centre of the forehead of all the three faces, a fact that gives the direct contradiction to the hypothesis that such figures are representations of the Trimūrtis, Brahmā, Vishṇu and Śiva. All three heads bear on them *jaṭāmakuṭas*, but that of the right head is composed of a large number of ringlets in which are seen snakes and a skull. The eyes of this face are oblique and staring and its mouth is gaping. This is surely the face of Aghōra. In this sculpture, one of the right hands is held in the *sarpa-mudrā* pose, another keeps something resembling a book (?) and the third an *akshamālā ;* whereas the left hands carry a *mātuḷuṅga*, a *kapāla* and a *sarpa*.

A comparison of this piece of sculpture with the magnificent carving at Elephanta gives the clue to the objects that should have been held by the now broken hands of the latter sculpture.

(iv) EKĀDAŚA RUDRAS.

We have already seen how Rudra was produced from the frown of Brahmā (or Vishṇu), and how he divided into eleven minor Rudras, who went by the collective name of the Ekādaśa-Rudras. The names of these eleven emanations of Rudra, according to the *Aṁśumadbhēdāgama*, are

1. Mahādēva,
2. Śiva,
3. Śaṅkara,
4. Nīlalōhita,
5. Īśāna,
6. Vijaya,
7. Bhīma,
8. Dēvadēva,
9. Bhavōdbhava,
10. Rudra, and
11. Kapālīśa.

The general characteristics of the images of these deities are first given in the authority quoted above and in the *Śilparatna*. It is stated in these works that the images of all these aspects of Śiva should have three eyes, four arms, *jaṭāmakuṭas* and be of white colour; they should be draped also in white clothes and be standing erect (*samabhaṅga*) on a *padmapīṭha.* They should be adorned with all ornaments and with garlands composed of all flowers and they should keep their front right hand in the *abhaya* and the front left hand in the *varada* poses, while they should carry in the back right hand the *paraśu* and in the back left hand the *mṛiga.*

The enumeration of the names of the Rudras are quite different in the *Viśvakarma-śilpa* and the *Rūpamaṇḍana.* In the former the names are given as

1. Aja,
2. Ēkapāda,
3. Ahirbudhnya,
4. Virūpāksha,
5. Rēvata,
6. Hara,
7. Bahurūpa,
8. Tryambaka,
9. Surēśvara,
10. Jayanta, and
11. Aparājita.

Whereas, the latter gives the following as the list of the names of these deities :—

1. Tatpurusha,
2. Aghōra,

3. Īśāna,
4. Vāmadēva,
5. Sadyōjāta,
6. Mrityunjaya.
7. Kiraṇāksha,
8. Śrīkaṇṭha,
9. Ahirbudhnya,
10. Virūpāksha,
11. Bahurūpa, and
12. Tryambaka.

The two works give the descriptions of the images of each of these eleven deities. According to the *Viśvakarma-śilpa*, Aja has sixteen arms. In the right hands he keeps the *śūla*, *aṅkuśa*, *kapāla*, *ḍamaru*, *sarpa*, *mudgara*, *akshamālā* and *sudarśana* (*chakra*) ; of the left hands, one is held in the *tarjanī* pose, while the others carry the *gadā*, *khaṭvāṅga*, *paṭṭiśa* (a sharp edged iron rod), *ghaṇṭa*, *śakti*, *paraśu* and *kamaṇḍalu*.

Ēkapāda keeps in his left hand the *khaṭvāṅga*, *bāṇa*, *chakra*, *ḍamaru*, *mudgara*, *varada*, *akshamālā*, and *śūla* ; while the right hands keep the *dhanus*, *ghaṇṭa*, *kapāla*, *kaumudi* (*ardha-chandra?*), *tarjanī*, *ghaṭa*, *paraśu* and *chakra* (śakti?). It is stated that the worship of this deity secures to the votary all material enjoyments.

Ahirbudhnya keeps in his right hands the *gadā*, *chakra*, *khaḍga*, *ḍamaru*, *mudgara*, *śūla*, *aṅkuśa* and *akshamālā ;* and in the left hands the *tōmara* (an iron club), *paṭṭiśa*, *kavacha* (shield), *kapāla*, *tarjanī*, *ghaṭa*, *śakti* and *paraśu* ; or, there may be in one of the left hands a sword as in the right hand.

Virūpāksha holds in his right hands the *khaḍga*, *śūla*, *damaru*, *aṅkuśa*, *sarpa*, *chakra*, *gadā* and *akshamālā* ; and in the left hands, the *khēṭaka*, *khaṭvāṅga*, *śakti*, *paraśu*, *tarjanī*, *ghaṭa*, *ghaṇṭa*, and *kapāla.*

Rēvata carries in the right hands the *dhanus*, *khaḍga*, *śūla*, *gadā*, *sarpa*, *chakra*, *aṅkuśa* and *akshamālā* ; and in the left hands the *dhanus* (?), *khēṭaka*, *khaṭvāṅga*, *ghaṇṭa*, *tarjanī*, *paraśu*, *paṭṭiśa* and *pātra*. This aspect of Rudra grants, like Sūrya, all the goods of the world to his worshippers.

Hara bears in his right hands the *mudgara*, *ḍamaru*, *śūla*, *aṅkuśa*, *gadā*, *sarpa* and *akshamālā*, (the object in the remaining hand is not mentioned); and in the left hands, *paṭṭiśa*, *tōmara*, *śakti*, *paraśu*, *tarjanī*, *ghaṭa*, *khaṭvāṅga* and *paṭṭikā* (?).

Bahurūpa keeps in the right hands the *ḍamaru*, *chakra*, *sarpa*, *śūla*, *aṅkuśa*, *kaumudi* and *akshamālā* (the eighth object is not mentioned) ;

and in the left hands the *ghaṇṭa*, *kapāla*, *khaṭvāṅga*, *tarjanī*, *kamaṇḍalu*, *dhanus*, *paraśu* and *paṭṭiśa*.

Tryambaka carries in his right hands the *chakra*, *ḍamaru*, *mudgara*, *bāṇa*, *śūla*, *aṅkuśa*, *sarpa* and *akshamālā*; and in the left ones, the *gadā*, *khaṭvāṅga*, *pātra*, *dhanus*, *tarjanī*, *ghaṭa*, *paraśu* and *paṭṭiśa*.

Surēśvara holds in his right hands the *ḍamaru*, *chakra*, *śūla*, *aṅkuśa*, *bāṇa*, *mudgara* and *dhanus* (the object in the eighth hand is not mentioned) and in the left hands the *padma*, *paraśu*, *ghaṇṭa*, *paṭṭiśa*, *tarjanī*, *dhanus*, *khaṭvāṅga* and *pātra*.

Jayanta keeps in his right hands the *aṅkuśa*, *chakra*, *mudgara*, *śūla*, *sarpa*, *ḍamaru*, *bāṇa* and *akshamālā*; and in the left ones the *gadā*, *khaṭvāṅga*, *paraśu*, *kapāla*, *śakti*, *tarjanī*, *dhanus* and *kamaṇḍalu*.

And Aparājita carries in his right hands the *tōmara*, *khaḍga*, *aṅkuśa*, *śula*, *sarpa*, *chakra*, *ḍamaru* and *akshamālā*; and in the left hands the *śakti*, *khēṭaka*, *gadā*, *pātra*, *tarjanī*, *paṭṭiśa*, *padma* and *ghaṇṭa*.

The objects mentioned as being held in the hands of the various deities are required to be held in the order in which they are mentioned, beginning from the topmost hand to the lowest.

MISCELLANEOUS ASPECTS OF ŚIVA.

Five of the eleven Rudras enumerated in the *Rūpāmaṇḍana* have already been described under the head Pañchabrahmās. Descriptions of the sixth, seventh and the eighth are also given in this work, but not of the remaining three others.

Mṛityuñjaya, the sixth Rudra, should wear a garland of skulls on his head, be of white complexion, clad in garments made of tiger's skin, and carrying in two out of three of his right hands the *triśūla* and the *akshamālā*, and of the left hands two should hold the *kapāla* and the *kamaṇḍalu* while the remaining right hand and the left hand should be kept in the *yōga-mudrā* pose.

Kiraṇāksha, the seventh Rudra, has four arms and three eyes. One of his hands is held in the *abhaya* pose, and the others carry the *śukla-pāda* (white light-rays?), an *akshamālā* and a book.

Śrīkaṇṭha should be clad in embroidered clothes (*chitravastra*), and ornamented with all ornaments including an *yajñōpavīta* of superior workmanship (*chitra-yajñōpavīta*) and must be very good looking. He has four arms and only one face. In his hands he should be carrying the *khaḍga*, the *dhanus*, the *bāṇa* and the *kheṭaka*.

As has already been stated above, the three remaining Rudras are not described.

(v) VIDYĒSVARAS.

Just as the weaver is the efficient cause (*nimittakāraṇa*), the Nishkalā-Śiva is the efficient cause of the universe composed of the moveable and immoveable objects. The immoveable objects consist of such things as the mountains, and the moveable, of things like *paśu* (here used in the technical sense of animals endowed with souls; man covered with ignorance). Souls have *sūkshma-śarīras* (subtle bodies) and *bhuvana śariras* (material regional bodies). The *bhuvanas* or regions are of two kinds, namely, the *suddha* (pure) and the *asuddha* (impure) *bhuvanas*. These *bhuvanas* and *kalās* and their residents are appended below in the foot note [1]. The *bhuvanas* or the regions have been created by Paramaśiva for the enjoyment of the *paśus* or embodied souls. The souls that live in the pure regions are pure in their nature and those that live in the impure regions are impure. The *paśus* are

(1) An abstract of the *kalā*, *tatva*, *bhuvana*, *varṇa*, *pada* and *mantra* of the Śaiva-śāstras which are interdependent upon each other are tabulated below for the information of those who are curious about this system of philosophy which has not yet obtained that amount of publicity which it deserves :—

divided into three classes: *viz.*, the *vijñānakalas*, the *praḷayākalas* and the *sakalas*. Those that are enveloped

Kalās.	Tatvas.	No. of Bhuvanas.	Names of the Bhuvanas.
	i. *Śuddha-tatvas.*		
(*a*) Śāntyātītakalā.	1. Śivatatva ...	10	Anāśrita, Anātha, Ananta, Vyōmarūpiṇī, Vyāpinī, Ūrdhvagāmanī, Mōchikā, Rōchikā, Dīpikā and Indhikā. (Five of these are Sākta-bhuvanas and the remaining five Nādōrdhva-bhuvanas.
	2. Śakti-tatva ...	5	Śāntyātītā, Śānti, Vidyā, Pratishṭā, and Nivṛitti. (These are called the Baindavapuras).
	Total ...	15	
(*b*) Śāntikalā.	3. Sadāśivatatva ...	1	Sadāśivabhuvana.
	4. Īśvaratatva ...	8	Śikhaṇḍi, Śrīkaṇṭha, Trimūrti, Ēkanētra, Śivōttama, Sūkshma and Ananta.
	5. Śuddhavidyā-tatva.	9	Manōnmanī, Sarvabhūtadamanī, Balapramathanī, Balavikaraṇī, Kalavikaraṇī, Kālī, Raudrī, Jyēshṭhā and Vāmā.
	Total ...	18	
	ii. *Śuddhāśuddha-tatvas.*		
(*c*) Vidyā-kalā.	6. Māyā ...	8	Angushṭhamātra, Īśāna, Ēkēkshaṇa, Ēkapiṅgala, Udbhava, Bhava, Vāmadēva and Mahādyuti.
	7. Kāla ...	2	Śikhēśa and Ēkavīra.
	8. Kalā ...	2	Pañchāntaka and Śūra.
	9. Vidyā ...	2	Piṅga and Jyōti.

by that kind of ignorance known as *mala* only are called the *vijñānakalas*; those with *mala* and *māyā*

Kalās.	Tatvas.	No. of Bhuvanas.	Names of the Bhuvanas.
(c) Vidyā-kalā.	10. Niyati ...	2	Saṁvarta and Krōdha.
	11. Rāga ...	5	Ēkaśiva, Ananta, Aja, Umāpati and Prachaṇḍa.
	12. Purusha ...	6	Ēkavīra, Īśāna, Bhava Īśa, Ugra, Bhīma and Vāma.
	Total ...	27	
	iii. *Aśuddhatatvas.*		
(d) Pratishṭhākalā.	13. Prakṛiti ...	8	Śrīkaṇṭha, Auma, Kaumāra, Vaishṇava, Brāhma, Bhairava, Kṛita and Akṛita.
	14. Buddhi ...	8	Brāhma, Prajēśa, Saumya, Aindra, Gandharva, Yaksha, Rākshasa and Piśācha.
	15. Ahaṅkāra ...	1	Sthalēśvara.
	16. Manas 17. Śrōtra 18. Tvak 19. Chakshus 20. Jihvā 21. Nāsi	1	Sthūlēśvara.
	22. Vāk 23. Pāṇi 24. Pāda 25. Pāyu 26. Upastha	1	Śaṅkukarṇa.
	27. Śabda 28. Sparśa 29. Rūpa 30. Rasa 31. Gandha	5	Kālañjara, Maṇḍalēśvara, Mākōṭa, Drāviṇḍa and Chhakalāṇḍa.

are called the *praḷayākalas* and those with all three kinds of ignorance, *mala*, *māyā* and *karma* are called

Kalās.	Tatvas.	No. of Bhuvanas.	Names of the Bhuvanas.
(*d*) Pratishṭhākalā.	32. Ākāśa ...	8	Sthānu, Svarṇāksha, Bhadrakarṇa, Gōkarṇa, Mahālaya, Avimukta, Rudrakōṭi and Vastra-Olpāda.
	33. Vāyu ...	8	Bhīmēśvara, Mahēndra, Aṭṭahāsa, Vimalēśa, Nala, Nākala, Kuruk-shētra and Gayā.
	34. Tējas ...	8	Bhairava, Kēdāra, Mahā-kāla, Madhyamēśa, Āmrātaka, Jalpēśa, Śrīśaila and Hariś-chandra.
	35. Jala ...	8	Lakuḷīśa, Pārabhūti Ḍiṇḍi, Muṇḍi, Vidhi, Pushkara, Naimiśa, Prabhāsa and Amarēśa.
	Total ...	56	
(*e*) Niv-ṛittikalā.	36. Pṛithvi ...	108	From Bhadrakālī to Kālāgni.(1)
	Grand Total ...	224	

(1) In the *Uttara-Kāmikāgama* the *bhuvanas* are enumerated as follows :—

कपालीशादयः प्राच्यामग्निरुद्रादयोऽनले ।
याम्याद्या दक्षिणे भागे निर्ऋत्याद्याश्च नैर्ऋते ॥
बलाद्या वारुणे भागे शीघ्राद्या वायुगोचरे ।
उत्तरे तु निधीशाद्या ईशे विद्याधिपादयः ॥
वृषादयस्त्वधोभागे शम्भुमुख्या नभोगताः ।
भुवनानां शतं चाष्टाधिकमेवं तु विन्यसेत् ॥

the *sakalas*. The *mala* envelope, if in the stage of leaving the person, is said to have undergone *paripakva*. The *vijñānakala* souls that have their *mala* in a high state of *paripakva* are those of the eight *Vidyeśvaras* and next to them come the *Mantrēśvaras*. Having been given pure body, deeds, *bhuvanas* and enjoyments (*śuddha tanu*, *karaṇa*, *bhuvana*, *bhōga*), these slowly get rid of their *mala*, by the destructive action of Śiva. These Vidyēśvaras are the beings through whom the lower order of beings should attain higher evolutionary stages. They are eight in number and

---

Besides Kalā, Tatva and Bhuvana, there are three more entities, namely, Varṇa, Pada and Mantra. All these six are dependent on one another; thus, *tatva* depends upon *kalā*, *bhuvana* on *tatva* and so on. It is said in the *Siddhānta-sārāvaḷi* that the *tatvas* from Pṛithvī (No. 36) to Māyā (No. 6) are called *Ātma-tatvas*; those from Śuddhavidyā (No. 5) to Sadāśivatatva (No. 3) are *Vidyātatvas* and the remaining, Śakti and Śiva *tatvas* are *Śiva-tatvas*. Analysing the above we get,

Mantras are in number			11
Padas	„	„	81
Varṇas	„	„	51
Bhuvanas	„	„	224
Tatvas	„	„	36 and
Kalās	„	„	5

have different colours. Their names and colours are given below in a tabular form.

No.	Name.	Colour.
1	Anantēśa	Blood-red.
2	Sūkshma	White.
3	Śivōttama	Blue.
4	Ēkanētra	Yellow.
5	Ēkarudra	Black.
6	Trimūrti	Crimson.
7	Śrīkaṇṭha	Another kind of red, and
8	Śikhaṇḍi.	Dark-brown.

Their figures should have each one face set with three eyes, adorned with a *jaṭāmakuṭa*, *yajñōpavīta* and all other ornaments. According to the *Pūrva-Kāraṇāgama* they should carry in their back hands the *śūla* and the *ṭaṅka* and keep their front ones in the *varada* and *abhaya* poses. But the *Vishṇudharmōttara* states that their front hands should be kept in the *añjali* pose, and the back ones should carry the *bāṇa* and the *triśūla*. Detailed descriptions of each of these Vidyēśvaras are found in the *Aṁśumadbhēdāgama*.

According to this authority, Ananta has a handsome, pacific appearance; a single face with three eyes in it; four arms; has the red colour of the shoe-flower; is adorned with a *karaṇḍa-makuṭa* and all other ornaments; he is to be standing upon a *padmapīṭha* and clothed in white garments. Two of his hands are held in the *varada* and *abhaya* poses and the other two keep in them the *śūla* and *ṭaṅka*.

Trimūrti (Ēkapāda), Ēkanētra and Ēkarudra are, (according to the *Aṁśumadbhēdāgama*), alike and their description is given under Ēkanētra below. A more elaborate description of Ēkapāda-Trimūrti and other forms of Trimūrtis is found in the *Uttara-Kāraṇāgama*. According to this Ēkapāda-Trimūrti should be standing erect (*samabhaṅga*) with only one leg upon a *padma-pīṭha*. This member of the class of Vidyēśvaras is also pacific. The colour of the deity is clear as the crystal and he has three eyes and four arms; the two front hands are held in the *varada* and the *abhaya* poses, while the two back hands keep the *ṭanka* and *śūla* or *mṛiga*. His ears may be adorned with either ordinary *kuṇḍalas* or those set with pearls and his head with a *jaṭā-makuṭa* and there should be all other ornaments in their appropriate places on the person of this deity.

From the right and left of this erect figure of Śiva should be seen emerging those of Brahmā and Vishṇu respectively. In sculpture they ought to be shown above the waist and must have each a leg kept bent and held up above the ground level. Brahmā, as usual, should have four faces and four arms. The two front hands should be shown as held in the *añjali* pose and the other two as carrying the *sruk* and the *kamaṇḍalu*. Similarly, Vishṇu should have four arms of which the front two are folded and held in the *añjali* pose and the back hands should hold the *śaṅkha* and the *chakra*. The head of Vishṇu should be adorned with the *kirīṭamakuṭa*. The whole of this composite piece of sculpture should be surrounded by a single *prabhāmaṇḍala*. It is stated in another *Āgama* (*Uttara-Kāmikāgama*) that the figures of Brahmā and Vishṇu should be sculptured according to the *tālamāna* (proportions) prescribed for female deities.

Another way in which Trimūrti may be represented is this: Brahmā and Vishṇu may be sculptured as issuing from either side of a large *liṅga*. Thirdly, they may be represented each one separately with all their characteristics and as standing side by side on three separate *padma-pīṭhas*.

Fourthly, there may be three shrines in a temple each separated from the other and in these there may be set up in the middle shrine a *linga* and in the right and left the shrines for Brahmā and Vishṇu respectively. Fifthly, in a temple consisting of three contiguous shrines (triforium) they may be set up as in the previous case. The central figure may be also Nṛitta or other forms of Śiva.

Illustrations are not wanting of the Ēkapāda-Trimūrti. In all important Śiva temples of S. India, we meet with this image in some place or other, at least carved upon pillars. An excellent specimen of it is found in the temple at Tiruvoṟṟiyūr, whose photograph has been reproduced in the Introduction to Vol. I of this work. (See Pl. F, fig. 1.) Fig. 1, Pl. XCIX, is another piece of sculpture which is found in the Śiva temple at Jambukēśvaram; this is almost identical with that of Tiruvoṟṟiyūr. In addition to the three *mūrtis*, Brahmā, Vishṇu and Śiva, we have in this instance the figures of a *haṁsa*, a bull and a Garuḍa, the vehicles respectively of Brahmā, Śiva and Vishṇu. There is also the figure of a *yōgi* standing on the right with a *jaṭābandha* on his head carrying in his left hand a *daṇḍa* and keeping his right hand in the attitude of praising the Trimūrti. For the third mode of representation of the Trimūrtis see Pls. LXII, fig. 1 and LXXIV of Vol. I. Temples containing separate shrines for Brahmā, Vishṇu and Śiva are found in many parts of the Travancore State; for example there is the Valiya-chālai temple at Trivandram and the temple at Tiruvallam. The triforium temples are common features of the Chālukya-Hoysaḷa style of architecture. As examples of this I may quote the splendid temple of Dakshiṇakēdārēśvara at Baḷigāmi, the temple at Sōmanāthapura and the Kēdārēśvara temple at Haḷebīḍu. All these temples have their ground plan resembling roughly the ace of the "clubs" of the playing cards, the three circular portions representing the three shrines and the tail the front *maṇḍapa*, which is common to all the three shrines. In these temples we generally see two *liṅgas* in two shrines and a figure of Vishṇu in the remaining third shrine. One of the *liṅgas* represents Brahmā and the other Śiva. (See Epigraphia Carnatika, Vol. V, of Hassan District, for the photograph of the Kēdārēśvara temple):

Sūkshma has a pacific appearance, is of blue complexion and has three eyes and four arms. He is clothed in garments embroidered with gold lace and adorned with all ornaments. The front hands of Sūkshma are held in the *varada* and *abhaya* poses, while the back hands carry the *ṭaṅka* and the *śūla*.

Śrīkaṇṭha has also four arms in two of which he carries the *śūla* and the *ṭaṅka* and holds the others in the *varada* and *abhaya* poses: he is standing upon a *padmapīṭha* and is draped in red garments.

Śivōttama is of white complexion, has four arms and two eyes, is adorned with a *karaṇḍa-makuṭa* and with other appropriate ornaments and is clothed in white garments. He bears on his chest a white *yajñōpavīta*. Keeping his front hands in the *varada* and *abhaya* poses, and carrying in his back hands the *śūla* and the *pāśa*, he stands erect (*samabhaṅga*) on a *padma-pīṭha*.

Śikhaṇḍi of dark complexion is a pacific deity having four arms; he is adorned with a *karaṇḍa-makuṭa* and all other ornaments and is draped in red clothes. His front hands are held in the *varada* and the *abhaya* poses, while the back ones keep in them the *khaḍga* and the *khēṭaka*.

Ēkanētra has three eyes and a pacific look and bears on his head a *jaṭāmakuṭa*. He is clothed in white silk garments and is adorned with all ornaments. Two of his hands are in the *varada* and the *abhaya* poses, while the two remaining ones are carrying the *śula* and the *ṭaṅka*.

Ēkarudra resembles in all respects Ēkanētra described above.

In conjunction with the Śaktis, Vāmā, Jyēshṭhā Raudrī, Kāḷī, Kalavikaraṇī, Balavikaraṇī, Balapramathanī and Sarvabhūtadamanī, the Vidyēśvaras are made by Paramaśiva to create the universe. It may be noted that all these eight aspects of Śiva pacific in their nature and are residents of the pure regions (Śuddhabhuvanas).

(vi). MŪRTYASHṬAKA.

The eight forms of Śiva which go by the names of Bhava, Śarva, Īśāna, Paśupati, Ugra, Rudra, Bhīma and Mahādēva are grouped under the collective name of the Mūrtyashṭaka. We have already seen how these names were received in succession by Śiva when he was first produced by Prajāpati and how the eight aspects represented by the names given above became the lords of the various *tatvas* such as fire, air, earth, etc. (See also Vol. I, pp. 398-400.)

We learn from the *Liṅga-purāṇa* that Śiva is to the universe what clay and the potter are to the pot, namely the *upādāna kāraṇa* (material cause) and the *nimitta kāraṇa* (instrumental or generative cause). Such a Being manifests himself in five different forms.

He who is the soul of the universe is called Īśāna. The illusory (*māyā*) material world is Tatpurusha; *Buddhi* with its eight components beginning from *dharma* is Aghōra; Vāmadēva pervades the whole of the universe in the form of *ahaṅkara* and the *manas-tatva* (mind) is Sadyōjāta.

The *Sūta-saṁhitā* also conveys the same notion about the nature of the five aspects of Śiva known as the Pañcha-brahmās; it states that the universe is pervaded by the Pañcha-brahmās and the man who is able to realise this attains liberation from bondage (*saṁsara*). Īśāna is the *ākāśa*, Tatpurusha air, Aghōra fire, Vāmadēva water, and Sadyōjāta earth. But Śrīkaṇṭhāśivāchārya views them somewhat differently; in his *Brahma-mīmāṁsa-bhāshya* he tells us that Sadāśiva is sound (*śabda*), *Īśvara* touch (*sparśa*), Rudra form (*rūpa*), Vishṇu taste (*rasa*) and Brahmā smell (*gandha*).

According to the *Liṅga-purāṇa*, *jñana*, *ichchhā* and *kṛiyā* are the three eyes of Paramēśvara. The desire to create that first arose in the mind of Paramēśvara is called the *Śiva-tatva*, which is also known as the *ichchhā-śakti-tatva.* When there are both the *jñāna-śakti* and the *kṛiyāśakti* blended in Paramēśvara he goes by the name of Sadāśiva when the former *śakti* is predominant and Mahēśvara when the latter *śakti* is predominant and Śuddha-vidyā when they are both equally balanced. When Īśvara absorbs in himself the universe he is known as the Purusha and Saṁsāri when he has manifested himself in the form of the gross material universe.

Thus, it is seen that the exact idea involved in viewing Mahēśvara as of five aspects is explained by each authority in its own way; however, the majority of them agree in taking the aspects as the manifestations of the Supreme deity in the elements of nature such as fire, air, earth, etc.

These eight deities are required to be represented in sculpture and set up in Śiva temples. The general description of these images is found in the *Vishṇudharmōttara* and the *Pūrva-Kāraṇāgama* : the *Aṁśumadbhēdāgama* gives the separate descriptions of a few of the *ashṭa-mūrtis.* In the first authority the eight *mūrtis* are said to resemble Śiva, wearing on their head *jaṭāmakuṭas* embellished with the crescent moon, adorned with appropriate ornaments and carrying in two of their hands the *khaṭvāṅga* and the *triśūla* and keeping the other hands in the *varada* and the *abhaya* poses. This description is amplified by the addition of a few more details by the *Pūrva-Kāraṇāgama*. It states that they should all have three eyes and be draped in red silk garments and that their colours are respectively white, black, red, *kṛishṇa* (a kind of blue, or slate colour), pale pink, dark-brown (as the colour of musk or *kastūrī*), coral red and deep blue.

According to the *Aṁśumadbhēdāgama*, Śarva should have the white colour of the *śaṅkha* or of the moon and be of a pacific appearance. On his head there should be the *jaṭāmakuṭa* in which is tied a crescent moon; the other parts of his body should be adorned with all the ornaments appropriate to them. In the back hands he should be carrying the *khaḍga* and the *khēṭaka* and his front hands should be in the *varada* and *abhaya* poses and he should be standing upon a *padmapīṭha*. Bhīma is the terrific aspect among the eight *mūrtis* of Śiva. His complexion is deep red; his appearance must be frightful and there should also be side tusks. He should be clothed in white garments, adorned with a *jaṭā-makuṭa*, and all other ornaments. His two hands must be carrying the *śūla* and the *pāśa* and the remaining two should be held in the *varada* and the *abhaya* poses. It is stated that Mahādēva should be shaped like Paśupati; Paśupati should be sculptured like Śarva and set up in a temple. And Bhava's description is exactly similar to that of Bhīma, excepting that Bhava is a pacific aspect, and consequently has a calm, peaceful look and is without the side tusks, the criterion and concomitant of the *ugra* or terrific aspects; the descriptions of the other deities belonging to this group are not found in my copy of the *Aṁśumadbhēdāgama*.

As far as it is known, there do not exist any sculptured representations of the groups, the Ēkādaśa-Rudras, the Vidyēśvaras or the Mūrtyashṭaka, at least in any one of the South Indian temples and I do not know if in Northern India these are found anywhere, either receiving *pūjā* or not.

(vii). LOCAL LEGENDS AND IMAGES BASED UPON STHALAMĀHĀTMYAS.

Besides the various aspects of Śiva described in this and the previous chapters, which are common to the whole of India and are recognized by the Purāṇas, Itihāsas, etc., there are very many images which are met with in different temples and which are associated with certain legends peculiar to each of these temples. For instance, at Jambukēśvara near Śrīraṅgam, an elephant and a spider are said to have worshipped Śiva in a grove of white *jambu* tree; we meet with sculptured representations of an elephant pouring with its trunk the water which it had brought from the river Kāvērī on the head of a *liṅga* and a spider weaving its web in a corner to protect the *liṅga* from the rays of the sun. The legend in connection with Ēkāmranāthasvāmin of Kāñchi is that the goddess Parvatī made a penance to Śiva standing on one leg, with hands uplifted on the head in the *añjali* pose; Śiva being pleased with her devotions appeared to her under an *āmra* (mango) tree. These pieces of sculpture peculiar to each place are the outcome of the *sthala-māhātmya* written generally at some later period of the history of the temple and is usually based upon some imaginary event that had occurred in it. The one *māhātmya* that has contributed very largely to the multiplication of images of Śiva is the *Hālāsya-māhātmya* or the one pertaining to the god Śiva at Madura, the capital of the Pāṇḍyas. The god Sundarēśvara (the name of the God Śiva enshrined in Madura) is said to have indulged in sixty-four *līlās* or sports, which are also narrated in later works such as *Śivalīlārṇava*. In all these *līlās*, Śiva assumed human and other forms for the purpose of succouring help to some one in need of

PLATE CXX.

Fig. 1. Pārvatī doing penance: Stone: Paṭṭīśvaram.

Fig. 2. Pārvatī embracing the linga.

[To face page 409]

it. For example, reference may be made to legends according to which he was once pleased to grant heaven to a pious crane; he taught the *Mṛityuñjaya-mantra* to a black-bird to protect itself and its species from the aggressions of stronger species; he once took pity upon a litter of motherless pigs and acted the part of their mother and eventually caused them to be re-born as the sons of a human being and bestowed upon them the office of the ministers of the Pāṇḍya king and so on. All these sports of Śiva at Madura are materialised into stone sculptures which are to be seen everywhere in the extensive temple not only of Madura but also in temples situated in many places adjoining Madura. Since the local legends are so many and the sculptures representing these are numberless, it is practically impossible to deal with them in a work dealing with images which are of universal acceptance.

Two illustrations are however added to give the reader a notion about the nature of such representations. The first, figs. 1 and 2, Pl. CXX, is one symbolising the legend connected with the Ēkāmranāthasvāmin temple at Conjeevaram. Pārvatī, according to this legend, was doing penance on the bed of the river Vēgavatī; she had set up a *liṅga* and was offering worship to it daily with intense piety. To disturb her penance with a view to test her mental firmness, god Śiva suddenly sent freshes in the river Vēgavatī so as to sweep away the *liṅga* and the other objects of worship set up by Pārvatī. When thus suddenly beset with difficulties, Parvatī, not knowing how to avert them, hugged the *liṅga* to her bosom, so that if it was swept out, she might also perish with it. Śiva, pleased with the firmness of devotion of Pārvatī, appeared to her in person under a mango tree (which stood singly, *ēkāmmra*) and was joined with his consort. In fig. 1, Pl. CXX, Pārvatī is seen doing penance and fig. 2 on the same plate shows her hugging passionately the *liṅga* symbol when it was threatened to be washed away in the flood.

The second illustration, fig. 2, Pl. CXIX, is of Śiva who took the form of a sow to suckle a number of the young ones of a pig which was killed in a hunt and which were dying for want of succour. Here, Śiva is represented with the usual four arms in two of which he is seen carrying the *paraśu* and the *mriga*, while with two others he is seen hugging a number of little pigs, which are drinking lustily the milk from the teats of their foster-mother, while some are squeaking and rolling down on the earth

PLATE CXIX.

Fig. 1. Ēkapādamūrti : Stone : Jambukēśvara (Śrīraṅgam island).

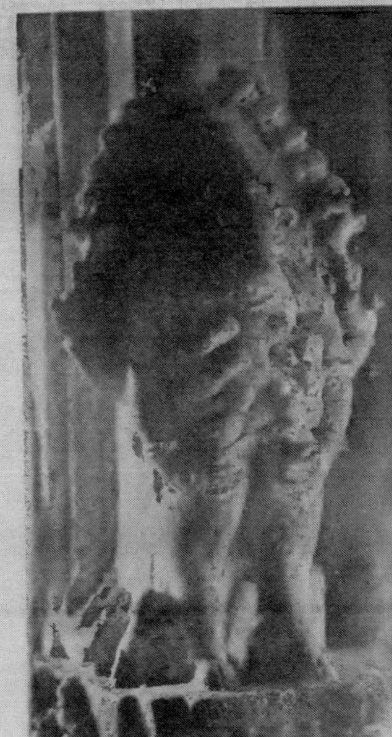

Fig. 2. Śiva as a sow suckling its young ones : Stone : Tirupparaṉkuṉṟam.

[To face page 410]

for drawing the attention of the foster-parent to their hungry condition. The photograph reproduced here is that of a piece of sculpture to be found in the Śiva temple at Tirupparaṇkuṉṟam near Madura.

SUBRAHMANYA.

SUBRAHMANYA.

SUBRAHMANYA is almost exclusively a South Indian deity. There is not a village, however small, which does not possess a shrine for Subrahmaṇya. In fact the popularity of this deity with the South Indian is so great as to induce him to build shrines for him in all places such as towns, villages, gardens, mountain tops and other odd places. Strangely enough Subrahmaṇya is less known and less worshipped in Northern India; there are not many temples of this god in Northern India. In Bengal it is stated that he is worshipped by disreputable women on certain occasions, while in the Bombay Presidency no *sumaṅgali* (a woman whose husband is alive) would visit the temple of Kārttikēyasvāmin (Subrahmaṇya).

The birth of Kārttikēya or Subrahmaṇya is given at some length in the Bālakāṇḍa of the *Rāmāyaṇa*. Śiva, after he was married to Umā, began to indulge in gratifying his love towards her; a thousand years of the gods passed thus but no issue was born. The gods in the meanwhile becoming alarmed that the offspring which might be born to Mahādēva would be of an extraordinary character, entreated him to practise austerity. Śiva acceded to their prayer but inquired what would become of the seed which he had already discharged. The gods replied that this should be received by the earth and Agni and Vāyu should enter it. Agni accordingly entered it and produced a white mountain, where Kārttikēya was born. Out of gratitude, the gods worshipped Śiva; the consort of Śiva cursed the gods that their wives should become barren, because she was denied the pleasure of becoming a mother.

In another place in the same work the birth of Kārttikēya is described differently. While Śiva, the lord of the gods, was performing penance, the other gods went to Brahmā and asked him to provide them with a general in the place of Śiva, their former commander, who had since taken to austerities. To this Brahmā replied that in consequence of the curse of Umā no sons could be born to the gods; but he suggested that Agni could beget a son on Gaṅgā and that the offspring might become the general of the gods. In obedience to the advice of Brahmā, the gods went to the mount Kailāsa and appointed Agni to carry out their wish. Agni accordingly consorted with Gaṅgā and begot Kārttikēya.

The Vana-parvan of the *Mahābhārata* has another account of the birth of Kārttikēya. Indra, whose army (*dēvasēna*) was defeated by the *dānavas*, was meditating upon his reverses, when he heard the cry of a female calling for help and invoking a husband to afford her protection. Indra seeing that she had been seized by the demon Kēśin remonstrated with him. But the *asura* did not heed it but hurled his club against Indra. Indra cut it off with his *vajra* and Kēśin was finally defeated and driven away. Indra then learnt from the woman he had rescued that she was called Dēvasēna (the army of the gods) and that she had a sister named Daityasēna (the army of the demons) and that they both were the daughters of Prajāpati. She added that her sister liked Kēśin, but she herself did not; therefore she requested Indra to secure for her a proper husband who would be able to overcome all the enemies of the gods. Indra took Dēvasēna to Brahmā and desired him to provide her with a valorous husband; Brahmā promised that the help-mate of Dēvasēna would soon be born, under the circumstances described below.

Vasishṭha and other *ṛishis* performed an *yājña* to which the gods headed by Indra went to receive oblations. Agni, being invoked, descended from the sun, entered the fire, received oblations of the *ṛishis* and presented them to the gods. Then he beheld the wives of the *ṛishis* and became perturbed by desires. His heart felt distressed because he failed to obtain the wives of these brāhmaṇas; he therefore resolved to abandon his corporeal form and went away to the forest. Meanwhile, Svāhā, the daughter of Daksha, who was loving Agni from her youth, discovering the cause of Agni's discomfiture resolved to take the forms of the wives of the *ṛishis* and to present herself to Agni. Assuming first the form of Śivā, the wife of Āṅgirasa, Svāhā addressed Agni thus: "Agni, you ought to love me, who am troubled with love for you. I am the wife of the *ṛishi* Āṅgirasa. If you will not do so, look upon me as dead". Agni embraced her with joy and delighted her. Assuming the form of a Gāruḍi bird to avoid detection, Svāhā issued from the forest and beholding a white mountain surrounded by palisades of arrows, guarded by seven-hooded snakes and rākshasas and others, went quickly to its summit which was difficult of access and threw the seed into a golden receptacle. Thus did this goddess enjoy the company of Agni by assuming successively the forms of the wives of the *ṛishis*. But she could not take the divine form of Arundhati, the wife of Vasishṭha, owing to the power of the latter's austerity and her obedience to her husband. Six times was the seed of Agni thrown by the enamoured Svāhā into the receptacle from the *pratipada* day (the first day of a fortnight). The collected seed which was discharged (*skanna*) by Agni generated a son and gave to the child the character of Skanda. Kumāra was born with six heads, twelve arms, ears, eyes and feet, one neck and one belly. He was made the commander of the army of the gods and Dēvasēna was married to him.

The wives of the six *ṛishis* who were discarded on suspicion by their husbands repaired to Skanda and complained to him that they were unjustly abandoned by their husbands and consequently became degraded from their former position and entreated him to secure for them heaven (*svarga*). Skanda granted them their desire and kept them with him. Svāhā then approached Skanda and informed him that she was his genuine mother and then told him that from her childhood she loved Agni but that her love was unrequited by him and desired that she should somehow be made to live perpetually with Agni. Skanda conferred this boon upon her saying that whatever oblations of brāhmaṇas was introduced by hymns, they should always lift it and throw it in the fire saying 'Svāhā' and that Agni should dwell continually with her.

Then Prajāpati asked Skanda to go to Mahādēva, the vexer of Tripura. Addressing Skanda as the unconquered, Prajāpati informed him that he had been produced for the good of the gods and of all the world by Rudra who had entered Agni and Umā who had entered into Svāhā. Skanda was received with due honour by the bull-bannered Rudra with his consort Umā.

It is stated about Skanda that because he was honoured by Rudra he was the son of Rudra. Again the brāhmaṇas call Agni Rudra; consequently Kārttikēya is the son of Rudra; the seed which was discharged by Rudra became a white mountain and this seed of Agni was formed by the Kṛittikās on the white mountain. Skanda, that most eminent deity, being born of Agni, who was Rudra and from Svāhā and the six wives of the *ṛishis* was the son of Rudra. Thus then it will be seen a sort of confusion arose about the real parentage of Skanda and attempts are made to establish the identity of Agni with Rudra. This identity is based upon the Vēdic assertions that Agni is the same as Rudra.

Almost the same account is given in all the later works such as the *Kumārasambhava*, etc.

The *āgamas* state that the temple for Subrahmaṇya may be constructed on all sides of a town except the east and it might face any direction. These temples may be built in capital cities, in towns, villages, on the tops of mountains, on the banks of rivers, in gardens, forests or under large trees. They may stand separately as a *svayampradhāna* temple or be attached to some others, such as that of Śiva. Different kinds of central shrines are prescribed for the temple of Subrahmaṇya; these may contain from one to seven *talas* (storeys) and may be surrounded by *prākāras* or circuits and adorned with *maṇḍapas* or pavilions, and other adjuncts. As usual the size of the shrine of this god is also determined with reference to the height of the image to be set up in it. The temples of Subrahmaṇya are to be adorned with either peacocks or elephants placed in the corners of the *vimāna*, where generally Garuḍa or Nandi is seen in the temple of Vishṇu or Śiva respectively.

In a *svayampradhāna* temple of Subrahmaṇya there are required to be set up eight *parivāradēvatas*, namely, Yakshēndra, Rākshasēndra, Piśāchēndra, Bhūtarāṭ, Gandharva, Kinnara, Daityanāyaka and Dānavādhipa. The figures of these are to be placed on the eight cardinal points of the *prākāra*; Yakshēndra being on the east, Rākshasēndra on the south-east and so on. These Parivāra-dēvatās are to be sculptured as having two or four arms and they should be of dark complexion and terrific look. If they have four arms, two of the hands are to be held in the *varada* and the *abhaya* poses, while the remaining two should carry the *khaḍga* and the *khēṭaka*. But if they have only two arms, the hands should keep the *khaḍga* and the *khēṭaka*.

Besides the *parivāra-dēvatās* mentioned above, the temple of Subrahmaṇya is required to have eight *śarīra-pālakās* or body-guards. They are named Shaṇmukha, Śaktipāṇi, Kārttikēya, Guha, Skanda, Mayūravāhana, Sēnāni and Śaktihastavān. They are also, like the *parivāra-dēvatās*, required to be represented with four or two arms; if they have four arms, two hands out of the four should be held on the chest in the *añjali* pose and the remaining two are to keep in them the *vajra* and the *padma*. The *śarīra-pālakās* may have one or six faces and must be located on the eight cardinal points beginning from the east as in the case of the *parivāra-dēvatās*, but perhaps in a second *āvaraṇa*. If they cannot be represented regularly by sculptured figures, at least *pīṭhas* representing them must be set up, with a peacock or an elephant kept in front of them.

The *Kumāra-tantra* mentions a much larger number of *parivāra-dēvatās*; eight, twelve, sixteen or thirty-two *dēvatas* are prescribed in it. If eight *devatas* are to be set up, we are told that on the east, facing the deity, should be the figure of an elephant that on the south-east, Śāsta; in the south, Brahmā; on the south-west, the Sapta-mātṛikās; on the west, Jyēshṭhā; on the north-west Durgā; on the north, Kshētrapa and on the north-east, Sumitraka. The names of the *parivāra-dēvatas* * of the groups of twelve, etc., are given in the foot-note below.

---

* The names of the twelve *parivāra-dēvatās* are, the elephant, Sūrya, Śāsta, Brahmā, Yama, Sapta-mātṛikās, Varuṇa, Agastya, Durgā, Nārada, Śrīśa and Sumitra. The following are the names of the sixteen *parivāra-dēvatās* :—the elephant, Brahmā, Agastya, Nārada, Sumitraka, Śukra, Bṛihaspati, Durgā, Ditī, Aditī, Chandra, Sūrya, Śāsta, Mahālakshmī and Bhāratī and the Sapta-mātṛikās.

To make up the thirty-three *parivāra-dēvatas*, the following are added to the above mentioned sixteen deities, namely, the Ashṭa-dikpālakas, Sudēha, Surēśa, Sumukha, Bhṛiṅgi, Vásuki, Ashṭavara (vakra ?) Bhṛiṅgi (Bhṛigu ?) Daksha-Prajāpati, Vīrabhadra, Śukra,, Bhū, Jyēshṭha and two others.

In the north-east corner of the temple of Subrahmaṇya should be set up either the image of Skanda-Chaṇḍa or the famous Sākalya-pīṭha. Skanda-Chaṇḍa might have four or two arms; in the first case, the two front hands are to be held in the *abhaya* and the *varada* poses respectively, while the back ones should carry the *vajrāyudha* and a lotus flower.

The image of Subrahmaṇya is seen sculptured in different ways. We have instances of standing and seated figures of this deity; some have six faces while others only one; some have two arms while others have from four to twelve arms; sometimes the image of Subrahmaṇya is seen with that of one Śakti (goddess) and often with two. He is further represented as a boy who has not undergone the *upanayana* (or the initiation) ceremony or as one who has undergone it. Then again he appears as a youth of resplendent beauty. The seated figure is either on a *padmāsana* or on a peacock. It is laid down as a rule that if the figure is a seated one, it should have only two arms; if a standing one, four; and lastly, if it is seated upon a peacock, it may have six, eight or twelve arms. The sitting posture is recommended for representing the *yōga* (*dhruva*) *bēra*, the standing posture for the *bhōga* (*utsava*) *bēras* and the figure seated on vehicles for *dhyāna bēras* (images meant for fixing one's thoughts upon and meditating). The image with two arms is said to be *sātvik*, one with four arms *rājasik* and one with more arms than four *tāmasik* in nature.

Subrahmaṇya with two arms may be sculptured in any one of the five following manners:—

(i) in the first mode the image might keep in the right hand a *padma* and the left hand may be resting upon the hip (*kaṭyavalambita*);

(ii) in the second mode the right hand may be held in the *abhaya* pose and the left in the *kaṭyavalambita* pose;

(iii) in the third mode the right hand may carry a *daṇḍa* and the left hand may be in the *kaṭyavalambita* pose;

(iv) in the fourth mode the right hand may carry the *śaktyāyudha* and the left the *vajra*, and

(v) in the fifth mode the right hand may carry a *śaktyāyudha* and the left a *kukkuṭa* (a fowl).

In the case of the figure of Subrahmaṇya with four arms the hands are required to be kept in any one of the seven poses and to carry articles as given in the following table :—

No.	Right Hands.		Left Hands.	
	I.	II.	I.	II.
a.	Abhaya ...	Śakti ...	Varada ...	Vajra.
b.	Abhaya ...	Akshamālā...	Varada ...	Kamaṇḍalu.
c.	Abhaya ...	Akshamālā...	Kaṭyavalambita	Kamaṇḍalu.
d.	Abhaya ...	Śakti ...	Kaṭyavalambita	Kukkuṭa.
e.	Abhaya ...	Śakti ...	Akshamālā ...	Kukkuṭa.
f.	Abhaya ...	Śakti ...	Kaṭyavalambita	Kamaṇḍalu.
g.	Khaḍga ...	Śakti ...	Kheṭaka ...	Kukkuṭa.

Subrahmaṇya with two or four arms is said to be capable of giving *siddhi* to his worshippers.

The figure of Subrahmaṇya with six arms should have in its right hands *abhaya*, *khaḍga* and *śakti*; and in the left hands *khēṭaka*, *akshamālā* and *kukkuṭa*. The image of Subrahmaṇya with eight arms should be represented as carrying in its hands the *vajra*, *śakti*, *abhaya*, *varada*, *khaḍga*, *khēṭaka*, *bāṇa* and *dhanus*; or, they may keep the *padma*, *vajra*, *śakti*, *abhaya*, *varada*, *khaḍga*, *khēṭaka* and *pāśa*.

Subrahmaṇya with twelve arms may be sculptured in six different ways; the following table furnishes the information regarding the poses of the hands and the objects carried in them :—

No.	I.	II.	III.	IV.	V.	VI.
a.	Śakti ...	Bāṇa ...	Khaḍga ...	Dhvaja ...	Gadā ...	Abhaya.
b.	Do. ...	Do. ...	Do. ...	Chakra ...	Pāśa ...	Prasāritahasta.
c.	Do. ...	Dhvaja ...	Do. ...	Do. ...	Do. ...	Abhaya.
d.	Do. ...	Do. ...	Do. ...	Padma ...	Abhaya ...	Bāṇa.
e.	Do. ...	Vajra ...	Chakra ...	Pāśa ...	Aṅkuśa ...	Gadā.
f.	Do. ...	Bāṇa ...	Khaḍga ...	Abhaya ...	Dhanus ...	Khēṭaka.

No.	VII.	VIII.	IX.	X.	XI.	XII.
a.	Vajra ...	Dhanus ...	Khēṭaka ...	Padma ...	Śūla ...	Varada.
b.	? ...	Śaṅkha ...	Kukkuṭa ...	Dhanus ...	Daṇḍa ...	Hala.
c.	Vajra ...	Dhanus ...	Khēṭaka ...	Kukkuṭa ...	Aṅkuśa ...	Varada.
d.	Do ...	Pāśa ...	Do. ...	Daṇḍa ...	Do. ...	Do.
e.	Śūla. ...	Abhaya ...	Padma ...	Do. ...	Do. ...	Do.
f.	Do. ...	Kukkuṭa ...	Chakra ...	Pāśa ...	? ...	Do.

The *āgamas* mentioned the appropriate forms of the image of Subrahmaṇya that should be set up in temples erected for that deity in towns of different kinds * the image that must grace a temple

* According to the *Kāmikāgama* towns are divided into the following classes according to its residents, etc.:—

The village resided in by learned brāhmaṇas is called a *maṅgala* or an *agrahāra*. The place which has a mixed population of brāhmaṇas and other castes is said to be *grāma*. The place where a rich landlord lives with only his tenants and dependants is called a *kuṭika* or an *ēkabhōga*; (*kuṭika* is a Tamil word, *kuḍi*, rendered thus in Sanskrit). That portion of a *pura* (town) which is inhabited by brāhmaṇas and surrounded by their gardens is called a *kharvaṭa*. A place full of trading population of all classes and is visited by maritime people of other nations and is situated on the sea-coast is called a *paṭṭaṇa*. The suburb in a *vana* (forest) or *rājya* solely inhabited by Śūdras is called either a *kaṇṭaka*, *khēṭaka* or *grāma*. The capital of a subordinate chief is called a *śibira* and the town where the elephants and horses of the king are stationed is a *sēnasthāna* and that where the king lives and has a large population of all classes, and is provided with many secret passages is called a *sēnāmukha*. That portion of a town where travellers and *sannyāsins* are fed and lodged is called a *maṭha*. The town where large military forces are stationed is a *vidyāsthāna*; if the latter has in it the palace of the king also, it goes by the name of *rājadhāni*. Those places which adjoin *grāmas*, etc., are known by the names of *kubja* (Tam. *kuppam*) and *chērika* (Tam. *chēri*). The quarters occupied by weavers in a *grāma*, etc., is a *nagari*.

constructed for this deity in the *rājadhāni* (the capital city) of a reigning sovereign is to be one with six faces, six arms, twelve eyes and twelve or six ears. It should keep in its hands the *śakti*, *khaḍga*, *akshamālā*, *abhaya*, *kukkuṭa* and *khēṭaka*. The image that should be set up in a *grāma* or a *prāsāda* (palace) should have twelve arms; the right hands of this image should carry the *śakti*, *musala*, *khaḍga*, *chakra*, *pāśa* and *abhaya*; and the left hands, the *vajra*, *dhanus*, *khēṭaka*, *śikhi-dhvaja* (a banner made of peacock feathers), *aṅkuśa* and *varada*. (See Pl. CXXVIII.) This figure should be of the colour of the rising sun and be draped in red clothes and be adorned with a *karaṇḍa-makuṭa*, and the *yajñōpavīta* and be seated on a peacock with, on either side, a figure of a *dēvī*. Though different types of images of Subrahmaṇya are prescribed for consecration in different kinds of villages there is no positive objection to any of the five types of the image of this deity, namely, those with two, four, six, eight or twelve arms, being set up in any kind of town.

Subrahmaṇya is known by several names, the chief among them are Kārttikēya, Shaṇmukha, or Shaḍānana, Śaravaṇabhava or Sarajanman, Sēnāni, Tārakajit, Krauñchabhēttā, Gaṅgāputra, Guha, Agnibhū, Skanda and Svāminātha. Most of his epithets have reference to the circumstances of his birth. Śiva cast his seed into Agni who being unable to bear it cast it into the river Ganges; hence Skanda is called Agnibhū and Gaṅgāputra. The seed was then transferred to the six Kṛittikas when they went to bathe in the Ganges, each of whom therefore conceived and begot a son; all these children afterwards became combined in one being having six heads and twelve arms and eyes. Hence he became known by the names of Kārttikēya, Shaṇmukha and Shaḍānana. According to another account the seed of Śiva was cast by the river Ganges into a thicket of reeds (*śara*) and the boy who came out of the thicket of grass came to be known as the Śarajanman. Subrahmaṇya pierced the Krauñcha mountain and hence he was called Krauñchabhētta. He commanded the army of the *dēvas* against the *asura* Tāraka whom he vanquished and killed. Therefore he got the names Dēvasēnāpati and Tārakāri. He is called Guha because he lived in a receptacle for six days before he was fully formed. Because he was born from the discharged seed (*skanna*) of Śiva he was known as Skanda.

The most characteristic weapon of Subrahmaṇya is the *śakti*; the *Mārkaṇḍeya-purāṇa* gives a short account of the origin of this weapon thus: Sūrya (the sun) was once so powerful that his heat was causing damage to the world. Viśvakarman, the celestial mechanic, contrived to abstract a portion of the solar glory and rendered him innocuous. 'From the power taken away from Sūrya, Viśvakarman fashioned' the *śaktyāyudha* for the use of Subrahmaṇya. It is worth noting that a portion of the solar glory was transferred to Subrahmaṇya, who, according to the *Bhavishyat-purāṇa*, took his seat near Sūrya when the *daityas* attacked him and when the gods rallied round him for his support. The same *purāṇa* informs us that the *dvārapālakas* of Subrahmaṇya are Sūrya under the name of Rājña and Śiva under the name of Srausha. These facts coupled with the information regarding the origin of Subrahmaṇya distinctly point to its origin to the sun-myth. We saw in the first instance that Agni was invoked by the *ṛishis* for receiving the oblations in their *yajña* and that he descended from the sun; the *Mahābhārata* states that on the day the *ṛishis* began their *yajña* the sun and the moon were together, that is, the day was a new-moon day; beginning from the *pratipada* day the seed of Agni was gathered for six days and on the *shashṭhi tithi* Subrahmaṇya of the colour of the rising sun came into existence. His *dvārapālakas*, we saw above, are Sūrya and Śiva (who is the same as Agni or Rudra).

A *dhyāna-ślōka* current in some parts of S. India actually describes him as Sūrya. All these facts clearly point to the sun-myth as the origin of Subrahmaṇya; his six heads perhaps represent the six *ṛitus* or seasons, the twelve arms, the twelve months; the *kukkuṭa* or the fowl the harbinger of the rising sun and the peacock whose feathers display a marvellous blending of all colours represents the luminous glory of the sun; the *śaktyāyudha* is also of solar origin.

Corresponding to the various names of Subrahmaṇya are images whose descriptions are found in almost all the *āgamas*. The following are some of the important aspects of Subrahmaṇya dealt with in the *Kumāra-tantra*, *viz.*,

i. Śaktidhara,	ix. Shaṇmukha,
ii. Skanda,	x. Tārakāri,
iii. Sēnāpati,	xi. Sēnāni,
iv. Subrahmaṇya,	xii. Brahma-śāsta,
v. Gajavāhana,	xiii. Vaḷḷi-kalyāṇa-sundaramūrti,
vi. Śaravaṇabhava,	xiv. Bālasvāmi,
vii. Kārttikēya,	xv. Krauñchabhētta and
viii. Kumāra,	xvi. Śikhivāhana.

To this list are added a few more by the *Śrītattvanidhi*; the descriptions of these are given briefly below.

Śaktidhara : This aspect of Subrahmaṇya should have a single face and only two arms. The left hand should bear a *vajra* and the right one the *śakti;* the latter weapon is said to represent the *ichchhā*, *jñāna* and *kṛiyā śaktis*. The following description of Jñānaśakti-Subrahmaṇya is found in the *Śrītatvanidhi*: this form of the deity should have only one face and four arms and his head adorned with a *jaṭāmakuṭa* ornamented with rubies, he should wear a garland of cactus flowers, and his body should be smeared with a paste of sandal and there must be on his chest a white *yajñōpavīta*. In three out of the four hands there should be the *śakti*, *kukkuṭa* and *vajra* and the fourth hand should be held in the *abhaya* pose. It is therein stated that this aspect of Subrahmaṇya is the embodiment of *jñāna-śakti*.

Skanda : According to the *Kumāra-tantra* this aspect should be represented with one face and two arms and should be of the colour of the lotus. The loins are to be bound by a broad belt and the only clothing which this figure should possess is the *kaupīna*. The right hand should keep a *daṇḍa* while the left one should rest upon the hip (*kaṭyavalambita*). This aspect of Subrahmaṇya is popularly known as the Paḷaniyāṇḍavar. This is the description which is given in the *Śrītatvanidhi* for Vēlāyudha-Subrahmaṇya. This latter work, however, gives quite a different description of Skanda which is as follows. This aspect of Subrahmaṇya is required to possess, as in the previous one, one face set with two eyes, and four arms. He should be seated upon a lotus flower (*padmāsana*). His head is to be surrounded by a *prabhā-maṇḍala;* on the head there should be the usual *karaṇḍa-makuṭa* adorned with a wreath of flowers; there must also be ornaments made of rubies and on the waist a broad girdle of fine workmanship. The front two hands should be kept in the *varada* and the *abhaya* poses while the back hands should carry the *kukkuṭa* and the *vajra.* The colour of this aspect of the deity is said to be that of smoke.

Sēnāpati: This aspect should have the brilliance of the sun and should possess six faces and twelve eyes. One of the arms of Sēnāpati should pass round the waist of his *dēvī,* who should be seated upon his left lap; the corresponding right hand should keep a lotus. The other hands should hold the following objects in them: *śūla, khēṭaka, vajra, dhanus, gadā, ghaṇṭā, kukkuṭa* and *abhaya.*

Under the name Dēvasēnāpati, the *Śrītatvanidhi* gives the following description: He should have one face, two eyes and four arms : two of the hands should be held in the *abhaya* and *varada* poses respectively and the remaining two should carry the *śaṅkha* and the *chakra ;* the colour of this aspect of Subrahmaṇya is said to be black. He should be adorned with all ornaments, and should have a white *yajñōpavīta* and his body should have a coating of finely smelling sandal paste. The face must be very pretty and a smile must be playing about his lips.

Subrahmaṇya : This aspect of Skanda should be of the colour of *kuṅkuma* (saffron) and be adorned with *kēyūra*, *hāra* and other ornaments. One of the right hands should be held in the *abhaya* and in the rest must be the *śakti*, *kukkuṭa*, and a *padma*. The colour of this aspect of the deity should be that of the rising sun and that of the sandal paste and the clothing red. Or, the figure may have only two arms of which one should rest upon the hip (*kaṭyavalambita*) and the other hand be held in the *abhaya* pose.

Gajavāhana has also only one face, two eyes and four arms ; in one of the left hands he should hold the *kukkuṭa* while the other should be kept in the *varada* pose ; in one of the right hands there should be the *śakti* and the other should be held in the *abhaya* pose.

Śaravaṇabhava should have six heads, twelve eyes and twelve arms. Two of his hands are to be in the *abhaya* and the *varada* poses while the remaining ones should carry in them the *śakti*, *ghaṇṭa*, *dhvaja*, *padma*, *kukkuṭa*, *pāśa*, *daṇḍa*, *ṭaṅka*, *bāṇa* and *dhanus*. The complexion of this aspect is yellow; the face should resemble a full-blown lotus.

The *Srītatvanidhi*, as usual, gives an entirely different description of Śaravaṇabhava. According to this authority Śaravaṇabhava should have only one face, three eyes and six arms, be of the colour of the rising sun and be seated upon a lion. The body should be covered with ashes (*bhasma* or *vibhūti*). There should be in the hands flowery arrows, a bow made of sugar-cane, *khaḍga*, *khēṭaka*, *vajra* and the *kukkuṭa*.

Kārttikēya should have six faces and six arms and be of the colour of the rising sun. Two of his front hands should be kept in the *abhaya* and the *varada* poses, while the rest should carry *vajra*, *khēṭaka*, *śakti* and *khaḍga*.

According to the *Śrītatvanidhi* Kārttikēya should have one face with three eyes, ten arms and the complexion of the rising sun. There should be a fruit (or leaf) of the *bilvā* tree on the head and in the right hands the *śūla*, the *chakra*, the *aṅkuśa*, and *abhaya*; in the left hands the *tōmara*, the *pāśa*, the *śaṅkha*, and the *vajra* and *varada*. He should have his peacock vehicle by his side. The complexion of this aspect of Subrahmaṇya should also be that of the rising sun.

Kumāra should hold in his right hands the *śakti* and the *khaḍga* and in the left ones *kukkuṭa* and the *khēṭaka*. The *Srītatvanidhi* substitutes the *abhaya* and *varada* in the place of *khaḍga* and *khēṭaka* in the above description.

Shaṇmukha: The colour of Shaṇmukha should be that of *kuṅkuma* (saffron) and he should be seated on the peacock. As his name indicates he should have six faces, twelve eyes and twelve arms; in the right hands he should have the *śakti*, *bāṇa*, the *khaḍga*, *dhvaja*, *gadā* and *abhaya*; and in the left ones *dhanus*, *vajra*, *padma*, *kaṭaka-hasta* and *varada* (and one more object which is perhaps the *khēṭaka*). Shaṇmukha is here mentioned as the nephew of Vishṇu. The *Srītatvanidhi* mentions the *śaṅkha*, *chakra*, *kukkuṭa*, *pāśa* and *hala* as among the objects held by the hands of Shaṇmukha. It also states that on either side of Shaṇmukha there should be standing two *dēvīs* called Jayā and Vijayā.

Tārakāri : The figure of Tārakāri is required to be sculptured with twelve arms, in the hands of which there should be the *aṅkuśa*, *dhvaja*, *khaḍga*, *kaṭaka-hasta*, *abhaya*, *pāśa*, *chakra*, *musala*, *śakti* *vajra*, *varada* and *khēṭaka.* The colour of Tārakāri, is described as equal to a crore of Aruṇas shining at the same time. According to the *Śrītatvanidhi*, Tārakāri should have only one face and three eyes and he should be seated upon an elephant carrying in two of the right hands the *khaḍga* and the *śakti* and one of them held in the *abhaya* pose ; one of the left hands should be in the *varada* pose and the remaining hands should keep the *khēṭaka* and the *akshamālā.*

Krauñchabhēttā : This aspect of Subrahmaṇya should have six faces and eight arms. In the right hands there should be the *khaḍga*, *śakti*, *abhaya* and *bāṇa ;* and in the left ones *varada*, *vajra*, *dhanus* and *khēṭaka.* His complexion is to be that of the lotus flower.

Krauñchabhēttā according to the *Śrītatvanidhi* should be represented with a single face and four arms and three eyes. Two of the hands should be kept in the *varada* and *abhaya* poses and the remaining hands should carry flowery arrows and a bow made of sugarcane ; or, the front two hands should be shown as breaking the Krauñcha mountain. There should be near him his peacock vehicle.

Sēnāni should also possess twelve arms and twelve eyes; the hands should have in them *khaḍga*, *chakra*, *aṅkuśa*, *śakti*, *abhaya*, *śūla*, *varada*, *padma*, *daṇḍa and gadā*.

Brahma-śāstā : This is the aspect of Subrahmaṇya in which he put down the pride of Brahmā by exposing his ignorance of the Vēdas. He should be represented with a single face and four arms; he should have only two eyes. In the back hands there should be the *akshamālā* and the *kamaṇḍalu* and the front hands should be held in the *varada* and *abhaya* poses. The colour of Brahma-śāstā should be the red of the lotus flower.

Bālasvāmi is the aspect of Subrahmaṇya as a child. If he is sculptured as standing by the side of his parents, as in the Sōmāskanda aspect of Śiva, he should be represented as a child carrying a lotus in each hand; if, however, he is shown separately, he may be sculptured with a *padma* in his right hand and with the left hand resting upon the hip (*kaṭyavalambita*). The colour of this aspect is also red.

Śikhivāhana is to be of the colour of coral and to have a single face and four arms. In one of the hands there should be held the *śakti* and in the other the *vajra*, while the remaining ones should be held in the *abhaya* and the *varada* poses respectively. He is said to be the destroyer of the enemies of the gods.

Vaḷḷikalyāṇasundara: In this aspect Subrahmaṇya is sculptured as being married to Vaḷḷi. He should be represented in this case as carrying in the back right hand the *akshamālā* and the front hand should be held in the *abhaya* pose; the front left hand should rest upon the hip and the back hand should carry a *kamaṇḍalu.* Brahmā with a *sruva* in his hand should be shown as officiating in the ceremonies in front of the fire that should be sculptured as burning in a *kuṇḍa.* Vishṇu should keep in his hands a water-vessel ready to pour water in the act of giving the girl in marriage to the bridegroom. A host of gods and goddesses should be shown as offering praises to the married couple. Both the bride and the groom should be adorned with all ornaments appropriate to the occasion. The colour of Subrahmaṇya in this aspect also is red.

The *Śrītatvanidhi* adds the description of the following aspects of Subrahmaṇya, namely, Agnijāta-Subrahmaṇya, Saurabhēya-S., Gāṅgēya-S. Guha-S., Brahmachāri-S., and Dēśika-S.

Agnijāta-Subrahmaṇya should have two faces, eight arms and a white complexion ; his neck should be of black colour; he should carry in three out of the four right hands the *sruva*, an *akshamālā* and a *khaḍga* and the remaining hand should be kept in the *svastika* pose ; in three of the left hands there should be the *vajra*, *kukkuṭa*, *khēṭaka* and an *ājya-pātra* (vessel of ghee or clarified butter). He should be sculptured as engaged in the act of offering fire sacrifice.

Saurabhēya-Subrahmaṇya should have four faces, eight eyes and eight arms and should be seated upon a *kamalāsana ;* in the right hands there should be the *śakti*, a lotus, flowery arrows and *abhaya ;* and in the left hands *vajra*, a bow made of sugar-cane, a *śūla*, and *varada.* He should be standing with his right leg kept firmly on the ground and the left leg somewhat bent. His colour should be that of the lotus flower.

Gāṅgēya-Subrāhmaṇya is required to be represented with a single face, three eyes and four arms. The head must be adorned with a *karaṇḍa-makuṭa ;* he should be standing upon a *makara* (a kind of fish) and should be carrying a flag on which is painted a *kukkuṭa*, and should be adorned with *nīlōtpala* flowers. In his right hands should be a *paraśu* and a *pūrṇa-kumbha* (a vessel filled with water); in the left hands he should keep an *araṇi* (a piece of wood which is used in generating fire by friction) and a *kukkuṭa.* The colour of this aspect of Subrahmaṇya is that of gold.

It might be noticed that in all these aspects the descriptions are such as to suit the nature of the aspect; for example Subrahmaṇya, the son of Agni, is said to have two faces, the same number as possessed by Agni; he carries an *ājya-pātra sruva* and other objects necessary for making fire-offerings. Similarly, in the case of the Gāṅgēya-Subrahmaṇya, or Subrahmaṇya the son of Gaṅgā, he is required, like Gaṅgā, to be standing upon a *makara*, carry a *pūrṇakumbha* and adorned with *nīlōtpala* or water-lilies, objects characteristic of rivers.

Guha-Subrahmaṇya should have one face, three eyes and four arms. His head should be adorned with a *kirīṭa* made of gold set with rubies. In the right hands there should be the *vajra* and the *śula* and the left hands should be held in the *varada* and the *abhaya* poses. The colour of Guha is black and that of his clothes white. His Dēvī should be by his side and they should look like a newly married couple.

Brahmachāri-Subrahmaṇya : Subrahmaṇya in this aspect should have two eyes, two arms and be standing upon a *padma.* He must have a tuft of hair on his head, a *yajnōpavīta*, *mauñji* (grass girdle) and *kaupīna.* The right leg should be firmly placed upon the *padma* and the left one slightly bent and rested upon it. In the right hand there should be a *daṇḍa* and in the left a *vajra.* His complexion should be red.

Dēśika-Subrahmaṇya : This is the aspect in which *Subrahmaṇya* taught Śiva, his own father, the significance of the sacred syllable *ōm.* As a teacher he should be represented as possessing one face, six arms and as seated upon the peacock. His head should be adorned with a *karaṇḍa-makuṭa ;* two of his hands should carry the *śakti*, one an *akshamālā* and two others kept in the *varada* and the *abhaya* poses ; the remaining hand should perhaps be held in the *chinmudrā* pose. Śiva in the aspect of a disciple is called the Śishya-bhāva-mūrti. The *Mānasāra* gives a description of the form of Śishyabhāvamūrti. Śiva should be seated in front of his teacher Subrahmaṇya cross-legged, with one of his right hands kept closing his mouth and another kept on the chest in the *jñāna-mudrā* pose ; the other two hands should carry the *ṭaṅka* and the *mṛiga.* He should have a white complexion and his face should resemble the full-moon. His head should be adorned with a crescent moon. Pārvatī, his consort, should also be standing by his side.

Pls. CXXI-CXXIX illustrate the various aspects of Subrahmaṇya. Fig. 1, Pl. CXXI, belongs to the collection of the late Mr. M. K. Nārāyaṇasvāmi Ayyar and represents Skanda or Vēlāyudha-Subrahmaṇya. In the right hand of the image is a *daṇḍa* and a *sakti* is kept resting on his right arm. The left hand rests upon the hip. The image is clothed with only a *kaupīna* and wears the ornaments generally worn by boys. This is a modern piece of work.

Fig. 2 on the same plate is the photograph of the image of Kumāra belonging to the Śiva temple at Tiruppālatturai. The image has four arms; in the right hand at the back there is the *śakti* and in the back left hand the *vajra;* the front right and the left hands are kept in the *abhaya* and the *varada* poses respectively. A *śaktyāyudha* rests upon the right front arm.

Pl. CXXII is the reproduction of the photograph of Subrahmaṇya with his two consorts Dēvasēna and Vaḷḷi to be found in the Nāgēśvarasvāmin temple at Kumbhakōṇam. It is precisely similar to the figure of the Tiruppālatturai temple. Herein, Subrahmaṇya has behind him his peacock.

Fig. 1. Skanda or Vēlāyudha-Subrahmaṇya :

Fig. 2. Kumāra : Bronze :

[To face page 444]

Vaḷḷi. Subrahmaṇya. Dēvasēnā.

Subrahmaṇya with his consorts Dēvasēna and Vaḷḷī:
Stone: Kumbhakōṇam.

[To face page 444]

Mahāvaḷḷi. Subrahmaṇya. Dēvasēnā.

Subrahmaṇya with his consorts Dēvasēnā and Vaḷḷi:
Bronze: Tiruvoṟṟiyūr.

[To face page 445]

PLATE CXXIV.

Subrahmaṇya : Stone : Ellora.

[To face page 445]

The description of the Dēvīs of Subrahmaṇya is given as follows in the *Kumāra-tantra* : Mahāvalli should be of black complexion and should have a smiling face. She should stand with her right leg kept firmly on the ground and the left leg kept somewhat bent and placed on it. She should be holding in her left hand a *padma* (lotus) and her right hand should be hanging by her side. The complexion of Dēvasēna is red and she should also have a smiling face and standing with her left leg kept firmly on the ground and the right one somewhat bent. She should carry in her right hand a *nīlōtpala* flower, and the left one should be hanging. These descriptions are rigidly observed in the sculpture of the Nāgēśvarasvamin temple.

Pl. CXXIII is exactly similar to the previous one. The original of this sculpture is in the Śiva temple at Tiruvoṟṟiyūr and is executed very skilfully.

The photograph reproduced on Pl. CXXIV is that of a piece of sculpture belonging to one of the rock temples at Ellora. The central figure, Subrahmaṇya, has four arms and a single face. The front right hand which is broken seems to have held the *śakti*, whose head is visible near the figures of a Dēva and his Dēvī sculptured on the upper left corner. The back right hand rests upon the hip ;

the front left hand carries a *kukkuṭa* and the back left hand embraces the peacock which stands to the left of Subrahmaṇya. There are on either side a goat-headed attendant of Subrahmaṇya; one of these must be Daksha-Prajāpati, who is said to be one of the *parivāra-dēvatās* of Subrahmaṇya. The figure on the left has its left arm crossed against its chest and keeps its right one as if going to close his mouth,—attitudes which show a great deal of reverence. The figure on the left of Subrahmaṇya has its left hand resting upon its hip and keeps something in its right hand. On either side of the figure of Subrahmaṇya and soring in the air are two Dēvas with their Dēvīs praising him. The central figure of Subrahmaṇya has an *yajñōpavīta*, a *udarabandha* and a fine *hāra;* the ears are adorned with two different kinds of *kuṇḍalas* and the head is surmounted with a *karaṇḍa-makuṭa*, round which there is a *prabhā-maṇḍala*.

Pl. CXXV is the photograph of Subrahmaṇya with his consorts and resembles the other two photographs described above. The only difference consists in that the figure of Subrahmaṇya in this instance bears the *śakti* and the *kukkuṭa* in its back right and left hands respectively, while, as in the other instances, the front right and left hands are kept in the *abhaya* and the *varada* poses

PLATE CXXV.

Subrahmaṇya with his consorts Dēvasēnā and Vaḷḷī:
Stone: Kumbhakōṇam.

[To face page 446]

PLATE CXXVI.

Fig. 1. Subrahmaṇya with his two consorts : Ivory : Trivandram.

Fig. 2. Sikhivāhana : Stone : Kumbhakōṇam.

Fig. 3. Sēnāpati : Stone : Madras Museum.

[To face page 447]

PLATE CXXVII.

Shaṇmukha : Stone : Paṭṭiśvaram.

[To face page 447]

respectively. The person of Subrahmaṇya is elaborately adorned with all sorts of ornaments.

Fig. 1, Pl. CXXVI is a piece of ivory carving executed in the School of Arts at Trivandram and closely resembles the previous sculpture. Fig. 2 on the same plate represents Subrahmaṇya as seated upon the peacock; the right leg is hanging while the left one is bent and rested upon the peacock. The front hands are in the *abhaya* and the *varada* poses, and the back hands keep in them the *śakti* and the *vajra*. Fig. 3 on the same plate portrays Subrahmaṇya as seated upon the peacock, embracing his consort with his right arm and keeping in his left hand a bow; whereas the Dēvi embraces her lord with her left arm and carries in her right hand an arrow. Fig. 2 may be taken as Śikhīvāhana and fig. 3 as Sēnāpati.

Pl. CXXVII illustrates the description of Shaṇmukha. This beautifully carved figure belongs to the Śiva temple at Paṭṭīśvaram. It has twelve arms of which two are held in the *abhaya* and the *varada* poses and the remaining ones carry the *śakti*, *ṭaṅka*, *chakra*, *khaḍga* and *musala* (or pāśa?) and *vajra*, *dhanus*, *bāṇa*, *khēṭaka* and *śaṅkha*. The figure has six heads of which three are visible in the photograph. Behind the figure of Subrahmaṇya is his peacock.

Pl. CXXVIII is almost similar to the previous one; in addition to the weapons mentioned in the last plate, there is in this a *śaktyāyudha* made separately and kept leaning on the back arms. The *padmāsana* upon which this image stands is hexagonal, specially so made to agree with the six faced nature of the deity for whom it serves as a pedestal.

Pl. CXXVIII*a* is a piece of sculpture which is to be found in the temple at Aihoḷe and represents Tārakāri. In this Subrahmaṇya is seen riding a peacock and spiritedly attacking the fallen Tārakāsura with his *śaktyāyudha* which he wields with his right hand. The left hand carries the *vajra.* On either side of Subrahmaṇya are two Dēvas in the *ālīḍhāsana* posture, flying in the air and praising him. Above and on either side of the central figure are two persons carrying offerings and flower garlands.

Pl. CXXIX is a fine piece of sculpture to be seen in the front *maṇḍapa* of the temple of Śiva at Tirupparankunṟam near Madura. It represents the scene of the marriage of Subrahmaṇya with Dēvasēna. Subrahmaṇya is standing on the right with his right hand stretched out to receive the water which Indra is ready to pour from a water vessel, standing behind Dēvasēna on the left.

PLATE CXXVIII.

Shaṇmukha Bronze: Nallúr.

[To face page 448]

PLATE CXXVIIIa.

Tārakāri-Subrahmaṇya : Stone : Aihoḷe.

[To face page 418]

PLATE CXXIX.

Dēvasēnā-Kalyāṇasundaramūrti : Stone : Tirupparaṅkuṉṟam.

[To face page 448]

Subrahmaṇya has in the front left hand a lotus and in the back left one the *śakti;* it is not apparent from the photograph what other object is held in the back right hand.

Indra is seen keeping in the right hand the *ṭaṅka* and in the left the *vajra* and with his right hand he is pouring water into the hand of Subrahmaṇya.

Brahmā is seated in a countersunk surface below doing *hōma* (fire offerings) in connection with the marriage of Subrahmaṇya.

The modesty of the bride is very well portrayed in this piece of sculpture.

The *Kumāra-tantra* gives the description of the *dvārapālakas* of the shrine of Subrahmaṇya. They are called Sudēha and Sumukha; both of these are said to be brāhmaṇas. They should be represented with one face and two or four arms. If they possess two arms only, the right hand should be held in the *abhaya* pose and the left hand should keep a *gadā.* If they have four arms, the back hands should keep in them the *vajra* and the *śakti* and the front hands as in the case of the two-armed figure. One of these should be of red complexion and the other black; they must be adorned with all ornaments and should have side-tusks. Their head must have the *karaṇḍa-makuṭas.*

Sudēha should be to the right and Sumukha to the left of the entrance.

Another attendant of Subrahmaṇya is called Sumitra. His story is given thus in the *Kumāra-tantra.* There once lived a good brāhmaṇa named Svarṇāksha in Kāśi; he had a son named Sumitra who had been worshipping Skanda in due form during his three consecutive births. Subrahmaṇya was pleased with his devotion to himself (Subrahmaṇya) and gave him the name Sumitra (a good friend) and made him the head of the *gaṇas* and gave him a place near him. Then follows a description of the image of Sumitra; Sumitra should be sculptured according to the *uttama-nava-tāla* measure, with two eyes, two arms and a red complexion. He should have a fine looking face and should be youthful possessing side-tusks. The head should be covered with a *karaṇḍa-makuṭa* hiding his tuft of hair or a *jaṭā-makuṭa.* The right hand should carry the *śakti* and the left hand should be kept on the hip (*kaṭyavalambita*). Or, the hands may be kept in the *añjali* pose on the chest. He may be sculptured either as seated or as standing on a *padmāsana.*

Pl. CXXX is the reproduction of the photograph of Sumukha the left gate-keeper of the shrine of Subrahmaṇya in the great Śiva temple at

Dvārapālaka of the Subrahmaṇya shrine : Stone : Tanjore.

[To face page 450]

Tanjore. The front right hand of the image bears a short sword, while the front left hand carries a shield ; the back right hand is in the *sūchi* pose and the back left hand in the *vismaya* pose. The right leg of the figure of Sumukha rests upon the head of a lion, and the left foot of the image stands upon a *padmāsana*. It is one of the finest pieces of sculpture to be found in the Brihadīśvara temple at Tanjore.

NANDIKESVARA OR ADHIKA-RANANDI.

NANDIKĒŚVARA OR ADHIKĀRANANDIN.

At the entrance into many an important temple of Śiva in Southern India one meets with a pair of images, of which one is a male figure and the other a female one, the consort of the former. The male figure is shaped exactly like that of Śiva in the aspect of Chandraśēkharamūrti. It is seen standing upon a *padmāsana* and carrying in its back hands the *paraśu* and the *mṛiga* ; but, unlike the figure of Chandraśēkharamūrti, which keeps its front hands in the *varada* and the *abhaya* poses, that of Adhikāranandin has them folded on the chest in the *añjali* pose. The figure of Adhikāranandin is sometimes mistaken by the less informed persons for that of Śiva.

Three different accounts are found of the origin of Adhikāranandin. According to the *Śiva-mahāpurāṇa*, he was the son of the *ṛishi* Sālaṅkāyana ; the following account is given of him by this authority : Sālaṅkāyana, who was long without a son, was doing penance under a *sāla* tree in a place called Sālagrāma. Appreciating his austerities, Vishṇu appeared before him and asked him to request for any boon he desired. The *ṛishi* prayed that he may be blessed with a son of great virtue. Immediately after this request was made, a person sprang from the right of Vishṇu, who resembled Śiva in every way. He was given the name Nandikēśvara. The *purāṇa* adds that this was the forty-ninth birth of Nandikēśvara.

A second account of the birth of Nandikēśvara runs as follows: in the Trētā-yuga, a *ṛishi* named Nandi was performing a severe penance on the peak called Muñjavān on the Mandara mountain. Śiva pleased with the devotion of Nandi presented himself before the *ṛishi*. The latter requested Śiva to grant him the boons that he should have unshakeable faith in and love for Śiva, as also that he should be made the head of the *gaṇas*. Śiva granted him the boons with pleasure and disappeared. Indra and the other gods were overjoyed to see the bliss that befell the *ṛishi* Nandi and praised him for his good fortune.

The *Liṅga-purāṇa* has a third account of the origin of Nandikēśvara. A blind *ṛishi* named Silāda was practising penance with a desire to obtain an immortal son, not born of human beings.

Indra becoming pleased with the austerities of this *ṛishi* resolved to fulfil the *ṛishi's* desire and approached him and told him that no one but Śiva could grant him what he wanted and directed him to address his penances to that deity. He did as advised by Indra, and Śiva pleased with him, promised that he would himself be born to the *ṛishi* as his son ; thereby he intended to satisfy Brahmā also who was desirous of Śiva taking a human incarnation. After some time, Silāda was engaged in a sacrifice (*yāga*) ; a lad proceeded from the room in which the *ṛishi* Silāda was performing the *yāga* ; he looked precisely like Śiva, with a *jaṭā-makuṭa* on his head, three eyes and four arms. He was carrying in his hands the *śūla*, the *ṭaṅka*, the *gadā* and the *vajra*. Because Silāda became pleased with the fulfilment of his desire by the appearance of this, his son born not by human agency, Śiva gave the lad the name Nandi and disappeared.

Then Silāda and his son Nandi repaired to the former's *āśrama*. There the boy lost his superhuman form and became quite like any ordinary mortal. Though feeling sorry for the change, Silāda performed on his son the usual ceremony such as *upanayana*, when the boy attained the seventh year of age ; he soon became well versed in the Vēdas. Some time after, two *ṛishis* named Mitra and Varuṇa came to the *āśrama* of the *ṛishi* Silāda as his guests; these gazed intently at Nandi and perceived through their mental vision that the life of the boy was to come to an end in one year more. They informed this sad news to the father of the boy. The *ṛishi* and his father Sālaṅkāyana sank in despair on hearing the prognostication of their guests, and swooned. But, Nandikēśvara, though internally perturbed, began to meditate upon Śiva so intently that the latter appeared to him and took hold of him in his arms and threw round his neck the flower garland which was hanging round his own neck. Forthwith the boy was changed into a being endowed with three eyes, ten arms and appearance which exactly resembled Śiva. The latter blessed this metamorphosed Nandi to be free from old age and death and also anointed him as the head of his *gaṇas* and married him to Suyaśa, the daughter of the Maruts.

The name Nandikēśvara, 'the tawny coloured dwarf' and a follower of Śiva occurs in the *Rāmāyaṇa* (V. 17, Sec. 16 of the Uttara-kāṇḍa). There he is stated to be another manifestation of Śiva (*apara tanuh*) and that when he was keeping guard over the Kailāsa, Rāvaṇa, the lord of Laṅkā and of the Rākshasas, came driving in his ærial car and wanted to cross the abode of Śiva. But he was promptly stopped by Nandikēśvara. Upon this Rāvaṇa made contemptuous remarks concerning the monkey-face of Nandikēśvara. Incensed at the insult offered to him, he cursed Rāvaṇa that beings possessing the same shape as himself and of similar energy (that is, monkeys) would destroy the race of Rāvaṇa.

Nandikēśvara is mentioned also in the *Bhāgavata-purāṇa*. During the *yāga* that Daksha-prajāpati was performing, he spoke tauntingly of Śiva. Nandi grew angry at the insult offered to his lord Siva and pronounced maledictions against Daksha and the other revilers of Śiva.

The *Vishṇudharmōttara* gives the following description of Nandikēśvara. He should have three eyes and four arms and a red complexion. His garments should be made of tiger's skin; in one of his hands there should be the *triśūla* and in another the *bhindi;* a third hand should be held over his head and the fourth held as though he is commanding a host of people. His gaze should suggest that he is seeing objects at a great distance and regulating the large crowd of devotees resorting to offer worship to Śiva.

Nandikēśvara is more often represented as a bull than as a bull-faced human being or as a duplicate of Śiva. The former is kept lying in front of the central shrine of all Śiva temples.

An illustration of Adhikāra-Nandin is given on Pl. CXXXI. The original of the photograph therein reproduced is in the temple of Śiva at Vaḻuvūr. It is sculptured precisely like Śiva in the aspect of Chandraśēkharamūrti, carrying the *paraśu* and the *mriga* in the back right and left hands respectively, and standing upon a *padmāsana ;* but unlike Chandraśēkharamūrti who keeps the front right and left hands in the *abhaya* and the *varada* poses, Nandikēśvara has them folded on the chest in the *añjali* pose. The body has three slight bends in it (*tribhanga*). On his head are the *jaṭā-makuṭa* and the Gaṅgā and the crescent moon.

Pl. CXXXII is the photograph of the bronze Nandi in the Śiva temple at Pañchanadikkuḷam ; it is an ordinary bull couchant and is placed in the *mahāmaṇḍapa* of the Śiva temples generally.

PLATE CXXXI.

Adhikāra-Nandin : Bronze : Vaḻuvūr.

[To face page 460]

PLATE CXXXII.

Nandi : Bronze : Pañchanadikkuḷam : (Tanjore Dt.).

[To face page 460]

CHANDESVARA.

CHAṆḌĒŚVARA.

THE story of Chaṇḍēśvara, how he worshipped Śiva and attained to the position of the leader of the *bhūtagaṇas* of Śiva, has been given already under Chaṇḍēśānugrahamūrti. The image of Chaṇḍēśvara is essential in a Śiva temple and should be set up in the north-east corner with reference to the central shrine of the temple.

The image of Chaṇḍēśvara may be set up in a shrine unattached to any temple, or as one of the *parivārā-dēvatas* or attendant deities in a Śiva temple. In the first instance, the shrine of Chaṇḍēśvara is said to be *svatantra* and in the second *paratantra*. The *svatantra* temple of Chaṇḍēśvara may be situated in any of the eight directions (north, north-east, etc.) or in the centre of towns and villages. The temple of Chaṇḍēśvara may range in size from a mere shrine of one cubit cube to a magnificent temple with a base of thirty cubits square, surmounted by a *vimāna* of one to seven *talas* or storeys in height, ornamented with the figures of Chaṇḍēśvara or any other deity on the corners of each *tala* (storey); or, there might be in these corners figures of Nandi, the bull couchant. In the case of the temple of *svatantra* Chaṇḍēśvara, it is required to face any one of the directions except the north; this temple should have *prākāras*, *maṇḍapas*, etc., in proportion to the dimensions of the central shrine.

Surrounding the central shrine there should be eight *parivara-mūrtis*, named Rudrabhakta, Rudra-Chaṇḍa, Chaṇḍama, Mahābala, Vīrya, Ṭaṅkapāni, Īśasēvaka and Rudrakōpaja. They should all be of white complexion, big-bodied and with the pair of front hands held in the *añjali* pose and the back pair carrying in them *ṭaṅkas*. They may be represented either as standing or seated in the *vīrāsana* attitude and draped in elephant skins; they should have terrific countenances. Instead of Rudra-bhakta and others, Indra and the other Dikpālakas may be made the *parivāras* of the temple of Chaṇḍēśvara. They may be represented as actual anthropomorphic figures or with simple *pīṭhas* (as in the case of the Sapta-Mātṛikās, see Vol. I, Pl. CXX). In front of the temple of Chaṇḍēśvara there should be, as in Śiva's temples, a Nandi or couchant bull, and at the main entrance of the temple there should be two gate-keepers named Chaṇḍānuga and Chaṇḍabhṛitya. These two should be sculptured with two arms and carrying clubs in their hands; sometimes they may be dispensed with also.

The figure of Chaṇḍēśvara should be fashioned according to the *madhyama* or *adhama-daśa-tāla vidhi* as is given in *Pratimālakshaṇa* or instructions given for the making of images; different descriptions are found in the *āgamas* for making the image of Chaṇḍēśvara. In the first instance, we see it stated that it might be sculptured as seated upon a *padmāsana;* its look should be terrific, as if fire would burst out of its face; the colour of Chaṇḍēśvara should be jet black and there must be a *sarpayajñōpavīta* on its body. The head should be adorned with a *jaṭā-makuṭa*, in which there should be the crescent of the moon, as in the case of Śiva. Chaṇḍēśvara, according to this description, should have four faces, four arms and twelve eyes. In the right hands there should be the *akshamālā* and the *triśūla* and in the left hands the *ṭaṅka* and the *kamaṇḍalu*.

A second description of the image of Chaṇḍēśvara is as follows. The complexion of this deity should be conch-white; there should be three eyes and four arms and in the *jaṭā-makuṭa* the crescent moon. The figure of the deity should be seated in the *vīrāsana* posture and should carry in its back hands the *dhanus* called the *Pināka* and the *bāṇa* called the *Amōgha*, while the front hands should be kept in the *varada* and *abhaya* poses.

According to the third description, Chaṇḍēśvara may be represented as either standing or sitting, with only a pair of arms but with three eyes. The colour of the body is here also required to be inky-black. As in the other cases there should be the *jaṭā-makuṭa* on the head. If the figure is made a seated one, the right leg should be hanging below the seat and the left leg should be bent and rested upon the seat. The left hand may either be placed on the left thigh or held in the *varada* pose. In the right hand there may be a *ṭaṅka;* or both hands may carry *ṭaṅkas;* or both hands may be folded on the chest in the *añjali* pose. Or, the figure may be sculptured as seated in the *utkuṭikāsana* posture with the head slightly bowed down as in deep sorrow, but with a face full of peace.

In the fourth mode of representing Chaṇḍēśvara, he must be sculptured as having four arms three of which should be carrying the *ṭaṅka*, the *pāśa* and the *śūla* and the remaining one held in the *abhaya* pose.

" In the descriptions found in the works of the Siṁhaḷadēśa (Ceylon) * it is stated", so says the *Kāmikāgama*, " that Chaṇḍēśvara should be represented in the Kṛitayuga with eight arms, in the Trētāyuga with six, in the Dvāparayuga with four and in the Kaliyuga with two only. But", the same authority adds, "no such thing is mentioned in the works of the other countries".

Again, Chaṇḍēśvara may be shown singly or with his consort Dharmanīti. If his Dēvī is also sculptured, she should be adorned with all ornaments and should carry a *nīlōtpala* in her hands. Her colour is also to be black.

The *Kāraṇāgama* states that Prachaṇḍachaṇḍa, Vikrāntachaṇḍa, Vibhuchaṇḍa, Vīrachaṇḍa and another whose name is not given came from the Pañchabrahmās. The stewardship of the house of Śiva was bestowed in the Kṛitayuga upon Prachaṇḍachaṇḍa, in the Trētāyuga upon Vikrāntachaṇḍa, in

---

* This is clear evidence that there existed in Ceylon the worship not only of Buddha but of the various deities of the Hindu cults and that there existed text-books in that country also containing descriptions of images, which sometimes differed from the readings of those on the continent of India. Evidently some of those Buddha *āgamas* quoted by Dr. Anandakumārasami in his " Simhalese Art " belong to the category of works referred to in the *Kāmikāgama*.

the Dvāparayuga upon Vibhuchaṇḍa and in the Kaliyuga upon Vīrachaṇḍa.

In the case of *paratantra* Chaṇḍēśvara his shrine should be facing the south and, as has been already mentioned, be situated on the north-east corner of the first *prākāra* of the Śiva temple. According to the *Kāraṇāgama* the *paratantra* Chaṇḍēśvara may have three eyes and four arms or only two eyes and two arms, be terrific in appearance, and have a *jaṭā-makuṭa* on the head. Of the four hands two are to be kept in the *abhaya* and *varada* poses and the remaining two should carry the *pāśa* and the *paraśu*. If however there are only two hands, one of them should be in the *varada* pose and the other should carry a *ṭaṅka*. There should be a white *yajñōpavīta* on the body which should be adorned with all ornaments also. The figure of Chaṇḍēśvara may be either standing or sitting.

Two illustrations are given on Pl. CXXXIII. The very well-executed original stone sculpture is placed in a very dark corner of the *maṇḍapa* in front of the central shrine of the Śiva temple at Tiruvoṟṟiyūr. It is seated in the *vīrāsana* posture and it carries a *paraśu* in its right hand, the left one resting upon the left lap. There is a figure of Chaṇḍēśvara carved on the north of the central

Fig. 1. Chaṇḍēśvara (seated) :
Stone : Tiruvoṟṟiyūr.

Fig. 2. Chaṇḍēśvara (standing) :
Bronze : Marudāntanallūr.

[To face page 468]

shrine of the Śaiva cave callea Dhumar Lena in Ellora; it has been mistaken by Dr. Burgess for "Śiva as a *yōgi* or ascetic, with a club in his left hand, and seated on a lotus."

The second illustration is of the standing Chaṇḍēśvara: it belongs to the temple at Marudāntanallūr. The figure has only two arms and the hands are held in the *añjali* pose. A *ṭaṅka* rests on the left arm.

BHAKTAS.

BHAKTAS.

BHAKTAS or devotees whose images are also enjoined to be set up for worship in temples may belong to the Brāhmaṇa, Kshatriya, Vaiśya or the Śūdra caste; or of mixed castes; males or females; they may be *āchāryas* or crowned monarchs; living or dead. All that is wanted to apotheosise them is that they should be bhaktas or acknowledged devotees. Such devotees should be worshipped in images. These images may be set up either in separate temples (*svayam-pradhāna*) or in the temples of some deity whose devotee the bhakta happens to be, as a dependent on that deity (an *aṅga*). As instances of the former may be pointed out the temple of Kaṇṇappa Nāyānar, the hunter saint, on the hill at Kāḷahasti; and of Kulaśēkhara Āḻvār at Mannārkōyil near Ambāsamudram. The attendant or *aṅga* class of images are found in all important temples of S. India. The well-known sixty-three (*Aṟuvattu-mūvar*) Śaiva saints and the twelve Āḻvārs or Vaishṇava saints of Drāviḍa are seen invariably in Śaiva and Vaishṇava temples in S. India.

A *svayam-pradhāna* or independent temple of a bhakta may be constructed on the top of a hill, on the bank of a river, in *vanas* (gardens) and in *grāmas* (towns). The *aṅga* or dependent class of bhaktas are required by the *āgamas* to be set up near the place where flower-garlands for the use of the temple are made. The first class of images may have *parivāras* or attendants, while the latter should not possess any for the obvious reason, namely, that they are themselves depending upon others.

Bhaktas may be represented by anthropomorphic figures, or, in the case of Śaiva bhaktas, as Śivaliṅgas, or occasionally also in the form of Śiva himself. But in the case of Vaishṇava bhaktas they are generally represented as actual human beings just as they appeared when they were living. The images may be made of stone, clay, metal, wood or gems. They may be carved in half relief or in the round (*ardha-chitra* or *chitrābhāsa*). They should be sculptured according to the *ashṭa-tāla* measure, either as standing or as seated on a *padmāsana* or a *siṁhāsana*. They may be sculptured with or without a tuft of hair on their head; if they are shown with a tuft it should be neatly done up in a knot on the top of the head;

PLATE CXXXV.

Kāḍavarkōṉ. Śirāḷaṉ. Śiṟuttoṇḍar. Queen of Kāḍavarkōṉ.

A few of the Śaiva Saints: Bronze: Tiruchcheṅgāṭṭaṅguḍi.

[To face page 475]

if they are not to possess a tuft of hair, their head should be shown as clean shaven. If the devotee is a crowned monarch or a ruling chief he should be sculptured with a *kirīṭa* or *karaṇḍa-makuṭa* on his head. The bhaktas may be made to carry in their hands any object which is generally associated with them or they may have their hands held in the *añjali* pose, or the attitude of worship. They may be sculptured as singing, dancing or doing *pūjā*. They should be adorned with all ornaments and if the bhakta is a female, she should be decked with such ornaments as are appropriate to her sex.

The following are the lists of the Śaiva and Vaishṇava saints of S. India :—

I. ŚAIVA SAINTS.

No.	Name.	Caste.	Occupation.	Place of birth.
1	Tirujñānasamban-dha.	Brāh-maṇa.	Temple priest.	Shiyāli (Tanjore).
2	Tillai Brāhmaṇas ...	Do.	Do.	Chidambaram.
3	Kalaya-nāyanār ...	Do.	Do.	Tirukkaḍavūr.
4	Muruga-nāyanār ...	Do.		Tiruppugalūr.
5	Rudra-Paśupati ...	Do.		Talaiyūr.
6	Śiṟappuliyār ...	Do.		
7	Gaṇanāthar ...	Do.		
8	Pūśalār ...	Do.		
9	Chaṇḍēśar ...	Do.		Śēyñalūr.
10	Sōmāśimāṟaṇār ...	Do.		
11	Naminandiyār ...	Do.		Ēmappērūr.

No.	Name.	Caste.	Occupation.	Native place.
12	Appūdiyaḍigaḷ ...	Brāhmaṇa.		Tiṅgaḷūr.
13	Nīlanakkar ...	Do.		Tiruchchāttamaṅgai.
14	Sundaramūrti ...	Do.		Tiruveṇṇainallūr.
15	Pugaḻttuṇaiyār ...	Āmātya.		
16	Śiṟuttoṇḍar ...	Do.		Tiruchcheṅgāṭṭaṅguḍi.
17	Kō-Chcheṅgaṇṇāṉ .	Crowned monarch.		
18	Pugaḻchchōḻar ...	Do.		
19	Aruṇmāṉiyār ...	Do.		
20	Iḍaṅgaḻiyār ...	Do.		
21	Ṉeḍumāṟaṉ ...	Do.		
22	Śēramāṉperumāḷ ...	Do.		Tiruvañjaikkaḷam.
23	Narasiṅgamuṉaiyaraiyar.	Ruling Chief. (Kshatriya).		Ruling with Tirukkōvalūr as his capital.
24	Kūṟṟuvar ...	Do.		
25	Kaḻaṟ-chiṅgar ...	Do.		
26	Meypporuḷār ...	Do.		
27	Aiyaḍigaḷ ...	Do.		
28	Kāraikkālammaiyār	Vaiśya.		Kāraikkāl.
29	Mūrtināyanār ...	Do.		Madurai.
30	Kalikkāmaṉār ...	Do.		
31	Amarnīdiyār ...	Do.		Paḻaiyāṟai.
32	Iyaṟpagai ...	Do.		Kāvirippūmpaṭṭiṉam.
33	Mūrkkanāyanār ...	Veḷḷāḷa.		
34	Śeṟuttuṇaiyār ...	Do.		
35	Vāyilār ...	Do.		
36	Kōṭpuliyār ...	Do.		
37	Śaktiyār ...	Do.		
38	Arivāṭṭāyaṉār ...	Do.		Kaṇamaṅgai.
39	Iḷaiyāṉguḍimāṟaṉār	Do.		Iḷaiyāṉguḍi.

No.	Name.	Caste.	Occupation.	Native place.
40	Śākkiyar ...	Vellāla.		
41	Māṇakkañjārar ...	Do.		Kañjaṉūr.
42	Viṟaṉ-minḍar ...	Do.		
43	Muṉaiyaḍuvār ...	Do.		Tiruchcheṅguṉṟūr.
44	Ēyarkōṉ-Kalikkāmaṉār.	Do.		Perumaṅgalam.
45	Tirunāvukkaraśu (Appar).	Do.		Tiruvāmūr.
46	Tirumūlar ...	Cowherd.		Sattaṉūr.
47	Āṉāyar ...	Do.		Maṅgalavūr.
48	Tirunīlakaṇḍar ...	Potter.		Chidambaram (Tillai).
49	Tirunīlakaṇḍattu Pāṇaṉ.	Pāṇaṉ.		
50	Atibattanāyaṉār ...	Fisherman.		Nāgapaṭaṇam
51	Kaṇṇappa-nāyaṉār..	Vēḍaṉ (hunter).		Kāḷahasti (Uḍuppūr).
52	Ēṉadināyaṉār ...	Shāṇāṉ. (Toddy-drawer).		Eyiṉaṉūr.
53	Nēśanāyanār ...	Śāliyar, (weaver).		Kampili.
54	Tirunāḷaippōvār (Nandaṉār).	Paṟaiyaṉ.	Field labour.	Ādaṉūr.
55	Tirukkuṟipput toṇḍar.	Washerman.		Kāñchi.
56	Kaliyaṉār ...	Oil-monger.		
57	Kulachchiṟaiyār ...	Prime-minister to the Pāṇḍya king.		Maṇamēṟkuḍi.
58	Milalaikkuṟumbar ...	(Kuṟumbaṉ.)		Miḻalai.

No.	Name.	Caste.	Occupation.	Native place.
59	Daṇḍiyaḍigaḷ ...			Tiruvārūr.
60	Kaṇampullar ...			
61	Eribattar ...			
62	Kāriyār ...			
63	Sundaramūrti ...	Brāhmaṇa.		Tirunāvalūr.

VAISHNAVA BHAKTAS.

No.	Name.	Caste.	Occupation.	Native place.
1	Periyāḻvār (Vishṇuchitta).	Brāhmaṇ.	Making flower garlands.	Śrivilliputtūr.
2	Āṇḍāl (Gōdā) ...	Do. (woman).	Do.	Do
3	Poygaiyāḻvār ...	Brāhmaṇa.	Yōgi.	Conjeevaram.
4	Pēyāḻvār ...	Do.	Do.	Mylapore.
5	Bhūtattāḻvār ...	Do.	Do.	Mahābalipuram.
6	Nammāḻvār (Śaṭakōpa).	Śūdra.	Do.	Āḻvār-Tirunagari.
7	Tirumaṅgaiyāḻvār .	Kallar. (Robber).	(1) Waylaying and robbing. (2) Service to temples.	Tiruvāli.
8	Toṇḍaradippoḍiyālvār.	Brāhman.	Making flower garlands.	Maṇḍaṅguḍi
9	Tiruppāṇālvār ...	Pāṇan.	Singing.	Uṟaiyūr.
10	Madurakaviyāḻvār .	Brāhmaṇa.	Serving. Nammālvār	Tirukkōḷūr.
11	Tirumaliśaiyālvār .	Do.	Yōgi.	Tirumaḷiśai.
12	Kulaśēkharāḻvār ...	Kshatriya.	Crowned monarch.	Tiruvañjaikkaḷam.

Besides the Śaiva saints above enumerated, there are counted many more at the present time; that is, after that list of sixty-three was drawn up by Sundaramūrti-Nāyanār, many others of saintly nature came into being and though they could not be placed in the older list, are still held in as much esteem as the older saints. Such are, for instance, Māṇikkavāchakar, Karuvūrttēvar, Kaṇḍāradittar, Tirumāḷigaittēvar, Śēndanār, Chēdiyarāyar, Purushōttamanambi, Tiruvāliyamudanār, Pūndurutti-kāḍanambi, Meykaṇḍadēvar and others. Images are set up for these persons also, along with the sixty-three; that is why we see in many Śiva temples not sixty-three, but about seventy-three images of *bhaktas*. The number of *bhaktas* cannot be limited, since any number of these might be added at any time.

Similarly, in Vaishṇava temples of S. India, which are almost always under the management of the Śrīvaishṇavas, are seen often more than twelve figures of saints. The additional ones are of subsequent *āchāryas*, like Rāmānuja, Maṇavāḷa-māmunigaḷ, Vēṅkaṭanātha Dēśika, etc.

It might be observed that Kulaśēkharāḻvār, a crowned monarch, has a *makuṭa* on his head, according to the rules laid down above (see Pl. CXXXVI). We see also that Kaṇṇappa-nāyanār has his hair tied up in a fine knot on the crown of the head (see Pl. CXXXIV), and certain *brāhmaṇa* saints, with a small tuft of hair on the crown, as in the case of Vishṇuchitta (Periyāḻvār), Toṇḍaradippoḍi and Madurakavi, in our illustrations (Pl. CXXXVI).

Again, certain characteristic features mark particular saints; for instance, Apparsvāmigaḷ is at once recognised by a staff, with a triangular metallic piece, at its end, intended for removing grass grown in temples; for, he had undertaken to do that service in all temples he visited (see Pl. CXXXVII, fig. 3). Tirujñānasambandha among the Śaiva (See fig., Pl. CXXXVII) and Tiruppāṇāḻvār among the Vaishṇava saints (Pl. CXXXVI) would easily be recognised by the cymbals they have in their hands. Tirumaṅgai, by the sword and shield; and Māṇikkavāchakar, by the book in his hands, (fig. 2, Pl. CXXXVII and Pl. CXXXVIII).

For the history of these Śaiva and Vaishṇava saints, the readers are referred to the *Periyapurāṇam* in Tamiḻ ,—for, this has not as yet been rendered in English by any one,—and Mr. A. Gōvindāchārya's 'Lives of Drāviḍa Saints' in English, respectively.

We learn from the writings of the Śrīvaishṇavas that in the days of Rāmānuja and later,

Kaṇṇappa Nāyanār : Bronze : Madras Museum.

[To face page 460]

PLATE CXXXVI.

ĀḺVĀRS OR ŚRĪVAISHṆAVA SAINTS—Bronze: Tāḍikkombu.

Madhurakavi-yāḻvār. Tirumaḻiśai-yāḻvār. Tiruppā-ṇāḻvār. Tirumaṅgai-yāḻvār.(?) Nammāḻvār. (O Rāmānuja (or Uḍaiyavar). Garuḍa.

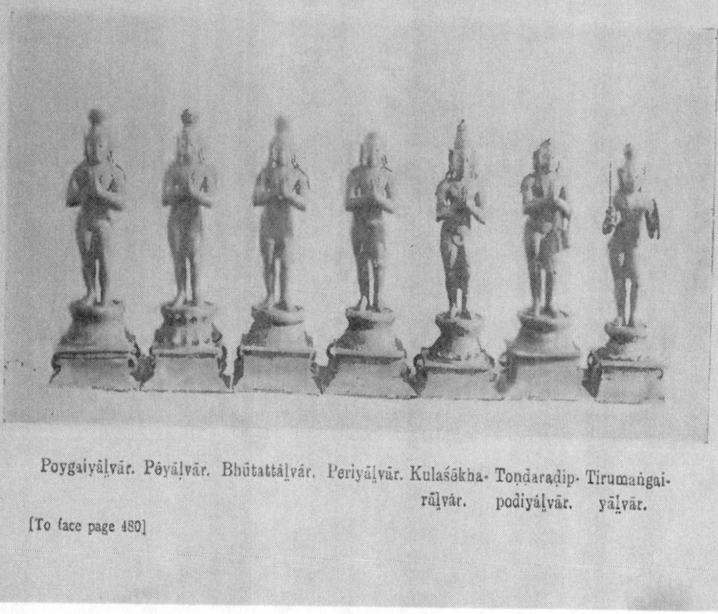

Poygaiyāḻvār. Pêyāḻvār. Bhūtattāḻvār. Periyāḻvār. Kulaśēkha-rāḻvār. Toṇḍaraḍip-podiyāḻvār. Tirumaṅgai-yāḻvār.

[To face page 480]

PLATE CXXXVII.

Fig. 1. Tirujñānasambandha : Padmanābhapuram.

Fig. 2. Māṇikkavāchakar.

Fig. 3. Apparsvāmigaḷ.

Tiruchcheṅgōḍu.

Fig. 4. Sundaramūrti : Bronze : Padmanābhapuram.

[To face page 480]

PLATE CXXXVIII.

Māṇikkavāchakar : Bronze : *Viśvakarma* (Dr. A. K. K.).

[To face page 480]

people were owning slaves and that the latter had their names tattooed on their chests in token of their condition. Some sold themselves to others as slaves in times of famine. When once they became slaves, they were bound to serve their masters with the utmost fidelity; in short, they had to become practically members of the family of their masters and personally interest themselves in the welfare of their families; in other words the slaves became the bhaktas of their masters. As a concrete instance of this custom might be pointed out the life-size images of the Vijayanagara kings Kṛishṇadēvarāya and Veṅkaṭapatidēvarāya and the queens of the former, Chinnādēvī and Tirumaladēvī, which are set up in the temple of Veṅkaṭēśa on the Tirumalai hill at Tirupati. These were apparently set up in their life-time as the paleography of the writing on their chests indicates. These devotees of Veṅkaṭēśa inscribed themselves as the slaves of the Lord of Tirumala and thereby bound themselves to do everything for the welfare of the temple and in testimony whereof they seem to have caused their images being set up in the temple with their names engraved on their chests, so that the images might be ever worshipping their own favourite god Veṅkatēśa (see *Viśvakarma*).

ARYA OR HARIHARAPUTRA.

ĀRYA OR HARIHARAPUTRA.

THE deity Ārya, Śāsta or Hariharaputra, so well known to the Drāviḍas is not familiar to the inhabitants of Northern India; even in the Drāviḍa country he is the favourite only of the Malayāḷam people. The country of the latter possesses as large a number of temples of Śāsta as the Tamil country has of Subrahmaṇya and it is an invariable rule in the Malayāḷam country that in every temple, be it of Śiva or of Vishṇu, there must be in its south-west corner a shrine for Śāsta. He is considered by them as the guardian of the land and as such eight mountain tops along the Western Ghats are surmounted by eight temples in which are set up eight images of Śāsta to protect the country on the west of the mountain ranges, inhabited by the Malayāḷis, from all external evils and misfortunes. In this country he is better known as Śāsta than as Hariharaputra or Ārya. In the Tamil country he is known by the name Hariharaputra or more frequently Ayyanār (a modification of Ārya). That Śāsta should have been a very common name and the deity was perhaps once better known by that name in the Tamil country is deducible from the fact that in all examples in Grammars of declension, inflexion, etc., the subject of a sentence is Śāttan (Śāsta), just as the Sanskrit Grammarians usually employ the name of Dēvadatta. The name Śāsta or its corruption is not borne by men in the Tamil country, but one can meet with persons of that name by scores in the Malayāḷam country.

This deity which is very peculiar to the Drāviḍa country does not appear to have been known to the region north of the Gōdāvarī. In no early Sanskrit work is the deity mentioned. Even the dictionaries do not record this name and give its origin. In the *Vishṇupurāṇa* we hear that, Vishṇu, seeing that there ensued a quarrel between the Dēvas and Asuras over the distribution of the *amṛita* (ambrosia) obtained by churning the ocean of milk, assumed the form of a charming damsel, distributed the precious article among the Dēvas, the Asuras being all the while dazed by the enchanting beauty of the maiden and oblivious of the cause of their quarrel. It is in the *Śrī Bhāgavata* that we learn, for the first time that Hara fell in love with Vishṇu in his form of Mōhinī. From the union between Hara and Hari, Ārya, Śāsta or Hariharaputra is said to have been born. The *Suprabhēdāgama* very distinctly mentions that Śāsta was born of Mōhinī, the form assumed by Vishṇu for the purpose of distributing the *amṛita* among the gods when it was churned from the milk-ocean, by the union with her of Hara. That this is a deity peculiarly Dravidian and has been taken into the fold of the Āryan pantheon at a later period goes without contradiction. At present Hariharaputra is treated in the Tamil country as a village deity and is mostly worshipped by the lower classes and the *pūja* in the temple of Hariharaputra or Ayyanār (or Ayyanārappan) is performed by a Śūdra. The *Pādmasaṁhitā* states that the *pūja* in the temple of Ārya should be performed by a Pāraśava; we know from other sources that a Pāraśava is an *anulōma* born of a Brāhmaṇa father and a Śūdra mother. But somehow Ayyanār, like the more *tāmasic* forms of Dēvi such as Kāḷi, which are worshipped by the lower classes in the Tamil country, is made *pūja* to by the Brāhmaṇas in Malabar.

This deity is called Śāsta because he is able to control and rule over the whole world; etymologically therefore, the word means a ruler of a country, and is sometimes applied to teachers and fathers. The *Amarakōśa* applies the name to Buddha also. The Tamil Nighaṇṭus call him by the additional names Sātavāhana, the rider of the white elephant, Kāri, the wielder of the weapon known as *śeṇḍu*, the consort of Pūraṇa and Pushkalā, the protector of Dharma and Yōgi; they also state that the vehicle of Śāsta is the elephant and the crest of his banner a cock. The names, rider of the white elephant, Yōgi, the protector of Dharma coupled with the significance of Buddha applied to Śāsta in the *Amarakōśa* incline one to conclude that Buddha as conceived and worshipped in the Tamil country was ultimately included in the Hindu Pantheon and a Purāṇic story invented for his origin at a later period of the history of Hindu Iconology. The name Śātavāhana is also very noteworthy as it has been assumed by a dynasty of powerful kings of the earlier centuries of the Christian era.

The descriptions of the image of Śāsta or Ārya are found given in the *Amśumadbhēdāgama*, the *Suprabhēdāgama* and the *Kāraṇāgama*. The figure of Śāsta should have four arms and three eyes, and a peaceful countenance; its colour should be golden yellow and it should be draped in silk garments. It must be seated upon a *padmāsana*. The front right and left hands should be held in the *abhaya* and *varada* poses respectively and the back right and left hands should carry a *khaḍga* and a *khēṭaka* respectively. This is the description given in the *Aṁśumadbhēdāgama.* The *Suprabhēdāgama* has a very different description altogether; it states that the figure of Śāsta should have only two arms and two eyes and a dark complexion. It should be adorned with all ornaments and a white *yajñōpavīta.* The arms and legs should be kept folded: in the right hand there should be a crooked stick (known in Tamil as the *śeṇḍu*) and in the left fruits and tender leaves of plants (*pallava*). The body of this deity should be like that of a *bhūta*, with a big belly. The hair on his head should be jet black in colour. Śāsta should be represented as playing with dogs, sheep and fowls. He has two wives named Madanā and Varṇanī; the figures of these should be sculptured one on either side of that of Śāsta, with large breasts and adorned with all ornaments. To the left of Śāsta there should be the figure of Damanaka—who he is, is not mentioned—of ill-looking features.

The *Kāraṇāgama* agrees with the *Aṁśumadbhēdāgama* in taking Sāsta as the son of Mōhinī by Hara, but states, with *Suprabhēdāgama*, that Sāsta should have only two arms and two eyes, and a dark complexion. Śāsta should be seated on a *pīṭha*, with his left leg hanging down the seat and the right one folded and rested upon the seat vertically. On the knee of this latter leg should rest the elbow of the stretched left arm. In the right hand there should be a *vajradaṇḍa*, which is a crooked stick (note the *vajra* a characteristic weapon of the Bauddha Bōdhisatva). The figure of Śāsta should be of youthful and peaceful appearance. The hair of his head should be like blue-black ink and be spread out. His vehicle is the elephant as also is the crest on his banner. He should have by his side a blitheful damsel. At the end of the description, it is mentioned that the colour of Śāsta might be blue, white or dark, his vehicle the bull, that he might have four arms and that the crest on his banner a cock.

The same authority states that if Ārya is to be represented as a *Yōgi* he should be sculptured as seated in *yōgāsana ;* if as a student of the Vēdas, he should wear a *pavitra* (a ring made of *kuśa* grass) on his fingers, and wear his upper cloth on his shoulder in the *upavīta* fashion and be seated in the *vīrāsana* posture. If Sāsta is to be shown as seated in the *sukhāsana* fashion, the posture should be what is known as *sukhāsana*, the right foot of the bent right leg resting upon the thigh of the left leg which should be hanging. The gaze of Sukhāsana-Ārya should be fixed on his right foot.

PLATE CXXXIX.

Fig. 1. Śāstā : Bronze : Śāstānkōṭṭai.

Fig. 2. Śāstā : Stone : Tiruppaṛaiyāṛu.

[To face page 490]

PLATE CXL.

Fig. 1. Gajārūḍha Śāstā : Bronze : Vaḻuvūr.

Fig. 2. Śāstā : Bronze : Tiruppālatturai.

[To face page 491]

Four photographs are given in illustration of the images of Śāsta. Fig. 2, Pl. CXXXIX is the photograph of an image to be found in the Śiva temple at Tiruppaṟaiyāṟu in N. Travancore. This image is seated with its right leg bent and rested in a vertical position and the left leg bent and rested in a horizontal position on the seat. The right hand of the figure is in the *varada* pose and rests upon the right thigh; the left arm which is slightly bent is made to rest upon the left thigh. The image is adorned with all kinds of ornaments. This is the Vīrāsana-Ārya. The second photograph fig. 2, Pl. CXL is of a bronze image belonging to the temple at Tiruppālatturai in the Tanjore district. This image is also seated in the *vīrāsana* posture, with his left arm, which is stretched out, resting upon the knee of the left leg which is bent and kept resting vertically on the seat. The right leg is hanging down the seat which is a *padmāsana*. The right hand is held in the *kaṭaka* pose, to receive in it a *śeṇḍu* stick. The hair on the head of this image is spread out fan-wise in a circle. The third photograph fig. 1, Pl. CXL, is of another bronze image to be found in the temple at Vaḻuvūr also in the Tanjore district. It represents Śāsta as seated upon an elephant which has on each side a double tusk unlike the mundane elephant. The figure of Śāsta in this instance is sculptured exactly like the image of Tiruppālatturai. The fourth illustration fig. 1, Pl. CXXXIX, the original of which is enshrined in the temple at Śāstānkōṭṭai in Travancore is of a standing figure of Śāsta. Here, he is represented with a pair of arms, which carry the *dhanus* and *bāṇa* respectively and as standing erect. On the two upright posts of the highly ornamented *prabhāvaḷi* are sculptured the two *dēvīs* of Śāsta, the right one of them carrying, as usual in the case of an image attended by two *dēvīs*, a *padma* and the left one a *nīlōtpala* flower.

KSHETRAPALA.

KSHĒTRAPĀLA.

FOR the protection of the towns and villages from evil deities and from bad men, the shrine of the Kshētrapāla should be in the north-east corner of the town or village, the image of the Kshētrapāla being set up and *pūjā* offered to it systematically. It is best (*uttama*) for the shrine to face the west; it may face the south, but it is not very good to do so (*madhyama*) and to make it face the east is the worst (*adhama*).

The image of the Kshētrapāla should be always a nude standing one with three eyes; it may possess two, four, six or eight arms. The *sātvika* image has either two or four arms; the *rājasa* six arms and the *tāmasa* eight. In the *sātvika* form alone, the image, though it might possess side tusks should be of pacific look, whereas, in the other cases, it should be of terrific look only. Similarly, the colour of the body differs in different aspects of the Kshētrapāla; it is white if the image is a *sātvika* one; it is red if it is *rājasa* and black if it is *tāmasa*.

In the case of the *sāṭvīka-mūrti*, if the image of Kshētrapāla has only two arms, there should be the *triśūla* in its right hand and a *kapāla* in its left. On the other hand, if there are four arms, there must be the *khaḍga* in the back right hand, and the *ghaṇṭa* in the back left hand, or *śūla* and *kapāla* or *śūla* and *ghaṇṭa* respectively. The two front hands should be held in the *varada* and *abhaya* poses.

In the case of the *rājasamūrti* the image of Kshētrapāla should carry in its three right hands the *triśūla*, the *khaḍga* and the *ghaṇṭa* and in its three left hands the *khēṭaka*, the *kapāla* and the *nāga-pāśa*. And, in the case of the *tāmasamūrti*, there should be, in addition to the articles mentioned above, the *dhanus* in the additional fourth right hand and the *bāṇa* in the additional fourth left hand.

All the three aspects of the Kshētrapāla should have the hair on the head standing erect all round the head and of blazing red colour; the figure must be standing erect (*samabhaṅga*) on a *padmapīṭha* and be adorned with different kinds of snake ornaments. As has been observed above, nudity is the most characteristic feature in all these images. Such is the description contained in the *Aṁśumadbhēdāgama.*

The *Suprabhēdāgama* and the *Kāraṇāgama* have each some slight variations in their description of Kshētrapāla. The former authority mentions that the image of Kshētrapāla should be adorned with a *nāga-yajñōpavīta* on its body and a garland of skulls on the head; that the eyes should be circular in shape and that if the image has four arms, there should be the *triśūla* and the *khaḍga* in the right hands and the *kapāla* and the *khēṭaka* in the left hands; if there are six arms, in the additional right hand there should be a *nāgapāśa* and in the additional left hand the *tōmara* (a weapon); and if there are eight arms, together with the articles mentioned above, the additional right hand should carry a *ḍamaru* and the additional left one the *khaṭvāṅga.*

The *Kāraṇāgama* agrees with the above descriptions in all details except in regard to the articles held by the image which has eight arms; in this case, according to this authority, there should be in seven out of the eight hands the *kapāla*, the *śūla*, the *ghaṇṭā*, the *pāśa*, *agni*, the *ṭaṇka* and the *khaṭvāṇga* and the remaining hand should be held in the *abhaya* pose.

Aghōraśivāchārya in his *Vighnēśvara-pratishṭhāvidhi*, gives a *dhyāna-ślōka* in which the dog is said to be the vehicle of Kshētrapāla.(1) The Tamil *Nighaṇṭus* agree with this authority in this respect; the *Piṅgala-nighaṇṭu* distinctly mentions that Kañchuka, Kāri, Mukta, Nirvāṇi, Siddha, Kapāli, Vaṭuka and Bhairava are the other names of Kshētrapāla. From this it will be evident that the so-called Kshētrapāla is no other than Bhairava described elsewhere and therefore need not have been treated here in a separate chapter; but since the *āgamas* deal with this aspect of Śiva, which is said to be his one-ten-thousandth part, under a separate head and in a separate chapter, the arrangement of the *āgamas* is here followed strictly (See figs. 1 and 2, Pl. CXLI).

---

(1) दंष्ट्रिणं चोग्ररूपञ्च यज्ञरक्षाधिकारिणम् ।
श्वानवाहं ज्वलत्केशं क्षेत्रपालमहं भजे ॥

Fig. 1. Kshētrapāla : Stone : Ajmere : Merwara.

Fig. 2. Kshētrapāla : Stone : Haḷebīḍu.

[To face page 498]

BRAHMA.

BRAHMĀ.

THE history of Brahmā has incidentally been given here and there in the first volume of this work as also in a previous portion of the present one. It has already been stated that Brahmā was born in a golden egg and was therefore known as Hiraṇyagarbha; that he sprang from the waters and the ether; that he took the form of a boar and lifted up the earth from the ocean; that he took the *avatār* of a fish; that he was born from the lotus that issued from the navel of Vishṇu; that he was the father of Daksha and other Prajāpatis (patriarchs), that he disputed the superiority of Vishṇu over himself and that when, in connection with the dispute, Śiva appeared between them in the form of a pillar of fire, he (Brahmā) went up to search for its upper end and failed to do so; that he was born to the *ṛishi* Atri and his wife Anasūya as one of the aspects of Dattātrēya; that he served as a charioteer of Śiva when the latter attacked the Tripurāsuras; and that he acted as *purōhita* (officiating priest) in the marriage of Śiva and also of Subrahmaṇya; and many other things have also been mentioned about him.

It is well-known that Brahmā (who is to be carefully distinguished from Brahma in the neuter gender) is a member of the later Hindu Trinity; but he is not held now in such great importance as the other two members of the Trinity. No temples are dedicated for his exclusive worship, nor is there any sect or class owing special and exclusive allegiance to him; in other words, there is no Brahmā cult as we have the Vaishṇava and the Śaiva cults with a large number of adherents, ever quarrelling over the superiority of their own particular sect or god. Hence it is believed by some people that Brahmā is offered no *pūjā* on earth now, and is not worshipped at all. This opinion is far from the truth. As has been elsewhere remarked, there exists (and should exist), no temple which has not got all the three members of the Trinity, be it a Śiva's temple or Vishṇu's. The niche on the northern wall of the central shrine of the Vishṇu's or Śiva's temple should contain an image of Brahmā and must receive daily *pūjā*. He is one of the most important of the *parivāra-dēvatās* of the first *prākāra* of a Vishṇu or Śiva temple. Nor are instances of a separate temple dedicated exclusively to Brahmā wanting in India, though they are very few and far between. Even such a very late production on images and temples like the *Rūpamaṇḍana* has got a complete description of a temple of Brahmā and mentions its *parivāra-dēvatas*, the *dvārapālakas* etc., facts which clearly indicate that the building of separate temples for Brahmā had not yet become unknown. Elaborate descriptions of the images of Brahmā are found in almost all works of authority.

The Rūpamaṇḍana says that the four peaceful looking faces of Brahmā are symbolic of the four Vēdas, the four Yugas, and the four Varṇas. Formerly Brahmā had five heads, but one of them was cut off by Śiva. The four heads should be respectively facing the four quarters. Brahmā should have four arms; he may be standing, seated on either a *padmāsanā* or a *haṁsa* (swan). The *Śilparatna* mentions another seat called the *lamba-kūrchāsana* for Brahmā; the phrase literally means a seat composed of long grass; it perhaps is meant to indicate a seat or mat made of grass. If he is to be represented as seated, he should be shown in the *yōgāsana* posture; if standing, then on a *padma-pīṭha*. The complexion of Brahmā should be chrome-yellow and the colour of his eyes a mixture of red and yellow (orange). On his head should be a *jaṭā-makuṭa* and he should be adorned with all ornaments; there should be on his chest a white *yajñōpavīta*. His body should be covered with a coat of white sandal paste and he should be wearing a garland of white flowers. A *kaṭisūtra* (or waist-band) should go round the loins. The undergarments should consist of white clothes and the upper portion of the body should be covered with a deer's skin worn in the *upavīta* fashion. There should be golden or ruby *kuṇḍalas* in the ears. The *Suprabhēdāgama* states that the colour of *jaṭās* on his head should be of red colour and the *Śilparatna* and the *Vishṇupurāṇa* would have the colour of Brahmā white and crimson respectively. The hands of Brahmā may carry the following articles or may be held in the following poses:—

(1) There may be the *akshamālā* and the *kūrcha* (a handful of *kuśa* grass) in the right hands and *kuśa* and *kamaṇḍalu* in the left hands; or

(2) the *sruk* and the *sruva* in the right hands and the *ājya-sthāli* (ghee-pot) and *kuśa* grass in the left ones; or

(3) the front two hands may be held in the *abhaya* and *varada* poses the back hands carrying

PLATE CXLII.

Brahmā : Bronze : Madras Museum.

[To face page 504]

PLATE CXLIII.

Fig. 1. Brahmā : Stone : Tiruvoṟṟiyūr.

Fig. 2. Brahmā : Stone : Madras Museum.

[To face page 505]

the *akshamālā* and the *kamaṇḍalu* (See Pl. CXLII); or

(4) the front right hand may be placed with its palm facing below on the palm of the front left hand which is facing above and both resting upon the crossed legs; and the back hands carrying, as in the former case, an *akshamālā* and a *kamaṇḍalu*; or

(5) the front right hand may be in the *varada* pose, the back right hand carrying a *sruva* and the back left hand a *sruk* and the front left hand a *kamaṇḍalu* (See fig. 2, Pl. CXLIII); or

(6) the front right hand should keep an *akshhmālā*, the back right hand a *sruk*, the back left hand a *pustaka* (book) and the front left hand a *kamaṇḍalu*.

The *Vishṇupurāṇa* requires that Brahmā's eyes should be closed as in the attitude of *dhyāna* or meditation and the *Rūpamaṇḍana* prescribes a beard for him. The former authority also adds that he should be seated in a chariot drawn by seven swans. To the right and left of Brahmā should be his consorts Sarasvatī and Sāvitrī respectively. Their persons should be adorned with all ornaments and they must be naturally also very beautiful; or, it is enough to represent

Sāvitrī alone with Brahmā seated on his left side or on his left lap. According to the *Śilparatna* there ought to be four *Vēdas* and the *ājya-sthāli* placed in front of Brahmā and he should be surrounded on all sides by *ṛishis*.

The *Rūpamaṇḍana* gives the following description of Sāvitrī; she should have four faces and four arms; in the hands she should carry an *akshamālā*, a book, a *padma* and a *kamaṇḍalu*. She is a deity who is meant to bestow all good to the Śrōtriya Brāhmaṇas.

In a temple exclusively dedicated to Brahmā, there should be set up in the central shrine that aspect of his, named Viśvakarma. In this form Brahmā has, as usual, four heads and four arms; in his hands there should be the *akshamālā*, a book, a bundle of *kuśa* grass (?) and a *kamaṇḍalu;* and he should be seated upon a swan (See Pl. CXLIV). The following *parivāra-dēvatas* are required to be set up in the eight quarters beginning from the east and going round clockwise, namely, Ādiśēsha, Gaṇēśa, the Mātṛikās, Indra, Jalaśāyi, Pārvatī and Rudra, the Navagṛahas and Lakshmī respectively. Below is given a table mentioning the names of the Dvārapālakas of the temple of Brahmā and the articles held by them in their hands :—

PLATE CXLIV.

Brahmā : Stone : Aihole.

[To face page 506]

No.	Name.	Objects held in the			
		Right hands.		Left hands.	
1	Satya	Padma	Sruk	Pustaka	Daṇḍa
2	Sadharma	Pustaka	Daṇḍa	Padma	Sruk
3	Priyōdbhava	Akshamālā	Padma	Āgama (Pustaka)	Daṇḍa
4	Yajña	Daṇḍa	Āgama	Sruk	Kavacha
5	Vijaya	Akshamālā	Gadā	Khēṭaka	Daṇḍa
6	Yajñabhadra	Do.	Do.	...	Do.
7	Sarvakāmika	Do.	Pāśa	Aṅkuśa	Do.
8	Vibhava	Daṇḍa	Aṅkuśa	Pāśa	Padma

All these eight Dvārapālakas should be represented as of terrific nature and with beards. There should be *makuṭas* on their heads. A large number of *ṛishis* also with moustaches and *jaṭas*, carrying in their hands the *akshamālā* and the *kamaṇḍalu*, should be seated in the temple of Brahmā and be meditating upon him.

Nine photographs are given in illustration of the images of Brahmā ; the originals belong to the various parts of India and are of different varieties; they exhibit the general natural characteristics of the country to which each belongs. Of these, the picture on Pl. CXLIV, is that of Brahmā found in the Śiva temple at Aihoḷe in the Bijāpūr district of the Bombay Presidency. Brahmā is here seated upon a *padmāsana* with his left leg hanging and the right one kept bent and supported on the seat. He has in his front right hand an *akshamālā*, in the back right hand a *pāśa* (?), in the back left hand a *kamaṇḍalu* and the front left hand is kept in the *varada* pose. He wears *jaṭāmakuṭas* on his heads and has an *yajñōpavīta*, *kaṭisūtra* and other ornaments. To the right and left are two women (whose arms alone are visible in the photograph) carrying flower garlands held over the head of Brahmā; probably they represent the goddesses Sarasvatī and Sāvitrī. At the base of the seat and on the left is seated a *ṛishi* with his hands held in the *añjali* pose (these alone are visible in the picture) and correspondingly on the right is a *hāmsa* (whose tail, one wing and one leg alone are visible in the photograph).

The second photograph, (Pl. CXLV), is that of a sculpture to be found in Sopāra in the Ṭhāṇa district of the same Presidency. It is a standing figure of Brahmā. As in other pieces of sculpture, this one also has a pointed beard for the middle face only. On the head are *jaṭāmakuṭas* and a *yajñōpavīta* graces his body; there are also the *kaṭisūtra* and other ornaments. In the right front hand of the image is held apparently a lotus; in the back right hand, is the *sruk*, in the back left hand a *kūrcha* and in the front left hand

PLATE CXLV.

Brahmā : Stone : Sōpāra, Ṭhaṇa District.

[To face page 508]

PLATE CXLVI.

Brahmā : Stone : Aihoḷe.

[To face page 508]

PLATE CXLVII.

Brahmā : Stone : Haḷebīḍu.

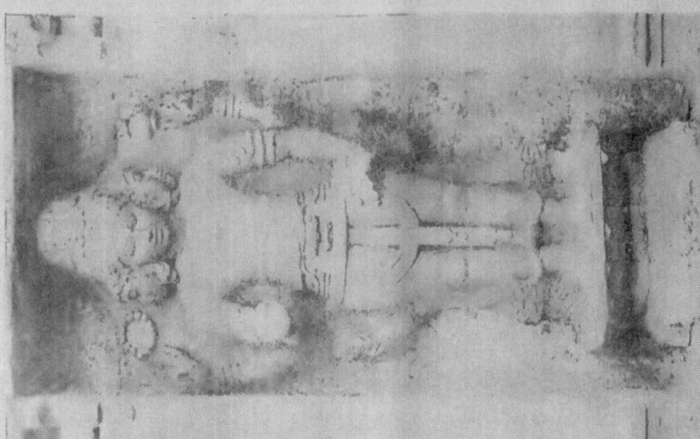

Brahmā : Stone : Kumbhakōṇam.

[To face page 609]

PLATE CXLVIII.

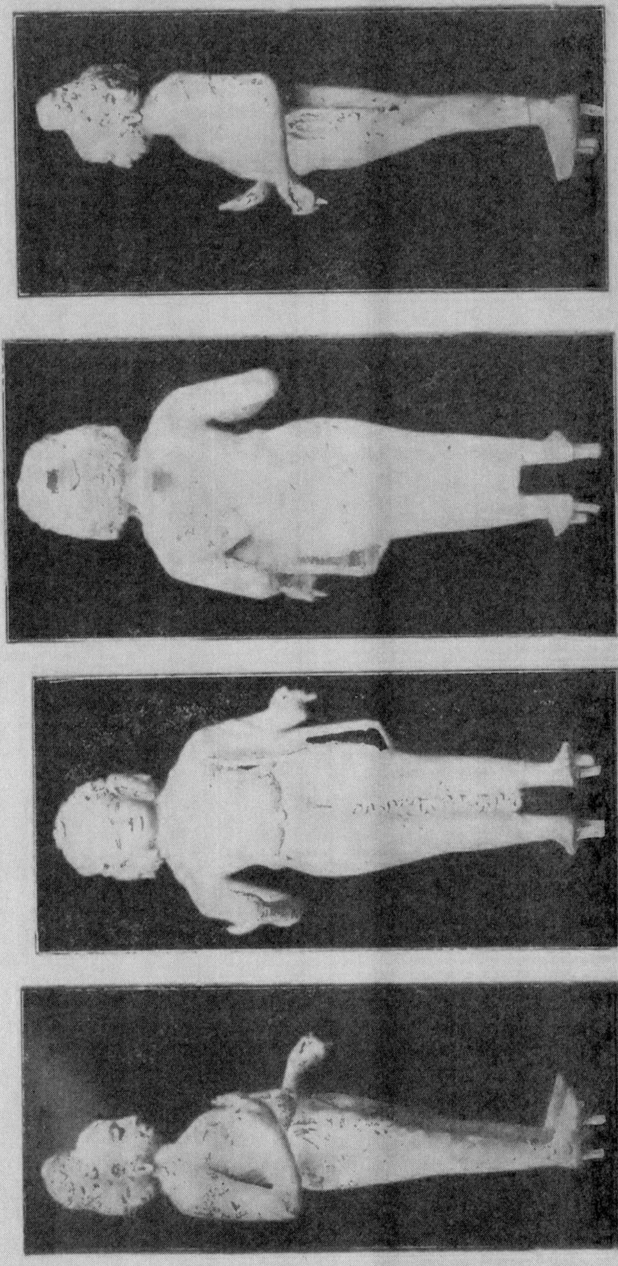

Right view.

Front view.

Back view.

Left view.

Brahmā : Bronze : Karachi Museum, Sind.

[To face page 509]

a *kamaṇḍalu.* On either side of the figure of Brahmā stands a female figure, apparently carrying in their hands bundles of *kuśa* grass. To the left of Brahmā is his vehicle, the swan, and to the right a *brahmachārin* boy. Here, the figure of Brahmā has a big belly, which is bound up, with a *udarabandha.* Fig. 2, Pl. CXLIII is exactly similar to the Sopāra sculpture, but belongs to the Chālukya-Hoysaḷa style.

The illustration, fig. 1, (Pl. CXLVII), comes from the Nāgēśvarasvāmin temple at Kumbhakōṇam. It is almost like the Sopāra figure; the points of difference being that the central face has not got a beard; the front right hand is in the *abhaya* pose and the back right carries an*a kshamālā;* the back left hand has a *kamaṇḍalu* and the front left hand is resting upon the thigh (*kaṭyavalambita hāsta*). The workmanship is excellent and the effect is very pleasing.

The next plate, (Pl. CXLVIII) contains the photographs of the front, back and the side views of a very beautiful figure of Brahmā; they were supplied to me by the Superintendent of Archæology of the Western Circle. This figure of Brahmā is peculiar in that it has only two arms instead of four as required by the *āgamas:* the right one of these is held bent with the palm turned inwards. What this hand-pose indicates is not plain. The other arm is also bent and is carrying a *kamaṇḍalu*, whose neck alone now remains in the sculpture. On the heads are *jaṭāmakuṭas* and the underwear is a fine cloth whose folds and creases are beautifully arranged by the artist. On the left shoulder is thrown in an artistic manner a deer-skin, the head and forelegs of the deer being well visible in the side view. On the whole this piece of old sculpture is an excellent specimen of the art of India.

The next illustration (Pl. CXLIV) is also from Aihoḷe. Brahmā is seated in the centre on a swan. He has in his hands an *akshamālā*, a lotus (?), the *kūrcha* and a *kamaṇḍalu*. Surrounding him are *ṛishis*, three on either side, a young boy is taking lotus flowers in his hands to Brahmā and another is seen on the top right hand corner of the panel. The *ṛishis* are here represented as being very emaciated presumably by reason of their austerities. The photograph next reproduced is that of an image of Brahmā to be found in the Madras Museum. It belongs to the Chālukya-Hoysaḷa School and is a standing image, carrying in its hands an *akshamālā*, *sruva*, *pāśa* and *kamaṇḍalu*. Here all the faces of Brahmā have pointed beards.

The original of the next photograph, fig. 2, Pl. CXLVII, is in the Hoysaḷēśvara temple at Haḷebīḍu and is of the later Hoysaḷa period. It is also a standing figure, under a very artistically and delicately carved umbrella and *prabhāvaḷi* and ornamented with beautifully executed ornaments. It carries in its hands an *akshmālā*, a *pāśa* the *sruk* and the *sruva* and a *kamaṇḍalu.* On either side of Brahmā stands a woman carrying a *chāmara* (chauri); perhaps they represent Sarasvatī and Sāvitrī.

In the Madras Museum is preserved a beautiful bronze image of Brahmā seated under a *prabhāvaḷi*, whose photograph is reproduced in Pl. CXLII; this image has *kirīṭamakuṭas* instead of *jaṭāmakuṭas* on the heads. The front right hand is held in the *abhaya* pose and the front left hand in the *varada* pose; while the back right hand carries an *akshamālā* and the back left hand a *kamaṇḍalu.* Bronze images of Brahmā are very rare and especially the one like the Madras Museum image, which is an *utsava-vigraha*, is met with very rarely, if at all. This image clearly points to the existence of Brahmā worship, even with grand festivals and processions, as would appear to be unmistakably evidenced by this *utśava-vigraha.*

The next illustration, fig. 1, Pl. CXLIII, is from the temple at Tiruvoṟṟiyūr. The original is found in the niche in the north wall of the shrine of Gauḷēśvara in the Śiva temple at that place. It belongs to the latter part of the eleventh century A. D. and does not differ from the Kumbhakōṇam image.

The last illustration, Pl. CXLIX, is the reproduction of the photograph of the figure of Brahmā found in the north niche of the central shrine of the Śiva temple at Tiruvadi. In its back right hand, is the *akshamālā ;* the front right one seems to have been held in the *abhaya* pose; the back left hand and the front left one are carrying the *kamaṇḍalu* and a book respectively. It is one of the finest pieces of sculpture of Southern India.

PLATE CXLIX.

Brahmā: Stone: Tiruvadi.

[To face page 512]

THE DIKPALAKAS.

THE DIKPĀLAKAS.

According to Hindu mythology, the eight quarters of the universe are governed by the eight guardian deities beginning with Indra and hence these eight deities are known by the name of Dikpālakas. These deities are:—

1. Indra, the lord of the east,
2. Agni, the Lord of the south-east,
3. Yama, of the south,
4. Nirṛuti, of the south-west,
5. Varuṇa, of the west,
6. Vāyu, of the north-west,
7. Kubēra, of the north and
8. Īśāna, of the north-east.

It might be noticed that all these eight deities held prominent positions in the Vēdic period, long before Vishṇu and Śiva of the modern Trinity, became supreme in Hindu mythology; and the former are now obliged to be content with the more modest situation of the guardianship of the quarters of the universe. It therefore becomes necessary to trace the history of the degradation, so to speak, of these deities from the exalted positions held by them during the Vēdic times.

INDRA.

The word Indra, is derived from Indha, meaning *kindler* says the *Śatapatha-Brāhmaṇa.* In the *Ṛig-vēda* he is distinctly mentioned as one born without a fellow : (*tvam anapir Indra janushasanadasi*) and as one without a rival (*aśatrur Indra jajñishē*). In the *Taittiriya saṁhitā* Indra is seen contesting his supremacy with Vishṇu, the Yajñapurusha. The same *Śatapatha-Brāhmaṇa* mentions that Indra, Agni and Sūrya strove hard to secure the supreme positions among the gods and succeeded : this statement gives us an insight into the origin of the Trimūrtis of the later times. In the *Ṛig-vēda* Indra is described as the wielder of the *vajra* (or iron thunderbolt), encompassing the sky and the waters, and reaching up to heaven and is said to have fixed the earth, the luminaries, propped up the sky and so on, and that these acts were all done under the exhilarating influence of the drink quaffed off from three cups. Though praised as unequalled by other gods or mortals, Indra is not a self-existent being but was born of a mother (*Ṛig-vēda.* x 134, 1).

It has already been stated that the *vajra* was shaped for Indra by Tvashṭri from the bones of Dadhīcha. With the *vajra* he killed the *asura* named Vṛitra. While he, as the chief of the gods, churned the ocean of milk in company with the *asuras*, the white elephant named *Airāvata*, came out of it and this was taken for himself by Indra. The name of the wife of Indra is Indrāṇī or Śachi. In the *Mahābhārata*, Indra is said to be the father of Arjuna and to have a thousand eyes (or *yōnis*) spread all over his body because he seduced Ahalya, the wife of the *ṛishi* Gautama. He is also classed, as we know, as one of the twelve Ādityas.

It is thus seen how Indra, one of the supreme gods of the Vēdic period, deteriorated into the chief of the minor gods, the leader of the army of the gods and finally into one of the guardian deities of the eight regions. He was receiving from the human beings some sort of worship on earth, but Kṛishṇa was the first to put a stop to it. It was on this occasion that Indra caused havoc in *Gōkula* by sending down torrents of rain and it was also then that Kṛishṇa protected the cowherds and their belongings by lifting up the Gōvardhana mountain. In spite of Kṛishṇa's protest against the worship of Indra, it was still existing in the 7th to the 10th centuries of the Christian era.

The *Śilappadigāram*, that remarkable gem of dramatic epic of the Tamil language, has a chapter describing how the annual festival of Indra was celebrated in Kāvirippūm-paṭṭinam, the metropolis of the Chōḷas: it states that the festival began on the Paurṇimā of the solar month Vaiśākha and was continued for twenty-eight days. The date of this work has been determined to be the middle of the eighth century A.D. In an inscription belonging to the reign of Parāntaka Chōḷa I to be found in Toṇḍamānāṟṟūr near Kaḷahasti, mention is made of the details of the arrangements made for celebrating the festival for Indra. The custom of offering *pūjā*, and *a fortiori* of celebrating festivals, to Indra does not obtain at the present day.

The Vēdic deity Indra plays also an important part in the Buddhist and Jaina religious lore. The description of Śakra, as given on p. 78 of Beal's *Catena of Buddhist Scriptures* is almost exactly the same as that given in Hindu works.

As has been already stated, Indra is the lord of the eastern direction and therefore the image of the deity is to be placed on the eastern side, when a group of the Dikpālakas is set up. The places where such a group is generally placed in a Hindu temple are the ceiling of the front *maṇḍapa*, the eight corners of one of the upper-storeys of the *vimāna* if it has more storeys than one, and, if the temple has more than one *prākāra*, in one of them.

The description of the image of Indra, as also of the other *Dikpālakas* is contained in almost all the *āgamas* and in the *Bṛihat-saṁhiṭā* and *Vishṇu-dharmōttara*. It is stated in the *Aṁśumadbhēdāgama* that the colour of the image of Indra should be dark and that it should have two eyes and two arms; the image should possess very handsome features and be adorned with the *kirīṭa*, *kuṇḍalas*, *hāra*, *kēyūra* and other ornaments and be draped in red garments (delicate textured Chinese cloths ?). Indra should carry in his right hand the *śakti* and in the left the *aṅkuśa*. The neck of the figure of Indra should be thick and the belly rather big; the image might be sitting or standing upon a *siṁhāsana* or be seated upon his elephant, the Airāvata.

To the left of the figure of Indra should be seated that of his consort Indrāṇī, decorated with all ornaments and carrying an *utpala* flower in the hand, and the features should be those of a gay and joyful young woman. On either side of this celestial pair should be represented two Gandharva women waving multicoloured *chāmaras*.

Some of the other authorities have practically the same description but differ in stating that the articles held in the hand by Indra are the *vajra* and *aṅkuśa* or a *nīlōtpala* flower ; while the others state that the colour of Indra should be white and that he should have a third eye lying horizontally in the middle of the forehead and four arms,—one of the right hands of which is to carry the *vajra*, the other right hand a *padma*, while one of the left arms should be passed round the figure of Indrāṇī as in embracing and the remaining left hand should carry the *aṅkuśa*.

Indrāṇī should be of the colour of gold and be clad in blue garments. She should have two arms of which one should be embracing Indra and the other hand should carry a *santāna-mañjari*. The *Vishṇudharmōttara* adds that she should be seated upon the left lap of herlord.

The elephant Airāvata should have four tusks, two on either side.

Two photographs are reproduced in illustration of the description of the figure of Indra. The first figure Pl. CL, is to be found in Chidambaram. Indra is seated upon his Airāvata and has four arms, the front two hands are in the *abhaya* and *varada* poses and the back hands carry the *aṅkuśa* and the *vajra*. The second one, fig. 1, Pl. CLI, is seated on a *bhadrapīṭha* and has four arms. The front right hand is kept in the *varada* pose and holds in it an *akshamālā ;* the front left hand

Indra: Stone: Chidambaram.

[To face page 520]

PLATE CLI.

Fig. 1. Indra: Stone:

Fig. 2. Vâyu: Stone: Chidambaram.

[To face page 520]

carries a *kamaṇḍalu* and the back right and left hands hold the *aṅkuśa* and the *vajra* respectively. The head is adorned with a *jaṭāmakuṭa* and a number of necklaces and an *yajñōpavita* adorns the chest.

AGNI.

Agni was also a very important deity in the Vēdic age and with Indra and Sūrya formed the Triad of that period. As with Indra this principal deity came, in course of time, to occupy a very minor place in the Hindu Pantheon. He was the most adorable to all *hōtris*, he it was who knew the proper seasons to worship the gods with oblations, he was the medium through whom the gods received their share of offerings and he was believed to be concealing himself in waters or plants. He was the lord of the house, the resplendent guest of the house and is friendly to man. He was also a terror to the *rākshasas* and *yātudhānas*, whom he crushed between his iron teeth. His birth is accounted for in various ways. He is said to have been brought down from the sky, generated by Indra between two clouds, by Dyaus and in the waters. He has a triple existence, namely, as fire on earth, as lightning in the atmosphere and as the sun in the sky and that the sun entered into him at night and emerged out of him at dawn. Agni was actually generated in the Vēdic age by the rubbing of one piece of wood with another vigorously: the lower piece was called the *araṇi* and the child thus born, that is, the fire, was found to consume its own mother, the wood. The description of Agni as he was conceived by the Vēdic bards is that he had two heads, four horns, three feet and seven arms.

Later on Agni is identified definitely with Rudra and Śiva and is therefore considered to be the father of Kārttikēya. He becomes the destroyer among the later trinity and he is also considered to be capable of conferring blessings upon humanity; truly does Agni (fire) destroy everything if not handled properly and is therefore a source of damage to man; also he is an excellent friend of man conferring the boon of removing all obnoxious matter, perishing or decaying matter by burning them down and rendering the surroundings of human dwellings clean and healthy. At present Agni occupies a minor position as the medium or agency for conveying the offerings, made through him, to gods. His wife is Svāhā.

We have a fine description of Agni of the later period given in the *Harivaṁśa*. There he is represented as draped in black clothes, has the smoke for his standard and head-gear and carries a flaming spear. His chariot is drawn by horses of red colour and the winds are the wheels of his chariot. He has a ram as his pet animal and he is more often shown as riding this animal instead of in a chariot as described above. The following is the *Āgamic* description of Agni :

Agni should be of red colour, with four arms and three eyes and the hair or *jaṭā* of the head which should also be of red colour, standing on end and forming a sort of *prabhāmaṇḍala.* He should be seated upon a ram. The front two hands should be held in the *varada* and *abhaya* poses, while in the back right hand there should be the *sruk* and in the back left hand the *śakti.* If he is represented as having only two arms, they should carry the *sruk* and *śakti* respectively. According to another authority, Agni should be of the colour of molten gold or the red colour of the rising sun and be clad in red garments ; he should have also moustaches and a *yajñōpavīta.* In his hands he should keep the *akshamālā* and the *kamaṇḍalu.* Where he is represented as possessing four arms, the *Vishṇu-dharmōttara* states, he should carry in his right hands the flames of fire (*jvālās*) and the *triśūla* and in one of the left hands the *akshamālā*, while the remaining left hand should be embracing his wife Svāhā. It also adds that Agni should have four sharp tusks and that his chariot should be drawn by four parrots and that the banner on it should be the smoke (*dhūmakētu*). The driver of the chariot of Agni is Vāyu. His consort Svāhā should be clothed in red garments, be smeared with *kuṅkuma* (saffron paste) and be adorned with *mātra* (?) and be carrying a *ratna-pātra* in her hand (that is, a vessel containing gems or one set with gems).

According to a third authority the colour of Agni should be yellow like that of Brahmā and he should also be represented like Brahmā with golden coloured *jaṭās* and eyes of yellow colour: he is to be carrying in his hands the *akshamālā* and the *śaktiyāyudha* and be seated upon a seat known as the *arddha-chandrāsana*.

Two illustrations of the figure of Agni are given on Pls. CLII and figure 2, CLIII. The first figure is found in the Śiva temple at Kaṇḍiyūr in Travancore. It has two heads which are of the goat, seven arms and three legs. Of the seven arms four are on the right side and three on the left. The second figure belongs to the Śiva temple at Chidambaram and is almost similar to the first figure. Instead of the faces being those of goats, as in the first figure, they are human in this case and a bull (not a ram as required by the *āgamas*) is sculptured behind Agni as his vehicle.

PLATE CLII.

Agni : Stone : Kaṇḍiyūr (Travancore).

[To face page 524]

Fig. 1. Yama: Stone: Chidambaram.

Fig. 2. Agni: Stone: Chidambaram.

[To face page 524]

THE DIKPĀLAKAS.

YAMA OR VAIVASVATA.

Yama is also a deity of some celebrity of the Vēdic period. In the *Ṛigvēda* he is mentioned as the son of Vivasvat and of Śaraṇyū, the daughter of Tvashṭri, with a twin sister named Yami. This sister of his importuned him to become her husband, but he successfully resisted the incestuous offer. He was the first man who died, reached the other world and showed others the path to that world. He guides other men thither, and assembles them in a house which is secured to them for ever. He is, however, nowhere in the Vēdic period, represented as a punisher of sins ; nevertheless he is still an object of terror. He has two dogs each with four eyes and wide nostrils which guard the road to this last abode of the mortals. In one place he is actually identified with death.

In the later day mythology he is reduced to the situation of the guardian of the region of the deceased, and, as the presiding deity of the place, he is invested with the powers of appraising the quality and quantity of the sin committed by each soul and meting out proportioned punishments: as the dispenser of justice he is also known as Dharmarāja. He is said to be the father of Dharma, the eldest of the five Pāṇḍavas. The following description of the image of Yama occurs in the Sanskrit authorities :

Yama should be of dark colour, resembling the rain-cloud, with two arms, fire-coloured eyes and sharp side-tusks. He should be adorned with a *kirīṭa-makuṭa* and other ornaments, a red flower garland and be covered over with red sandal-paste and draped in red garments. He may be seated either on a *siṁhāsana* or on a he-buffalo. His hands should bear a *khaḍga* and a *khēṭaka* or a fruit and tender leaves or *daṇḍa* and *pāśa*.

On either side of Yama should be standing Mṛityu and Saṁhitā, with terrific faces and of dazzling blue and red colours respectively. Besides these there should be also two women waving *chāmaras* on either side of Yama. In front of Yama should be standing two Brāhmaṇas called Dharma and Adharma, as also at the door, Chitragupta and Kālī, all clothed in red garments. Yama should be surrounded by the *dēvas*, *asuras*, *dharmis* (those who have done good acts) and *pāpis* (sinners) ever worshipping him.

The *Vishṇudharmōttara* states that the colour of Yama's garments is golden yellow and that, seated on his left lap, there should be his consort *Dhūmōrṇā* whose complexion is that of the *nīlōt-pala* flower. Yama has four arms, while his consort has only two. In his right hand Yama keeps the *daṇḍa* and the *khaḍga* and in the left hand a flaming *triśūla* and the *akshamālā*. The right arm of *Dhūmōrṇā* is to be passed behind Yama in embrace with the left hand bearing a pomegranate fruit. On the right side stands Chitragupta dressed like the Westerners (*āpīchyavēsha*); he is to be of fine looks and to carry in his right hand a stile and in the left a palm leaf for recording the acts of the mortals. To the left of Yama stands Kāla of terrific appearance and armed with the *pāśa*.

The figure of Yama whose photograph is given on Pl. CLIII is found in the Śiva temple at Chidambaram. It has two arms; the right hand carries a *pāśa* and the left a *gada*. There is a small *karaṇḍa-makuṭa* on the head and a number of ornaments on the person. His vehicle, a bull, is standing behind him.

NIRṚUTI.

Nirṛuti is also a deity of the Vedic period; though mention is made of this deity in the *Ṛigvēda*, neither the Vedic nor later literatnre throws much light on it. In the dictionaries Nirṛuti is said to be Alakshmī, (Jyēshṭhādēvi), a *rākshasa*, etc. In later mythology Nirṛuti is made the guardian of the south-western region of the universe and an elaborate description of this divinity is given in the *āgamas* and other authoritative works.

Nirṛuti is said to be of blue colour, with a large body draped in yellow garments and seated either on a *bhadrapīṭha*, a lion or riding on the shoulders of a man.(1) The *Vishṇudharmōttara* states that he must be seated on an ass, bearing a *daṇḍa* in his hand. He should have a terrific appearance with ill-looking eyes, gaping mouth, exposing teeth and side tusks, and the hair on the head standing on end. However, he should be adorned with all ornaments and with garlands composed of all flowers and be surrounded by Rākshasas and seven *Apsaras* women. He should have two arms; in the right hand there should be a sword and in the left one a shield. According to the *Vishṇudharmōttara* Nirṛuti has four consorts named Dēvī, Kṛishṇāṅgī, Kṛishṇāvadanā and Kṛishṇapāśa and these should also be with him. The *Apsaras* ladies surrounding Nirṛuti should be clothed with silk garments, and should be of handsome looks, with smiling countenances, large breasts and glutials, thick thighs and slender waists; they should smear different kinds of sweet smelling scents on their bodies.

(1) *Nara-vāhana* is the characteristic vehicle of Kubēra.

Fig. 1. Kubēra : Stone : Dohad Panch Mahals.

Fig. 2. Nirṛuti : Ahōbilam.

[To face page 528]

One illustration of Nirṛuti is given in fig. 2, on Pl. CLIV. Herein Nirṛuti is seen riding upon the shoulders of a man and carrying a *daṇḍa* in his right hand.

VARUṆA.

Varuṇa was no doubt an important deity of the Vēdic period; he belonged to the triad, Indra, Varuṇa and Agni. He is praised often in company with Indra or Mitra as the possessor of illimitable resources and as upholding the heaven and the earth. He is the lord of the rain, the water and the sea. Except for the fact that he is the guardian of the west, he is practically overlooked in modern mythology. At the present when the rain fails he is invoked by *mantras* and *pūjā* and prayed to send down showers.

Varuṇa is of white colour, is draped in yellow garments and possesses a pacific look. His head should be adorned with a *karaṇḍa-makuṭa* and all other ornaments and should be wearing on his person an *yajñōpavīta*. He should be represented as of strong constitution and as seated or standing upon a fish or *makara* (a kind of aquatic animal, more mythical than real) or a crocodile. He may be represented as possessing two or four arms; if shown with two arms only, one hand should be in the *varada* pose and the other should be carrying a *pāśa*; if with four, one of the hands should be in the *varada* pose, while the remaining ones should carry the *pāśa*, a snake and a *kamaṇḍalu*.

As usual, the *Vishṇudharmōttara* has a different description from those found in the *āgamas*. It states that Varuṇa should be seated in a chariot drawn by seven *haṁsas*; his colour is like the *vaiḍūrya* (a precious gem) and he must be draped in white garments and adorned with ornaments set with pearls and necklaces composed of the same material. He should have a slightly hanging belly and four arms. Over his head there should be a white umbrella and on his left the fish banner. In the right hands of Varuṇa there should be the *padma* and the *pāśa* and in the left hands the *śaṅkha* and the *ratna-pātra*. A very good looking consort of his should be seated on his left lap with a *nīlōtpala* in her left hand and her right arm embracing Varuṇa, her lord.

To the right and left respectively of Varuṇa should be standing the river goddesses Gaṅgā and Yamunā. Gaṅgā of moon-like white colour and possessing a pretty face should be standing on a *matsya* or *makara*, with a *chāmara* in one hand and a *padma* in the other, and Yamunā, also possessing good looks and having the colour of the

PLATE CLV.

Fig. 1. Gaṅgā : Stone : Fig. 2. Yamunā : Stone :
Tigova : Jabulpur District, Central Provinces.

[To face page 531]

PLATE CLVI.

Gate of a Temple with Gangā and Yamunā on the jambs:
Stone: Kharod, Bilāspūr District, Central Provinces.

[To face page 531]

nīlōtpala flower, should be standing on a tortoise with a *chāmara* in one hand and a *nīlōtpala* in the other.

Varuṇa being the lord of the ocean he is represented in the descriptions as keeping with him the *padma*, the *śaṅkha* and a vessel containing *ratnas* (or gems)—the sea being believed by the Hindus to be the repository of gems—and as being attended upon by the river goddesses.

Illustrations of the river goddesses, Gaṅgā and Yamunā are given on Pls. CLV and CLVI. Fig. 1, Pl. CLV represents Gaṅgā; she is standing upon a *makara* under the shade of a tree. Her right elbow rests upon the shoulder of a female attendant, while the left hand carries some object which is not quite clear in the photograph. Two more dwarfish attendants are on her left side. Yamunā is represented in fig. 2 on the same plate. She also stands under a tree one of whose branches she holds by her left hand. The right hand is held in the *sūchi* pose. She is standing upon a *kūrma* (tortoise). On either side of her is an attendant. Pl. CLVI is a very finely carved gate-way of a ruined temple of Śiva at Kharod, in the Bilāspūr district of the Central Province. On the jambs of this gate are sculptured Gaṅgā and Yamunā; Gaṅgā stands on the proper right and Yamunā on the proper left. They both carry *pūrna-kumbha* or pots full of water.

VĀYU.

Vāyu is also a Vēdic, elemental deity. His place is in the air. He is said to have Indra as his charioteer or his companion in his chariot; however, he does not occupy any very prominent place in the Vēdas. He is called the son-in-law of Tvashṭri and is reputed to be handsome looking in appearance. Maruts or winds are not associated somehow with Vāyu, though in one instance he is said to have given birth to them by the rivers of heaven.

In the later mythology he is assigned the guardianship of the north-west region of the universe. He is said, in the *Mahābhārata*, to be the father of Bhīma; as also of Hanumān. The Mādhvas believe that their Āchārya, Ānandatīrtha, is an incarnation of Vāyu.

Vāyu should be a youthful person of powerful constitution, of black colour and possessing two or four arms. His eyes must be of red colour and his garments, white. He should have a wavy-curved brow and be adorned with all ornaments. In his right hand it is stated, there should be a *dhvaja* (banner) and in the left a *daṇḍa*. It might also mean that the right hand should be held in the *patāka-hasta* pose. Some authorities prescribe the *aṅkuśa* in the right hand of this deity. His hair should be dishevelled and he may be seated either on a *siṁhāsana* or on a deer; the latter is more often me with in sculptures as the vehicle of Vāyu. He should also appear to be in a haste to move very quickly. The *Vishṇudharmōttara* states that the colour both of the body and of the garment of Vāyu should be sky-blue and that he should carry in his hands the *chakra* and a *dhvaja*. Vāyu should have his mouth open. To his left should be seated his consort.

DHANADA OR KUBĒRA.

The words Dhanada or Kubēra literally mean the giver of wealth or a person with a deformed body. The story of Kubēra who is also known by the name of Vaiśrāvaṇa is given in the *Uttara-kāṇḍa* of the *Rāmāyaṇa* thus:—Brahmā begot a mind-born son named Pulastya; the latter had a son named Gaviputra-Vaiśrāvaṇa. This Vaiśrāvaṇa left his father and joined Brahmā, who granted him, in return for his devotion to himself, immortality and lordship over riches and installed him in Laṅkā as his capital. Pulastya, incensed at the faithlessness of his first son, made one portion of his self be born as Viśravas, who looked with disdain upon his ungrateful brother Vaiśrāvaṇa. Vaiśrāvaṇa wishing to pacify his father presented him with three good looking Rākshasīs named Pushpōtkaṭa, Mālinī and Rākā. By Pushpōtkaṭa Pulastya had two sons Rāvana and Kumbhakarṇa; by Mālinī, Vibhīshaṇa; by Rākā, Khara and Sūrpanakhā. These later born sons of Pulastya being envious of Vaiśrāvaṇa's prosperity practised austerities; pleased with them Brahmā conferred upon Rāvaṇa the boon of possessing at will any number of heads and shapes, and of being invincible except by men. Having obtained these powers Rāvaṇa came to Laṅkā, expelled Vaiśrāvaṇa and made himself the master of the place. Kubēra retired to the hill Gandhamādana. Elsewhere Vaiśrāvaṇa, Rāvaṇa and others are said to be the sons of Viśravas and also that Kailāsa became the abode of Kubēra and that his wife was Riddhī. It is somewhat strange to hear in the *Rāmāyaṇa* that Mahādēva went to the Kailāsa to pay a visit to Kubēra, when it is remembered that the Kailāsa is believed to be the abode especially of Mahādēva.

Another account of the origin of Dhanada is to be found in the *Varāhapurāṇa*. When Brahmā entertained the desire to create the universe, a shower of lime-stones began to pour forth from his face attended with a hurricane. After sometime the fury of the storm broke down and everything became calm by the wish of Brahmā. He asked the mass of stones which thus fell from him to assume the form of a divine person of peaceful countenance and appointed him as the Lord of Wealth and commanded him to be also the guardian of the riches of the gods.

In the Buddhist literature and mythology also Kubēra is the god of riches and the guardian deity of the northern region of the universe. He is also the lord over the *Yakshas* and is the husband of Hāritī. He has also the name Vaiśrāvaṇa (whose Prākṛit form Vassāvaṇa, is current in Ceylon) and Jambhala.

The *āgamas* also recognise him as the master of the *Yakshas* and describe his figure as follows :— The colour of Kubēra according to one authority should be golden yellow and according to another crimson ; the colour of his underwear is to be red, and the upper garment, white. His person should be adorned with all ornaments, including a *kirīṭa*, or a *karaṇḍa-makuṭa*, *kuṇḍalas* and necklaces composed of a series of golden coins. He should be good looking, or even terrific looking and possessing either two or four arms : if the arms are only two, the hands may be kept in the *varada* and *abhaya* poses or the left hand may keep in it a *gadā* : if, on the contrary, he has four arms one of them should be embracing his consort Vibhavā and another one embracing Vṛiddhi, seated on the left and right laps respectively of Kubēra ; the remaining hands should carry the *gadā* and the *śakti*. The *Vishṇudharmōttara* states that his left eye should be of yellowish brown colour (*piṅgala*), that he should be dressed in the fashion of the westerners (*āpīchyavēsha*), that his body should be protected with an armour, that he should have a pair of moustaches and that there should also be side-tusks in his mouth. All the authorities are uniform in asserting that Kubēra should have a rather big and slightly pendant belly. He may be seated on a *padmapīṭha* or be driving in a chariot drawn by men or even directly seated on the shoulders of a man. The *Aṁśumadbhēdāgama* states that the vehicle of Kubēra is a ram. To the right and left of Kubēra there should be respectively the Śaṅkhanidhi and the Padmanidhi whose descriptions are as follows: these two personifications should resemble in shape the *bhūtas*, that is, with short limbs attached to a large trunk and surmounted by a large face, carrying in their hands lotus flowers. They should be draped in white clothes, adorned with *karaṇḍa-makuṭas* and placed upon *padmapīṭhas*. In another place it is stated that he should be surrounded by the eight kinds of wealth and by a number of *Yakshas*.

The two goddesses Vibhavā and Vṛiddhī should in their turn be embracing Dhanada each by one arm and carrying in the other hand a *ratna-pātra*.

The *Rūpamaṇḍana* prescribes the elephant as the *vāhana* of Kubēra and states that his four hands should carry the *gadā*, a purse containing money, a pomegranate fruit and a *kamaṇḍalu*.

In the Buddhist mythology, Kubēra is sculptured exactly as in the Hindu representation; but he is immediately recognised as Kubēra by a mongoose which is generally also shown either as sitting upon his left lap or placed on his left side. (See Figs. 196 and 199* in V. A. Smith's *History of Fine Art in India and Ceylon*).

ĪŚĀNA.

The lord of the north-east region of the universe is Īśāna. From the description given of him, we know he is the same as Mahādēva or Śiva. Īśāna should have three eyes, a pacific appearance, white complexion and should be draped in white

---

* Mr. V.A. Smith calls this male figure 'Sarasvati enthroned' evidently through oversight. The mangoose in the left hand of the figure, and the three ornamented pots of treasure placed under its feet clearly show that the sculpture represents Kubēra.

garments and in tiger's skin. His head should be adorned with a *jaṭā-makuṭa*, his chest should bear an ordinary white *yajñōpavīta* or a *nāga-yajñōpavīta* and otherwise also adorned with all ornaments. There should be the crescent moon on the *jaṭā-makuṭa*. He may be seated either on a *padmāsana* or better upon a white bull. If he is represented with only two arms, his hands must carry a *triśūla* and a *kapāla* or one of the hands (the left one generally) might be in the *varada* pose; if, however, he has four hands, the two front ones should be sculptured as playing upon a *vīṇā* and the others are to be held in the *varada* and *abhaya* poses. This description seems to be incorrect; for the *vīṇā* must be held only by the hands of the front pair of arms, which are also the very hands that are necessarily to be in the *varada* and *abhaya* poses.

THE ASVINI-DEVATAS.

THE AŚVINI-DĒVATĀS.

THE twin-gods, the Aśvini-dēvatās, were playing an important part in the Vēdic period. Yāska says in his *Nirukta* that these gods Aśvins were so-called because they pervaded everything (*vyaśnuvātē*), one of them with moisture and the other with light; but Aurṇavabha derives the name from *aśva*, a horse. Who these gods were the commentators of the Vēdas themselves are not able to answer; some say these were personifications of heaven and earth; others of day and night and yet others, the sun and moon. Prof. Roth thinks that they represent Indra and Āditya and that they are the harbingers of the Dawn to usher whose existence they hurry on in their chariot. In the *Ṛigvēda* they are said to be the sons of Vivasvat and Śaraṇyū in one place, of the sky in another and of the ocean in a third. The *Taittirīya-saṁhitā* calls them the youngest of the gods and the brothers of Ushas. They are also associated with Sūryā, the daughter of the sun, and are held to be young, beautiful, bright and agile and as wearing lotus garlands; they were possessed of wonderful therapeutic power and are said to have helped many with this power of theirs. We have already seen that they restored the head of Yajña-Nārāyaṇa which was accidentally severed. They are described as always riding in a chariot drawn by fleet horses. Nothing very definite about these gods or their position in the Vēdic mythology is known and yet it is a well-known fact that they are very often invoked in the Vēdic literature.

In the *Purāṇic* period different stories are given for the origin of the Aśvins. For example, the *Varāhapurāṇa* gives the following account of the birth of the Aśvins. Sūrya (the sun) married the girl named Saṁjñā who was offered by Tvashṭa and begot through her Yama and Yamunā. Saṁjñā, however, was able to bear no more the heat of Sūrya and resolved to run away from him. Leaving behind her her shadow (*chhāya*) and assuming the form of a horse (*baḍaba*) repaired to Uttarakuru. By Chhāyā, Sūrya had two children named Śani and Tapatī. All the children of Sūrya were ill-treated by Chhāyā and Yama and Śani complained against her to their father. For this they were cursed by Chhāyā as the effect of which Yama had become the lord of the *prētas*, but the hard lot was mitigated by the intercession of the father who made him even in this accursed state to be the god of Dharma and be also one of the Lōkapālas, guarding the southern quarter of the Universe; and Śani obtained powerfully evil eyes through the curse of Chhāyā. After all these events were over, Sūrya learnt that Saṁjñā was living as a mare in Uttarakuru, went there in the form of a stallion, joined her and begot the twin children named the Aśvins, who are, in this account, held to be the personifications of *prāṇa* and *apāna*, the two vital airs which sustain animal life. In the cosmic evolution, these gods came into existence on the *dvitīyā tithi*. With the help of their father Sūrya they obtained a place among the gods and became the custodians of the *amṛita* and physicians to the celestials. The Aśvins are known by the name of Nāśatyas. Curiously enough these deities, little understood by even the Vēdic commentators, have received a great deal of consideration in the hands of the authors of the various *Āgamas*. In fact, a number of *Āgamas* contain a description of the images of the Aśvini-dēvatās. It is highly doubtful if ever they were sculptured and set up in temples, for at the present time we do not hear of the existence of such images anywhere in India, as *svayampradhāna* deities. No doubt they are carved on the same block of stone as was used for the sculpturing of the image of the sun, as attendants of this latter deity. The following description of the images of the Aśvins is found in the *Aṁśumadbhēdāgama*. These gods should be represented as horse-faced and be seated together upon a *siṁhāsana*. They should be adorned with a *jaṭā-makuṭa* on the head, the *yajñōpavīta*, garlands of yellow flowers, and with all other ornaments. The colour of their body is to be red, like the flower of the pomegranate tree. The Aśvins should have lotus-like beautiful eyes and each only a pair of arms; in the left hand they should keep each a book, while their right hands should be held in the *abhaya* pose. The right legs of the gods should be hanging below the seat, while the left one must be folded and rested upon it. The names of these gods are given as Nāśatya and Dasra. On either side of the Aśvins should be the figures of the females called Mṛita-sañjīvinī and Viśalyakaraṇī waving chauris (*chāmaras*). The colour of these goddesses is said to be brown.

On the left of the Aśvins there should be the figures of Danvantari and Ātrēya, adorned with all ornaments, draped in black garments and carrying in their hands a sword and a shield each. Their colour should be yellow and red respectively.

In the *Suprabhēdāgama* it is stated that the colours of the Aśvins are white and yellow respectively and that they ought to be clothed in white garments and should have turbans on their heads. The *Pūrvakāraṇāgama* which also contains their description does not differ materially from the above two authorities. But the *Vishṇu-dharmōttara* gives a somewhat different description. It substitutes instead of the *abhaya* pose required by the *Āgamas* a vessel containing drugs (*ōshadhis*) in their right hands. On the right and left of these gods are to be standing, according to this authority, two goddesses named Rūpa-sampat and Ākṛiti of great beauty and of white (?) and grass green colours respectively, bearing in their hands vessels set with gems ; and these must be dressed in white garments.

Illustrations of the Aśvini-dēvatās might be seen on the sculpture of Sūrya reproduced on Pl. XC, fig. 3, of Volume I of this work.

DEMI-GODS.

DEMI-GODS.

HINDU mythology includes in its fold a number of minor gods such as the *ṛishis*, *pitṛis* and *nāgas.* A brief account and the description of the images of these will be given in the following paragraphs. The figures of *ṛishis*, *apsarasas* and others are, according to the *āgamas*, required to be placed in Hindu temples, and as such are not mere mythological curiosities having theoretical existences and possessing imaginary descriptions. We meet with their representations here and there in temples and the description of these is not to be considered out of place in a work of this kind. Besides, the present compilation being a close following of the *āgamas* both in arrangement and description, the existence of the descriptions of these demi-gods in the *āgamas* necessitates the incorporation of such descriptions in the present publication also. Among the heading the demi-gods are included in this chapter the following:—

1. Vasus,
2. Nāgadēva and the Nāgas,
3. Sādhyas,
4. Asuras,
5. Apsarasas,

6. Piśāchas,
7. Vētāḷas,
8. Pitṛis,
9. Ṛishis,
10. Gandharvas and
11. Marutgaṇas.

(i) VASUS.

In the *Ṛigvēda*, the number of gods is said to be thirty-three which is composed of the eight Vasus, eleven Rudras, twelve Ādityas and the heaven and the earth. According to the *Rāmāyaṇa* all the thirty-three gods were the sons of Aditi, while according to the *Mahābhārata* they were the attendants upon the sun and were worshipping him.

We learn from the *Śrī Bhāgavata* that in the sixth Manvantara, Daksha had by his wife Asikni sixty daughters. He married them to the Prajāpatis. Dharma obtained thus ten daughters of Daksha, of whom one, Vasu, begot the eight Vasus. Once upon a time, says the *Dēvībhāgavata* the Vasus with their respective wives went out enjoying pleasure and reached the *āśrama* (hermitage) of Vasishṭha. The wife of Dyau one of the Vasus seeing the celestial cow named Nandinī in the abode of Vasishṭha, asked her husband about the nature of the cow and who her owner was. He informed her that it belonged to Vasishṭha and had the rare quality of giving milk which was able to make those that drank it live eternally young and of sound health. The wife of Dyau requested her husband to carry away the cow to their residence, for she wanted her human friend, the daughter of the king Uśīnara, to drink the milk of Nandinī and to live long in unfading youth and sound health. The Vasu robbed Vasishṭha of his cow and was conducting her to his home; the *ṛishi* perceiving through his mental eye the mischief perpetrated by the Vasu, cursed all the Vasus to become human beings. Thereupon the Vasus hurried to the *āśrama* of Vasishṭha to beg for his pardon and to request him to restore them once again to the state of gods. He promised that the other Vasus except Dyau would regain their celestial condition after the lapse of a year; Dyau alone should continue to be a human being for a long time. Disgusted with the human existence that was soon to come upon them and to divest themselves of it in an honourable way, they requested the river goddess Gaṅgā to be temporarily born on the earth as a woman, to become the wife of the king Śantanu and beget them as her children, whom, they requested, she should throw away into the river one after another as they were born. To this Gaṅgā agreed and the Vasus were born to her and being disposed of as requested by them, they then reached their former position in heaven.

The names of the eight Vasus are given in a majority of the authorities as follows:—Dhara, Dhruva, Sōma, Āpa, Anala, Anila, Pratyusha and Prabhāsa. In one work the name of Savitṛi is substituted for Āpa in the above list. The general features of the images of the Vasus are that they should have each two arms, two eyes, and be of red colour; they should be clothed in yellow garments and be adorned with *karaṇḍa-makuṭas.* They should have side tusks, terrific look, sinuous brows and fine hair. As in the case of all other images these should also be adorned with all ornaments. They may either be seated or standing and should be carrying in their hands the *khaḍga* and the *khēṭaka* respectively. The *Suprabhēdāgama*, among the Śaivāgamas, and the *Viśvakarma-śāstra* agree in stating that the colour of the Vasus is golden yellow and the latter prescribes beautifully embroidered red garments for the images of their demi-gods. The *Viśvakarma-śāstra* gives detailed descriptions of each one of the Vasus. According to this authority the images of the Vasus ought to possess four arms. In the following table are given the various articles carried in their hands by the eight Vasus.

No.	Names of the Vasus.	Right hands.		Left hands.		REMARKS.
		Front.	Back.	Front.	Back.	
1	Dhara ...	Padma ...	Akshamālā	Hala ...	Śakti ...	Notice the fact that the back left hand has uniformly the *śakti*, which is made the insepar-able concomitant of the Vasus, ac-cording to this authority.
2	Dhruva ...	Kamalāksha-mālā.	Chakra ...	Kamaṇḍalu.	Śakti ...	
3	Sōma ...	Padma ...	A rosary of pearls.	Aṅkuśa ...	Śakti ...	
4	Āpa ...	Hala ...	Śakti (?) ...	Aṅkuśa ...	Śakti ...	
5	Anila ...	Aṅkuśa ...	Akshamālā.	Śakti ...	Upavīta (?)	
6	Anala ...	Akshamālā.	Sruva ...	Kapāla ...	Śakti ...	
7	Pratyusha ...	Khaḍga ...	Aṅkuśa ...	Khēṭaka ...	Śakti ...	
8	Prabhāsa ...	Daṇḍa ...	Kapāla ...	Aṅkuśa ...	Śakti ...	

(ii) NAGADEVA AND THE NAGAS.

The Nāgas are, according to the *purāṇic* authorities, a race of serpents who inhabited the *Pātāḷa-lōka* or the nether regions. The *Mahābhārata* and the *Varāhapurāṇa* give the origin of the Nāgas. By Dākshayaṇī, the daughter of Daksha, Kaśyapa begot the seven serpents beginning with Vāsuki. Their progeny increased and the world was flooded with serpents to the great detriment of man. The latter complained to Brahmā about the hardship caused to them by the serpents. Brahmā summoned the serpents to his presence and cursed them to be ruined by the imprecations of their mother which she uttered in the Svāyam bhuva-manvantara and banished them to the *Pātāḷa-lōka* with the command that they should not bite any human beings, except those who were predestined to die a premature death and those that were really bad. We learn from the *Mahābhārata* that the Nāgas were the sons of Kadru and Kaśyapa, that they induced their step-brother Vainatēya (Garuḍa) to fetch for them the *amṛita* (ambrosia) preserved in the kingdom of Indra, that they were made to grant freedom to Vinata and her sons from the voluntary bondage they had entered into under Kadru, that they were deprived of the *amṛita* brought down by Garuḍa, that Indra carried it away once again to his abode, that by licking the *kuśa* grass on which the vessel of *amṛita* was placed they had their tongues split in twain and other accounts. In historical times, portions of India were inhabited by a race of men who went by the name of the Nāgas and they are said to have formed the majority of persons who joined the newly started Buddhistic religion. Some scholars of Malabar are inclined to believe that the modern Nāyars (Śudras) of Malabar might be descendants of the early Nāgas, a name which, in modern times might have been corrupted into Nāyars. The hypothesis is more fictitious and fanciful, than real and tenable.

The Nāgas are believed to have been born on the Pañchamī *tithi* of the bright half of the month Śrāvaṇa and the whole of India offers *pūjās* to the Nāgas on this day, except the Draviḍa brāhmaṇas ; in Southern India the Mahrāṭa and the Kannaḍa women observe the previous day, the *chaturthi*, also as sacred to the Nāgas, a custom which is nowhere seen to be observed. It is a common sight all over India to meet with the Nāga images set up under big pipal trees by scores and worshipped occasionally. Childless people take a vow to set up the images of Nāgas in anticipation of being blessed with children and celebrate the Nāgapratishṭhā ceremony with great pomp and at great expenditure.

A description is found in the *Aṁśumadbhēdāgama* of Nāgadēva, which appears to be that of the chief of the Nāgas. It states that the image of Nāgadēva should have three eyes, four arms, a beautiful countenance and be of red colour. The image should be adorned with a *karaṇḍa-makuṭa* on its head and all other ornaments on its person and should be standing upon a *padma-pīṭha.* The hands of the front arms should be kept in the *varada* and *abhaya* poses, while the back hands should be keeping each a snake in it. Over the head of Nāgarāja should be a hood of a five headed cobra and he must be draped in white clothes.

The *Śilparatna* adds that the Nāgas should be half human and half serpentine in shape, the lower part, below the navel being that of a snake. Their heads must be covered with hoods having one, three, five or seven heads and they should have split tongues like those of snakes. In their hands they must carry a sword and a shield respectively. The *Maya-śilpa* gives the detailed descriptions of the seven great Nāgas, Vāsuki,

Fig. 1. Nāga and Nāginī: Stone: Haḷebīḍu.

Fig. 2. Nāgiṇi: Stone: Madras Museum.

[To face page 557]

Takshaka, Kārkōṭaka, Padma, Mahāpadma, Śaṅkhapāla and Kuḷika as follows :—

The colour of Vāsuki is pearl-white ; that of Takshaka glistening red and he must have on his hood the mark of the *svastika*. The colour of Kārkōṭaka is black and on his hood there should be three white stripes ; Padma is of the rosy hue of the lotus flower, with a white streak and adorned with coral ornaments. The colour of Mahāpadma is white with the mark of *triśūla* on his hood ; whereas that of Śaṅkhapāla, is yellow with a white streak on his hood ; the colour of Kuḷika is also red and his hood bears the mark of the crescent moon. All these seven great serpents should have two tongues and two arms and a hood with seven heads held over their human heads bearing on them gems. They must all be clad in one or three coats and carry in their hands an *akshamālā* and a *kamaṇḍalu*.

Two photographs are reproduced in illustration of the descriptions given above. Fig. 1, Pl. CLVII, is the photograph of the Nāga and Nāgiṇī to be found in the Hoysaḷēśvara temple at Haḷebīḍu. The lower parts of these are in the form of snakes and are entwined with each other. The head of the Nāga has over it a hood of cobra with seven heads, whereas that of the Nāgiṇī one of three heads. The

Nāga bears in his right hand a sword and is embracing with his left arm his consort. The Nāginī bears a lotus flower in her left hand and embraces with her right arm her consort. The human head of the Nāga is adorned with a *karaṇḍa-makuṭa* and that of the Nāginī with a knot of hair.

Fig. 2 on the same plate is that of a piece of sculpture of a Nāginī preserved in the Madras Museum. As in the previous instance the Nāginī has her lower half that of the snake. She has on her head a *karaṇḍa-makuṭa* which is covered by a cobra hood with three heads in it. She carries a sword and a shield in her right and left hands respectively.

(iii) SĀDHYAS.

According to the *Nirukta* the word *Sādhya* means a ray of light. The gods who abide in the sky and absorb water and other liquids are said to be the *Sādhyas*. They are said to be adorable even by the gods.

The Sādhyas are twelve in number and are named, according to the *Agnipurāṇa*, Māna, Manta, Prāṇa, Nara, Apāna, Vīryavān, Vinirbhaya, Naya, Daṁśa, Nārāyaṇa, Vṛisha and Prabhi. These are said to be the sons of Dharma and were great souls (*mahātmas*). The images of Sādhyas should be represented as seated upon *padmāsanas* and as carrying in their hands the *akshamālā* and the *kamaṇḍalu.*

(iv) ASURAS.

The Asuras and Rākshasas are very old demi-gods. They are often mentioned in the Vēdic period. The *Nirukta* says that the word *asura* implies a cloud that sprinkles water. The dark mass of cloud was evidently personified into a wicked being which required to be chastened by Indra to pour down rain. The *asuras* are included in the Pañchajana which, according to the *Nirukta* was composed of the Gandharvas, the Pitṛis, the Dēvas, the Asuras and the Rākshasas ; but Śāyaṇa enumerates them as the gods, men, serpents, Gandharvas including the Apsarasas and the Pitris. From the *Taittirīyasaṁhitā* we learn that the earth once belonged to the *asuras* and the gods had only a very small place on it. The gods asked the *asuras* for more, upon which the *asuras* desired to know how much of the land they would require. The Dēvas replied "as much as this she-jackal can go round in three steps." The *asuras* consented to grant this request of the Dēvas and Indra assumed for the occasion the form of a she-jackal and stepped round the whole of the earth in three strides. Then again we learn from the *Śatapatha Brāhmaṇa* that the gods became distinguished from the *asuras* under the following circumstances: being the descendants of Prajāpati, they both obtained their father's inheritance, namely, speech,—true and false; they both spoke truth and falsehood. The gods then abandoned falsehood and took exclusively to truth. As a consequence, the gods became weaker and poorer. The poet admits naively that truth certainly reduces people at first to the conditions mentioned above, but that the gods ultimately became prosperous. The *asuras*, on the other hand, took to falsehood and indulged solely in it. Truth became in after-times the triple science (*trayīvidyā*). In other ways also the *asuras* sank lower in status than their brothers the *dēvas*. In striving to attain higher positions, the *asuras* did not know to whom they should offer their oblations and through presumption went on taking them into their own mouths, whereas the gods offered the oblations to each other. Because of their presumption, the *asuras* were overcome by the *dēvas*. In the Aitihāsic period the Rākshasas are often described as dark, ugly, impure people, addicted to man-eating.

The images of *asuras* are required to be made in a variety of forms with terrific appearances, having fearful side tusks, ugly eyes surmounted with curling awkward brows, and carrying several

Fig. 1. Dvārapālaka of the Śiva Temple: Stone: Kāvēripākkam.

Fig. 2. Apsaras: Stone: Śrinivāsanallūr.

[To face page 561]

kinds of weapons. They should be adorned with all ornaments, including the *kirīṭa* and the *kuṇḍalas.*

(v) APSARASAS.

The *Apsarasas* are so called because they are said to have sprung from the waters when the ocean was churned for obtaining ambrosia (*amṛita*). They are believed to be celestial nymphs with no one as their particular husbands and that they were courting human heroes as they ascended the heaven. In the *Uttara-kāṇḍa* of the *Rāmāyaṇa* we are told that Rāvaṇa considered the *apsarasas* as mere courtezans, without any husbands and with this conviction he ravished against her protestations Rambhā, the most beautiful of all the *apsarasas*, even though she pointed to him that she being the wife of Naḷakuvēra, the son of his (Rāvaṇa's) brother Kubēra. The *apsarasas* are said to be seven in number and the names of the most important of these are given as Rambhā, Vipulā, Urvasī, and Tilōttama.

In sculpturing the images of the *apsarasas* they should be represented as having slender waists, large gluteals and well developed busts. They should all look very pretty with a smiling countenance and adorned with all ornaments and draped in silk garments. They must be standing erect (*sama-bhaṅga*) on *bhadra-pīṭhas.*

(vi) PIŚĀCHAS.

Who this class of beings are is not clearly known; but that they are known to have been referred to from very early times is evident from literature. Their images are required to be represented as of extremely emaciated appearance, with the knobs of the bones jutting out and the veins visible under the surface of the skins; they must be composed of the bones, tendons and skin only. The hair on their head should be stiff and spread out.

(vii) VĒTĀḶAS.

Another obscure class of beings are the Vētāḷas, whose descriptions in the *āgamas* are not very different from those of the Piśāchas. The only difference between them is that the latter should be tall in stature, with parched up belly and projecting cheek-bones.

(viii) PITṚIS.

Hiraṇyagarbha Manu had Marīchī and other sons; the sons of these latter are known as the Pitṛis or Pitṛigaṇas. Mention is made of seven such *gaṇas* and they are as follows :—

(*a*) Virāṭ's sons were the Pitṛis of the Sādhyas and were called the Sōmasad.

(*b*) Marīchi's sons, those of the Dēvatas and were called the Agnishvātta.

(*c*) Atri's sons, those of the Daityas, Dānavas, Yakshas, Gandharvas, Uragas and the Rākshasas and were called the Barhishad.

(*d*) Kavi's (Śukrāchārya's) sons, those of the Brāhmaṇas and were called the Sōmapa.

(*e*) Aṅgiras' sons, those of Kshatriyas and were called the Havirbhuja.

(*f*) Pulastya's sons, those of the Vaiśyas and were called the Ājyapa, and

(*g*) Vasishṭha's sons, those of the Śūdras and were called the Sukalins.

In giving the description of the Pitṛis, the *āgamas* state that they are three in number and that they must be seated either on the same wooden seat or on a *bhadra-pīṭha ;* the three *pitṛis* are the father, the grandfather and the great grandfather. These must be sculptured as old but good looking and strong people of yellow colour, draped in yellow garments and wearing each an *yajñōpavīta.* On their head must be the *kēśa-bandha* and they should be adorned with all ornaments: their body should be smeared with ashes (*bhasma*). They should have nice teeth and have with them a walking stick and an umbrella. The *pitṛis* should have only two arms of which the left one should be kept stretched out on the knee of the bent left leg; the right hand should be held in the *sūchi-hasta* pose. The *Vishṇudharmōttara* states that the *pitṛis* should be seated upon *kuśāsana* (mat made of *kuśa* or on spread out *kuśa* grass) and that they should carry the *piṇḍapātra* or the vessel to receive the rice-balls offered to them by their living descendants.

(ix) ṚISHIS.

The word *ṛishi*, according to the *Nirukta*, means the rays of the sun and these are said to be seven in number. By an extension of meaning the term came to be applied to the *ṛishis*, the seers; just as the sun's rays spread everywhere and disclose the existence of all things, the seers or the *ṛishis* are able to perceive everything. Again, the *Śatapatha Brāhmaṇa* considers the *ṛishis* as breaths and derives the word *ṛishi* thus: "In as much as before all this Universe, they, desiring this Universe, were worn out (*arishan*) with toil and austerity therefore they are *ṛishis*." Later on, the *ṛishis* were regarded as those who had reached the other end (*pāragas*) of *jñāna* and *saṁsāra*. The origin of the *ṛishis* according to the *Nirukta* is as follows:—Brahmā took some dirt from his body and sacrificed it to the fire. From the flames there emanated the *ṛishi* Bhṛigu (=fried in the fire). After the fire subsided, another *ṛishi* arose from the live charcoal (*aṅgāra*) and was therefore called Āṅgiras. A third *ṛishi* was predicted to be born after the two former from the same fire and was called Atri; the name Atri is also capable of meaning *not-three* and hence that the number of *ṛishis* was not going to stop with three and that some more were to be born from the *kuṇḍa* (fire-pit). When the *agni* was removed and the *kuṇḍa* dug out a *ṛishi* came into existence from the place where the *kuṇḍa* stood. He was known as Vaikhānasa. The *Brahmāṇḍapurāṇa* gives a slightly different account of the birth of the *ṛishis*. Marīchi was born first; at the time of the *yāga* was born Kratu. A third came into existence saying *aham tritīya*, I am the third, and was hence known as Atri. Then again a fourth with thick hair was born and was called Pulastya; a fifth with flowing hair and called Pulaha was next born. From the heap of coins and other *dakshiṇas* (presents) placed in the *yāga-śālā* (sacrificial ground) was born another *ṛishi* and he was called Vasishṭha. All these were the mind-begotten sons of Brahmā and it is from these all other beings including the Pitṛis were generated.

The *ṛishis* are grouped into seven classes. Vyāsa and others are called the Mahāṛishis; Bhēla and others, the Paramaṛishis; Kaṇva and others, the Dēvaṛishis; Vasishṭha and others, the Brahmaṛishis; Śuśruta and others, the Śrutaṛishis; Ṛituparṇa and others, the Rājaṛishis and Jaimini and others, the Kāṇḍaṛishis.

The names of the seven *ṛishis* differ from *manvantara* to *manvantara.*

Jñāna or opinion is of two kinds, *vidyā* (true) and *avidyā* (false); the former of these arises from perception, inference and recollection and the infallible intuition peculiar to the *ṛishis.* The *ṛishis* possessed an intuition which was peculiarly their own and was shared slightly by the ordinary mortals. We learn that the *ṛishis* who lived of old and who conversed about sacred truths with the gods directly, led a conjugal life; whenever they wanted anything they approached straight the gods with metrical composition in praise of these gods; thus supernatural powers came to be attributed to these sages. The *ṛishis* seem also to be divided into the ancient and the modern, the former being Bhṛigu, Āṅgiras and others. It is worth noting that the *ṛishis* were called also *kavis* (poets) *mēdhāvins* (wise men), *vipra* (learned men) *vipaśchit*, *vēdhas*, (words meaning also the learned men), *muni* (the thoughtful), etc.

The *āgamas* give the names of the seven *ṛishis* differently; thus, the *Aṁśumadbhēdāgama* has Manu, Agastya, Vasishṭha, Gautama, Āṅgiras, Viśvāmitra and Bhāradvāja; whereas the *Suprabhēdāgama* enumerates them as Bhṛigu, Vasishṭha, Pulastya, Pulaha, Kratu, Kaśyapa, Kauśika and Āṅgiras; and the *Pūrvakāraṇāgama*, Agastya, Pulastya, Viśvāmitra, Parāśara, Jamadagni, Vālmīki and Sanatkumāra. We have perhaps to understand that each of these authorities gives the names as they obtained in different *Manvantaras*.

The images of the *ṛishis* should be sculptured as either seated or standing on a *padma-pīṭha*; they must be shown as peaceful old people with flowing beards reaching up to the chest, with *jaṭāmakuṭas* on their heads, *yajñōpavītas*, and with their foreheads marked with three streaks of *vibhūti* (*bhasma* or ashes). They may have in their hands a walking stick and an umbrella or they may keep the right hands in the *jñāna-mudrā* pose and rest the left arms on the knee of the left leg which must be bent and resting upon the seat. They should be clothed in garments made of barks of trees, which should be held in position by *kaṭi-sūtrâs*; their upper wear should be white clothes.

(x) GANDHARVAS.

Another class of semi-divine beings are the Gandharvas. In the *Atharvaṇa Vēda* they are said to be a class of gods, hairy, like monkeys or dogs ; they assume at will handsome appearances to seduce the females of this earth. Therefore they are invoked so that they may not indulge in this sort of wrong act but live with their own wives. The Gandharvas are believed to be deities who know the secrets of the divine truths and reveal them to the world. As we have already seen they are included in the class of Pañchajanas and Śāyaṇa links them with Apsarasas: according to him they are the males of a class of divine beings whose females were the Apsarasas. In the *Atharvaṇa Vēda* the Gandharvas are said to be 6333 in number. Of the eight different systems of marriage, according to the classification of the Āryas, one is the Gandharva system. This corresponds practically to the European and other similar systems, namely, a man and a woman falling in love with each other and entering into the life of man and wife until by mutual consent they separate or till the lifetime of one of the contracting parties, in other words the alliance is not a religious sacrament but a sort of contract. Hence the repudiation by Rāvaṇa of the protests of Rambhā whom he seduced and who was not willing to consort with him. The description of the images of Gandharvas is not met with in the *āgamas* and is, therefore, not possible to be given authoritatively.

(xi) THE MARUT-GANAS.

In the Vēdic period the Maruts are said variously to be the children of the earth under the name of Priśni and Rudra and as children of the ocean: they are said to behave like sons to Indra. Rudra and Priśni are said to have begotten these in their assumed forms of a bull and a cow. Generally they were very friendly to Indra and with their help strengthened him against Vṛitrāsura. Only in a very few instances they are described as having abandoned Indra and left him to kill Vṛitrā single-handed. The Maruts are the gods of the tempest and as such are sometimes included in the thirty-three gods and sometimes counted as outside this number; in some places they are said to be thrice sixty and in others as only twenty-seven in number. They were the favourite deities of some *ṛishis* who have sung high praises about them. In these they are extolled as having spears resting upon their shoulders wearing anklets, golden ornaments and helmets, seated upon resplendent cars drawn by spotted deer and carrying light in their hands; they are ever engaged in gathering rain-clouds and compelling them to discharge their contents. Divested of the poetic element and viewed in the ordinary sense, the Maruts are gusts of wind personified; they are as fleet as deer and are really ever busy in gathering rain-clouds and helping Indra the god of the atmosphere.

The *Aṁśumadbhēdāgama* contains a description of the images of these Maruts. They should all be of handsome looks, dark in complexion and possessing two arms and standing upon *padmapīṭhas.* They should be draped in white silk garments, adorned with all ornaments and flowers and should have luxuriantly growing hair on their heads.

APPENDIX A.

PLATE CLIX.

The Figure of Naṭarāja showing the relative positions of the limbs.

[To face page 573]

APPENDIX A.

The detailed measurements of the distances of the various limbs from the *madhyasūtra*, of the dancing Śiva-Naṭarāja are given in the *Kāmikāgama* and the *Kāraṇāgama*. The texts pertaining to this portion are not free from errors; therefore it is apprehended that some of the measurements may perhaps be incorrect. However, they are given below in the accompanying table.

Distances measured.	According to the	
	Kāraṇāgama	Kāmikāgama
The *madhya-sūtra* should pass from a distance 8½ *yavas* removed from the centre of the forehead, through a position tangential to the right wing of the nose and the centre of the projecting ankle bone of the right leg which is planted upon the figure of the *Apasmāra-pūrusha*. This rule is according to the *Kārāṇagama*. The *Kāmikāgama* says: The		

Distances measured.	According to the	
	Kāraṇāgama	Kāmikāgama.
madhya-sūtra shall pass through the head, the forehead, the side of the right wing of the nose, the right side of the navel and the centre of the projecting bone of the ankle.		
The horizontal distance of the centre of the forehead from this *sūtra*.		2 aṅgulas.
The distance between this *sūtra* and the *hikkā-sūtra* (measured along the line of sight of the observer, *i.e.*, vertically to the plane of the paper).		3 ,,
The distance of the right arm-pit from this *sūtra*.	18 aṅgulas.(?)	
The distance of the left arm-pit.	8 ,,	
The width of the neck on the left of this *sūtra*.		5 ,,
The width of the neck on the right.		4 ,,
The beginning (from the shoulder) of the left arm held in the *gajahasta* pose should be situated from this *sūtra* at a distance of		3 ,,
The left hand bearing *agni* should be lifted as high as the *hikkā-sūtra*.		
The right hand carrying the *ḍamaru* and held in the *sūchi* pose should be at the height of the *karṇa-sūtra*.		This hand is required to be one *aṅgula* above the *karṇa-sūtra*.

APPENDIX A.

Distances measured.	According to the	
	Kāraṇāgama	Kāmikāgama
The distance between the wrists of the hands bearing *agni* and the *ḍamaru* respectively from the shoulder.	24 aṅgulas.	
The distance between the middle of the forearm of the hand held in the *abhaya* pose and the forearm of the *daṇḍa-hasta* (*gaja-hasta*).		17 aṅgulas.
There should be, according to the *Kāraṇāgama*, the *sarpavalaya* round the middle of the fore-arm, the hand of which is held in the *abhaya* pose; and there must be an upper-garment of tiger's skin thrown on the shoulder between the two left arms.		
The distance between the tip of the thumb of the *abhaya-hasta* and the nipple of the right breast.		2 "
The shortest distance between the wrist of the *abhaya-hasta* and the *daṇḍa hasta*.		6 "
The width of the portion of the abdomen on the right of the *madhya-sūtra*.	4 aṅgulas.	8 "
Do. on the left.	13 "	12 "
The distance (measured on the right side) of the navel from the *madhya-sūtra*.	1 "	
The root of the penis is situated on the left of this *sūtra* at a distance of	14 "	

Distances measured.	According to the	
	Kāraṅāgama	Kāmikāgama
The back side of the buttocks is situated on the left side of this *sūtra* at a distance of	7 aṅgulas	17 aṅgulas
The *madhyasutra* should touch the *śrōṇi* and the left thigh and divide its width into two portions : the length of the portion on the right.		17 „ (7?)
Do. on the left.		9 „
The knee of the raised leg should reach the height of the navel, according to the *Kāranāgama* and *śroṇi*, according to the *Kāmikāgama*.		
The sole of the lifted leg should be just above the knee of the standing leg, according to the *Kāranagama* and up to the level of the knee, according to the *Kāmikāgama*.		
The distance between the sole of the lifted leg and the knee of the standing leg.	34 „(?)	24 „
The distance between the wrist of the *daṇḍa hasta* and the knee of the lifted leg.	1 yava (?)	14 „
The distance between the middle of the thigh of the left leg and the navel.		9 „
The distance from the *madhyasūtra* of the knee of the bent, standing right leg.	10 aṅgulas.	12, 10 or 9 aṅgulas.

From the fact that the *madhyasūtra* is required to touch the middle, practically, of the head, the *śrōṇi*, the right thigh and the centre of the ankle, we see that the line drawn from the centre of gravity of the heavy figures of Śiva-Naṭarāja is made to fall exactly in the centre of the base, which is generally a broad *padmapīṭha*, mounted upon a *bhadrapīṭha*. The perfect stability of the image is thus secured. The projecting limbs such as the two out-stretched arms, the uplifted leg and the back of the body are so symmetrically arranged with reference to this line as to counterpoise each other and not interfere in any way with the stability. Now, if the image were to stand upon only one leg without any other support, there would be the danger of the superincumbent weight acting detrimentally to the strength of the statue; the frail leg may break at the ankle, if the image sustains any accident. To avert such a possibility, the presence of the *prabhā-maṇḍala* is insisted upon; the out-stretched arms, the large number of *jaṭās* issuing from the head, a long, flowing strip of cloth which is tied round the middle of the body and the crown of the head are made to touch the *prabhāmaṇḍala* and are attached to it, thus affording perfect protection from the danger of breaking at the ankle. It might also be noticed that, as a general rule, (a more or less perfect one), the two out-stretched hands and the foot of the standing leg are made to lie on the three apices of an inverted equilateral triangle and are practically also on the same plane as that of the *prabhāmaṇḍala*. The height of mathematical calculation as regards distances and masses in the making of perfectly stable and strong images is, it might be stated, attained in the casting of the often bulky and large images of Śiva-Naṭarāja.

॥ प्रतिमालक्षणानि ॥

APPENDIX B.

प्रतिमालक्षणानि ।

लिङ्गलक्षणम् ।

लिङ्गं स्थावरजङ्गमाख्यभिदया द्वेधा तु पूर्वं पुनः
षड्भेदं क्षणिकादिभेदवशतः तत्रापि चार्काश्विनौ ।
अष्टाष्टापि च सप्तधा च नवधा भेदाः क्रमात्स्युः पुनः
प्रोक्तं मानुषके पुनर्दशविधं धारामुखाद्यैर्भवेत् ॥

व्या–लिङ्गं भूतानि लयमस्मिन् गच्छन्तीति लिङ्गम् ।

तदुक्तं सुप्रभेदे—

लयं गच्छन्ति भूतानि संहारे निखिलं यतः ।
सृष्टिकाले पुनस्सृष्टिं तस्माल्लिङ्गमुदाहृतम् ॥ इति ॥

एतल्लिङ्गं स्थावरजङ्गमाख्यभिदया स्थावरं जङ्गमं चेत्याख्या यस्याः, भिदया भेदः तया, द्वेधा स्थावरं जङ्गममिति द्विधेत्यर्थः ।

तदुक्तं कारणे—

अतः परं प्रवक्ष्यामि लिङ्गलक्षणमुत्तमम् ।
स्थावरं जङ्गमं चैव द्विविधं लिङ्गमुच्यते ॥
शिलामयं तु यद्रूपमजविष्णुहरैर्युतम् ।
त्रिसूत्रं मुकुलैर्युक्तं स्थावरं लिङ्गमुच्यते ॥
शेषाण्यन्यानि सर्वाणि जङ्गमं लिङ्गमुच्यते । इति ॥

तत्पुनः द्विविधमपि पुनः क्षणिकादिभेदवशतः क्षणिकमृन्मय रत्नजलोहजदारुजशैलजभेदात् षड्भेदम् ।

क्षणिकलिङ्गम् ।

तथोक्तं सुप्रभेदे—

क्षणिकं चैव मृल्लोहरत्नजं दारुजं तथा ।
शैलजं चैव विघ्नेश ! षड्भेदं लिङ्गमुच्यते ॥
शिलामयं तु यद्रूपमजविष्णुहरैर्युतम् ।
त्रिसूत्रं पुष्कलैर्युक्तं स्थावरं लिङ्गमुच्यते ॥
शेषाण्यन्यानि सर्वाणि जङ्गमं लिङ्गमुच्यते । इति ॥

तेषामपि भेदानाह ' तत्रापि चेति '। अर्क—द्वादशभेदतः, अश्विनौ द्वौ भेदौ, वसु[1] अष्टभेदाः, पुनरप्यष्टभेदाः, सप्तधा सप्तभेदाः, नवधा नवभेदाः, एवं क्रमात्स्युः । तथा चोक्तं सुप्रभेदे—

क्षणिकं द्वादशं प्रोक्तं मृन्मयं द्विविधं पुनः ।
दारुजं चाष्टधा प्रोक्तमष्टधा लोहजं स्मृतम् ॥
सप्तधा रत्नजं चैव शैलजं तु चतुर्विधम् ।
रत्नजं लोहजं चैव बाणलिङ्गं चलं स्मृतम् ॥
शैलजं चाचलं प्रोक्तं मृन्मयं दारुजं तथा ।

एतेषां लक्षणं फलं चापि सुप्रभेदे—

क्षणिकानां फलं वक्ष्ये सैकतं मोक्षकांक्षिणाम् ।
तण्डुलं विभवार्थीनामन्नमन्नप्रदं स्मृतम् ॥

---

१. मूले अष्टेति पदं दृश्यते ।

नदीमृद्भूमिलाभं स्याद्रोमयं रोगनाशनम् ।
नवनीतं मनोह्लादं रुद्राक्षं ज्ञानवर्धनम् ॥
गन्धं सौभाग्यकांक्षीणां कूर्चं मुक्त्यर्थिनां स्मृतम् ।
आयुष्यवर्धनं पुष्पं गुलमिष्टार्थसिद्धिदम् ॥
पैष्टं पुष्टिप्रदं प्रोक्तं क्षणिकानां फलं भवेत् ।
एतेषां चैव लिङ्गानां न प्रमाणं न च स्थितिः ॥

[मृन्मयलिङ्गलक्षणम् *॥]

मृन्मयं राज्यफलदं पक्वापक्वप्रभेदकम् ।
शुद्धदेशे मृदं ग्राह्य पूजाभागं सयोनिकम् ॥
कृत्वा दग्धमिदं प्रोक्तं पक्वापक्वमिहोच्यते[1] ।

कामिके—

श्वेतां च मृदमादाय पयस्तैलदधिघृतम् ।
यवगोधूमचूर्णं च पयोवृक्षत्वचान्वितम् ॥
विमलेन सुगन्धेन चूर्णान्यालोड्य संमृदा ।
श्रीवेष्टकं सर्जरसं तथा गुग्गुलुशर्कराः ॥
पंञ्चनिर्यासंसंयुक्तमथ लोकप्रसिद्धिदम् ।
एतेषां सङ्ख्यया तुल्यं मृदं गृह्णीत देशिकः ॥

सुप्रभेदे—

चूर्णैरालोड्य सुमृदा मासपक्षोषितं तथा ।
रत्नबीजसमायुक्तं पक्वं लिङ्गं समाचरेत् ॥

---

१. 'तत्रापक्व'मिति सुप्रभेदपाठः ।

[लोहजलिङ्गम् *।]

लोहजाष्टभेदा यथा—

सौवर्णं राजतं ताम्रं कांस्यमारकूटं तथा ।
आयसं सीसकं चैव त्रपुकं चेति लोहजम् ॥

[लोहजलिङ्गफलम् *।]

सौवर्णं श्रीप्रदं प्रोक्तं राजतं राज्यसिद्धिदम् ।
ताम्रं पुत्रप्रदं चैव विद्वेषं कांस्यमेव च ॥
आरकूटं तथोच्चाटे क्षयकारकमायसम् ।
सीसजं रोगहरणं त्रपुरायुष्यवर्धनम् ॥
एवं तु लोहजं प्रोक्तं ततो रत्नजमुच्यते ।

[रत्नजलिङ्गम् *।]

मौक्तिकं च प्रवालं च वैडूर्यं स्फटिकं तथा ॥
पुष्यं मरतकं नीलं रत्नजं संप्रकीर्तितम् ।
लोहरत्नादिके लिङ्गे पूजाभागं सपीठकम् ॥
यथालाभप्रमाणेन स्फटिकादीनि कारयेत् ।
स्फटिकादिषु कर्तव्या त्रिभागैरेव पीठिका ॥
तथायामसुविस्तारपिण्डिका शुभदा स्मृता ।
एकाङ्गुलं समारभ्य आ चतुर्विंशदङ्गुलान् ॥
लोहजं लिङ्गमित्याहुर्लक्षणोद्धारणं विना ।

[दारुजलिङ्गम् ॥*]

दारुजाष्टकं यथा—

शमीमधूकमण्डूककर्णिकारं तथैव च ।
तिन्दुकार्जुनकौ चैव पिप्पलोदुम्बरं तथा ॥

कामिके बहव उक्ताः यथा—

खदिरश्चन्दनस्सालो मधूकस्सरलो मतः ।
बिल्वः कदम्बबदरौ देवदारुश्च शिंशुपा ॥

पनसार्जुनावशोकश्च क्षीरिणो रक्तचन्दनः ।
स्निग्धसाराश्च ये वृक्षाः पयसान्ये तु मध्यमाः ॥ इति ॥

[शैलजलिङ्गम् ।]

शैलजं च ब्राह्मणादिचतुर्वर्णानुसारेण चतुर्विधम् ।

सुप्रभेदे—

शिलापि च सुविज्ञेया जातिभेदात्परिक्षयेत्[1]।
श्वेता रक्ता तथा पीता कृष्णा चेति चतुर्विधा ॥

गोक्षीरशङ्खवर्णाभा ब्राह्मणानां प्रशस्यते ।
जपाबन्धूकपुष्पाभा नृपाणां प्रोच्यते क्रमात् ॥

रजनीस्वर्णसदृशा वैश्यानां तु प्रशस्यते ।
माषगुग्गुलुसङ्काशा शूद्राणां तु समृद्धिदा ॥

सर्वेषां तु शिला कृष्णा सर्वसंपत्करी स्मृता ।
सा चोषररजःक्लिन्ना तप्ता चार्कस्य रश्मिभिः ॥

---

१. 'जातिभेदपरिक्षणैः' इति भवितव्यम् ।

अग्निदग्धान्ययुक्ता या वर्जयेत्तां प्रयत्नतः । इति ॥

एतद्दारुशिलाश्च दारुशिलासंग्रहप्रकरणोक्तप्रकारेण ग्रहीतव्याः ।

शैलजे नवभेदा यथा ।

सुप्रभेदे—

दिव्यं स्वायम्भुवं पूर्वं दैवतं गाणपं तथा ।
आसुरं सुरलिङ्गं च आर्षं राक्षसकं तथा ॥
मानुषं बाणलिङ्गं च लिङ्गं नवविधं भवेत् ।

एतेषां लक्षणं यथा—

पताका झर्झराकारा रुद्राक्षाकृतिरेव च ।
आज्यं वा मधुगन्धं वा पातालात्पर्वताकृतिः ॥
इत्येतल्लक्षणं प्रोक्तं लिङ्गं स्वायम्भुवस्य तु ।
दिव्यं स्वायम्भुवं पूर्वमुत्तमोत्तममेव च ॥
दैवतं गाणपं प्रोक्तं मध्यमोत्तममेव च ।
आसुरं सुरलिङ्गं च आर्षं चैवाधमोत्तमम् ॥
मानुषं लिङ्गमेवोक्तं मध्यमं त्वधमं भवेत् ।
बाणलिङ्गस्य नैवोक्तं लक्षणं तु विसर्जयेत् ॥

मकुटे—

दैविकं चार्षकं चैव गाणपं मानुषं तथा ।
एवं चतुर्विधं लिङ्गं दैविके लक्षणं शृणु ॥
दीपाकारं भवेल्लिङ्गं निम्नोन्नतसमन्वितम् ।
रेखाकोटरसंयुक्तं टङ्कशूलसमन्वितम् ॥

यवोन्नतमुखे धारा कराञ्जलिपुटाकृति ।
ब्रह्मसूत्रविहीनं च दैविकं तदिहोच्यते ॥
कूष्माण्डस्य फलाकारं मातुलङ्गफलाकृति ।
उर्वारुकफलाकारं कपित्थस्य फलाकृति ॥
तालीफलवदाकारं गाणपं लिङ्गमुच्यते ।
मूलंस्थूलं भवेल्लिङ्गं नालिकेरफलाकृति ॥
लिङ्गमार्षमाख्यातं ब्रह्मसूत्रविवर्जितम् ।
द्वारं वा गर्भमानं वा हस्तमानमथापि वा ॥
शिवशास्त्रोक्तमार्गेण शिरोवर्तनया युतम् ।
ब्रह्मसूत्रसमायुक्तमेतन्मानुषमुच्यते ॥

कामिके—

स्वायम्भुवं बाणलिङ्गं दैविकं चार्षकं त्विति ।
गाणपं मानुषं लिङ्गं षट्प्रकारं प्रकीर्तितम् ॥
यत्स्वेनैवोत्थितं लिङ्गं स्वायम्भुवमुदाहृतम् ।
शिवेन संस्कृतं यत्तु बाणलिङ्गमुदाहृतम् ॥
दैवेन स्थापितं दैवमार्षकमृषिपूजितम् ।
गणैस्संस्थापितं लिङ्गं गाणपं तदुदाहृतम् ॥
मानुषं मनुजैश्शिष्टैः स्थापितं तदुदाहृतम् । इति ॥

मानुषलिङ्गे (द्वा) दशभेदा यथा—

लिङ्गनिर्णये——

समलिङ्गं वर्धमानं शैवाधिकं च स्वस्तिकम् ।
सार्वदेशिकलिङ्गं च त्रैराशिकसहस्रकम् ॥

धारालिङ्गं च शैवेष्टथं मुखलिङ्गमुदाहृतम् ।
लिङ्गं च दशभेदं स्यान्मानुषे तत्प्रकीर्तितम् ॥

किरणे—

स्वयमुद्भूतलिङ्गस्य स्थापितस्य महर्षिभिः ।
दवैर्वा स्थापितस्यापि रूपमानं न विद्यते ॥
तल्लिङ्गाकृतिरूपेण नामभेदः पृथक् पृथक् ।
ज्ञातव्यः फलदश्चायं साधकेन यथार्थकः ॥

....

सार्वदेशिकंलिङ्गलक्षणं यथा कारणे—

सार्वदेशिकलिङ्गानि कथ्यन्ते गर्भमानतः ।
प्रासादगर्भमाने तु पञ्चांशे त्रिभिरुत्तमम् ॥
नवांशे पञ्चभिर्मध्यं भवत्यर्धेन कन्यसम् ।
तदवान्तरभेदेन भवन्त्यन्यानि षट् पुनः ॥
तत्तन्मन्दिरमानेन त्रयस्त्रिंशत्प्रमाणकम् ।
विंशत्यंशे कृते गर्भे दशांशमधमं भवेत् ॥
एकादशांशैर्मध्यं स्याद्भागैर्वा दशभिर्वरः ।
मध्यमे षड्विभागेन नवलिङ्गोदयस्तु वा ॥
गर्भं तु नवधा कृत्वा नवलिङ्गोच्छ्रयस्तु वा ।
अधमं गर्भपातं वा त्रिभागं चोत्तमं भवेत् ॥
मध्यमेऽष्टविभागे तु तत्तदन्तरभेदतः ।
त्रयस्त्रिंशत्प्रमाणानि लिङ्गानि कथितानि च ॥

अथवा गर्भगेहस्य त्र्यंशैकमधमं भवेत् ।
गर्भार्धं मध्यमं ज्ञेयं पञ्चत्रिंशत्परं[१] मतम् ॥

पूर्ववन्मध्यमं कृत्वा त्रयस्त्रिंशद्भवन्ति हि ।
एकहस्तं समारभ्य चैकांशेन विवर्धनात् ॥

नवहस्तप्रमाणान्तं मानं स्याल्लिङ्गदैर्घ्यकैः ।
एकविंशतिभागेन गर्भगेहे विभाजिते ॥

त्रयोदशांशकं श्रेष्ठं दशांशमधमं भवेत् ।
पूर्ववन्मध्यमं कृत्वा त्रयस्त्रिंशत्प्रमाणकम् ॥

लिङ्गायामे विकारांशे चतुर्द्विकरसंहितः ।
सत्रिभागशरैर्लिङ्गविस्तारं परिकीर्तितम् ॥

गायत्र्यंशे तु लिङ्गोच्चे पञ्चभिर्वा तु विस्तरः ।
अथवाष्टादशांशे तु लिङ्गोच्चे पञ्चभागकम् ॥

चतुर्भागोऽथवा लिङ्गविस्तारः परिकीर्तितः ।
दैर्घ्यं त्रिस्सप्तधा कृत्वा रसभूताब्धिभागतः ॥

विस्तारः कथितश्शास्त्रे लिङ्गानां मुनिपुङ्गवाः ! ।
द्वारस्तम्भाधिकश्चैव मानं लिङ्गे समूह्यताम् ॥

(जीर्णोद्धारदशके ।)

लिङ्गमानाद्धिमानं वा लिङ्गं वा हर्म्यमानतः ॥ ३६ ॥

गर्भमध्ये च सूत्रात्तु वामेऽर्चालिङ्गमेव वा ।
स्थापयेत्किञ्चिदंशं तु आश्रयित्वा विचक्षणः ॥ ३७ ॥

---

१ 'पञ्चत्र्यंशं पर' मिति भवितव्यम् ।

त्रिसप्तांशे कृते द्वारे महांशे मध्यमे भवेत् ।
कृत्वा षडंशकं तच्च वामे द्व्यंशं व्यपोह्य च ॥ ३८ ॥
तदंशमग्रे नीत्वा तु प्रागुदग्गतसूत्रकम् ।
तद्ब्रह्मसूत्रमित्युक्तं तत्सूत्रं शिवमध्यमम् ॥ ३९ ॥
गर्भार्धमधमं श्रेष्ठं पञ्चत्र्यंशं शिवायतम् ।
भवन्ति नव मानानि तयोर्मध्येऽष्टभाजिते ॥ ४० ॥
श्रेष्ठमध्यकनिष्ठानि त्रित्रिभेदानि तानि हि ।
नागरे नागरस्योक्तं मानं लिङ्गस्य मन्दिरे ॥ ४१ ॥
विकारांशे तदायामे भूतगङ्गाग्निविस्तरम् ।
जयदं पौष्टिकं सार्वकामिकं नागरे विदुः ॥ ४२ ॥
गर्भे त्रिसप्तभागे तु दशांशं द्राविडेऽधमम् ।
त्रयोदशांशकं श्रेष्ठं गर्भेऽष्टांशे तु पूर्ववत् ॥ ४३ ॥
त्रिस्सप्तांशे निजायामे षट्पञ्चचतुरंशकम् ।
जयदादिविशालं तत्पूर्ववद्द्राविडे मतम् ॥ ४४ ॥
वेसरे पञ्चपञ्चांशे गर्भागारे विमानके ।
त्रयोदशांशके हीनं श्रेष्ठं स्यात् षोडशांशकम् ॥ ४५ ॥
तयोर्मध्येऽष्टभागे तु नवलिङ्गानि पूर्ववत् ।
पञ्चपञ्चांशके दैर्घ्ये वसुधातुरसांशके ॥ ४६ ॥
वेसरस्योदितं व्यासं पूर्ववज्जयदादिकम् ।
विकारपरितो भूतव्यासः सर्वत्र कीर्तितः ॥ ४७ ॥
गर्भमानमिदं प्रोक्तं हस्तमानं तु वच्म्यहम् ।
आरभ्यैककरं नन्दहस्तान्तं षट्षडङ्गुलैः ॥ ४८ ॥

वृद्ध्यायतास्त्रयस्त्रिंशत्सङ्ख्या लिङ्गस्य कीर्तिताः ।
पञ्चारत्निविमानाद्या द्वादशक्ष्माद्यसद्मनः ॥ ४९ ॥
क्रमेणैव त्रयस्त्रिंशत्सङ्ख्या तासां विधीयते ।
केचित् त्र्यङ्गुलवृद्ध्या तु वदन्त्येकादिहस्ततः ॥ ५० ॥
आयादिसम्पदामर्थं मानादेकाङ्गुलक्षयात् ।
प्रवृद्ध्योत्तुङ्गमातव्यं तत्र दोषो न विद्यते ॥ ५१ ॥
............ष्याङ्गुलमूलाद् द्व्यर्धाष्टककलाङ्गुलैः ।
वृद्ध्या लिङ्गायतं शस्तं प्रत्येकं नवमानकम् ॥ ५२ ॥
क्षुद्राल्पमध्यमोत्कृष्टहर्म्याणामुदितं क्रमात् ।
द्वारोदयसमं श्रेष्ठं त्रिभागोनं कनिष्ठकम् ॥ ५३ ॥
स्तम्भोत्सेधनवांशे तु मुनिभूतांशकोदयम् ।
तत्तद्गर्भेऽष्टधा भक्ते नवलिङ्गोदयाः स्मृताः ॥ ५४ ॥
नागरादिषु सौधेषु प्रोक्तव्यासानि पूर्ववत् ।
प्रासादशिखरग्रीवस्तूप्यधिष्ठानमानकैः ॥ ५५ ॥
केचिद्वदन्ति मुनयः कुम्भयोन्यादयो वराः ।

லிங்கப்பிரமாணத்தாலே விமானம் கொள்ளுதல், அன்றிக்கே விமானம் முற்படச்சமையில் விமானப்பிரமாணத்தாலே லிங்கப்பிரமாணம் கொள்வான். (36)

கர்ப்பகிருஹத்தில் மய்யத்தில் இடத்தே சிறிது அம்சத்தை அடுத்த லிங்கத்தையாதல் ஸ்தாபிப்பான். அந்த அம்சம் கொள்ளும்படி. (37)

விமானத்தில் துவார விஸ்தாரத்தை இருபத்திஒரு அம்சம் செய்து இதில் நடுவில் அம்சத்தை ஆறம்சம் செய்து இதில் மய்யத்திலேனின்றும் இவிடத்தை இரண டம்சத்தை விட்டு அந்தம்சத்தில் முடிவில் நூலே கீழ்மே லான நூலாகவும் தென் வடலான நூலாகவும் அறிவான். இந்த நூலே பிரம்மசூத்திர மென்றறிக. இந்த நூல்தானே சிவ ஸ்ூத்ரமாம் என்றறிக. சிவசூத்திரமென்றது லிங்கத் தில் மய்யமென்றபடி ; லிங்கப் பிரமாணம் கொள்ளும்படி. (39)

கர்ப்ப கிருஹ விஸ்தாரத்தில் செம்பாதி பிரமாணம் கொண்டலிங்கத்தின் நீளம் அதமப்பிரமாணமாம். கர்ப்ப கிருஹ விஸ்தாரத்தை அஞ்சு அம்சம் செய்து இதில் மூன்றம்சம் கொண்டலிங்கப் பிரமாணத்தை உத்தமமென் றறிவான் உத்தமப்பிரமாணத்துக்கும் அதமப்பிரமாணத் துக்கும் இடை நீளத்தை எட்டு செய்து ஒன்பது லிங்க மாம். (40)

இந்த ஒன்பது லிங்கப்பிரமாணம் கொள்ளும்படி உத்தமோத்தமம், உத்தமமத்தியமம், உத்தமாதமம் என்ற மூன்றும், மத்தியமோத்தமம், மத்தியமமத்தியமம், மத்திய மாதமம், என்ற மூன்றும் அதமோத்தமம்,அதமமத்தியமம், அதமாதமம் என்றும் மூன்றும் ஆக பிரமாணம் ஒன்பதாக அறிவான். ($40\frac{1}{2}$)

நாகரமான பிராஸாதத்தில் நாகரலிங்கத்துக்கு பிரமாணம் சொல்லப்பட்டது. (41)

அந்த லிங்கத்தினுடைய நீளத்தை பதினாறு அம்சம் செய்து இதில் அஞ்சம்சமான விஸ்தாரத்தை ஜயதமென் றறிவான். நாலம்சம் கொண்ட விஸ்தாரத்தை பௌஷ்டிக மென்றறிவான். மூன்றம்சம்கொண்ட விஸ்தாரத்தை ஸார் வகாமிகமென்றறிவான். (42)

திராவிடப்பிராஸதத்திலே கர்ப்பகிருஹ விஸ்தாரத்தை இருபத்திஒரு அம்சம் செய்து பத்தம்சம் கொண்டது அதமம், பதின்மூன்றம்சம் கொண்டது உத்தமம். உத்தமப் பிரமாணத்துக்கும் அதமப்பிரமாணத்துக்கும் நடுவில் நீளத்தை எட்டம்சம் செய்து ஒன்பது பிரமாணம் லிங்காயாமம் கொள்ளுக. இந்தப்பிரமாணம் ஒன்பதையும் முன்பு போலே உத்தமமத்யமாதமமாகக் கொள்ளுவான். (44)

இப்படிக்குச்சொன்ன லிங்காயாமத்தை இருபத்திஒரு அம்சம் செய்து இதில் ஆறம்சமான விஸ்தாரத்தை ஜயத மென்றும் அஞ்சம்சம்கொண்ட விஸ்தாரத்தை பௌஷ்டிக மென்றும் நாலம்சம்கொண்ட விஸ்தாரத்தை ஸார்வகாமிக மென்றும் அறிவான். திராவிட லிங்கப்பிரமாணம் சொல்லப்பட்டது. (44)

வேஸரமான விமானத்தில் கர்ப்பகிருஹவிஸ்தாரத்தை இருபதம்சம் செய்து இதில் பதின் மூன்றம்சமகொண்ட லிங்காயாமம் அதமம். பதினுறம்சம்கொண்ட லிங்காயாமம் உத்தமம். உத்தமப்பிரமாணத்திற்கும் அதமப்பிரமாணத்துக்கும இடையிலம்சத்தை எட்டம்சம் செய்து ஒன்பது பிரமாணமாம். இதில் உத்தமாதமமத்தியமங்களை முன் போலே அறிக. (45½)

இந்த வேஸரலிங்கத்தினுடைய நீளத்தை இருபத்தி அஞ்சு அம்சம் செய்து எட்டம்சம் ஏழம்சம் லிங்க விஸ்தாரம் கொள்ளுக. (46½)

சுற்றளவெ பதினுலு (பதினுறு ?) செய்து இதில் அஞ்சம்சம்செய்து அகலமாக எல்லாவிடத்திலும் அறிக. (47)

இப்படி கர்ப்பகிருஹ பிரமாணம் சொல்லப்பட்டது. இதுக்கு மேல் ஹஸ்தபிரமாணம் சொல்லப்படுகிறது. (47½)

ஒரு முழம் துடங்கி ஒன்பது முழம் அறுதியாக ஆறுறு விரலேற்ற முப்பத்துமூன்று பிரமாணமாம். இந்த

முப்பத்துமூன்று பிரமாணமும் லிங்கப்பிரமாணம் சொல்லப்பட்டது. (48½)

அஞ்சு முழம் பிரமாணமான பிராஸாதம் துடங்கி பன்னிரண்டு நிலமறுதியான பிராஸாதத்திற்கு சொல்லப் பட்டது; ஹஸ்தப்பிரமாண மறுதியாக இந்தப் பிரமாணம் முப்பத்திமூன்றும் கொள்ளும்படி. அஞ்சு முழமான பிராஸாதத்திற்கு ஒரு முழமான லிங்கம் பிரதிஷ்டிப்பான். ஏழு முழமான பிராஸாதத்திற்கு ஒன்றேமுக்கால் முழம் பிரமாணமான லிங்கத்தைப் பிரதிஷ்டிப்பான். ஒன்பது முழமான பிராஸாதத்திற்கு ஒன்றரை முழம்பிரமாணமான லிங்கத்தை ஸ்தாபிப்பான். பதினொரு முழம் பிரமாண மான பிராஸாதத்திற்கு ஒரு முழம் பிரமாணமான லிங்க த்தை பிரதிஷ்டிப்பான். ஏழு முழமான பிராஸாதத்திற்கு ஒன்றேகால் முழப்பிரமாண லிங்கத்தை ஸ்தாபிப்பான். பதினொரு முழம் பிரமாணமான பிராஸாதத்துக்கு ஒன்றே முக்கால் முழம் கொண்ட லிங்கத்தை ஸ்தாபிப்பான். பதின்மூன்று முழம் பிரமாணமான பிராஸாதத்துக்கு இரண்டு முழம் பிரமாணமான லிங்கத்தை ஸ்தாபிப்பான் இப்படி ஒன்பது முழப்பிரமாணமறுதியாக லிங்கத்தை ஸ்தாபிப்பான். (49½)

ஒரு முழம் துடங்கி ஒன்பது பிரமாணமறுதியாக மும்மூன்று விரலாலென்று சிலர் சொல்லா நின்றார்கள். மும்மூன்று விரலாலும் ஏற்றலாம். (50)

இப்படிக்குக்கொண்ட பிரமாணத்துக்கு ஆயாதி சுத்தி செய்கைக்கு ஒரு விரல் குறைந்து கொள்ளுதல் ஒரு விரல் ஏற்றம் கொள்ளுதல் செய்வான். இதில் தோஷமில்லை யென்றிக. (51)

இருபத்திஅஞ்சு விரல் துடங்கி ஒன்பது பிரமாண மறுதியாக எட்டு விரலேற்றிக்கொள்ளுக. உத்தமப் பிரா

ஸாதத்திற்கு லிங்கப்பிரமாணம் இருபத்தஞ்சு விரல் துடங்கி ஒன்பது பிரமாணமறுதியாக பதினாறு விரலா லேற்றிக்கொள்ளுக. (52½)

துவாரத்தினுடைய உத்ஸேதத்தோடொக்கக்கொண்ட லிங்கப்பிரமாணத்தை உத்தமமென்றறிக. துவாரோத் ஸேதத்தில் மூன்றிலொன்று குறையக்கொண்ட லிங்கப் பிரமாணத்தை அதமமென்றறிக. (53)

கால் நீளத்தை ஒன்பது செய்து ஏழம்சம் கொண்ட லிங்கப்பிரமாணத்தை உத்தமமென்றறிவான். அஞ்சம்சம் கொண்ட பிரமாணத்தை அதமமென்றறிவான். (53½)

கர்ப்பகிருஹப்பிரமாணத்தில் சொன்னப்போலே துவா ரப்பிரமாணத்திலும் சொன்ன உத்தமப்பிரமாணத்துக்கும் அதமப்பிரமாணத்துக்கும் நடுவு நீளத்தை எட்டு செய்ய ஒன்பது பிரமாணமாம். உத்தமமத்திமாதமங்களை கர்ப்ப கிருஹ பிரமாணத்தில் சொன்னப்போலே துவாரப்பிர மாணத்திலும் ஸ்தம்ப பிரமாணத்திலும் சொன்னாப் போலே அறிக.

துவாரப்பிரமாணத்தாலும் லிங்கப்பிரமாணத்தாலும் கொண்ட லிங்காயாமத்துக்குக்கொண்ட விஸ்தாரத்தை நாகரப்பிராஸாதம் முதலானவற்றில் கொண்டலிங்காய யாமத்தால்கொண்ட விஸ்தாரம்போலே கொள்க. (54½)

பிராஸாதங்களுடைய அதிஷ்டானம் சிகரம் கழுத்து ஸ்தூபி இவற்றாலும் கர்ப்பகிருஹப்பிரமாணம்போலே லிங் கப்பிரமாணம் கொள்ளுவான் என்று அகஸ்தியபகவான் முதலான சில ரிஷிகள் சொல்லுவார்கள். ஆதலால் அதிஷ் டான பிரமாணத்தாலும் கழுத்தினுடைய பிரமாணத்தா லும் லிங்கத்துக்கு பிரமாணம் கொள்க. (55½)

(मयमते त्रयस्त्रिंशाध्याये ॥)

आढ्यादिलिङ्गभेदाः ।

सार्धांशावसुसार्धसिन्धुचरणोनागाद्रिसाङ्घ्र्यष्टको-

दन्वन्मङ्गलनन्ददिक्फणिनगैस्त्र्यंशोन्नातिस्त्र्यष्टके ।

दैर्घ्ये चेद्विकृतौ रसाक्षजलधित्र्यंशान्वितेष्वंशकै-

राढ्यानाढ्यसुरेढ्यसर्वसमके लिङ्गे विदुर्विस्तृतिम् ॥

(सिद्धान्तसारावल्यां चर्यापादे ॥)

लिङ्गायामे विकारांशे चतुर्भूतरसैः क्रमात् ।

सत्रिभागैस्त्रिरंशैस्तु सुरेढ्यानाढ्यके द्विजाः ! ॥

आढ्यं सर्वसमं लिङ्गं विशिष्टं परिकीर्तितम् ।

तेषां तन्मध्यमेऽष्टांशे प्रत्येकं नवधा भजेत् ॥

(कामिकागमे द्विषष्टितमपटले ॥)

समलिङ्गम् ।

लिङ्गायामे त्रिभागे तु एकांशं चतुरश्रकम् ।

मध्ये व्योमं तु वस्वश्रं [वृत्तं चाप्येक*] मंशकम् ॥

समलिङ्गमिति ख्यातं विप्रादीनां तु ऋद्धिदम् ।

(अंशुमद्भेदागमे एकपञ्चाशपटले ॥)

आद्यं तु सर्वतोभद्रं द्वितीयं वर्धमानकम् ।

शिवाधिकं तृतीयं स्याच्चतुर्थं स्वस्तिकं भवेत् ॥

अथ जगदमराणां सर्वतोभद्रमिष्टं
सुखदमवनिपानां वृद्धिदं वर्धमानम् ।
धनदमिह विशां वै शम्भुभागाधिकं य-
च्छुभदमथ परेषां स्वस्तिकं तच्चतुर्णाम् ॥

त्रिंशद्भागे सर्वतोभद्रलिङ्गे मूले मध्ये ..... दशांशं क्रमेण ।
वृत्तं तुल्यं सर्वतः शम्भुभागं विप्राणां तद्भूपतीनां प्रशस्तम् ॥

முதல் ஸர்வதோபத்ரலிங்கமாம். இரண்டாவது வர்த்தமானலிங்கம். மூன்றாவது சிவாதிகலிங்கம். நாலாவது ஸ்வஸ்திகலிங்கமென்றறிக. (70½)

பிராம்மணருக்கு ஸர்வதோபத்ரலிங்கமாம்; அவர்களுக்கு சுகத்தை கொடுக்கும் ராஜாக்களுக்கு வர்த்தமான லிங்கமாம்; அவர்களுக்கு விர்த்தியைக்கொடுக்கும். வைசியர்களுக்கு சிவாதிக லிங்கமாம்; அவர்களுக்கு தனத்தைக் கொடுக்கும். சூத்திரர்களுக்கு ஸ்வஸ்திக லிங்கமாம்; அவர்களுக்கு விருத்தியைக் கொடுக்கும் என்றறிக. (71½)

ஸர்வதோபத்ரமான லிங்கத்தினுடைய நீளத்தை முப்பது செய்து அடியிலே பத்தும் நடுவிலே பத்தும் தலையிலே பத்தும் அம்சமுமாகக் கொள்வான். அந்த லிங்கமானது அடியிலே நின்று தலையளவும் விருத்தமாயிருப்பது. இந்த லிங்கம் பிராமணர்களுக்கும் ராஜாக்களுக்கும் சொல்லப் பட்டது. (72½)

(मयमते त्रयस्त्रिंशाध्याये ॥)

प्रतिमालक्षणानि ।

चतुरश्रमधोभागमष्टाश्रं मध्यमं तथा ।
तदूर्ध्वं वृत्तमेव स्यात्त्रिभागं सर्वतस्समम् ॥
समलिङ्गमिति प्रोक्तं वर्धमानमतः शृणु ।

(सुप्रभेदागमे त्रयस्त्रिंशाध्याये ॥)

वर्धमानालिङ्गम् ।

भानुद्व्यंशे तथायामे सप्तांशं चतुरश्रकम् ।
अष्टाश्रमष्टभागेन नवांशं वृत्तमुच्यते ॥
षट्सप्तवसुभागं वा पञ्चषट्सप्त [भागकम्*] ।
चतुष्पञ्चषडंशं वा वर्धमानं चतुर्विधम् ॥

(अंशुमद्भेदागमे एकपञ्चाशपटले ॥)

वेदभूतरसभागिकैरथो भूतषण्मुनिपदैरतःपरम् ।
षट्कसप्तवसुभागया ततः सप्तनागनव भागया पुनः ॥(७३$\frac{१}{२}$)
वर्धमानमुदितं चतुर्विधं ब्रह्मविष्णुशिव ...... क्रमात् ।
सर्वसंपदुपवर्धनप्रदं पुत्रवृद्धिदमिदं महीभृताम् ॥

வர்த்தமான லிங்கத்தினுடைய நீளத்தை பதினைஞ்சு செய்து பிரும்மபாகம் நாலம்சமும் விஷ்ணுபாகம் அஞ்சம்சமும் ருத்திரபாகம் ஆறு அம்சமுமாகக் கொள்ளுக. அன்றியே லிங்கத்தினுடைய நீளத்தை பதினெட்டுக் கூறு செய்து பிரும்மபாகம் அஞ்சம்சமும் விஷ்ணுபாகம் ஆறம்சமும் ருத்திரபாகம் ஏழும்சமும் கொள்ளுவான். [அன்றியே லிங்கத்தினுடைய நீளத்தை இருபத்தியொரு கூறு செய்து பிரும்மபாகம் ஆறம்சமும் விஷ்ணுபாகம்

ஏழும்சமும் ருத்திரபாகம் எட்டம்சமும் கொள்ளுவான் *]
அன்றியே லிங்கத்தினுடைய நீளத்தை இருபத்திநாலம்சம்
செய்து பிரம்மபாகம் ஏழும்சமும் விஷ்ணுபாகம் எட்டம்
சமும் ருத்ர பாகம் ஒன்பதம்சமும் கொள்ளுவான். ஆக
வர்த்தமானத்துக்கு நாலுபடி சொல்லப்பட்டது. இந்த
லிங்கமானது ராஜாக்களுக்கு வெற்றியையும் முடிவில்லாத
ஸர்வஸம்பத்தையும் கொடுக்குமென்றறிக. (74½)

(मयमते त्रयस्त्रिंशाध्याये ॥)

चतुःपञ्चषडंशं तु पञ्चषट्सप्तभागिकम् ।
[षट्सप्ताष्टांशकं सप्तभागाष्टनवभागिकम् ॥*]
वर्धमानमिति प्रोक्तं विप्रादीनामनुक्रमात् ।

(पूर्वकारणागमे नवमपटले ॥)

चतुर्विंशति चायामे सप्तांशं चतुरश्रकम् ।
अष्टाश्रमष्टभागेन नवांशेनैव वृत्तकम् ॥
वर्धमानमिदं लिङ्गं शिवाधिकमतः परम् ।

(सुप्रभेदागमे त्रयस्त्रिंशाध्याये ॥)

शैवाधिक्यलिङ्गम् ।

लिङ्गायामे दशांशे तु गुणांशं चतुरश्रकम् ।
वस्वश्रं चैव तत्तुल्यं युगांशं स्याच्छिवांशकम् ॥
शैवाधिक्यमिदं ख्यातमथवान्यत्प्रकारतः ।
वेदवेदशरांशं वा पञ्चपञ्चषडंशकम् ॥
षट्षट्सप्तांशकैर्वाथ शैवाधिक्यं चतुर्विधम् ।

(अंशुमद्भेदागमे एकपञ्चाशपटले ॥)

सप्तसप्तवसुभागया ततः पञ्चपञ्चकषडंशकैरपि ।
वेदवेदशरभागया ततो बन्ध[बन्ध*] युगभागया पुरः ॥
उक्तमत्र हि मया चतुर्विधं तच्छिवाधिकमजाधिभागिकैः ।
सर्ववस्तुदमिदं विशामलं सर्ववर्णयमिनामुदीरितम् ॥

சிவாதிகலிங்கத்தினுடைய நீளத்தை இருபத்திரண்டம்சம் செய்து பிரம்மபாகம் ஏழம்சம் (செய்து) விஷ்ணு பாகம் ஏழம்சமும் ருத்திரபாகம் எட்டம்சமும் கொள்வான். அன்றியே லிங்கத்தினுடைய நீளத்தை பத்தம்சம் செய்து பிரம்மபாகம் மூன்றம்சமும் விஷ்ணுபாகம் மூன்றம்சமும் ருத்திர பாகம் நாலம்சமுமாகக் கொள்வான். சிவாதிகலிங்கம் இப்படிச் சொல்லப்பட்டது. இந்த லிங்கம் வைசியருக்கும் அந்த வம்சத்தில் தபஸ்விகளுக்கும் சொல்லப்பட்டது. இது இவர்களுக்கு ஸர்வ வஸ்துக்களையும் கொடுக்குமென்றறிக.

(मयमते त्रयस्त्रिंशाध्याये ॥)

सप्तसप्ताष्टभागंतु पञ्चपञ्चषडंशकम् ।
वेदवेदशरांशं तु गुणानलयुगांशकम् ॥
एवं शिवाधिकं प्रोक्तं द्विजादीनां क्रमाद्गृहे ।

(पूर्वकारणागमे नवमपटले ॥)

आयामं दशधा कृत्वा चतुरश्रं त्रिभागतः ।
अष्टाश्रं च त्रिभागेन चतुरंशेन वृत्तकम् ॥
शिवाधिकमिदं शस्तं भुक्तिमुक्तिफलप्रदम् ।

(सुप्रभेदागमे त्रयस्त्रिंशाध्याये ॥)

स्वस्तिकलिङ्गम्

लिङ्गायामे नवांशे तु चतुरश्रं द्विभागया ।

वस्वश्रं तु गुणांशेन वेदांशं वृत्तमुच्यते ॥

(अंशुमद्भेदागमे एकपञ्चाशपटले ॥)

उक्तायामे स्वास्तिके ...... भागे मूले द्व्यंशं मध्यभागे गुणांशम् ।

पूजाभागे चातुरंशं क्रमेण चोक्तं शूद्रे सर्वकामप्रदं तत् ॥

ஸ்வஸ்திகலிங்கத்தினுடைய நீளத்தை ஒன்பதம்சம் செய்து பிரம்மபாகம் அடியிலே இரண்டம்சமும் விஷ்ணு பாகம் நடுவே மூன்றம்சமும் பூஜாலிங்கம் நாலம்சமும் கொள்வான். இந்த லிங்கம் சூத்திருக்கும் எல்லாருக்கும் நன்மையைக் கொடுக்கும்.

(मयमते त्रयस्त्रिंशाध्याये ॥)

नवधा लिङ्गमानेन द्व्यंशं मध्ये गुणांशकम् ।

वृत्ते युगांशकं दैर्घ्यं शूद्रेऽप्येतच्च शस्यते ॥

(कामिकागमे द्विषष्टितमपटले ॥)

धारालिङ्गम् ।

धारालिङ्गे ....सर्वलिङ्गे मतं

तलाश्रं वा कलाश्रं युगाश्रम् ।

तस्मादूर्ध्वे द्वैगुणसधारं

धारालिङ्गं सर्ववर्णे प्रशस्तम् ॥

முன்பு சொல்லப்பட்ட லிங்கங்களிலும் தாராலிங்கம் செய்யலாம். அந்த தாராலிங்கம் இருக்கும்படி : பிரும்ம பாகம் அஷ்டாச்ரம் ஆதல் பதினறு அம்சத்தால் சதுரச்ரமாயிருப்பது. பிரும்ம பாகத்தில் அச்ரத்தில் இரட்டி அச்ரமாயிருப்பது விஷ்ணுபாகம். விஷ்ணுபாகத்தில் அச்ரத்தில் இரட்டி அச்ரமாயிருப்பது ருத்திரபாகம். அந்த அச்ரங்கள் தாரையாயிருப்பது அந்த லிங்கத்தை தாராலிங்க மென்றறிவான். அந்த லிங்கம் எல்லா ஜாதிகளுக்குமாம் என்று சொல்லப்பட்டது. (80½)

(मयमते त्रयस्त्रिंशाध्याये ॥)

धारालिङ्गमथो वक्ष्ये श्रूयतां तु प्रजापते! ।
पादादूर्ध्वकपर्यन्तं धारालिङ्गं प्रशस्तकम् ॥
अधो वेदाश्रकं कुर्यात्तदूर्ध्वे त्वष्टधारया ।
ऊर्ध्वे षोडशधाराच्च भोगार्थी लभते सुखम् ॥
एतद्द्विज महाप्राज्ञ! सर्वकामप्रसाधनम् ।

(पूर्वकारणागमे नवमपटले ॥)

पञ्चधारास्सप्तधारा नव(धारा) द्वादशधारकाः ।
धाराष्षोडशविंशच्च त्रिरष्टावाष्टविंशतिः ॥

(सुप्रभेदागमे त्रयस्त्रिंशाध्याये ॥)

पूर्वोक्तसमलिङ्गे च धारालिङ्गं विकल्पितम् ।
चतुरश्रं द्विरष्टाश्रं तन्मूले परिकल्पयेत् ॥
वैष्णवांशे (तु) च शैवांशे धाराद्विद्विगुणीकृते ।
सर्वेषामपि लिङ्गानां धारालिङ्गं त्रिधा मतम् ॥

मूलेऽष्टाश्रं वा कलाश्रं युगाश्रं तस्मादूर्ध्वं तद्युगास्स्युश्च धाराः।

एवं पूर्वाचार्यकै (स) रीश्वरस्य प्रोक्तं धारालिङ्गमेतत्त्रिधैव ॥

(शिल्परत्ने एकोनत्रिंशाध्याये ॥)

सहस्रलिङ्गम् ।

पूजाभागे सर्वतोभद्रलिङ्गे धारालिङ्गं पञ्चपञ्चक्रमेण ।

एकैकस्यामष्टमं चोपरिष्टात्साहस्रं तद्रेखया लिङ्गमुक्तम् ॥

ஸஹஸ்ரலிங்கம் இருக்கும்படி முன்பு சொல்லப்பட்ட ஸர்வதோபத்ரலிங்கத்தில் பூஜாபாகத்தில் இருபத்தியஞ்சு தாரையாய் கீறி ஒரு தாரைக்கு நாற்பது ரேகையாக மேலே மேலே கீறி ஆயிரலிங்கமாம். இந்த லிங்கம் ஸர்வ காமியங்களையும் கொடுக்குமென்றறிவான். (81½)

(मयमते त्रयस्त्रिंशाध्याये ॥)

सर्वतोभद्रलिङ्गेषु धाराः स्युः पञ्चविंशतिः ।

सप्तपर्णदलाकारास्समास्सर्वास्समान्तराः ॥

एकैकस्यां तु धारायां चत्वारिंशत्प्रसंख्यया ।

कुर्यात्समानि लिङ्गानि स्यात्तल्लिङ्गसहस्रकम् ॥

(शिल्परत्ने एकोनत्रिंशाध्याये ॥)

समखण्डे शिवायामे रुद्रभागविनिर्मिते ।

एकाधिकनवत्यंशे विषमांशनिवेशितम् ॥

सैकसाहस्रलिङ्गानां नवभागोच्चमेव वा ।

(कामिकागमे द्विषष्टितमपटले ॥)

त्रैराशिकलिङ्गम् ।

रसमुनिवसुभागे वृत्तकेऽष्टाश्रकेऽन्ते
परिधिरथ नवांशे लिङ्गतुङ्गे तु भूयः ।
त्रिभिरथ गुणभागैश्च त्रिभिस्तुङ्गमानं
द्व्यजहरिहरभागे तत्तु(तत्) त्रैराशिकं स्यात् ॥

பிரும்மபாகம் ஆறம்சமும் [விஷ்ணுபாகம் ஏழம்சமும்*] ருத்ரபாகம் எட்டம்ச[மு*]மான லிங்கத்தில் சுற்றளவை ஒன்பதம்சம் செய்து பிரம்மபாகம் மூன்றம்சமும் விஷ்ணுபாகம் மூன்றம்சமும் ருத்திரபாகம் மூன்றம்சமுமாக ச்செய்வான். இத்தை திரைராசிக லிங்க மென்றறிவான். (82½)

(मयमते त्रयस्त्रिंशाध्याये ॥)

अग्रे मूले च मध्ये च प्रमाणं सर्वतस्समम् ।
आयामं नवधा कृत्वा वृत्तं षड्भागमुच्यते ॥
सप्तभागमथाष्टाश्रं तुर्याश्रं वसुभागिकम् ।
त्रैराशिकमिति ज्ञेयं धनधान्यसुखावहम् ॥

(पूर्वकारणागमे नवमपटले ॥)

प्रतिमालक्षणानि ।

अर्चनं नवधा कृत्वा ब्रह्माद्यास्त्रिविभागतः ।
षट्सप्ताष्टकभागैस्तु नाहो रुद्रादिषु क्रमात् ॥
त्रैराशिकमिदं लिङ्गं शूद्राणां तत्प्रशस्यते ।

(जीर्णोद्धारदशके कामिकवचनम् ॥)

लिङ्गोत्सेधे तु नन्दांशे षट्सप्तवसुभागकैः ।
ब्रह्मविष्ण्वीशभागानां क्रमान्नाहाः प्रकीर्तिताः ॥
लिङ्गं त्रैराशिकं नाम भवेत् सर्वसमे तु तत् ।

(शिल्परत्ने एकोनत्रिंशाध्याये ॥)

कृत्वा नवांशं लिङ्गोच्चं बन्धबन्धगुणांशकम् ।
षट्सप्ताष्टकनाहं तु वृत्तेऽष्टाश्रे युगाश्रके ॥
त्रैराशिकमिदं शास्त्रे स्वस्तिकमधुनोच्यते ।

(कामिकागमे द्विषष्टितमपटले ॥)

मुखलिङ्गम् ।

मुखलिङ्गं त्रिवक्त्रं स्यादेकवक्त्रं चतुर्मुखम् ।
सन्मुखं चैकवक्त्रं स्यात् त्रिवक्त्रे पृष्ठके न हि ॥
पश्चिमास्यं स्थितं शुभ्रं कुङ्कुमाभं तथोत्तरे ।
याम्यं कृष्णकरालं स्यात्प्राच्यां दीप्ताग्निसन्निभम् ॥

सद्यो वामं तथाघोरं तत्पुरुषं चतुर्थकम् ।

पञ्चमं च तथेशानं योगिनामप्यगोचरम् ॥

(रूपमण्डने ॥)

मुखलिङ्गं ततो वक्ष्ये सर्वकामार्थसाधनम् ।

पूजाभागं समस्तं तु द्विषष्टयंशं भजेत्क्रमात् ॥

त्रयोदशाङ्गुलार्धं तु मुखमेकं प्रकीर्तितम् ।

शराननं चतुर्वक्त्रं त्रिवक्त्रं चैकवक्त्रकम् ॥

चतुर्दिक्षु चतुर्वक्त्रं त्रिवक्त्रं पृष्ठहीनकम् ।

कुर्वेकवक्त्रमूर्ध्वे तु मुखमानेन बुद्धिमन्! ॥

मकुटेनोर्ध्ववक्त्रं तु त्रयोदशार्धाङ्गुलेन तु ।

ग्रीवामूलात् स्तनान्तं स्यादर्धाधिकं त्रयोदश ॥

स्तनसूत्रावधिर्यावत् कारयेद् द्विभुजान्वितम् ।

प्रतिमालक्षणोक्तेन मार्गेणैव समाचरेत् ॥

शेषं लिङ्गवदाकारं कारयेल्लक्षणान्वितम् ।

वक्त्रलिङ्गप्रमाणं तु प्रोक्तं पीठमथो शृणु ॥

(कारणागमे नवमपटले ॥)

लिङ्गशिरोवर्तनम् ।

शिरसो वर्तनमधुना लिङ्गानां वक्ष्यते क्रमशः ।

छत्राभा त्रपुषाभा कुक्कुटकाण्डार्धचन्द्रसदृशाभाः ॥ ९०½ ॥

बुद्बुदसदृशाः पञ्चैवोद्दिष्टा वर्तना मुनिभिः ।

व्यासे षोडशभागे लिङ्गस्यैकं द्विगुणयुगांशेषु ॥ ९१½ ॥

सांलम्ब्याधोभागानुभयोरपि पार्श्वयोः क्रमशः ।

छत्राभानि शिरांसि च चत्वारीह प्रवर्तन्ते विधिना ॥ ९२½ ॥

समलिङ्गे प्रथमे द्वे शैवाधिकालिङ्गके तृतीयं स्यात् ।

चतुरंशेषु यदुक्तं तत्प्रोक्तं वर्धमानासु ॥ ९३½ ॥

सङ्करमन्योन्यं वा शुभहं स्याद्वर्तनानां च ।

उच्चार्धं कुक्कुटजं त्र्यंशैकांशेन्दुखण्डनिभा ॥

बुद्बुदसदृशा सार्धं त्र्यंशं व्यासेऽष्टभागे तु ।

सर्वेषामपि वैतास्सामान्या वर्तनास्तु लिङ्गानाम् ॥ ९५½ ॥

शिरोवर्तभागत्र्यंशैकं चाधिरोप्य निजतुङ्गे ।

लिङ्गायामयुते तेषां भागयुते तेन सार्धमतः ॥

इन्द्वश्विनिगुणभागाः प्रोक्तास्सर्वेष्वपि क्रमशः ।

अपरे मध्यमलिङ्गे श्रेष्ठे लिङ्गे ततः शिरोमानम् ॥

लिङ्गानां शिरसीप्सितांशमुभयोः संलम्ब्य पार्श्वद्वयोः

कृत्वा मत्स्ययुतं तदास्यजघनान्निष्क्रान्तसूत्रद्वयोः ।

तस्माद्यत्र[च*]संयुतिर्मतिमता बिन्दुत्रयाढ्यं तथा

कर्तव्यं बहुवर्तनास्वभिमतं सोपायमीशोदितम् ॥

லிங்கங்களுக்கு சிரோவர்த்தனம் சொல்லப்படுகிறது. (90)

குடைப்புறம்போலேயாதல் திரபுஷம்போலேயாயிருக்குதல் கோழிமுட்டைபோலே இருக்குதல் அர்த்தசந்திரனைப்போலே இருக்குதல் நீரில் குமிழிபோலே இருக்குதல் ஆக சிரோ வர்த்தனம் அஞ்சுபடி சொல்லப்பட்டது. (91)

லிங்கங்களினுடைய விஸ்தாரத்தை பதினறம்சம் செய்து ஓரம்சம் இரண்டம்சம் மூன்றம்சம் நாலம்சம் சிரஸ்ஸின் கீழே இரண்டு பார்சுவத்திலும் நாற்றிச் சாய்ப்பான். ஆக சத்ராகாரமான சிரோ வர்த்தனம் நாலு படி சொல்லப்பட்டது. (92½)

ஸர்வதோபத்ரலிங்கத்துக்கு ஓரம்சமும் இரண்டம்சமும் கொள்வான். சிவாதிகலிங்கத்துக்கு மூன்றம்சம் கொள்ளுவான். வர்த்தமானலிங்கத்துக்கு நாலம்சம் கொள்ளுவான் என்று சொல்லப்பட்டது. (93½)

இந்தக்கிரமம் அன்றிக்கே இந்தஅம்சங்கள் ஒன்றுக்கொன்று கலசுமாமாகில் அந்த சிரோவர்த்தனம் கர்த்தாவுக்குப் பொல்லாங்கைக் கொடுக்குமென்று சொல்லப்பட்டது. (94)

குக்குடாண்டமான சிரோவர்த்தனத்தை உயரத்தில் பார்த்துக் கொள்ளுவானென்று அர்த்த சந்திரமான சிரோவர்த்தனத்தை மூன்றத்தொன்று கொள்ளுவானென்று சொல்லப்பட்டது. (94½)

நீர்க் குமிழிபோலே இருக்கும் சிரோவர்த்தனத்துக்கு லிங்கவிஸ்தாரத்தை எட்டம்சம் செய்து மூன்றரை அம்சம் கொள்ளுவானென்று சொல்லப்பட்டது. (95)

இந்த சிரோவர்த்தனத்தை மூன்று லிங்கங்களுக்கும் ஸாமான்யமென்று சொல்லப்பட்டது. (95½)

சிரோவர்த்தனும்சத்தில் மூன்றிலொன்று லிங்கோத் ஸேதத்தில் ஏற்றிக்கொள்ளுவான். லிங்காயாமத்தில் கூடினதிலும் ஆறுபாகம் கூடினதிலும் ஏறட்டுக் கட்டுவான். ஓரம்சம் இரண்டம்சம் மூன்றம்சம் எல்லா லிங்கத்துக்கும் கிரமத்தாலே சொல்லப்பட்டது. அதமலிங்கங்களுக்கும் மத்யமலிங்கத்துக்கும் உத்தமலிங்கத்துக்கும் சிரோமான மேற்றிக்கொள்ளும்படி அடவே சொல்லப்பட்டது. (97½)

லிங்கங்களுடைய சிரோவர்த்தனமாகச் சொன்ன அம்சத்தை பார்ச்வங்கள் இரண்டிலும் கீழே நாத்தி அவிட மிரண்டும் மீனுக வீசி மீனங்களுடைய முகத்திலும் வாலிலும் புறப்பட்ட நூல் இரண்டுகளிலே கூட்டி மூன்று பிந்துவாம். அவ்வளவிலே சிரோவர்த்தனத்தை சயிப்பானென்று சிவனாலே சொல்லப்பட்டது. (98½)

(मयमते त्रयस्त्रिंशाध्याये ॥)

कुर्वीत त्रपुषीफलाग्रसदृशं छत्रोपमं मस्तकं

बालेन्द्वाकृतिकुक्कुटाण्डसदृशं विप्रादिवर्णक्रमात् ।

भेदास्सर्वसमांशकप्रभृतयो नाहप्रभेदान्विताः

तेप्येते क्रमतः स्यु.......तदनुलोमाङ्गीक्रातिश्चेष्यते ॥

विस्तारं शिवलिङ्गमूर्ध्नि वसुनन्दादित्यरुद्रांशकं

कृत्वा तत्क्रमतो विशोध्य परितो व्येकद्विलोकांशकान् ।

कृत्वात्यष्टितिथिप्रकृत्यतिधृतिख्यातांशयुक्तं क्रमात्
पूजाभागमिहोक्तभागमुपरिष्टाच्छोधयेद्वर्णिषु ॥

तन्मस्तके नवविभागतया विभक्ते
भागं विशोध्य परितश्शिवभागदैर्घ्यम् ।
द्वात्रिंशदंशकतया परिकल्प्य भागा-
नेकैकशो द्विजमुखेषु विशोधयेद्वा ॥

छत्राभं त्रपुषाकारं कुक्कुटाण्डनिभं तथा ।
अर्धेन्दुसदृशं चाथ बुद्बुदाभं तु पञ्चमम् ॥

सर्वेषामपि लिङ्गानां शिरसो वर्तनक्रमम् ।
लिङ्गव्यासात् षोडशांशमेकद्वित्रियवाधिकम् ॥

आरोप्येकेध[1]स्संलम्ब्य लिङ्गस्योभयपार्श्वयोः ।
वर्तयन्तत्र चत्वारि च्छत्राभानि भवन्ति हि ॥

प्रथमं च द्वितीयं च समलिङ्गं नियोजयेत् ।
शिवाधिके तृतीयं तु चतुर्थं वर्धमानके ॥

वर्तनं सङ्करं नैव कुर्यात्तदशुभं यतः ।
षडंशे लिङ्गविस्तारे सार्धत्र्यंशेन वर्तयेत् ॥

---

१ 'आरोप्य चाधः' इति स्यात् ।

त्रपुषाभशिरस्सिद्ध्यै रामांशैः कुक्कुटाण्डकम् ।
लिङ्गव्यासतृतीयांशवर्धनादर्धचन्द्रकम् ॥

लिङ्गव्यासेऽष्टधा भक्ते सार्धांशत्रयवर्धनात् ।
बुद्बुदाभस्य लिङ्गस्य शिरस्सिध्यति शोभनम् ॥

लिङ्गानां शिरसीप्सितांशमुभयोस्संलम्ब्य तत्पार्श्वयोः
कृत्वा मत्स्ययुगं तदास्यजघनान्निष्क्रान्तसूत्रद्वयोः ।
तस्माद्यत्र च संयुतिर्मतिमता बिन्दुत्रयाढ्यं यथा
तत्त[त्व]र्तयितव्यमत्र बहुधा सोपाय ईशोदितम् ॥

(शिल्परत्ने एकोनत्रिंशाध्याये ॥)

शिरोवर्तनभागे तु चतुर्थे वा षडंशके ॥
एकं द्वयं त्रयं दद्याद् ब्रह्मभागात्क्रमेण तु ।
शिरोवर्तनभागस्य त्र्यंशं पूजांशकोपरि ॥

लिङ्गायामेऽथवारोप्य षड्भागे तु तदुच्छ्रये ।
एकांशं योजयेद्धीमान् लिङ्गे द्व्यंशं तु मध्यमे ॥
त्रिभागमुत्तमे लिङ्गे योजयेद्वा द्विजोत्तमाः ! ।
केवलं वा शिरोमानमधिरोप्य विवर्तयेत् ॥

शिरसा मिश्रितं भागं पार्श्वयोरवलम्ब्य च ।
वृत्तद्वयं तु तन्मानादुभयोः पार्श्वयोर्नयेत् ॥

ऊर्ध्वदेशे शिरोमध्ये तृतीयं मण्डलं न्यसेत् ।
मण्डलैश्च त्रिभिर्मत्स्यद्वयमत्रोपजायते ॥

तन्मत्स्याननपुच्छस्थसूत्रयोर्यत्र सङ्गतिः ।
तत्र स्थित्वा त्रिभिर्वास्य वर्तनीयं शिरश्शुभम् ॥

(कामिकागमे द्विषष्टितमपटले ॥)

लिङ्गपीठम् ।

लिङ्गनाहसमपीठविस्तरं विस्तृतस्य शरवेदतुङ्गकम् ।
विस्तृतार्धसमगोमुखान्तकं गोमुखान्तसमकण्ठनाहकम् ॥

(सकलागमसारसङ्ग्रहे ॥)

त्रिगुणं लिङ्गविस्तारं त्रिगुणार्धं चतुर्गुणम् ।
त्रिविधस्त्वधमादिस्तु पीठविस्तारमुच्यते ॥

विष्णुभागस्य चोत्सेधं पीठोत्सेधं विधीयते ।
अथवा ब्रह्मभागस्य चाष्टांशेन समन्वितम् ॥

पद्मपीठं भद्रपीठं वेदिका परिमण्डलम् ।
पीठं चतुर्विधं प्रोक्तं लक्षणं शृणु सांप्रतम् ॥

कृत्वा षोडश चोत्सेधं द्व्यंशेन च तु पट्टिका ।
पञ्चभागं तदूर्ध्वाब्जं दलैष्षोडशभिर्युतम् ॥

दलमर्धाङ्गुलोत्सेधं पद्मपीठमिहोच्यते ।
द्विभागं मध्यवृत्तं तु समन्तात्सदृढं (?) दृढम् ॥

चतुर्भिरूर्ध्वपद्मं तु द्विभागेनोर्ध्वपट्टिका ।
तदूर्ध्वे तु ततः कुर्यादेकांशं घृतवारिणा ॥

पीठतारत्रिभागैकं नालं कुर्यात्तथोत्तरे ।
तत्तारस्य चतुर्थांशं तदर्धार्धमथादिकम् ॥

द्विगुणं त्रिगुणं मूलं तद(म)ग्रं चार्धनाशनम् ।
विस्तारस्य चतुर्थांशादर्धादर्धमथापि वा ॥

जलमार्गं त्रिभागैकं कुर्यात्तत्र विशेषतः ।
एवं तु पद्मपीठं हि भद्रपीठमथ शृणु ॥

पूर्ववत् षोडशांशं तु कृत्वोत्सेधं विधानतः ।
भागेनोपानमेकेन चतुर्भिर्जगतीभवेत् ॥

कुमदं तु त्रिभिर्भागैरेकेनैव तु पट्टिका ।
कण्ठं कुर्यात्त्रिभिर्भागैरेकांशेन तु पट्टिका ॥

महापट्टिका द्व्यंशा तु एकेन घृतवारिणी ।
भद्रपीठं समाख्यातं वेदिपीठमथोच्यते ॥

पीठोत्सेधे नवांशे तु द्वियंशेन तु पट्टिका ।
चतार्भिः कण्ठतुङ्गं तु व्यंशेनैवोर्ध्वपट्टिका ॥

घृतवार्येकभागं तु समन्ताच्चतुरश्रकम् ।
वेदिपीठं समाख्यातं परिमण्डलमुच्यते ॥
भद्रमेव हि वृत्तं स्यादेतद्वै परिमण्डलम् ।
तेष्वाकांशसमं वापि त्रिपादं वार्धमेव वा ॥
पीठाङ्गानां प्रवेशं च तथा निर्गमनं पुनः ।
सकलानां च लिङ्गानां सामान्यं पीठलक्षणम् ॥

(सुप्रभेदागमे त्रयस्त्रिंशपटले ॥)

स्त्रीशिलां तु परिग्राह्य पीठं कुर्याद्विशेषतः ।
लिङ्गविस्तारमानेन त्रिगुणं पीठविस्तृतम् ॥
कण्ठद्विगुणमेवं वा त्रिगुणं पीठविस्तृतम् ।
कण्ठस्य द्विगुणार्धं वा लिङ्गदैर्घ्यसमं तु वा ॥
गर्भगेहं त्रिधा भज्य भागैकं पीठविस्तृतम् ।
लिङ्गमानेन हर्म्यं स्यात् लिङ्गमानेन पिण्डिका ॥
पूर्वाकृतिर्यथा पीठं तथा कुर्यात्पुनः पुनः ।
अन्याकृतिर्न कर्तव्या कृता चेत्कर्तृनाशिनी ॥
वेदाश्राष्टाश्रमानं तु विभजेदष्टधा पुनः ।
गुणभागमधस्त्यक्त्वा बाणांशं पीठिकोच्छ्रयम् ॥
ब्राह्मवैष्णवमानं तु षोडशांशेन भाजयेत् ।
सप्तभागमधो मुक्त्वा ग्रहांशं पिण्डिकोच्छ्रयम् ॥

पीठोत्सेधं तु यन्मानं विकारांशेन भाजयेत् ।
पक्षांशं पट्टिका प्रोक्ता बाणांशं पद्मपिण्डकम् ॥

अंशद्वयेन वृत्तं स्याद्वेदांशमूर्ध्वपद्मकम् ।
तस्योर्ध्वे पट्टिका द्वाभ्यामंशेन घृतवारिणी ॥

पीठतारत्रिभागैकं नालनिर्गममुच्यते ।
तत्समं मूलविस्तारं तत्त्रिभागैकमग्रतः ॥

उत्तरे जलमार्गं स्यात्सोमस्याभिमुखं भवेत् ।
मध्ये खातं त्रिभागैकं क्रमेण कृशता भवेत् ॥

एवं तु पद्मपीठं स्याद्भद्रपीठमथोच्यते ।
पूर्ववत् षोडशांशेन पीठोत्सेधं भजेत्ततः ॥

व्योमांशं पादुकोत्सेधं वेदांशं जगती भवेत् ।
अग्न्यंशं वृत्तमित्युक्तं भागैकेन तु पट्टिका ॥

गुणांशं कण्ठमित्युक्तं भागैकेन तु पट्टिका ।
महापट्टिद्वयांशेन घृतवारि तथांशकम् ॥

एवं स्याद्भद्रपीठं तु सर्वलिङ्गेषु योग्यकम् ।
एकविंशतिभागेन पीठोत्सेधं विभाजयेत् ॥

अंशेन पादुकां कुर्याच्चतुर्धा जगतीं कुरु ।
कण्ठमेकेन कर्तव्यं पद्ममेकांशमेव च ॥

तत्कुम्भं त्रिभिरंशैश्च पद्ममेकांशमेव च ।
कुर्यादेकेन कम्पं तु पक्षांशेनैव कण्ठकम् ॥

कम्पमेकेन कर्तव्यं पद्ममेकेन कारयेत् ।
महापट्टि द्विभागाभ्यां पद्ममेकांशकेन तु ॥

तस्योर्ध्वे पट्टिकैकेन घृतवारि तथांशकम् ।
विजयं नाम पीठं तु सर्वशान्तिकरं परम् ॥

विभजेत्पिण्डिकोत्सेधं अष्टादशविभागतः ।
एकेन पादुकां कुर्यादध्यर्धं कम्पपद्मयोः ॥

जगती चतुरंशं स्याद्वर्णांशेनैव वप्रकम् ।
तदूर्ध्वे कम्पमेकांशं द्वाभ्यां वै पट्टिका भवेत् ॥

पद्ममेकेन कर्तव्यमर्धेन घृतवारिणा ।
स्वायम्भुवमिति प्रोक्तं सर्वदेवेषु योग्यकम् ॥

विकारांशेन विभजेद्भागेनोपानमुच्यते ।
पद्मपिण्डी द्विभागेन कम्पमेकेन कारयेत् ॥

सप्तांशं कण्ठमित्युक्तं द्वाभ्यां वै कम्पपद्मकौ ।
अध्यर्धेन महापट्टी पद्ममर्धेन कारयेत् ॥

कम्पमर्धेन कर्तव्यमर्धेन घृतवारिणा ।
स्थण्डिलं स्यादिदं पीठं सर्वदेवेषु पूजितम् ॥

भागार्धं तत्त्रिपादं वा समं वा शेषनिर्गमम् ।
मूलादष्टांशमग्रे तु हीनं स्यात्पद्मपीठके ॥

सर्वेषामेव पीठानामुपानात्पीठविस्तरम् ।
पीठिकालक्षणं प्रोक्तं पादशैलविधिं शृणु ॥

(पूर्वकारणागमे नवमपटले ॥)

निष्कलानां तु लिङ्गानां सकलानामथाधुना ।
सामान्येन विधानेन वक्ष्येऽहं पीठलक्षणम् ॥ १ ॥

जात्यैकया विधातव्यं नेष्टमन्योन्यसङ्करम् ।
आहुश्शैले द्रुमे केचित् पीठं पक्केष्टकामयम् ॥ २ ॥

लोहजं मणिलिङ्गानां लोहजानां तु पैण्डिकम् ।
आदाय स्त्रीशिलां सम्यक् पीठं लि स्य निर्मितम् ॥ ३ ॥

நிஷ்கலமான லிங்கங்களுக்கும் பிரதிமைகளுக்கும் ஸாமான்ய விதியாலே பீடலக்ஷணம் சொல்லக்கடவேன். (1)

பீடத்தை லிங்கத்துக்கொத்த ஜாதியாகக்கொள்ளுவான். ஒன்றுக்கொன்று கலந்து செய்யலாகாது. (1½)

சிலையாலுண்டான லிங்கத்திலும் விருக்ஷஜமான லிங்கத்திலும் பீடத்தைச்சுட்டசெங்கலாலே கட்டுவானென்று சிலர் சொல்லுவார்கள். (2)

ஸ்படிகம் முதலான மணிலிங்கங்களுக்கும் லோஹஜமான லிங்கங்களுக்கும் பீடங்களை லோஹஜமாகவே கொள்ளுவான். (2½)

சிலாமயமான லிங்கத்துக்கு ஸ்திரீ சிலையாலே பீடத்தை நிர்மிப்பான். (3)

पूजांशद्विगुणं हीनं श्रेष्ठं लिङ्गोन्नतेः समम् ।
......ते पीठविस्तारास्तयोर्मध्येऽष्टभाजिते ॥ ४ ॥

उत्तमा मध्यमा हीनास्त्रिभिर्भेदाः प्रकीर्तिताः ।
अथवा लिङ्गतुङ्गार्धं हीनं पादोनकं वरम् ॥ ५ ॥

तयोर्मध्येऽष्टभागे तु ....सानि पूर्ववत् ।
विष्कम्भं त्रिगुणं वाथ नाहतुल्यविशालकम् ॥ ६ ॥

பீடம் பூஜாம்சத்திலிரட்டி அதமம். ஒன்ருன லிங்கோத்ஸேதம் உத்தமம். மத்தியமத்துக்கும் உத்தம பிரமாணத்துக்கும் நடுவே எட்டம்சம் செய்ய ஒன்பது பிரமாணமாம். ஆக பீட விஸ்தாரங்கள் ஒன்பது படி சொல்லப்பட்டது.

உத்தமோத்தமம் உத்தமமத்தியமம் உத்தமாதமம், மத்யமோத்தமம் மத்யமமத்யமம் மத்யமாதமம், அதமோத்தமம் அதமமத்தியமம் அதமாதமம் ஆக ஒன்பது பிரமாணத்தையுமறிவான்.

லிங்கோத்ஸேதத்தில் பாதி அதமம். லிங்கோத்ஸேதத்தில் முக்கால்............உத்தம பிரமாணம். இந்த இரண்டு பிரமாணத்துக்கு நடுவு எட்டம்சம் செய்வான். பத்து பீடவிஸ்தாரத்துக்கு பிரமாணமாம்; உத்தமம். இந்த பிரமாணத்தில் உததம மத்யமாதமங்களை முன்பு போலே அறிவான். ($5\frac{1}{2}$)

அன்றிக்கே லிங்கவிஸ்தாரத்தில் மும்மடங்கு ஆதல் லிங்கத்தில் சுற்றளவு ஆதல் பீடவிஸ்தாரமாக சொல்லப்பட்டது. (6)

विष्कम्भकर्णाद्द्विगुणं सार्धद्विगुणं तु वै ।
पीठविस्तारमुद्दिष्टं स्वाष्टांशोनमथोपरि ॥ ७ ॥

मण्डनाय स्वविस्ताराष्टांशेनैवाधिकं ततः ।
सर्वेषामपि पीठानां जन्मान्तं मूलविस्तृतम् ॥ ८ ॥

अग्रव्यासं महापट्टिकान्तं सम्यक् प्रकीर्तितम् ।
विष्णुभागसमोत्सेधं सपादं सार्धमेव वा ॥ ९ ॥

चतुरश्रं च वस्वश्रं षडश्रं द्वादशाश्रकम् ।
द्विरष्टाश्रं सुवृत्तं च तेषामेवायतान्यपि ॥ १० ॥

லிங்கவிஸ்தாரத்தில் தன்னில் சதுரித்து அந்த கர்ணத்தில் இரட்டியாதல் இரண்டரையாதல் மும்மடங்கு பீடவிஸ்தாரமென்று சொல்லப்பட்டது. இந்தப்பீடவிஸ்தாரங்களில் எட்டிலொன்று பீடத்துக்கு மேல்குறைந்திருப்பது. (7)

அலங்காரத்தின் பொருட்டு முன்புசொன்னவிஸ்தாரத்தில் எட்டிலொன்று ஏற்றி பீடவிஸ்தாரம் கொள்க. எல்லாபிரமாணங்களும் சொன்ன விஸ்தாரபிரமாணமுமாக உபானத்திலே கொள்வான். (8)

அக்ரவிஸ்தாரபிரமாணத்தை மஹாபட்டிகையறுதி கொள்வான் என்று அழகியதாக சொல்லப்பட்டது. பீடோத்ஸேதம் விஷ்ணுபாகத்தின்மேலே ஒன்றுகால் ஒன்றரையாதல் பீடத்துக்கு உத்ஸேதப். கொள்ளுவான் என்ற சொல்லப்பட்டது. (9)

त्रिकोणमर्धचन्द्रं च चतुर्दशनिभानि वै ।
समानि यानि लिङ्गस्य चाहुः पीठं च संज्ञकम् ॥११॥
आयतान्यासनानीति निष्कलानां वदन्ति वै ।
त्रिकोणमर्धचन्द्रं च निष्कले सकले क्रमात् ॥ १२ ॥
भद्रपीठं च चन्द्रं च वज्रपीठं महाम्बुजम् ।
श्रीकरं (विकरं) पद्मपीठं च महावज्रं च सौम्यकम् ॥ १३ ॥
श्रीकामार्थमिति प्रोक्ता नाम्नैता नव पीठिकाः ।
स्वनामाकृतियुक्त्या तु त्रिकोणार्धेन्दुसंयुते ॥ १४ ॥

சதுரச்ரம், ஆயதசதுரச்ரம், அஷ்டாச்ரம், ஆயதமான அஷ்டாச்ரம், ஷடச்ரம், ஆயதமான ஷடச்ரம், துவாதசாச்ரம், ஆயதமான துவாதசாச்ரம் ஷோடசாச்ரம் ஆயதமான ஷோடசாச்ரம் விருத்தம் ஆயதவிருத்தம் மூன்றுகோணம் அர்த்தசந்திரன் ஆக பதினுலுபடி பீடத்துக்கு வடிவு சொல்லப்பட்டது. (11)

நீளமான பீடங்களை நிஷ்கலமான லிங்கங்களுக்கு ஆஸனமென்று சொல்லுவார்கள். நிஷ்களத்துக்கு திரிகோணபீடமும் சகளத்துக்கு அர்த்தசந்திரனும் கொள்வானென்று சொல்லப்பட்டது. (12)

பத்ரபீடம், பத்மம், மஹாம்புஜம், ஸ்ரீகரம், பத்மபீடம், மஹாவஜ்ரம், ஸௌம்யகம், ஸ்ரீகாம்யம் ஆகப்பீடத்துக்கு..........சொல்லப்பட்டது. (13½)

திரிகோணத்திலும் அர்த்தசந்திரனிலும் தன்னுடைய நாமத்துக்கிடாக யுக்தியினாலே கொள்வான். (14)

पीठिकानामलङ्कारं क्रमशो वक्ष्यतेऽधुना ।

गृहीतोत्सेधमानांशवशेन विविधेन च ॥ १५ ॥

त्रिःपञ्चांशे व्यंशि जन्मं युगांशं वप्रस्योर्ध्वं...........

....व्यंशं क्षेपणं चार्धमूर्ध्वे सार्धग्रीवं पूर्ववत्क्षेपणोच्चम् ॥ १६ ॥

व्यंशं पट्टं स्नेहवार्यर्धभागं तत्सामान्यं भद्रपीठं स्वहृष्टम् ।

विप्रोर्वीभृद्वैश्यकानां परेषां श्रीसौभाग्यारोग्यभोग्यप्रदायि ॥ १७ ॥

द्विरष्टभागेऽश्विनिबाणनेत्रैर्युगांशनेत्रेन्दुभिरत्र पट्टम् ।

......पं च वृत्तं च दलं च पट्टं स्यात्पद्मपीठं घृतवारियुक्तम् ॥ १८ ॥

நிச்சயித்துக்கொண்டபலபடியான உத்ஸேத பிரமாணத்தாலே அடைவே பீடங்களுக்கு அலங்காரம் சொல்லப்படுகிறது. (15)

பீடத்தினுடைய உயரத்தை பதினஞ்சு அம்சம் செய்து இதில் உபாநம் இரண்டு, நாலம்சம் ஜகதி, ஓரம்சம் குமுதகம், அரையம்சம் கம்பு, இரண்டம்சம் குமுதகம், அரையம்சம் கம்பு, ஒன்றரை அம்சம் கண்டம். அரையம்சம் கம்பு இரண்டம்சம் பட்டிகை ஒன்றரையம்சம் ஸ்நேஹ வாரி ஆக அம்சம் பதினஞ்சு. இது பத்து பத்ரபீடத்துக்கு அலங்காரம். இந்த பீடம் பிராமணருக்கும் ராஜாக்களுக்கும், செட்டிகளுக்கும் வெள்ளாளருக்கும் ஸ்ரீயையும் ஸௌபாக்கியத்தையும் ஆரோக்கியத்தையும் போக்யத்தையும் கொடுக்குமென்று சொல்லப்பட்டது. (17)

பத்மபீடமென்கிற பீடத்தினுடைய உத்ஸேதத்தை பதினறம்சம் செய்து இதில் இரண்டம்சம் உபாநம் அஞ்சம்சம் எழுதகம் இரண்டம்சம் பட்டிகை ஓரம்சம் கிருத வாரி ஆக அம்சம் பதினறு. (18)

द्विसप्तांशे सार्धमर्धं गुणार्धं जन्मं निम्नं पङ्कजं तत्क्रमेण ।
पट्टं निम्नं चार्धमर्धं तु भागं वज्रं निम्नं कम्पकं पूर्ववत् स्यात् ॥१९॥
त्र्यंशं पद्मं निम्नमर्धं तदूर्ध्वे ह्यध्यर्धांशा पट्टिकाज्यार्धभागा ।
एतत्पीठं वज्रपद्मं हि नाम्ना सामान्यं तत्सर्वलिङ्गेषु शस्तम् ॥ २० ॥
त्रिषड्भागैर्व्यर्धवेदांशकार्धैस्सार्धव्यर्धार्धकार्धानलांशैः ।
अर्धाध्यर्धार्धांशकैर्जन्ममब्जं पट्टं निम्नं पङ्कजं वृत्तमब्जम् ॥ २१ ॥
निम्नं पट्टं पङ्क........श्रीपट्टं तत्स्नेहभारं क्रमेण ।
ए.........सम्यगुक्तं महाब्जं चित्रं सद्भिः पौरुषे चार्षकेऽपि ॥२२॥

வஜ்ரபத்மமென்று பேரையுடைய பீடத்தில் உத்ஸேதத்தை பதினலம்சம் செய்து இதில் ஒன்றரையம்சம் உபாநம் அரையம்சம் நிம்னம். மூன்றரையம்சம் எழுதகம். இதன் மேல் அரையம்சம் பட்டம்.......யம்சம் நிம்னம் ஓரம்சம் வஜ்ரம் அரையம்சம் நிம்னம் அரையம்சம் கம்பு மூன்றம்சம் எழுதகம். அரையம்சம் நிம்நம் ஒன்றரையம்சம் பட்டிகை அரையம்சம் கிருதவாரி. ஆக அம்சம் பதினலு இந்த வஜ்ரபீடத்தை எல்லா லிங்கங்களுக்கும் கொள்வானென்று சொல்லப்பட்டது. (20)

மஹாப்ஜமென்று நாமத்தோடுகூடிய பீடோத்ஸேதத்தை பதினெட்டம்சம் செய்து இதில் ஒன்றரையம்சம் எழுதகம். மூன்றம்சம் குமதகம். அரையம்சம் எழுதகம். அரையம்சம் கம்பு. அரையம்சம் பத்மம். ஒன்றரையம்சம் பட்டிகை கிருதவாரி யரையம்சம் ஆக அம்சம் பதினெட்டு இந்த மஹாபத்ம பீடம் ஆர்ஷலிங்கத்துக்கும் மாநுஷலிங்கத்துக்கும் ஆமென்று சொல்லப்பட்டது. (22)

लब्धोत्सेधे षोडशांशेंऽशि जन्म त्र्यंशं पद्मं पद्मतुङ्गं युगांशम् ।
हृद्भागार्धं द्व्यंशि वृत्तं धगर्धं पद्मं त्र्यंशं पट्टिका सार्धभागा ॥ २३ ॥
अर्धांशं तत्स्नेहवार्यर्धघातं तावद्व्यासं त्र्यंशकं वा युगांशम् ।
नालव्यासं निर्गमं त[स्य*]त्र्यंशं कुर्यादग्रं श्रीकरं श्रीकरं तत् ॥ २४ ॥
अध्यर्धार्धद्व्यर्धकार्धार्धकार्धैः पक्षार्धैर्द्व्यर्धैः खुरं निम्नमब्जम् ।
पट्टं निम्नं पट्टमब्जं तु निम्नं पट्टं निम्नं पीठपद्मं दशांशे ॥ २५ ॥
त्रिःपञ्चांशे लब्धतुङ्गे स चार्धेऽर्धाद्व्यर्धं सार्धेन्दुभागैः ।
अर्धद्व्यर्धाद्व्यर्धकार्धैः क्रमेण जन्मं निम्नं पट्टकं तत्क्रमेण ॥ २६ ॥

ஸ்ரீகரமென்று நாமத்தையுடைய பீடோத்ஸேதத்தை பதிநாறம்சம் செய்து இதிலோரம்சம் உபாநம், மூன்றம்சம் மஹோபாநம் நாலம்சம் பத்மம், அரையம்சம் கம்பு, இரண்டம்சம் விருத்தம் அரையம்சம் கம்பு மூன்றம்சம் பத்மம். ஒன்றரையம்சம் பட்டிகை அரையம்சம் கிருதவாரி. ஆக அம்சம் பதிநாறு. கிருதவாரியினுடைய தாழ்ச்சியும் அரையம்சம். பீடவிஸ்தாரத்தில் மூன்றிலொன்று நாலிலொன்று நாளவிஸ்தாரம் கொள்வது. நாளக்கழுத்தி பீடவிஸ்தாரத்தில் மூன்றிலொன்று கொள்க. நாளத்தில் விஸ்தாரம் நாளத்தினுடைய மூலவிஸ்தாரத்தில் மூன்றிலொன்ருகக் கொள்க. என்று சொல்லப்பட்டது. இது கர்த்தாவுக்கு ஸ்ரீயைக்கொடுக்கும். (24)

பீடபத்மம் தசாம்சம் என்றது. பீடபத்மமென்று நாமதேயத்தையுடைத்தான பீடோத்ஸேதத்தை பத்தம்சம்செய்து இதில் ஒன்றரையம்சம் உபாநம். அரையம்சம் நிம்னம். இரண்டரையம்சம் பத்மம். அரையம்சம் கம்பு

जन्मं निम्नं पङ्कजं पट्टकं तद्वज्रं वृत्तं (तत्)क्षेपणं कञ्जमूर्ध्वे ।

पट्टं निम्नं तन्महावज्रमुक्तं........................ ॥ २७ ॥

वज्रं वृत्तं तुङ्गनाम्ना तदेव सौम्यं पीठं सम्पदायुष्करं स्यात् ।

द्विषड्भागे चन्द्रनेत्रार्धभागैः सार्धार्धैः सार्धसार्धार्धकार्धैः ॥ २८ ॥

अध्यर्धेनार्धेन निम्नं तु वप्रं निम्नं पद्मं धृग्धलं वृत्तमब्जम् ।

धृक्पद्मं तत्पट्टिकानिम्नपट्टं श्रीकामं तल्लब्धतुङ्गे मयोक्तम् ॥ २९ ॥

அரையம்சம் நிம்னம். அரையம்சம் பட்டம் இரண்டம்சம் பத்மம் அரையம்சம் நிம்னம் ஓரம்சம் பட்டிகை அரையம்சம் கிருதவாரி ஆக அம்சம் பத்து.

மஹாவஜ்ரமென்று பேரையுடையத்தான பீடோத்ஸேதத்தை பதினஞ்சம்சம்செய்து இதில் ஒன்றரையம்சம் உபாநம் அரையம்சம் நிம்னம், நாலம்சம் பத்மம். அரையம்சம் பட்டம். ஓரம்சம் கண்டம். ஒன்றரையம்சம்...... ஓரம்சம் கண்டம் அரையம்சம் கம்பு இரண்டம்சம் பத்மம். ஒன்றரை அரையம்சம் கிருதவாரி ஆக அம்சம் பதினஞ்சு மஹாவஜ்ர பீடம் சொல்லப்பட்டது. (27)

இந்த மஹாவஜ்ரபீடத்தில் வஜ்ரம்விருத்தமாக ஸௌம்யபீடமென்று நாமமாம். இந்த ஸௌம்யபீடமானது கர்த்தாவுக்கு ஸர்வஸம்பத்தைக் கொடுக்கும், ஸௌம்யபீடமும் சொல்லப்பட்டது.

ஸ்ரீகாம்யமென்று நாமதேயத்தை யுடைத்தான பீடோத்ஸேதத்தை பன்னிரண்டுசெய்து இதில் ஓரம்சம்

धाम्नि प्रोक्तान्यप्याधिष्ठानकानीत्यन्यप्यस्मिन्मण्डनीयानि युक्त्या ।

यथाबलं यथाशोभं यथायुक्ति प्रवेशनम् ।
निर्गमं सर्वपीठानां अङ्गानां परिकल्पयेत्[1] ॥ ३० ॥

க்ஷுத்ரோபாநம். இரண்டம்சம் ஜகதி. அரையம்சம் நிம்னம். ஓரம்சம் பத்மம். ஒன்றரையம்சம் பட்டிகை அரையம்சம் கிருதவாரி ஆக அம்சம் பன்னிரண்டு. இப்படி ஸ்ரீகாம்யபீடம் சொல்லப்பட்டது.

பிராஸாதங்களில்கொண்ட அதிஷ்டானங்களில் அலங்காரம்போல பீடங்களுக்கும் கொள்ளலாமென்று சொல்லப் பட்டது.

இந்த பீடாலங்காரங்களுடைய அம்சங்களில் சுருப் புக்களும் பிறப்பாடும் இவ்வங்கங்களுடைய பலத்துக்கீடா கவும் சோபைக்கீடாகவும் யுக்திக்கீடாகவும் கொள்வான். இந்த அங்கங்களை யழகியதாக கல்பிப்பான்.

(मयमते चतुस्त्रिंशाध्याये ॥)

---

१ अस्मिन् पीठलक्षणे मूलव्याख्यानयोः लेखकप्रमादजनितं वर्णलोप पङ्क्तिलोपादिकमुपलभ्यते ॥

लिङ्गोद्भवादिचतुर्मूर्तयः ।

लिङ्गोद्भवादिचतुर्मूर्तयः ।

लिङ्गोद्भवमूर्तिः ।

अथ वक्ष्ये विशेषेण लिङ्गोद्भवविधिं शृणु ।
लिङ्गाकारस्य मध्ये तु चन्द्रशेखरमूर्तिवत् ॥

नळकात्तलपर्यन्तं लिङ्गे शूलसमन्वितम् ।
ब्रह्मापि हंसरूपेण ऊर्ध्वे वै वामपार्श्वके ॥

विष्णुर्वराहरूपेण दक्षिणेंऽशे त्वधोगतः ।
विष्णुर्दक्षिणपार्श्वे तु वामपार्श्वे पितामहः ॥

हृदयेऽञ्जलिसंयुक्तौ स्थितौ लिङ्गं समीक्ष्य च ।
रक्तश्यामहिरण्याभा ईशविष्णुपितामहाः ॥

एवं लिङ्गोद्भवं ख्यातं वृक्षसङ्ग्रहणं ततः ।

(अंशुमद्भेदागमे षट्सप्ततितमपटले ॥)

पूर्ववत्कारयेत्सम्यक् चन्द्रशेखरमूर्तिनम् ।
लिङ्गाधः शर्वजान्वन्तभागं नेन्द्रियगोचरम् ॥

लिङ्गोर्ध्वाधःप्रदेशे तु हंससूकरमाचरेत् ।
बिम्बस्याननमानेन कारयेद्धंसमादरात् ॥

बिम्बाद्विमुखमानेन भूकृष्टास्यं तु सूकरम् ।
ब्रह्माविष्णू द्विपार्श्वस्थौ नतौ तस्यानुकूलकौ ॥

तिर्यग्गतसुपादौ तौ सर्वावयवसुन्दरौ ।
लिङ्गोद्भवस्त्विति ख्यातो ब्रह्माविष्ण्वभिनान्दितः ॥

ब्रह्माविष्णुविहीनो वा हंससूकरसंयुतः ।

(उत्तरकामिकागमे पञ्चाशत्तमपटले ॥)

लिङ्गं कृत्वोर्ध्वतो ब्रह्मा हंसरूपं तथैव च ।
विष्णुं वराहवक्त्रं तु लिङ्गस्याधः प्रकल्पयेत् ॥

हृदयेऽञ्जलिसंयुक्तौ ब्रह्मविष्णू च पार्श्वयोः ।
लिङ्गमध्ये तु कर्तव्यं पूर्ववच्चन्द्रशेखरम् ॥

अदृश्या तस्य पादाब्जौ तथैव मकुटं यथा ।

(सुप्रभेदागमे चतुस्त्रिंशत्तमपटले ॥)

अथ लिङ्गोद्भवं वक्ष्ये लिङ्गाकारस्य मध्यतः ।
नलकात् पादस्य तलं लिङ्गे शूलसमायुतम् ॥

चन्द्रशेखरवत्सर्वं कारयेत्सुन्दराकृतिम् ।
ब्रह्मा तु हंसरूपेण ऊर्ध्वगो वामपार्श्वतः ॥

विष्णुर्वराहरूपेण दक्षिणांशे त्वधोगतः ।
हृदयेऽञ्जलिसंयुक्तौ रक्तश्यामनिभौ परम् ॥

वीक्षमाणौ परं लिङ्गमिदं लिङ्गोद्भवं स्मृतम् ।

(शिल्परत्ने द्वाविंशपटले ॥)

आयामं यत्तु लिङ्गस्य भूतांशं विभजेत्ततः ।
ऊर्ध्वे व्योमांशकं त्यक्त्वा मूले चैव तथा भवेत् ॥
तन्मध्ये कारयेद्धीमांश्चन्द्रशेखरमूर्तिताम् ।
अजविष्णू द्विपार्श्वे द्वौ नमस्कृत्वानुकूलकौ ॥
धर्मांशं विभजेल्लिङ्गं शरांशमुदयान्तयोः ।
लिङ्गोर्ध्वे कारयेद्धंसमधस्तात्सूकराननम् ॥
विष्णुं सङ्कल्पयेदुर्वीमाननेनैव कर्षितम् ।
बिम्बस्य द्विमुखेनैव हंसरूपं तु कारयेत् ॥
ऋज्वागतिस्थितिं वामाद्वरदाभयहस्तकम् ।
कृष्णापरशुसंयुक्तं कारयेदिन्दुशेखरम् ॥
अधोभागे तु भागेन जान्वन्तं तु न दृश्यकम् ।
एवं लिङ्गोद्भवं कुर्याच्चन्द्रशेखरमुच्यते ॥

(कारणागमे एकादशपटले ॥)

लिङ्गाकारस्य मध्ये तु चन्द्रशेखरवत्स्थितम् ।
नलकाधस्स्थितं पादं लिङ्गोद्भवसमन्वितम् ॥
विरिञ्चिर्हंसरूपेण चोर्ध्वगो वामपार्श्वके ।
दक्षे वराहरूपस्य रूपेणाधोगतो हरिः ॥

प्रतिमालक्षणानि ।

वामदक्षिणपार्श्वस्थौ कृताञ्जलिसमन्वितौ ।
स्वरूपेण द्विपादस्थावजविष्णू विभोः परे ॥
एवं लिङ्गावतारं तु सर्वशान्तिकरं सदा ।

तुङ्गाङ्गविस्तृतिनतांसकलम्बमानैस्संपन्नचिह्नभुजभूषणवर्णभेदैः ।
शोभान्वितं शुभकरं सकलप्रजानामैश्वर्यसङ्घपरिवृद्धिकरं विदध्यात् ॥

(श्रीतत्वनिधौ ॥)

चन्द्रशेखरमूर्तिः ।

इन्दुमौलिप्रतिष्ठां तु वक्ष्ये लक्षणपूर्विकाम् ।
आपाद्य च शिलादीनि तैः कुर्य्यात्प्रतिमां गुरुः ॥
चतुर्भुजस्त्रिनेत्रश्च समपात्स्थानके स्थितः ।
वराभयसमायुक्तपूर्वस्थकरपल्लवः ॥
वरदं वामहस्ते स्यादभयं दक्षिणे करे ।
वरदं यदि तं कुर्य्यादथान्यस्सिंहकर्णिकः ॥
ऊरुस्पृष्टकरो वापि कटको वा विधीयते ।
मृगटङ्ककरावन्यौ दोस्सीमान्तं व्यवस्थितौ ॥
मृगटङ्कौ तु कर्णान्तौ कर्त्तरीसंव्यवस्थितौ ।
पराङ्मुखोऽभिमुखो वा मृगष्टङ्कः पराङ्मुखः ॥
रत्नपत्रिकया वापि शङ्खपत्रिकयापि वा ।
पद्मपत्रिकया वापि शोभितं वामकर्णकम् ॥

सव्यं मकरसिंहाख्यपत्रकुण्डलकैर्युतम् ।
पृष्ठतः कर्णपर्यन्तं केशवर्तिविलम्बनम् ॥
पार्श्वयोर्बाहुमूलात्तु जटाग्राणां विलम्बनम् ।
हारयुग्ग्रीवसंयुक्तं तथा कर्णिकयान्वितम् ॥
वक्षस्स्थलं प्रकर्तव्यं भुजाः केयूरसंयुताः ।
सुपत्रवलयोपेतास्सर्वरत्नोपशोभिताः ॥
मुक्तादामविलम्बाश्च तदग्रं मणिभूषणम् ।
कराग्रं कटकोपेतमङ्गुल्यो मुद्रिकान्विताः ॥
छन्नवीरोत्तरीयोपवीतैस्सोदरबन्धनः ।
समस्तरत्नपाशाढ्यकृत्तिमाननदामभिः ॥
संयुक्तकटिसूत्रोऽन्तः पादजालकसंयुतः ।
चन्द्रशेखर एवं स्याद्देव्या च सहितो न वा ॥
सापीहाभिन्नपीठा वा देवेनालिङ्गिताथवा ।
तयालिङ्गितदेवो वा अन्योन्यालिङ्गितस्तु वा ॥
आलिङ्गनयुतो वा स्यान्निरालिङ्गोऽथवा मतः ।

(उत्तरकामिकागमे अष्टाचत्वारिंशत्तमपटले ॥)

ऋज्वागतं तु तं देवं मृगं परशुधारिणम् ।
कृत्त्यम्बरधरं देवं कर्तव्यं चन्द्रशेखरम् ॥

(सुप्रभेदागमे चतुस्त्रिंशत्तमपटले ॥)

प्रतिमालक्षणानि ।

लिङ्गं च विष्णुरूपं च विना कुर्विन्दुशेखरम् ।

(पूर्वकारणागमे एकादशपटले ॥)

अभयवरदहस्तं सौम्यशृङ्गारभावं
विपुलवदननेत्रं चन्द्रबिम्बांशमौलिम् ।
ऋजुतनुसमपादस्थानकं विद्रुमाभं
हरिणपरशुपाणिं पद्मपीठोपरिस्थम् ॥

एतत्पार्श्वस्थगौरी ।

श्यामां त्रिनेत्रां द्विभुजां त्रिभङ्गीं सव्यापसव्यस्थितकुञ्चिताङ्घ्रिम् ।
सव्ये तु नीलोत्पलचारुहस्तां देवस्य वामस्थितपद्मपीठाम् ॥

(श्रीतत्वनिधौ ॥)

केवलमूर्तिः ।

अभयं दक्षिणं हस्तं वरदं वाममुच्यते ।
वरदं वामहस्तं तु अधोमुखं प्रकल्पयेत् ॥
तलमूलं कटिस्पृष्टं मेढ्राग्रान्तं तु तत्करे ।
ऊर्ध्ववक्त्रं तु वरदं पृष्ठं नाभिसमोद्धृतम् ॥
आर्जवं राजसं भावं कल्पयेद्द्विजसत्तम ! ।
कर्तरी परहस्ते द्वौ टङ्कं वै दक्षिणे करे ॥
हरिणी च बाह्यवक्त्रं वाभ्यन्तरमुखं तु वा ।
जटामकुटसंयुक्तं दक्षिणार्धेन्दुसंयुतम् ॥

वामेन्दुशेखरं वाथ प्रवालसदृशप्रभम् ।
त्रिनेत्रं सौम्यवदनं सर्वाभरणभूषणम् ॥

पीताम्बरं तथा देवं वस्त्राग्रौ नलकान्तगौ ।
उभयोः पार्श्वयोरेवमम्बरं तूरुमध्यगम् ॥

(अंशुमद्भेदागमे त्रिषष्टितमपटले ॥)

केवलं गौरिसहितमालिङ्गं च त्रिधा भवेत् ।
केवलं समपादं तु स्थान [कं परि*] कल्पयेत् ॥

अभयं दक्षिणं हस्तं वरदं वाममुच्यते ।
हरिणी वामहस्ते तु टङ्कं वै दक्षिणे करे ॥

जटामकुटसंयुक्तं दक्षिणेर्धेन्दुशेखरम् ।
वामेन्दुशेखरं वाथ प्रवालसदृशप्रभम् ॥

त्रिनेत्रं सौम्यवदनं सर्वाभरणभूषितम् ।
पीताम्बरधरं देवं वस्त्राग्रे नलकान्तगौ ॥

उभयोः पार्श्वयोरेवं मध्यतश्चोरुमध्यगम् ।

(शिल्परत्ने द्वाविंशपटले ॥)

पाशुपतमूर्तिः ।

अथ वक्ष्ये विशेषेण पाशुपतस्य लक्षणम् ।
समपादं स्थानकं स्याच्चन्द्रशेखरमूर्तिवत् ॥

त्रिनेत्रं चतुर्भुजं सौम्यमूर्ध्वकेशं महातनुम् ।
अभयं शूलहस्तं च दक्षिणे तु करद्वयम् ॥
वरदं चाक्षमालां च वामपार्श्वे करद्वयम् ।
प्रवालसदृशप्रख्यं सौम्यनेत्रातिशीतलम् ॥
सर्वाभरणसंयुक्तं किंचित्प्रहसिताननम् ।
नित्योत्सवाय बिम्बं तत्स्थानकं वासनं तु वा ॥

(अंशुमद्भेदागमे एकसप्ततितमपटले ॥)

अथ पाशुपतं वक्ष्ये चन्द्रशेखरवत्स्थितम् ।
चतुर्भुजं त्रिनेत्रं चाप्यूर्ध्वकेशं महातनुम् ॥
दक्षिणेऽभयकं शूलं कपालं वरदं परे ।
प्रवालसदृशप्रख्यं सर्वाभरणभूषितम् ॥

(शिल्परत्ने द्वाविंशपटले) ॥

बलिभर्तुः प्रतिष्ठां तु वक्ष्ये तल्लक्षणं तु वै ।
नित्योत्सवे तु कथितं सूत्राद्यं चेन्दुमौलिवत् ॥
प्रायश्चित्तादिके वाथ सर्वकामप्रसिद्धये ।
नित्योत्सवेऽपि तच्छ्रेष्ठं तं मन्त्रैश्च विशेषतः ॥

(उत्तरकामिकागमे त्रिपञ्चाशत्तमपटले ॥)

रौद्रपाशुपतमूर्तिः ।

तदेवाग्निसमं वर्णं रक्ताक्षं कुटिलभ्रुवम् ।
तीक्ष्णदंष्ट्रासमायुक्तं व्यालयज्ञोपवीतिनम् ॥
ज्वालानलशिखाकारमतिरक्तकवस्त्रधृ ।
शूलं त्वधोमुखं धृत्वा कपालं वरदोद्धृतम् ॥
अथवाभयं विना शूलमूलं धृत्वा तु तत्करे ।
शूलाग्रं वरदेनैव गृह्य तिर्य्यग्गतोद्धृतम् ॥
दक्षिणे त्वपरे हस्ते टङ्कं खड्गं च वामके ।
रौद्रं पाशुपतं ह्येतद्धिलिलिङ्गे तु पूजितम् ॥
एतन्मूर्तिं सकृद् ध्यायेत्सर्वशत्रुविनाशनम् ।
एतत्तु रौद्रमूर्तिं तु प्रतिमां तु न कारयेत् ॥

(अंशुमद्भेदागमे एकसप्ततितमपटले ॥)

अथातस्संप्रवक्ष्यामि अस्त्रराजस्य पूजनम् ।
चतुर्भुजं त्रिनेत्रं च शिखाकूटसमुज्वलम् ॥
वामसव्ये च शूलं तु वरदाभयहस्तकम् ।
रौद्रपाशुपतं ह्येवं बलिबिम्बं तथोच्यते ॥

(सुप्रभेदागमे द्विपञ्चाशत्तमपटले ॥)

पाशुपतास्त्रमूर्तिः ॥

चतुर्वक्त्रं चतुर्बाहुं सूर्यकोटिसमप्रभम् ।
संहाराभं सुमूर्धानं प्रतिवक्त्रं त्रिलोचनम् ॥
दीप्तदन्ताग्रकेशभ्रश्मश्रुभीमं महाबलम् ।
शक्तिमुद्गरशङ्खासीन्दधानं सोमसूत्रिणम् ॥
साङ्गं पाशुपतं शस्त्रं भजे पद्मासने स्थितम् ।

(श्रीतत्वनिधौ ॥)

सुखासनादिमूर्तयः ।

सुखासनादिमूर्तयः ।

सुखासनमूर्तिः ।

मेरुपर्वतपार्श्वे तु मुनीनामाश्रमे तथा ।
दिगम्बरं तु मां दृष्ट्वा तेषां स्त्रीणां भ्रमोऽस्ति वै ॥

तं ज्ञात्वा मुनयस्सर्वे जुहुवुस्त्वाभिचारिकम् ।
तन्मध्ये ह्युदितानीह नागं कृष्णमृगं तथा ॥

अपस्मारं च परशुमुक्षं व्याघ्रं हरिं तथा ।
करोटिं तु महाभीममेवमाद्या गता मयि ॥

नागं मृगं च परशुं क्रीडार्थं धारितं मया ।
पादाधस्तादपस्मारं करोटिं शिरसोपरि ॥

सिंहव्याघ्रौ तदा हत्वा तच्चर्म धारितं मया ।
तदुक्षं वाहनं भूत्वा मम प्रियकरं सदा ॥

महोदधेर्विषं कण्ठे सोमार्धं शेखरे धृतम् ।
बकपुष्पं जटाभारे मया नृत्तेऽवधारितम् ॥

समानमन्यत्सर्वासां प्रतिमानां विशेषतः ।
त्रिनेत्रं चतुर्भुजं सौम्यं बालेन्दुकृतशेखरम् ॥

धुस्तूरभुजगोपेतं जटामकुटमण्डितम् ।
व्याघ्रचर्माम्बरं चैव हारकेयूरसंयुतम् ॥

यज्ञोपवीतसंयुक्तं कुण्डलाभ्यामलङ्कृतम् ।
मूर्तीनां द्वादशानां तु सामान्यमिदमीरितम् ॥

अतः परं विशेषस्तु क्रमशो वक्ष्यतेऽधुना ।
आसने तु सुखासीनं मृगीपरशुधारिणम् ॥

अभयं दक्षिणे हस्ते वरदं वामहस्तके ।
कटकं वा सुखासीनमुमास्कन्दौ च वर्जितम् ॥

एवं सुखासनं प्रोक्तमुमासहितमुच्यते ।

(सुप्रभेदागमे चतुस्त्रिंशत्तमपटले ॥)

आर्जवं राजसं भावं भद्रपीठोपरिस्थितम् ।
वामाङ्घ्रिं शाययेत्पीठे दक्षिणाङ्घ्रिं तु लम्बयेत् ॥

जागतं(?) तु सुखासीनं प्रवालसदृशप्रभम् ।
त्रिनेत्रं तु प्रसन्नास्यं संपन्नं राजसैर्गुणैः ॥

व्याघ्राजिनवरोपेतं दुकूलवसनान्वितम् ।
दक्षिणे परशुं वामे कृष्णं हस्ते समुद्धृतम् ॥

अभयं दक्षिणे वामे कटकं सिंहकर्णवत् ।
दक्षिणे मकराख्यं वा कुण्डलं सिंहमेव वा ॥

पत्रकुण्डलमन्यत्र वामकर्णे विशेषतः ।
अथवा कर्णयुगले वृत्तकुण्डलकं न्यसेत् ॥
जटामकुटसंयुक्तं नानाभरणभूषितम् ।
यज्ञोपवीतसंयुक्तं सर्पराट्कङ्कणान्वितम् ॥
एवं सुखासनं प्रोक्तं राजराष्ट्रसुखावहम् ।

(शिल्परत्ने द्वाविंशाध्याये ॥)

चतुर्भुजं त्रिनेत्रं च जटामकुटसंयुतम् ।
अभयं दक्षिणं हस्तं वरदं वामहस्तकम् ॥
कृष्णापरशुसंयुक्तं वामदक्षिणहस्तयोः ।
शयनं दक्षिणं पादं वामपादं तु लम्बितम् ॥
उमासहितवत्सर्वं स्कन्दगौरीविवर्जितम् ।

(पूर्वकारणागमे एकादशपटले ॥)

उमासहितमूर्तिः ।

केवलं त्वेवमाख्यातं वामे गौरीसमायुतम् ।
तद्गौरीसहितं ख्यातं भिन्नपीठैकमेव वा ॥

(अंशुमद्भेदागमे त्रिषष्टितमपटले ॥)

केवलं त्वेवमाख्यातं वामे गौरीसमन्वितम् ।
भिन्नपीठे विशेषेण तद्गौरीसहितं विदुः ॥

(शिल्परत्ने द्वाविंशपटले ॥)

आलिङ्गमूर्तिः ।

तदेव भङ्गसंयुक्तं देवीदेवौ परस्परम् ।
देवो वरदहस्तेन देवी वै...पराश्रितम् ॥

...स्तनाभ्यन्तरे वामपार्श्वमालिङ्गनं कुरु ।
पार्श्वसूत्रात्पुरो वामबाहुमालिङ्गनं तु वा ॥

देवी दक्षिणहस्तेन शम्भोर्दक्षिणपार्श्वतः ।
कटिसूत्रोपरि स्पृष्ट्वा पुष्पं वामकरे धृता ॥

अथवा प्राग्वदेवेशो देव्यास्तु दक्षिणे करे ।
रक्तोत्पलं परिग्राह्य वामहस्तं प्रलम्बिता ॥

एवमालिङ्गमूर्तिं च विधामार्गेण कल्पयेत् ।
सर्वाभरणसंयुक्तं प्रभामण्डलमण्डितम् ॥

चन्द्रशेखरमाख्यातं वृषारूढमथ शृणु ।

(अंशुमद्भेदागमे त्रिषष्टितमपटले ॥)

देवो वरदहस्तेन देवीं तत्पार्श्वमाश्रिताम् ।
स्तनाभ्यन्तरे वामपार्श्वमालिङ्गनं कुरु ॥

पार्श्वसूत्रात्पुरो वामबाहुमालिङ्गनं तु वा ।
देवी दक्षिणहस्तेन शम्भोर्दक्षिणपार्श्वतः ॥

कटिसूत्रोपरि तथा वामे पुष्पधृता करे ।
अथवा प्राग्वदेवेशो देवी रक्तोत्पलान्विता ॥

करे तु दक्षिणे वामहस्तमात्रं प्रलम्बयेत् ।
एवमालिङ्गमूर्तिं तु त्रिधा मार्गेण कल्पयेत् ॥
एवं पञ्चविधं प्रोक्तं चन्द्रशेखरमूर्तिनम् ।

(शिल्परत्ने द्वाविंशपटले ॥)

सोमास्कन्दः ।

वक्ष्यामि सोमोमास्कन्दसुखेशस्थापनं परम् ।
तल्लक्षणसमायुक्तं तच्चेदानीं प्रकथ्यते ॥
चतुर्भुजस्त्रिनेत्रश्च जटामकुटमण्डितः ।
सर्वाभरणसंयुक्तो वरदाभयहस्तकः ॥
कृष्णापरशुयुक्तोर्ध्ववामेतरकरान्वितः ।
असव्यसव्यकर्णस्थपत्रिकानक्रकुण्डलः ॥
सोपवीतः प्रसन्नात्मा शायितासव्यपात्तलः ।
सालम्बदक्षपादेन वामे गौर्या च संयुतः ॥
सर्वलक्षणसंयुक्तस्सर्वाभरणभूषितः ।
वामे देव्या समायुक्तस्तदध्यायप्रसिद्धया ॥
ससोमस्सोम एव स्यात्सोमास्कन्दविधिर्भवेत् ।
देवोच्चदशभागैकभागेनाथ द्विभागतः ॥
त्रिवेदभागैर्वा कुर्य्यात् स्कन्दं तन्मध्यमे गुरुः ।
द्विनेत्रस्सद्विबाहुश्च करण्डमकुटान्वितः ॥

कर्णयोर्नक्रपिण्डेन सर्वाभरणभूषितः ।
दक्षभागकरस्थाब्जः प्रसारितकरोऽपरः ॥

द्विहस्तपङ्कजो वाथ नृत्तरूपयुतोऽथवा ।
देव्यूरुसंस्थितो वापि निष्पङ्कजकरोऽथवा ॥

आसीनो वा स्थितो वापि स्कन्दस्त्वेवं प्रकीर्तितः ।
स्कन्दोमारहितस्त्वेष एवं स्यात्तु सुखासनः ॥

सोमे च सोमास्कन्दे च सुखेशे लक्षणं मतम् ।

(उत्तरकामिकागमे सप्तचत्वारिंशत्तमपटले ॥)

सहासने ह्युमादेवीं सुसौम्यवदनोज्ज्वलाम् ।
द्विभुजां पद्महस्तां तु मकुटाभरणान्विताम् ॥

कटकाख्यधरां वामे प्रसारितमथापि वा ।
उमाबाहुस्तनान्तं वा मानं वै षण्मुखस्य तु ॥

कण्ठे शूलसमायुक्तं छन्नवीरसमायुतम् ।
उमाशङ्करयोर्मध्ये स्कन्दं वै बालरूपिणम् ॥

आसनं स्थानकं वापि वरदं कटकान्वितम् ।
कृत्वा सुखासनं यद्वत् पूर्ववत्परमेश्वरम् ॥

देवस्य मुखमन्वीक्ष्य किञ्चिद् गौरीं तु कारयेत् ।

(सुप्रभेदागमे चतुस्त्रिंशत्तमपटले ॥)

अथ वक्ष्ये विशेषेण सोमास्कन्देश्वरं परम् ।
सुखासनं यथा प्रोक्तं तथा देवो विधीयते ॥
देवस्य वामपार्श्वे तु पार्वती च सहासने ।
शाययेद्दक्षिणं पादं वामपादं प्रलम्बयेत् ॥
वरदं वामहस्ते तु दक्षिणे चोत्पलं करे ।
दूर्वाश्यामनिभा देवी सर्वाभरणभूषिता ॥
रक्ताम्बरधरा हारमकुटोज्वलन्विता ।
वामोरुबाह्ये पीठे तु वामहस्ततलं न्यसेत् ॥
प्रह्वदुत्पलसंयुक्तमन्यमेवं करोतु वा ।
देवीदेवेशयोर्मध्ये स्थापयेत्स्कन्दमूर्तिनम् ॥
केशान्ते वापिकोपेतं करण्डमकुटोज्वलम् ।
उभयोर्हस्तयोः पुष्पं वामे वरदमेव वा ॥
कटकं वाथ तद्धस्ते सिंहकर्णमथापि वा ।
अथवा पुस्तकं दक्षहस्ते वामे पुरोक्तवत् ॥
कटिसूत्रयुतं नग्नं बाहुभूषणभूषितम् ।
आसीनं वा स्थितं वाथ नृत्तं वा स्कन्दमाचरेत् ॥
नृत्तं चेत् फलवद्वामहस्तमन्यत्र सूचिकम् ।
अथवा वामहस्तं तु फलं त्यक्त्वा प्रसारयेत् ॥
वक्ष्यमाणविधानेन स्कन्दनृत्तं समाचरेत् ।

(शिल्परत्ने द्वाविंशपटले ॥)

चतुर्भुजं त्रिनेत्रं च जटामकुटसंयुतम् ।
सर्वाभरणसंयुक्तं वरदाभयहस्तकम् ॥

कृष्णापरशुसंयुक्तं दक्षिणे वामकेऽपि च ।
पत्रं तु वामकर्णे तु दक्षिणे कुण्डलं भवेत् ॥

उपवीतधरं चैव शयनं वामपादकम् ।
लम्बितं दक्षिणं पादं वामे गौरीसमायुतम् ॥

तयोर्मध्ये स्थितस्स्कन्दस्सर्वलक्षणसंयुतः ।
ब्रह्मविष्णू द्विपार्श्वाभ्यां देवीभ्यां युक्तभोगदम् ॥

देवस्य बाहुसीमान्तं देव्यास्त्वायाममुच्यते ।
द्विबाहुका द्विनेत्री च करण्डमकुटान्विता ॥

सर्वाभरणसंयुक्ता दुकूलवसनान्विता ।
शयनं दक्षिणं पादं वामपादं तु लम्बितम् ॥

कटकं दक्षिणं हस्तं वरदं वामहस्तकम् ।
बेरायामं तु विभजेदष्टधा चैव भागिकम् ॥

द्विभागं वा गुहायामं बाहु(ल ?)रूपेण कल्पयेत् ।
द्विभुजश्च द्विनेत्रश्च सर्वाभरणभूषितः ॥

कटकं दक्षिणे हस्ते वामहस्तं प्रलम्बितम् ।
आसीनो वा स्थितो वापि कारयेत्तु गुहं ततः ॥

पद्मपीठोर्ध्वके वापि केवलं पीठकोपरि ।
भवानीसहितं ह्येवं वृषवाहनमुच्यते ॥

(पूर्वकारणागमे एकादशपटले ॥)

उमामहेश्वरौ ।

युग्मं स्त्रीपुरुषं कार्यमुमेशौ दिव्यरूपिणौ ।
अष्टवक्त्रं तु देवेशं जटाचन्द्रार्धभूषितम् ॥
द्विपाणिं द्विभुजां देवीं सुमध्यां सुपयोधराम् ।
वामपाणिं तु देवस्य देव्यास्स्कन्धे नियोजयेत् ॥
दक्षिणं तु करं शम्भोरुत्पलेन विभूषितम् ।
देव्यास्तु दक्षिणं पाणिं स्कन्धे देवस्य कल्पयेत् ॥
वामपाणौ तथा देव्या दर्पणं दापयेच्छुभम् ।

(विष्णुधर्मोत्तरे ॥)

उमामहेश्वरं वक्ष्ये उमया सह शङ्करम् ।
मातुलिङ्गं त्रिशूलं च धत्ते दक्षिणे करे ॥
आलिङ्गन्वामहस्तेन नागेन्द्रं द्वितीये करे ।
हरस्कन्धे उमाहस्तो दर्पणं द्वितीये करे ॥
अधस्ताद्वृषभं कुर्यात्कुमारं च गणेश्वरम् ।
भृङ्गिरिटिं तथा कुर्यान्निर्मांसं नृत्यसंस्थितम् ।

(रूपमण्डने ॥)

सपरिवारोमामहेश्वरः ।

वामे शैलसुता पुरस्तु वृषभः पश्चात्सुरेन्द्रादयो
दैत्यारिश्च विधिश्च पार्श्वदलयोर्वाय्वादिकोणेषु च ।
भृङ्गी नारदबाणभैरवगजास्यस्कन्दवीरेश्वरा
मध्ये शुभ्रसरोजकोमलरुचं शम्भुं भजे पाण्डुरम् ॥

(श्रीतत्वनिधौ)

संहारमूर्तयः ।

संहारमूर्तयः ।

कामान्तकः ।

अग्रे तु दक्षिणामूर्तेर्योगनिष्ठस्य मन्मथम् ।
कुर्यात्तु पतितं दृष्टिपातादेव च तत्क्षणात् ॥

भक्त्वा दशांशं देवोच्चमेकाद्यासप्तभागिकम् ।
मन्मथोत्सेधमुद्दिष्टं स तु हेमविभूषितः ॥

शुद्धजाम्बूनदप्रख्यः पुष्पपञ्चेषुसंयुतः ।
मीनकेतुस्तथैवेक्षुकार्मुकः क्र(र ?)तिसंयुतः ॥

देवभागवसन्ताख्यमित्रयुक्तोऽतिसुन्दरः ।
लम्भिनी तापिनी चैव वेदिनी द्राविणी तथा ॥

मारिणीति शराख्यास्स्युर्धनुर्वामे शराः परे ।
मन्मथो मित्रयुक्तो वा युतो वैकशरेण तु ॥

(उत्तरकामिकागमे सप्तपञ्चाशत्तमपटले ॥)

उग्ररूपं तु कामारिं पार्श्वे कामं प्रपातितम् ।
कार्यं कामरिपुं ह्येवं वक्ष्येऽहं कालनाशनम् ॥

(सुप्रभेदागमे चतुस्त्रिंशत्तमपटले ॥)

त्रिनेत्रं चतुर्भुजं देवं जटामकुटमण्डितम् ।
उग्रदृष्टिसमायुक्तमक्षमालोरगन्धरम् ॥

दक्षिणे तु पताका च वामहस्तं तु सूचिका ।
एतदेव विशेषं तु शेषं व्याख्यानमूर्तिवत् ॥

बेरायामरसांशाच्च त्रिभागं मन्मथायतम् ।
पीठस्थो वा रथस्थो वा कामः काञ्चनसन्निभः ॥

सर्वभूषणभूष्यं च दिव्यरूपसमन्वितम् ।
पुष्पैश्चैव शरैर्युक्तमिक्षुचापं च षड्ध्वजम् (?) ॥

मदरागवसन्तैश्च हेमबान्धवसंयुतम् ।
तापिनी दहनी विश्वमोहिनी विश्वमर्दनी ॥

मादिनी नाम निर्दिष्टास्तस्य पञ्चशरा इमे ।
कार्मुकं वामहस्ते तु बाणं तु सव्यहस्तके ॥

देवस्याभिमुखं कुर्यात्कामरूपं प्रपातितम् ।
कामनिग्रहमेवं स्याच्छृणु वैवाह्यमूर्तिनम् ।

(पूर्वकारणागमे एकादशपटले ॥)

गजासुरसंहारमूर्तिः ।

अथ वक्ष्ये विशेषेण गजहामूर्तिलक्षणम् ।
सर्वाभरणसंयुक्तं चतुर्दोश्चाष्ट एव वा ॥

चतुर्भुजं चेत् पाशं च गजचर्मं च दक्षिणे ।
गजश्रृङ्गं च चर्मं च वामपार्श्वे करद्वये ॥
चतुर्भुजं समाख्यातमष्टहस्तमथोच्यते ।
शूलं डमरुकं पाशं गजचर्मं च दक्षिणे ॥
गजश्रृङ्गं कपालं च गजचर्मं च विस्मयम् ।
एवं पार्श्वे तु चत्वारो हस्तमेवं प्रकल्पयेत् ॥
शम्भोर्वामाङ्घ्र्यधस्तात्तु गजस्यैव तु मस्तकम् ।
मकुटस्योपरिष्टात्तु गजपुच्छं प्रकल्पयेत् ॥
पार्श्वयोर्गजपादांस्तु यथायुक्त्या तु कल्पयेत् ।
प्रभामण्डलवच्छेषं गजचर्मं प्रकल्पयेत् ॥
व्याघ्रचर्माम्बरोपेतं दुकूलवसनान्वितम् ।
सर्वालङ्कारसंयुक्तमतिरक्तसमप्रभम् ॥
एवं तु गजहामूर्तिं प्रथमं तु विधीयते ।
शूलं खड्गं तथा चर्मं गजश्रृङ्गं च दक्षिणे ॥
कपालं खेटकं घण्टां गजचर्म च वामके ।
सुस्थितं वामपादं तु गजस्य मस्तकोपरि ॥
उद्धृतं दक्षिणं पादं तिर्य्यगुत्कुटिकं भवेत् ।
एवं द्विविधरील्या तु गजहामूर्तिरुच्यते ॥
स्कन्दोद्धृताप्युमादेवी शम्भोर्वामे भयान्विता ।

(अंशुमद्भेदागमे सप्ततितमपटले ॥)

गजहामूर्तिनं वक्ष्ये सर्वाभरणभूषितम् ।
पाशं च गजचर्म च दक्षपार्श्वकरद्वये ॥

गजस्य शृङ्गं चर्म च वामपार्श्वे करद्वये ।
शूलं डमरुकं पाशं गजचर्म च दक्षिणे ॥

गजशृङ्गं कपालं च पाशं चर्म च वामतः ।
शम्भोर्वामे ब्य(माङ्घ्य ?)धस्तात्तु गजमस्तकमेव हि ॥

मकुटस्योपरिष्टात्तु गजपुच्छं प्रकल्पयेत् ।
पार्श्वयोर्गळ(ज?)पादं तु यथा युक्त्या तु कारयेत् ॥

प्रभामण्डलवच्छेषं गजचर्म प्रकल्पयेत् ।
व्याघ्रचर्माम्बरोपेतं दुकूलवसनान्वितम् ॥

सर्वाभरणसंयुक्तमतिरक्तप्रभान्वितम् ।
सुस्थितं वामपादं तु गजवीरस्य मस्तके ॥

उद्धृतं दाक्षिणं पादं कक्षसूत्रान्तु(न्त?)माचरेत् ।
गौरी स्कन्दं समुद्धृत्य शम्भोर्वामे भयान्विता ॥

अथवा शूलखड्गौ च गजदन्तं च चर्म च ।
दक्षिणे वामतः कुर्यात् कपालं खेटकं पुनः ॥

घण्टां च गजचर्म च कैरिति...वामतः ।

(शिल्परत्ने द्वाविंशपटले ॥)

कालारिमूर्तिः

अथ वक्ष्ये विशेषेण कालहामूर्तिलक्षणम् ।
देवस्य दक्षिणं पादं पद्मपीठोपरिस्थितम् ॥

प्रथमनृत्तमूर्तेस्तु दक्षिणस्थितपादवत् ।
वामपादं तदुद्धृत्य कुञ्चितं तलमुद्धृतम् ॥

अङ्गुष्ठमुद्धृताङ्घ्रेस्तु कालस्य हृदये न्यसेत् ।
दंष्ट्रास्यं च त्रिनेत्रं च जटामकुटमण्डितम् ॥

चतुर्भुजसमायुक्तमष्टहस्तमथापि वा ।
दक्षिणे पूर्वहस्तं तु शूलं कर्णान्तमुद्धृतम् ॥

दक्षिणे परहस्तं तु परशुं वरदं तथा ।
वामे पूर्वकरं नाभिसीमान्तं सूच्यधोमुखम् ॥

वामे त्वपरहस्तं तु विस्मयं परिकल्पयेत् ।
हिक्कासूत्रसमं टङ्ककरं त्वभ्यन्तरं मुखम् ॥

उष्णीषान्तं समुद्धृत्य विस्मयेऽनामिकाग्रकम् ।
कर्णान्तं मणिबन्धान्तं शूलहस्तसमान्तकम् ॥

चतुर्दोर्ष्वेवमाख्यातमष्टहस्तमथ श्रृणु ।
शूलं परशु वज्रं च खड्गं दक्षिणहस्तके ॥

विस्मयं खेटकं पाशं सूचीहस्तं तु वामके ।
विद्रुमस्य निभाकारं सर्वाभरणभूषितम् ॥

कालहामूर्तिमाख्यातमधस्तात्काल उच्यते ।
द्विभुजं च द्विपादं च सदंष्ट्रं पाशपाणिनम् ॥

करण्डमकुटोपेतमसृग्धाराविकीर्णितम् ।
महाभयसमायुक्तं सपाशहृदयाञ्जलिम् ॥

विकीर्णपादं मां दृष्ट्वा शाययेदूर्ध्ववक्त्रकम् ।
कालहामूर्तिमेवं तु प्रोक्तं लिङ्गोद्भवं ततः ॥

(अंशुमद्भेदागमे षट्सप्ततितमपटले ॥)

कुञ्चितासव्यपादस्तु व्याघ्रचर्माम्बरान्वितः ।
ततोद्धृतसदक्षाङ्घ्रिस्तीक्ष्णदंष्ट्रोग्रनासिकः ॥

दक्षहस्तस्थशूलो वा वामहस्तस्थसूचिकः ।
दक्षहस्तस्थपरशुर्नागपाशोऽथवा मृगः ॥

कटाक्षदृष्टिर्देवस्य कालदेहव्यवस्थितः ।
शूलं ह्यधोमुखं प्रोक्तं कालकु(ग?)ण्डस्थमेव वा ॥

कालं तु पतितं कुर्य्याच्च(दु?)त्प्लुताक्षं तु मूर्छितम् ।
मुद्गरं र(उद्गिरद्र?)क्तवक्त्रं च तथा लोहितमूर्धजम् ॥

शूलपाशकरं चैव विकीर्णचरणान्वितम् ।
दंष्ट्राकरालवदनं रक्तभ्रूरक्तलोचनम् ॥

देवस्य(स्य?) नाभिमानेन नवतालेन कारयेत् ।
कृताञ्जलिपुटं वापि कारयेत्कालमादरात् ॥

अथवाथ हराल्लिङ्गान्निर्गतात्पतितं नयेत् ।
कालान्त(लं तं ?) लिङ्गमानाद्यं लिङ्गोद्भूतोक्तवन्नयेत् ॥

त्रिभङ्गेन स्थितश्चान्योऽधोमुखो भस्मविग्रहः ।
बद्धपुष्पाञ्जलिः पार्श्वे मार्कण्डेयः स्थितो वरः ॥

कर्तव्यः कालतो भू(भी ?)तस्सन्तुष्टो न हरेण तु ।
मार्कण्डेयेन मानेन युक्तो वा वर्जितस्तु वा ॥

अपस्मारशरीरस्थचरणेन युतो न वा ।
कालारिरेवमाख्यातो मन्मथान्तक उच्यते ॥

(उत्तरकामिकागमे सप्तपञ्चाशत्तमपटले ॥)

दक्षिणे तु करे शूलं वामे सूच्यङ्गुलि स्मृतम् ।
पादं कालस्य हृदये न्यस्त्वैवं(स्यैवं ?) पादसंस्थितम् ॥
कालनाशमिदं प्रोक्तं लिङ्गोत्पत्तिमतः परम् ।

(सुप्रभेदागमे चतुस्त्रिंशत्तमपटले ॥)

कालारिं कारयेदीशं नताङ्गं वामतो मनाक् ।
सुस्थितं दक्षिणं पादं पद्मपीठेऽन्यमङ्घ्रिकम् ॥

दक्षिणे पूर्वहस्ते तु शूलं कर्णान्तमुद्धृतम् ।
दक्षिणे परहस्ते तु परशु वरदं तु वा ॥

वामे पूर्वकरं नाभिसूत्रान्ते सूचिमाचरेत् ।
वामे तु परहस्ते तु विस्मयं परिकल्पयेत् ॥

उष्णीषान्तं समुद्धृत्य विस्मयेऽनामिकाग्रकम् ।
शूलं परशुवज्रौ च खड्गं दक्षिणहस्तके ॥

विस्मयं खेटकं पाशं सूचीहस्तं च वामके ।
शुद्धविद्रुमसङ्काशं सर्वाभरणसंयुतम् ॥

अधस्तात्कारयेत्कालं द्विभुजं पाशहस्तकम् ।
करण्डमकुटोपेतं सदंष्ट्रं विकृताननम् ॥

असृग्धारासमायुक्तं महाभयसमन्वितम् ।
हृदयाञ्जलिसंयुक्तं विकीर्णाङ्घ्रिद्वयं पुनः ॥

(शिल्परत्ने द्वाविंशपटले ॥)

चतुर्भुजं त्रिनेत्रं च जटामकुटसंयुतम् ।
उद्धृतं दक्षिणं पादं वामपादं तु कुञ्चितम् ॥

व्याघ्रचर्माम्बरोपेतं तीक्ष्णनासोग्रदंष्ट्रकम् ।
दक्षिणे तु करे शूलं सूचिहस्तं तु वामके ॥

परशुं दक्षिणे हस्ते नागपाशं तु वामके ।
अधोमुखं भवेच्छूलं दृष्टिर्वै कालदेहके ॥

अपरे तु द्विहस्तौ तु कटकाविति कीर्तितौ ।
दोस्समं कटकाग्रं तु द्व्यन्तरं तु यवं भवेत् ॥

(पूर्वकारणागमे एकादशपटले ॥)

त्रिपुरान्तकमूर्तिः । (१)

त्रिपुरान्तकमूर्तेस्तु लक्षणं वक्ष्यतेऽधुना ।
दक्षिणं सुस्थितं पादं वामपादं तु कुञ्चितम् ॥

दक्षिणे पूर्वहस्तोर्ध्वे नाभिसूत्रावसानकम् ।
सिंहकर्णं तु तद्धस्तं बाणमध्यं तु पीडितम् ॥

बाणायामं तु तत्सप्तत्यङ्गुलं तु विधीयते ।
कनिष्ठिकापरीणाहं देवेशस्य करस्य तु ॥

वामहस्ते धनुर्धृत्वा कक्षान्तं तत्करोर्ध्वकम् ।
पूर्णमुष्टिस्तु नाहं स्यान्मध्यादग्रौ क्रमात्कृशौ ॥

अग्रमर्धाङ्गुलव्यासं वृत्तं वर्णैर्विचित्रितम् ।
बाणनाहत्रिभागैकं रज्जुनाहं तु तन्तुना ॥

धनोर्दीर्घाष्टभागे तु सप्तांशं रज्जुदीर्घकम् ।
तद्दीर्घस्यानुकूलं तु धनोर्वक्रमुदाहृतम् ॥

त्रिवक्रसहितं वाथ बालचन्द्राभमेव वा ।
धनुराकृतिरेवं स्यात् दारुजं लोहजं तु वा ॥

कर्तरी परहस्तौ तु टङ्ककृष्णमृगान्वितौ ।
गङ्गं(टङ्कं ?) दक्षिणहस्ते तु वामहस्ते मृगं धृतम् ॥

जटामकुटसंयुक्तं सर्वाभरणभूषितम् ।
प्रवालसदृशप्रख्यं वामे गौरीसमायुतम् ॥

त्रिपुरान्तकमूर्तेस्तु प्रथमं लक्षणं त्विदम् ।

(अंशुमद्भेदागमे सप्तषष्टितमपटले ॥)

पुरारिस्थापनं वक्ष्ये तदादौ लक्षणं च वै ।
चतुर्भुजास्त्रिनेत्रश्च जटामकुटसंयुतः ॥
समभाग(भङ्ग ?)युतस्सम्यक् स्थापकेन समन्वितः ।
सव्यकर्णस्थमकरकुण्डलेन समन्वितः ॥
कृष्णापरशुसंयुक्तपरहस्तद्वयान्वितः ।
धनुर्बाणयुतोपेतवामेतरकरान्वितः ॥
परहस्तोज्झितो वाथ द्विहस्तस्त्रिपुरान्तकः ।
कुर्यात्सलक्षणं वाथ वामभागे तु पार्वतीम् ॥
एवं कृत्वा पुरारिं तु प्रतिष्ठां कारयेत्ततः ।

(उत्तरकामिकागमे एकोनपञ्चाशत्तमपटले ॥)

धनुर्बाणसमायुक्तं कृष्णा परशुधारिणम् ।
उमया सहितं देवं कृत्वा तत्त्रिपुरान्तकम् ॥

(सुप्रभेदागमे चतुस्त्रिंशत्तमपटले ॥)

अथाष्टधा प्रवक्ष्यामि त्रिपुरान्तकमूर्तिनम् ।
दक्षिणं सुस्थितं पादं वामपादं तु कुञ्चितम् ॥
दक्षिणे पूर्वहस्तं तु नाभिसूत्रावसानके ।
सिंहकर्णं तु तद्धस्तं बाणमध्यनिपीडितम् ॥

वामहस्ते धनुर्धृत्वा कक्षान्तोर्ध्वं समुद्धृते ।
कर्तरी परहस्तौ द्वौ टङ्ककृष्णमृगास्थितौ(गान्वितौ ?)

टङ्कं तु दक्षिणे वामे कृष्णसारङ्गमेव हि ।
जटामकुटसंयुक्तं सर्वाभरणभूषितम् ॥
प्रवालसदृशप्रख्यं वामे गौरीसमायुतम् ।
इदं प्रथममाख्यातं द्वितीयं तु ततः परम् ॥

(शिल्परत्ने द्वाविंशपटले ॥)

चतुर्भुजं त्रिनेत्रं च जटामकुटसंयुतम् ।
सर्वाभरणसंयुक्तं दिव्याम्बरसमायुतम् ॥
पत्रं तु वामकर्णे तु दक्षिणे कुण्डलान्वितम् ।
धनुर्बाणसमायुक्तं कृष्णापरशुसंयुतम् ॥
उपवीतसमायुक्तं सभङ्गस्थानकं कुरु ।
वृषवाहनवच्छेषं कारयेत्तु विचक्षणः

(पूर्वकारणागमे एकादशपटले ॥)

त्रिपुरान्तकमूर्तिः । (२)

तदेव वामपादं तु अपस्मारोपरिस्थितम् ।
शेषं प्रागिव कर्तव्यं द्वितीयं लक्षणं भवेत् ॥

(अंशुमद्भेदागमे सप्तषष्टितमपटले ॥)

तदेव वामपादं तदपस्मारोपरिस्थितम् ।
शेषं प्रथमतुल्यं हि तृतीयमथ वक्ष्यते ॥

(शिल्परत्ने द्वाविंशपटले ॥)

त्रिपुरान्तकमूर्तिः । (३)

सुस्थितं वामपादं तु दक्षिणं कुञ्चितं भवेत् ।
शेषं प्रागिव कर्तव्यं सूत्रं त्वितरपार्श्वगम् ॥

तृतीयं लक्षणं प्रोक्तं चतुर्थं लक्षणं शृणु ।

(अंशुमद्भेदागमे सप्तषष्टितमपटले ॥)

सुस्थितं वामपादं तु दक्षिणं कुञ्चितं भवेत् ।
शेषं प्रागिव कर्तव्यं चतुर्थं तु ततः परम् ॥

(शिल्परत्ने द्वाविंशपटले ॥)

त्रिपुरान्तकमूर्तिः । (४)

तदेव वामपादं तु अपस्मारोपरिस्थितम् ।
प्रागिवैव विशेषं तु चतुर्थं लक्षणं भवेत् ॥

(अंशुमद्भेदागमे सप्तषष्टितमपटले ॥)

तदेव वामपादं तदपस्मारोपरिस्थितम् ।

(शिल्परत्ने द्वाविंशपटले ॥)

त्रिपुरान्तकमूर्तिः । (५)

तदेव पूर्वहस्तौ द्वौ कटकौ हृदि सीमगौ ।
वामदक्षिणहस्तौ द्वौ क्रमादूर्ध्वमधोमुखम् ॥
बाणमूलधृतं सव्यं वामं बाणाग्रकं धृतम् ।
परे तु दक्षिणे टङ्कं धनुस्तद्वामहस्तके ॥
तद्धस्ते तु मृगं वाथ वामे गौरीसमायुतम् ।
अपस्मारं विना पादं नतं प्रागिव सूत्रकम् ॥
एवं चतुर्भुजोपेतं मूर्तिं पञ्चविधं भवेत् ।

(अंशुमद्भेदागमे सप्तषष्टितमपटले ॥)

तदेव पूर्वहस्तौ द्वौ कटकौ हृदि सीमगौ ।
वामं दक्षिणकं हस्तं क्रमादूर्ध्वमधोमुखम् ॥
बाणमूलधृतं सव्यं अन्यबाननोद्धृतम् (?) ।
परे दक्षिणके टङ्कं धनुषं वामहस्तके ॥
तद्धस्ते तु मृगं वाथ वामे गौरीसमायुतम् ।
अपस्मारं विना कार्यं पञ्चमं समुदाहृतम् ॥

(शिल्परत्ने द्वाविंशपटले॥)

त्रिपुरान्तकमूर्तिः । (६)

अतिभङ्गनतोपेतमष्टहस्तसमन्वितम् ।
बाणं च परशुं खड्गं वज्रं वै दक्षिणे करे ॥

धनुषं विस्मयं हस्तं खेटकं कटकं तु वा ।
वामहस्ते समाख्यातं पूर्वसूत्रात्करान्तकम् ॥
यथाशोभनतं तुङ्गं कल्पयेद् गौरिसंयुतम् ।

(अंशुमद्भेदागमे सप्तषष्टपटले ॥)

षष्ठमिष्टं च बाणं च पाशं खड्गं च दक्षिणे ।
धनुषं विस्मयं खेटं कुक्कुटं(कटकं ?) वामहस्तके ॥
यथाशोभं तथा कुर्याद्वामे गौरीसमायुतम् ।

(शिल्परत्ने द्वाविंशपटले ॥)

त्रिपुरान्तकमूर्तिः । (७)

षष्ठमं ह्येवमाख्यातं सप्तमं दशदोर्युतम् ।
बाणं चक्रं तथा शूलं टङ्कं वज्रं च दक्षिणे ॥
धनुश्शङ्खं तथा सूची विस्मयं खेटकं तथा ।

(अंशुमद्भेदागमे सप्तषष्टितमपटले ॥)

सप्तमे दक्षिणे बाणं चक्रं शूलं ततः परम् ।
टङ्कं वज्रं तथा वामे धनुषं सूचिविस्मये ॥
खेटान्द्र............सर्वं पूर्ववदाचरेत् ।

(शिल्परत्ने द्वाविंशपटले ॥)

त्रिपुरान्तकमूर्तिः । (८)

तदेव दक्षिणं जानु ततो(लो?)परि निधापयेत् ।
तत्पूर्वे वामपादं तु तलं न्यस्त्वा रथोपरि ॥
रथं तु मुकुळोपेतं मुकुळं रज्जुना वृतम् ।
मुकुळाभ्यन्तरे ब्रह्मा चतुर्वक्त्रश्चतुर्भुजः ॥
तस्य दक्षिणहस्तौ द्वौ वेणुदण्डं कमण्डलुम् ।
कुण्डिका पद्मपाशं च वामहस्तद्वयोद्धृतम् ॥
रथस्य मुकुळाधस्ताद्वृषभं श्वेतवर्णकम् ।
रथं पवनमार्गेण कल्पयेत्कल्पवित्तमः ॥
त्रिपुरान्तकमाख्यातमष्टभेदं द्विजोत्तम! ।
प्रवालसदृशं वर्णं सत्वराजसमिश्रितम् ॥
सर्वाभरणसंयुक्तमेकवक्त्रं त्रिनेत्रकम् ।
तस्य वामेऽप्युमादेवीं प्रागुक्तविधिना कुरु ॥
सामान्यलक्षणं वर्ण्यं त्रिपुरान्तकमूर्तिनः ।

(अंशुमद्भेदागमे सप्तषष्टपटले ॥)

एवमेवाष्टमं कुर्याद्वसुधोपरि विन्यसेत् ।
दक्षिणाङ्घ्रिस्तथा जानु वामपादतलं पुनः ॥
पुरस्स्थितरथस्योर्ध्वे विन्यसेत्तु यथोचितम् ।
रथं तु मुकुलोपेतं मुकुलं कज्ज(रज्जु?)नावृतम् ॥

मुकुलाभ्यन्तरे ब्रह्मा चतुर्वक्त्रश्चतुर्भुजः ।
तस्य दक्षिणहस्तौ द्वौ वेणुदण्डं कमण्डलुम् ॥
कुण्डिकां पद्मपाशं च वामहस्तद्वयोद्धृतम् ।
रथस्य मुकुलाधस्ताद्वृषभं श्वेतवर्णकम् ॥

(शिल्परत्ने द्वाविंशपटले ॥)

शरभेशः ।

शरभेशप्रतिष्ठां तु वक्ष्ये लक्षणपूर्विकाम् ।
पक्ष्याकारं सुवर्णाभं पक्षद्वयसमन्वितम् ॥
ऊर्ध्वपक्षसमायुक्तं रक्तनेत्रद्वयान्वितम् ।
पादैस्सिंहपदाकारैश्चतुर्भिश्च समन्वितम् ॥
सुतीक्ष्णनखसंयुक्तैरूर्ध्वस्थैर्वेदपादकैः ।
दिव्यलाङ्गूलसंयुक्तं सुविकीर्णजटान्विम् ॥
कन्धरोर्ध्वनराकारं दिव्यमौलिसमायुतम् ।
सिंहास्यं भीमदंष्ट्रं च भीमविक्रमसंयुतम् ॥
हरन्तं नरसिंहं तु जगत्संहरणोद्धृतम् ।
कृताञ्जलिपुटोपेतं निश्चेष्टितमहातनुम् ॥
नरदेहं तदूर्ध्वास्यं विष्णुं पद्मदलेक्षणम् ।
पादाभ्यामम्बरस्थाभ्यां कुक्षिस्थाभ्यां च तस्य तु ॥
गगनाभिमुखं देवं कारयेच्छरभेश्वरम् ।

(उत्तरकामिकागमे चतुःपञ्चाशत्तमपटले ॥)

शरभमूर्तिः ।

महामेरुसमाकारमष्टपादं रविप्रभम् ।
द्वात्रिंशद्बाहुसंयुक्तं सूर्यसोमाग्निलोचनम् ॥
दुर्गाकालद्विपक्षं च सुतीक्ष्णघनगर्जितम् ।
ऊर्ध्वकेशं महाबाहुं नानालङ्कारभूषितम् ॥
वज्रमुष्ट्यभयं चक्रं शार्क्तिं दण्डाङ्कुशौ तथा ।
खड्गखट्वाङ्गपरशूनक्षमालास्थिशूलकम् ॥
धनुश्च मुसलं चाग्निं दधानं दक्षिणैः करैः ।
वरदं पाशहस्तं च गदां बाणध्वजौ तथा ॥
क्रकचं क्रोडशङ्खौ च खेटं नागं च पङ्कजम् ।
कपालं पुस्तकं कुन्तं दुर्गाश्लिष्टकराम्बुजम् ॥
हलं वामे दधानं च भीषणं करपङ्कजैः ।
दंष्ट्रोल्लासं महासिंहजटाच्छटनिपीडितम् ॥

(श्रीतत्वनिधौ ॥)

ब्रह्मशिरश्छेत्तृमूर्तिः ।

गौरवर्णं त्रिनेत्रं च जटामौलिविराजितम् ।
ताटङ्कं कुण्डलं सव्यवामश्रुत्योश्च बिभ्रतम् ॥
व्याघ्रचर्माम्बरधरं चतुर्भुजसमन्वितम् ।
वज्रं परशुपूर्वांसं वामे ब्रह्मकरोटिकम् ॥

अपरे शूलहस्तं च शेषं पूर्वोक्तवत्कुरु ।

(श्रीतत्वनिधौ ॥)

भैरवः ।

अथातो रूपनिर्माणं वक्ष्येऽहं भैरवस्य तु ।
लम्बोदरं तु कर्तव्यं वृत्तपिङ्गललोचनम् ॥

दंष्ट्राकरालवदनं फुल्लनासापुटं तथा ।
कपालम(मा ?)लिनं रौद्रं सर्वतस्सर्पभूषणम् ॥

व्यालेन त्रासयन्तं च देवीं पर्वतनन्दिनीम् ।
सजलाम्बुदसङ्काशं गजचर्मोत्तरच्छदम् ॥

बहुभिर्बाहुभिर्व्याप्तं सर्वायुधविभूषणम् ।
बृहत्सालप्रतीकाशैस्तथा तीक्ष्णनखैश्शुभैः ॥

साचीकृतमिदं रूपं भैरवस्य प्रकीर्तितम् ।

(विष्णुधर्मोत्तरे ॥)

वटुकभैरवः ।

खट्वाङ्गमांसपाशं च शूलं च दधतं करैः ।
डमरुं च कपालं च वरदं भुजगं तथा ॥

आत्मवर्णसमोपेतसारमेयसमन्वितम् ।
ध्यात्वा जपेत्सुसंहृष्टः सर्वान्कामानवाप्नुयात् ॥

(रूपमण्डने ॥)

प्रतिमालक्षणानि ।

विकीर्णलोहितजटं त्रिनेत्रं रक्तविग्रहम् ।
शूलं कपालं पाशं च डमरुं दधतं करैः ॥
नानारूपैः पिशाचैश्च नानारूपगणैर्वृतम् ।
श्वानारूढं च निर्वाणं वटुकं भैरवं भजे ॥
(वटुकभैरवकल्पे ॥)

स्वर्णाकर्षणभैरवः ।

पीतवर्णं चतुर्बाहुं त्रिनेत्रं पीतवाससम् ।
अक्षय्यस्वर्णमाणिक्यगणपूरितपात्रकम् ॥
अंसाहितमहाशूलचामरं तोमरोद्वहम् ।
सन्ततं चिन्तयेद्भक्त्या भैरवं सर्वसिद्धिदम् ॥
नानाभरणशोभाढ्यमानन्दसुखरूपिणम् ।
मदोन्मत्तं सदानन्दं सर्वदेवनमस्कृतम् ॥
एवं ध्यायेच्च मन्त्रज्ञः स्वर्णाकर्षणभैरवम् ।
(श्रीतत्वनिधौ ॥)

अष्टाष्टभैरवाः ।

इतः परं प्रवक्ष्यामि श्रृणु राजन्नशेषतः ।
अष्टाष्टकमिदं पुण्यं भैरवाणामभीष्टदम् ॥
पूर्ववद्वर्णतो ध्याने ध्येयं सर्वैः पृथक्पृथक् ।

प्रतिमालक्षणानि ।

प्रथमाष्टकम् ।

आद्याष्टकं सुवर्णाभं त्रिशूलं डमरुं तथा ॥
पाशं चासिं दधानं च ध्यायेत्सर्वाङ्गसुन्दरम् ।

द्वितीयाष्टकम् ।

अथ द्वितीयकं ध्यायेदक्षमालामथाङ्कुशम् ।
दधानं पुस्तकं वीणां सुखेतमणिभूषणम् ॥

तृतीयाष्टकम् ।

ज्वालां शक्तिं गदां कुन्तं दधानं नीलवर्णकम् ।
ध्यायेत्तृतीयं शुभदमष्टकं शुभलक्षणम् ॥

चतुर्थाष्टकम् ।

खड्गं खेटं पट्टसं च दधानं परशुं तथा ।
धूम्रवर्णमभिप्रेतं ध्यायेदष्टकमादरात् ॥

पञ्चमाष्टकम् ।

कुन्तं खेटं च परिघं भिण्डिपालं तथैव च ।
पञ्चमाष्टकमेतद्धि श्वेतं स्यात्सुमनोहरम् ॥

षष्ठसप्तमाष्टमाष्टकानि ।

पीतष्षष्ठमृषीरक्तमष्टमं च तटित्प्रभम् ।
पञ्चमाष्टकमेतद्धि श्वेतं स्यात्सुमनोहरम् ॥
कुन्तादिकं समं प्रोक्तं षडारभ्याष्टमान्तकम् ।

अष्टाष्टभैरवनामानि ।

असिताङ्गो विशालाक्षो मार्ताण्डो मोदकप्रियः ।
स्वच्छन्दो विघ्नसंतुष्टः खेचरः सचराचरः ॥

रुरुश्च क्रोडदंष्ट्रश्च तथैव च जटाधरः ।
विश्वरूपो विरूपाक्षो नानारूपधरः परः ॥

वज्रहस्तो महाकायश्चण्डश्च प्रलयान्तकः ।
भूमिकम्पो नीलकण्ठो विष्णुश्च कुलपालकः ॥

मुण्डपालः कामपालः क्रोधो वै पिङ्गलेक्षणः ।
अभ्ररूपो धरापालः कुटिलो मन्त्रनायकः ॥

रुद्रः पितामहाख्यश्चाप्युन्मत्तो वटुनायकः ।
शङ्करो भूतवेतालत्रिणेत्रस्त्रिपुरान्तकः ॥

वरदः पर्वतावासः कपालः शशिभूषणः ।
हस्तिचर्माम्बरधरो योगीशो ब्रह्मराक्षसः ॥

सर्वज्ञः सर्वदेवेशः सर्वभूतहृदिस्थितः ।
भीषणाख्यो भयहरः सर्वज्ञाख्यस्तथैव च ॥

कालाग्निश्च महारौद्रो दक्षिणो मुखरोऽस्थिरः ।
संहारश्चातिरिक्ताङ्गः कालाग्निश्च प्रियङ्करः ॥

घोरनादो विशालाक्षो योगीशो दक्षसंस्थितः ।

(श्रीतत्वनिधौ)

वीरभद्रमूर्तिः ।

चतुर्भुजं त्रिणेत्रं च जटामकुटसंयुतम् ।
दक्षिणे खड्गबाणौ च वामे चापं गदां धरम् ॥
दंष्ट्राकरालवदनं भीमं भैरवगर्जितम् ।
रुण्डमालासमायुक्तं पादुकोपरिसुस्थितम् ॥
भद्रकालीसमायुक्तं करालं हृदि विन्यसेत् ।

दक्षब्रह्मस्वरूपम् ।

वीरस्य दक्षभागे तु दक्षब्रह्माणमास्थितम् ।
अजवक्त्रं द्विनयनं शृङ्गद्वयविभूषितम् ॥
नमस्काराञ्जलिं विप्रं शिवध्यानपरायणम् ।
(श्रीतत्वनिधौ ॥)

अथ वक्ष्ये विशेषेण वीरभद्रेश्वरं शृणु ।
महापातकदोषघ्नं सर्वपीडानिवारणम् ॥
वीरभद्रमिति ख्यातं दक्षयज्ञहरं परम् ।
चतुर्भुजं त्रिणेत्रं च ज्वालाकेशं सुदंष्ट्रिणम् ॥
घण्टामालाधरं घोरं शिरोमालाविभूषितम् ।
वृश्चिकाभरणं चैव नागयज्ञोपवीतिनम् ॥
नूपुरं विमलं तद्वत्पादौ पादुकभूषितौ ।
नीलकण्ठं च त्र्यक्षं च ऊरुकञ्चुकसंयुतम् ॥

खड्गखेटधनुर्बाणं कपालं भिण्डिपालकम् ।

रक्तवर्णसमायुक्तमुग्रदृष्टिभयङ्करम् ॥

एवं ध्यात्वा विशेषेण प्रतिष्ठां कारयेत्ततः ।

(उत्तरकारणागमे ॥)

जलन्धरहरमूर्तिः ।

रक्ताभमुग्रनयनं द्विभुजं च त्रिनेत्रकम् ।

उपवीतसमायुक्तं सर्वालङ्कारशोभितम् ॥

पादयोः पादुकायुक्तं किञ्चिद्वै गमनोन्मुखम् ।

दक्षहस्ते स्थितं छत्रं वामे पूर्णकमण्डलुम् ॥

सुविकीर्णजटाभारं गङ्गाचन्द्रसमन्वितम् ।

कर्णकुण्डलसंयुक्तं हारनूपुरसंयुतम् ॥

द्विभुजं च त्रिनेत्रं च किरीटकटकान्वितम् ।

सर्वालङ्कारसंयुक्तं कक्षे खड्गसमन्वितम् ॥

कृताञ्जलिपुटोपेतहस्ते चक्रं दधं परम् ।

जलन्धरमथ प्रोक्तम् ॥

(श्रीतत्वनिधौ ॥)

मल्लारिशिवः ।

मकुटमणिमयूखप्रोज्झिताशेषरत्नं

विमलशशिकलाङ्कं सुन्दरेन्दीवराक्षम् ।

अनुकृतशशितेजःकुण्डलं चारुहासं
प्रकटदशनशोभानिर्जितानेकहीरम् ॥
अभिनवमणिमुक्ताहारचाम्पेयमाला-
विविधकुसुमगुच्छैः शोभिवक्षस्स्थलाढ्यम् ।
सफणपवनभुग्दोर्दण्डभूषाभिरामं
करडमरुनिनादैः पूरितद्योखगर्भम् ॥
त्रिभुवनभवनेशं पीतकौशेयवासं
दनुजदहनदक्षं प्रस्फुरत्खड्गहस्तम् ।
भुजगफणसुगुप्तैर्भूषणैर्न्यस्तभूषं
प्रणतसुरकिरीटव्याप्तपादारविन्दम् ॥
सितहयवरपत्रं हारसंभूषिताङ्गं
परिवृतमतिघोरैः सप्तभिस्सारमेयैः ।
कनकगिरिसमाभं नैशचूर्णाभिरामं
सकलनिगमगुह्यं नौमि मल्लारिदेवम् ॥

(मल्लारिमाहात्म्ये ॥)

अष्टभुजाघोरमूर्तिः ।

अथ वक्ष्ये विशेषेण सर्वलोकैकपावनम् ।
सर्वयुद्धजयं चैव ब्रह्महत्यादिनाशनम् ॥

महापातकदोषघ्नं गुरुद्रोहनिवारणम् ।
शिवद्रव्यापहारं च उपपातकनाशनम् ॥
सर्वैश्वर्याभिवृद्ध्यर्थं परमोक्षनिरासनम् ।
अघोरास्त्रेश्वरं भीमं स्थापनं वक्ष्यते शृणु ॥
त्रिनेत्राष्टभुजं भीममुग्रदंष्ट्राकरालकम् ।
कालमेघसमं घोरं रक्तवस्त्रसमन्वितम् ॥
ज्वालाकेशसमायुक्तं कृशानुनयनैर्युतम् ।
अर्धचन्द्राकृतिं भस्म ललाटोपरिशोभितम् ॥
भुजाभ्यां त्रिशिखा तिर्यक् वेतालं खड्गमेव च ।
डमरुं च कपालं च खेटकं खड्गमेव च ॥
रक्तवस्त्राम्बरोपेतं रक्तपुष्पसमन्वितम् ।
रक्ताभरणसंयुक्तं खड्गमालाविभूषितम् ॥
शिरोमालाविभूष्यं च नागयज्ञोपवीतिनम् ।
वृश्चिकाभरणं कण्ठे कालाग्निसदृशप्रभम् ॥
एवं ध्यात्वा महाघोरं द्वात्रिंशल्लक्षणान्वितम् ।
पद्मपीठोपरिस्थं च समीपे वृषभं तथा ॥
एवं संकल्प्य विधिवत् प्रतिष्ठां कारयेत्ततः ।

(उत्तरकारणागमे ॥)

द्वात्रिंशद्भुजाघोरमूर्तिः ।

एकवक्त्रं सदानन्दं द्वात्रिंशद्भुजसंयुतम् ।
जटामकुटसंयुक्तं त्रिनेत्रं चन्द्रशेखरम् ॥

अभयं खड्गशूलं च चक्रं डमरुकं तथा ।
दधानमस्थिबाणौ च गदां पद्मं कपालकम् ॥

ज्ञानमुद्रां कुन्तहस्तमङ्कुशं चाक्षमालिकाम् ।
खट्वाङ्गं परशुं चैव दधानं दक्षिणैः करैः ॥

वरं च फलकं चैव टङ्कं पाशं च मुद्गरम् ।
नागमग्निं मृगं घण्टां धनुश्च कटिहस्तकम् ॥

रत्नं च कुमुदं कुम्भं मुसलं पुस्तकं तथा ।
एतदायुधसंयुक्तं रुण्डमालाविभूषितम् ॥

कालमुण्डस्य शिरसि स्थितं सर्वाभयप्रदम् ।

(शिवतत्वरत्नाकरे ॥)

दशभुजाघोरमूर्तिः ।

परशुं डमरुं खड्गखेटौ बाणशरासने ।
शूलं कपालमभयवरौ दधतमिष्टदम् ॥

त्रिलोचनं भीषणास्यं नीलाङ्गं रक्तवाससम् ।
अहिभूषि[त*]सर्वाङ्गं तमघोरमुपास्महे ॥

(पाञ्चरात्रे ॥)

प्रतिमालक्षणानि ।

महाकालो घनश्यामः काल्यालिङ्गितविग्रहः ।
श्यामकञ्चुकधारी च मदारुणविलोचनः ॥
ब्रह्माण्डचषके पूर्णं पिबन्विश्वरसासवम् ।
महाकालीं घनश्यामामनङ्गार्द्रामपाङ्गयन् ॥
सिंहासने समासीनः कल्याणकलनात्मके ।
कालमृत्युमुखैर्युक्तस्सर्वलोकैकभक्षकः ॥
ललिताध्यानसंपन्नो ललितापूजनोत्सुकः ।
वितन्वन्ललिताभक्तेष्वायुषो दीर्घदीर्घताम् ॥

(ललितोपाख्याने ॥)

अनुग्रहमूर्तयः

अनुग्रहमूर्तयः ।

चण्डेशानुग्रहमूर्तिः ।

अथ वक्ष्ये विशेषेण चण्डेशानुग्रहं परम् ।
उमासहितवत्सर्वं वामे किंचिन्नताननम् ॥

दक्षिणे त्वभयं वर्ज्य तद्धस्तं वरदं भवेत् ।
वामे तु कटकं वर्ज्य तं न्यस्त्वा चण्डमूर्धनि ॥

हृदयेऽञ्जलिसंयुक्तश्चण्डेशो भक्तिसंयुतः ।
आसीनः पद्मपीठे तु चण्डेशस्स्वर्णसन्निभः ॥

देवीदेवेशयोर्मध्ये स्कन्दमूर्तिं विना बुधाः ! ।
चण्डेशानुग्रहं ख्यातं दक्षिणामूर्तिरुच्यते ॥

(अंशुमद्भेदागमे पञ्चसप्ततितमपटले ॥)

उमया सहितस्याथ चन्द्रशेखरमूर्तिनः ।
वामे वा दक्षिणे वापि कारयेद्देशिकोत्तमः ॥

एवं(देवं ?) जानूरुनाभ्यन्तस्तनवक्षोगलास्यगम् ।
सुखासीनं स्थितं वापि कृताञ्जलिपुटान्वितम् ॥

देवेक्षणसमोपेतं मद्भक्तं चण्डनायकम् ।
सर्वाङ्गसुन्दरं कुर्य्यात्कनिष्ठदशतालतः ॥

मालाग्रं देववरदे कटकेनेतरेण तु ।
देवशिरसि चण्डस्य मालया परिवेष्टयेत् ॥

(उत्तरकामिकागमे पञ्चपञ्चाशत्तमपटले ॥)

चण्डेशानुग्रहं देवमुमास्कन्दवदाचरेत् ।
वाम(मे ?) किंचिन्नतं चास्यं दक्षिणे त्वभयं विना ॥

तद्धस्ते वरदं कार्यं वामे तु कुटं(कटकं ?) विना ।
चण्डेशमूर्ध्नि विन्यस्य तद्धस्तं करुणान्वितम् ॥

हृदयेऽञ्जलिसंयुक्तश्चण्डेशो भक्तिसंयुतः ।
आसनाधस्त्वु(?)पासीनो भक्तिमान् स्वर्णसन्निभः ॥

(शिल्परत्ने द्वाविंशपटले ॥)

उमासहितवत्सर्वं स्कन्देनैव विना कुरु ।
किंचिदस्मिन् विशेषोऽस्ति तं विशेषं शृणु द्विजाः ! ॥

कटकं दक्षिणे हस्तं वरदं वामहस्तके ।
देवस्य पुरभागं तु चण्डेशं तु प्रकल्पयेत् ॥

देवस्य बाहुमात्रेण चण्डेशायाममुच्यते ।
कृताञ्जलिपुटोपेतं चासीनं प्रतिवक्त्रकम् ॥

देवाशिरसि चण्डस्य मालया परिभूषयन् ।

चण्डेशानुग्रहं प्रोक्तं मुखलिङ्गं पुरोक्तवत् ॥

(पूर्वकारणागमे एकादशपटले ॥)

विष्ण्वनुग्रहः ॥

नन्दीशानुग्रहस्त्वेवं तद्वद्विष्णुप्रसादकृत् ।

हित्वा नन्दीश्वरं तस्मिन्विष्णुं तल्लक्षणान्वितम् ॥

सचक्राञ्जलिहस्तं च शङ्खाब्जापरहस्तकम् ।

कारयेद्देव एष स्याच्चक्रदो विष्णुमूर्तिनः ॥

कारयेदेवमेवान्यप्रसादाभिमुखं शिवम् ।

(उत्तरकामिकागमे पञ्चपञ्चाशत्तमपटले ॥)

विष्णुस्त्वीशपुरःस्थितोऽञ्जलिकरो देवस्य पादाब्जयो-

स्संस्थाप्याक्षिलसत्सुमाल्यमनिशं पीताम्बरं कौस्तुभम् ।

यस्तस्मै दयया परं पशुपतिं पद्माक्ष इत्याख्यया

टङ्कं कृष्णमृगं वरं च दधतं चक्रप्रदं तं भजे ॥

एकवक्त्रं त्रिनेत्रं च जटामकुटसंयुतम् ।

दधमेणं च परशुं वरं च चैव वामके ॥

दक्षिणे चक्रसंयुक्तं दातृरूपमिहोच्यते ।
देवस्य वामभागे तु श्यामरूपं सुसंस्थितम् ॥
सर्वाभरणसंयुक्तं पीतवस्त्रोत्तरीयकम् ।
शङ्खचक्रसमायुक्तमुत्तरे चाञ्जलिं न्यसेत् ॥
एवं लक्षणसंयुक्तं विष्णुरूपमिहोच्यते ।

(श्रीतत्वनिधौ ॥)

अथातस्संप्रवक्ष्यामि सर्वभूतहिताय च ।
चक्रदानस्वरूपं तु शृणु (ष्व) शरवणोद्भव ! ॥
त्रिनेत्रं चतुर्भुजं शान्तं जटामकुटमण्डितम् ।
वामपादं तु शयनं लम्बितं सव्यपादकम् ॥
टङ्कं रथाङ्गं सव्ये च वर(दं) कृष्णमृगं तथा ।
वामे विष्णुसमायुक्तं कृताञ्जलिपुटान्वितम् ॥
वामे गौरीसमायुक्तमुत्तरे परमेष्ठिनम् ।
सर्वावयवसंयुक्तं सर्वलक्षणसंयुतम् ॥
पद्मपुष्पं समभ्यर्च्य हरिणा नेत्रपूजितम् ।
प्रभामण्डलमध्यस्थं शिरश्चक्रसमायुतम् ॥
एवं कल्प्य विशेषेण प्रतिष्ठां शृणु षण्मुख ! ।

(उत्तरकारणागमे ॥)

नन्दीशानुग्रहः ।

नन्दीश्वरप्रसादे तु विशेषः कश्चिदिष्यते ।
द्विनेत्रं द्विभुजं शान्तं कृताञ्जलिपुटान्वितम् ॥

सुविकीर्णजटोपेतं जटामकुटकान्वितम् ।
आभङ्गसहितं कुर्य्यादागमश्रवणोन्मुखम् ॥

नन्दीश्वरप्रसन्नं तु कारयेत्पूर्वमानतः ।

(उत्तरकामिकागमे पञ्चपञ्चाशत्तमपटले ॥)

विघ्नेश्वरवरप्रसन्नमूर्तिः ।

चतुर्भुजं त्रिनेत्रं च जटामकुटसंयुतम् ।
अभयं शिरसि न्यस्य वरदं वामहस्तके ॥

कृष्णापरशुसंयुक्तं विघ्नेशो दक्षिणे स्थितः ।
शयानं दक्षिणं पादं दधं वामं तु लम्बितम् ॥

सर्वाभरणसंयुक्तं श्यामवर्णं सुशोभितम् ।
देवस्य वामपार्श्वे तु देवीं प्रहसिताननाम् ॥

सर्वालङ्कारसंयुक्तां सव्ये तूत्पलधारिणीम् ।
वामे वरदसंयुक्तां द्विभुजां च त्रिनेत्रकाम् ॥

दक्षिणे शयितं पादं दधं वामे तु लम्बितम् ।
एकपीठस्थितां देवीमुमास्कन्दोक्तवत्कुरु ॥

विघ्नेशं रक्तवर्णं च किरीटमकुटान्वितम् ।
नमस्काराञ्जलिकरं पाशाङ्कुशसमन्वितम् ॥
सर्वलक्षणसंयुक्तं सर्वाभीष्टफलप्रदम् ।
विघ्नप्रसादमित्युक्तं............... ॥

(श्रीतत्वनिधौ ॥)

अथातस्संप्रवक्ष्यामि विघ्नेशानुग्रहं परम् ।
सर्वभूतहितं पुण्यं सर्वाभीष्टप्रदायकम् ॥
सर्वविघ्नविनाशार्थं कारयेद्देशिकोत्तमः ।
त्रिनेत्रं चतुर्भुजं शान्तं कुण्डलाभरणोज्वलम् ॥
बकपुष्पसुकेशं च स्तबकं चूलिकाकृतिम् ।
बकपत्रसमायुक्तं बकपुष्पसमन्वितम् ॥
आरग्वधस्रजं चैव स्तबकेन परिप्लुतम् ।
अङ्कुशं त्वक्षमालां च भसितं वरदं तथा ॥
वामे गौरीसमायुक्तं सव्यभागे गजाननम् ।
गजाननस्य काले तु भसितं धार्य पाणिना ॥
दिव्यच्छत्रसमायुक्तं सर्वावयवसुन्दरम् ।
एवं संकल्प्य विधिवत्प्रतिष्ठां कारयेत्ततः ॥

(उत्तरकारणागमे ॥)

किरातार्जुनमूर्तिः ।

चतुर्भुजं त्रिनेत्रं च जटामकुटसंयुतम् ।
सर्वाभरणसंयुक्तं दिव्याम्बरसमावृतम् ॥

धनुर्बाणयुतं रक्तं कृष्णापरशुसंयुतम् ।
उपवीतसमायुक्तं समभङ्गतनुं कुरु ॥
वामे गौरीसमायुक्तं दक्षिणे त्वर्जुनं स्थितम् ।

अर्जुनस्वरूपम् ।

एकवक्त्रं द्विनयनं जटामकुटसंयुतम् ।
सर्बाभरणसंयुक्तं कृताञ्जलिपुटं स्थितम् ॥
एवं किरातमाख्यातम्............ ।

(श्रीतत्वनिधौ ॥)

नृत्तमूर्तयः ।

नृत्तमूर्तयः ।

नृत्तमूर्तिः । (१)

नृत्तमष्टशतं भेदं तेष्वादौ नव उच्यते[१] ।
उत्तमं दशतालेन सर्वाङ्गं परिकल्पयेत् ॥

ऊर्ध्वकुक्षिं स्पृशेत्पूर्वसूत्रमेवं प्रकल्पयेत् ।
तत्सूत्राड्डोलबाह्वग्रमर्धाधिककलाङ्गुलम् ॥

तस्मादपरबाह्वग्रं युगाङ्गुलमुदाहृतम् ।
तस्मादग्निकराग्रान्तं सार्धत्रिंशाङ्गुलं तु वा ॥

हिक्कासूत्रसमोद्धृत्य तद्धस्ते मध्यमाग्रके ।
तद्धस्ततलमध्ये वा मध्याङ्गुलाग्रपर्वके ॥

मध्यपर्वेऽथवोद्धृत्य त्वनलं पात्रसंयुतम् ।
पात्रं विनाऽथवा त्वग्निं पञ्चांशं विस्तृतं भवेत् ॥

दक्षिणे पूर्वसूत्रात्तु बाह्वग्रं विंशदङ्गुलम् ।
तस्माड्डमरुके हस्ते मणिबन्धस्य बाह्यकम् ॥

---

१ 'नृत्तमष्टदशं ह्येवा तेष्वादौ नवमुच्यते' इति पाठान्तरम् ।

अष्टविंशतिमात्रं वा त्रिंशदङ्गुलमेव वा ।
दक्षिणे पूर्वहस्तं तु अभयं परिकल्पयेत् ॥
तन्मध्यमाङ्गुलाग्रं तु हिक्कासूत्रसमोद्धृतम् ।
अभये प्रकोष्ठमध्ये भुजङ्गवलयं न्यसेत् ॥
प्रकोष्ठमध्यनाहस्य सपादं तस्य दैर्घ्यकम् ।
तद्दीर्घाद्दुपरिख्यातं फणं भान्वङ्गुलं भवेत् ॥
सप्ताङ्गुलविशालं तु घनं चैकाङ्गुलं भवेत् ।
पुरस्स्थितान्समीक्ष्यं तु जिह्वाद्वयसमन्वितम् ॥
भुजङ्गवलयं ह्येवं कल्पयेत्कल्पवित्तमः ।
उद्धृताङ्घ्रेस्तु जानूर्ध्वनाभिसूत्रसमं भवेत् ॥
सुविकीर्णजटाभारं पञ्चषं सप्त एव वा ।
रुद्रसङ्ख्याथवा विप्र ! उभयोः पार्श्वयोस्तथा ॥
जटाभारं पुष्पमाल्यैरलङ्कृत्य विशेषतः ।
नागं चैवार्कपुष्पं च दुर्धूर(धुस्तूर ?)कुसुमं तथा ॥
हसितशीर्षकं १ चैव करोटी रत्नबन्धितम् ।
भूषयित्वा तु मकुटे दक्षिणेऽर्धेन्दुशेखरम् ॥
सिन्दूरालङ्कृतोरस्कमक्षमालावलम्बितम् ।
भस्मोद्धूलितसर्वाङ्गं किंचित्प्रहसिताननम् ॥

---

१ 'हसति शिरसीक'मिति आदर्शान्तरपाठः ॥

यज्ञोपवीतसंयुक्तमुरस्सूत्रसमन्वितम् ।
व्याघ्रीचर्म्माम्बरोपेतमूरुत्रिंशावसानकम् ॥

पादौ नूपुरसंयुक्तौ सर्वाभरणभूषितः ।
हस्तपादाङ्गुलास्सर्वे रत्नहेमाङ्गुलीयकाः ॥

मध्याङ्गुला विवर्ज्यास्तु शेषास्तु मुद्रिकान्विताः ।
दक्षिणं कुञ्चितं पादमपस्मारोपरि स्थितम् ॥

त्रिर्य्यक्पादतलं न्यस्त्वा नृत्तं कुर्य्यान्महेश्वरः ।
वामपादेतोद्धृत्य[1] तिर्य्यक् तद्दक्षिणानुगम् ॥

डोलहस्तमथावर्त्य त्वपस्मारमथोच्यते ।
शम्भोस्सव्ये शिरः स्थाप्य वामे पादौ विकीर्णकौ ॥

तन्मुखं तु समुद्धृत्य व्याललीलासमन्वितम् ।
व्यालं वै वामहस्ते तु दक्षिणं तस्य मुद्रया ॥

तस्य श्यामनिभाकारमपस्मारं द्विजोत्तम ! ।
तस्य पार्श्वेऽप्युमादेवीं प्रागुक्तविधिना कुरु ॥

इदं स्यात्प्रथमं नृत्तं सर्वलोकहितावहम् ।

(अंशुमद्भेदागमे पञ्चषष्टपटले ॥)

नृत्तमूर्तिप्रतिष्ठां तु वक्ष्ये तल्लक्षणान्विताम् ।
चतुर्भुजस्त्रिनेत्रश्च संविकीर्णजटायुतः ॥

---

१ ‘ वामपादं ततोद्धृत्ये ’ति पाठान्तरम् ।

जटामकुटसंयुक्तो वक्रनागफणावृतः ।
पृष्ठगाः पार्श्वगास्तास्स्युः पञ्चाद्येकैकवृद्धितः ॥
त्रिंशत्सङ्ख्यावसानास्स्युर्जटास्तास्सान्तरालकाः ।
धुर्द्धूरा(धुस्तूरा ?)रग्वधार्कादिपुष्पयुक्तास्सपिङ्गलाः ॥
कृताञ्जलिपुटोपेतजाह्नव्या दक्षिणस्थया ।
बालचन्द्रेण संयुक्तो वामपार्श्वस्थितेन च ॥
युक्तो वकुलमालाभिर्मुक्तादामोरगादिभिः ।
व्याघ्राजिनाम्बरो दीप्तस्सर्वाभरणभूषितः ॥
वामदोर्मूलमालम्बिद्वीपिचर्माम्बरान्वितः ।
दिव्याम्बरान्वितो वापि मृगाजिनयुतोऽपिवा ॥
कस्थ[1]ब्रह्मकपालेन नानापुष्पैरलङ्कृतः ।
धृतवाराहत(द ?)न्ताग्र[2]श्शार्दूलनखकच्छपः ॥
शाङ्खिकैर्मणिभिः प्रोतमालया हृदि भूषितः ।
स्थितो दक्षिणपादेन वामेनोपरिवर्तिना ॥
कुञ्चितावर्तमानाङ्घ्रिसुप्रसारितसत्करः ।
अम्बिकामुखबिम्बाब्जभ्रमरीकृतलोचनः ॥
आबद्धकिङ्किणीयुक्तस्तद्वन्नूपुरशोभितः ।
वामदक्षिणकर्णाढ्यपत्रिकानक्रकुण्डलः ॥

---

१ 'अपि माष'मिति न्यायेन करस्थेतिपदे रेफो निरस्त इति संभाव्यते ।
२ 'दंष्ट्राग्रः' इति पाठान्तरम् ।

दक्षाभयकरस्थेन भुजङ्गेनोत्फणेन च ।
वामापरकरस्थेन वह्निना दक्षकेन तु ॥
डिण्डिमेन समायुक्त उपवीतेन संयुतः ।
गोक्षीरधवलप्रख्य आदित्याङ्गुलभङ्गयुक् ॥
नानासर्पसमायुक्तस्त्वपस्मारोपरि स्थितः ।
मूर्ध्नो ललाटदक्षस्थं ना सादक्षपुटस्थितम् ॥
नाभेर्दक्षिणतो गुल्फमध्ये सूत्रं प्रसारयेत् ।
ललाटमध्यं सूत्रात्तु द्विमात्रमिति कीर्तितम् ॥
हिक्कासूत्रद्वयोर्मध्ये त्रिमात्रमिति कीर्तितम् ।
श्रोणिवामोरुसंस्पृष्टं तत्सूत्रमिह संमतम् ॥
सूत्रगुल्फद्वयोर्मध्यमेकाङ्गुलमिति स्मृतम् ।
सूत्राद्धि नतजान्वन्तं भानुदिङ्नन्दमात्रकम् ॥
तत्सूत्राद्वामपृष्ठान्तं सप्ताधिकदशाङ्गुलम् ।
तत्सूत्राद्वामजान्वेकचत्वारिंशदशाङ्गुलम् (?) ॥
सूत्राद्दक्षिणतः कुक्षिरष्टाङ्गुल उदाहृतः ।
सूत्रात्तु सव्यकुक्षिस्तु त्र्यङ्गुल इति स्मृतम् ॥
ऊरोर्दक्षिणतस्सूत्रं सप्ताधिकदशाङ्गुलम् ।
सूत्रात्तद्वामभागे तु नवमात्रमुदाहृतम् ॥
सूत्रात्तु वामकण्ठस्तु पञ्चाङ्गुल उदाहृतः ।
सूत्रात्तु दक्षकण्ठे तद्भाग इत्यभिधीयते ॥

सूत्रात्तु वामबाह्वन्तं त्र्यङ्गुलक्षयसंयुतम् ।
अथवान्यप्रकारेण सूत्रपातोऽभिधीयते ॥
कनीनिकान्तं तन्मूर्ध्नः तद्वन्नासापुटान्ततः ।
नाभेश्च दक्षवामान्तं स्थिताङ्घ्रेर्गुल्फमध्यमम् ॥
स्पृष्ट्वा यत्पतितं सूत्रं मध्यसूत्रमुदाहृतम् ।
सूत्राद्वाममुखं पञ्च[मा*]त्रं कण्ठं त्रिमात्रकम् ॥
बाह्वन्ते तिथिमात्रं स्यान्नवमात्रं तु कक्षगम् ।
मध्योदरेऽष्टमात्रं स्यात् श्रोणी विश्वाङ्गुलेन च ॥
कटिस्तिथ्यङ्गुलेन स्यादन्यत्र षष्टिमात्रकः ।
नवमात्रं तदूरु स्यात्पार्ष्ण्यन्तं वेदतुङ्ग[क*]म् ॥
सप्ताङ्गुलं मुखं नेत्रं कण्ठस्स्याद्रसमात्रकम् ।
बाह्वन्ते तु त्रिमात्रं स्यात्कक्षान्ते विश्वमात्रकम् ॥
मुन्यङ्गुलं भवेत्कुक्षौ श्रोण्यां स्याद्युगमात्रकम् ।
कट्यां च वेदमात्रं स्याज्जानुरष्टाङ्गुलं भवेत् ॥
पादाग्रे मुखमात्रं स्यादेवं बुद्ध्वा समाचरेत् ।
स्थितजानुसमं विद्याद्वर्तिताङ्घ्रेस्समुच्छ्रयम् ॥
तत्पार्ष्णिजान्वोर्द्विमुखव्यन्तरं परिकीर्तितम् ।
श्रोणीसमुच्छ्रयं वामजानोरुद्धरणं मतम् ॥
तदूरुमध्यान्नाभेश्च अन्तरं नवमात्रकम् ।
तज्जानोर्दण्डहस्तस्य मणिबन्धान्तरं मनुः ॥

तस्मादभयहस्तस्य मणिबन्धो रसाङ्गुलः ।
तस्य चाङ्गुष्ठमूलान्तात्स्तनाक्षव्यन्तरं मतम् ॥
ततो(द्दो?)स्समं तलोच्चं स्यात्तद्बाह्वोर्मध्यमात्पुनः ।
सप्तादशाङ्गुलं विद्याद्दण्डहस्तस्य को(कू?)र्परम् ॥
भुजान्तं साग्निहस्तोच्चं सोग्निः पञ्चाङ्गुलोच्छ्रयः ।
विस्तारः कोलकस्तस्य शिखाभिस्तिसृभिर्युतः ॥
धृताडमरुको हस्तो कर्णोच्चादङ्गुलोऽधिकः ।
साग्नि डमरुकायामो भूतैस्तु मुखविस्तृतिः ॥
कोलको मध्यविस्तारः परितस्सूत्रयन्त्रितः ।
एकजिह्वासमायुक्तो गम्भीरध्वनिसंयुतः ॥
बाह्वास्तु मणिबन्धान्तं चतुस्त्रिंशत्तथापरम् ।
अपस्मारोच्छ्रयं भानुरुद्रनन्दाष्टमात्रकैः ॥
देवस्य वक्त्रमानेन स्यादपस्मारमानकम् ।
वक्त्रद्वयं समारभ्य पञ्चवक्त्रावसानकम् ॥
वक्त्रार्धमानवृद्ध्या तु सप्तमानमुदाहृतम् ।
चतुस्तालेन कर्तव्यमपस्मारो द्विजोत्तमाः! ॥
उष्णीषात्पादपर्यन्तं षडष्टांशं विभाजयेत् ।
उष्णीषात्केशपर्यन्तं कोलकं चेति कीर्तितम् ॥
केशान्ताद्धनुपर्यन्तमष्टभागमिति स्मृतम् ।
गलमर्धाङ्गुलं प्रोक्तमध्यर्धः कर्ण उच्यते ॥

षडङ्गुल इति प्रोक्तो हिक्कादिहृदयान्ततः ।
तथैव तस्मान्नाभ्यन्तं षडङ्गुलमिति स्मृतम् ॥
तस्मात्तु मेढ्रमूलान्तं कौशिकाङ्गुलमुच्यते ।
ऊर्वायामं तु सप्तांशं जानूत्सेधो द्विमात्रकः ॥
जङ्घायामस्तु सप्तांशः पादोत्सेधो द्विमात्रकः ।
द्विभुजश्च द्विनेत्रश्च ऊर्ध्ववक्त्रस्त्वधोमुखः ॥
व्यालं वै वामहस्ते तु तस्य मूर्धा तु दक्षिणे ।
आवृतालङ्कृता भङ्गी सव्यपार्श्वशिरोयुतः ॥
देवस्य वक्त्रमानेन जाह्नव्यायाम उच्यते ।
द्विभुजा च त्रि(द्वि?)नेत्रा च करण्डमकुटान्विता ॥
सर्वाभरणसंयुक्ता कृताञ्जलिपुटान्विता ।
ऊर्द्ध्वभागादधोभागं तोयाकारेण कारयेत् ॥
गङ्गादेव्यानया देवस्संयुक्तो वा विवर्जितः ।
प्रभावकाशं विस्तारो दशाधिकशताङ्गुलम् ॥
सप्तत्रिंशच्छतायामतद्दण्डो भागविस्तरः ।
एकाद्यदशपर्यन्तमात्रैरूनाधिकापि वा ॥
व्यङ्गुलादङ्गुलर्ध्या तु बालचन्द्रस्तु सप्तधा ।
तद्वशात्पार्श्वगां देवीं कल्पयेत्तद्विधानतः ॥
कुर्य्याद्भृङ्गीरटिं (भृङ्गिरिटिं?) वाथ भद्रकालीमथापि वा ।
भुजङ्गत्रास आख्यातो भुजङ्गललितस्ततः ॥

भुजङ्गत्रासवत्सर्वं विशेषः कश्चिदस्ति हि ।
उद्धृतस्य तलं कुर्यात्स्थितजानूर्ध्वतः क्रमात् ॥

द्विमात्रं वा त्रिमात्रं वा चतुर्मात्रमथापि वा ।
भुजङ्गललितः ख्यातस्तद्वैरव इहोच्यते ॥

भुजङ्गत्रासवत्सर्वं विशेषस्तत्र चोच्यते ।
उद्धृतं दक्षिणं पादं वामपादं तु वा नयेत् ॥

स पादो देहमध्यस्थ ऊर्द्ध्वपादतलान्वितः ।
चतुर्भुजोऽष्टहस्तो वा नानादिव्यास्त्रभूषितः ॥

शिलादिद्रव्यमासाद्य कुर्य्यादेवं नटेश्वरम् ।

(उत्तरकामिकागमे षट्चत्वारिंशत्तमपटले ॥)

नृत्तार्धोद्धृतवामाङ्घ्रिजानु नाभिसमोत्थितम् ।
पादाङ्गुष्ठसमो जानु जान्वङ्गुष्ठसमोद्धृतम् ॥

प्रसार्य वामहस्तं च दण्डव दयोपरि ।
अभयं दक्षिणं हस्तं शेषं डमरुकान्वितम् ॥

कण्ठसीमान्तमुद्धृत्य यथाशोभं प्रकल्पयेत् ।
साग्निकं वामहस्तं तु बाहुसीमान्तमुद्धृतम् ॥

पादाधस्स्थमपस्मारं सर्पक्रीडासमन्वितम् ।
धुस्तूरकं करोटिं च गङ्गेन्दुबकपिञ्छकम् ॥

तिस्रः पञ्चजटास्सप्त प्रसार्य कुसुमोज्वलाः ।
सव्ये त्वेवं तथा वामे दीप्ताग्निसदृशोज्वलाः ॥
नृत्तरूपमिदं वत्स ! सर्वशान्त्यर्थमुच्यते ।

(सुप्रभेदागमे चतुस्त्रिंशत्तमपटले ॥)

नृत्तमष्टाशतविधं तत्रादौ नव कथ्यते ।
भानुरुद्रदशांशं वा तुङ्गं नृत्तनतं भवेत् ॥
हिक्कासमानमुन्नम्य दक्षहस्ताङ्गुलाग्रकम् ।
त स्ततलमध्ये वा मध्यमाङ्गुलिकाग्रके ॥
तन्मध्यपर्वगं वाथ वह्निं पात्रगतं तु वा ।
पात्रं विनाथवा कुर्यादपरे डमरुं तथा ॥
दक्षिणे त्वन्यहस्ते स्यादभयं पूर्वमुक्तवत् ।
अभये प्रकोष्ठमध्ये तु भुजङ्गवलयं न्यसेत् ॥
डोलायमानं तद्वामहस्तं कुर्याद्यथोचितम् ।
स्थिताङ्घ्रिजानोर्वामाङ्घ्रिजानुनीत्रं कलाङ्गुलम् ॥
सुविकीर्य जटाभारं नानानागविचित्रितम् ।
करोटिकाभिर्दुर्द्धूर(धुस्तूर ?)कुसुमैश्च भुजङ्गमैः ॥
भूषितं मकुटं कुर्याद् दक्षिणेऽर्धेन्दुशेखरम् ।
सिन्दूरालङ्कृतोत्तंसमक्षमालावलम्बितम् ॥

भस्मधूलितसर्वाङ्गं किंचित्प्रहसिताननम् ।
यज्ञोपवीतादियुतं व्याघ्रचर्मोम्बरान्वितम् ॥

दक्षिणं कुञ्चितं पादमपस्मारोपरि स्थितम् ।
चतुस्तालेन कर्तव्यमपस्मारं प्रमाणतः ॥

शम्भोस्सव्यगतं तस्य शिरः कुर्यादधोमुखम् ।
पादौ विकीर्ण्य(र्ये ?) हस्ताभ्यां व्याललीलामुदान्वितम् ॥

व्यालं वै वामहस्ते वा दक्षिणं मुद्रयान्वितम् ।
सस्यश्यामनिभं कुर्यादपस्मारं विशेषतः ॥

पद्मपीठमधः कुर्यात्कलाङ्गुलसमुच्छ्रयम् ।
तच्चतुर्गुणविस्तारं प्रभामण्डलसंयुतम् ॥

रविमण्डलवृत्तं तु प्रभामण्डलमत्र तु ।
तत्र वामेऽप्युमादेवीं प्रागुक्तविधिना कुरु ॥

एतत्स्यात्प्रथमं नृत्तं सर्वलोकहितावहम् ।

(शिल्परत्ने द्वाविंशपटले ॥)

चतुर्भुजं त्रिनेत्रं च सुविकीर्णजटान्वितम् ।
कुररीवक्ष(?)संयुक्तं बर्हिपिञ्छसमन्वितम् ॥

मौलेर्दक्षे तु [1]धुर्तूरमर्धचन्द्रसमन्वितम् ।
दक्षिणे तु जटाग्रे तु जाह्नवीमभिवन्दिताम् ॥

---

१. धुस्तूरपदं धुर्तूर इति दुर्दूर इति च कारणाद्यागमेषु बहुत्र प्रयुज्यते ।

पत्रं तु वामकर्णे तु दक्षिणे नक्रकुण्डलम् ।
सर्वाभरणसंयुक्तमुपवीतसमन्वितम् ॥

व्याघ्राजिनाम्बरोपेतं पादकिङ्किणिशोभितम् ।
जगत्प्र(गजप्र?)सारितं वामे दक्षिणेऽभयहस्तकम् ॥

डमरुं सव्यहस्ते तु वह्निर्वै वामहस्तके ।
वक्रं तु दक्षिणं पादमपस्मारोपरि स्थितम् ॥

उद्धृतं वामपादं तु पादाग्रं दक्षिणानुगम् ।
ललाटमध्यं दक्षे तु हित्वा सार्धाष्टकं यवम् ॥

तस्मात्तु लम्बयेत्सूत्रं दक्षनासापुटान्तकात् ।
दक्षिणाङ्घ्रेस्तु गुल्फस्य मध्यमादेव पातितम् ॥

तत्सूत्रकक्षयोर्मध्ये ऊरुस्स्मृत्यङ्गुलं भवेत् ।
तत्सूत्रकक्षयोरन्तर्वामोरोर्वसुमात्रकम् ॥

तत्सूत्राद्दक्षिणे ग्रीवा षडङ्गुलमिति स्मृतम् ।
तत्सूत्राद्वामके ग्रीवा गुणाङ्गुलमुदाहृतम् ॥

तत्सूत्राद्दक्षिणे नाभेर्व्यन्तरं चाङ्गुलं भवेत् ।
तत्सूत्रान्मेढ्रमूलान्ताद्वामभागमिति स्मृतम् ॥

वामा स्फिक्पिण्डिका सूत्रात्सप्तानामङ्गुलं भवेत् ।
तत्सूत्राद्वक्रपादस्य जानुकं तु दशा ङ्गुलम् ॥

दक्षिणे बाहुसीमान्ताद्धिक्कासूत्रस्य मध्यमम् ।
(यवद्वयसमायुक्तं विंशदङ्गुलं चेति कीर्तितम् ॥)

यवद्वयाधिकं विंशदङ्गुलं चेति कीर्तितम् ।
हिक्कामध्यं समारभ्य दोस्सीमान्तं तु वामके ॥

यवद्वयसमायुक्तं सप्तादशाङ्गुलं भवेत् ।
नाभेर्दक्षिणके कुक्षितारं भागमिति स्मृतम् ॥

नाभेर्वामे तु कुक्षौ च तारं त्रयोदशाङ्गुलम् ।
वरदाग्निधरं हस्तं दोस्समं चेति कीर्तितम् ॥

शरमात्रं पावकोत्सेधं विस्तारं तु गुणाङ्गुलम् ।
त्रिशिखाभिस्समायुक्तं कल्पयेत्तलमध्यमे ॥

बाहोश्च मणिबन्धाच्च चतुस्त्रिंशदङ्गुलं भवेत् ।
डमरुकोपेतहस्तं तु सूचीहस्तमिति स्मृतम् ॥

तत्सूचिहस्तकस्योर्ध्वं कर्णोर्ध्वसममुच्यते ।
बाहोश्च मणिबन्धाच्च चतुर्विंशदङ्गुलं भवेत् ॥

वामाङ्घ्रेश्चैव जानूर्ध्वं नाभेस्तु सममुच्यते ।
वामाङ्घ्रेः पार्ष्णिकाधश्च वक्राङ्घ्रेर्जानुकोपरि ॥

तत्समं त्विति विज्ञेयं तत्पार्ष्णेर्जानुकान्ततः ।
चतुस्त्रिंशतिमात्रं तु व्यन्तरं चेति कीर्तितम् ॥

मणिबन्धकजान्वोश्च व्यन्तरं तु यवं भवेत् ।
दोर्मूलान्तसमं चैव अभयाग्रं प्रकीर्तितम् ॥

मणिबन्धकबाहोश्च व्यन्तरं तु यमं भवेत् ।
तस्य कूर्परमध्ये तु व्यालं तत्रैव विन्यसेत् ॥

चूचुकं नाभिकामूला द्ध्यन्तरं[१] तु यमं(त्वं?)भवेत् ।
सव्यस्य वामसूत्रस्य मध्याद्वै पार्श्वयोस्तयोः ॥
वामबाहुद्वयोर्मध्ये शार्दूलाजिनकं न्यसेत् ।
त्रिवक्त्रायाममानेन अपस्मारं ततः कुरु ॥
चतुस्तालप्रमाणेन भूतरूपेण कारयेत् ।
तस्यैव वामपार्श्वे तु देवीं कुर्यात्सलक्षणम् ॥
भुजङ्गत्रासमेवं तु भिक्षाटनमथ शृणु ।

(पूर्वकारणागमे ॥)

नृत्तमूर्तिः । (२)

तदेव दक्षिणे पार्श्वे जटाग्रे जाह्नवी भवेत् ।
स्त्रीमानोक्ताङ्गसम्पूर्णं हृदयेऽञ्जलिसंयुतम् ॥
एवं जाह्नविसंयुक्तं नृत्तं यत्तद्द्वितीयकम् ।

(अंशुमद्भेदागमे पञ्चषष्टितमपटले ॥)

तदेव दक्षिणे पार्श्वे जटाग्रे जाह्नवी भवेत् ।
शम्भोरुच्चाङ्गुलेनैव षोडशाङ्गुलमुन्नतम् ॥
स्त्रीमानोक्ताङ्गसंपूर्णा हृदयेऽञ्जलिसंयुता ।
एवं जाह्नविसंयुक्तं नृत्तं यत्तद् द्वितीयकम् ॥

(शिल्परत्ने द्वाविंशपटले ॥)

---

१. सूचिकानामिकामूलध्यन्तरमिति स्यात् ।

नृत्तमूर्तिः । (३)

तदेव वामपादं तु अपस्मारोपरि स्थितम् ।
उद्धृतं दक्षिणं पादं वामात्तुङ्गं प्रसारयेत् ॥
शेषं प्रागिव कर्तव्यं नृत्तं...तुस्तृतीयकम् ।

(अंशुमद्भेदागमे पञ्चषष्टितमपटले ॥)

नृत्तमूर्तिः । (४)

सुविकीर्णजटाभारं जटामकुटमण्डितम् ।
जटामकुट(मण्डल ?)संयुक्तं शेषं प्रथमनृत्तवत् ॥
चतुर्थं नृत्तमेतत्स्यात् सर्वप्राणिहितावहम् ।

(अंशुमद्भेदागमे पञ्चषष्टपटले ॥)

अनुकीर्णजटाभारं जटामकुटमण्डितम् ।
जटामण्डलयुक्तं वा चतुर्थेऽन्यद्यथादिमम् ॥

(शिल्परत्ने द्वाविंशपटले ॥)

नृत्तमूर्तिः । (५)

उष्णीषोर्ध्वकसीमान्तं सव्यपादं समुद्धृतम् ।
सुवक्रं वामपादं तु अपस्मारोपरि स्थितम् ॥
भुजाष्टकसमायुक्तमेतत्पञ्चममुच्यते ।
अभयं शूलपाशं च डमरुं दक्षिणे करे ॥

कपालं चाग्निपात्रं च घण्टां हस्तिकरोपमम् ।
गजहस्तोपमं हस्तं प्रसार्य्यं दक्षिणानुगम् ॥

यत्तत्प्रथमनृत्तस्य पूर्वसूत्रं प्रसारयेत् ।
पञ्चमं नृत्तमेवं स्यात्ततष्षष्ठं वदाम्यहम् ॥

अंशुमद्भेदागमे पञ्चषष्टपटले ॥

उष्णीषोर्ध्वैकमात्रान्तं सव्यपादं समुद्धरेत् ।
सवक्रं वामपादं तदपस्मारोपरिस्थितम् ॥

(उप) भुजाष्टकसं [आ*] युक्तमेतत्पञ्चममुच्यते ।
अभयं शूलपाशौ च डमरुं दक्षिणे करे ॥

कपालं चाग्निपात्रं च घण्टां[१] हस्तिकरोपमम् ।

(शिल्परत्ने द्वाविंशपटले ॥)

नृत्तमूर्तिः । (६)

दोर्भिष्षोडशभिर्युक्तं वामे गौरीसमायुतम् ।
स्कन्दधृग्वामहस्तेन सव्यहस्तोद्धृताञ्जलिः ॥

स्कन्दोभयकराभ्यां तु मातुस्तनकदाहृतम्[२] ।
एवं गौरी समीक्ष्येशं भीतातिस्नेहविस्मयात् ॥

---

१ 'तालिण्डुकरोपम 'मिति पाठान्तरम् ॥ २ 'हस्ताभ्यामुद्धृतं स्कंधं स्तनं तस्य प्रसारितम्' इति पाठान्तरम् । 'निपीड्य वे' ति शिल्परत्नगतार्धेन समनन्तरस्थितेन भवितव्यमिति प्रतिभाति ।

अभयं डमरुं चैव वज्रं शूलं तथैव च ।
पाशं टङ्कं तथा दण्डं नागं वै दक्षिणे करे ॥

अभयं शूलपाशं च खड्गं डमरुकं ध्वजम् ।
वेतालं सूचिहस्तं च दक्षिणेऽष्टकरं भवेत् ॥

सव्यानुगकरं डोलं वामं चैव गजोपमम् ।
अनलं मिथुनं चैव वलयं केतुरेव च ॥

घण्टा खेटकपालं च वामपार्श्वेऽष्टहस्तके ।
अनलं गजहस्ताभं खेटकं विस्मयं तथा ॥

घण्टां चैव कपालं च क्षुरिका सूचिमेव च ।
वामे त्वष्टभुजं ख्यातं शेषं पञ्चमनृत्तवत् ॥

पादौ पंचमनृत्तं स्यात् यत्तत्तद्वद्विधीयते ।
षष्ठमं ह्येवमाख्यातं सप्तमं शृणु सुव्रत! ॥

(अंशुमद्भेदागमे पञ्चषष्टितमपटले ॥)

दोर्भिष्षडङ्गसंयुक्तं[1] वामे गौरीसमायुतम् ।
स्कन्दो भयात्कराभ्यां तु मातुः स्तनद्वदोदरात् ॥

निपीड्य वा कराभ्यां तु वामभागोद्धृताञ्जलिम् ।
एवं गौरी निरीक्ष्येशं भीत्यातिस्नेहविस्मयात् ॥

---

१ 'दोर्भिष्षोडशभिर्युक्त' मिति भवितव्यम् ।

अभयं डमरुं चैव वज्रं शूलं तथैव च ।
पाशं टङ्कं तथा दण्डं नागं वै दक्षिणे करे ॥

सजानुगकरं डोलं वामं गजकरोपमम् ।
अङ्कु(न ?)लं मिथुनं चैव वलयं केतुरेब च ॥

घण्टां चैत्र कपालं च वामपार्श्वेऽष्टहस्तके ।
पादौ पञ्चमनृत्तस्य विधिवत्तद्विधीयते ॥

(शिल्परत्ने द्वाविंशपटले ॥)

नृत्तमूर्तिः । (७)

त्रिनेत्रं चाष्टहस्तं च सुविकीर्णजटायुतम् ।
कुञ्चितं वामपादं तु अपस्मारोपरि स्थितम् ॥

उद्धृतं दक्षिणं पादं चाङ्गुष्ठं चाग्रसीमगम् ।
अभयं शूलपाशं च डमरुं दक्षिणे करे ॥

कपालं चाग्निपात्रं च तथा विस्मयहस्तकम् ।
गजहस्तोपमं हस्तं सव्यासव्यानुगं तथा ॥

नतमानं दशांशं स्यात् वामे गौरीसमायुतम् ।
सप्तमं नृत्तमाख्यातं जगदार्तिविनाशनम् ॥

(अंशुमद्भेदागमे पञ्चषष्टपटले ॥)

नृत्तमूर्तिः । (८)

तदेव षड्भुजोपेतमभयं डमरुं तथा ।
शूलं दक्षिणपार्श्वे तु कपालं विस्मयं तथा ॥
गजहस्तोपमं वामे सूत्रं प्राग्वत्तदष्टमम् ।
पञ्चमस्य च नृत्तस्य षष्ठमस्य च .... स्मृता ॥
नेत्रद्वयमिति ख्यातं शेषाणां तु त्रिनेत्रकम् ।

(अंशुमद्भेदागमे पञ्चषष्टपटले ॥)

नृत्तमूर्तिः । (९)

चतुर्भुजं त्रिनेत्रं च जटामकुटसंयुतम् ।
अभयं डमरुं सव्ये वामेऽग्निर्गजहस्तवत् ॥
अपस्मारं विना पीठे वामाङ्घ्रिं कुञ्चितं स्थितम् ।
तत्तत्पुरस्स्थितं पीठे सव्यपादकनिष्ठिका ॥
तत्पादं कुञ्चितं युक्त्या सूत्रं युक्त्या तु लम्बयेत् ।
नवमं नृत्तमाख्यातं गङ्गाधरमथ श्रृणु ॥

(अंशुमद्भेदागमे पञ्चषष्टपटले ॥)

दक्षिणामूर्तिभेदाः ।

दक्षिणामूर्तिभेदाः

व्याख्यानदक्षिणामूर्तिः ।

अथ वक्ष्ये विशेषेण दक्षिणामूर्तिलक्षणम् ।
लम्बयेद्दक्षिणं पादं वामाङ्घ्रिर्नलकाग्रकम् ॥

सव्योर्वग्रे निधातव्यं वामपादं तु शाययेद् ।
नतमध्यर्धमात्रं स्याच्चतुर्भुजसमन्वितम् ॥

दक्षिणे पूर्वहस्तं तु ज्ञानमुद्रां तु धारयेत् ।
दक्षिणे परहस्तं तु अक्षमालाधरं परम् ॥

वरदं वामहस्तं स्याद्दण्डहस्तमथापि वा ।
वामजानूपरिष्टात्तु वरदे तलपृष्ठकम् ॥

वामजानूपरिष्टात्तु दण्डं चेत्कूर्परं न्यसेत् ।
वामे तु परहस्ते तु वह्निं वा व्यालमेव वा ॥

अर्धार्जवक्त्रं[१] सर्वाङ्गमार्जवं स्फटिकोपमम् ।
विकीर्णमूर्धजं वापि जटामण्डलमेव वा ॥

---

१ 'अर्धार्जवक्त्र' मित्यर्धस्य 'अर्थेन्द्रवक्त्रसर्वाङ्गममदा स्फटिकोपमम्' इति पाठान्तरम् ।

......बद्धमूर्ध्नि वा जटामकुटमेव वा ।
चतुर्भुजस्त्रिनेत्रस्तु कुन्देन्दुधवलप्रभः ॥
श्वेतविद्रुमहेमाभश्श्यामाभो वा प्रकीर्तितः ।
व्याघ्रचर्माम्बरो वापि दिव्याम्बरधरस्तु वा ॥
उत्तरीयसमोपेतश्शुक्लयज्ञोपवीतकः ।
विकीर्णमूर्धजो वापि जटामकुट एव वा ॥
पट्टिकाबन्धनो वापि सत्करोटिकया युतः ।
धुर्धूरारग्वधैर्नागपत्रैश्चन्द्रेण मण्डितः ॥
पञ्चमुद्रासमोपेतो गङ्गाकिङ्किणिसंयुतः ।
अधस्ताद्वटवृक्षस्य शैलादूर्ध्वं श्रितः पुनः ॥
व्याघ्रचर्मोपरिष्टात्तु स्थितो वीरासनोऽथवा ।
लम्बितं दक्षिणं पादं तज्जानूपरि संस्थितम् ॥
वामाङ्घ्रिनलकं कुर्यात्सव्यहस्तं तु मुद्रया ।
सन्दर्शसंज्ञयोपेतो वामहस्तस्थपुस्तकः ॥
अथवा नागसंयुक्तो वामहस्तस्समीरितः ।
वरदं तं विजानीयाज्जानुस्थमणिबन्धकः ॥
दण्डहस्तो यदा स स्यात्प्रकोष्ठं[१] जानुसंस्थितम् ।
विकसत्पद्मसङ्काशस्त्वधस्ताद्विस्तृताङ्गुलिः ॥

१ 'दण्डहस्ते यदा स स्याद्' इति पाठान्तरम् ।

परहस्तद्वये चाक्षमालाज्वालासमन्वितः ।
पद्मं वा चोत्पलं वापि व्यालं वामे तु कल्पयेत् ॥
कटकौ तौ प्रकर्तव्यौ प्रसन्नसमलोचनः ।
नासाग्रदृष्टियुग्वामहस्तो वा स्यात्सुपुस्तकः ॥
सजटामकुटा देवचूचुकास्यगलान्तकाः ।
तत्तत्कलासमोपेताश्शुक्लयज्ञोपवीतिनः ॥
शुक्लाद्यम्बरसंयुक्ता भस्मरुद्राक्षसंयुताः ।
कौशिकः काश्यपश्श्यामस्त्वितरौ पीतवर्णकौ ॥
रक्तवर्णो भरद्वाजो धूम्राभावत्रिगौतमौ ।
एषामेकद्वयं वापि त्रयं वा पार्श्वयोर्न्यसेत् ॥
व्याख्यानमूर्तिरेवं स्याद्गेयमूर्तिस्ततो मतः ।
(उत्तरकामिकागमे एकपञ्चाशत्तमपटले ॥)

दक्षिणामूर्तिमीशानं कुर्याद्वटतरोरधः ।
लम्बयेद्दक्षिणं पादं वामाङ्घ्रेर्नलकाग्रकम् ॥
सममेवं विधातव्यं वामपादं तु शाययेत् ।
दक्षिणे पूर्वहस्ते तु ज्ञानमुद्रां तु धारयेत् ॥
दक्षिणे परहस्ते तु कारयेदक्षमालिकाम् ।
वरदं वामहस्ते तु दण्डं वा परिकीर्तितम् ॥
वामजानूपरिष्टात्तु दण्डं चेत्कूर्परं न्यसेत् ।
वामे परकरे तत्र वह्निं वा मृगमेव वा ॥

विकीर्णमूर्धजं वापि जटामण्डलसंयुतम् ।
जटाभिर्बद्धमूर्तिर्वा जटामकुटशोभितम् ॥
शुद्धस्फटिकसङ्काशं................ ।
वामे धुर्द्दूर(धुस्तूर?)पुष्पं च नागं च शिरसि स्मृतम् ॥
दक्षिणेन्दुकलायुक्तं सर्वाभरणभूषितम् ।
सितवस्त्रोत्तरीयं च सितयज्ञोपवीतिनम् ॥
व्याघ्रचर्माम्बरोपेतं त्रिनेत्रं क्लेशवर्जितम् ।
रुद्राक्षं कण्ठमालां च हृन्मालां च विधापयेत् ॥
नारदो जमदग्निश्च वसिष्ठो दक्षपार्श्वके ।
भारद्वाजश्च शुनकस्त्वगस्त्यो वामपार्श्वके ॥
वन्दितैः किन्नराद्यैस्तु सेवितं भक्तिसंयुतैः ।
अपस्मारोपरिष्टात्तु लम्बपादतलं न्यसेत् ॥
धर्मव्याख्यानमूर्तिः स्यादेवं सर्वशुभावहम् ।

(शिल्परत्ने द्वाविंशपटले ॥)

दक्षेण मुद्रां प्रतिपादयन्तं सिताक्षसूत्रं च तथोर्ध्वभागे ।
वामे च पुस्तामखिलागमाद्यां बिभ्राणमूर्ध्वेन सुधाधरं च ॥
सिताम्बुजस्थं सितवर्णमीशं सिताम्बरालेपनमिन्दुमौलिम् ।
ज्ञानं मुनिभ्यः प्रतिपादयन्तं तं दक्षिणामूर्तिमुदाहरन्ति ॥

(विष्णुधर्मोत्तरे ॥)

प्रतिमालक्षणानि ।

चतुर्भुजं त्रिनेत्रं च द्वीपिचर्माम्बरान्वितम् ।
आवृतालङ्कृता भङ्गी शश्यर्ककुसुमान्वितम् ॥

सद(न्दं ?)शं दक्षिणं हस्तं पुस्तकं त्वामहस्तके ।
सव्यके चाक्षमालां च व्यालं वै वामहस्तके ॥

पादाग्रे दृष्टिपातं तु किंचिद्भङ्गसमायुतम् ।
लम्बितं दक्षिणं पादं तस्योर्वग्रस्य चोपरि ॥

वामपादस्य नलकं संयुतं कारयेत्सुधीः ।
हिक्कामध्यं समारभ्य कटके मणिबन्धकात् ॥

व्यन्तरं त्रियवं प्रोक्तमृषिसङ्घैस्समावृतम् ।
अगस्त्यश्च पुलस्त्यश्च विश्वामित्रोऽङ्गिरास्तथा ॥

एवं व्याख्यानमूर्तिं तु गेयमूर्तिं शृणुष्वथ ।

(पूर्वकारणागमे एकादशपटले ॥)

ज्ञानदक्षिणामूर्तिः ।

तदेव वीणाहीनं तु ज्ञानमुद्राभयान्वितम् ।
वामं प्रसारितं हस्तं वामजानूरुकूर्परम् ॥

दक्षिणे त्वपरे चाक्षमाला वामेऽब्जमुत्पलम् ।
शुद्धश्वेतनिभं वर्णं शेषं पूर्ववदाचरेत् ॥

ज्ञानमूर्तिरिति ख्यातं सर्वकारणकारणम् ।

(अंशुमद्भेदागमे पञ्चसप्ततितमपटले ॥)

अथवा पूर्वहस्ताभ्यां ज्ञानमुद्राभयौ धृतौ ।
वामं प्रसारितं वाथ वामजानूर्ध्वकूर्परे ॥

अपरे दक्षिणे त्वक्षमालामुत्पलमन्यतः ।
ज्ञानमूर्तिरिति ख्यातं सर्वकारणकारणम् ॥

(शिल्परत्ने द्वाविंशपटले ॥)

योगदक्षिणामूर्तिः ।

अन्योन्याङ्घ्रितलं विप्र! स्फिक्पिण्डाधः प्रकल्पयेत् ।
ज्ञानमुद्रां हृदि स्थाने त्वभ्यन्तरमुखं करम् ॥

वरदं वामहस्तं तु मेढ्रपीठोपरि न्यसेत् ।
अपरे दक्षिणे चाक्षमालाब्जं वामहस्तके ॥

नासाग्रं तु समीक्ष्याक्षमार्जवं सूत्रदेहकौ ।
अपरे तु जटालम्ब्य ऋषिभिस्सेवितं परम् ॥

योगमूर्तिरिति ख्यातं ध्याने दुःखनिवृत्तिदम् ।
लम्बयेद्दक्षिणं पादं वाममुत्कुटिका(त्कटुका?)सनम् ॥

योगपट्टिकयाबध्य देहं चोत्कुटिका(त्कटुका?)ङ्घ्रिकम् ।
प्रसार्य्य वामहस्तं तु वामजानूपरि द्विज! ॥

प्रागिवैव कृतं शेषं सोऽप्येवं योगमूर्ति वै ।
ऊरुमूर्ध्नि समाश्रित्य अन्योन्यं पादपार्ष्णिकौ ॥

योगपट्टिकयोपेतं जङ्घामध्ये द्विजोत्तम ! ।
प्रसार्य्य पूर्वहस्तौ द्वौ जानूपरि निधापितौ ॥

अपरे दक्षिणे चाक्षमाला वामे कमण्डलुम् ।
जटामण्डलसंयुक्तं ततश्चन्द्रशेखरम् ॥

नीलग्रीवासमायुक्तं शङ्खकुन्देन्दुसन्निभम् ।
अपरे शाययेदुक्षं नानासर्पविभूषितम् ॥

ह्न्मा.....................रुद्राक्षैस्तु[१] ।
एवं त्वनेकभेदेन दक्षिणामूर्तिरुच्यते ॥

(अंशुमद्भेदागमे पञ्चसप्ततितमपटले ॥)

व्याख्यानसहितस्त्वेव सन्दर्शस्य समास्ययुक् ।
तत्राक्षिपातयोगेन सदाकुञ्चितलोचनः ॥

प्रसृतो वामहस्तस्याद्योगमूर्तिरयं मतः ।
अथ कुञ्चितवामाङ्घ्रियुग्मास्फिग्गतपार्ष्णिकः ॥

उद्धृतं तस्य जान्वग्रं दण्डकूर्परकान्तयुक् ।
सदंस(सन्दर्श ?)दृष्टिपातश्च आभङ्गं चैव पूर्ववत् ॥

नानामृगैस्तु संकीर्णं नानाव्यालैस्तु संयुतः ।
नानामुनिगणैस्सार्धं सिद्धविद्याधरैरपि ॥

---

१ 'अपरेचाययेत्रृक्षो नानासर्पविभूषितः । हन्माला कर्णमालाध्या दूर्वत्रृश्चे विराजितम् ॥' इति पाठान्तरम् ।

भूतैश्च किन्नरैरन्यैः पुष्पवृक्षैश्च मण्डितम् ।
शैलं कुर्यात्तु तत्पार्श्वे वटवृक्षस्तु शाद्वलः ॥

फलशाखोपशाखाढ्यो नानापक्षिसमायुतः ।
तन्मूले दक्षिणे छायानिषण्णः कू(कृ ?)पया युतः ॥

रत्नोपशोभिते पीठे व्याघ्रचर्मोत्तरछदे ।
आसीनो मुनिभिस्सम्यक् कौशिकादिभिरादरात् ॥

शिवद्विजकुलस्यादिभूतैस्तु परितस्स्थितैः ।
आगमाहितचेतोभिः परमेशेन दीक्षितैः ॥

एवं तु दक्षिणामूर्तेर्मूर्तिभेदा उदाहृताः ।
आसीनो वा स्थितो वापि ऋषिभिस्संवृतो न वा ॥

वटवृक्षविहीनो वा भूताद्यावृत एव वा ।
भूतस्थलम्बपादो वा दक्षिणेशस्समीरितः ॥

(उत्तरकामिकागमे एकपञ्चाशत्तमपटले ॥)

अन्योन्याङ्घ्रितलं सम्यक् स्फिक्पिण्डाधः प्रकल्पयेत् ।
ज्ञानमुद्रां हृदि स्थाने त्वभ्यन्तरमुखं करम् ॥

वरदं वामहस्तं तु मेढ्रपीठोपरि न्यसेत् ।
अपरे चोत्पलं चाक्षमालां पूर्ववदाचरेत् ॥

नासाग्रं स्वं समीक्ष्य स्वमार्जवं देहमाचरेत् ।
सुविकीर्णजटायुक्तं योगमूर्तिरिति स्मृतम् ॥

लम्बयेद्दक्षिणं पादं वाममुत्कुटि(त्कटु ?)कासनम् ।
संबद्धय योगपट्टेन देहोत्कुटि(त्कटु ?)काङ्घ्रिकौ ॥
प्रसार्य वामहस्तं तु वामजानूपरि स्थितम् ।
एतच्च योगमूर्तिस्स्याच्छेषं पूर्ववदाचरेत् ॥
ऊरुमूलं समाश्रित्य अन्योन्याबद्धपार्ष्णिकम् ।
योगपट्टिकयोपेतं जङ्घामध्ये विशेषतः ॥
प्रसार्य पूर्वहस्तौ द्वौ जानूपरि निधापितौ ।
अपरे दक्षिणे वाक्षमालां वाम(मे?)कमण्डलुम् ॥
जटामण्डलसंयुक्तं करोव्यर्धेन्दुशेखरम् ।
नीलग्रीवासमायुक्तं शङ्खकुन्देन्दुसन्निभम् ॥
योगमूर्तिविशेषाख्यं शेषं प्रागिव कारयेत् ।

(शिल्परत्ने द्वाविंशपटले ॥)

वीणाधरदक्षिणामूर्तिः ॥

तदेव वामपादेनोत्कुटि(त्कटु?)कासनसंयुतम् ।
पूर्वहस्तद्वयोर्वीणाधृतं युक्त्या द्विजोत्तम! ॥
शेषं प्रागिव कर्तव्यमेतद्वीणाधरं भवेत् ।

(अंशुमद्भेदागमे पञ्चसप्ततितमपटले ॥)

ऊर्ध्वाधोमध्यकटकौ तस्यां सर्पकरावुभौ ।
वीणा तु दक्षिणे वाग्रे(दक्षिणोर्वग्रे?)ऽदक्षिणे कटक(के?)स्थितः॥

दक्षिणे कटकं चोरुस्थितायां विनिवेशयेत् ।

(उत्तरकामिकागमे एकपञ्चाशत्तमपटले ॥)

तदेव वामपादेनोत्कुटिकासनसंयुतम् ।
पूर्वहस्तद्वये वीणा चेत्तद्वीणाधरं स्मृतम् ॥

(शिल्परत्ने द्वाविंशपटले ॥)

कटकं दक्षिणं हस्तमधोमुखं तदुच्यते ।
वामहस्तं तु कटकमूर्ध्ववक्त्रं तदुच्यते ॥
तन्त्रीं निवेशयेदूरुकाग्रे दक्षिणपादके ।
वामहस्तस्य कटके सव्यहस्तं तथोपरि ॥
ऊरुबाह्यं त्रिमात्रं तु कटकोर्ध्वे युगाङ्गुलम् ।
दण्डायाममिति प्रोक्तं विस्तारं तु द्विमात्रकम् ॥
वा(ला?)बुवक्त्रं तु षण्मात्रमुत्सेधं तु तदर्धकम् ।
एतदेव विशेषं तु शेषं पूर्वोक्तवद्भवेत् ॥
दक्षिणामूर्तिरेवं स्याच्छृणु मन्मथनिग्रहम् ।

(पूर्वकारणागमे एकादशपटले ॥)

कङ्कालमूर्तिभिक्षाटनमूर्ती ।

कङ्कालमूर्तिभिक्षाटनमूर्ती ।

कङ्कालमूर्तिः ।

अथ कङ्कालमूर्तेस्तु लक्षणं वक्ष्यतेऽधुना ।
पादौ तु पादुकोपेतौ वामपादं तु सुस्थितम् ॥

गमनापेक्षया सव्यपादमीषत्समुद्धृतम् ।
शुद्धश्वेतनिभं वर्णं सर्वाभरणभूषितम् ॥

रक्तकञ्चुकबद्धाङ्गं जटामकुटमण्डितम् ।
धुर्धूरपुष्पनागं च वामे सव्येन्दुशेखरम् ॥

हसितं वक्त्रसन्धार्य्यं सुगेयगणसेवितम् ।
किंचित्प्रकाशितान्तस्स्थदशनांशुविलासितम् ॥

गेयश्रृङ्गारसंयुक्तमास्यमेवं प्रकल्पयेत् ।
कर्णौ कुण्डलसंयुक्तौ वामे शङ्खदलं तु वा ॥

पूर्वहस्तद्वयोर्वामे डंक(ढक्का?)कसव्ये प्रहारकम् ।
दक्षिणं हिमं वक्त्व्यातं(हरिणीवक्त्रे व्यापितं?) सिंहकर्णवत् ॥

वामहस्ते तु पिञ्छं च कङ्कालास्थि च धारयेत् ।
तदस्थ्याकृति निर्मांसं द्विपादं द्विकरान्वितम् ॥

कृष्णश्यामनिभाकारमरे(मपाने?) दण्डवेशनम् ।
दण्डे कङ्कालपादौ द्वौ रज्जुना बन्धयेद्बुधः ॥
केतुकिङ्किणिनेत्राभ्यां निष्क्रान्तरुधिरं तु वा ।
एतत्कङ्कालनाम्ना तु वामस्कन्धोपरि न्यसेत् ॥
अनेकभूतैर्जायाभिस्सेवितं त्वादरान्वितैः ।
बलिपात्रधृतं भूतं वामेऽग्रे गमनान्वितम् ॥
दर्व्या त्वन्नं तु तत्पात्रे निधायाकृतिजायया ।
किञ्चित्प्रकाशितं योनिसंयुक्तानतवाससा ॥
संभ्रान्तमनसोपेता जायास्सर्वास्त्वनेकशः ।
व्याघ्रचर्माम्बरोपेतं दुकूलवसनान्वितम् ॥
दक्षिणे कटिपार्श्वे तु छुरिकां चैव बन्धयेत् ।
उभयोः पार्श्वयोर्हस्तं नानानागविभूषितम् ॥
ऋषिभिर्देवगन्धर्वसिद्धविद्याधरादिभिः ।
हृदयेऽञ्जलिसंयुक्तैस्संभ्रान्तमनसान्वितैः ॥
आत्मानीतस्वमानान्तं सेवितं तैः सुपूजितम् ।
वीधी(थी?)स्संमार्जयेद्वायुः पर्जन्यो जलसेचनम् ॥
पुष्पवृष्टिकृतो देवा ऋषयः स्तोत्रपाठकाः ।
ऋग्यजुस्सामाथर्वैश्च स्तुति कुर्यात्पदेपदे ॥
चर्मबन्धं च कंसं च कदम्बं सुषिरं तथा ।
श ध्वनिसमायुक्तं पञ्चशब्दा महारवे ॥

तुम्बुरुनारदादेश्च गेयकर्म सलक्षणम् ।
छत्रं धृत्वा रविश्चन्द्रश्चामरान्दिव्ययोषितः ॥
(अंशुमद्भेदागमे द्विसप्ततितमपटले ॥)

पादे पादुकसंयुक्तं चतुर्दोर्भिस्समन्वितम् ।
सयज्ञसूत्रं शान्तं च गमनोन्मुखमीश्वरम् ॥

आबद्धक्षुरिकं सौम्यं कपर्दमुकुटोज्ज्वलम् ।
क्षौमाम्बरं सितं कुर्यात्सुन्दरं तं विभूषणम् ॥

सशङ्खपत्रिका वामे दक्षिणे नक्रकुण्डलम् ।
दक्षिणं कुञ्चितं पादं वामपादं तु सुस्थितम् ॥

समभङ्गयुतं वापि कान्तियुक्तनिजाङ्गकम् ।
प्रहरं दक्षिणे हस्ते ढक्कां वामे तु पूर्वयोः ॥

सव्यमध्याङ्गुलाग्रं तु कृष्णाजिह्वाग्रगं भवेत् ।
वामे करे परे पिञ्छदण्डकं कालदण्डकम् ॥

उभयोर्दण्डयोर्मूलं स्कन्धमूलोपरि स्थितम् ।
नानागणसमायुक्तं नानाभूतसमाकुलम् ॥

स्वसव्ये भूतमूर्धस्थबलिपात्रेण संयुतम् ।
नानारूपधरैर्भूतैरनेकैः परिवारितम् ॥

भेरिकाकाहळाद्याढ्यैर्गानृत्तरवाकुलैः ।
योषितश्चानवद्याङ्ग्यो मत्प्रेक्षावश्यमोहिताः ॥

स्रस्तभूषणवस्त्राद्या बलिदानसमुन्मुखाः ।
आशीर्वादान्विताः काश्चित् काश्चिदालिङ्गनोन्मुखाः ॥
योषितो देववक्षास्यस्तननाभ्यन्तसीमकाः ।

(उत्तरकामिकागमे द्विपञ्चाशत्तमपटले ॥)

कङ्कालमूर्तिनं वक्ष्ये पादयोः पादुकान्वितम् ।
सुस्थितं वामपादं तु गमनापेक्षयापरम् ॥
पादमीषत्समुद्धृत्य करोत्वधिकसुन्दरम् ।
शुद्धश्वेतनिभं चारु सर्वाभरणभूषितम् ॥
रत्नकञ्चुकबद्धाङ्गं जटामकुटमण्डितम् ।
धुर्द्धूरपुष्पं नागं च वामे दक्षेन्दुशेखरम् ॥
किंचित्प्रकाशितान्तस्स्थदशनांशुविराजितम् ।
दक्षिणं हरिणीवक्त्रे व्यापितं सिंहकर्णवत् ॥
वामहस्ते च दण्डं तु कङ्कालास्थि च धारयेत् ।
तदस्यस्थातु(स्थ्याकृतिः?) निर्मांसं द्विपादं द्विकरान्वितम् ॥
कृष्णश्यामनिभाकारमपाने दण्डवेशनम् ।
दण्डे कङ्कालपादौ द्वौ रज्जुना बन्धयेद्बुधः ॥
केतुदण्डेन नेत्राभ्यां निष्क्रान्तं रुधिरं तु वा ।
एवं कङ्कालदण्डं तु वामस्कन्धोपरि न्यसेत् ॥
बलिपात्रधृतं भूतं वामेऽग्रे गमनान्वितम् ।
दक्षिणेऽन्नं तु तत्पार्श्वे निधाय कृतजायया ॥

किंचित्प्रकाशितं योनिसंयुतानतवाससा ।
संभ्रान्तमनसोपेतं जायास्सर्वास्त्वनेकशः ॥
व्याघ्रचर्माम्बरोपेतं दुकूलवसनान्वितम् ।
दक्षिणे कटिपार्श्वे तु क्षुरिकाश्चैव बन्धयेत् ॥
क्षुरिका हैमसंकाशा रूपबंधसमन्विता ।
यक्षकिन्नरासिद्धाद्यैस्सेवितं पूजितं नुतम् ॥
चामरैरर्कचन्द्राभ्यां वीजितं रत्नभूषितैः ।
अण्डानां सुस्थितार्थं तु सर्वलोकोपकारकम् ॥
कङ्कालमोचनार्थं तु स्यात् कङ्ककाभिधः ।
(शिल्परत्ने द्वाविंशपटले ॥)

चतुर्भुजं त्रिनेत्रं च कपर्दमकुटान्वितम् ।
पादे पादुकसंयुक्तं किंचिद्वै गमनोन्मुखम् ॥
सर्वाभरणसंयुक्तं यज्ञसूत्रोपशोभितम् ।
शङ्खं तु वामकर्णे तु दक्षिणेन च कुण्डलम् ॥
क्षौमवस्त्रधरं कुर्याद्दक्षिणे क्षुरिकायुधम् ।
डमरुं वामहस्ते तु प्रहरं दक्षिणे करे ॥
कङ्कालदण्डमूलं तु पिञ्छदण्डस्य मूलकम् ।
वामे त्वपरहस्तेन सङ्गृहीतं तु कल्पयेत् ॥
उभयोर्दण्डकाग्रं तु अंसकोपरि विन्यसेत् ।
कृष्णामुखगतं हस्तं दक्षिणेऽपरहस्तकम् ॥

नानानागसमायुक्तं किंचित्प्रहसिताननम् ।
बलिपात्रधरं भूतदेवं वामे तु कारयेत् ॥

भिक्षादानोन्मुखस्त्रीभिर्मोहिताभिस्समाकुलम् ।
नानाभूतसमायुक्तं नानालीलासमन्वितम् ॥

ढक्कासंयुक्तहस्तं तु वरदं चेति कीर्तितम् ।
हरिणीजिह्वया हस्तस्याग्रमालेपितं कुरु ॥

कङ्कालधारिणं हस्तं कटकं चेति कीर्तितम् ।
कक्षतुल्यं तु तस्याग्रं यमं दोर्मणिबन्धयोः ॥

बिम्बस्य त्रिमुखं वापि सार्धत्रिमुखमेव वा ।
कारयेद्भूतरूपाणि पञ्चतालेन बुद्धिमान् ॥

देवस्तनसमोच्चं वा कक्षोच्चं वा विशेषतः ।
नारीस्संकल्पयेद्धीमानुभयोः पार्श्वयोरपि ॥

(पूर्वकारणागमे एकादशपटले ॥)

भिक्षाटनमूर्तिः ।

अथ वक्ष्ये विशेषेण भिक्षाटनमहेश्वरम् ।
पादौ पादुकसंयुक्तौ वामपादं तु सुस्थितम् ॥

ईषदुद्धृत्य सव्यं तु पादं तु गमनोत्सुकम् ।
ललाटमध्यमासव्ये नवाष्टौ वा यवान्तरे ॥

पादौ पादुकसंयुक्तौ पादुकारहितौ तु वा ।
सुविकीर्णजटाभारं जटामण्डलमेव वा ॥

वृत्तबन्धजटा वाथ नग्नरूपं नताननम् ।
ललाटपट्टसंयुक्तं करेधृत्वे(रोत्वर्धे ?)न्दुशेखरम् ॥

सर्वाभरणसंयुक्तं कटिसूत्रविवर्जितम् ।
शुद्धश्वेतनिभं वर्णं नानानागविभूषितम् ॥

दक्षिणे पूर्वहस्तं तु मृगस्यास्यान्तिकं भवेत् ।
वामे तु पूर्वहस्तं तु वरदं स्यात्कपालधृक् ॥

दक्षिणे परहस्ते च डमरुं च धरेद्द्विज ! ।
वामे तु शिखिपिञ्छं च कर्तव्यं त्वतिशीतलम् ॥

सितवस्त्रोत्तरीयं च नागेन कटिवेष्टितम् ।
श्वेतयज्ञोपवीतं तु नीलकण्ठं त्रिपुण्ड्रधृक् ॥

पद्मपीठोपरिष्टात्तु शेषं कङ्कालरूपवत् ।

(अंशुमद्भेदागमे चतुस्सप्ततितमपटले ॥)

एष एव परो दवो नग्नः कङ्कालवर्जितः ।
विकीर्णोभयपार्श्वस्थजटालकविभूषितः ॥

कटिदेशे प्रकर्तव्यः फणिसूत्रेण वेष्टितः ।
सत्कपालं च वरदं वामहस्तं तु कल्पयेत् ॥

दिव्यढक्कासमायुक्तं वामस्थमपरं करम् ।
शिखिपिञ्छधरं कुर्यात्सव्यस्थमपरं करम् ॥

व्यालपार्श्वस्थितः कार्यः पूर्वसव्यो मृगास्यगः ।
सव्यं कोणसमायुक्तमथवा परिकल्पयेत् ॥
कपालहस्तपृष्ठं तु नाभिदघ्नं प्रकल्पयेत् ।
डमरूच्चं तु कर्णान्तं तद्धस्तमणिबन्धनात् ॥
कर्णान्तं षोडशैर्मात्रैः शेषं कङ्कालवद्भवेत् ।
भिक्षाटनो हरः प्रोक्तः पृथग्विष्णुयुतो न वा ॥

(उत्तरकामिकागमे द्विपञ्चाशत्तमपटले ॥)

सृष्टिमूर्तेः कपालं तु स्थितिमूर्तेः कलेबरम् ।
डमरुकसमोपेतं भस्मसर्पैरलङ्कृतम् ॥
कण्ठे(स्कन्धे ?) शूलसमायुक्तं छन्नवीरसमायुतम् ।
पादुकोपरि पादौ च सर्वभूतसमावृतम् ॥
एवं भिक्षाटनं वत्स ! कामनाशमथ शृणु ।

(सुप्रभेदागमे चतुस्त्रिंशत्तमपटले ॥)

अथ भिक्षाटनं वक्ष्ये पादौ पादुकसंयुतौ ।
सुस्थितं वामपादं तु गन्तुं दक्षिणमुद्धृतम् ॥
सुविकीर्णजटाभारं जटामण्डलमेव वा ।
विवृथ(वृत्त ?)बन्धजटा वाथ उपानरहितं तु वा ॥
ललाटपट्टसंयुक्तं करोत्वर्धेन्दुशेखरम् ।
सर्वाभरणसंयुक्तं को(क ?)टिसूत्रविवार्जितम् ॥

शुद्धश्वेतनिभं प्रोक्तं नानानागविभूषितम् ।
दक्षिणं पूर्वहस्तं तु मृगस्यास्यान्तिकं भवेत् ॥

वामे तु पूर्वहस्तं तु वरदं तु कपालधृक् ।
दक्षिणे परहस्ते तु डमरुं चर्म्मघटितम् ॥

वामे तु शिखिपिञ्छं तु सितवस्त्रोत्तरीयकम् ।
श्वेतयज्ञोपवीतं तु कटौ नागेन वेष्टितम् ॥

नीलकण्ठं त्रिपुण्ड्राढ्यं पद्मपीठोपरि स्थितम् ।
कङ्कालमूर्तिवच्छेषं सर्वमत्र विशेषतः ॥

(शिल्परत्ने द्वाविंशपटले ॥)

त्रिनेत्रं चतुर्भुजं नग्नरूपं किंचित्स्मिताननम् ।
आवृतालङ्कृताभङ्गी पादे पादुकसंयुतम् ॥

दक्षिणे तु कराग्रं तु हरिणास्यानुगं भवेत् ।
दक्षिणापरहस्तं तु डमरुकयुतं भवेत् ॥

वामे कपालहस्तं तु अपरं पिञ्छधारिणम् ।
कुञ्चितं दक्षिणं पादं वामपादं तु स्वास्तिकम् (सुस्थितम् ?) ॥

सभङ्गस्थानकं कुयार्द् गमनोन्मुखरूपकम् ।
कपालोपेतहस्तस्य पृष्ठं नाभिसमं भवेत् ॥

शेषं सर्वं विशेषेण कङ्कालस्योक्तवद्भवेत् ।

(कारणागमे एकादशपटले ॥)

गङ्गाधरादिमूर्तयः ।

गङ्गाधरादिमूर्तयः ।

गङ्गाधरः ।

गङ्गाधरमहं वक्ष्ये संक्षेपाच्छृणु सुव्रत ! ।
सुस्थितं दक्षिणं पादं वामपादं तु कुञ्चितम् ॥

दाक्षिणे पूर्वहस्तं तु वरं देव्याननाश्रितम् ।
वामे तु पूर्वहस्तेन देवीमालिङ्गनं कुरु ॥

दक्षिणे परहस्तं तु जटाजाह्नविसंयुतम् ।
उष्णीषान्तं समद्धृत्य वामे कृष्णमृगं धृतम् ॥

देवस्य वामपार्श्वे तु गौरी विरहितानना ।
सुस्थितं वामपादं तु कुञ्चितं दक्षिणं भवेत् ॥

प्रसार्य दक्षिणं हस्तं वामहस्तं तु पुष्पधृक् ।
अथवा दक्षिणं हस्तं प्रकोष्ठं तिर्य्यगन्तं भवेत् ॥

श्रोण्यधस्तात्तलं लम्ब्य वस्त्रं धृतमिवाकृतिः ।
भागीरथीं दक्षपार्श्वे ऋषिभिः प्रार्थितेश्वरम् ॥

गङ्गाधराकृतिर्ह्येवं ततो वै त्रिपुरान्तकम् ।

(अंशुमद्भेदागमे षट्षष्टपटले ॥)

गङ्गाधरप्रतिष्ठां तु वक्ष्ये तल्लक्षणान्विताम् ।

चतुर्भुजस्त्रिनेत्रश्च जटामकुटमण्डितः ॥

दक्षिणाभयहस्तस्थोऽप्यन्यत्र कटकामुखः ।

तेन हस्तेन धृत्वैकां जटां गङ्गासमन्विताम् ॥

संस्थितस्तु प्रसन्नात्मा कृष्णापरशुसंयुतः ।

जटायुक्तकरोच्चं तु कर्णस्योर्ध्वसमं भवेत् ॥

तदन्तरं तु द्विमुखमाभङ्गेन समन्वितम् ।

इन्दुशेखरवच्छेषं कर्तव्यं मुनिपुङ्गवाः ! ॥

देवस्य वामभागे तु देवीं कुर्यात्सलक्षणाम् ।

कुर्याद् भगीरथं देवं नाभ्यास्थस्यन(स्यस्तन?)सीमगम् ॥

गलान्तं वाष्टतालेन विलम्बितजटान्वितम् ।

वल्कलाम्बरसंयुक्तं हृन्मस्तककृताञ्जलिम् ॥

द्विनेत्रं च द्विबाहुं तमेवं गङ्गाधरो भवेत् ।

(उत्तरकामिकागमे त्रिषष्टितमपटले ॥)

गङ्गाधरमहं वक्ष्ये सर्वलोकसुखावहम् ।

सुस्थितं दक्षिणं पादं वामपादं तु कुञ्चितम् ॥

विश्लिष्यं स्याज्जटाबन्धं वामे त्वीषन्नताननम् ।

दक्षिणे पूर्वहस्ते तु वरदं दक्षिणेन(बामेन?) तु ॥

देवीमुपाश्रितेनैव देवीमालिङ्ग्य कारयेत् ।
दक्षिणापरहस्तेनोद्धृत्योष्णीषसीमकम् ॥
स्पृशेज्जटागतां गङ्गां वामेन मृगमुद्धरेत् ।
देवस्य वामपार्श्वे तु देवी विरहिताननना ॥
सुस्थितं वामपादं तु कुञ्चितं दाक्षिणं भवेत् ।
प्रसार्य दक्षिणं हस्तं वामहस्तं तु पुष्पधृक् ॥
सर्वाभरणसंयुक्तौ सर्वालङ्कारसंयुतौ ।
भगीरथं दक्षिणे तु पार्श्वे मुनिवरान्वितम् ॥

(शिल्परत्ने द्वाविंशपटले ॥)

चतुर्भुजं त्रिनेत्रं च कपर्दमकुटान्वितम् ।
अभयं दक्षिणं हस्तं कटकं वामहस्तकम् ॥
कपर्दमकुटं तेन गृहीतं जाह्नवीयुतम् ।
वामदक्षिणहस्तौ तु कृष्णापरशुसंयुतम् ॥
अभयं पूर्ववत्प्रोक्तं कपर्दोपेतहस्तकम् ।
तस्य वामे भवानीं तु कारयेल्लक्षणान्विताम् ॥
जान्वन्तं वापि नाभ्यन्तं भागीरथ्यास्तु मानकम् ।
प्रलम्बकजटोपेतमुष्णीषं जल(मुष्णीषाञ्जलि ?)हस्तकम् ॥
द्विभुजं च त्रिनेत्रं च वल्कलाम्बरसंयुतम् ।
एवं गङ्गाधरं प्रोक्तं चण्डेशानुग्रहं शृणु ॥

(पूर्वकारणागमे एकादशपटले ॥)

अर्धनारीश्वरः ।

अथार्धनारीमूर्तिं तु वक्ष्येऽहं शृणु सुव्रत ! ।
चतुर्भुजं वा द्विभुजं द्विविधं परिकीर्त्तितम् ॥

सुस्थितं दक्षिणं पादमितरं कुञ्चितं भवेत् ।
वामेऽर्धं पार्वतीरूपं दक्षिणेऽर्धं महेश्वरम् ॥

अभयं परशुं सव्यहस्तौ तत्तु शिवांशकम् ।
वृषमूर्ध्नि च विन्यस्तं कूर्परं वामहस्तके ॥

तदन्यद्वामहस्तं तु कटकं पुष्पहस्तकम् ।
द्विभुजे वरदं पूर्वं परहस्तं तु पुष्पधृक् ॥

शिवस्याभरणं सव्ये वामे स्त्रीभूषणं मतम् ।
पुंस्तनं दक्षिणे पार्श्वे वामे नारीपयोधरम् ॥

अथवा कुञ्चितं सव्यं वामपादं तु सुस्थितम् ।
सव्यं शूलधरं हस्तं वामं पुष्पधरं करम् ॥

वरदं दक्षिणं हस्तं वृषमूर्ध्नि तु कूर्परम्[१] ।
कपालं दक्षिणे हस्ते वामहस्तं प्रसारितम् ॥

दक्षिणे रौद्रदृष्टिस्स्यात् वामपार्श्वे तु शीतलम् ।
दुकूलं चोरुमध्यस्थं सव्यं गुल्पमन्यकम्[२] ॥

---

१ 'वरदं दक्षिणं हस्तमन्योऽक्षिशिरपूर्वक' मिति पाठान्तरम् ।
२ 'सव्यं गुल्फन्तमन्यक' मिति पाठान्तरम् ।

एवं समासतः प्रोक्तमर्धनारीश्वरं परम् ।
(अंशुमद्भेदागमे एकोनसप्ततितमपटले ॥)

उमार्धं वामभागं तु हरार्धं दक्षिणं वपुः ।
सजटामकुटं दक्षं शश्यर्धाङ्कितमग्रजाः ! ॥
करण्डमकुटं वाममलकेन समन्वितम् ।
ललाटं दक्षिणे भागे नयनार्धेन संयुतम् ॥
पत्रं तु वामकर्णे स्याद्वालिकेनापि संयुतम् ।
सनक्रकुण्डलं सव्ये तं विना वाथ कारयेत् ॥
सव्ये टङ्काभये हस्ते उत्पलं वामगे करे ।
देव्यध्यायोदितास्त्रं वा दर्पणासक्तलोचनम् ॥
उमाभागं स्तनोपेतं चित्रवस्त्रपरिच्छदम् ।
व्याघ्राजिनाम्बरं सव्यपादं कुञ्चितमिष्यते ॥
सुस्थितं वामचरणं नूपुरेणाप्यलङ्कृतम् ।
वामं मरतकाभं स्याद्दक्षिणं मणिसन्निभम् ॥
चन्द्रशेखरवच्छेषं कर्तव्यं हि मुनीश्वराः ।
(उत्तरकामिकागमे षष्टितमपटले ॥)

दक्षिणार्धे हरं चैव वामार्धे पार्वती तथा ।
दक्षिणं कुञ्चितं पादं वामपादमृजु स्थितम् ॥
हरस्य दक्षिणे हस्ते कूर्परं वृषके स्थितम् ।
प्रकोष्ठे शुकसंयुक्तं हरं परशुसंयुतम् ॥

वामे कटकहस्तं तु दक्षिणे त्वभयं स्मृतम् ।
श्यामवर्णमुखां देवीं रक्तवर्णं हरं तथा ॥
व्याघ्रचर्माम्बरं देवं पार्वतीं क्षौमधारिणीम् ।

(सुप्रभेदागमे चतुस्त्रिंशत्तमपटले ॥)

अर्धनारीश्वरं वक्ष्ये सुस्थितं दक्षिणाङ्घ्रिकम् ।
कुञ्चितं वामपादं तु सर्वाभरणभूषितम् ॥
वामार्धं पार्वतीरूपं दक्षिणार्धं महेश्वरम् ।
अभयं परशुं दक्षहस्ते वामगतं भुजम् ॥
वृषस्य मूर्ध्नि विन्यस्तकूर्परं चारु सुन्दरम् ।
पुष्पधृक्कटकं त्वन्यं चतुर्भुजमिदं स्मृतम् ॥

(शिल्परत्ने द्वाविंशपटले ॥)

अर्धनारीश्वरो देवः कथ्यते लक्षणान्वितः ।
दक्षिणं पुरुषाकारं वामं योषिन्मयं वपुः ॥
त्रिशूलं दक्षिणे हस्ते वामहस्ते च दर्पणम् ।
उत्पलं वा प्रकुर्वीत केयूरवलयान्विते ॥
कर्णे तु दक्षिणे नागं वामे कर्णे तु कुण्डलम् ।
जटाभारो दक्षिणे स्यादर्धचन्द्रार्धभूषितः ॥
कुन्तलान् कबरीभारान्वामभागेन विन्यसेत् ।
ललाटे लोचनस्यार्धं तिलकार्धं प्रकल्पयेत् ॥

विशालं दक्षिणं वक्षो वामं पीनपयोधरम् ।
द्वीपिचर्मपरीधानं दक्षिणं जघनस्थलम् ॥

वामे लम्बपरीधानं कटिसूत्रत्रयान्वितम् ।
वामस्य दक्षिणं पादं पद्मस्योपरि कल्पयेत् ॥

तस्यार्धं च तथा वामं नूपुरालङ्कृतं लिखेत् ।

(शिल्परत्नसंयोजिते कस्मिंश्चिद् ग्रन्थे ॥)

अर्धं देवस्य नारी तु कर्तव्या शुभलक्षणा ।
अर्धं तु पुरुषः कार्यस्सर्वलक्षणभूषितः ॥

ईश्वरार्धे जटाजूटं कर्तव्यं चन्द्रभूषितम् ।
उमार्धे तिलकं कुर्यात् सीमन्तमलकं तथा ॥

भस्मोद्धूलितमर्धं तु अर्धं कुङ्कुमभूषितम् ।
नागोपवीतिनं चार्धमर्धं हारविभूषितम् ॥

वामार्धे तु स्तनं कुर्यात् घनं पीनं सुवर्तुलम् ।
उमार्धे तु प्रकर्तव्यं सुवस्त्रेण च वेष्टितम् ॥

मेखलां दापयेत्तत्र वज्रवैडूर्यभूषिताम् ।
ऊर्ध्वलिङ्गं महेशार्धं सर्पमेखलमण्डितम् ॥

पादं च देवदेवस्य समपद्मोपरि स्थितम् ।
सालक्तकं स्मृतं वाममञ्जनेन(म्मञ्जीरेण?) विभूषितम् ॥

त्रिशूलमक्षसूत्रं च भुजयोस्सव्ययोस्स्मृतम् ।
दर्पणं चोत्पलं कार्यं भुजयोरपसव्ययोः ॥

(विष्णुधर्मोत्तरे ॥)

सबालेन्दुजटाभारमैशमर्धं तु दक्षिणम् ।
उमार्धं वामभागे तु सीमन्तातिलकालकम् ॥

नयनार्धं ललाटे तु संयुक्तं दक्षिणांशके ।
दक्षिणे कुण्डलं कर्णे वामकर्णे तु पत्रकम् ॥

कुटिलं पालिकां वामे टङ्काभयौ च दक्षिणे ।
उत्पलं वामहस्ते तु केयूरकटकान्वितम् ॥

उमांशे तु स्तनं कुर्यात् वह(बह्वा?)कारधरं तु वा ।
श्रोण्यर्धं दक्षिणे शम्भोर्व्याघ्रचर्मकृताम्बरम् ॥

उमार्धं कटिसूत्रान्तं चित्रवस्त्रपरिच्छदम् ।
नूपुरालङ्कृतं वामे सव्यपादं तु कुञ्चितम् ॥

आभङ्गेन तथा कुर्यात्सार्धनारीश्वरं वपुः ।

(पूर्वकारणागमे एकादशपटले ॥)

हर्यर्धमूर्तिः ॥

अर्धनारीश्वरो ह्येवं हर्यर्धं शृणुत द्विजाः ! ।
प्राग्वत्कृत्वा महेशार्धं विष्णवर्धमितरत्र च ॥

भुजद्वययुतं शङ्खकटकस्तत्र संमतः ।
पीताम्बरसमोपेतं सर्वाभरणसंयुतम् ॥
हर्यर्धमेवं ब्रह्मादिभागं चैवं समाचरेत् ।
(उत्तरकामिकागमे षष्टितमपटले ॥

पीताम्बरधरं विष्णुं व्याघ्रचर्माम्बरं हरम् ।
विष्णुं किरीटसंयुक्तं शङ्करं तु जटान्वितम् ॥
श्यामवर्णं हरिं चैव शङ्करं युक्तरूपिणम् ।
हरिरर्धमिदं प्रोक्तं भिक्षाटनमतः परम् ॥
(सुप्रभेदागमे चतुस्त्रिंशत्तमपटले ॥)

अथ वक्ष्ये हरिहरं सुस्थितं समपादकम् ।
दक्षिणे त्वभयं वामे कटकं तूरुसंयुतम् ॥
परशुं दक्षिणे वामे शङ्खं तु परहस्तके ।
वाममर्धं हरिं कुर्य्याद्धरमन्यार्धमाचरेत् ॥
क्रमाच्छ्यामप्रवालाभमुभयोचितभूषणम् ।
दक्षिणे व्युग्रदृष्टिस्स्याद्वामे शीतलनेत्रकम् ॥
किंचित्प्रकाशितोर्ध्वाक्षं दक्षिणार्धे ललाटके ।
शिरश्चक्रसमायुक्तं तस्य लक्षणमुच्यते ॥
रुद्राङ्गुलविशालं तु तद्वानांशे गतं नम् (?) ।
सुवृत्तं चक्रवत्तन्तु पद्माकृतिरथापि वा ॥

शिरश्चक्रविशालस्य सप्तभागैकभागिकम् ।
शिरश्चक्रस्य नालस्य विस्तारं परिकीर्तितम् ॥
चक्रतारत्रिभागैकं चक्रादाशिरसोऽन्तरम् ।
अग्राल्ललाटपट्टस्य शिरश्चक्रस्य नालकम् ॥
गुणाङ्गुले तु कव्यूर्ध्वे चक्रनालस्थितिर्भवेत् ।
चक्राद् गुणांशमालम्ब्य पुष्पमाला तु मध्यमात् ॥
सर्वेषामपि देवानां देवीनामेवमाचरेत् ।

(शिल्परत्ने द्वाविंशपटले ॥)

देवं हरिहरं वक्ष्ये सर्वपातकनाशनम् ।
दक्षिणे शङ्करस्यार्धमर्धं विष्णोश्च वामतः ॥
बालेन्दुभूषितः कार्यो जटाभारस्तु दक्षिणे ।
नानारत्नमयं द्रव्यं किरीटं वामभागतः ॥
दक्षिणं सर्पराजेन भूषितं कर्णमालिखेत् ।
मकराकारकं दिव्यं कुण्डलं वामकर्णतः ॥
वरदो दक्षिणो हस्तो द्वितीयश्शूलभृत्तदा ।
कर्तव्यौ वामभागे तु शङ्खचक्रगदाधरौ ॥
दक्षिणे वसनं कार्यं द्वीपिचर्ममयं शुभम् ।
पीताम्बरमयं भव्यं जघनं सव्यमालिखेत् ॥
वामपादः प्रकर्तव्यो नानारत्नविभूषितः ।
दक्षिणाङ्घ्रिः प्रकर्तव्यो भुजगेन्द्रविभूषितः ॥

प्रतिमालक्षणानि ।

शीतांशुधवलः कार्यश्शिवभागो विचक्षणैः ।
अतसीपुष्पसंकाशो विष्णोर्भागो विरच्यते ॥

(शिल्परत्नसंयोजिते कस्मिंश्चिद् ग्रन्थे ॥)

कार्यं हरिहरस्यापि दक्षिणार्धं सदाशिवः ।
वाममर्धं हृषीकेशश्श्वेतनीलाकृतिः क्रमात् ॥
वरत्रिशूलचक्राब्जधारिणो बाहवः क्रमात् ।
दक्षिणे वृषभः पार्श्वे वामभागे विहङ्गराट् ॥

(विष्णुधर्मोत्तरे ॥)

ईशार्धं पूर्ववत्प्रोक्तं विष्ण्वर्धे मकुटं नयेत् ।
वामे तु द्विभुजोपेतं केयूरकटकोज्ज्वलम् ॥
स्यान्नक्रकुण्डलं कर्णे कटकं शङ्खहस्तकम् ।
अर्धपीताम्बरोपेतं भूषणैर्भूषणार्हकैः ॥
ऋज्वागतं तथा सर्वं चन्द्रशेखरवत्कुरु ।
हरिरर्धमिदं प्रोक्तं सुखासनमथ श्रृणु ॥

(पूर्वकारणागमे एकादशपटले ॥)

कल्याणसुन्दरः ।

अथ वक्ष्ये विशेषेण कल्याणसुन्दरं ततः ।
सुस्थितं वामपादं तु दक्षिणं कुञ्चितं भवेत् ॥

दक्षिणं पूर्वहस्तं तु गौरीदक्षिणहस्तधृक् ।

वरदं वामहस्तं तु परहस्तद्वयोस्ततः ॥

दक्षिणे परशुं वामे धृतं कृष्णमृगं परम् ।

जटामकुटसंयुक्तं सर्वाभरणभूषितम् ॥

देहं प्रवालवर्णाभं देवेशस्य विशेषतः ।

सव्ये श्यामनिभा देवी प्राग्वन्मानादिसंयुता ॥

उत्पलं वामहस्ते तु धृतं दक्षिणहस्तकम् ।

शम्भोर्हस्तेन संग्राह्यं लज्जालम्बाननान्विता ॥

पार्वत्यनुगता श्रीर्भूस्सर्वाभरणभूषिते ।

हस्ताभ्यां संस्पृशेदेते गौर्यायास्तु कटीं द्विज ! ॥

देवाग्रे कारयेत्कुण्डे होमकर्म प्रजापतिः ।

शम्भोर्वै स्तनसीमान्तं प्रजेशस्योदयं भवेत् ॥

चतुर्भुजं चतुर्वक्त्रं सर्वाभरणभूषितम् ।

कुण्डिका चाक्षमाला च वामदक्षिणतः परे ॥

स्रुक्स्रवौ पूर्वहस्तौ द्वौ धृतौ वामेतरौ क्रमात् ।

उत्तराभिमुखासीनः पद्मपीठे प्रजापतिः ॥

प्रागग्रौ देविदेवेशौ देवी देवस्य दक्षिणे ।

दक्षिणाभिमुखो विष्णुर्होमस्योत्तरतास्स्थितः ॥

शम्भोर्वै नासिसीमान्तं श्रेष्ठं अ......स्तनान्तकम्[१] ।

श्यामवर्णं समभङ्गं शङ्खचक्रं परे करे ॥

हिरण्यकरकेणापः पूर्वहस्तद्वयोरपि ।

सङ्गृह्य वरदे हस्ते दद्यादुकपूर्वकम् ॥

अनादिगोत्रसम्भूतस्स शिवः परमेश्वरः ।

आदिगोत्रामिमां गौरीं तवैवास्माद्ददाम्यहम् ॥

इत्युक्त्वा वरदे हस्ते दद्याद्भक्त्योदकं हरिः ।

अष्टविद्येशलोकेशास्सिद्धयक्षगणादयः ॥

ऋषयश्चैव गन्धर्वा मातरश्चान्यदेवताः ।

तत्तच्छक्तिसमोपेता हृदयेऽञ्जलिसंयुताः ॥

सम्भ्रान्तमनसोपेतास्संवीक्ष्य परितस्स्थिताः ।

एवं कल्याणमूर्तिस्तु अर्धनारीश्वरं ततः ॥

(अंशुमद्भेदागमेऽष्टषष्टपटले ॥)

जटामकुटसंयुक्तश्चन्द्रार्धकृतशेखरः ।

त्रिदृक् चतुर्भुजश्चैव नवयौवनगष्टुतः[२] ॥

समभङ्गयुतो देवः स्थानकस्थः प्रकीर्तितः ।

सकुञ्चत्सव्यसत्पादस्थितसव्येतराङ्घ्रिकः ॥

---

१ 'शम्भोर्वै नासिसीमान्तं श्रेष्ठायामं स्तनान्तक' मिति पाठान्तरम् । एतदनन्तरं 'ययोर्मध्येऽष्टवाभाज्यं नवधात् केशवोदयम्' इत्यादर्शान्तरे वर्तते ।
२ 'नवयौवनगर्वित' इति पाठान्तरम् ।

इन्दुशेखरहस्ताभपरहस्तद्वयान्वितः ।
जलसङ्ग्रहणे योग्यवरवामकरान्वितः ॥

स्वदक्षिणगृहीतो वा दक्षहस्तः प्रसन्नधीः ।
पूर्ववत्कथितं देव्या मानं विप्रोत्तमास्त्विह ॥

देवीदृगास्यचिबुककक्षचूचुकमानता ।
तद्देव्यपरभागस्था श्रीदेवी सर्वलक्षणैः ॥

युक्ता देविकटिस्पृष्टकराभ्यामपि संयुता ।
देवोच्चदशभागैकभागादेकादशावधि ॥

भागमानयुतः श्यामः किरीटमकुटान्वितः ।
ग्रहीतशङ्खचक्रश्च हस्ताभ्यां धृतयापि च[1] ॥

तोयकुण्डिकयोपेतो विष्णुरेष उदाहृतः ।
तदूर्ध्वे दक्षिणं हस्तं धारापाताय कल्पितम् ॥

हरेरुक्तप्रमाणेन ब्रह्माणमपि कारयेत् ।
चतुर्मुखं चतुर्बाहुं जटामकुटमण्डितम् ॥

होमोन्मुखं प्रसन्नं तं कुङ्कुमक्षोदसन्निभम् ।
मौञ्जीमेखलयोपेतं सोपवीतोत्तरीयकम् ॥

वामेतरकरावूर्ध्वौ कमण्डल्वक्षधारकौ ।
वराभयकरौ पूर्वौ स्यातां तौ दक्षिणेतरौ ॥

---

१ ‘ धृतवापि च ’ इति पाठान्तरम् ।

सूचिपादाक्रियो(सूचीपताकयो ?)पेतावन्यौ तु कटकामुखौ[१] ।
ब्रह्मरूपमिति ख्यातं तथा पद्मासनस्थितम् ॥
देवस्याङ्गुलमानेन द्वाविंशत्यङ्गुलो भवेत् ।
अग्निकुण्डस्य विष्कम्भस्त्रिमेखलयुतस्य च ॥
मेखलैकाङ्गुला प्रोक्ता प्रत्येकं मुनिपुङ्गवाः ! ।
द्वादशाङ्गुलविस्तारदैर्घ्या सा सप्तजिह्वकः ॥
पञ्चजिह्वायुतो वाग्निः कुण्डमध्यस्थितस्त्वयम् ।
(उत्तरकामिकागमे अष्टपञ्चशत्तमपटले ॥)

अथ कल्याणमूर्तस्तु लक्षणं सर्वमङ्गलम् ।
सुस्थितं वामपादं तु दक्षिणं कुञ्चितं भवेत् ॥
दक्षिणं पूर्वहस्तं तु गौरीदक्षिणहस्तधृक् ।
वरदं वामहस्तं तु परहस्तद्वये तथा ॥
दक्षिणे परशुं वामे तथा कृष्णमृगं परम् ।
जटामकुटसंयुक्तं सर्वाभरणभूषितम् ॥
देहं प्रवालवर्णाभं देवेशस्य विशेषतः ।
तत्र श्यामनिभा देवी प्राग्वन्मादिन(मानादि?)संयुता ॥
उत्पलं वामहस्ते तु धृत्वा दक्षिणहस्तकम् ।
शम्भोर्हस्तेन सङ्ग्राह्यं लज्जाभरणसंयुता ॥

---

१ 'खवपातकरोपेता.' विति पाठान्तरम् ।

पार्वतीमनुगा श्रीर्भूस्सर्वाभरणभूषिता ।
हस्ताभ्यां संस्पृशेदेवं गौरीमपि करद्वये ॥

देवाग्रे कारयेत्कुण्डे तत्र होमं प्रजापतिः ।
शम्भोर्वै स्तनसीमान्तं प्रजेशस्योदयं तथा ॥

चतुर्भुजं चतुर्वक्त्रं सर्वाभरणभूषितम् ।
प्रागग्रौ देविदेवेशौ देवी देवस्य दक्षिणे ॥

दक्षिणाभिमुखो विष्णुर्होमस्योत्तरदिक्स्थितः ।
शम्भोर्वै नाभिसीमान्तं श्रेष्ठं स्तनतलोन्नतम् ॥

कन्यतं(सं?) तु तयोर्मध्ये पूर्ववन्नवधा स्मृतम् ।
श्यामवर्णसमायुक्तं शङ्खचक्रौ परे करे ॥

हिरण्यकरकेणापः पूर्वहस्तद्वयेन तु ।
संगृह्य वरदे हस्ते दद्यादुकपूर्वकम् ॥

अष्टलोकेशविद्येशास्सिद्धयक्षगणादयः ।
ऋषयश्चैव गन्धर्वा मातरश्चान्यदेवताः ॥

तत्तच्छक्तिसमोपेता हृदयाञ्जलिसंयुताः ।
संभ्रान्तमनसोपेतास्संवीक्ष्य परितस्स्थिताः ॥

(शिल्परत्ने द्वाविंशपटले ॥)

सचन्द्रार्धजटामौलिसौम्यं प्रथमयौवनम् ।
चतुर्भुजं त्रिनेत्रं च हारकेयूरभूषितम् ॥

मेखलोदरबन्धं च क्षौमवस्त्रधरं शुभम् ।
वासुकिः कुण्डलं काञ्ची तक्षको हारपुष्करम् ॥
किं च त्रिभङ्गिकं कायं दक्षपादं तु कुञ्चितम् ।
वरदं वामहस्तं तु कृष्णापरशुहस्तकम् ॥
देवस्य दक्षहस्ते तु देवीहस्तं तु संयुतम् ।
नास्यन्तं वापि चास्यान्तं हिक्कासूत्रसमं तु वा ॥
पीनोरःपीतगन्धां (पीनगण्डां) च पीनस्तनसमन्विताम् ।
द्विबाहुकां द्विनेत्रां च सर्वाभरणभूषिताम् ॥
दुकूलवसनां देवीं कुर्याद्देवस्य सव्यके ।
देवस्यायाममानं तु विभजेद् द्वादशाङ्गुलम् ॥
रुद्रांशं वा नवांशं वा वस्वंशं वैकहीनकम् ।
आयामं तद्वरेः प्रोक्तं तस्य बाहुसमन्वितम् ॥
चिबुकान्तं वाथ कक्षान्तं लक्ष्म्यायामं प्रकीर्तितम् ।
विष्णुबिम्बसमं वापि तद्वस्वंशैकहीनकम् ॥
सप्तभागैकहीनं वा रसांशैकविहीनकम् ।
अजायाममिदं तस्य चतुर्भागैकभागता ॥
अग्निज्वालोच्छ्रयं प्रोक्तं तस्यार्धं विस्तृतं भवेत् ।
देवीलक्षणमेवं स्याल्लक्ष्म्याश्च लक्षणं श्रृणु ॥
नागहस्तसमौ बाहू केयूरकटकोज्वलौ ।
शोभनाम्बरसंपन्ना श्रोणी च विपुला तथा ॥

मेखला अक्षिसूत्राङ्गा उमापार्श्वेवगार्थता (?) ।
एवं लक्ष्मीस्समाख्याता विष्णुरूपमथोच्यते ॥
किरीटमकुटोपेतं कटिसूत्रोदरबन्धनम् ।
केयूरकटकं चैव यज्ञसूत्रसमन्वितम् ॥
लम्बसूत्रसमायुक्तं पीताम्बरसमायुतम् ।
मकरंकुण्डलोपेतं श्रीवत्सं वक्षसि स्थितम् ॥
शङ्खचक्रधरं कुण्डं हस्तद्वयेन धारिणम् ।
जलधारोन्मुखं किंचिद्वक्रेणैव समायुतम् ॥
विष्णुरूपं समाख्यातं ब्रह्मरूपमथ श्रृणु ।
चतुर्भुजं(मुखं?) चतुर्बाहुं कमण्डल्वक्षधारिणम् ॥
यज्ञसूत्रोत्तरीयं तु जटामकुटसंयुतम् ।
सव्यहस्तेऽक्षमालां च वामहस्ते कमण्डलुम् ॥
स्रुवं दक्षिणहस्ते तु पताका वामहस्तके ।
अम्बुजासनकासीनं ब्रह्माणं होमसंमुखम् ॥
एवं वैवाह्यमुद्दिष्टमुमया सहितं श्रृणु ।

(पूर्वकारणागमे एकादशपटले ॥)

वृषवाहनमूर्तिः ।

वृषवाहनमूर्तेस्तु लक्षणं वक्ष्यतेऽधुना ।
दक्षिणं सुस्थितं[१] पादं वामपादं तु कुञ्चितम् ॥

---

१ 'स्वस्तिक' मिति पाठान्तरम् ।

वृषस्य मस्तकोर्ध्वे तु न्यसे(स्ये?)द्वै वामकूर्परम् ।
हिक्कासूत्रादधो विप्र! कला वा द्विर्नवाङ्गुलम् ॥
तस्मादासनसीमकं वृषस्योच्छ्र्यं ख्यातम्[१] ।
पक्षषोडशमात्रं वा नतं तत्सिंहकर्णवत् ॥
वक्रदण्डायुधं तस्मिन् कल्पयेत्तु चलाचलम् ।
स्थिताङ्घ्रिजानूर्ध्वसीमाद्धिक्कासूत्रान्तमुन्नतम् ॥
कनिष्ठिकापरीणाहमग्रं वक्रत्रयान्वितम् ।
लोहजं दारुजं वाथ वक्रदण्डैवमाचरेत् ॥
परहस्तद्वयोश्चैव टङ्ककृष्णमृगं धरेत् ।
टङ्कं दक्षिणहस्ते तु वामहस्ते मृगं धरेत् ॥
जटामकुटसंयुक्तं जटाभारं तु लम्बितम् ।
जटाबन्धशिरो वापि कर्तुरिच्छावशान्नयेत् ॥
सर्वाभरणसंयुक्तं रक्ताभं रक्तवाससम् ।
वामपार्श्वे त्वु(ह्यु?)मादेवी दक्षिणे वा विशेषतः ॥
सुस्थितं दक्षिणं पादं वामपादं तु कुञ्चितम् ।
उत्पलं दक्षिणे हस्ते वामहस्तं प्रसारितम् ॥

---

१ 'वामकोर्परलम्बस्या तस्मादास्तनसीमकम् । वृषभस्योच्छ्र्यं ख्यातं पादस्थाकधीताङ्गुलम् ।' इति पाठान्तरम् ।

श्रीमानोक्तविधानेन उमादेवीं तु कारयेत् ।
वृषवाहनमाख्यातं नृत्तमूर्तिमथ शृणु ॥

(अंशुमद्भेदागमे चतुष्षष्टपटले ॥)

वृषारूढप्रतिष्ठां तु वक्ष्ये तल्लक्षणान्विताम् ।
चतुर्भुजेस्त्रिनेत्रस्तु जटामकुटसंयुतः ॥

परशुर्दक्षिणे हस्ते वामहस्ते मृगो भवेत् ।
पूर्वदाक्षिणहस्तस्तु कटको वक्रदण्डयुक् ॥

अस्य सव्यप्रकोष्ठं तु विन्यसेद्वृषमस्तके ।
स हस्तो हंसपक्षो वा पतकाधोमुखस्तु वा ॥

तन्मध्यमाङ्गुलाग्रेण नाभिसूत्रसमं भवेत् ।
तस्यैवा दक्षिणे देवीं कारयेल्लक्षणान्विताम् ॥

अथ स्वदक्षिणे गौरीयुक्तो वा मूर्त्यपेक्षया ।
आयुधव्यतिरिक्तैस्स्वैरङ्गैस्तु विपरीतकैः ॥

संयुक्तो वा वृषारूढस्त्वेवं मुक्तिप्रदो भवेत् ।
पृष्ठस्थो वृषभः कार्य्यो देवजानूरुकोच्छ्रयः ॥

मेढ्रान्तो नाभिसीमान्तश्शेषं सर्वं तु पूर्ववत् ।

(उत्तरकामिकागमे द्विषष्टितममटले ॥)

वृषारूढमथो वक्ष्ये वृषभं पृष्ठतस्स्थितम् ।
उमारुद्रौ स्थितौ कृत्वा कूर्परं वृषमस्तके ॥

मृगं परशुसंयुक्तं कर्तव्यं वृषवाहनम् ।

(सुप्रभेदागमे चतुस्त्रिंशत्तमपटले ॥)

दक्षिणं सुस्थितं पादं वामपादं तु कुञ्चितम् ।
वृषस्य मस्तकोर्ध्वे तु न्यस्येद्वै वामकोर्परम् ॥

तस्य दक्षिणहस्ते तु वक्रदण्डमुदाहृतम् ।
कनिष्ठाङ्गुलिपरीणाहं मध्ये वक्रत्रयान्वितम् ॥

लोहजं दारुजं वापि वक्रदण्डं प्रकल्पयेत् ।
परहस्तद्वयोश्चैव टङ्कं कृष्णमृगं न्यसेत् ॥

जटामकुटयुक्तं वा जटाभारं तु लम्बितम् ।
जटाबन्धशिरो वापि कर्तरिम्ना(कर्तुरिच्छा?)नुसारतः ॥

सर्वाभरणसंयुक्तं रक्ताभं रक्तवाससम् ।
वामपार्श्वे तु वा देवी दक्षिणे वा विशेषतः ॥

सुस्थितं दक्षिणं पादं वामपादं तु कुञ्चितम् ।
उत्पलं दक्षिणे हस्ते वामहस्तं प्रलम्बितम् ॥

(शिल्परत्ने द्वाविंशपटले ॥)

गौरीश्वरौ स्थितौ पीठे वृषभं पृष्ठतस्स्थितम् ।
त्रिनेत्रं चतुर्भुजं चैव जटामकुटसंयुतम् ॥

दिव्याम्बरधरो देवस्सर्वाभरणभूषितः ।
परशुं दक्षिणे हस्ते वामे कृष्णसमन्वितम् ॥

कटकं दक्षिणे हस्तं वृषभस्यैव मस्तके ।
वामहस्ते प्रकोष्ठं तु स्थापितं कुरु बुद्धिमान् ॥
तस्यैव वामभागे तु देवीं कुर्याद्विचक्षणः ।
वृषारूढमिदं प्रोक्तं त्रिपुरारिं शृणुष्वथ ॥

(पूर्वकारणागमे एकादशपटले ॥)

विषापहारमूर्तिः ।

एकवक्त्रं त्रिनयनं जटामकुटसंयुतम् ।
चतुर्बाहुं सुरक्तं समृगं परशुधारिणम् ॥
दक्षहस्ते गरं धृत्वा पानोन्मुखमदेक्षणम् ।
वरदं वामहस्ते तु सर्वालङ्कारसंयुतम् ॥
देवस्य वामपार्श्वे तु देवीं चैव तु कारयेत् ।

श्यामां द्विनेत्रां द्विभुजां त्रिभङ्गीं
सव्यापसव्यस्थितकुञ्चिताङ्घ्रिम् ।
कण्ठे निपीड्यस्थितसव्यलम्बां
चिन्ताकुलामीश्वरतुष्टिदात्रीम् ॥

पीतवस्त्रां द्विनयनां वाञ्छितार्थफलप्रदां ।

(श्रीतत्वनिधौ ॥)

अथातस्संप्रवक्ष्यामि विषापहरणेश्वरम् ।
चतुर्भुजं त्रिनेत्रं च किञ्चिद्दंष्ट्रकरालनम्(क ?) ॥

जटारत्ननिभं विद्यात् पूर्णचन्द्रनिभाकृतिम् ।
त्रिशूलं गण्डिकां चैव गोकर्णाकृति दक्षिणे ॥

कपालं वामहस्ते च वामे गौरीसमायुतम् ।
वामपादं तु शयनं लम्बितं सव्यपादकम् ॥

महोक्षस्थं महाभीमं कालकूटविषाशनम् ।
कण्ठमध्ये महाकालमाबध्य गौरिपाणिना ॥
व्याघ्रचर्माम्बरधरं किङ्किणीमालयावृतम् ।
वृश्चिकाभरणोपेतं सर्वाभरणभूषितम् ॥

एवं महेश्वरं ध्यात्वा प्रतिष्ठां साधकोत्तमः ।

(उत्तरकारणागमे ॥)

सदाशिवादिमूर्तयः ।

सदाशिवादिमूर्तयः ।

सदाशिवः ।

सदेशस्थापनं वक्ष्ये तल्लक्षणपुरस्सरम् ।
द्रव्यैश्शिलादिभिः कुर्य्यात्पूर्वोक्तैस्तं विशेषतः ॥

बद्धपद्मासनं श्वेतं स्थितं पञ्चास्यसंयुतम् ।
पिङ्गलाभजटाचूडं (जूटं ?) दशदोर्दण्डमण्डितम् ॥

अभयं च प्रसादं च तथा शक्तिं त्रिशूलकम् ।
खट्वाङ्गं दक्षभागस्थैर्वहन्तं करपल्लवैः ॥

भुजङ्गं चाक्षमालां च डमरुं नीलपङ्कजम् ।
बीजापूरं(बीजपूरं ?) च वामस्थैर्वहन्तं सुप्रसन्नकम् ॥

अर्चनाध्यायसंसिद्धध्यानान्तरयुतं तु वा ।
इच्छाज्ञानक्रियाशक्तित्रयसंक्लृप्तलोचनम् ॥

ज्ञानचन्द्रकलायुक्तं कलावर्षोपलक्षितम् ।
ब्रह्मसूत्रादिकं कार्य्यं सुवेशः प्रतिमोदितम् ॥

एवं सदाशिवः कार्यो मनोन्मन्या समन्वितः ।

(उत्तरकामिकागमे त्रिचत्वारिंशत्तमपटले ॥)

महासदाशिवमूर्तिः ।

प्रसन्नपञ्चविंशकस्फुटाननं जटाधरं
सुपञ्चसप्ततीक्षणं कपोलकुण्डलाङ्कितम् ।
शतार्धहस्तभूषितं वराभयान्वितं सितं
भुजङ्गभूषणं परं भजे महासदाशिवम् ॥

(मानसारे ॥)

ईशानादयः ।

ईशस्तत्पुरुषाघोरवामजातक्रमेण तु ।
सितपीतकृष्णरक्ताश्चतुर्वर्णाः प्रकीर्तिताः ॥
पञ्चवक्त्रास्स्मृतास्सर्वे दशदोर्दण्डभूषिताः ।
खड्गखेटधनुर्बाणकमण्डल्वक्षसूत्रिणः ॥
वराभयकरोपेताश्शूलपङ्कजपाणयः ।

(विष्णुधर्मोत्तरे ॥)

ईशानः ।

शुद्धस्फटिकसङ्काशो जटाचन्द्रविभूषितः ।
अक्षत्रिशूलहस्तश्च कपालं वामतोऽभयम् ॥

(रूपमण्डने ॥)

वेदाभयेष्टाङ्कुशपाशटङ्ककपालढक्काक्षकशूलपाणिः ।
सितद्युतिः पञ्चमुखोऽवतान्मामीशान ऊर्ध्वं परमप्रकाशः ॥

(शैवे कारणागमे ॥)

तत्पुरुषः ।

पीताम्बरस्तत्पुरुषः पीतयज्ञोपवीतवान् ।
मातुलिङ्गं करे वामेऽक्षमाला दक्षिणे तथा ॥

(रूपमण्डने ॥)

प्रदीप्तविद्युत्कनकावभासो विद्यावराभीतिकुठारपाणिः ।
चतुर्मुखस्तत्पुरुषस्त्रिनेत्रः प्राच्यां स्थितो रक्षतु मामजस्त्रम् ॥

(शैवे कारणागमे ॥)

अघोरः ।

दंष्ट्राकरालवदनं सर्पशीर्षं त्रिलोचनम् ।
रुण्डमालाधरं देवं सर्पकुण्डलमण्डिताम् ॥
भुजङ्गकेयूरधरं सर्पहारोपवीतिनम् ।
यो वस्ते कटिसूत्रं च गले वृश्चिकमालिकाम् ॥
नीलोत्पलदलश्यामं अतसीपुष्पसन्निभम् ।
पिङ्गाक्षं पिङ्गजटिलं शशाङ्ककृतशेखरम् ॥
तक्षकः पुष्टिकश्चैव पादयोस्तस्य नूपुरौ ।
अघोररूपकं कुर्यात्कालरूपमिवापरम् ॥
महावीर्यं महोत्साहमष्टबाहुं महाबलम् ।
त्रासयन्तं रिपोस्सङ्घं निवेशो यत्र भूतले ॥
खट्वाङ्गं च कपालं च खेटकं पाश एव च ।
वामहस्तेषु कर्तव्यमिदं शस्त्रचतुष्टयम् ॥

त्रिशूलं परशुः खड्गो दण्डश्चैवारिमर्दनः ।
शस्त्राण्येतानि चत्वारि दक्षिणेषु करेषु च ॥

(रूपमण्डने)

कुठारखेटाङ्कुशपाशशूलकपालढक्काक्षगुणान्दधानः ।
चतुर्मुखो नीलरुचिस्त्रिनेत्रः पायादघोरो दिशि दक्षिणस्याम् ॥

(शैवे कारणागमे ॥)

वामदेवः ।

रक्ताम्बरधरं देवं रक्तयज्ञोपवीतिनम् ।
रक्तोष्णीषं रक्तनेत्रं रक्तमाल्यानुलेपनम् ॥

जटाचन्द्रधरं कुर्यात्त्रिनेत्रं तुङ्गनासिकम् ।
वामदेवं महाबाहुं खड्गखेटकधारिणम् ॥

सर्वालङ्कारसंयुक्तं रक्तकुण्डलधारिणम् ।

(रूपमण्डने ॥)

वराक्षमालाभयटङ्कहस्तस्सरोजकिञ्जल्कसमानवर्णः ।
त्रिलोचनश्चारुचतुर्मुखो मां पायादुदीच्यां दिशि वामदेवः ॥

(शैवे कारणागमे ॥)

सद्योजातः ।

शुक्लाम्बरधरं देवं शुक्लमाल्यानुलेपनम् ।
जटाभारयुतं कुर्य्याद्बालेन्दुकृतशेखरम् ॥

प्रतिमालक्षणानि ।

त्रिलोचनं सौम्यमुखं कुण्डलाभ्यामलङ्कृतम् ।
सद्योजातं महोत्साहं वरदाभयपाणिकम् ॥

(रूपमण्डने)

कुन्देन्दुशङ्खस्फटिकावभासो वेदाक्षमालावरदाभयाङ्कः ।
त्र्यक्षश्चतुर्वक्त्र उरुप्रभावस्सद्योऽधिजातोऽवतु मां प्रतीच्याम् ॥

(शैवे कारणागमे ॥)

महेशः ।

पञ्चमूर्धं चतुर्वक्त्रं नेत्रैर्द्वादशभिर्युतम् ।
चतुरास्यं चतुर्नासी वसुश्रोत्रं चतुर्गळम् ॥

तनुरेतद्द्विपादं हि सायुधं दशबाहुकम् ।
शुद्धस्फटिकसङ्काशं सूर्यकोटिसमप्रभम् ॥

चन्द्रांशुहिमशीतं च सर्वाभरणभूषितम् ।
शुक्लाम्बरधरं देवं शुक्लयज्ञोपवीतिनम् ॥

अभयं शूलपरशुं वज्रं खड्गं च दक्षिणे ।
खेटकाङ्कुशपाशं च घण्टां वरदवामके ॥

कुर्यादेवं महेशं तु शक्तेस्तु लक्षणं शृणु ।
चतुर्भुजां त्रिनेत्रां च सर्वालङ्कारसंयुताम् ॥

नितम्बतटविस्तीर्णां मध्यक्षामां स्तनोन्नताम् ।
दक्षिणे चोत्पलोपेतां वामहस्ते स्रजं धरीम् ॥

वरदाभयहस्तां वै दुकूलवसनान्विताम् ।
करण्डमकुटोपेतामीश्वरस्य तु वामके ॥
पीठे चैकासने युक्तां तत्प्रभामण्डले स्थिताम् ।
चन्द्रार्काग्निप्रतीकाशां जगन्मङ्गलकारकाम् ॥
कारयेदीश्वरीमेवं वामादीनां शृणुष्वहि ।
(सुप्रभेदागमे चतुस्त्रिंशत्तमपटले ॥)

रुद्राः ।

चतुर्भुजास्त्रिनेत्राश्च जटामकुटमण्डिताः ।
शुक्लवस्त्रधरास्सर्वे शुक्लवर्णाः प्रकीर्त्तिताः ॥
सपादस्थानकास्सर्वे पद्मपीठोपरि स्थिताः ।
सर्वाभरणसंयुक्ताः सर्वपुष्पैरलङ्कृताः ॥
अभयं परशुं सव्ये कृष्णं वरद वामके ।
महादेवश्शिवो रुद्रः शङ्करो नीललोहितः ॥
ईशानो विजयो भीमो देवदेवो भवोद्भवः ।
कपालीशश्च विज्ञेया रुद्रा एकादशाः (?) पराः ॥
(अंशुमद्भेदागमे एकोनपञ्चाशपटले ॥)

अजः ।

अथ रुद्रान् प्रवक्ष्यामि बाहुषोडशकान्वितान् ।
अजनामा महारुद्रो धत्ते शूलमथाङ्कुशम् ॥

कपालं डमरुं सर्पं मुद्गरं च सुदर्शनम् ।
अक्षसूत्रमधो दक्षे तथा वामे कराष्टके ॥

तर्जनीमूर्ध्वतस्तत्र खट्वाङ्गं तदधःकरे ।
गदां च पट्टिशं घण्टां शक्तिपरशुकुण्डिकाः ॥

एकपादः ।

एकपादाभिधो बिभ्रत् क्ष्वेडादः स्याद्दहन् शरम् ।
चक्रं डमरुकं शूलं मुद्गरं तदधो वरम् ॥
अक्षसूत्रमधो वामे खट्वाङ्गं चोर्ध्वहस्तके ।
धनुर्घण्टां कपालं च कौमुदीं तर्जनीं घटम् ॥
परशुं चक्रमाधत्ते क्रमाद्बाह्वष्टके त्विति ।
अनेकभोगसंपत्तिं कुरुते यजनात्सदा ॥

(विश्वकर्मशास्त्रे ॥)

ध्यायेत्कोटिरविप्रभं त्रिनयनं शीतांशुगङ्गाधरं
हस्ते टङ्कमृगं वराभयकरं पादैकयुक्तं विभुम् ।
शंभोर्दक्षिणवामकक्षभुजयोर्ब्रह्माच्युताभ्यां स्थितं
तत्तल्लक्षणमायुधैः परिवृतं हस्तद्वयाढ्यांजलिम् ॥
ब्रह्माण्डप्रलये सुसंस्थितपदं ब्रह्माण्डमध्यस्थितं
ह्येवं लक्षणसंयुतं पुरहरं पादैकमूर्तीकृतम् ।

एकपादमिति ख्यातं सुखासीनम्। रक्तवर्णः। पक्षान्तरे श्वेतवर्णोऽपि प्रसिद्धः ।

(श्रीतत्त्वनिधौ ॥)

अहिर्बुध्नः ।

अहिर्बुध्नो गदां चक्रं चासिं डमरुमुद्गरौ ।
शूलाङ्कुशाक्षमालाश्च दक्षोर्ध्वाधःकरैः क्रमात् ॥

तोमरं पट्टिशं चर्म कपालं तर्जनीं घटम् ।
शक्तिं परशुकं वामे दक्षवद्धारयत्यसिम् ॥

विरूपाक्षः ।

विरूपाक्षस्ततः खड्गं शूलं डमरुकाङ्कुशौ ।
सर्पं चक्रं गदामक्षसूत्रं बिभ्रत्कराष्टके ॥

खेटं खट्वाङ्गकं शक्तिं परशुं तर्जनीं घटम् ।
घण्टाकपालकौ चेति वामोर्ध्वादिकराष्टके ॥

रेवतः ।

रेवतो दक्षिणे चापं खड्गशूलं गदामहिम् ।
चक्राङ्कुशाक्षमालास्तु धारयन्नूर्ध्वमादितः ॥

धनु(धनुः ?)खेटं च खट्वाङ्गं घण्टातर्जनिकां ततः ।
परशुं पट्टिशं पात्रं वामबाहु[ष्ट*]केऽर्कवत् ॥

सर्वसंपकरोत्येष (संपत्करो ह्येष ?) जायते वार्चनाद्ध्रुवम् ।

हरः ।

हराख्यो मुद्गरं चैव डमरुं शूलमङ्कुशम् ।
गदासर्पाक्षसूत्राणि धारयन् दक्षिणोर्ध्वतः ॥

पट्टिशं तोमरं शक्तिं परशुं तर्जनीं घटम् ।
खट्वाङ्गं पट्टिकां चेति वामोर्ध्वादिक्रमेण तु ॥

बहुरूपः ।

बहुरूपो दधद्दक्षे डमरुं च सुदर्शनम् ।
सर्पं शूलाङ्कुशौ चैव कौमुदीं जपमालिकाम् ॥
घण्टाकपालखट्वाङ्गं तर्जनीं कुण्डिकां धनुः ।
परशुं पट्टिशं चैव वामोर्ध्वादिकराष्टके ॥

त्र्यम्बकः ।

त्र्यम्बकोऽपि दधच्चक्रं डमरुं मुद्गरं शरम् ।
शूलाङ्कुशाहिजाप्यं च दक्षोर्ध्वादिक्रमेण हि ॥
गदाखट्वाङ्गपात्राणि कार्मुकं तर्जनीघटौ ।
परशुं पट्टिशं चैव वामोर्ध्वादिकराष्टके ॥

सुरेश्वरः ।

सुरेश्वरो हि डमरुं चक्रं शूलाङ्कुशावपि ।
शरं च मुद्गरं चापं दक्षबाह्वष्टके त्विति ॥
पङ्कजं परशुं घण्टां पट्टिशं तर्जनीं धनुः ।
खट्वाङ्गं कारयेत्पात्रं वामेऽष्टकरपल्लवे ॥

जयन्तः ।

जयन्तो दशमो रुद्रोऽप्यङ्कुशं चक्रमुद्गरौ ।
शूलाहिडमरुं बाणमक्षसूत्रं यमे त्विति ॥
गदाखट्वाङ्गपरशुं कपालं शक्तिं तर्जनीम् ।
धनुः कुण्डीमथोर्ध्वादिवामबाह्वष्टके दधत् ॥

अपराजितः ।

अथापराजितो दक्षे तोमरं खड्गमङ्कुशम् ।
शूलाहिचक्रडमरुमक्षमालां दधत्क्रमात् ॥
शक्तिं खेटं गदां पात्रं तर्जनीं पट्टिशं कजम् ।
घण्टामुत्तरतश्चाथ धारयन्नूर्ध्वमादितः ॥
अजैकपादहिर्बुध्नो विरूपाक्षश्च रेवतः ।
हरश्च बहुरूपश्च त्र्यम्बकश्च सुरेश्वरः ॥
रुद्रा एकादश प्रोक्ता जयन्तश्चापराजितः ।

(विश्वकर्मशास्त्रे ॥)

मृत्युञ्जयः ।

कपालमालिनं श्वेतं शशाङ्ककृतशेखरम् ।
व्याघ्रचर्मधरं मृत्युञ्जयं नागेन्द्रभूषितम् ॥
त्रिशूलमक्षमाला च दक्षयोः करयोस्स्मृतः ।
कपालं कुण्डिकां वामे योगमुद्राकरद्वयः ॥

किरणाक्षः ।

चतुर्भुजो महाबाहुः शुक्लपादाक्षपाणिकः ।
पुस्तकाभयहस्तोऽसौ किरणाक्षस्त्रिलोचनः ॥

श्रीकण्ठः ।

चित्रवस्त्रधरं कुर्याच्चित्रयज्ञोपवीतिनम् ।
चित्ररूपं महेशानं चित्रैश्वर्यसमन्वितम् ॥
चतुर्बाहुं चैकवक्त्रं सर्वालङ्कारभूषितम् ।
खड्गं धनुः शरं खेटं श्रीकण्ठं बिभ्रतं भुजैः ॥

(रूपमण्डने ॥)

विद्येश्वराः ।

दिग्वर्णा जटिलस्त्र्यक्षाश्शरत्रिशूलधारिणः ।
पुटाञ्जलिकरास्सर्वे विद्येशाश्चैकवक्त्रकाः ॥
अनन्तश्च त्रिमूर्तिश्च सूक्ष्मः श्रीकण्ठ एव च ।
शिवश्शिखण्ड्येकनेत्र एकरुद्रश्च ते क्रमात् ॥

(विष्णुधर्मोत्तरे ॥)

अनन्तेशस्तथा सूक्ष्मश्शिवोत्तमश्चैकनेत्रकः ।
एकरुद्रस्त्रिमूर्तिश्च श्रीकण्ठश्च शिखण्डिनः ॥
अष्टविद्येश्वरा ह्येते त्रिनेत्राश्च चतुर्भुजाः ।
अभयंवरदोपेताष्टङ्कशूलधरास्तथा ॥
रक्तकुन्दस्तथा नीलं पीतं कृष्णं च कुङ्कुमम् ।
अरुणं भिन्नाञ्जनप्रख्यं क्रमाद्विद्येशवर्णकम् ॥
जटामकुटसंयुक्ता उपवीतसमन्विताः ।
सर्वाभरणसंयुक्ताश्शान्तवक्त्रसमन्विताः ॥
विद्येशाकृतिरेवं स्याद् दिक्पालाकृतिरुच्यते ।

(पूर्वकारणागमे चतुर्दशपटले ॥)

अनन्तः ।

अनन्तश्चतुर्भुजस्सौम्यस्सर्वाभरणभूषितः ।
जपापुष्पनिभाकारः करण्डमकुटान्वितः ॥

सितवस्त्रधरः शान्तास्त्रिनेत्रः पद्मसंस्थितः ।
अभयवरदोपेतो गङ्गा(टङ्क ?)शूलधरश्शुचिः ॥

त्रिमूर्तिः ।

एकरुद्रमिवात्रैव त्रिमूर्तिं चैव कारयेत् ।

(अंशुमद्भेदागमे एकोनपञ्चाशपटले ॥)

रक्तवर्णस्त्रिनेत्रश्च वरदाभयहस्तकः ।
कृष्णापरशुसंयुक्तो जटामकुटमण्डितः ॥

ऋज्वागतस्तथैकेन पादेनापि समन्वितः ।
दक्षिणोत्तरयोश्चैव पार्श्वयोरुभयोरपि ॥

कटिप्रदेशादूर्ध्वे तु ब्रह्मविष्णूर्ध्वकाययुक् ।
स्त्रीमानवत्तयोर्मानं ब्रह्मविष्ण्वोस्तु कल्पयेत् ॥

कृताञ्जलिपुटावेकपादयुक्तौ च वा मतौ ।
अथवा शिवलिङ्गस्य पार्श्वयोन्तर्गतौ कृतौ ॥

अथवा तौ पृथक् स्थाप्यावेकविष्टरमास्थितौ ।
अथवा मध्यमे लिङ्गं पृथगालयसंस्थितम् ॥

तस्य सव्येऽप्यसव्ये च ब्रह्मविष्णू तथा मतौ ।
पृथग्धामस्थिता वैकधामस्था वा त्रिमूर्तयः ॥

संश्लिष्टधामयुक्ता वा ब्रह्मविष्णुशिवा मताः ।
पूर्वास्याः पश्चिमास्या वा परिवारादिसंयुताः ॥

भिन्नप्राकारगा वापि एकप्राकारसंस्थिताः ।
नृत्तमूर्त्यादिदेवा वा स्थापनीयास्तु मध्यमे ॥
एवं लक्षणमादिष्टं प्रतिष्ठाविधिरुच्यते ।

(उत्तरकामिकागमे एकषष्टितमपटले ॥)

सूक्ष्मः ।

सूक्ष्मो नीलनिभश्शान्तो हेमवस्त्रधरः परः ।
चतुर्भुजस्त्रिनेत्रश्च सर्वाभरणभूषितः ॥
अभयवरदोपेतटङ्कशूलधरस्तथा ।

श्रीकण्ठः ।

अभयवरदोपेतटङ्कशूलधरः परः ।
रक्तवस्त्रसमायुक्तः पद्मपीठोपरि स्थितः ॥
श्रीकण्ठं ह्येवमाख्यातं नागदेवमथोच्यते ।

शिवोत्तमः ।

शिवोत्तमः श्वेतवर्णश्चतुर्दोर्भिस्समन्वितः ।
सर्वाभरणसंयुक्तश्शुक्लवासोपवीतकः ॥
नेत्रद्वयसमायुक्तः करण्डमकुटान्वितः ।
अभयवरदोपेतश्शूलपाशधरश्शुचिः ॥
पद्मपीठोपरिष्ठात्तु स्थानकस्समपादकः ।

शिखण्डी ।

शिखण्डिस्त्वञ्जनाभस्तु चतुर्भुजसमन्वितः ।
करण्डमकुटोपेतस्सर्वाभरणभूषितः ॥

रक्तवस्त्रधरश्शान्तस्त्वभयवरदान्वितः ।
खड्गखेटकसंयुक्तः पद्मपीठोपरिस्थितः ॥

एकनेत्रः ।

एकनेत्रश्चतुर्बाहुर्नेत्रत्रयसमन्वितः ।
क्षौमवस्त्रधरश्शान्तो.........कसमप्रभः ॥

जटामकुटसंयुक्तस्सर्वाभरणभूषितः ।
अभयवरदोपेतष्टङ्कशूलसमन्वितः ॥

एकरुद्रः ।

एकाक्षसदृशं त्वेकरुद्रं कुर्य्याद्विशेषतः ।

(अंशुमद्भेदागमे एकोनपञ्चाशपटले ॥)

मूर्त्यष्टकम् ।

शर्वो भीमो महादेवो रुद्रः पशुपतिर्भवः ।
उग्र ईशान इत्यष्टौ मूर्तयश्शिवसन्निभाः ॥

मृगाङ्कचूडामणयो जटामण्डलमण्डिताः ।
त्रिनेत्रा वरखट्वाङ्गत्रिशूलवरपाणयः ॥

(विष्णुधर्मोत्तरे ॥)

भवश्शर्वस्तथेशानपशुपत्युग्रकस्तथा ।
रुद्रो भीमो महादेवः कीर्तितास्त्वष्टमूर्तयः ॥

चतुर्भुजास्त्रिनेत्राश्च जटामकुटधारिणः ।
अभयंवरदोपेताष्टङ्कक्रुष्णधरास्स्मृताः ॥

सर्वाभरणसंयुक्ता रक्तक्षौमधरा इमे ।
शुक्लं श्यामं च रक्तं च कृष्णं गोक्षीरसान्निभम् ॥

काश्मीरं विद्रुमं नीलं भवादीनां तु वर्णकम् ।
अष्टमूर्त्याकृतिर्ह्येवं वसूनामाकृतिं शृणु ॥

(पूर्वकारणागमे चतुर्दशपटले ॥)

शर्वः ।

शर्वश्चतुर्भुजश्शान्तस्सर्वाभरणभूषितः ।
जटामकुटसंयुक्तश्शङ्खकुन्देन्दुसन्निभः ॥

अभयवरदोपेतः खड्गखेटकधारितः ।
पद्मपीठोपरिष्टात्तु स्थानकश्शर्व एव हि ॥

भीमः ।

भीमश्चतुर्भुजो रौद्रस्सर्वाभरणभूषितः ।
जटामकुटसंयुक्तो व्यातिरिक्त(ह्यतिरक्त ?)समप्रभः ॥

अभयं वरदं चैव शूलं पाशं च धारयेत् ।
सितवस्त्रधरश्चैव रौद्रदृष्टिस्सदंष्ट्रकः ॥

26

पशुपतिः ।

पशुपतिं शर्ववत्कृत्वा स्थापयेद्देशिकोत्तमः ।

भवः ।

भवश्चतुर्भुजश्शान्तो जटामकुटमण्डितः ।

अतिरक्तसमप्रख्यस्सर्वाभरणभूषितः ॥

अभयवरदोपेतः शूलपाशधरो भवः ।

(अंशुमद्भेदागमे एकोनपञ्चाशपटले ॥)

सुब्रह्मण्यमूर्तिभेदाः ।

सुब्रह्मण्यमूर्तिभेदाः ।

षण्मुखः ।

अथ वक्ष्ये विशेषेण षण्मुखस्य तु लक्षणम् ।
पञ्चतालोत्तमेनैव[1] स्कन्दं कुर्याद्विशेषतः ॥

द्विभुजं वा चतुर्हस्तं षड्भुजं भानुहस्तकम् ।
शक्तिबाणं च पाशं प्रसारितम्[2] ॥

सव्ये वामे तु पिञ्छं च खेटकं कुक्कुटं तथा ।
धनुर्दण्डं हलं चैव भानुहस्तान्यतोद्धृतम्[3] ॥

षड्भुजे त्वभयं खड्गं शक्तिर्दक्षिणपार्श्वके ।
खेटकं चाक्षमाला च कुक्कुटं वामहस्तके ॥

चतुर्भुजेऽभयं शक्तिर्दक्षिणे तु करद्वयम्(ये ?) ।
कुक्कुटं चाक्षमाला च वामहस्तोद्धृतं शुभम् ॥

द्विभुजे कुक्कुटं वामे शक्तिर्दक्षिणहस्तके ।
अत्रानुक्तं तु तत्सर्वमुमास्कन्दोक्तवत्कुरु ॥

(अंशुमद्भेदागमे एकोनपञ्चाशपटले ॥)

---

१ उत्तमपञ्चतालेनेत्यर्थः । २ 'शक्तिं वाणं च खड्गं च चक्रं प्रासं प्रसारितम्' इति पाठान्तरम् । ३ 'भानुहस्तान्विते स्थितम्' इति पाठान्तरम् ।

गुहस्य स्थापनं वक्ष्ये तल्लक्षणपुरस्सरम् ।
पुरादेर्मध्यमे वाग्नौ यमे वा मध्यमे तयोः ॥

नैर्ऋते वरुणे वायौ सोमे शर्वेऽथवा भवेत् ।
अन्तरालेऽथवा तेषां शिवधाम्न्येत्रमेव वा ॥

अन्यदेवालयेऽप्येवमथवा पर्वतोपरि ।
पर्वतस्यान्तिके वापि नद्युद्यानादिकेऽथवा ॥

राजधान्यादिके वाथ पुण्यक्षेत्रे गृहेषु वा ।
प्रासादमण्डपादीनां देशे पुण्यतरुष्वथ ॥

कुमारालय इष्टस्स्याद्धामलक्षणलक्षितः ।
अथैकादित्रयस्त्रिंशद्धस्तविस्तारसंयुतः ॥

त्रेतायां नवहस्तोर्ध्वं विस्तारो नेष्यते द्विजाः ! ।
दिङ्न्यस्तस्कन्दरूपाढ्यः केवलो वा तदालयः ॥

रुद्रोमाविघ्नरूपाढ्यस्त्वथवा हंसकोणयुक् ।
गजकोणे(। ?)ऽथवा स स्यात् केवलो वा गुहालयः ॥

एकभूम्यादिसप्तान्ततलेष्विष्टतलान्वितः ।
शिवोक्तमार्गसंक्लृप्तगर्भाद्येष्टकयान्वितः ॥

तद्वन्मूर्धेष्टकास्थूपिप्रतिष्ठाभ्यां समायुतः ।
धाम्नस्संस्थापनेनाढ्यः प्रागुक्तविधिना सह ॥

प्रागुक्तमण्डपाद्यैश्च प्राकाराद्यैश्च मण्डितः ।
पूर्वास्यः पश्चिमास्यो वा दक्षोत्तरमुखस्तु वा ॥

परिवारामरैर्युक्तः कथ्यन्ते ते प्रसङ्गतः ।
यक्षेन्द्रो राक्षसेन्द्रश्च पिशाचेन्द्रश्च भूतराट् ॥

गन्धर्वः किन्नरो दैत्यनायको दानवाधिपः ।
क्रमात्पूर्वादिशर्वान्तस्थिता एते चतुर्भुजाः ॥

वरदाभयसंयुक्ताः खड्गखेटसमन्विताः ।
खड्गखेटसमायुक्ता द्विभुजा वाञ्जनप्रभाः ॥

भीमरूपास्सुशान्ता वा बद्धकेशास्तु वा मताः ।
शकुनी पूतना चैव रेवती चार्धपूतना ॥

वक्त्रमाण्डिनि शान्ता च[1] एता देवाष्टमूर्तयः ।
षण्मुखश्शक्तिपाणिश्च कार्तिकेयो गुहस्ततः ॥

स्कन्दो मयूरवाहस्स्यात्सेनानीश्शक्तिहस्तवान् ।
एते वा मूर्तिपास्तस्य कृताञ्जलिपुटान्विताः ॥

वज्रपद्मधरास्सर्वे स्कन्दोक्ता राक्ष(कृलक्ष्म?)संयुताः ।
चतुर्भुजा द्विहस्ता वा षड्वक्त्राश्चैकवक्त्रकाः ॥

एते वा परितस्स्थाप्याः क्रमात्पूर्वादियोगतः ।
इन्द्रादीन्वाष्टपीठं वा मयूरं वाग्रतो गजम् ॥

विघ्नेशं क्षेत्रपं भानुं महापीठं प्रकल्पयेत् ।
बलिपीठं च शर्वोक्तान्परिवारांस्तु वा न्यसेत् ॥

---

१ 'वक्त्रमण्डुनी शान्ता च' इति पाठान्तरम् ।

बलिपीठं (ठ?) दलेष्विन्द्रपूर्वान्मध्ये ग्रहेश्वराः ।
द्वारपौ कल्पयेद् द्वारे श्यामरक्तनिभौ क्रमात् ॥
दक्षवामगतौ द्वाराद् द्विभुजौ वा चतुर्भुजौ ।
खड्गखेटधरौ सूचिमुद्राविस्मयसंयुतौ ॥
श्यामाभौ रक्तवर्णौ वा सितकृष्णौ भयङ्करौ ।
जयाख्यविजयाख्यौ द्वौ द्वारपौ विकृताननौ ॥
ईशाने कल्पयेत्स्कन्दचण्डं वेदकरं वरम् ।
अभयं वज्रपद्मे च वहन्तं द्विभुजं तु वा ॥
शाकल्यसंज्ञया ख्यातं तदर्थं पीठमेव वा ।
लक्षणं तस्य संक्षेपाच्छृणुध्वं द्विजसत्तमाः ! ॥
द्रव्यैश्शिलादिभिः कुर्यात्प्रतिमालक्षणोदितैः ।
प्रतिमालक्षणे प्रोक्तं विश्वमानं गुहस्य तु ॥
योजनीयं द्विजा गर्भद्वारस्तम्भादिसंयुतम् ।
द्विभुजश्च द्विनेत्रश्च सुब्रह्मण्यस्सुसुन्दरः ॥
पद्मधृक् सव्यसत्पाणिर्लम्बितेतरसत्करः ।
बालरूपी प्रतिष्ठाप्यो ग्रामस्यैवाभिवृद्धये ॥
द्विहस्तो यज्ञसूत्राढ्यस्सशिखस्सत्रिमेखलः ।
कौपीनदण्डधृक्सव्यपाणिः कट्याश्रितोऽपरः ॥
स्थाप्योऽयं ज्ञानदस्स्कन्दः पर्वतेषु वनादिषु ।
चतुर्भुजस्त्रिनेत्रश्च कर्णयोः पत्रपिण्डयुक् ॥

नक्रकुण्डलयुक्तो वा ह्यक्षशक्तिकरद्वयः ।
वरदाभयसंयुक्तश्शक्तिद्वययुतो न वा ॥

शक्त्यैकया युतो वा स्यात्तयोर्लक्षणमुच्यते ।
द्विनेत्रे द्विभुजे शान्ते पद्मोत्पलकरद्वये ॥

श्यामरक्तनिभे सव्यवामपार्श्वे व्यवस्थिते ।
गौरीलक्षणसंयुक्ते कल्पयेत्तु शिवानने ॥

गजेति गजवल्लीति नाम्ना ख्याते(ते अति ?)तिसुन्दरे ।
इत्थं लक्षणयुक् स्थाप्यः पुरे वा नगरेऽपि वा ॥

षडाननश्च षड्बाहुरर्कश्रोत्रेक्षणान्वितः ।
षट्कर्णस्त्वर्क[क *]र्णो वा षड्भिर्मौलिभिरान्वितः ॥

सशक्तिस्साभयस्सासिस्साक्षमालस्सकुक्कुटः ।
सखेटकस्त्वयं स्थाप्यो वृद्धये राजधानिके ॥

रक्ताम्बरसमायुक्तो बालचन्द्रसमप्रभः ।
करण्डमकुटोपेतो नेत्रत्रयसमन्वितः ॥

शक्तिं च मुसलं खड्गं चक्रं पाशाभये वहन् ।
दक्षिणेऽदक्षिणे वज्रं कार्मुकं खेटकं तथा ॥

मयूरं च ध्वजं चैवमङ्कुशं वरदं वहन् ।
सोपवीतो मयूरस्थश्शक्तिद्वयसमायुतः ॥

ग्रामादौ स्थापनीयोऽयं प्रासादादौ च सिद्धये ।
एवं पञ्चविधः स्कन्दविभागस्स्थानभेदतः ॥

द्वापरे स्यान्न वान्यत्र सर्वे सर्वत्र वा मताः ।

(उत्तरकामिकागमे चतुष्षष्टितमपटले ॥)

अथातस्संप्रवक्ष्यामि स्कन्दस्य स्थापनं परम् ।
तस्योद्भवं समासेन शृणु पूर्वं गजानन ! ॥
देहत्यागेऽपि तां दृष्ट्वा तद्योगमहमभ्यसन् ।
सती चाङ्गं पुनर्गत्वा सुता हिमवतस्तथा[१] ॥
गिरिपार्श्वे तपः कृत्वा तत्सुता पार्वती भवेत् ।
आवयोस्सङ्गमं(: ?) तत्र देवैस्संप्रार्थितो यतः ॥
रेतो वह्निस्तु संग्राह्य क्षिप्त्वा शरवणे च तु ।
तस्माच्छरवणोभावो नाम इत्यपि कीर्तितः ॥
षट्कृत्तिकायां स्थपनं(स्तन्यपानात् ?) षण्मुखस्त्वभिधीयते ।
तेनैव कार्तिकेयस्तु बालहीनां हि तद्भवेत्(लानां हितकृद् भवेत्?) ॥
प्रासादं विधिवत्कृत्वा प्रतिमां तदनन्तरम् ।
शिलामृद्दारुलोहैर्वा नवतालेन मानयेत् ॥
द्विहस्तो वा चतुर्बाहुरष्टबाहुरथापि वा ।
द्विभुजं पद्महस्तं तु वज्रं शक्तिं तथापरे ॥

---

१ आदर्शान्तरे एतदनन्तरं 'षट्कृत्तिकास्तन्यपानात् षण्मुखस्त्वभिधीयते । तेनैव कार्तिकेयस्तु बालानां हितकृद् भवेत्' इति वर्तते । न तु 'गिरिपार्श्वे तपः कृत्वे' त्यादिवचनानि ॥

अभयं वरदं पूर्वे चतुर्बाहुरिति स्मृतम् ।
खड्गखेटकमूर्ध्वे तु पाशं पद्मं तथाष्टकम् ॥
आसनं स्थानकं वापि यानं वै त्रिविधं तथा ।
आसनं द्विभुजं प्रोक्तं स्थानकं स्याच्चतुर्भुजम् ॥
यानमष्टभुजे कुर्यात् स्थापनं परिवारके ।
स्कन्दं पद्मगजारूढमुपवीतसमन्वितम् ॥
दाडिमीपुष्पसङ्काशं सर्वाभरणभूषितम् ।
सर्वलक्षणसंयुक्तं पूर्वोक्तेन विधानतः ॥
विद्यामेधा च सहिते शुक्लश्यामनिभे तथा ।
सर्वालङ्कारसंयुक्ते द्विभुजे पद्मधारिके ॥

(सुप्रभेदागमे चतुश्चत्वारिंशत्तमपटले ॥)

चतुर्भुजं द्विबाहुं च शान्तं सिद्धिप्रदं स्मृतम् ।
द्विभुजश्च चतुर्बाहुष्षड्भुजोऽष्टभुजः पुनः ॥
द्विषड्भुजः पञ्च भेदा एतेषां लक्षणं शृणु ।
द्विहस्ते पञ्चभेदोऽस्ति कटिबद्धाभयं तु वा ॥
पद्मधृक् सक(?)बद्धं वा दण्डेन कटिबद्धकम् ।
शक्तिवज्रधरं वापि शक्तिकुक्कुटमेव च ॥
चतुर्भुजस्सप्तभेदं वज्रशक्तिवराभयम् ।
अभयं वरदं पश्चादक्षमालाकमण्डलुम् ॥

ततो वै कुण्डि अक्षस्सृक् कटिबन्धाभयान्वितम् ।
पश्चादभीतिवरदं शक्तिकुक्कुटसंयुतम् ॥

ततोऽभयं च शक्तिं च कुक्कुटं चाक्षमालिकाम् ।
शक्तिं कमण्डलुं पश्चात् कटिबद्धाभयं तु वा ॥

पश्चात् कुक्कुटशक्तिभ्यामसिखेटसमायुतम् ।
षड्भुजे त्वभयं खड्गं शक्तिं दक्षिणपाणिषु ॥

खेटकं चाक्षमालां च कुक्कुटं वामपाणिषु ।
अष्टबाहुं ततो वक्ष्ये वराभीवज्रशक्तयः ॥

खड्गखेटशरं चापं द्विषड्भुजमथ शृणु ।
द्विषड्भुजेति(पि ?)षड्भेदं तत्तद्भेदं वदाम्यहम् ॥

सव्ये शक्तिशरं खड्गध्वजं चैव गदाभयम् ।
वामे वज्रं धनुः खेटं पद्मं शूलं वरं पुनः ॥

शक्तिं बाणं च खड्गं च चक्रं पाशं प्रसारितम् ।
सव्ये वामेऽपि चक्रं च शङ्खं वै कुक्कुटं ततः ॥

धनुर्दण्डं हलं चैव विश्वामित्रमहामुने! ।
शक्तिं च मुसलं खड्गं चक्रं पाशं तथाभयम् ॥

वज्रं धनुर्ध्वजं खेटमङ्कुशं वरदं तु वा ।
शक्तिं खड्गं ध्वजं पद्मं कुक्कुटं प्रासदण्डके ॥

वराभयधनुर्बाणं टङ्कमेतैर्युतं तु वा ।
वज्रं शक्तिं च दण्डं च चक्रं पाशाङ्कुशं गदाम् ॥

शूलं च चक्रपद्मे च वरदाभयसंयुतम् ।
शक्तिं चर्ममसिं शूलं विशिखाभीतिकार्मुकम् ॥
चक्रं पाशं कुक्कुटं च वरदं द्वादशैः करैः ।
दधानं षण्मुखं शान्तं प्रतिवक्त्रं त्रिलोचनम् ॥
एवं विधानं षड्वक्त्रमेकास्यं वाथ कल्पयेत् ।
कुङ्कुमाभं द्वादशाक्षं सर्वाभरणभूषितम् ॥
आसनं स्थानकं वापि ध्यानकं(यानकं?) त्रिविधं स्मृतम् ।
आसनं द्विभुजं प्रोक्तं स्थानकं तु चतुर्भुजम् ॥
द्विषड्भुजं चाष्टबाहुं षड्बाहुं ध्यान(यान?)रूपकम् ।
योगं भोगं च यानं च बेरं तु त्रिविधं पुनः ॥
आसनं योगबेरं स्यात् स्थानकं भोगबेरकम् ।
ध्या(या?)नकं यानबेरं स्यान्नागरादिक्रमं तथा ॥
सात्विकं द्विभुजं बेरं राजसं स्याच्चतुर्भुजम् ।
तामसं द्वादशभुजमेवं स्यादर्चनाविधौ ॥
पीतं वा रक्तवर्णं वा श्यामवर्णमथापि वा ।
स्कन्दं पद्मासनस्थं वा मयूरारूढमेव वा ॥
गजेन्द्रयानकं वापि शक्त्येकासहितं तु वा ।
शक्तिं विनापि कर्तव्यं सोपवीतं सुयौवनम् ॥
शत(छन्न?)वीरसमायुक्तं पादनूपुरसंयुतम् ।
पत्रकर्णयुतं कान्तं नानाकुण्डलकं तु वा ॥

मन्दस्मितं बालवेषं शोभनाङ्गं शुभेक्षणम् ।
करण्डमकुटोपेतं सर्वलक्षणसंयुतम् ॥

शक्तिद्वययुतं वापि शक्त्यैकसहितं तु वा ।
शक्तिं विनापि कर्तव्यं योगबेरं तदीरितम् ॥

देव्योरुत्सेधमद्यैव शृणु कौशिक सुव्रत ! ।
कर्णान्तं वाथ(वास्य ?)सीमान्तं हन्वन्तं बाहुतुङ्गकम् ॥

हिक्कान्तं वा स्तनान्तं वा कल्पयेदुत्तमानि च ।
मध्यमंदशतालेन देव्यौ च परिकल्पयेत् ॥

महावल्ल्याकृतिं वक्ष्ये श्याममन्दस्मिताननम् ।
स्थितं वै सव्यपादं तु वामपादं तु कुञ्चितम् ॥

पद्मधृग्वामहस्तं च सव्यहस्तं प्रलम्बितम् ।
देवसेनाकृतिं वक्ष्ये रक्तं मन्दस्मिताननम् ॥

स्थितं वै वामपादं तु दक्षपादं तु कुञ्चितम् ।
उत्पलं सव्यहस्तं च वामहस्तं प्रलम्बितम् ॥

(कुमारतन्त्रागमे चतुर्विंशतितमपटले ॥)

विलिखेत् षण्मुखं देवं मयूरवरवाहनम् ।
तरुणादित्यसङ्काशं बालभूषणभूषितम् ॥

स्थानीये खेटके वापि कुमारो लिख्यते यदा ।
भुजान् द्वादश कुर्वीत खर्वटे चतुरो भुजान् ॥

ग्रामे वने द्विबाहुस्स्यादालेखनीयो विचक्षणैः।

(शिल्परत्ने पञ्चविंशपटले ॥)

स्कन्दः कुमाररूपश्शक्तिधरो बर्हिकेतुश्च।

(बृहत्संहितायामष्टापञ्चाशत्तमाध्याये ॥)

कुमारष्षण्मुखः कार्यश्शिखण्डकविभूषणः।
रक्ताम्बरधरः कार्यो मयूरवरवाहनः ॥

कुक्कुटश्च तथा घण्टा तस्य दक्षिणहस्तयोः।
पताका वैजयन्ती च शक्तिः कार्या च वामयोः ॥

(विष्णुधर्मोत्तरे ॥)

रक्ताम्बरसदृक्(सुदृक्?) स्तोकबालो बालार्कसन्निभः।
शिखण्डमणिको ग्रीवमांसलः प्रियदर्शनः ॥

शक्तिस्तु विलसत्खड्गचक्रपाशप्रसारितः।
दक्षिणेऽदक्षिणे रक्तचूडखेटककार्मुकः ॥

पताका पिञ्छिकामुष्टिस्तर्जनी च प्रसारिता।
गुहो द्वादशबाहुस्स्यात्पुरीखेटकपत्तने ॥

चतुर्दोर्भिर्वाथ षड्दोर्भिस्संयुक्तं परिकल्पयेत्।
सशक्तिस्सहय(साभयः?)ससासिस्साक्षमालस्सकुक्कुटः ॥

सखेटश्च सषड्बाहुश्चतुर्दोस्स्वस्ति(सासि?)खेटकः।
सशक्तिकुक्कुटस्स्वे(स्वे?)कवक्त्रकः कुङ्कुमच्छविः ॥

मयूरारोहसर्वत्र भ्रामराद्यद्विबाहुकः(?)।
वासिकाबद्धमकुटस्सुब्रह्मण्यस्सुसुन्दरः ॥

स्कन्दस्याकृतिरेवं तु आर्यस्याकृतिरुच्यते ।

(पूर्वकारणागमे त्रयोदशपटले ॥)

शक्तिधरः ।

एकास्यं द्विभुजं वामे वज्रं दक्षिणजे करे ।
इच्छाज्ञानक्रियाशक्तिरूपं शक्तिधरं भजे ॥

(कुमारतन्त्रागमे द्वितीयपटले ॥)

ज्ञानशक्तिसुब्रह्मण्यः ।

एकवक्त्रं द्विनेत्रं च जटामकुटसंयुतम् ।
श्वेतार्कपुष्पमालं च हेमरत्नकिरीटिनम् ॥
चतुर्भुजैर्वज्रशक्तिकुक्कुटाभयधारिणम् ।
दिव्यगन्धानुलिप्ताङ्गं शुक्लयज्ञोपवीतिनम् ॥
शिवशक्तिज्ञानयोगं ज्ञानशक्तिस्वरूपकम् ।
श्वेतवर्णः ॥

(श्रीतत्वनिधौ ॥)

स्कन्दः ।

कल्पद्रुमं प्रणमतां कमलारुणाभं
स्कन्दं भुजद्वयमनामयमेकवक्त्रम् ।
कात्यायनीसुतमहं कटिबद्धदाम१-
कौपीनदण्डधरदक्षिणहस्तमीडे ॥

(कुमारतन्त्रागमे द्वितीयपटले ॥)

१ 'वामहस्तं च' इति श्रीतत्वनिधिपाठः । 'वाम'मिति मानसारपाठः ।

स्कन्दसुब्रह्मण्यः ।

चतुर्भुजं द्विनेत्रं च श्वेतपद्मासनस्थितम् ।
कुक्कुटाभयवज्राणि दधतं वरदं करे ॥
किंचित्केशशिखाबद्धपुष्पमालाभिरावृतम् ।
मेखलाम्बरसंवीतं रत्नभूषणभूषितम् ॥
धूम्रवर्णप्रभं स्कन्दं प्रभामण्डलमाण्डितम् ।
स्कन्दरूपमिदं प्रोक्तम्................॥ धूम्रवर्णः ।

(श्रीतत्वनिधौ ॥)

सेनापतिः ।

नौम्यादित्यप्रदीप्तं द्विदशनयनकं षण्मुखं मन्दहासं
वामाङ्के सुस्थितायास्सरसिरुहधृतालिङ्गितायाः प्रियायाः ।
उत्तुङ्गोरुस्तनाग्रे विहित [1]करतलभीतिखेटा[2]दिशूल-
ह्रादिन्युद्दीप्तशक्तीध्वसनघन(?)गदाकुक्कुटाब्जेषुहस्तम् ॥

(कुमारतन्त्रागमे द्वितीयपटले ॥)

एकवक्त्रं द्विनयनं शङ्खचक्रवराभयान् ।
सर्वाभरणसंयुक्तं दिव्यगन्धानुलेपनम् ॥
श्यामवर्णं प्रभुं चैव शुक्लयज्ञोपवीतिनम् ।
सुस्मितं चारुवदनं देवसेनापतिं भजे ॥
श्यामवर्णः ।

(श्रीतत्वनिधौ ॥)

---

१ 'करतलोऽभीती'ति मानसारपाठः । २ 'खेटासिशूलाद्यादीप्तादीप्तशक्तिः स हरतु दुरितं कुक्कुटाब्जस्य युक्ता' इति मानसारपाठः ।

सुब्रह्मण्यः ।

सिन्दूरारुणमिन्दुकान्तिवदनं केयूरहारादिभि-
दिव्यैराभरणैर्विभूषिततनुं स्वर्गादिसौख्यप्रदम् ।
अम्भोजाभयशक्तिकुक्कुटधरं रक्ताङ्गरागांशुकं
सुब्रह्मण्यमुपास्महे प्रणमतां भीतिप्रणाशोद्यतम् ॥

अन्यच्च

एकवक्त्रं द्विदोर्दण्डं कटिबद्धाभयान्वितम् ।
तरुणारुणसङ्काशं सुब्रह्मण्यमुपास्महे ॥

(कुमारतन्त्रागमे द्वितीयपटले ॥)

गजवाहनः ।

एकाननं द्विनयनं वरकुक्कुटौ च
वामद्वये निशितशक्त्यभयद्वयं च ।
बिभ्राणमीश्वरसुतं तपनायुताभं
नित्यं नमामि गजवाहनमिष्टसिद्ध्यै ॥

(कुमारतन्त्रे द्वितीयपटले ॥)

शरवणभवः[1] ।

शक्तिं घण्टां ध्वजसरसिजे कुक्कुटं पाशदण्डौ
टङ्कं बाणं वरदमभयं कार्मुकं चोद्वहन्तम् ।
पीतं सौम्यं द्विदशनयनं देवसङ्घैरुपास्यं
साद्भिः पूज्यं शरवणभवं षण्मुखं भावयामि ॥

(कुमारतन्त्रागमे द्वितीयपटले ॥)

---

१. मानसारे खेटकृपाणयोरधिकतया, पाशस्थाने प्रासस्य च वर्णनमस्ति ।

षड्भुजं चैकवदनं बालसूर्यसमप्रभम् ।
सर्वाभरणसंयुक्तं सिंहस्थं दधतं भजे ॥
त्रिनेत्रं भसितोद्धूलं पुष्पबाणेक्षुकार्मुकम् ।
खड्गं खेटं च वज्रं च कुक्कुटध्वजधारिणम् ॥
शरजन्म समाख्यातं ॥ रक्तवर्णः ।

(श्रीतत्वनिधौ ॥)

कार्तिकेयः ।

वरदकुलिशखेटं वामहस्तत्रये च
दधतमभयशक्तिं खड्गमन्यत्त्रये च ।
तरुणरविसमाभं साधुभिः पूज्यमानं
कमलवदनषट्कं कार्त्तिकेयं नमामि ॥

(कुमारतन्त्रागमे द्वितीयपटले ॥)

त्रिनेत्रं दशहस्तं च मस्तके बिल्वधारिणम् ।
शक्तिं शूलं तथा चक्रमङ्कुशाभयमन्यके ॥
वरदं तोमरं पाशं शङ्खं वज्रं च वामके ।
मयूरवाहनारूढं सर्वाभरणभूषितम् ॥
बालसूर्यप्रतीकाशं कार्तिकेयं शिवात्मजम् ।
रक्तवर्णः ।

(श्रीतत्वनिधौ ॥)

कुमारः ।

सव्यद्वये निशितशक्त्यासिमादधानं
वामद्वयेऽभिमतकुक्कुटखेटकं त्वाम्[1] ।
वल्लीपतिं विबुधलोचनपूर्णचन्द्रं
कल्याणदाननिरतं कलये कुमारम् ॥

(कुमारतन्त्रागमे द्वितीयपटले ॥)

चतुर्भुजं चैकवक्त्रं करण्डमकुटान्वितम् ।
शक्तिं चाभयदं दक्षे सव्ये वरदवज्रके ॥
पद्मपुष्पं धरं कण्ठे देवं बालस्वरूपकम् ।
रक्तवर्णः ।

(श्रीतत्वनिधौ ॥)

षण्मुखः ।

वन्दे सिन्दूरकान्तिं शरविपिनभवं श्रीमयूराधिरूढं
षड्वक्त्रं देवसैन्यं मधुरिपुतनयावल्लभं द्वादशाक्षम् ।
शक्तिं बाणं कृपाणं ध्वजमपि च गदां चाभयं सव्यहस्ते
चापं वज्रं सरोजं कटकमपि वरं शूलमन्यैर्दधानम् ॥

(कुमारतन्त्रागमे द्वितीयपटले ॥)

शक्तिं शरं च खड्गं च चक्रं पाशाभयौ तथा ।
कुक्कुटं च धनुः खेटं शङ्खं[2] धत्ते हलं वरम् ॥

---

१ 'हरितकुक्कुटखेटकं चे'ति मानसारपाठः । २ मानसारे शङ्खहलयोस्स्थाने कुलिशाङ्कुशयोः पाठः दृश्यते ।

मयूरवाहनोपेतं सर्वलक्षणसंयुतम् ।
जया[1] च विजया चैव वामदक्षिणपार्श्वयोः ॥
सर्वालङ्कारसंयुक्तं सर्वाभरणभूषितम् ।
षण्मुखं चेति विख्यातं............ ॥
रक्तवर्णः ।

(श्रीतत्वनिधौ)

तारकारिः ।

वरदमङ्कुशध्वजे च कटकौ चापवज्र-
मभयपाशचक्रखड्गमुसलशक्तिमन्वहम् ।
द्विदशपाणिभिर्दधानमरुणकोटिसन्निभं
भजत तारकारिमत्र भवविनाशकारणम् ॥

(कुमारतन्त्रागमे द्वितीयपटले ॥)

एकवक्त्रं त्रिनयनं गजपृष्ठोपरि स्थितम् ।
षण्मुखं चाभयं खड्गं शक्तिं वामेतरे दधम् ॥
खेटकं चाक्षमालां च कुक्कुटं वामहस्तके ।
तारकारिं भजे ख्यातम्............... ॥
रक्तवर्णः ।

(श्रीतत्त्वनिधौ ॥)

---

१ 'गजाम्बया च वल्ल्या चे'ति मानसारपाठः ।

सेनानीः ।

अभयमसिरथाङ्ग[1] चाङ्कुशं शक्तिशूलं
वरदकुलिशपाशं पद्मदण्डौ गदां च ।
दधतमुभयपक्षद्वादशायामहस्तै-
र्द्विदशकमलनेत्रं देवसेनान्यमीडे ॥

ब्रह्मशास्ता ।

वामे करे च युगले करकुण्डिके च
सव्येऽक्षसूत्रमभयं दधतं विशाखम् ।
वल्ल्या युतं वनजलोचनमेकवक्त्रं
वन्दामहे वनजसंभवशासितारम् ॥

वल्लीकल्याणसुन्दरः ।

हस्तद्वन्द्वेऽक्षमालामभयमपि धृतं कुण्डिकां श्रोणिबन्धं
सव्ये वामे निषण्णस्स्रुवधृतविधिना हूयमानेन युक्तम् ।
सर्वालङ्कारयुक्तं जलकलशधृता विष्णुना चारुणाभं
वल्लीकल्याणमूर्तिं सकलसुरगणैस्स्तूयमानं प्रपद्ये ॥

बालस्वामी ।

पद्मसव्यकटिसंयुतवामं पद्मकान्तिनिभमेकमुखं च ।
बालवृद्धिकरमीश्वरसूनुं बालमुन्नतभुजं प्रणतोऽस्मि ॥

---

१ मानसारे 'असिरथाङ्गशूलपाशानां स्थाने वरदोभयशक्तिचापाः' पठ्यन्ते ॥

अन्यच्च,

एकवक्त्रं द्विनयनं पद्मद्वयकरद्वयम् ।
प्रियप्रियकरं वन्दे बालरूपं रविप्रभम् ॥

क्रौञ्चभेत्ता ।

अभयशितकृपाणौ[1] शक्तिबाणौ च सव्ये
वरदकुलिशचापं खेटकं चान्यहस्ते ।

दधतममरसेनानायकं चाष्टबाहुं
कमलवदनषट्कं क्रौञ्चभेत्तारमीडे ॥

(कुमारतन्त्रागमे द्वितीयपटले ॥)

चतुर्भुजं त्रिनेत्रं च स्थितं सिंहासनोपरि ।
वरदाभयसंयुक्तपुष्पबाणेक्षुकार्मुकम् ॥

मयूरवाहनारूढं नमस्ये रक्षणोन्मुखम् ।
क्रौञ्चभेदकरद्वन्द्वं क्रौञ्चभेदिस्वरूपकम् ॥
रक्तवर्णः ।

(श्रीतत्वनिधौ ॥)

शिखिवाहः ।

विद्रुमप्रभमेकमुखं विभुं वज्रशक्तिवरदाभयपाणिम् ।
देवलोकरिपुघ्नमविघ्नदं नौमि[2] रुद्रभवं शिखिवाहम् ॥

दाडिमीपुष्पसंकाशं गुञ्जाभं कुङ्कुमाकृतिम् ।
षड्वक्त्रसहितं देवं द्वादशाक्षं सुयौवनम् ॥

---

१ 'मसिधराङ्ग' मिति मानसारपाठः । २ 'युग्मशक्तिशिखिवाहनं गुहम्' इति मानसारपाठः ।

चतुर्भुजमुदाराङ्गं यज्ञसूत्रेण संयुतम् ।
वरदाभयसंयुक्तं कमण्डल्वक्षधारिणम् ॥
नक्रकुण्डलसंयुक्तं करण्डमकुटोज्ज्वलम् ।
हारकेयूरकटककटिसूत्रैर्विभूषितम् ॥
रत्नविद्रुमभूषाढ्यं नव(छन्न ?)वीरसमायुतम् ।
पादनूपुरसंयुक्तं सर्वाभरणभूषितम् ॥
सर्वलक्षणसंयुक्तं कुमारं शङ्करात्मजम् ।
महावल्लीदेवसेनायुक्तं सुरगणप्रियम् ॥
इत्थं रूपं यजेन्नित्यं सर्वलोकहितावहम् ।
चतुर्भुजं बालवेषं स्कन्दं कनकसप्रभम् ॥
शक्तिकुक्कुटहस्तं च वरदाभयसंयुतम् ।
विद्रुमानिभ द्विदशहस्त रविनेत्र शक्तिशरखड्गमभयध्वजगदां च ।
वामकरचापकुलिशाब्जवरशूलखेटधरसव्यकर षण्मुख! नमस्ते ॥

षड्वक्त्रं शिखिवाहनं त्रिनयनं रक्ताम्बरालङ्कृतं
शक्तिं चर्म च खड्गशूलविशिखाभीतिं धनुश्चक्रकम् ।
पाशं कुक्कुटमङ्कुशं च वरदं दोर्भिर्दधानं तथा
ध्यायेदीप्सितसिद्धिदं शशिधरं स्कन्दं सुराराधितम् ॥
लोकालोकान्धकारप्रतिहतकिरणैर्भानुकोटिप्रकाशं
भूमिन्यस्तैककोटीष्वसनमपि शरं लम्बमानोर्ध्वकायम् ।
हस्ताभ्यां चेतराभ्यां धृतमथ कुलिशं शक्तिमम्भोरुहाक्षं
सर्वालङ्कारयुक्तं भजत सुरपुरीपालकं बाहुलेयम् ॥

(कुमारतन्त्रागमे द्वितीयपटले ॥)

चतुर्भुजं चैकवक्त्रं त्रिनेत्रमभयं वरम् ।
पाशाङ्कुशदधं चैव ज्वालाकेशशिखण्डकम् ॥

इन्द्रनीलरथारूढं रक्तोत्पलसमप्रभम् ।
चतुर्दशादिभवनं शिखिवाहनमाचरेत् ॥

रक्तवर्णः ।

अग्निजातसुब्रह्मण्यः ।

द्विमुखं चाष्टबाहुं च श्वेतं वा श्यामकन्धरम् ।
स्रुवाक्षमालां खड्गं च स्वस्तिकं दक्षिणे करे ॥

कुक्कुटं खेटकं वज्रमाज्यपात्रं तु वामके ।
अग्निहोत्रविधिं देवमग्निजातस्वरूपकम् ॥

नीलवर्णः । (?)

सौरभेयसुब्रह्मण्यः ।

चतुर्वक्त्राष्टनयनं भुजाष्टकमलासनम् ।
कुञ्चितं वामपादं च सुस्थितं दक्षिणं पदम् ॥

शक्त्युत्पले पुष्पबाणमभयं दक्षिणे करे ।
वज्रं चेक्षुधनुश्शूलं वरदं वामके दधम् ॥

पद्मपुष्पनिभं चैव सौरभेयस्वरूपकम् ।

पाटलवर्णः ।

गाङ्गेयसुब्रह्मण्यः ।

एकवक्त्रं त्रिनयनं दाडिमीकुसुमप्रभम् ।
करण्डमकुटोपेतं कुक्कुटध्वजधारिणम् ॥
नीलोत्पलधरं वन्दे मकरारूढमव्ययम् ।
परशुं पूर्णकुम्भं च सव्यहस्ते तु धारिणम् ॥
अरणिं कुक्कुटं वामे गाङ्गेयसमरूपकम् ।
पाटलवर्णः ।

गुहसुब्रह्मण्यः ।

चतुर्भुजं त्रिनेत्रं च हेमरत्नकिरीटिनम् ।
शूलं वज्रं धरं सव्ये वराभयकमन्यके ॥
श्वेतवस्त्रधरं देवं सर्वेषां रक्षणोन्मुखम् ।
जायया वामपार्श्वे तु कल्याणोत्सवविग्रहम् ॥
पादाम्बुजं हृदि ध्यात्वा गुहरूपं समाश्रये ।
श्यामवर्णः ।

ब्रह्मचारिसुब्रह्मण्यः ।

द्विनेत्रं द्विभुजं चैव बालसूर्यधरं प्रभुम् ।
दक्षभागे दण्डहस्तं वज्रवामोरुहस्तकम् ॥
सव्यापसव्यपादं तु स्थितं वा कुञ्चितं तु वा ।
शिखायज्ञोपवीताढ्यं मौञ्जीकौपीनसंयुतम् ॥

मेखलोपरिविड्याणं रक्तपद्मोपरि स्थितम् ।
दिव्यरूपधरं देवं ब्रह्मचारिणमाश्रये ॥

रक्तवर्णः ।

देशिकसुब्रह्मण्यः ।

षड्भुजं चैकवदनं करण्डमकुटान्वितम् ।
शक्तिहस्तद्वयं चैव जपमालाधरं शुभम् ॥
मयूरवाहनारूढं वराभयकराम्बुजम् ।
इत्येवं विधिवद् ध्यायेच्छिवदेवस्य देशिकम् ॥
रक्तवर्णः ।

(श्रीतत्वनिधौ ॥)

सुब्रह्मण्यद्वारपालकौ ।

सुदेहसुमुखौ विप्रौ गुहस्य द्वारपालकौ ।
एकवक्त्रौ द्विबाहू च गदाभयकरौ स्मृतौ ॥
चतुर्भुजौ चेत्तस्योर्ध्वे वज्रशक्तिधरौ तथा ।
रक्तश्यामलवर्णाढ्यौ सर्वाभरणभूषितौ ॥
सुदंष्ट्रौ स्मितवक्त्रौ च करण्डमकुटोज्वलौ ।
दक्षिणे तु सुदेहं च सुमुखं च तथोत्तरे ॥

(कुमारतन्त्रागमे पञ्चमपटले ॥)

सुमित्रः ।

सुमित्रस्थापनं वक्ष्ये शृणु कौशिक सुव्रत! ।
उक्त्वैव जननं पूर्वे(वं ?) प्रतिष्ठां च ततः परम् ॥

वसिष्ठगोत्रः स्वर्णाक्षपुत्रः काशीपुरे वसन् ।
त्रिजन्मसु पुरा स्कन्दं समभ्यर्च्य यथाविधि ॥

सुमित्र इति सेनान्या प्रोक्तः प्रीतेन देवलः ।
सुब्रह्मण्यस्य सामीप्ये गाणपत्यमवाप्तवान् ॥

उत्तमंनवतालेन सुमित्रं कारयेद् बुधः ।
द्विनेत्रं द्विभुजं रक्तं सुवक्त्रं च सुयौवनम् ॥

दक्षिणे शक्तिहस्तं च वामं च कटिबन्धनम् ।
अलकं ज्योतिसंयुक्तं दंष्ट्रिणं रुचिराननम् ॥

करण्डमकुटं वापि जटामकुटमेव वा ।
हस्तौ मुकुलवद् बद्धौ दक्षिणं शक्तिसंयुतम् ॥

सर्वाभरणसंयुक्तमासनं स्थानकं तु वा ।
यज्ञोपवीतसंयुक्तं पद्मपीठोपरि स्थितम् ॥

इत्थं रूपं सुमित्रस्य गुहेन विहितं पुरा ।

मारतन्त्रागमे द्विचत्वारिंशत्तमपटले ॥)

नन्द्यादयः ।

नन्द्यादयः ।

नन्दी ।

नन्दी कार्यस्त्रिनेत्रस्तु चतुर्बाहुर्महाभुजः ।
सिन्दूरारुणसङ्काशो व्याघ्रचर्मपरिच्छदः ॥
त्रिशूलभिन्दिपालौ च करयोस्तस्य कारयेत् ।
शिरोगतं तृतीयं तु तर्जयन्तं तथापरम् ॥
आलोकयानं कर्तव्यं दूरादागामिनं जनम् ।

(विष्णुधर्मोत्तरे ॥)

बिभ्राणं परशुं मृगं करतले ईशप्रमाणाञ्जलिं
भस्मोद्धूलितपाण्डुरं शशिकलागंगाकपर्दोज्ज्वलं ।
परियायत्रिपुरान्तकं प्रथमतः श्रेष्ठं गणैर्वन्दितं
ब्रह्मेन्द्राच्युतपूजिताङ्घ्रिकमलं श्रीनन्दिकेशं भजे ॥

चण्डेशः ।

चण्डेशस्थापनं वक्ष्ये तल्लक्षणपुरस्सरम् ।
परस्वतन्त्रभेदेन द्विविधं तच्च संमतम् ॥
पुरादौ मध्यमे वाष्टदिक्षु चण्डेश्वरालयः ।
धामेशानेऽथ सौम्ये वा सोमेशेन्द्रान्तरेऽथवा ॥

अन्तमण्डलदेशे[1]ऽन्तर्हारायां वेष्टशालके ।
अथैकादित्रयस्त्रिंशद्धस्तविस्तारसंयुतः ॥
धामलक्षणसंसिद्धधामेनापि समन्वितः ।
एकादिसप्तभूम्यन्तं भूमिभागसमन्वितः ॥
धामोक्ताकारसंयुक्तो दिक्षु चण्डेश्वरान्वितः ।
इष्टदेवान्वितो वा स्यात्केवलो वा वृषान्वितः ॥
प्रागुक्तविधिनानीतगर्भाद्येष्टकया युतः ।
मूर्धेष्टकासमायुक्तः स्थूपिस्थापनसंयुतः ॥
दक्षिणद्वारसंयुक्तः पराङ्गश्चेन्मुनीश्वराः ! ।
स्वतन्त्रस्थापने दक्षपूर्वपश्चिमदिङ्मुखः ॥
दिङ्न्यस्तामरविन्यस्तमध्यकुम्भयुतेन च ।
धामसंस्थापनेनाढ्यः प्रागुक्तविधिना सह ॥
प्रागुक्तगर्भमानाद्यं सर्वमत्र प्रयोज्यताम् ।
प्राकारमण्डपोपेतः परितः परिवारयुक् ॥
रुद्रभक्तस्ततो रुद्रचण्डश्चण्डप एव च ।
महाबलस्तथाविर्य(वीर्य ?)ष्टङ्कपाणीशसेवकौ[2] ॥
रुद्रकोपज इत्यष्टमूर्तयः परिवारगाः ।
एते श्वेता महाकायाः कृताञ्जलिपुटान्विताः ॥

---

[1] 'अन्तर्मण्डलदशे' इति पाठान्तरम् । [2] 'महाबलास्तथा विप्रा' इति पाठान्तरम् ।

सटङ्कास्तद्विहीना वा वीराद्यासनसंस्थिताः ।
कृत्तिवासोऽन्विता वाथ चण्डरूपधरास्तु वा ॥
इन्द्राद्या वा तदर्धं(र्थं ?)तु पीठं वा पूर्वतो वृषः ।
बलिपीठादिपीठान्तं पूर्ववत्कल्पयेत्तु वा ॥
द्वारस्थौ द्वारपौ कार्यौ द्विकरौ दण्डधारकौ ।
चण्डानुगश्चण्डभूत्यौ[1](भृत्यो ?) नेष्टौ वा देशिकाग्रजाः ! ॥
द्रव्यैश्शिलादिभिः कार्यः पूर्ववल्लक्षणान्वितः ।
मध्येन दशतालेन दशतालाधमेन वा ॥
प्रतिमालक्षणप्रोक्तमानेनायादिसंयुतः[2] ।
बद्धपद्मासनश्चण्डनाथो दुर्दर्शभीषणः ॥
व्यालयज्ञोपवीती च मुखोद्गीर्णमहानलः ।
करालकज्जलाभासो जटिलश्चन्द्रशेखरः ॥
चतुर्वक्त्रश्चतुर्बाहुश्चाक्षमालात्रिशूलवान् ।
टङ्कं कमण्डलुं वामे भानुरक्तार्कलोचनः ॥
अथवा शङ्खवर्णाभश्चतुर्बाहुस्त्रिलोचनः ।
चन्द्रार्धमण्डितः कृत्तिवासा वीरासनस्थितः ॥
पिनाकामोघबाणाभ्यां व्यग्रपाणितलद्वयः ।
वराभयप्रदानाभ्यामन्यत्र परिमण्डितः ॥

---

१ 'चण्डभृत्यौ' इति पाठान्तरम् । २ 'मानेनायदिसंयुतः' इति पाठान्तरम् ।

अथवा द्विभुजश्शुक्लवस्त्रस्त्र्यक्षोऽञ्जनप्रभः ।
जटामकुटयुक्तो वा तुलसीकृतमूर्धजः(?) ॥

स्थानको वासनस्थो वा शयितासव्यपात्तलः ।
सलम्बसव्यपादस्तु वामहस्तभु(स्तु ?)जानुगः ॥

वरहस्तोऽथवा स स्यादितरष्टङ्कसंयुतः ।
वामेतरकरष्टङ्कयुक्तोऽञ्जलिपुटोऽथवा ॥

शङ्करेक्षणसंपन्नश्शोकनम्रशिरास्तु वा ।
उत्कुटासनयुक शान्तो जटिलष्टङ्कधृक्करः ॥

एवं वा चण्डनाथस्तु कार्यस्त्विष्टासनान्वितः ।
अथवाभयटङ्काभ्यां पाशशूलद्वयेन तु ॥

चतुर्भुजस्तु वा कार्यश्शङ्कराज्ञानुपालकः ।
विशेषस्सिंहले देशे कश्चिदत्राभिधीयते ॥

क्रेतायां(कृतेऽय ?)मष्टहस्तस्स्यात्त्रेतायां[1] षड्भुजो मतः ।
द्वापरे च चतुर्हस्तः कलौ तु द्विकरो मतः ॥

अन्यदेशे तु सर्वत्र विभागो नायमीरितः ।
अथवा चण्डनाथस्तु देव्या तु सहितो न वा ॥

सा देवी श्यामला हस्तद्वयाखिलविभूषिता ।
धर्मनील्याख्यया ख्याता धृतनीलोत्पला वरा ॥

---

१ 'कृतयामि' ति पाठान्तरम् ।

एवमापाद्य बेरं तु मनुभिस्स्थापनं नयेत् ।

(उत्तरकामिकागमे पञ्चषष्टितमपटले ॥)

अथातस्संप्रवक्ष्यामि चण्डेशस्थापनं परम् ।
उद्भवं प्रथमं तस्य द्वितीयं स्थापनं क्रमात् ॥

रुद्रस्यैव तु रुद्रांशं तत्सर्वं चण्डनामतः ।
गणेशावरणे स्थित्वा दशांशेनायुतेन तु ॥

प्रचण्डादिर्विनिष्क्रान्ता पञ्चमूर्तिर्विधानतः ।
प्रचण्डचण्डः प्रथमं ततो विक्रान्तचण्डकः ॥

तृतीयो विभुचण्डस्तु वीरचण्डश्चतुर्थकः ।
एवं वै पञ्चचण्डेशाः पञ्चब्रह्मसमुद्भवाः ॥

कृतयुगाधिपत्यं तु प्रचण्डमिदमुच्यते ।
विक्रान्तचण्डनामा तु त्रेतायामधिपस्स्मृतः ॥

द्वापरे चाधिपत्यं हि विभुश्चण्डेश उच्यते ।
कलौ तु वीरचण्डेशस्वा(स्या?)धिपत्यं प्रकीर्तितम् ॥

एवं [वै*] पञ्चभेदेन चण्डनाम विधीयते ।
आलयस्यैशदिग्भागे विमानं पूर्ववत्क्रमात् ॥

त्रिनेत्रं चतुर्भुजं वापि द्विनेत्रं द्विभुजं तु वा ।
भीमं जटासमायुक्तं सर्वाभरणभूषितम् ॥

अभयं शान्तदेहं(?) च पाशं वै परशुं तथा ।
द्विभुजं यदि कर्तुं चेच्छान्त(?)टङ्कयुतं तथा ॥
शुक्लयज्ञोपवीतं च शुक्लाम्बरधरं तथा ।
स्थानकं चासनं प्रोक्तं पूर्वोक्तविधिना ततः ॥
(सुप्रभेदागमे सप्तचत्वारिंशत्तमपटले ॥)

चण्डश्च चण्डेश्वरो रक्तश्वेतमिश्रश्च विस्तरः ।
द्विबाहुस्सजटाजूटशेखरः कर्णकुण्डलः ॥
धृतयज्ञोपवीतश्च शुक्लाम्बरधरश्शुचिः ।
सर्वभूषणसंभूष्यष्टङ्कपाणिरथापि वा ॥
अर्धचन्द्रासनासीनः पुष्पमालावलम्बितः ।
चण्डेशस्याकृतिर्ह्येवं क्षेत्रपालाकृतिं शृणु ॥
(पूर्वकारणागमे त्रयोदशपटले ॥)

शिवभक्ताः ।

वक्ष्यामि शिवभक्तानां प्रतिष्ठां भोगमोक्षदाम् ।
ब्राह्मणा क्षत्रिया वैश्याश्शूद्रा वा ह्यन्तरालजाः ॥
स्त्रियो वा गुरवश्चैषामभिषिक्तो नृपोऽथवा ।
शिवभक्तिसमोपेता जीवन्तो वा मृतास्तु वा ॥
तेषां प्रतिकृतिं कृत्वा प्रतिष्ठाप्य समर्चयेत् ।
स्वप्रधानं पराङ्गं च द्विविधं स्थापनं मतम् ॥

ग्रामादौ वा नदीतीरे पुष्करिण्यास्तटेऽपि वा ।
वने चोपवने वापि पर्वते वा मनोरमे ॥

स्थानेऽन्यत्र च कर्तव्यं स्वप्रधानस्य मन्दिरम् ।
देवालयान्तस्सालादौ तत्र कल्पितमन्दिरे ॥

परिवारसमोपेतं स्वप्रधानं प्रकीर्तितम् ।
देवालयादौ सर्वत्र मालिकामण्डपादिषु ॥

परिवारविहीनं यत्कल्पितं त्वङ्गमिष्यते ।
तदर्थं शिवलिङ्गं वा प्रतिमा वा शिवस्य तु ॥

स्कन्दनन्द्यादिरूपं वा मृतप्रतिकृतिं तु वा ।
कुर्यादायादिसंयुक्तं शिलाद्यैरुक्तवस्तुभिः ॥

शैलं लोहं तथा वार्क्षं मृन्मयं मणिजं तु वा ।
अर्धचित्रमथाभासं पटादिपरिकल्पितम् ॥

लिङ्गं चेत्तद्विधानोक्त्या प्रतिमा च तथैव च ।
तदुक्ततालभेदेन१ कर्तव्यं स्याद् द्विजोत्तमाः ! ॥

मृतप्रतिकृतिं चोक्तामष्टतालेन कारयेत् ।
आसीनं स्थानकं वापि वाहनारूढमेव वा ॥

आसने स्थानके वाथ पद्मसिंहासनं तु वा ।
अधस्तात्कल्पयेद्विद्वानुभयं वा विधीयताम् ॥

---

१ 'तद्रक्ततालभेदेने 'ति पाठान्तरम् ।

यथेष्टासनयुक्तं वा समाश्रं वा यथाश्रकम् ।
आसनोन्मानविस्तारायामं तद्वदलंकृतिम् ॥

प्रतिमोक्तप्रकारेण प्रागुक्तविधिना नयेत् ।
शिखी वा बद्धकेशी वा मुण्डितो जटिलोऽथवा ॥

अभिषिक्तो नृपश्चेत्तु किरीटमकुटान्वितः ।
यथेष्टायुधयुक्तो वा नमस्कारयुतोऽथवा ॥

सर्वलक्षणसंपन्नस्सर्वाभरणभूषितः ।
गायका नृत्तयुक्ता वा पूजका वा यथेष्टकाः ॥

स्त्रियश्चेत्तस्यानुरूपेण[1] भूषणैरुपभूषिताः ।
एवं लक्षणमाख्यातं प्रतिष्ठाद्यं निगद्यते ॥

(उत्तरकामिकागमे षट्षष्टितमपटले ॥)

आर्य्यः ।

आर्य्यश्चतुर्भुजश्शान्तस्त्रिनेत्रः पद्मसंस्थितः ।
हिरण्यसदृशप्रख्यो दुकूलवसनान्वितः ॥

अभयवरदोपेतः खड्गखेटकधारितः ।
सुस्थितः पद्मपीठे तु आर्य्यमेवं प्रकल्पयेत् ॥

(अंशुमद्भेदागमे एकोनपञ्चाशपटले ॥)

---

१ स्त्रियश्चेदित्यर्धमादर्शान्तरे नास्ति ।

अथातस्संप्रवक्ष्यामि शास्तृस्थापनमुत्तमम् ।
शास्ता सर्वस्य लोकस्य तस्माच्छास्तेति चोच्यते ॥

समुद्रमथने काले परिगृह्यामृतं तथा ।
हरिर्बभूव स्त्रीरूपा मोहिनीनाम नामतः ॥

तां मोहिनीमहं दृष्ट्वा संगतोऽस्मि कदाचन ।
जातस्तदा महाशास्ता मेध्याहाम्रवतीश्वराः ॥

द्विनेत्रं द्विभुजं कृत्वा सर्वाभरणभूषितम् ।
श्यामवर्णयुतं तेषां शुक्लयज्ञोपवीतिनम् ॥

श्वानकुक्कुटमेषाद्यैः क्रीडन्तं सर्वसिद्धिदम् ।
मदनावर्णनीदेवौ[१](व्यौ?) पीतौरस(नोरस?)समन्वितौ(ते?) ॥

सर्वाभरणसंयुक्तौ(क्ते?) पार्श्वयोर्विन्यसेत्ततः ।
वामे दमनकं[२] न्यस्त्वा तद्वेषं विकृतं स्मृतम् ॥

द्विभुजं दक्षिणे हस्ते चक्रदण्डमथेश्वरम् ।
फलपल्लवहस्तं च कुञ्चिताङ्घ्रिकरद्वयम् ॥

भूताकारं बृहत्कुक्षिं नीलालकविभूषितम् ।
शास्तुश्च लक्षणं प्रोक्तं स्थापनं शृणु तत्वतः ॥

(सुप्रभेदागमे त्रिपञ्चाशत्तमपटले ॥)

---

१ 'पनकापर्णिनौ देव्यै' इति पाठान्तरम् । २ 'वामधे मनकं न्यस्ता' इति पाठान्तरम् ।

मोहिनीतनयश्शान्तो द्विबाहुश्श्यामसन्निभः ।
पीठालम्बितशायितौ वामदक्षिणपादकौ ॥
वामाङ्घ्रिजानुकोर्ध्वे तु वामहस्तं स्थितं कुरु ।
मण्डलीभूतदण्डाग्रो वज्रदण्डधरो युवा ॥
स्निग्धनीलाञ्जनाकीर्णकुन्दलीभूतभूध्वजः(न्तलीभूतमूर्धजः?) ।
गजवाहनकेतुस्स्याद्विलासी सविलासिनी ॥
नीलश्वेताश्ववृषभवाहनो वा चतुर्भुजः ।
रक्तचूडध्वजो वापि सर्वत्र परिकीर्तितः ॥
ज्ञानी योगासनासीनो वेदाध्यायी पवित्रकः ।
सोभयांसोपवीतस्स्यान्न्यूनावीरासनास्थितः ॥
लीलाविगीतभावी स्यात्सुर(ख?)भावी सुखासनः ।
वामोरूपरि विन्यस्त(स्ता?)वामपादतलेक्षणः ॥
आर्यस्याकृतिरेवं तु शक्रस्याकृतिरुच्यते ।

(पूर्वकारणागमे त्रयोदशपटले ॥)

क्षेत्रपालः ।

त्रिविधः क्षेत्रपालस्तु सात्विको राजसस्तमः ।
श्वेतं रक्तमथो कृष्णं सात्विकादिगुणं भवेत् ॥
द्विभुजं वा चतुर्बाहु शान्तं सात्विकमुच्यते ।
षड्बाहु चोग्रवदनमुग्रं स्याद्राजसं स्मृतम् ॥

तामसं चाष्टबाहुं च एते वै समपादकाः ।
स्थानकं पद्मपीठे तु भद्रपीठे तु वा यथा ॥
शूलं दक्षिणहस्ते तु कपालमितरे धृतम् ।
द्विभुजं ह्येवमाख्यातं चतुर्हस्तमथोच्यते ॥
परहस्ते तु सव्ये तु खड्गं घण्टां तदन्यके ।
अथवा पूर्वहस्ते तु अभयं वरदान्वितौ ॥
पूर्ववत्परहस्तौ द्वौ घण्टां वा वामहस्तके ।
सात्विकं ह्येवमाख्यातं राजसं शृणु सुव्रत ! ॥
शूलं खड्गं च घण्टां च दक्षिणे [तु*] करत्रये ।
खेटकं च कपालं च नागं वा पाशवामके ॥
तामसे तु धनुर्बाणं दक्षिणेऽदक्षिणे धृतम् ।
शेषं राजसवत्ख्यातं रक्तकेशोर्ध्वमण्डलम् ॥
उग्रदृष्टिसमायुक्तं नानानागविभूषितम् ।
त्रिनेत्रं नग्नरूपं च क्षेत्रपालं प्रकल्पयेत् ॥

(अंशुमद्भेदागमे एकोनपञ्चाशपटले ॥)

अथातस्संप्रवक्ष्यामि क्षेत्रेशस्य विधिक्रमम् ।
ईश्वरस्यायुतांशेन क्ष(क्षे ?)त्रपालोद्भवं तथा ॥
ग्रामादावैशदिग्भागे लोकरक्षार्थकारणम् ।
प्रासादं प्रतिमां तत्र पूर्वोक्तविधिना तथा ॥

द्वारं तु पश्चिमे मुख्यं दक्षिणे मध्यमं स्मृतम् ।
कन्यसं चेन्द्रदिग्द्वारं प्रतिमालक्षणं ततः ॥

चतुर्भुजं त्रिनेत्रं वा षड्भुजं चाष्टहस्तकम् ।
सुदंष्ट्रं भैरवाकारं कृष्णवर्णं दिगम्बरम् ॥

सर्पयज्ञोपवीतं च शिरोमालाकरोटिकम् ।
ऊर्ध्वकेशं सुवृत्ताक्षं नागाभरणभूषितम् ॥

त्रिशूलं दक्षिणे हस्ते वामहस्ते कपालकम् ।
खड्गं च दक्षिणे हस्ते वामहस्ते तु खेटकम् ॥

एवं चतुर्भुजं विद्धि षड्भुजं च ततः शृणु ।
नागं च दक्षिणे पाणौ तोमरं वामहस्तके ॥

प्रागुक्तायुधसंयुक्तं षड्भुजं त्विति कीर्तितम् ।
शूलं डमरुखट्वाङ्गं दक्षिणे वामहस्तके ॥

एवमष्टभुजं प्रोक्तं षड्भुजायुधसन्निभम् ।

(सुप्रभेदागमे पञ्चाशत्तमपटले ॥)

रक्तोग्रेक्षणः कालमेघवर्णो वापि महाबली ।
द्विबाहुर्वा चतुर्बाहुरष्टबाहुरथापि वा ॥

कपालशूलो द्विभुजो घण्टापाशसमायुतः ।
चतुर्बाहुः क्रमात्क्षेत्रपालो वामे च दक्षिणे ॥

अग्निटङ्कौ च खट्वाङ्गं भयमष्टभुजे क्रमात् ।
रक्तपद्मासनारूढः श्यामवर्णोग्ररूपकः ॥
विसृतोर्ध्वो(र्ध्व ?) रक्तकेशः कुञ्चितभ्रूसविभ्रमः ।
नग्नरूप(पः ?)शिरोमालाभूषितस्तीक्ष्णदंष्ट्रकः ॥

(पूर्वकारणागमे त्रयोदशपटले ॥)

ब्रह्मा ।

चतुर्भुजश्चतुर्वक्त्रो हरितालसमप्रभः ।
जटामकुटसंयुक्तः पिङ्गाक्षस्सर्वभूषणः ॥
कृष्णाजिनोत्तरीयश्च यज्ञसूत्रसमन्वितः ।
शुक्लवस्त्रधरश्शान्तः कटिसूत्रसमन्वितः ॥
शुक्लमाल्यानुलेपश्च कर्णकुण्डलमण्डितः ।
दक्षिणे चाक्षमाला च कूर्चं चैव तु धारयेत् ॥
कमण्डलुकुश(शं ?) वामे दक्षिणे स्रुक्स्रुवौ तलः (?) ।
आज्यस्थालीं कुशांचैव(श्चैव ?) वामहस्ते तु धारयेत् ॥
अभयवरदोपेतौ पूर्वहस्तौ द्विजोत्तम ! ।
आसने तूभयाङ्घ्रिश्च शाययेत्तु ततः परम् ॥
मेढ्रमूलोपरिष्टात्तु वामहस्तोर्ध्ववक्त्रकम् ।
सव्यहस्तं च तस्योर्ध्वे तदन्यास्यं च कारयेत् ॥

दक्षिणे चाक्षमालां च वामहस्ते कमण्डलुम् ।
सरस्वती दक्षभागे सावित्री वामभागके ॥
आसीनो वा स्थितो वापि पद्मपीठोपरि स्थितः ।

(अंशुमद्भेदागमे एकोनपञ्चाशपटले ॥)

चतर्मुखं चतुर्बाहुं कमण्डल्वक्षधारिणम् ।
रक्तवर्णजटायुक्तं कृत्वा ब्रह्माणमुज्वलम् ॥
सावित्रीं वामपार्श्वे तु सर्वालङ्कारसंयुताम् ।
एवं चतुर्मुखं कुर्याज्जगत्सृष्टिकरं शुभम् ॥

(सुप्रभेदागमे चतुस्त्रिंशत्तमपटले ॥)

लिखेच्चतुर्मुखं देवं चतुर्बाहुं शुभेक्षणम् ।
रत्नकुण्डलसंयुक्तं लम्बकूर्चोपरि स्थितम् ॥
कृष्णाजिनधरं गौरं शुक्लाम्बरविराजितम् ।
दक्षिणं वरदं हस्तं तत्रान्यांशुभ (न्यंस्रुव?) धारिणम् ॥
कमण्डलुधरं वामं तथान्यं संयुतं शु(स्रु?)चा ।
बिभ्राणं चतुरो वेदान् पुरतश्चास्य विन्यसेत् ॥
वामे पार्श्वे तु सावित्रीं दक्षिणे तु सरस्वतीम् ।
आज्यस्थालीं पुरोभागे महिषीश्च(महर्षींश्च ?) समन्ततः ॥

हंसारूढं लिखेत्क्वापि क्वचिच्च कमलासनम् ।
स्रष्टारं सर्वलोकानां ब्रह्माणं परिकल्पयेत् ॥

(शिल्परत्ने पञ्चविंशपटले ॥)

ब्रह्मा कमण्डलुकरश्चतुर्मुखः पङ्कजासनस्थश्च ।

(बृहत्संहितायामष्टापञ्चाशत्तमाध्याये ॥)

ब्रह्माणं कारयेद्विद्वान् देवं सौम्यं चतुर्भुजम् ।
बद्धपद्मासनं तुष्टं तथा कृष्णाजिनाम्बरम् ॥
जटाधरं चतुर्बाहुं सप्तहंसरथस्थितम् ।
वामे न्यस्तेतरकरं तस्यैकं दोर्युगं भवेत् ॥
एत(क?)स्मिन् दक्षिणे पाणावक्षमाला तथा शुभा ।
कमण्डलुं द्वितीये च सर्वाभरणधारिणम् ॥
सर्वलक्षणयुक्तस्य शान्तिरूपस्य पार्थिव! ।
पद्मपत्रदलाग्राभं ध्यानसंमीलितेक्षणम् ॥
अर्चायां कारयेदेवं चित्रे वा वास्तुकर्मणि ।

(विष्णुपुराणे ॥)

पद्मपत्रासनस्थश्च ब्रह्मा कार्यश्चतुर्मुखः ।
सावित्री तस्य कर्तव्या वामोत्सङ्गगता तथा ॥

(आदित्यपुराणे ॥)

ऋग्वेदादि प्रभेदेन कृतादियुगभेदतः।
विप्रादिवर्णभेदेन चतुर्वक्त्रं चतुर्भुजं॥
दक्षिणाधः करात्स्रष्टा जपमालां तथा स्रुचम्।
पुस्तं कमण्डलुं धत्ते सकूर्चःकमलासनः॥
अक्षसूत्रं पुस्तकं च धत्ते पद्मं कमण्डलुम्।
चतुर्वक्त्रा तु सावित्री श्रोत्रियाणां गृहे हिता॥

(रूपमण्डने॥)

जटिलाः श्मश्रुलाः शान्ता आसीना ध्यानतत्पराः।
कमण्डल्वक्षसूत्राभ्यां संयुक्ता ऋषयस्स्मृताः॥
विश्वकर्मा चतुर्बाहुरक्षमालां च पुस्तकम्।
कं वा(बुं?) कमण्डलुं धत्ते त्रिनेत्रो हंसवाहनः॥
आग्नेय्यां तु गणेशस्स्यान्मातृस्थानं च दक्षिणे।
नैरृत्ये तु सहस्राक्षं वारुण्यां जलशायिनम्॥
वायव्ये पार्वतीरुद्रौ ग्रहांश्चैवोत्तरे न्यसेत्।
ऐशान्ये कमलादेवीं प्राच्यां तु धरणीधरम्॥

इति ब्रह्मायतनम्।

ब्रह्मप्रतीहाराः।

ब्रह्मणोऽष्टौ प्रतीहारान् कथयिष्याम्यनुक्रमात्।
पु(प?)रुषाकारगम्भीराः सकूर्चा मकुटोज्ज्वलाः॥

पद्मं स्रुक्पुस्तकं दण्डं सत्यो वामेऽथ दक्षिणे ।
सव्यापसव्ये करके शेषं प्राग्वत्सधर्मकः ॥

अक्षं पद्मागमौ दण्डं करैर्धत्ते प्रियोद्भवः ।
दण्डागमस्रुक्फलकैर्यज्ञः स्यादायुधैः शुभैः ॥

अक्षसूत्रगदाखेटदण्डैर्विजयनामकः ।
अधोहस्तापसव्येन खेटकं यज्ञभद्रकः ॥

अक्षः पाशाङ्कुशौ दण्डो भवे स्यात्सार्वकामिकः ।
दण्डाङ्कुशपाशपद्मैर्विभवस्सर्वशान्तिदः ॥

इति ब्रह्मप्रतीहाराः ।

(रूपमण्डने ॥)

दिक्पालाः ।

दिक्पालाः ।

इन्द्रः ।

श्यामवर्ण(र्णं) द्विहस्तं च रक्ताम्बरधरं शुभम् ।
किरीटमकुटोपेतं सर्वाभरणभूषितम् ॥

शक्तिर्दक्षिणहस्ते तु वामहस्तेऽङ्कुशं धृतम् ।
विशालोदरग्रीवं च वामे शचीसमन्वितम् ॥

द्विनेत्रं सौम्यवदनं सिंहासनोपरि स्थितम् ।
आसीनं वा प्रकर्त्तव्यं गजारूढमथापि वा ॥

इन्द्रमेवं समाख्यातमश्विन्यौ च प्रवक्ष्यते ।

(अंशुमद्भेदागमे एकोनपञ्चाशपटले ॥)

इन्द्रमैन्द्रे तु मतिमांस्त्विन्द्रो वज्राङ्कुशोधरात्[1] ।
श्यामाङ्गं तु गजारूढमप्सरोगणसंयुतम् ॥

(सुप्रभेदागमे अष्टचत्वारिंशत्तमपटले ॥)

सुरराजं प्रवक्ष्येऽहमैरावतसमाश्रितम् ।
किरीटकुण्डलधरं भुजद्वयसमन्वितम् ॥

---

१ 'वज्राङ्कुशौ दधत्' इति पाठान्तरम् ।

कुलिशं दक्षिणे पाणौ वामहस्ते तथोत्पलम् ।
दिव्यरत्नविभूषाढ्यं दिव्यचीनांशुकैर्युतम् ॥
चित्रचामरधारिण्यौ स्त्रियौ पार्श्वे प्रकल्पयेत् ।
सिंहासनस्थमथवा लिखेद् गन्धर्वसंयुतम् ॥
इन्द्राणीं वामतस्तस्य लिखेदुत्पलधारिणीम् ।
दिव्यश्रृङ्गारसंयुक्तामिन्द्रवक्त्रावलोकिनीम् ॥

(शिल्परत्नसंयोजिते कस्मिंश्चिद् ग्रन्थे ॥)

शुक्लश्चतुर्विषाणो द्विपो महेन्द्रस्य वज्रपाणित्वं च ।
तिर्यग्ललाटसंस्थं तृतीयमपि लोचनं चिह्नम् ॥

(बृहत्संहितायामष्टापञ्चाशत्तमाध्याये ॥)

चतुर्दन्ते गजे सक्तः श्वेतः कार्यस्सुरेश्वरः ।
वामोत्सङ्गगता कार्या तस्य भार्या शची नृप ! ॥
नीलवस्त्रा सुवर्णाभा सर्वाभरणवांस्तथा ।
तिर्यग्ललाटकस्ताक्ष्र्यः(स्याक्षः ?) कर्तव्यश्च विभूषितः ॥
शक्रश्चतुर्भुजः कार्यो द्विभुजा च तथा शशी(ची ?) ।
पद्माङ्कुशौ च कर्तव्यौ वामदक्षिणहस्तयोः ॥
वामं शचीपृष्ठगतं द्वितीयं वज्रसंयुतम् ।
वामे शच्याः करे कार्या रम्या सन्तानमञ्जरी ॥

दक्षिणं पृष्ठविन्यस्तं देवराजस्य कारयेत् ।

(विष्णुधर्मोत्तरे ॥)

वज्रपाणिर्महावीरस्सिंहस्कन्धोऽवलीलधृक् ।

ललाटोरस्स्थलायामपीवरोरुर्महोदरः ॥

प्रसन्नवदनश्श्यामवर्णो रक्ताम्बरस्सुखी ।

किरीटकुण्डली हारकेयूरादिविभूषितः ॥

पृथुशिरोगजारूढो देवराजश्शचीपतिः ।

शक्रस्याकृतिरेवं तु चण्डेशस्याकृतिं शृणु ॥

(पूर्वकारणागमे त्रयोदशपटले ॥)

वरं वराङ्कुशौ चैव कुण्डीं धत्ते करैस्तु यः ।

गजारूढः सहस्राक्ष इन्द्रः पूर्वदिशाधिपः ॥

(रूपमण्डने ॥)

वह्निः ।

वच्मीह वह्निरूपं तु रक्तवर्णं चतुर्भुजम् ।

वरदाभयहस्तं च................ ॥

शक्तिस्स्यादपरे वामे दक्षिणे तु स्रुचं धरम् ।

एकाननं त्रिनेत्रं च रक्तकेशोर्ध्वमेव च ॥

वह्निरूपं समाख्यातमेवं धामनि विन्यसेत् ।

(सुप्रभेदागमे एकचत्वारिंशत्तमपटले ॥)

कृत्वा चाग्निमजारूढं रक्ताभं रक्तलोचनम् ।
शिखाभिरूर्ध्वगाभिश्च युक्ति(क्तं ?)शक्तिस्रुवं धरम् ॥

(सुप्रभेदागमे अष्टचत्वारिंशत्तमपटले ॥)

वह्नेस्स्वरूपं वक्ष्यामि शुद्धकाञ्चनसुप्रभम् ।
अर्धचन्द्रासनगतं रक्तवस्त्रविराजितम् ॥
लोहितं वा प्रकुर्वीत बालार्कसमतेजसम् ।
युक्तं यज्ञोपवीतेन लम्बकूर्चेन शोभितम् ॥
मेषपृष्ठस्थितं देवं भुजद्वयसमन्वितम् ।
दक्षिणे चाक्षसूत्रं स्यात् करे वामे कमण्डलुः ॥
स्वाहादेवी कृता पार्श्वे कुङ्कुमेन विलेपिता ।
अरुणैरम्बरैर्भव्या लेख्या मात्र (?) विभूषिता ॥
कुण्डस्थो वा प्रकर्तव्यो हव्यवाहो विचक्षणैः ।
ज्वालाभिस्सप्तशीर्षेण शोभमानो महाद्युतिः ॥

(शिल्परत्नसंयोजिते कस्मिंश्चिद् ग्रन्थे)

रक्तं जटाधरं वह्निं कारयेद्धूम्रवाससम् ।
ज्वालामालाकुलं सौम्यं त्रिनेत्रं श्मश्रुधारिणम् ॥
चतुर्बाहुं चतुर्दंष्ट्रं देवेशं वायुसारथिम् ।
चतुर्भिश्च शुकैर्युक्ते धूमाचिह्नरथे स्थितम् ॥

वामोत्सङ्गगता स्वाहा शक्रस्येव शची भवेत् ।
रत्नपात्रकरा देवी वह्नेर्दक्षिणहस्तयोः ॥
ज्वालात्रिशूले कर्तव्ये त्वक्षमाल्यं च वामके ।
(विष्णुधर्मोत्तरे ॥)

अर्धचन्द्रासनासीनो ब्रह्मरूपो हुताशनः ।
प्रज्वलत्काञ्चनज्योतिः पिङ्गलः पिङ्गलोचनः ॥
हेमकूर्चाग्रसदृशस्वरूपं च शिरोरुहम् ।
तरुणादित्यसंकाशं तद्वस्त्रमुपवीतकम् ॥
अक्षमाला च शक्तिश्च दक्षिणेऽदक्षिणेऽपि च ।
ज्वालामालाकुलं तीव्रं पार्श्वस्थान्य(स्थं ह्यं ?)शुमण्डलम् ॥
मेषारूढं च कुण्डस्थो योगपट्टेन वेष्टितम् ।
दक्षिणे तु स्थिता स्वाहा रत्नकुण्डलमाण्डिता ॥
अग्नेराकृतिरेवं स्याच्छृणु वैवस्वताकृतिम् ।
(पूर्वकारणागमे चतुर्दशपटले ॥)

वरदः शक्तिहस्तश्च समृणालकमण्डलुः ।
ज्वालापुञ्जनिभो देवो मेषारूढो हुताशनः ॥
(रूपमण्डने ॥)

वैवस्वतः ।

द्विभुजः कृष्णवर्णस्तु खड्गखेटकधारिणी ।
करालदंष्ट्रवदनो रक्तमाल्यानुलेपनः ॥

रक्तवस्त्रधरोग्रश्च किरीटमकुटान्वितः ।
दीप्ताग्निसदृशाक्षश्च महामहिषवाहनः ॥

यमस्त्वेवं हि पार्श्वस्थौ तमिस्रौ चोग्रवक्त्रकौ ।
चित्रगुप्तः कलिश्चैव द्वारपार्श्वे तु संस्थितौ ॥

कृष्णश्यामनिभौ तौ च रक्तवस्त्रसिता(धरा ?) वुभौ ।
पीठपार्श्वस्थितौ मृत्युसहितादु(संहितौ व्यु ?)ग्रतेजसौ ॥

नीललोहितसङ्काशौ द्वौ चामरधृते स्त्रियौ ।
पुरतः संस्थितौ विप्रौ धर्माधर्म समाह्वयौ[1] ॥

यमस्सिंहासनासीनो महिषारोहितस्तु वा ।
यमलक्षणमाख्यातं रोहिणीलक्षणं शृणु ॥

(अंशुमद्भेदागमे एकोनपञ्चाशपटले ॥)

यमं सुदण्डहस्तं तु महिषासनसंस्थितम् ।
करालं कालवर्णं च फलपल्लवपाणिनम् ॥

(सुप्रभेदागमे अष्टचत्वारिंशत्तमपटले ॥)

पितृराजं प्रवक्ष्यामि नीलाञ्जनसमच्छविम् ।
दण्डं पाशं धनुर्दोर्भ्यां प्रदीप्ताग्निविलोचनम् ॥

महामहिषमारूढं सिंहासनमथापि वा ।
मृत्युना चित्रगुप्तेन पार्श्वयोरुपशोभितम् ॥

---

१ 'धर्मशर्म समाह्वया' विति पाठान्तरम् ।

करालैः किंकरैश्चैव सुरासुरगणैस्तथा ।
धर्मिभिः पापिभिश्चैव सेव्यमानं निरन्तरम् ॥

(शिल्परत्नसंयोजिते कस्मिंश्चिद् ग्रन्थे ॥)

सजलाम्बुदसच्छायस्तप्तचामीकराम्बरः ।
महिषस्थश्च कर्तव्यस्सर्वाभरणवान् यमः ॥
नीलोत्पलाभां धूम्रोर्णां(धूमोर्णां?) वामोत्सङ्गे च कारयेत् ।
धूम्रोर्णा(धूमोर्णा?) द्विभुजा कार्या यमः कार्यश्चतुर्भुजः ॥
दण्डखड्गावुभौ कार्यौ यमदक्षिणहस्तयोः ।
ज्वाला त्रिशूला कर्तव्या त्वक्षमाला च वामके ॥
दण्डोपरि मुखं कार्यं ज्वालामालाविभूषणम् ।
धूम्रोर्णा(धूमोर्णा?)दक्षिणो हस्तो यमपृष्ठगतो भवेत् ॥
वामे तस्याः करे कार्यं मातुलुङ्गं सुदर्शनम् ।
पार्श्वे तु दक्षिणे तस्य चित्रगुप्तं तु कारयेत् ॥
औदीच्यवेषं स्वाकारं द्विभुजं सौम्यदर्शनम् ।
दक्षिणे लेखनी तस्य वामे पत्रं तु कारयेत् ॥
वामे पाशधरः कार्यः कालो विकटदर्शनः ।

(विष्णुधर्मोत्तरे ॥)

दण्डपाणिर्महादीप्तः कालाञ्जनसमच्छविः ।
महामहिषिकारूढो दीप्ताग्निसमलोचनः ॥

(पूर्वकारणागमे चतुर्दशपटले ॥)

लेखनीं पुस्तकं धत्ते कुक्कुटं दण्डमेव च ।
महामहिषमारूढो यमः कृष्णाङ्ग ईरितः ॥

(रूपमण्डने ॥)

निर्ऋतिः ।

निर्ऋतिर्नीलवर्णस्तु द्विभुजश्च महातनुः ।
खड्गं दक्षिणहस्तेन वामहस्तेन खेटकम् ॥

पीतवस्त्रधरं रौद्रं करालास्यं च दंष्ट्रिणम् ।
सर्वाभरणसंयुक्तं नानापुष्पैरलङ्कृतम् ॥

दुकूलवसनास्सर्वाः पीनोरुजघनस्तनाः ।
मध्यक्षामातिसौम्याश्च किञ्चित्प्रहसिताननाः ॥

नानागन्धानुलिप्ताङ्गा भद्रपीठोपरि स्थिताः ।
समभङ्गसमायुक्तास्सप्तसङ्ख्याप्सरास्स्मृताः ॥

अप्सरैश्च समायुक्तो निर्ऋतिश्च विशेषतः ।
निर्ऋतिस्त्वेवमाख्यातं वरुणस्त्वथ वक्ष्यते ॥

(अंशुमद्भेदागमे एकोनपञ्चाशपटले ॥)

खड्गखेटकसंयुक्तं निर्ऋतिश्यामवर्णकम् ।
करालं विकृताकारं सिंहारूढं द्विनेत्रकम् ॥

(सुप्रभेदागमे अष्टचत्वारिंशत्तमपटले ॥)

राक्षसं संप्रवक्ष्यामि नैर्ऋते स्थितम् ।
नरयानसमारूढं रक्षि(क्षो ?)भिर्बहुभिश्श्रितम् ॥
कालमेघसमाभासं खड्गखेटकधारिणम् ।
पीतवस्त्रपरीधानं स्वर्णभूषाविभूषितम् ॥

(शिल्परत्नसंयोजिते कस्मिंश्चिद् ग्रन्थे ॥)

विरूपाक्षो विवृत्ता(वृता ?)स्यः प्राशु(प्रांशु ?)दंष्ट्रोज्वलाननः ।
ऊर्ध्वकेशी खरस्थश्च द्विबाहुर्भीषणाननः ॥
कर्णेन कृष्णरक्ताङ्गः कृष्णाम्बरधरस्तथा ।
सर्वाभरणवान् दंष्ट्रासङ्कैर्दण्डधरस्तथा ॥
भार्याश्चतस्त्रः कर्तव्या देवी च निर्ऋतिस्तथा ।
कृष्णाङ्गी कृष्णवदना पाशहस्ता तु वामतः ॥

(विष्णुधर्मोत्तरे ॥)

राक्षसेशो विशालाक्षः पीतवस्त्रश्शवासनः ।
निर्ऋतिस्सुस्थितासीनः खड्गहस्तो महोज्वलः ॥
निर्ऋतेराकृतिर्ह्येवं वरुणस्याकृतिं शृणु ।

(पूर्वकारणागमे चतुर्दशपटले ॥)

खड्गं च खेटकं हस्तैः कर्त्तिकां वैरिमस्तकम् ।
दंष्ट्राकरालवदनं श्वानारूढश्च राक्षसः ॥

(रूपमण्डने ॥)

वरुणः ।

वरुणश्शुक्लवर्णस्तु द्विभुजः पाशहस्तकः ।
सर्वाभरणसंयुक्तः करण्डमकुटान्वितः ॥
पीतवस्त्रधरश्शान्तो महाबलसमन्वितः ।
यज्ञसूत्रसमायुक्तो मकरस्थानकासनः ॥

(अंशुमद्भेदागमे एकोनपञ्चाशपटले ॥)

वरुणं पाशहस्तं तु शुक्लवर्णसमप्रभम् ।
अन्यहस्तेन वरदं सर्वाभरणभूषितम् ॥

(सुप्रभेदागमे अष्टचत्वारिंशत्तमपटले ॥)

सप्तहंसे रथे कार्यो वरुणो यादसां पतिः ।
स्निग्धवैदूर्यसंकाशः श्वेताम्बरधरस्तथा ॥
किंचित्प्रलम्बजठरो मुक्ताहारविभूषितः ।
सर्वाभरणवान् राजन्! महादेवश्चतुर्भुजः ॥
वामभागगतं केतुं मकरं तस्य कारयेत् ।
छत्रं तु सुसितं मूर्ध्नि भार्या सर्वाङ्गसुन्दरी ॥
वामोत्सङ्गगता कार्या मध्ये तु द्विभुजा नृप! ।
उत्पलं कारयेद्वामे दक्षिणे(णं?) देवपृष्ठगम् ॥
पद्मपाशौ करे कार्यौ देवदक्षिणहस्तयोः ।
शङ्खं च रत्नपात्रं च वामयोस्तस्य कारयेत् ॥

भागे तु दक्षिणे गङ्गा मकरस्था सचामरा ।
देवी पद्मकरा कार्या चन्द्रगौरी वरानना ॥
वामे तु यमुना कार्या कूर्मसंस्था सचामरा ।
नीलोत्पलकरा सौम्या नीलनीरजसन्निभा ॥
(विष्णुधर्मोत्तरे ॥)

शङ्खकुन्देन्दुधवलः पाशहस्तो महाबलः ।
केयूरकुण्डली हारी पीतवासास्सुशोभनः ॥
आसीनो वा स्थितो वापि मकरे वरुणस्स्मृतः ।
(पूर्वकारणागमे चतुर्दशपटले ॥)

वरं पाशौ ब्यलं कुण्डी हस्तैर्बिभ्रत्क्रमाच्च यः ।
नक्रारूढः स कर्त्तव्यो वरुणः पश्चिमाश्रितः ॥
(रूपमण्डने ॥)

वायुः ।

द्विभुजस्तु महीवीर्य्यस्ताम्राक्षो धूम्रसन्निभः ।
ध्वजं वै दक्षिणे हस्ते वामहस्ते तु दण्डधृक् ॥
कुञ्चितभ्रूयुतो वायुः श्वेताम्बरविभूषितः ।
नानाभरणसंयुक्तः केशाढ्यः केशैस्तु सुविकीर्णकः ॥
सिंहासनोपरिष्ठात्तु शीघ्रयात्रोत्सुकः स्थितः ।
वायुरेवं समाख्यातो रुद्रलक्षणमुच्यते ॥
(अंशुमद्भेदागमे एकोनपञ्चाशपटले ॥)

अनिलं धूम्रवर्णं तु मृगारूढं ध्रवं (धृत ?)ध्वजम् ।
सव्येऽङ्कुशधरं श्यामं चात्मानं विधिवद् गतम् ॥

(सुप्रभेदागमे अष्टाचत्वारिंशत्तमपटले ॥)

समीरणं प्रवक्ष्यामि सूत्रहरिणवाहनम् ।
पीताम्बरधरं देवं चित्ररत्नविभूषितम् ॥

वरदं दक्षिणं हस्तं वामहस्तं पताकयम् (या ?) ।
बिभ्राणं कुण्डलोपेतं किरीटवरधारिणम् ॥

(शिल्परत्नसंयोजिते कस्मिंश्चिद् ग्रन्थे ॥)

वायुरम्बरवर्णस्तु तदाकाराम्बरो भवेत् ।
काष्ठपूरितचक्रस्तु द्विभुजो रूपसंयुतः ॥

गमनेच्छुश्शिवा भार्या तस्य कार्या च वामतः ।
कार्यो गृहीतचक्राङ्कः कराभ्यां पवनो द्विजः ॥

तथैव देवी कर्तव्या शिवा परमसुन्दरी ।
व्यावृतास्यस्तथा कार्यो देवो व्याकुलमूर्धजः ॥

(विष्णुधर्मोत्तरे ॥)

कुञ्चितभ्रूर्युवा वायुस्ताम्रदृग् धूम्रसन्निभः ।
अङ्कुशेन करो वीर्यश्शम्बराम्बरसंयुतः ॥

मृगारूढो विधातव्यस्सर्वाभरणभूषितः ।
एवं सदागतिस्सर्वव्यापकोऽयं समीरणः ॥

(पूर्वकारणागमे चतुर्दशपटले ॥)

वरं ध्वजं पताका च कमण्डलुकरैर्दधत् ।
मृगारूढो हरिद्धर्म्म(र्णः?) पवनो वायुदिक्पतिः ॥

(रूपमण्डने ॥)

धनदः ।

धनदस्सर्वयक्षेशस्सर्वाभरणभूषितः ।
तप्तकाञ्चनसङ्काशो हस्तद्वयसमन्वितः ॥

वरदाभयहस्तश्च गदां वै वामहस्तके ।
करण्डमकुटोपेतस्सितवासोत्तरीयकः ॥

दक्षभागे शङ्खनिधिर्वामे पद्मनिधिस्तथा ।
धनदस्य तु वामे तु देवीं कुर्यात्सलक्षणाम् ॥

पद्मपीठोपरिष्टात्तु द्विनेत्रो मेषवाहनः ।
रक्ताम्बरधरस्सौम्यश्शङ्खपद्मनिधिर्युतः ॥

शङ्खपद्मनिधी द्वौ च भूताकारौ महाबलौ ।
आसीनौ पद्मपीठे तु पद्महस्तौ द्विजोत्तम! ॥

करण्डमकुटोपेतौ सितावासोत्तरीयकौ ।
धनदं ह्येवमाख्यातं प्राग्वद्रुद्रांश्च कल्पयेत् ॥

(अंशुमद्भेदागमे एकोनपञ्चाशपटले ॥)

यक्षेशं तु गदाहस्तं श्यामरूपं भयावहम् ।
द्विबाहुं रक्तवस्त्राढ्यं रक्ताक्षं रक्तपाणिनम् ॥

(सुप्रभेदागमे अष्टचत्वारिंशत्तमपटले ॥)

हरमित्रं प्रवक्ष्यामि द्रव्यहारविभूषितम् ।
किरीटकुण्डलयुतं श्वेताम्बरविराजितम् ॥
नरयुक्तविमानस्थं गदापाणिं वरप्रदम् ।
महोदरं महाबाहुं गौरवर्णं मनोहरम् ॥
अष्टभिर्निधिभिर्युक्तं द्रविणव्यग्रपाणिभिः ।
समन्ताद् गुह्यकैर्युक्तं चित्रकर्मणि लेखयेत् ॥

(शिल्परत्नसंयोजिते कस्मिंश्चिद् ग्रन्थे ॥)

कर्तव्यः पद्मपत्राभो वरदो नरवाहनः ।
चामीकराभो वरदस्सर्वाभरणभूषितः ॥
लम्बोदरश्चतुर्बाहुर्वामपिङ्गललोचनः ।
आपीच्यवेषः कवची हारभारी मनोहरः ॥
द्वे च दंष्ट्रे मुखे तस्य कर्तव्ये श्मश्रुधारिणः ।
वामेन विभवा कार्या मौलिस्तस्यारिमर्दन! ॥
वामोत्सङ्गगता कार्या वृद्धिर्देवी वरप्रदा ।
देवपृष्ठगतं पाणिं द्विभुजायास्तु दक्षिणम् ॥
रत्नपात्रधरं कुर्याद्वामं रिपुनिषूदन! ।
गदाशक्ती च कर्तव्ये तस्य दक्षिणहस्तयोः ॥
सिंहार्कलक्षणं केतुं शिविकामपि पादयोः (?) ।
शङ्खपद्मनिधी कार्यौ सरूपौ निधिसंस्थितौ ॥

शङ्खपद्माञ्जलिक्रान्तं वदनं तस्य पार्श्वयोः (?) ।

(विष्णुधर्मोत्तरे ॥)

मकुटी कुण्डली हारी केयूरी नरवाहनः ।

यक्षराजः कुबेरोऽयं तप्तकाञ्चनसन्निभः ॥

शङ्खपद्मनिधीयुक्तो गदाहस्तो निधीश्वरः ।

(पूर्वकारणागमे चतुर्दशपटले ॥)

गदानिधीबीजपूरकमण्डलुधरः करैः ।

गजारूढः प्रकर्त्तव्यः सौम्ययो (?)नरवाहनः ॥

(रूपमण्डने ॥)

ईशः ।

ईशो वै द्विभुजश्शान्तस्सर्वाभरणभूषितः ।

जटामकुटसंयुक्तश्शुक्लवस्त्रद्युतिः स्थितः ॥

शुक्लयज्ञोपवीतश्च शुक्लपद्मोपरि स्थितः ।

शूलं दक्षिणहस्ते तु कपालं वामहस्तके ॥

ईशानमेत्रमाख्यातं ततो वै भास्कराकृतिः ।

(अंशुमद्भेदागमे एकोनपञ्चाशपटले ॥)

ईशानं तु चतुर्बाहुं त्रिनेत्रं तु जटाधरम् ।

शूलपाणिं वृषारूढं वरदाभयपाणिनम् ॥

(सुप्रभेदागमे अष्टचत्वारिंशत्तमपटले ॥)

ईशानं संप्रवक्ष्यामि शारदेन्दुसमप्रभम् ।
शुभ्रं वृषभमारूढं बालेन्दुकृतशेखरम् ॥

जटामण्डलभूषाढ्यं लोचनत्रयभूषितम् ।
त्रिशूलपाणिं वरदं व्याघ्रचर्माम्बरावृतम् ॥

मणिकुण्डलभूषाढ्यं नागयज्ञोपवीतिनम् ।
लिखेदेवंविधं देवं चित्रकं चित्रकोविदः ॥

(शिल्परत्नसंयोजिते कस्मिंश्चिद् ग्रन्थे ॥)

वृषारूढो महाराजो धवलः पिङ्गलेक्षणः ।
त्रिशूलपाणिरीशानस्त्रिनेत्रो लोकशङ्करः ॥

(पूर्वकारणागमे चतुर्दशपटले ॥)

वरं तथा त्रिशूलं च भागेद्र(?)बीजपूरकम् ।
बिभ्राणो वृषभारूढ ईशानो धवलद्युतिः ॥

(रूपमण्डने ॥)

अश्विन्यादिमूर्त्त्यन्तराणि ।

अश्विन्यादिमूर्त्यन्तराणि ।

अश्विनीदेवते ।

एकसिंहासनासीनावश्विन्यावश्वरूपिणौ ।
दाडिमीपुष्पसङ्काशावुभयौ सोपवीतिनौ ॥
फुल्लरक्तोत्पलाक्षौ च पीतस्त्रग्वस्त्रधारिणौ ।
नासत्योदस्रनामोक्त[1] जटामकुटधारिणौ ॥
करद्वयसमायुक्तौ श्रीभूषणविभूषितौ ।
अभयं दक्षिणं हस्तं पुस्तकं वामहस्तके ॥
लम्बितं दक्षिणं पादं वाममुत्कुटि(त्कटु?)कासनम् ।
देवानां भिषजावेतौ तौ चिकित्साविधायिनौ ॥
तयोश्च पार्श्वयोर्विप्र! दक्षिणेऽदक्षिणे क्रमात् ।
मृतसञ्जीविनी चैव संज्ञितौ(?) चामरोद्धृतौ ॥
पृष्ठे विशल्यकरणी द्वे स्त्रियोपेतपिङ्गलौ(?) ।
वामे धन्वन्तरिश्चैव आत्रेयश्च तथैव च ॥
पीतरक्तनिभावेतौ विधेयौ कृष्णवाससौ ।
खड्गखेटकहस्तौ तौ सर्वाभरणभूषितौ ॥

---

१ 'नासत्यदस्रनामाना' विति पाठान्तरम् ।

अश्विनाविति विख्यातौ वह्निः पूर्ववदेव हि ।

(अंशुमद्भेदागमे एकोनपञ्चाशपटले ॥)

नासत्यश्चैव दस्रश्च अश्विनौ तौ प्रकीर्तितौ ।

शुक्लवस्त्रधरोष्णीषौ पुस्तकाभयपाणिनौ ॥

सोत्तरीयौ सुरूपौ च शुक्लहेमनिभौ तथा ।

(सुप्रभेदागमे अष्टचत्वारिंशत्तमपटले ॥)

एकसिंहासनासीनावश्विनावश्वरूपिणौ ।

दाडिमीपुष्पसङ्काशावुभौ तौ सोपवीतकौ ॥

फुल्लरक्तोत्पलाक्षौ च पीतस्रग्वस्त्रधारिणौ ।

करद्वयसमायुक्तौ श्रीभूषणविभूषितौ ॥

अभयं दक्षिणे हस्ते वरदं वामहस्तके ।

लम्बितं दक्षिणं पादं वाममुत्कुटि(त्कटु?)कासनम् ॥

(शिल्परत्ने पञ्चविंशपटले ॥)

पद्मपत्रसवर्णाभौ पद्मपत्रसमाम्बरौ ।

द्विभुजौ देवभिषजौ कर्तव्यौ देहसंयुतौ ॥

सर्वाभरणसंपन्नौ विशेषाच्चारुलोचनौ ।

तयोरोषधयः कार्या दिव्या दक्षिणहस्तयोः ॥

वामयोः पुस्तके कार्ये दर्शनीये तथा नृप ! ।

एकस्य दक्षिणे पार्श्वे वामे चान्यस्य यादव ! ॥

नारीयुगं प्रकर्तव्यं सुरूपं चारुदर्शनम् ।
तयोश्च नामनी प्रोक्ते रूपसंपत्तथाकृतिः ॥

मधूकपुष्पसंकाशा रूपसंपत्प्रकीर्तिता ।
आकृतिः कथिता लोके शरकाण्डनिभा तथा ॥

रत्नभाण्डकरे कार्ये चन्द्रशुक्लाम्बरे तथा ।

(विष्णुधर्मोत्तरे ॥)

उभयोस्(यौ or यां?)सोपवीतौ तौ चूडामकुटधारिणौ ।
फुल्लरक्तोत्पलाक्षौ च पीतस्रक्शुक्लवस्त्रकौ ॥
अश्विन्याकृतिरेवं तु सूर्याकृतिं शृणुष्वथ ।

(पूर्वकारणागमे त्रयोदशपटले॥)

वसवः ।

धरो ध्रुवश्च सोमश्च आपस्त्वनल एव च ।
अनिलः प्रत्युषश्चैव प्रभावश्च तथैव च ॥

वसवश्चाष्टकास्त्वेते रक्तवर्णा द्विबाहवः ।
पीताम्बरधरास्सर्वे आसीनो वा स्थितोऽपि वा ॥

खड्गखेटकहस्तास्ते सर्वाभरणभूषिताः ।
करण्डमकुटोपेता रौद्रास्सर्वे प्रकीर्तिताः ॥

(अंशुमद्भेदागमे एकोनपञ्चाशपटले ॥)

धरो ध्रुवस्तथा सोमस्साविन्त्रस्त्वनिलोऽनलः ।
प्रत्युषश्च प्रभावश्च सुदंष्ट्रा भीमरूपकाः ॥
खड्गखेटकहस्तास्तु कुञ्चितभ्रूसुलोचनाः ।
सर्वाभरणसंयुक्ताश्चित्रवस्त्रधरास्तथा ॥
रक्तवस्त्रधराः पीताः प्रोक्ता वैवस्वतास्त्विह ।

(सुप्रभेदागमे अष्टचत्वारिंशत्तमपटले ॥)

अथातस्संप्रवक्ष्यामि वसुरूपाणि ते जय ! ।
पद्माक्षमालिके तस्य दक्षवामकरद्वये ॥
सीरशक्ती दधानोऽयं धराख्यो वसुरादिमः ।
मालां पुष्करबीजोत्थां चक्रं शक्तिं कमण्डलुम् ॥
दक्षाधरादिसिक्येन(?) यस्य स्युस्स ध्रुवो मतः ।
मुक्ताफलकृता माला पङ्कजं शक्तिरङ्कुशः ॥
स वसुः कीर्तितो वत्स ! सोमनामेति वै बुधैः ।
सव्यवामोर्ध्वगौ यस्य करौ स्तरशक्तिसंयुतौ ॥
सीराङ्कुशान्वितौ चाधः स भवेदापसंज्ञकः ।
अक्षमालोपवीत्यूर्ध्वे सृणिशक्तिकरावधः ॥
यस्य स्तस्सोऽनिलाख्यस्स्याच्छुभदः पञ्चमो वसुः ।
स्रुवाक्षमालिके दक्षे वामे शक्तिकपालभृत् ॥
सव्योर्ध्वादिक्रमाद्योऽसौ नलाख्यस्तु वसुस्स्मृतः ।
खड्गा(ड्गा ?)ङ्कुशधरस्सव्ये शक्तिखेटकरोऽन्यतः ॥

प्रत्यूषाख्यो वसुश्चायं सप्तमः परिकीर्तितः।
सव्ये दण्डकपालोऽसौ वामे तु सृणिशक्तिकः॥
शुभदः कीर्तितश्चायं प्रभासो वसुरष्टमः।
एते सर्वे समाख्याता नवकाञ्चनसन्निभाः॥
धरो ध्रुवश्च सोमस्त्या(श्चा?)पश्चैवानिलोऽनलः।
प्रत्यूषश्च प्रभासश्च वसवोऽष्टौ प्रकीर्तिताः॥

(विश्वकर्मशास्त्रे॥)

धरो धूम्रश्च सोमश्च आपश्चैवानिलोऽनलः।
प्रत्यूषश्च प्रभावश्च वसवश्चाष्ट एव च॥
द्विभुजाश्च द्विनेत्राश्च असिखेटकसंयुताः।
रक्तवर्णा इमे सर्वे पीतवस्त्रसमन्विताः॥
सर्वाभरणसंयुक्तास्स्निग्धकुन्तलमूर्धजाः।
वसूनामाकृतिर्ह्येवमश्वमूर्त्याकृतिं शृणु॥

(पूर्वकारणागमे चतुर्दशपटले॥)

नागदेवः।

त्रिनेत्रं चतुर्भुजं सौम्यं रक्ताभं सितवाससम्।
अभयवरदोपेतं परहस्ते तु नागधृक्॥
करण्डमकुटोपेतं नागं पञ्चफणान्वितम्।
सर्वाभरणसंयुक्तं पद्मपीठोपरि ।स्थितम्॥

(अंशुमद्भेदागमे एकोनपञ्चाशपटले॥)

नागाः ।

नागानां वक्ष्यते रूपं नाभेरूर्ध्वं नराकृतिः ।
सर्पाकारमधोभागं मस्तके भोगमण्डलम् ॥
एकं फणात्रयं वापि पञ्च वा सप्त वा नव ।
द्विजिह्वास्ते विधातव्याः खड्गचर्मकरैर्युताः ॥

(शिल्परत्ने पञ्चविंशाध्याये ॥)

श्वेतदेहश्च कर्तव्यस्स्फुरन्मौक्तिकसन्निभः ।
रक्ताङ्गस्स्वस्तिकोपेतस्सुतेजास्तक्षको महान् ॥
कृष्णः कार्कोटकः कण्ठे शुक्लरेखात्रयान्वितः ।
रक्तपद्मनिभः पद्मः शिरश्शुक्लस्सविद्रुमः ॥
शङ्खवर्णो महापद्मो मस्तके कृष्णशूलधृक् ।
हेमाभश्शङ्खपालस्स्यात् सितरेखाधरो गले ॥
कुलिको रक्तदेहस्तु चन्द्रार्धकृतमस्तकः ।
द्विजिह्वा वाङ्कुवत्सप्तफणामणिसमन्विताः ॥
अक्षसूत्रधरास्सर्वे कुण्डिकापुच्छसंयुताः ।
एकभोगाञ्चिभोगा वा ह्यतज्जातास्सुतादयः ॥

(मयः ॥)

साध्याः ।

साध्याः पद्मासनगताः कमण्डल्वक्षसूत्रिणः ।
धर्मपुत्रा महात्मानो द्वादशामरपूजिताः ॥

(ब्रह्माण्डपुराणे ॥)

असुराः ।

किरीटकुण्डलोपेतास्तीक्ष्णदंष्ट्रा भयानकाः ।
नानाशस्त्रधराः क्राक्षा दैत्यास्सुरगणाद्विषः ॥

दानवा विकृताकारा भ्रुकुटीकुटिलाननाः ।
करिभेन(?) च कुब्जेन मण्डिताश्शस्त्रपाणयः ॥

दंष्ट्राकरालवदना भ्रुकुटीकुटिलेक्षणाः ।
नानारूपा महाकाया नानाशस्त्रधरास्तथा ॥

(शिल्परत्ने पञ्चविंशाध्याये ॥)

अप्सरसः ।

रम्भा च विपुला चैव उर्वशी च तिलोत्तमा ।
मध्यक्षामसमायुक्ताः पीनोरुजघनस्तनाः ॥

(सुप्रभेदागमे अष्टचत्वारिंशत्तमपटले ॥)

दुकूलवसनास्सर्वाः पीनोरुजघनस्तनाः ।
मध्ये क्षौवादिवर्णाव(?)तिसौम्याश्च किंचित्प्रहसिताननाः ॥
नानालङ्कारसंयुक्ता भद्रपीठोपरि स्थिताः ।
समभङ्गसमायुक्तास्सप्तसङ्ख्याप्सरो(?) स्मृताः ॥

(शिल्परत्ने पञ्चविंशपटले ॥)

पिशाचाः ।

उत्पर्वकृशकायास्ते चर्मास्थिस्नायुविग्रहाः ।
ह्रस्वकीर्णशिरोजास्स्युः पिशाचाश्चित्रकर्मणि ॥

वेतालाः ।

ईदृक्का(शा?) एव वेताला दीर्घदेहाः कृशोदराः ।
कपोलैः पूर्व जैर्युक्ता लेखनीया मनीषिभिः ॥

(शिल्परत्ने पञ्चविंशाध्याये ॥)

पितरः ।

पितरः पीतवर्णाभाः वृद्धास्ते केशबन्धिताः ।
यज्ञसूत्रसमायुक्ता द्विभुजाः श्वेतवाससः ॥
नानाभरणसंयुक्ता भस्मोद्धूलितविग्रहाः ।
सितदन्तसमायुक्ताः सौम्यदृक्पातनान्विताः ॥
फलके भद्रपीठे वा पितरस्तु महात्मनः(?) ।
वामजानूपरिन्यस्तवामहस्तसमन्विताः ॥
सूची दक्षिणहस्ते तु पितरस्त्रय उच्यते(?) ।
पितरस्तु समाख्याताः शृणु वैवस्वतं ततः ॥

(अंशुमद्भेदागमे एकोनपञ्चाशपटले ॥)

पिता पितामहौ चैव(हश्चैव?) प्रपितामह एव च ।
पितरस्स्तूयमानास्तु तेषां वै लक्षणं शृणु ॥
सुदृढा पीतक(व?)र्णास्तु छत्रदण्डधरास्तथा ।
शुक्लवस्त्रैः परिच्छन्नाः कीर्तिताः पितरस्त्रयः ॥

(सुप्रभेदागमे अष्टचत्वारिंशत्तमपटले ॥)

पितरः पीतवर्णाभा द्विभुजाः श्वेतवाससः ।
यज्ञसूत्रसमायुक्तास्सौम्यदृग्वदनान्विताः ॥
फलके भद्रपीठे वा त्रयस्तु सहिताननाः(सनाः ?) ।

(शिल्परत्ने पञ्चविंशपटले ॥)

कुशपञ्चविष्टरस्थाः पितरः पिण्डपात्रिणः ।

(विष्णुधर्मोत्तरे ॥)

सप्तर्षयः ।

ऋषयः पीतवर्णास्तु नानावर्णान्विताम्बराः ।
वृद्धाश्च द्विभुजाश्शान्ता जटामकुटमण्डिताः ॥
चिबुका हृदयान्ताश्च उपवीतसमन्विताः ।
भस्मना च त्रिपुण्ड्रास्यास्स्थानका वासनास्तु वा ॥
दण्डं दक्षिणहस्ते तु छत्रं वामकरे धृतम् ।
छत्रदण्डं विना वापि सव्यं वै ज्ञानमुद्रिका ॥
वामजानूपरिन्यस्तवामहस्तसमन्विताः ।
मनुस्त्वगस्त्य इत्युक्तो वसिष्ठो गौतमस्तथा ॥
अङ्गिरास्स्याद्विश्वामित्रः भरद्वाज इति स्मृताः ।
एते वै सप्त ऋषयः कीर्तिताश्च विशेषतः ॥

(अंशुमद्भेदागमे एकोनपञ्चाशपटले ॥)

भृगुश्चैव वसिष्ठश्च पुलस्त्यः पुलहः क्रतुः ।
काश्यपः कौशिकश्चैव अङ्गिरा मुनयस्त्विमे ॥

सुवल्कला जटायुक्तास्सुमुखा दंशहस्तकाः ।
कव्या च मण्डिताकाराश्शुक्लवस्त्रधराश्शुभाः ॥

पिङ्गलाश्च सुनेत्राश्च पत्नयस्सप्त कीर्तिताः ।

(सुप्रभेदागमे अष्टाचत्वारिंशत्तमपटले ॥)

अगस्त्यश्च पुलस्त्यश्च विश्वामित्रः पराशरः ।
जमदग्निश्च वाल्मीकी सनत्कुमारश्च सप्त च ॥

शुक्लवस्त्रधरास्सर्वे शुक्लयज्ञोपवीतकाः ।
शुक्लवस्त्रोत्तरीयाश्च जटावल्कलसंयुताः ॥

कमण्डल्वक्षहस्ताश्च दीर्घश्मश्रुसमन्विताः ।
ऋषीणामाकृतिः प्रोक्ता अश्विन्याकृतिरुच्यते ॥

(पूर्वकारणागमे त्रयोदशपटले ॥)

कौशिकः ।

अगस्त्यवत्कौशिकं च स्थापयेत्स्थापकोत्तमः ।

भृगुः ।

भृगुः शुक्लनिभश्शान्तश्शुक्लवस्त्रधरस्तथा ।
करण्डमकुटोपेतो हस्तद्वयसमन्वितः ॥

अभयवरदोपेतस्सर्वाभरणभूषितः ।
स्थानकं वासनं वापि पद्मपीठे भृगुश्शुचिः ॥

मरुद्गणाः ।

मरुद्गणा धूम्रवर्णा द्विभुजात्यन्तसुन्दराः ।
केशभारसमायुक्तास्सर्वाभरणभूषिताः ॥

दुकूलवसनास्सर्वे नानापुष्पैरलङ्कृताः ।
अभयवरदोपेता टङ्कशूलसमन्विताः ॥

स्थानकाः पद्मपीठे तु शुक्लवस्त्रधराश्शुभाः ।
(अंशुमद्भेदागमे एकोनपञ्चाशपटले ॥)

INDEX.

INDEX.